Finger
Let's Call It

Let's Call It Finger

A History of North McNairy County & Finger, Tennessee & Its Surrounding Communities

John E. Talbott, J.D.

BRAYBREE
Publishing

Copyright © 2015 John E. Talbott, J.D.
All rights reserved

Published by BrayBree Publishing Company LLC
SECOND EDITION

No part of this book may be reproduced, stored in or introduced into a retrieval system or transmitted in any form or by any means (electronic, mechanical, photocopying, recording, or otherwise) without the prior written permission of the copyright owner.

The scanning, uploading, and distribution of this book on the Internet or through any other means is not permitted without permission from the copyright owner.

ISBN-13: 978-1-940127-03-3

Printed in the United States of America

BrayBree Publishing Company LLC
P.O. Box 1204
Dickson, Tennessee 37056-1204

Visit our website at www.braybreepublishing.com

*D*edicated to the pioneers who carved our beloved
community out of wilderness and set forth examples
we would do well to emulate and
to the children of our community today who might yet actually
honor that hardy and brave class of souls by yet building
anew on the ruins of the honored past.

ACKNOWLEDGEMENTS
TO THE FIRST EDITION

During the course of any work, a writer has many people who help him as he pursues his goal of writing. Without the help of many old friends and neighbors, much of this work would not exist. Many of those who have so willingly assisted me on this project have lived in north McNairy County and nearby for decades, while others left here decades ago to find greener grass elsewhere. Many made their way to California, Texas, and other western and northern states in the 1930s and 1940s. Others went to Memphis and Nashville to pursue a living. Regardless of their eventual destination, so many of these sons and daughters of McNairy County provided assistance to me. For that I will be forever grateful and thankful. I hope I have mentioned them all here on this page. If I have not, you know who you are and I hope you will please forgive me for my lapse of memory. This work is for you all and I hope you enjoy every word.

As with so many who make attempts to write and chronicle the history of an area, much time and effort is required and it is the family of the author who make the required sacrifices. For that I am grateful to my own family. My father, Ronald L. Talbott, has been extremely interested and involved in my research and writing, as has been my mother, Diane Talbott. They have been supportive and sincere in their efforts to ensure any success I mind find. My grandparents, Luther E. and Faye

(McIntyre) Talbott, have spent innumerable hours with me in the discussion and research of our area's history. Their constant support, reassurance and supply of information has been vital to the completion of this work. My wife, Michelle (Smith) Talbott, took quickly to my bad habits of trekking through woods to overgrown cemeteries, of turning pleasure trips into research missions, and spending hours upon hours visiting with elderly men and women and learning of the old ways. To her, I am thankful, for she is a true helpmate.

Finally, there are friends who are the same as family in your eyes. With them there are no lines between family and friends. The late Hayes Hayre, a distant relative and longtime friend, passed away in 2000. Hayes was a constant supporter and friend. Together we passed many hours walking the woods and old roads seeking out old house sites and graves. He was ever interested in the preservation of local history and lore and he was a faithful and good friend. Marvin Hand left the McNairy-Chester county area in the 1940s to pursue a new life in Hesperia, California. He found great success in the West and never forgot the land of his youth. In his old age and my days of youth, we became friends and neighbors who happened to live a thousand miles or so apart. Together we have shared many stories, moments, triumphs and despairs. He has followed my career and my pursuits with kind words of encouragement and enthusiastic support. Gracie (Plunk) Webster has spent a great deal of time helping me research this book. A constant friend, she has taken much work upon herself so that I could be free to write. So many items regarding education and schools and the old families of our area were the product of her effort and toil. She has been vital to the completion of this work in its present form. Laws Rushing Sr. has constantly encouraged me in my writing and reading. Many ideas have passed between the two of us over the years. Dean Charles DeWitt is not a native of Finger, but has constantly encouraged me in my interest in history and my love for writing. He was vital to my law school career, during which time the bulk of this volume was written. Finally, my thanks go to Dr. B.J. Naylor for his tutelage over the years and for supporting me in my first attempts to write. My experience writing *Fingerprints* with him was one of the most rewarding I have known. To these friends and so many more I am thankful.

ACKNOWLEDGEMENTS

My thanks goes to the following persons for supplying information and photographs: F.C. Mitchell of California, Omar DuBerry, Haven Garner, James L. Massey, Billy Frank Harris, Robert Beene, Glenn Naylor, Louise Murry, the late Albert Floyd, Leslie Floyd, Ben Davidson of Bingham, Illinois, Jerry Wilson Smith of Friendship, Tennessee; Professor Jim Hodges of Virginia, Robert Hodges of Texas, Gary O'Neal, Kevin D. McCann of Dickson, Tennessee, Florence Ward, Brian Neal Dickey, Vivian McIntyre, Lessie McIntyre, the late Lloyd Harris, Jim Montague of the Ned Ray McWherter Library and native of McNairy Station, the late Guy Brown, Mancel Kirk, Richard Leath, Merle Weatherford, the late Clifford Young, Genevieve (Scott) Bell, Vonnie Mae Garner, Ethel McIntyre, Roy McIntyre, Tanya Becker of El Sobrante, California, Billy Hugh Kirkpatrick, Don Lipford, Mildred Smith, and Ms. Ivy Cone.

ACKNOWLEDGEMENTS
TO THE SECOND EDITION

It is difficult to write new acknowledgments without first ratifying my original acknowledgments. As time has worked its will, most of those kind individuals have passed on into history as well and I miss them every one. After the publication of this work in 2003, several individuals were kind enough to contact me and offer additions to the information I had included in the book and in some cases provided me with first hand accounts of events I did recount. Therefore, I am very grateful to the late Robert Beene and the late Alice (McIntyre) McCaskill. Both were kind enough to further my knowledge of the area by providing their firsthand accounts of some events.

I was further aided after the publication of the first edition by friends such as the late Edgar Maurice "Molly" Stansell Sr. and Mr. L.A. Baucom. There were others who also those who provided critical assistance including Gary O'Neal. I also wish to acknowledge the hundreds of individuals who purchased some 800 copies of the first edition.

My circle of collaborators is slowly disappearing. This unfortunate tide cannot be turned back. Each year we lose another individual who possesses firsthand knowledge of the past. Those coming along simply are not connected to the past for they were not there but perhaps they will write their own story one day.

I do wish to thank my friend, cousin, and co-publisher, Kevin D. McCann, for his valuable assistance in setting up this book and offering every assistance, constructive criticism, and encouragement. Thank you also to Stephanie Howell for creating the index. Finally, I thank my wife, Michelle, and my three daughters, Ava, Claire, and Grace, for their patience while I worked to revise and update this work. When this book was originally published, I had no children. Today I am blessed with these three beautiful daughters and I am thankful to them and for them.

CONTENTS

Introduction to the First Edition	xv
Introduction to the Second Edition	xvii
CHAPTER ONE: The Land We Call Home	3
CHAPTER TWO: The Early Settlers of North McNairy County	12
CHAPTER THREE: The War Between the States	43
CHAPTER FOUR: The Education of North McNairy County	97
CHAPTER FIVE: The Birth of Business—Blacksmiths to Merchants	153
CHAPTER SIX: The Healing Arts—From Midwives and "Doctors by Experience" to Professional Physicians	205
CHAPTER SEVEN: Men and Women of Determination	225
CHAPTER EIGHT: Religion and the Pursuit of Faith	253
CHAPTER NINE: The Mysterious, the Unexplainable, and the Downright Tragic	277
CHAPTER TEN: Writings of Special Historical Note to North McNairy County	300
CHAPTER ELEVEN: The Burying Grounds of North McNairy County	352
Sources Consulted	465
Index	473
About the Author	513

INTRODUCTION
TO THE FIRST EDITION

It is the task of the historian to research, analyze, and write the history of a person, place, or event. Of course, to this simple explanation belong many caveats and explanations. Certainly, the process is not so simple. Great amounts of prejudice, uncertainty, and error often exist in the process and its finished product. Some historians are prolific and others are not, preferring a more cautious approach and a slower pace for the writing process. I, myself, do not claim to be a historian, but rather one who has a deep interest in the land of my childhood, that of my father and many of our fathers before us. This interest has always propelled me toward projects whose goal is the preservation of our local history.

My goal has been to tell the past to the present generation and leave these stories and historical sketches in written form so that future generations may learn. The names of those who have come before us should not be relegated merely to an engraven name on marble, limestone, or granite. We should seek to know more than their names and vital dates. We should seek out the facts, the tales, and the personal interest stories which might make these long-dead individuals once again come alive.

The reader might wonder what reward the author seeks to enjoy. That question may be answered in rather short order. I have already received my reward. Hours upon hours of hiking through densely wooded areas seeking out old homeplaces, overgrown cemeteries, and long abandoned wagon roads and fields. These hours and the adventures they have brought and presented have been a great reward in themselves. Still yet, I have had the honor and privilege of getting to know so many of our older generations who saw and lived through the transition of the horse and buggy days to the present age of technological advances and a fast-paced society. Having the opportunity to meet and become friends with so many of these good people has been a great blessing to me personally.

Yet there is much left to do. It is my personal hope and prayer that others will pick up the banner of preservation and history and carry on the crusade of knowledge and enlightenment. Each person's efforts are vital and may yield monumental contributions to other generations in the years to come. Regardless it is my sincerest hope that you may enjoy this work and the many stories and facts contained herein. Perhaps you will enjoy reading it as much I enjoyed writing it.

John E. Talbott
July 4, 2003

INTRODUCTION
TO THE SECOND EDITION

The old adage that "time flies" is no myth. Indeed it does fly. It seems that so many events have crowded themselves into the last eleven years since the first publication of this work. There have been additions, losses, births, deaths and the inescapable hand of time has wrought its many works. The acceptance of this work by so many people was overwhelming to me as its author. I never expected to have the pleasure and honor to realize that demand for this little work would long outlast its supply. In the last several years, I had many requests for the book but had none to provide. Finally, after years of toying with the idea of a revised edition, I decided to act.

Many old friends who assisted with this book or provided information or guidance or inspiration have long since passed from this life. With their deaths, great mental and emotional libraries were lost. As the years roll inevitably on, it seems to me that works of this nature are all the more needed to instruct and inform new generations of a past which they will never know otherwise. As that generation which includes my own children grows, they will be further removed from the pioneering spirit of those whose stories are recorded in this work. Still, I want my children and others of their generation to have the opportunity to learn of the past. History never ceases to be relevant.

As I write these lines, I am surrounded by three small and very active—if not rambunctious—daughters, asking questions and making the kinds of requests nine and eight-year old and eight-month old children make when their father is attempting to work. Again, time has wrought its changes and it gives me pause to chuckle and laugh about the changes it brings. I am certain I could not have written this book today as my attention is constantly diverted by inquisitive, precious, and too-soon-to-be grown little children. Still I can keep my thoughts long enough to make revisions.

Please accept this revised edition in the spirit that is intended. As in 2003, when the original was published, this book is put forth that all who love the Finger area and north McNairy County or have some connection to the area may find enjoyment, enlightenment and some degree of knowledge regarding our community's great and interesting past.

John E. Talbott
October 20, 2014

I have crossed Mississippi's
    brooks and rills
I have climbed Arkansas'
    pine clad hills
I have seen Missouri's fields
    of wheat
And Kentucky's blue grass
    meadows so neat
I have seen ladies in this State
    who are pretty and up to date
But no matter where I linger
    There are no so rare
as can compare
    With the lovely girls of Finger.

— W.P. Massey,
April 8, 1908

Mr. Massey served as postmaster of Finger
from June 13, 1895, to August 21, 1914

Let's Call It Finger

CHAPTER ONE

THE LAND WE CALL HOME

Brief geological history and description of north McNairy County—Description of the settlement process in nineteenth-century western Tennessee—The Jackson Purchase Treaty of 1818.

L and always tells a story. This statement has often been recited by those who hold a great respect for the earth and its many uses. When the term "earth" is applied, the concept of *terra firma* is implied. Perhaps as a man looks upon a mountain in the distance, he recalls the stories of his fathers, those of hard times, hard living, and hard work. Perhaps the farmer looks upon the fields "teeming" and explains to his son that the sweat and sacrifice his grandfathers and grandmothers poured out made that farm a going concern. Regardless of the story which was lived out upon that spot on this great globe, that spot tells a story. It tells a story when we make some mark, good or bad, upon it. It tells a story even when we have not altered it. It always tells a story.

As people differ on their politics, on their religion, and a number of other matters, so do they also differ on their view of the origins of our wonderful world. Those who adhere to the Genesis account of creation see the earth and its creatures as works wrought by the mighty hand of God, all completed in a particular and divine order. Heavens, earth, light, darkness, division of the water and the firmament, plants, seasons, sun, moon, stars, the foul, the fish, the cattle and the creeping things, then man, all from the craftsmanship of an omnipotent God, this according to Moses.[1] All in six days.[2] The view of the creationist was perhaps best summed up by the late William Jennings Bryan, defender of the common man, when he said, "I believe in the Rock of Ages, not the age of rocks."

Then there are the scientists and those who are "doubting Thomases." There is no plausible answer or explanation to corroborate the six day work of the Genesis account, according to the students and disciples of Darwin. To these skeptical yet inquisitive ones, whose faith is in the gospel of evolution, the story is not told in any ancient text written upon clay tablets or papyrus scroll. Rather, the story is told in the rocks, in the soil profiles, and in the fossil beds found buried deep in the soil or beneath the waters of the creeks. Their time frame is much longer than six days.

Therefore what did McNairy County look like at one time so very long ago? According to the scientists, the red clay hills and sandstones were covered by a sea. Beachfront property in Finger? Maybe, maybe not. That depends upon the extent of the waters. While only a few local residents, those of an especially curious and analytical nature, speculated upon the possibility of a large body of water, most never considered the reality of that possibility. Then came the discovery of fossil beds at Coon Creek, just east of Finger, in Leapwood.

Now if one believes strictly in the creation view, things now begin to get murky. Why? Because of what is buried in the creek bed of Coon Creek: clams, oysters, crabs, and mosasaurs.[3] Mosasaurs? We will come to that in just a moment. For now let us consider the presence of those clams, oysters, and crabs. You won't find them in Huggins Creek here in Finger. So how did they get to Leapwood?

---

1. *Genesis* 1:1-31. *The New Analytical Bible and Dictionary of the Bible* (Iowa Falls, IA: World Bible Publishers, 1973).

2. Many interpret days as referred to in Genesis as eras or series of years. Others hold to a literal translation.

3. Edward T. Luther, *Our Restless Earth: The Geologic Regions of Tennessee* (Knoxville: The University of Tennessee Press, 1977).

According to scientists, the waters of the seas rolled over what is now north McNairy County from about 550 million years ago until, at least, about 70 million years ago.[4] Since then, the area is said to have been marked by the Ice Ages. As an ice age ends and glaciers recede, they move ever so slowly across the surface of the earth, leaving a trail of erosion behind them. As for that mosasaur, it was a short-necked forty foot long predator of the seas, whose skeleton was found in Coon Creek.[5]

Now let us recap. One way or another, the land of north McNairy County obtained its features. If approached from the religious view, the surface of north McNairy County is such because the Heavenly Father designed it as such. If you gravitate toward the scientific view, then you see the event as rather a process, perhaps even a process accidental in nature. You would see it as a process of mountain-making, seas rising and receding, and Ice Ages coming and going. Regardless of the who or what, however, we and the land are here and that is all that matters for purposes of our discussion. So let us continue with our story.

How does the land of north McNairy County appear? Perhaps even that question must be examined in layers, bedrock, soil, vegetation and animal life. In 1882, General Marcus J. Wright wrote a practical description of the county.[6] From that description we will glean descriptions of our area. Wright said "the country immediately around Purdy is hilly and poor."[7] This is true farther north toward Finger. The "extreme northern part of the county is level or undulating, and the soil rich and productive."[8] This is the ancient area of Montezuma, now a portion of Chester County. The General also reported that the western side of the county was hilly.

McNairy County lies within the Gulf Coastal Plain of West Tennessee.[9] A look at a physiographic map of Tennessee shows McNairy

---

4. *Id.*

5. *Id.*

6. Marcus J. Wright and John E. Talbott, J.D. and Kevin D. McCann, editors. *Reminiscences of the Early Settlement and Early Settlers of McNairy County, Tennessee, 130th Anniversary Edition*. (Dickson, TN: BrayBree Publishing, 2012).

7. *Id.*

8. *Id.*

9. Robert E. Corlew, *Tennessee: A Short History* (Knoxville: The University of Tennessee Press, 1990).

County to be in an area of that plain that is labeled "clay hills."[10] This is apparent with just a glimpse at the northern section of McNairy County. In 1882, Wright reported the agricultural bounty consisted of cotton, wheat, oats, Indian corn, apples, peaches, peas, plums, cherries and grapes. He also declared the natural bounty of our county to consist of chiefly oak, hickory, ash, cypress, pine, and chestnut, in terms of native timbers.[11] Certainly that has changed to some degree. American chestnut trees, more properly known as *Castanea dentate*, no longer stand tall and strong in the South due to a blight known as *Endothia parasitica* that destroyed these nut bearing trees.[12] This blight was first noted in 1904 and had destroyed almost every specimen of the native chestnut tree by the middle of the twentieth century.[13] Cypress are primarily found in the swamps and bottoms of the southern parts of the county. However, throughout the twentieth century, there were oaks, hickories, and pines aplenty. Only recently has this vast natural wealth been greatly depleted by overexploitation, the product of clear cutting.

These natural treasures of vegetation provided a home, a meal, and a refuge from danger for thousands of animals, insects, and other almost minute forms of life. In the virgin forests of West Tennessee including that portion which would become north McNairy County, the wild berries, nuts, and herbs, along with the various types of wildlife which then roamed such as bear, turkey, deer and smaller game, fed the first Tennesseans.[14]

Therefore, let us ask an important question. Who were the first Tennesseans? Again we must start from the beginning. According to both historians and scientists, no human life existed in North America when the last glacial age began.[15] This would have been about 20,000 to

10. *Id.*

11. Wright, Talbott, McCann, *Reminiscences 130th Anniversary Edition.*

12. Eliot Wigginton, editor. *Foxfire 6: Shoemaking, Gourd Banjos and Songbows, One Hundred Toys and Games, Wooden Locks, A Water-Powered Sawmills and Other Affairs of Just Plain Living.* (New York: Anchor Press/Doubleday, 1980).

13. *Id.*

14. *Id.*

15. The reader must first presume that a glacial age existed. It is assumed by the author that a certain population holds to such theories and ideas and that others do not. Some embrace science to a fault and others dismiss without any educated study, a tragedy in itself. Other enlightened

30,000 years ago.[15] However, hunters from Asia, being nomadic peoples, followed the herds across a land bridge then connecting Siberia to Alaska.[17] Therefore, according to this theory, the first to roam the lands of Tennessee were the descendants of the above mentioned Asians.[18]

The land area now referred to as McNairy County was a part of that larger, boundary-free area of western Tennessee that was the Chickasaw lands. Of course, present-day West Tennessee was only itself a portion of the greater Chickasaw Territory, one which often overlapped with Cherokees and found itself a neighbor of the more fierce Choctaw. The great hunting area called West Tennessee provided food, shelter and a "home" to the Chickasaw long before Hernando de Soto and his Spaniards made their acquaintance around 1540.[19]

Certainly it would be a few generations later before the French and English could exercise the business skills of the Chickasaw in the ancient art of the trade. This relationship between traders and the Chickasaw had its roots in the late seventeenth century and as it grew, it delivered to the "native" population tools they could not have imagined in their own primitive era.[20] The Chickasaw, with few exceptions, had lived in relative seclusion and in a virgin forest insulating them from the brand of civilization being burned into the skin of the new state of Tennessee. The reader must remember that today's West Tennessee was yesteryear's west, plain and simple. To travel west of the Tennessee River was as great an adventurous feat as traveling west of the Mississippi River would be in a few years when Lewis and Clark made their now legendary scientific expedition.

Thus, the traders, both French and English, introduced this people to a new world of innovation and intrigue. Now the mighty men of the Chickasaw Nation could fight and hunt with tools far beyond the flint arrow and spear. Now the musket, the hatchet and the knife took

---

people make attempts to harmonize religion and science, made possible due in large part to the fact that God created both disciplines.

16. Corlew, *Tennessee: A Short History*.

17. Ronald N. Satz, *Tennessee's Indian Peoples: From White Contact to Removal, 1540-1840*. (Knoxville: University of Tennessee Press, 1979).

18. *Id.*

19. *Id.*

20. *Id.*

superior roles.[21] The women, who followed the pursuit of agriculture, now brandished iron hoes, axes, and other tools with which to make cultivation a less dreaded chore.[22]

Thus life went for the Chickasaw, a bevy of benefit for the new found art of trade with the Europeans. However, these new friends and their trinkets came with a terrible price. The competition for trade led to an escalation of tension and rivalry between the English and the French. Of course, as with any great conflict, all bystanders are subject to involvement, whether voluntary or not, and the effects involvement brings, ill or otherwise. In this case, the Chickasaw fell to the side of the British and soon began to make mischief with the French communication "system" established between trading posts.[23] However, such activities benefiting the British also brought about consequences for the Natives. The French played no games. Adopting a hard line on such intrigue, the French fought the Chickasaw for some time before the Chickasaw were forced to surrender at Memphis.[24] To some degree, this event would eventually weaken the Chickasaw as a nation.

In the latter half of the eighteenth century, the Chickasaw hold on West Tennessee remained relatively strong, but as the dawn of the nineteenth century approached, that hold would have but little time left. As white settlement continued in an east to west march consuming wilderness in the fires of civilization, West Tennessee became a prime target for the enterprising pioneers. In 1818, a two-man commission, consisting of none other than Isaac Shelby and Andrew Jackson, was formed for the purpose of gaining access to this rich wilderness between two great rivers.[25] These lands, it was explained to the Chickasaw, were given to Revolutionary War soldiers in 1783 by Virginia and North Carolina and could no longer be kept off limits to settlement.[26] With that, the Chickasaw acquiesced to the Jackson Purchase Treaty of 1818, which provided

21. *Id.*
22. *Id.*
23. Corlew, *Tennessee: A Short History*.
24. *Id.*
25. *Id.*
26. *Id.*

for payment to the Chickasaw Nation in annual installments of $300,000 for the next twenty years.[27]

Following this vitally important event, settlement's floodgates were thrown wide open. The ink on the treaty could scarcely have been dry when the speculators began to descend upon the area for the purpose of setting up the jurisdictional boundaries of new counties and preparing for the coming hordes of hungry men and women with hungry eyes and great ambitions.

Only five years following the treaty with the Chickasaw Nation, an act was presented to the Tennessee General Assembly providing for the establishment of a new county to be called McNairy. The land area in question was then the western portion of Hardin County, Tennessee. Our region was located within the Ninth Surveyor's District. The major body of water in the area that would become known as Finger was Huggins Creek, already named as such as early as 1823. It was referred to as Hugganses' Creek in the second deed to be recorded in the land records of McNairy County, Tennessee.[28] Likely, the name was given to the body of water by a surveyor in honor of someone. The act itself, consisting of five provisions, is reprinted below.[29]

CHAPTER XCVI
An Act to establish a new County west of Hardin County

> Be it enacted by the General Assembly of the State of Tennessee, that a county to be called and known by the name of McNairy, be, and the same is hereby established west of Hardin county; beginning at the southwest corner of Hardin county, running thence north with the west boundary of the same twenty-seven and one-half miles; thence west, passing the southeast corner of Madison county, to a point three miles west of the first range line in the ninth district; thence south parallel with said range line to the south boundary of this State; thence east on said boundary to the beginning.

27. *Id.*
28. McNairy County Register's of Deeds' Office, Deed Book A, page 2.
29. Wright, Talbott, McCann, *Reminiscences 130th Anniversary Edition.*

Be it enacted, that for the due administration of justice of said county, the Courts of Pleas and Quarter Sessions of said county and the Circuit Courts shall be held at the house of Abel V. Maury, near the centre of said county, until otherwise provided for by law, viz; The Courts of Pleas and Quarter Sessions on the 2d Mondays in January, April, July, and October, and the succeeding days, and the Circuit Courts on the 3d Mondays in May and November and the succeeding days, in each and every year, under the same rules, regulations and restrictions, and to have and exercise the same powers and jurisdiction that other Courts of judicature of like grades in this State now or hereafter may have.

Be it enacted, that the Sheriff of said county shall open and hold an election on the 1st Friday and Saturday in April next, at the place of holding Courts for said county, for the purpose of electing field officers for the militia of said county, under the same rules, regulations and restrictions as are pointed out by law in similar cases; and the militia of said county shall compose the eightieth regiment of Tennessee militia, and be attached to the eleventh brigade.

Be it enacted, that it shall be the duty of the commandant of said regiment, having been first commissioned and sworn according to law, to divide his regiment into such numbers of companies as he shall think best for the convenience of said companies, and it shall further be the duty of said commandant to issue writs of election for company officers according to law, as provided for in other cases of elections for captain and subaltern officers.

Be it enacted, that this Act shall take effect and be in force from and after the first day of January next.

JAMES FENTRESS,
Speaker of the House of Representatives.
R. WEAKLEY,
Speaker of the Senate.

A few important facts should be discussed before we continue our discourse on the history of northern McNairy County and the Finger area. The new county was named for Judge John McNairy. A native of North Carolina and a prominent jurist, he held the positions of Judge of the Superior Court of the Western District of Tennessee and Judge of the District Court of the United States for Tennessee. He died in 1833 in Nashville, Tennessee.[30] Pursuant to the Act, the first session of the county court was held in early 1824. From 1823 until the formation of Chester County in 1882, the county was comprised of 412,800 acres of land or 645 square miles.[31]

Now let us embark upon the adventure of telling the story of the history of north McNairy County and that area around what is now Finger. Certainly it is not so complete as one would like, but it is much fuller than has previously been published. Let us now imagine the trails walked by our ancestors and attempt to feel the range of emotions they must have known. So much is still to be discovered, but let us begin.

30. *Id.*
31. *Id.*

CHAPTER TWO

THE EARLY SETTLERS OF NORTH McNAIRY COUNTY

Introduction—The Early Families—Hodges—Kerby—Plunk—Anderson—Wisdom—Weaver—Ward—Ingraham—Walsh—Lane—Lowrance—Smith—McIntyre—Draper—Floyd—Putman— Randolph—Bulliner—Robbins.

F ollowing the 1818 Jackson Purchase Treaty, settlement began to occur. Hundreds of families began to make what has been deemed "the long trip over the mountains."[1] No one should make the mistake of thinking that only the men journeyed here first to clear the land and then send for the women and children. Should that have been the practice, perhaps the area would never have been settled. These early pioneers came with everything they possessed, including family. With a wagon or wagons loaded with every item of household use, every family heirloom (usually trusty tools of survival) and every stitch of linen, the families came, one after another, and often several families together. Usually the land to which they were coming was already theirs, in the form of a land grant or purchase. A family would often consist of mother, father, children, their spouses if married, and often elderly grandparents.

1. Ruth Helen Niemann, *The Glory of a Common Man: A Biography* (Self-published, 1976).

By way of example, the elderly mother of William Parrish Walker of the area now known as Jacks Creek, then just a short distance from the McNairy County line, displayed the true ruggedness of the early settler. William Parrish Walker moved to what was then Henderson County, Tennessee from Pittsylvania County, Virginia, leaving many loved ones far behind. At some point after his removal to the Jacks Creek area, his elderly mother paid him a visit from Virginia. She fell in with other travelers and rode an ox from Pittsylvania County, Virginia to Jacks Creek, Tennessee. Upon the conclusion of her visit, Ms. Walker rode her ox back to Virginia.[2]

The road to West Tennessee was not an easy one. Crossing unfamiliar territory and rough terrain was a usually once in a lifetime trek and for many good reasons. Though hostile Native American Indians were no longer a threat by the 1820s, disease and navigation of treacherous mountain paths presented the greatest dangers. Exposure to the elements and long arduous hours on the trail weakened the body and led often to sickness and sometimes death. The old roads are littered with the graves of the unknown, most often unmarked, but if marked at all, only with a sandstone or limestone marker. Coaxing and coercing teams of horses, mules and oxen over and through the mountains, hills and wilderness passages to western Tennessee was almost as difficult, if not more difficult, than clearing the land they were seeking.

Though a few of those hardy pioneers brought with them a number of slaves, there were very few. Few wealthy men and families came, for the "old country" seemed to be serving their needs well. This leads to the inevitable question of why so few wealthy families and their servants made the trip to a new land. The answer lies in the nature of these pioneers and the nature of their purpose for migration. These were not wealthy landowners seeking new frontiers. Rather these were poor farmers, for the most part, who were seeking opportunities to gain a place of their own on this green earth in their own name. These men and women owned little or no land back East. Some lived a meager existence in the towns of the Carolinas and Virginia, or were farmers who had grown restless and tired of the thin soils of the Highlands. They simply knew

---

2. Samuel Perkins Talbott-Hattie Cone Bray Family Papers. Private of Collection of John E. Talbott, Finger, Tennessee.

or at least hoped they would find deep soils and new opportunities in the west between the Mississippi River and the Tennessee River.

If opportunity was to become reality, hard work, persistence and faith had to take precedence over all other emotions. As these men and women set about their work, these states of mind had to be present. Therefore we come to the issue of the types of skill and work that had to be completed in order for the new settlers to be successful. That discussion is of utmost importance and even upon its completion we are hard pressed to understand their difficulties and frustrations.

Following the acquisition of the Chickasaw Purchase Territory, the large and expansive region needed to be surveyed and divided. One of the territorial surveyors was Major Benjamin Wright, who would later build the first cabin in the new settlement of Purdy. Major Wright also treated with the Native Americans and assisted in negotiated agreement with the Native American population then living, hunting and roaming the territory. Wright's son, Marcus Joseph Wright, later recalled the Natives calling on his father at their home.[3]

The first item of business in 1820 and following was to clear the land, as there were few open areas. In fact, the land was largely covered by what General Marcus J. Wright deemed the "large monarchs of an almost unbroken forest."[4] More that one purpose was served by clearing portions of the land. Small patches were cleared for the cultivation of crops and as a byproduct, white oak logs were available for building a cabin. One purpose served another.

For a number of years after the initial settlement of the area, the chore of clearing land was quite routine. First the undergrowth, whatever amount existed in these virgin forests, was cleared. With the use of a mattock and an axe, a tree would be ringed and scalped of its bark and damaged and this would lead to the death of the tree.[5] After a period of time, the tree would then be cut down and processed into logs. As often done today, the stumps were left until the roots had rotted and could be pried from the ground. Sometimes attempts were made to burn out

---

3. Wright, Talbott, McCann, *Reminiscences 130th Anniversary Edition*.

4. *Id.*

5. William E. Cox, *Hensley Settlement: A Mountain Community* (Philadelphia: Eastern National Park and Monument Association, 1978).

the stumps in order that planting and harvesting would be made easier. Whatever the methods, they were primitive and quite laborious.

It was most assuredly in and around the year 1820 that most settlers first laid their eyes upon the area now known as north McNairy County, although some have claimed and may very well have settled here in 1818. There comes, however, the question of what comprised north McNairy County in 1820, and it is a good and proper question. In fact, from 1823, the year the county was formed, until 1882, north McNairy County included many parts which now comprise Chester County.

In the vicinity of the present McNairy-Chester county line were great settlements which proudly stood as the northernmost points of settlement for a great new county in the first few years. General Wright spoke succinctly concerning the first years and first settlements of the county in his venerated work of 1882. He made mention of McNairy Station on the Mobile and Ohio Railroad, Bethel Springs on the same rail line, and Montezuma, near the Madison County line, a hamlet which refused the railroad.[6] However, there were a number of other settlements including Asaton, McIntyre's Crossing, Anderson's Store, Tinsley, White Plains, and Cotton Ridge.

This work will endeavor to fill in some of the gaps created by other works, by time, and the passing of so many knowledgeable citizens of our county. Because the county lost a certain section to the creation of Chester County, most histories tend to treat the great land cession as a wiping of the historical slate. The unfortunate tendency is to treat that section as if it had never existed within the bounds of our own great county. Therefore, some attempt will be made to fill in certain gaps.

Now we are brought to what most readers eagerly await, a mention of a familiar name, perhaps any name with which they can discover a connection. Therefore, we begin our discussion of the names, places, events, and activities that define who so many of us are today. Who were the Carolinians, the Virginians, and the Highlanders of Tennessee who etched out a new civilization in this rugged and wild land? They were your ancestors and mine. They were our own immediate forefathers.

Before we take the plunge in the high tides of history that swirl on the written page, we must take some matters into account. One must first understand that the author does not have access to every private family

6. Wright, Talbott, McCann, *Reminiscences 130th Anniversary Edition*.

history or collection of documents, photographs and other records. He had just those which have been shared and discussed with him through the years. There is also the dilemma of deciding what family or even what individual to discuss. Because so much time has passed, it becomes the job of the writer-historian to take on the role of detective and to determine to his own satisfaction who did what so long ago. Perhaps no two people will ever agree on the same account, but he must determine for himself the order of these things according to the evidence, and yet when new evidence surfaces later down the road, he may change his own mind. Here he presents a volume of information concerning many of these people, information which many, if not most, will never see otherwise. Therefore, enjoy!

The Early Settlers

We have been blessed in some small sense in that General Wright, as well as other reputable sources, long ago recorded the names of our early settlers in north McNairy County. These names are still present in today's north McNairy County lexicon as well as many more. We choose these because they were the first. Some of the names listed below are discussed further in this chapter, but others are not, instead individual members of other families are discussed in other appropriate chapters. The names of our early pioneers included Anderson, Beard, Bryant, Bulliner, Burkhead, Cason, Clayton, Clemons, Cobb, Deaton, Estes, Floyd, Fowler, Garner, Hallis, Hodges, Hurst, Ingraham, Jackson, Johnson, Jones, Kirby, Lane, Lowrance, Maness, McHolstead, McIntyre, Merchuson, Muse, O'Neal, Patterson, Plunk, Putman, Randolph, Rankin, Robinson, Robbins, Rowsey, Sells, Sipes (Cypes), Sheffield, Smith, Stewart, Wade, Walsh, Ward, Weaver, and Womble, among others.[7]

By 1860, a number of families had settled in the north McNairy County communities of Anderson's Store, Cotton Ridge, White Plains and McIntyre's Crossing. These families included: Ash, Ball, Barham, Barnes, Barrett, Blakeley, Brett (Britt), Brewer, Browder, Brown, Burkeens (Brickeens), Bullman, Curtis, Davidson, Davis, Dickey, Emmons, Ethridge, Farnsworth, Freeling, Gattis, Harris, Hendrix, Highsmith, Holder, Hughbanks, Inman, Keeter, Kirkpatrick, Lee, Long, Lott, Macon,

7. *Id.*

THE EARLY SETTLERS OF NORTH McNAIRY COUNTY

Malone, Mason, Massengill, McCallum, McCaskill, McCoy, Miller, Mills, Moore, Moser, Nailor (Naylor), Ozment (Ausment), Peoples, Phillips, Pickett, Pigram (Pegram), Pope, Reed, Robertson, Robeson, Rogers, Sewell, Stansell, Swaim, Tacker, Tedford, Tillmon (Tillman), Tisdale, Vires, Walker, White, Whitman, Worthington, Wright.[8]

It may never be established as fact the names of the first family or families who dared to dream of a new existence in what many of us now call "home." However, we have the stories of a number of families who very early made the arduous overland journey. Perhaps the first family to lay claim to settlement in this area was the Hodges' family. Of this interesting and somewhat peculiar family much will be discussed in the course of this work. Regardless, the various members of the Hodges' family claimed that their forebearer, Elisha Hodges, came to north McNairy County from Wilson County, Tennessee in 1818, the year of the treaty.[9] Elisha's settlement in this county, or the territory that would become this county, was in the company of his father, Jesse Hodges Sr., and other members of the family.

Elisha was a man of proud military accomplishment, indeed a legacy passed down to his sons, Elijah and Horry.[10] Elisha's military accolades and accomplishments would span at least three decades. He was commissioned an ensign in the State Militia on May 21, 1816.[11] Interestingly enough, the state capitol was located in Knoxville at that time. On January 12, 1832, Elisha was commissioned a captain of the 80th Regiment of the Tennessee Militia.[12] On January 9, 1836, he was commissioned a lieutenant colonel in the 80th Regiment.[13]

Despite all of Elisha's many accomplishments, it was Elisha's father, Jesse Hodges Sr., who was truly the first generation of this old family to migrate to McNairy County. Jesse was born on February 11, 1754, in

---

8. 1860 United States Federal Census.

9. *McNairy County Independent Appeal*, June 23, 1922.

10. Elijah James Hodges and Horry Hodges, both captains of the U.S. Sixth Tennessee Cavalry, are subjects of brief biographical sketches in Chapter Four of this work. Incidentally, this Horry Hodges was the uncle of the famed orator and educator Horry Hodges (1868–1940).

11. Military commission record contained in the Hodges' Family Papers, Private Collection of Ben Davidson, Ramsey, Illinois.

12. *Id.*

13. *Id.*

Halifax County, Virginia.[14] He married Elizabeth Collins on October 18, 1775, in Pittsylvania County, Virginia.[15] Jesse Hodges represented and was, indeed, a remnant of a quickly disappearing band of patriots who forged a new nation out of the fires of uncertainty and revolution.

In October of 1780, at the age of 26, Jesse joined the American Revolution as a volunteer.[16] He served in a company under the command of Captain William Dick, Lt. William Wilkerson, and Order Sergeant David Chism.[17] The following account of the company's activities were recorded in the "anonymous" record:

> The Company was organized and marched from Pittsylvania County, where he (Jesse) volunteered, to Halifax old Court House. There they joined a brigade commanded by Gen. Stephens and Col. Hayne Morgan, who were under the command of Gen. Greene. The Brigade was marched to various places in Virginia and North Carolina, eventually reaching Guilford County, North Carolina.
>
> Jesse Hodges was at Guilford only a short time where the army realized a need for wagons and teams. Learning that he had a team and wagon at home, the general sent him back to Pittsylvania County, Virginia, to get them. He was accompanied by three guards. He returned as soon as possible and was placed under Abner Wells, wagon master. Mr. Jamison was head wagon master. It was February 1781 when he rejoined the army with his wagon and team. He was with the army during the battles at Ramolis Mills and Guilford Court House and was ordered to drive his wagon and team to Troublesome Iron Works. The army followed the British across Deep River into South Carolina, and Jesse returned to his home in Pittsylvania County, Virginia, with a discharge which ended his first six-months tour of duty.
>
> Shortly after returning home, Jesse Hodges was again drafted for a six-months tour of duty under Capt. Thomas

---

14. Hodges' Family Papers. Private Collection of Ben Davidson, Ramsey, Illinois.
15. *Id.*
16. *Id.* The information contained in this record has been substantiated in other works and records.
17. *Id.*

Hudgers. He was mustered into service at Bucklier Tavern, Pittsylvania County, Virginia. He served 21 days of this enlistment and hired a cousin of his, James Casey, to serve out the balance of his time.[18]

Jesse continued to live in Pittsylvania County, Virginia, after the war until about 1797. He then relocated to Wilson County, Tennessee. Finally he moved to the area which would become north McNairy County in either 1818 or 1820. Jesse and Elizabeth had thirteen children; the first ten were born in Pittsylvania County, Virginia, and the last three in Wilson County, Tennessee. Their children were James C. Hodges, William Cayson Hodges, Jesse Hodges Jr., Josiah Hodges, Jeremiah Hodges, Marcus Hodges, France "Fanny" (Hodges) Hollis, Tabitha (Hodges) Barton, Elisha Hodges, Elijah Hodges, Thomas Collins Hodges, Elizabeth (Hodges) Ward and Harvey Hodges.[19] A few of these children would eventually settle permanently in north McNairy County or in other nearby counties.

Apparently Jesse and Elizabeth settled in the portion of McNairy County, which is now Chester County, close to present-day Mifflin. Prior to their deaths, Jesse and Elizabeth were living with their son William Cayson Hodges in present-day northern McNairy County. Elizabeth died on January 6, 1842, and Jesse followed her shortly thereafter on March 18, 1842. They lived to great ages for the time. Their exact burial site is currently unknown. However, there has been much speculation on the part of that family other interested individuals that Jesse and Elizabeth Hodges are buried in Mount Carmel Cemetery.

A number of the Hodges' family became actively involved in the affairs of McNairy County upon their settlement here. As mentioned, family sources asserted the family settled here in 1818.[20] Another source

18. As strange as it may seem today, during the time of the Revolutionary War and, at least, up to the end of the Civil War, it was common for men to hire replacements so they could return home and resume their business there.

19. If one is researching the Hodges' family, they must be constantly on guard not to confuse the various members of this family with another by the same name in a different generation. For example, there are numerous family members with the name Horry, Harvey, Elisha, and Elijah among others.

20. *McNairy County Independent Appeal*, June 23, 1922.

stated such settlement occurred between 1818 and 1822.[21] Some of the more active members of this family, including Captains Horry and Elijah Hodges and Dr. Henry Hodges and brother Horry, are discussed later in this work in their respective relevant sections. However, a few of the early members are discussed here.

Some of the children of Jesse Hodges Sr. did not settle or reside here at any time. The oldest son, James C. Hodges, a major in the War of 1812, drowned in the Cumberland River in September of that same year.[22] Others like Josiah settled in Henderson County (now Chester County), some of the girls married and remained in Wilson County, and still the fates of others are unknown.[23]

Yet still there was Elisha and William Cayson Hodges left to assist in molding the early days of McNairy County's future. One can only imagine the brunt borne by such sons who remained in the new territory to aid an elderly father in the quest to start anew. And yet there was a bigger goal than even that of familial relations. These sons who remained were, probably without realization, the new fathers of a new county and a new order.

William Cayson Hodges, the second son, was born in Pittsylvania County, Virginia, on September 22, 1778. He was married twice, first to Mary Douglas in 1811 and upon her death around 1815 or 1816, to Rebecca Calloway. He had at least six children.[24] They included William Cayson Hodges, Jr. (b. 1807), Jeremiah Hodges (b. 1810), James G. Hodges (January 22, 1815–1902), Tempa Hodges (b. 1819), Joseph H. Hodges (b. 1820), and a daughter whose name is lost to history. William Cayson Hodges died sometime after 1840. Although he may be buried in Mount Carmel Cemetery, this cannot be confirmed.

As for Elisha, he was born on November 24, 1794. He married Millie Ward (b. 1790) on July 28, 1814, in Wilson County. The couple had six children: Jesse C. Hodges, Tabitha (Hodges) White, John E.C. Hodges, Elisha M.R. Hodges, Captain Elijah J. Hodges, and Captain Horry Hodges. Elisha was among the first to purchase a lot in the

---

21. Newspaper clipping found among the papers of D. H. Lott. The historical items were found under the heading of "Good Springs" and were recorded by D. H. Lott.

22. Hodges' Family Papers. Private Collection of Ben Davidson of Ramsey, Illinois.

23. Id.

24. Id.

new town of Purdy in the early 1820s. A testament to his role in early McNairy County is his place on the Pioneer Monument erected by and large through the efforts of General Marcus Joseph Wright in 1904. It is believed that Elisha built the old Hodges' home which housed the family until the mid 1950s. Elisha died on September 1, 1847, and although his exact burial spot is currently unknown, most now believe he is buried in the Mount Carmel Cemetery.

It is vitally important the reader keep in mind these early families are not being presented and discussed in the order of their settlement in the county. Rather they are being presented indiscriminately as being among those first families. Also there are those families who early had a number of distinguished members who rendered service politically, religiously, militarily and otherwise. Having thus discussed the Hodges family, let us examine a dozen or so more active and influential families of north McNairy County.

The Kerby family was among the first mentioned as landowners in McNairy County land records. In fact, a Kerby had the distinction of being the firstborn white child in what would be McNairy County. Francis and Nancy Sparks Kerby brought a son, Hugh, into this world in December of 1821 near present-day Mt. Carmel Cemetery. Francis was born in 1788, and when he came to McNairy County, he settled north of present-day Finger, west of Huggins Creek. He was married to the former Nancy Sparks, who was born in 1790. The couple came very early to the county with their son John Kerby. Little else is known of the couple, but it is known they died in the period of the 1840s and were buried in the Kerby Cemetery north of Finger, now located on Westvaco lands.

Hugh Kerby, the pioneer child, served for a time as the postmaster of the Huggins Creek Post Office. He came to the post on June 7, 1854, succeeding James Wilson. However, the post office was discontinued on October 24, 1854. Hugh Kerby married Martha Jane Hendrix, the daughter of Richard Ivy Hendrix and Rebecca Cherry Hendrix. Hugh and Martha had two children, Nancy E. Kerby Lain and Alonzo Kerby. At Hugh's death in 1870, he was buried in Mount Carmel Cemetery. In the 1950s, a substantial monument was erected at Mount Carmel to Hugh's memory. The inscription on that stone reads as follows:

> First White Child
> Born in McNairy Co.
> HUGH KERBY
> 1821–1870
> In Memory Of Hugh Kerby Born Near
> The Spot Where Here He Is Buried
> The First White Child Born In The Land
> Which In 1823 Became McNairy County
> This Monument Is Erected By A Greatful [*sic*]
> People In Honor Of A Child Of
> The Wilderness Son If The Old
> Frontier Who With Others Of His Era
> Built For Us All A Citadel Of Liberty
> In A Beautiful Land

Hugh's brother, James "Hickory Jim" Kerby, was another of the first children born in the wilderness of McNairy County, pioneer children, if you will. He was born in 1824, the year after the county was officially established. He and his wife Emily (1829–1911) had a number of children including Mrs. Dovie (Kerby) Weaver. Hickory Jim died in 1878 and was buried in Refuge Cemetery.

One early family, a large family, which has not been discussed at length in previous works is the Plunk family.[25] This is a large and well-known family with branches all over McNairy County and the state of Tennessee. Unfortunately, a detailed history of this interesting family cannot be produced on these pages. Instead a small portion of their history will be presented in hopes that it will be of assistance to someone.

Dr. Peter Plunk is thought to have been born in Germany and then migrated to America. Although there has been speculation as to his wife's maiden name, it is known that her given name was Barbara. Dr. Plunk was an "herb doctor," most likely a doctor by virtue of experience and experiment, rather than by degree and licensure. He first acquired land in 1766 in Lincoln County, North Carolina. This property consisted of about 300 acres along Long Creek in present-day Gaston County, North Carolina. This particular tract of land was to be sold with the proceeds split among his seven daughters, this according to a 1789 document

---
25. The material in this sketch was provided by Gracie Webster and Marvin Hand.

purporting to be the will of Dr. Plunk. Regardless, Dr. Plunk bought an additional 450 acres on Lyles Creek near Conover, North Carolina, in present-day Catawba County, in 1785. Dr. Plunk called this farm home until his death in 1791. This farm was devised to his two sons, John and Jacob, with a life estate reserved to his widow, Barbara Plunk.

It was sometime after the death of Barbara Plunk in the early 1800s, most probably during the first decade, that steps were taken to begin a migration to western Tennessee. John Plunk sold his share of the Lyles Creek farm to Nicholas Carpenter in 1812. Carpenter was married to John's sister, Catherine Plunk. Jacob sold his 220 acre share for $1,000 to Elexius Conner on March 6, 1824. Following this transaction, the sons of Dr. Peter Plunk began their trek to wild western Tennessee.

According to family history and tradition, the brothers and other members of the Plunk family first settled in Madison County, near Pinson and the famous Native American Indian burial mounds. After a short period of time, the family moved to north McNairy County. Jacob and his wife Catherine and their seven sons and one daughter settled between present-day Bethel Springs and Finger. Brother John and his wife, Elizabeth, and their six sons and three daughters settled near Sweetlips Creek.

John was the older brother to Jacob, who was an "herb doctor" like their father. Tradition holds that the two brothers experienced a falling out over the issue of slavery. What distinguishes this dispute over a controversial issue which caused many such disputes is the time period within it must have occurred. Jacob, born around the year 1775, died in about 1828, a full thirty-three years before the beginning of the War Between the States. Upon Jacob's death, he was laid to rest in the present-day Plunk Cemetery where he lies today under a large beech tree. This burial would classify Plunk Cemetery as one of the older cemeteries in the county.

John Plunk, born around 1773, died sometime in the 1850s and was buried somewhere on his farm, now known as the Pickett farm. Several of Jacob's sons continued their occupation of the area with the passing years, which accounts for the term "Plunktown," which the area is often called. These sons included Joseph Plunk (1809–1885) and wife Nancy (Haley) Plunk, and David Plunk (1815–1883) and wife Anna

(Gage) Plunk. All four are buried in Plunk Cemetery, with Joseph and Nancy in unmarked graves.

Other early Plunks included Elisha Plunk, the son of George Plunk and the grandson of Jacob Plunk, who was a miller around Liberty in 1850. It was told that Elisha set out a pine tree by the corner of his smokehouse. What is significant about that tree, which has been gone since at least the 1950s, is that all of the natural pine growth around Liberty since that time supposedly sprang from that one planted pine tree. Elisha's son, the Reverend Hollie Plunk, recalled many decades ago that his father enjoyed hunting, fishing, and running a mill. Sometime after the 1850s, Elisha moved to Missouri, where he remained for 51 years, and finally in his old age, came home to die and be buried in the Mount Carmel Cemetery.[26] Other members of the Plunk family are profiled in other chapters of this work. This has been only a glimpse at this large and extended family.

Among the first families in McNairy County, one cannot overlook the hearty and enterprising Anderson family. Although this fine family only resided within the confines of the county for a few short decades, they left behind a namesake and a proud legacy for all. Their influence and industrious nature could be felt far from north McNairy County and benefited many then and still today.

William Taylor Anderson was born on May 24, 1804, in Sullivan County, Tennessee. He was the son of Thomas and Mary (Davidson) Anderson. According to a family historian, Thomas was born in Tennessee in 1779 and Mary, born in 1780, was a member of the "Chestnut Street, Philadelphia" Davidsons.[27] According to this same source, both are buried at Purdy, Tennessee, but that is incorrect. The mother, Mary (Davidson) Anderson, is buried in White Plains Cemetery near Tar Creek.[28] Most likely, Mr. Anderson is buried in one of the unmarked graves. For the Anderson family relative or otherwise interested reader, the family line can be traced as far back as follows: 1) James Anderson, born and raised in Ireland, 2) William Anderson, born in 1736 presumably in Ireland,

---

26. Other sources state that Elisha Plunk never moved back to north McNairy County, but was only visiting his son Dave Plunk and died while on a visit. His two wives are buried in Missouri.

27. Anderson Family Records File. Jack McConnico Memorial Library, Selmer, Tennessee.

28. See Chapter Eleven of this work for more details; this chapter deals with many of north McNairy County's small cemeteries.

emigrated to the English colonies and married Jane Brian of Virginia, and 3) Thomas Anderson, father of William Taylor Anderson.

According to General Wright, of Confederate fame, William Taylor Anderson was one of the "early settlers of McNairy County," and yet while a boy, his father moved to Bedford County, Tennessee, and settled near Wartrace on the Duck River.[29] In 1822, William left home to begin the difficult trek across the Cumberland Mountains to seek his own opportunities in western Tennessee.[30] He first came to Mount Pinson in Madison County and remained there with his uncle Samuel Anderson for about a year.[31] Although William's industrious and dedicated nature was evidenced by his accumulation of earthy financial wealth, he evidenced such tendencies early, before anyone could count him as wealthy. The year he spent at Mount Pinson, he toiled full-time for the purpose of clearing the land, earning a total of $50 that year.[32]

In late 1822, William moved again, this time to north McNairy County. Here he met a gentleman whose name has been overshadowed by the name of his son and thereby all but forgotten to local history. The man was James Wisdom, the father of William Sargent Wisdom, the county's first banker and financier. The elder Wisdom had already settled on Tar Creek with his family. More will be discussed regarding the Wisdoms in a following sketch.

Nevertheless, William would become very much a part of the Wisdom family. Sometime between 1822 and 1825, he married Mahala Wisdom, the daughter of James. To this union, thirteen children would be born. Those children were Mary Caroline Anderson (b. May 29, 1826), who married Joseph Lawton Rushing; Telitha Jane Anderson (b. May 13, 1828), who married William Walsh; E. Fay Eveline Anderson (b. May 15, 1831), who married Robert Stribling; Susan Anderson (b. January 30, 1833), who was married first to James Trice, then to J. Murchison; James Wisdom Anderson[33] (b. May 31, 1835), who married Ellen

---

29. Wright, Talbott, McCann, *Reminiscences 130th Anniversary Edition*.

30. *Id*.

31. *Id*.

32. *Id*.

33. James Wisdom Anderson and his brother-in-law, William K. Walsh, were both involved in the organization of the First National Bank (formerly Jackson Savings Bank) in 1874. James Wisdom Anderson served as President from 1873 to 1879 and William K. Walsh served as a director

Dunaway; Eleanor Anderson (b. March 13, 1837), who married Dr. Rufus Harris; Thomas Bryant Anderson (b. January 19, 1839), who married Puss Walker; William Harrison Anderson (died in infancy around 1840/41); George Sargent Anderson (b. November 25, 1842, d. December 31, 1862), who was killed at the Battle of Murfreesboro and is the subject of a later sketch; John Harrison Anderson (b. April 15, 1845), who married Sally Temple; Neil Publis Anderson (b. April 14, 1847), who married Lizzie Howard; Hugh Crump Anderson (b. February 2, 1851), who married Helen Bond; and Annette Anderson (b. August 8, 1852, d. May 24, 1860).[34]

Around the time of his marriage to Mahala, William formed a partnership with her brother, William S. Wisdom.[35] The two brothers-in-law engaged in the distillery business. After making some money from this profitable joint venture, William and Mahala relocated one mile south on the Purdy and Mifflin Road.[36] Here, he made his new settlement. The Anderson family lived in a tent until a cabin could be built.[37] Here, William engaged in farming the first few years and did well enough to travel back to Bedford County to retrieve his parents and bring them to his own house.

William was like many of his generation and time. Although he had no formal schooling or education, he picked up the basics on his own.[38] After working all day, he would study by light of the fire, lamp, or candle, until he was proficient in the three basics, ciphering, reading, and writing.[39] Between his settlement and the beginning of the War Between the States, William accumulated great wealth for his day. According to General Wright, "by hard work and rigid economy he [Anderson] accumulated a considerable estate, being worth at the beginning of the war

and later himself as President from 1879 to 1881. John L. Wisdom, a cousin of James Wisdom Anderson, served as President of the same bank from 1881 until 1890 and again from 1903 until 1909. Emma Inman Williams, *Historic Madison: The Story of Jackson and Madison County, Tennessee from Mound Builders to World War I* (Jackson, Tennessee: McCowat-Mercer Press, Inc., 1972), 325–326.

34. Anderson Family Records. Jack McConnico Memorial Library, Selmer, Tennessee.
35. Wright, Talbott, McCann, *Reminiscences 130th Anniversary Edition*.
36. *Id.*
37. *Id.* At this time, it was still probably just William and Mahala.
38. *Id.* William had a total of six weeks of school.
39. *Id.*

forty or fifty thousand dollars, consisting of a fine dwelling house, lands, Negroes, stocks, etc. He was a good farmer and always had plenty of everything around."[40]

William was certainly an active gentleman of the old order. His life, in many ways, revolved around the welfare of the local community and he found several ways to serve. He ran one of the few stores in the settlement and served as the postmaster of Anderson's Store, the community, from October 19, 1846, until April 30, 1857. The post office, was after all, located in William's store building. Due to his influence and prominence as the community's business leader, he became a natural choice for the community's political leader. The voting precinct for the Eighth Civil District was located in the store and William was elected both to the office of constable and magistrate, serving on the McNairy County Quarterly Court for several years. According to General Wright, William was one of the old line Whigs and served as a strong advocate for better education and for internal improvements in the state.[41]

As the War Between the States raged through McNairy County tearing families, farms, businesses, and lives apart, William was not spared. He was a Confederate supporter in a hotbed of Union activists. He lost a son to the lost cause of the Southern states at the battle of Murfreesboro and most everything else to the harsh and hot winds of war. He moved to Jackson, Tennessee, in 1869, as did many McNairy countians sympathetic to the cause of the Confederacy. He died at the age of 66 of pneumonia, on April 8, 1870.[42] His widow, Mahala, would live another twenty years, before joining her husband in the sweet haven of rest called Heaven in 1890. Despite these later disappointments, which were no fault of his own, William Taylor Anderson succeeded in being an advocate of settlement and growth. Anderson's Store is a name that has lived on, long past the community it identified.[43]

After the Anderson family relocated to Madison County, they became very involved in their new community. They were part of a larger migration of prominent McNairy County families to Jackson in Madison County following the end of the War Between the States. In 1872,

40. *Id.*
41. *Id.*
42. *Id.*
43. A further discussion of the Anderson's Store community will be found later in this work.

Mahala Anderson, James Wisdom Anderson, Thomas Bryant Anderson, Neil P. Anderson, Telitha Jane (Anderson) Walsh, Eveline (Anderson) Stribling, Hu C. Anderson, and Eleanor (Anderson) Harris were among those individuals who signed the Presbyterian Articles of Faith.[44] Of the forty-three individuals who signed that article, ten were members of the Anderson family. William T. Anderson and Mahala (Wisdom) Anderson and other members of this old family are buried in the Riverside Cemetery in Jackson, Tennessee.

On the other side of this grand union of William Taylor Anderson and Mahala Anderson is the venerable old Wisdom family. The name well fit the family. In the 1790s, James Wisdom and his family called Rockingham, North Carolina, their home. In fact, James Wisdom's most famous son, William Sargent Wisdom, was brought into this world at that place on July 14, 1796. However, like so many of his day, eager and hungry for new opportunities and new land, James Wisdom moved first to Anderson County, Tennessee, in 1809.

After approximately two years in Anderson County in 1811, he moved again, this time in a somewhat northwestern move. Then in 1820, James Wisdom uprooted his family once again and moved them to West Tennessee, a wilderness for the taming. The family first settled near present-day White Plains Cemetery which is today located on the farm of the late Marcus Barham. In fact, James was the recipient of a land grant.

It was on Tar Creek that many alliances and relationships began as James Wisdom's daughter married the young Anderson. Whether the name be Anderson or Wisdom, a number of fine men and women of ability have "sprung" forth from Mr. James Wisdom. James Wisdom lived out his last few years just a stone's throw from Tar Creek. He was no longer a young man when progress and toil brought him to the newly opened territory and the soon-to-be organized McNairy County. The venerable old James Wisdom, a pioneer and father of pioneers, died on March 13, 1828, and was buried in his settlement in what is commonly referred to as White Plains Cemetery. Though relatively young by today's standards, James Wisdom was in his fifty-fifth year, an advanced age in a time of hardship and very little medical innovation. His widow, Susannah Wisdom, lived another seven years, dying at the age of sixty in November of 1835. She also was buried on the little hill of White Plains.

44. Williams, *Historic Madison*, 309.

THE EARLY SETTLERS OF NORTH McNAIRY COUNTY   29

Interestingly, it appears that White Plains was more than originally thought a few years ago. According to amateur historian and Purdy native Ancell Walker Stovall, the Eighth Civil District "had a population in 1870 of 771 whites and 189 colored, a total of 960. The last land assessment was 22,063 acres, valued at $102,820. The voting place is White Plains and it gives a Republican majority in elections."[45] It was originally thought that the White Plains settlement and community had ceased to exist in the early 1830s after the Wisdoms and Andersons moved away from the Tar Creek settlement and to Purdy or on Purdy-Lexington Road to that area that would become known as Anderson's Store.

Further proof of the substantial nature of this early settlement at White Plains exists in the form of the early memoirs of the late General Marcus J. Wright.[46] Wright worked as a clerk in a store belonging to the Walsh brothers, C. Walsh and J.J. Walsh, at Cotton Ridge on Tar Creek. Wright mentioned having to walk from his residence to the store where he worked "selling goods and receiving and weighing cotton."[47] Apparently the store remained quite busy as General Wright spoke of working often until midnight.[48]

Another early north McNairy County family was the Weaver family, whose earliest known forefather was the blacksmith, Adam Weaver. Born in North Carolina in 1769, Adam Weaver eventually moved west, like so many other pioneers, and settled in Wilson County, Tennessee.[49] There has been much speculation as to the wife of Adam and whether a firm decision has been made regarding her identity is not known. Perhaps only good speculation remains still. In any event, the following three women are possible candidates: Sarah Tippett, Nancy Procter, or

45. Nancy Wardlow Kennedy, transcriber, *Notes of Ancil Walker Stovall: Including the Original Works of A.W. Stovall, Poetry and Speeches* (Selmer, Tennessee: Self-published, 2001), 10, 15.

46. In April 2012, the author discovered the document known as the early memoirs of General Marcus J. Wright. This document had been donated by the General's son, Howard P. Wright, to the Tennessee Historical Society for publication in the Society's historical magazine in 1938. However, the Society's magazine had ceased publication in 1937 and did begin publication of its historical quarterly until 1942. Thereafter, it appears that the memoirs just sat in the archives largely forgotten until 2012.

47. Wright, Talbott, McCann, *Reminiscences 130th Anniversary Edition*.

48. *Id*.

49. Kevin D. McCann, *The McCanns of McNairy County, Tennessee* (Ashland City, Tennessee: Self-published, 1993).

Martha Weaver.[50] The possibilities are as follows: In 1788, in Granville County, North Carolina, there is a marriage between an Adam Weaver and a Sarah Tippett. On October 15, 1793, in Rowan County, North Carolina, an Adam Weaver married a Nancy Proctor. Finally, there appears on the 1830 United States Census for McNairy County, Tennessee, the name of Martha Weaver, a woman between 50 and 60 years of age.[51] The actual identity of Adam Weaver's wife may never be known, but that of his earlier descendants can be.[52]

Adam Weaver received a ten acre grant in Williamson County, Tennessee, on October 26, 1811, and still owned the land as of 1815. The Weavers made their way to north McNairy County around the year 1825. General Wright recorded that John Weaver, son of Adam, came to McNairy County in 1825 and located in the Midwestern part of the county when a wilderness."[53] This area is the present-day community and area of Montezuma. Generations of Weavers have lived and died in this community.

The children of Adam Weaver numbered eleven, four sons and seven daughters.[54] The children are listed and discussed in order of their birth. Absalom Weaver was born in 1791. He married Elizabeth Rupard. John Weaver was born around the year 1792 and married Mary McMillan. Elizabeth Weaver was born sometime in the mid 1790s and married John Lynch on August 8, 1815, in Davidson County, Tennessee. She died sometime around 1848 in Perry County, Illinois. Fanny Weaver was born sometime around 1800 in North Carolina. Nothing else is known of her. Dedemiah Weaver was born around the year 1801 in North Carolina and married Jacob Green Crouse. Christina "Teny" Weaver was born sometime around the year 1811 in Tennessee and married William

---

50. Helen W. Williams, *The Weavers Beginning With Adam*. (Self-published, date unknown).

51. *Id.*

52. An October 8, 1990, letter to Faye (McIntyre) Talbott from Melba (McIntyre) Tullis of Texas states: "I do have the name of Adam Weaver's wife, she was Martha, and he was not from Rowan County, North Carolina, but another county. Deeds prove it and John was probably older than Absalom, as it seems so, when he bought land and sold it back in North Carolina after moving to Williamson County, Tennessee."

53. Wright, Talbott, McCann, *Reminiscences 130th Anniversary Edition*.

54. *Id.* General Wright stated that Weaver had twelve children, but listed only eleven himself. The information that follows is drawn from the author's research, Wright's account, and other family sources and research.

Russell. Lewis Weaver was born in Tennessee on February 27, 1813, and married Violet Nelson. Nancy Weaver was born in 1814 in Tennessee and married John R. Morris. Joshua Weaver was born in 1826 in Tennessee and married Martha Taylor. Finally, Adam Weaver had two daughters, whose names have never been identified and who apparently died relatively early in life.

Now let us examine some of the early branches of Adam Weaver's family more closely. As stated above, Absalom Weaver, presumably Adam's eldest son, was born in North Carolina on May 26, 1791, and married Elizabeth Rupard on July 3, 1819, in Williamson County, Tennessee.[55] Although it is definitely known that Absalom and Elizabeth were living in McNairy County by 1830, it is probable they were here with John in 1825 or shortly thereafter. Absalom died on December 25, 1839, in McNairy County. Elizabeth, born on May 4, 1804, lived on until February 15, 1884, when she passed away at the age of seventy-nine.[56]

The union between Absalom and Elizabeth produced ten children. Sarah Jane Weaver was born on July 7, 1820, in Tennessee and married Robert Thompson McIntyre around 1840, if not earlier. Sarah and Robert had seven children: Antione Jane (McIntyre) Stewart, Elizabeth (McIntyre) Massey, Isaac McKay McIntyre, Amanda (McIntyre) Dickey, John Absalom McIntyre, James Robert McIntyre, and Nancy Caroline McIntyre. Sarah died on January 12, 1875, and was buried in Mount Carmel Cemetery. Susan Weaver was born on February 15, 1822, in Tennessee. Adilude (Adilade) Weaver was born on May 29, 1824, in Tennessee. Lafayette D. Weaver was born on Fenruary 18, 1826, and married Elizabeth Parker on September 11, 1852. They had at least four children: Mary, Sarah, Emily, and an infant by 1860.

John G. Weaver was born on February 16, 1828, in Tennessee. He married Elizabeth A. Minton on December 31, 1865, in McNairy County. John served in the Confederate Thirty-first Tennessee Infantry during the War Between the States. John and Elizabeth had at least three children: William Weaver, who died in infancy; Asjona B. Weaver, a daughter born in 1867; and John A. Weaver, who was born on June 8, 1869, and died on February 21, 1871. John G. Weaver died on June 4,

---

55. McCann, *The McCanns of McNairy County*.

56. Bettye Sitton Reed, *My Three Sons: Volume III, Beene-McIntyre and Allied Lines*. (Privately published, 1985).

1901, and was laid to rest in Cave Springs Cemetery. Sinnai E. Weaver was born on September 1, 1830, in Tennessee and married John James McIntyre. They had at least three sons: James McIntyre, born in 1854, William McIntyre, born in 1858, and John McIntyre, born in 1860. They moved first to Dyer County and then to Lake County, Tennessee.

Elizabeth "Betsey" Weaver was born on July 18, 1832, in McNairy County. Nothing else is known of her. Absalom W. Weaver, Jr., was born on July 29, 1834. He served in the Confederate Thirty-first Tennessee Infantry, just as his brother John. He did not marry until several years after the War. Then in 1875, he married Tilda Emeline Henson in Hardeman County, Tennessee. She was born on March 8, 1856, and died on December 4, 1897, while giving birth to their thirteenth child. Their children were James Albert Weaver, Samuel Absalom Weaver, Susan Elizabeth Weaver, Nancy Adilude Weaver, John Perkins Weaver, William Thomas Weaver, George Allen Weaver, Ada Emeline Weaver, Catherine Alice Weaver, Joseph Harrison Weaver, Cordelia H. "Celia" Weaver, Robert Lee Weaver, and Emma Weaver. Absalom Weaver Jr., remarried to a woman fifty-two years his junior. He died of a heart attack on February 22, 1910, and was buried at Haltom's Chapel Cemetery.

William H. Weaver, born on August 25, 1836, in McNairy County. He married a woman named Margaret in 1855. They had at least one son, Joseph Absalom Weaver, born on June 23, 1859. Annis Weaver was born on December 19, 1838, in McNairy County. In a cemetery near present-day Montezuma, where Absalom Weaver Sr., is said to be buried, as well as his wife and other members of the family, there is an Annis Naylor. Although the author does not recall from memory the dates on the tombstone, it is quite possible and most probable that this is the same Annis Weaver, daughter of Absalom Weaver Sr.

As reported by General Wright, John Weaver, son of Adam Weaver, a soldier of the War of 1812, and wife Mary McMillan, had nine children of their own. They were: Isaac Weaver, who married Susan Muse; William Weaver, who married Sarah Pope; John Weaver, who married Carodis Pope; George Weaver, who married Susan Yates; Daniel Weaver, who married Lavinia Ward; Robert McMillan Weaver, who married Mary A. Highfield Womble; James Weaver, who married Susan James; Matthew Weaver; and Mary Weaver, who married Joel Pope. Although this sketch may seem somewhat tangled and quite lengthy, it does not do justice to this early family. There are many stories that go unrecorded in this account, which serves primarily to show the relationships and connections between the various members of this wide and extended family.

Another of the older families in the county is the Ward family. Unfortunately, not as much is known of the earlier history of this strong family, as little scholarship has been accomplished thus far.[57] The ancestors of the Ward family in McNairy County first settled in the northern section of the county near Mount Carmel in 1825. It was in November of that year that Matthew and Esther Ward moved into a tent on the hilltop now known as Mount Carmel Cemetery.[58] Here, Matthew set about the work and toil of setting out his fruit orchards and building "his humble home in the then wilderness."[59] According to one source, others joined Matthew Ward and a settlement was formed.[60] According to family sources, Matthew built his home in February, 1826, with the building of a one room log cabin northwest of Mount Carmel hill.

Among the children of these first settlers were Luke Ward, who was among those listed on the Pioneer Monument at Selmer, Duprina Ward, Lavina (Ward) Weaver, and Nathan Gilbert Ward. Nathan Gilbert Ward was born in 1821 and was married to Mary Ann (Loumiza) Ward. The couple had five children: John Brooks Ward, Nathan Richard Ward, John Clayton Ward, and Saphronia and Nicie Ward.

The family produced many good citizens whose influence has endured into the late twentieth century. It was through the line of Nathan Gilbert Ward and Mary Ann (Loumiza) Ward that many educators would eventually come, including Leonard Ward and Myrtle (Ward) Smith.

One of north McNairy County's earliest prominent settlers was a man whose family would eventually grow and extend into all parts of McNairy, Chester, Madison, and Shelby counties. Furthermore, most members of the family found prominence and success wherever they settled. This man was John S. Ingraham and his family included the Ingrahams and Ingrams. A fitting tribute to Ingraham and his determination to settle a strange and wild land is the placement of his name on

---

57. What is known has been gleaned from old newspaper accounts and a paper completed by the son of the late teacher Leonard Ward, Dennis Ward, himself a school teacher.

58. Dennis Ward, *Ward Family Genealogy*. (Circa 1986).

59. "Mount Carmel Memorial," *McNairy County Independent Appeal*, May 20, 1927.

60. *Id.*

the earlier mentioned 1904 Monument to the Early Settlers of McNairy County, which stands on the courthouse grounds in Selmer.

John S. Ingraham came to north McNairy County in the early 1820s. According to the eminent publisher Westin A. Goodspeed, John S. Ingraham was the son of James Ingraham and was a native of old Virginia. He relocated to Wayne County, Kentucky at an early age. Afterward, he was to become the third white settler in McNairy County subsequent to the opening of the territory after its purchase from the Chickasaw Nation. Ingraham had migrated to McNairy County immediately from Bedford County, Tennessee or so it appears. His son, James M. Ingraham, was born in Bedford County, Tennessee in 1815, some four years prior to the Chickasaw or Jackson Purchase Treaty.[61] James married a Miss Elizabeth Spencer, a native of Wilson County, Tennessee. The couple married in Madison County, Tennessee and subsequently relocated to McNairy County, Tennessee, where James was reared. Here, the couple's best known child would be born. That child was Lee H. Ingraham. Dr. Lee H. Ingraham will be treated more fully in Chapter Three of this work.

John S. Ingraham owned a large section of land along the present McCormick and Clarence Barham Roads. The area in which John and his wife, Rebecca (Hardin) Ingraham, lived is now known as the old Tom Barham or Ray Barham place. The old Ingraham home was located across the road from the present Barham house and just south of the old Ingraham family cemetery. The house was a story and a half with a stairway in between the rooms. What upstairs area existed to the house was similar. Like most homes of the time, if not all, the house was constructed of rough hewn logs to which weatherboard was later applied. The weatherboard was later painted red and the house became known far and wide as the "Red House." Located behind the house was the kitchen, which was connected to the main house by a breezeway. Such construction was essential to prevent kitchen fires from devastating the entire structure. Behind the house were the slave quarters and the smokehouse.

Unfortunately, Rebecca did not live long in her home or in McNairy County. She died on February 16, 1830, at the relatively young age of forty and was buried in what would become the Ingraham family cemetery. However, it must be remembered that such a frontier life was hard on a woman, especially after bearing a good number of children,

61. *Id.*

and it aged her quickly beyond her years. Rebecca (Hardin) Ingraham was most likely no different. With Rebecca's passing, John was left to raise their family of four sons and two daughters. He did so unmarried with no help, unless it was perhaps from the assistance of a female slave acting as a sort of nanny or "mammy." Eventually, however, John did remarry. Sometime, probably between 1845 and 1848, he married a woman who had been widowed herself, Margaret Butler. She brought with her to the Ingraham household four children of her own. They ranged in age from fifteen years to six years. Those children were Bennett Butler, Martha Butler, John C. Butler, and Joannah Butler. Then John and Margaret had three children of their own: Mary E. Ingraham, born in 1849; Celia L. Ingraham, born in 1851 and married to A.B. Person on May 11, 1873; and Granville Ingraham, born in 1853.[62]

The surviving records reveal something about John's dealings. Like many men of wealth, he bought and sold land and slaves as a common course of business. The following are examples from his business dealings. John bought a sixteen year old Negro boy from B.B. Adams for $750.00. Adams warranted the boy to be "sound, healthy, and sensible and a slave for life."[63] In other transactions, John bought a thirteen year old Negro boy named Jacob for $500.00 from James Wilson and an eleven year old Negro boy named Jack from Alexander H. Ingraham and Sally Basinger for $500.00.[64] Interestingly, John began giving property and slaves away to his children about the time he married Margaret Butler. On May 27, 1848, he gave his daughter Virginia A. Ingraham Walsh a Negro girl named Lucy Ann and his daughter Elizabeth Jane Ingraham a Negro girl named Mariah.[65] To his sons, he gave land. This was commonly done to show respect for the love and fidelity of a first family after the father had begun a second.

John S. Ingraham died at the age of sixty-five years, a relatively old age for the time, on August 28, 1855. He was buried next to Rebecca in the family cemetery.[66] At a time when land brought often no more than a

62. In regards to Mary E. Ingraham, there was a Mary E. who married O.D. Young on January 5, 1865, and another Mary E. who married Robert F. Carter on April 29, 1869.

63. *McNairy County Deed Book B*, 211.

64. *McNairy County Deed Book B*, 291, 341–342.

65. *McNairy County Deed Book C*, 267.

66. Goodspeed recorded John S. Ingraham's age at death as being seventy-one years of age.

dollar to a few dollars an acre, John S. Ingraham's real estate was valued at $3000 in 1850. This gives some indication to the extent of his real estate, this even after he had deeded a substantial portion to his children.

Another of the early families in north McNairy County was the Walsh family, who was related by marriage to the Ingrahams. The Walsh family hailed from Wilkes County, North Carolina. Brothers John and Jonathan Walsh came to McNairy County in 1827. John married Elizabeth Allen and from this union would come seven children, six sons and one daughter. They were William C. Walsh, who married Harriet Spencer; John Walsh, who died while still a young man; Madison Walsh, who married Martha Johnson; Thomas Walsh, who wed Katherine Kirby; Jefferson Walsh, who never married; Jesse Walsh, who married Virginia A. "Jennie" Ingraham, the daughter of John S. Ingraham; and Nancy Walsh, who became Mrs. A.M. Burton. This family was, by and large, of the Methodist persuasion and split in its politics.

The other Walsh brother to come to north McNairy County in its early days, Jonathan Walsh, married Winaford Kirby. To this couple was born ten children, six sons and four daughters. They were Henderson Walsh, who was married to Evaline Harrison; William K. Walsh, who married Telitha Anderson, the daughter of William Taylor Anderson; T.W. Walsh, who remained a bachelor; John L. Walsh, who wed Martha Murchison; J.F. Walsh, the husband of Elmira Rogers; E.T. Walsh, who married Virginia Kincaid; Elvire Walsh, the wife of Spencer Holbert; Sarah Walsh, who was married to Council Mayo; Julia Walsh, who became Mrs. W.D. Jopling; and Mary Walsh, who married R.G. Raney. This branch of the family was largely Presbyterian and likewise split in their political leanings.

Mostly this was a family of farmers and merchants. In 1850, William Walsh and Madison Walsh were listed on the U.S. Census as merchants and Edwin Walsh a clerk. In 1860, Jack Walsh was listed as a farmer. According to some sources, some members of the Walsh family eventually moved west. According to General Wright, "the old men lived to a ripe old age, died, and were buried in this county."[67] It is presumed he was referring to John and Jonathan Walsh, the subjects of his sketch and this sketch.

---

67. Wright, Talbott, McCann, *Reminiscences 130th Anniversary Edition*.

One of the early families whose prominence would grow was the Lane or Lain family. Thomas Lane was born in North Carolina on March 15, 1807. He was married to Jane A. (Holder) Lane and they had at least six children. They were Martha E. Lain, who married John F. Putman in 1866; James Simpson Lain, who was married to Nancy E. Kirby in 1866; William M. Lain, who wed Sarah A. Thomas in 1873, Nannie C. Robbins in 1879, and Susan V. Rhodes in 1897; Alexander C. Lane, who married Amanda C. Wilson in 1875 and Martha "Mattie" Croskery in 1880; Louisa D. Lain, who married Thomas Croskery in 1887; and Rueben G. Lain, who died just shy of his twentieth birthday.

Apparently Thomas Lane also had a brother by the name of Reuben Lane, for in 1837, the two sold twenty-five acres of land to Archibald Brown on the waters of Huggins' Creek. The reader will also note the two spellings of the name "Lane." On all of the tombstones at Mount Carmel Cemetery, with the exception of A.C. Lane, the name is spelled Lain. However, in old land deeds and grants and in much of the early scholarship on McNairy County's history, the name is spelled "Lane." Most of the family remained close to the Finger area and are buried in Mount Carmel Cemetery. Jane A. (Holder) Lane died on August 25, 1871, at the age of fifty. Thomas A. Lane died on November 15, 1886, and was buried at Mount Carmel. Other members of this family are treated more fully in other sections of this work.

One of the families whose name surfaces quite frequently in a examination of north McNairy County's early history is that of the Lowrance (Lorance) family. Abram (Abraham) Lorance came to north McNairy County in 1824 from Chatham County, North Carolina. He most likely settled on lands that he received through land grants, as he received more than one. He was said to have been the first person buried in Mount Carmel Cemetery, but that is now doubtful as he lived to a ripe old age and far past the establishment of the cemetery. It is conceivable he had an aged father whom he buried there shortly after their arrival, but that is pure speculation and no more. Among the members of his family were Elizabeth Lowrance, who married John Plunk, and Jacob Lowrance, the former trustee of McNairy County. In the mid 1830s, there was also a Nicholas Lowrance living in north McNairy County. It is possible that he left McNairy County at an early time. Little is known regarding Nicholas Lowrance with the exception of a few bills of sale and deeds of trust found in McNairy County register of deeds office. Jacob Lowrance, one of the best known members of this family, is treated more fully in Chapter Seven of this work.

Another early family of whom little is currently known is the Smith family. It is known that Hugh Smith settled in the northern section of the county near present-day Talleytown in present-day Chester County. Hugh was born on February 26, 1779. He was a man of apparent wealth for his day in that he owned eight Negro slaves in 1840. At that time, the price of slaves could range anywhere from five hundred to two thousand dollars. Little is known regarding Smith's family. James T. Smith, who was born on October 16, 1818, and was presumably a son of Hugh Smith, died on August 24, 1855, and was buried in the Smith-Ingraham portion of what is now New Oak Grove Cemetery. A couple of months later, on October 27, 1855, Hugh Smith passed away and was buried next to James. It is definitely known that Hugh had a son named William A. Smith, who died at the early age of twenty-four in 1862. The mother's name was S.W. Smith. A girl by the name of Margaret J.D. Smith was also buried within feet of Hugh. Their exact dates can be found in Chapter Eleven of this work.

One of the old families with whom the northern section of the county and its history and development are linked are the McIntyres of North Carolina. Like many families of the previous decade, they came over primitive roads and "highways" with little more than hope to sustain them. Still unlike many others families, this one was led by a widowed mother of five. Isaac McIntyre died on January 22, 1820, in Mecklenburg County, North Carolina. His widow, Elizabeth (Thompson) McIntyre, struggled the next few years to raise those five children. After years of struggle and frustration in North Carolina, Elizabeth moved her family across the mountains to western Tennessee. For a total of three hundred dollars, she bought fifty acres of land from John Brower in McNairy County on November 7, 1833. It was here that Elizabeth and her four sons settled.

Isaac and Elizabeth McIntyre's five children were Sarah "Sally" C. McIntyre, who married Peter E. Ross on March 11, 1830, in Mecklenburg County, North Carolina; John James McIntyre, who wed Sinnai E. Weaver, the daughter of Absalom Weaver Sr., and eventually settled in Lake County, Tennessee; Robert Thompson McIntyre, who married

Sarah Jane Weaver, the daughter of Absalom Weaver Sr., and is discussed in great detail in this work; Isaac McKay McIntyre; and William Cogbourne McIntyre, who eventually settled in Dyer County, Tennessee.

One is compelled to question themselves as to who Elizabeth knew in McNairy County. Did a neighbor from Mecklenburg County settle in McNairy County? Did a relative settle here previously? Did Elizabeth become so determined to leave North Carolina that she was willing to go anywhere for a fresh start regardless of the hardship or loneliness? These are valid questions. It is a difficult concept to fathom, a widow with four younger sons making such an arduous trek alone. We are certain of one thing: Elizabeth was dependent upon herself and four relatively young sons to make her new beginning as well as their own, for there appears to have been no safety net for them whatsoever in this new land.

Elizabeth and son William lived together while the others found mates, started families and moved away. Only Robert Thompson would stay in the county for the duration of his life and see most of his descendants remain here also. Elizabeth died in north McNairy County on January 8, 1858, while living with William. She was buried in Mount Carmel Cemetery. Only after her death did William move on to Dyer County, Tennessee.

Another family that came to north McNairy County at an early date was the Draper family. Draper family historians have stated they migrated to McNairy County around 1833 or 1834. This name would later remain in existence in north McNairy County around the turn of twentieth century but it was borne by the former black slaves of the white Draper family. John Draper and his mother, Joicy Draper, and family migrated to north McNairy County, Tennessee, from Person County, North Carolina. Joicy Draper, often also referred to as Joyce Draper, was born in Virginia in 1773. Her husband, Solomon Draper, was born sometime between 1765 and 1775 in Virginia. Solomon Draper appears to have died in Person County, North Carolina sometime between 1820 and 1830. By 1840, the Drapers had settled in north McNairy County. In 1840, John Draper had nine members in his household and two slaves. His mother owned eight slaves. By 1850, the family of John and Temperance Draper included: James (age 15), Mary (age 13), Henry (age 10), Elizabeth (age 8), Rufus (age 5), Paralee (age 2), Greene (age 23) and

John (age 18). Seventy-seven year old Joicy Draper was also living with them as well as nine year old William Walker.

What exactly happened to the Draper family here is not entirely known. We know that it is probable that both Joicy Draper and her son John Harrison Draper died in north McNairy County and were buried there. It is possible that the members of the family who died while living in McNairy County were buried in Mount Carmel Cemetery. We know that the Reverend Wilson A. McHolstead preached a funeral for a Mrs. Draper at Mount Carmel in 1887.[68] It is also known that Robert Thompson McIntyre owned certain land which he passed on to his daughter, Amanda (McIntyre) Dickey, known as the Draper land and houses. Regardless, it does appear that John Harrison Draper was deceased by 1868. In 1868, a Chancery Court lawsuit is on file in the McNairy County, Tennessee Chancery Court styled *John G. Wade and A.W. Skinner vs. C.P. Draper, James B. Draper, Buffern Y. Draper, Mary J. Draper, Thomas Wyblood, Paralee Draper, Mary F. Draper, George W. Draper & Remaining Heirs of John Draper, Deceased*. According to the court's notes, all of the defendants, i.e. the Drapers, were now residents of the state of Arkansas. Little is known after this lawsuit. It seems the Drapers moved on west to Arkansas after the War Between the States. Still, the name lived on the form of the black Draper family, the primary bearers of that name being old Gabriel "Gabe" Draper.

One of the last prominent families to settle in north McNairy County was the Floyd family. The Floyds are a family with long roots in this community and although there are few if any left here by the name, their descendants are many. Harmon Purdy Floyd was born in the northeast corner of South Carolina in either 1818 or 1819. According to his grandson, the poet and writer John Mason, "he made the long trip over the mountains" when he was twenty years old, making their arrival date in north McNairy County around 1838 or 1839.[69] According to Mason, coming with Harmon was his father Frederick Floyd and his grandmother Bullock, a native of the Horry District of South Carolina, and her slaves. However, more members of the family traveled here than those three. Let us examine what we can piece together of this family's early history.

---

68. *American Wesleyan*, November 8, 1881. Donna Watson, Assistant Director, Archives and Historical Library, The Wesleyan Church, Indianapolis, Indiana, to the author, June 30, 1994.

69. Neimann, *The Glory of a Common Man*.

Frederick Floyd was born on July 3, 1788, to James Floyd and wife Elizabeth (Page) Floyd. He married Sarah Bullock, who was born on July 22, 1792. Frederick appears to have been living in the Georgetown District when he married Sarah. Some revisionist Floyd family historians state that Frederick was actually married to a Sarah Pitman and that he married her in nearby Robeson County, North Carolina on February 20, 1809.[70]

When the family moved, bringing Sarah's mother, they also brought others of their children. Two daughters, Avy J.G. Floyd and Elizabeth H.M. Floyd, came also, as did another son Francis and his wife Eliza. Unfortunately either the trip or the new homeland was too difficult and laborious for both daughters, as neither survived long in north McNairy County. Elizabeth, who was born on May 15, 1827, passed away on May 20, 1839, just five days after her twelfth birthday. She became most likely the first person to be buried in a new cemetery to be called Floyd Cemetery. However, she would not be alone for long. Avy, who was born on December 8, 1812, and who was twenty-seven years old at the time, died on August 15, 1840. The sick and heart-broken father did not survive long. On October 19, 1840, at the age of fifty-two, Frederick Floyd passed away. Whether Mrs. Bullock died around that time or not is unknown, as her grave has yet to be found. It is most likely among the unmarked at Floyd Cemetery.

As difficult as it may have been, Sarah continued on. Around Christmas of 1840, she was blessed with a grandchild, named Frederick in honor of her husband, who would have been a grandfather. Unfortunately, the new child too was taken by death on March 25, 1841, at the tender age of three months. One can only imagine the strain and heartbreak of a home stricken with so many deaths in such a short time. Yet Harmon Purdy married not long after arriving in the county, surely bringing some amount of joy to the grieve stricken home. This family would eventually thrive and do well, with a great many offspring to prosper and carry on their good name.

The Putman family is another of north McNairy County's enigmatic families in that we know so very little about them. Yet we do know that they were apparently a respected family given their ties. Martin Putman

---

70. This account is held to by a Mr. Marty Grant who states such on his website http://martygrant.com. He attributes at least a portion of this information to a Mr. Fred Johnson.

was born on August 20, 1818, to Griggs and Sally Putman and was living in north McNairy County by 1840. There is some confusion as to whether he was born in North Carolina or Morgan County, Alabama. According to family historians, Martin married a woman by the name of Juda in or around the year 1839. According to the 1840 United States Census, Martin and his wife of less than one year, Juda Putman, were living in McNairy County. By 1850, Martin and Juda have five children. Again, according to family historians, Juda died between 1852 and 1854.

Martin and Juda's children were: John Franklin Putman (August 23, 1841–July 29, 1921), Tulitha Putman (March 25, 1843–March 8, 1900), Alie Putman (January 20, 1845–December 21, 1919), Harriet E. Putman (1847–?), William A. Putman (August 1849–February 1925), and Nancy E. Putman (August 11, 1854–November 5, 1924). As Martin and four of his children are buried in Mount Carmel Cemetery, it is also likely that Juda Putman is buried there as well. Neither Tulitha nor Alie ever married and remained spinsters to their death. Harriet married John M. Lowrance on January 27, 1867, in McNairy County, Tennessee. John M. Lowrance was the son of Jacob and Susana Lowrance. He and Harriet had at least one son, John L. Lowrance (March 28, 1872–November 9, 1973). Nancy E. Putman married Isom Christopher Buchanan "Buck" Naylor on March 4, 1880, with minister S.A. Norwood officiating.

John Franklin Putman married Martha E. Lain on December 23, 1866, and the couple had five children: William Harrison Putman, Louellen Putman, Mary Frances Putman, Thomas Franklin Putman, and Martin Ernest Putman. Old Martin Putman lived a long life seeing the county's development from just few years after its formation until his death on February 2, 1900. He was laid to rest in the old burying ground of Mount Carmel. Certain of Martin's children would survive into the 1920s.

Another old family whose impact was strong but long-lived is the Randolph family. This family could trace its McNairy County roots to John G. Randolph. This John Randolph was born in 1797 in the state of North Carolina but at an early age became a resident of Wilson County, Tennessee.[71] His father served in the War of 1812 and so did young John. Following his father's death during the war while at Pensacola,

---

71. Matt. Adams recorded in Wright's *Reminiscences* that Randolph was born in 1795, but his tombstone records his birth date as 1797.

Florida, John returned to Wilson County. John married Miss N. Gayle Wynne near Jackson, Tennessee, and migrated from Wilson County to McNairy County in 1838. He moved to the village of Montezuma in the Fourth Civil District. He was a farmer and large slaveholder. According to Matt. Adams in Wright's *Reminiscences of the Early Settlement and Early Settlers of McNairy County, Tennessee*, John G. Randolph "was a man of great energy and perseverance."[72]

John G. Randolph was a liberal supporter of educational and religious causes. A Methodist and a Democrat, John and wife Gayle had ten children: 1) Sarah Randolph married William Murchison; 2) Elizabeth "Lizzie" Randolph married Dr. Jesse McKinney; 3) John Randolph married Ruth Baskwell; 4) Samuel Randolph served in Newsome's Cavalry and perished in the War Between the States; 5) Martha Randolph who married T.L. Adams; 6) Mary Randolph[73] who died at the early age of 16 years; 7) Captain G.W. Randolph[74] who married Lula Moore; 8) Polk Randolph who married Bettie Duke; 9) Lavinia Randolph[75] who perished at the young age of seven years; and 10) Allie Randolph who married Dr. Larwill.[76] Following the death of his wife in 1878, John G. Randolph spent most of his time in Corinth, Mississippi with his daughter, Martha Adams, but died in Montezuma on February 24, 1880, while on business.

The Bulliner family lived in the Anderson's Store region of north McNairy County. Those buried in the area are found in the Mount Carmel Cemetery. The Bulliner family was listed by General Marcus J. Wright as being among the early families to have settled in the northern portion of the county. Those buried at Mount Carmel are marked as early as 1855. Perhaps there are earlier graves, but if so they are unmarked.

72. Wright, Talbott, McCann, *Reminiscences 130th Anniversary Edition*.

73. Mary L. Randolph was born on January 27, 1837, and died on June 2, 1853, and was buried in the Old Montezuma Cemetery. See Lewis P. Jones, *Cemeteries in Chester County* (Henderson, TN: White Printing Company, 1982).

74. The Reverend George W. Randolph was born on June 11, 1840, and died on February 25, 1911. According to her tombstone, Rev. Randolph's wife's name was Lelia V. Randolph. She was born on April 20, 1856, and died July 7, 1930. Both are buried in the old Montezuma Cemetery. See Jones, *Cemeteries in Chester County*.

75. Levena Ann Randolph died on January 18, 1850, and was buried in the old Montezuma Cemetery.

76. All of the genealogical information listed regarding the Randolph family was taken from Wright's *Reminiscences*. See Wright, Talbott, McCann, *Reminiscences 130th Anniversary Edition*.

Little is known of the Bulliner family but there is one interesting incident regarding this family. More interestingly, the event itself did not occur in McNairy County, but rather in the state of Illinois and the bodies were shipped home. The Bulliners had migrated from McNairy County, Tennessee to Williamson County, Illinois. This particular Illinois county was known as "Bloody Williamson" County. It was a county populated by natives of Tennessee, Kentucky, Virginia and the Carolinas, families who were "hot-blooded, proud, obstinate, jealous of family honor, and quick to resent an insult."[77] During the second-half of the nineteenth century, feuds and violence were common in Williamson County, Illinois. The Bulliner family was headed by two brothers and had migrated from McNairy County in 1865 during the last year of the War Between the States and afterward the Bulliners settled south of Crainville, Illinois, in Williamson County.[78]

The Bulliner family became involved what would become known as the "Bloody Vendetta."[79] The feud began when several members of the Bulliner family were playing cards in a tavern near Carbondale, Illinois, with a man by the name of Felix "Field" Henderson and Mr. Henderson hurled an insult at one of the Bulliners.[80] Mr. Henderson was badly beaten after calling one of the Bulliners "a damn lying son of a bitch" and following this incident, the Bulliners and the Hendersons became bitter feud enemies.[81]

According to historian Paul M. Angle, the Bulliner men were known as "honest, industrious and enterprising" and "big-boned, broad-shouldered, muscular, good-looking, and pleasant in manner, yet they could be most disagreeable to anyone who crossed them."[82] Like so many feuds in history, the feud between the two families simply smoldered and gained momentum while history awaited another incident to occur. While the ill will between the Bulliners and the Hendersons mounted, a farmer named George W. Sisney and one of George W. Bulliner's sons became

---

77. Paul M. Angle, *Bloody Williamson: A Chapter in American Lawlessness* (Chicago: University of Illinois Press, 1992), 73.

78. *Id.* at 74.

79. *Id.*

80. *Id.*

81. *Id.*

82. *Id.*

involved in a disagreement over a crop of oats.[83] The matter was heard in the courts and Sisney prevailed, but the two agreed to meet later and settle up their accounts.[84] Quickly, Sisney and Bulliner disagreed and the younger Bulliner man accused Sisney of perjury during the trial whereupon Sisney assaulted Bulliner knocking him to the ground.[85]

George Bulliner and his sons took after Sisney and fired upon him as he ran across an open field, hitting Sisney four times before he was able to reach shelter.[86] Each of the Bulliners involved were fined one hundred dollars each and Mr. Sisney brought a lawsuit against the Bulliner boys which was settled out of court and never brought to trial.[87] Eventually a number of Williamson County families developed vendettas against one another and each family had allies in other families as well as enemies. These families involved included the Crains, Sisneys, Hendersons, and Bulliners.[88] The Crains and the Bulliners were allied against the Hendersons and the Sisneys.[89] Between 1872 and 1873, a number of brawls occurred in which various members of these four families were involved and in each and every resulting criminal case, the defendants were either acquitted or the prosecution was dropped.[90]

On December 12, 1873, sixty-one year old George W. Bulliner set out on horseback toward Carbondale, Illinois, and later in the day, neighbors found Bulliner lying dead by the side of the road with his buckshot wounds in his back.[91] George Bulliner's body was brought back to north McNairy County and buried in Mount Carmel Cemetery near the grave of his mother, Rebecca Bulliner. A few months later, on or about March 29, 1874, two of George and Nancy Bulliner's sons were ambushed and

---

83. *Id*, 75.
84. *Id*.
85. *Id*.
86. *Id*.
87. *Id*.
88. *Id*.
89. *Id*.
90. *Id*.
91. *Id*.

were wounded.[92] David A. Bulliner was twenty-five years old at the time and was mortally wounded.[93]

On the morning of March 30, 1874, death was closing in around young David Bulliner. According to Williamson County's first county historian Milo Erwin, the scene of young Bulliner's death was as follows:

> The twilight shadow of death, cold and gray, came stealing on him. A supernatural lustre lighted up his eye, and illuminated the gathering darkness. At length his eyes closed, and an expression of ineffable placidity settled on his pallid lips, and he was no more.[94]

Just prior to his death, Bulliner identified his assailant as Tom Russell, a man who had no connection to the vendettas but whose affections for a woman was spurned in favor of one of the Bulliner sons.[95] Again, a Bulliner was brought back to Tennessee to be buried in Mount Carmel Cemetery just east of Finger. Eventually, after Bulliner's brother, Monroe Bulliner, was unable to identify Tom Russell as the murderer, Tom Russell was acquitted.[96]

The feud would continue for decades and more Bulliners would be involved. The entire affair or set of affairs resulted in a series of feuds that fed upon themselves. The entire affair has been carefully documented by Illinois State Historian Paul M. Angle (1900–1975) in his work, *Bloody Williamson: A Chapter in American Lawlessness.*

Another of the older families in north McNairy County included the family of William A. "Big Bill" Robbins. Mr. Robbins was born on December 2, 1800, in North Carolina. He was married to Miss Permelia T. Burton sometime around 1820. Mrs. Robbins was born in 1804. The couple had thirteen children: Joseph Leod Robbins (July 4, 1821–March 19, 1883), Betsy Robbins, Rebecca Anne Robbins, John Henry Robbins

---

92. *Id.*
93. *Id.*
94. *Id.*
95. *Id.*
96. *Id.*

(born circa 1829), William Crockett Robbins[97] (born circa 1831), Martha Jane Robbins, Bryant Robbins, Clayton Robbins, Maclin Robbins (born circa 1841), Katherine Robbins, Adeline Robbins, Marcus J. Robbins[98] (1846–1909) and Marion Robbins.[99] Mr. Robbins was a farmer and lived in the Anderson's Store community. Upon his death on April 20, 1883, Mr. Robbins was buried in the Old Oak Grove Cemetery near the present McNairy-Chester county line. Mrs. Robbins had died previously on March 12, 1873, and was buried in Old Oak Grove Cemetery as well.

This is a summary of the history of some of the early families in north McNairy County. Certainly there are more, who are just as worthy of praise and recognition as these. However, the author's research was contained to these and this due mostly to the reason that these families remained and were prominent in the succeeding years.

---

97. It is believed that William Crockett Robbins married Miss C.A. Wood on September 2, 1870, with M.J. Robbins acting as bondsman. R. Harold Cox, *Marriages of McNairy County, Tennessee: 1861–1911* (Selmer, TN: G & P Printing Services, 1989).

98. Marcus J. Robbins married Mary E. Hollis on December 16, 1868, with J.H. Anderson acting as bondsman and Justice of the Peace A.W. Skinner officiating. Mary E. Hollis Robbins died in 1928 and was buried in Old Oak Grove Cemetery.

99. Marion M. Robbins married Nancy M. Hardin on March 22, 1870, with W. Etheridge acting as bondsman and Justice of the Peace Tinsley Weaver officiating.

CHAPTER THREE

THE WAR BETWEEN THE STATES

History of slavery in north McNairy County—Loyalist activity and enlistment in the Union Army—Local action at Brown's Crossing—Home life during the war—The war in documents—Years of healing and reuniting—Prison experiences of Finis E. Miller—Biographical sketches of Hodges, Lain, Harris, Anderson, and others—The life and war experiences of General Mark Perrin Lowrey.

Flat, even fields of deep rich soil stretching farther than the eye can see. Large plantations with stately mansions full of household servants attending to the every need of the resident. No, not in north McNairy County. Perhaps the Delta or Georgia, but not north McNairy County. This was not the land of the genteel Southern planter. It was the hard scrabble land of subsistence farmers whose work was well-equal to that of a slave.

North McNairy County is well within the boundaries of a region of West Tennessee known as the "Poor Barrens." Here beneath the thin top soil lies layer upon layer of red clay, soapstone, and sandstone. The farmers of north McNairy County were, as a majority, small scale farmers. The labor force on the farm consisted of the farmer himself, with the help of his sons and daughters and the occasional boarder. The geography, terrain, and soil quality of north McNairy County made the institution of slavery in this area not only less feasible but almost impossible. To give an example of the contrast between McNairy County and its neighboring counties, consider the following facts. In 1830, slaveholders in McNairy County owned a combined 377 slaves as compared to the 3,000 to 4,000 slaves held in each of the three nearby counties of Hardeman, Fayette, and Madison.

In 1840, in north McNairy County, at least 15 slaveholders can be found, although there were surely a few others. The following were located in the United States Census for 1840: Joicy Draper (8 slaves), John Walsh (9 slaves), John Draper (2 slaves), William Taylor Anderson (4 slaves), James Wilson (3 slaves), Benjamin Sells (1 slave), James S. Hanks (1 slave), Andrew B. Craig (1 slave), Clinton L. Moore (1 slave), William Hendrix (4 slaves), William Cayson Hodges, Sr. (8 slaves), Jesse B. Aldridge (1 slave), Mark Dodd (4 slaves), Hugh Smith (8 slaves), and Nancy Kerby (1 slave).[1] Although this seems like a fairly large number of slaveholders, considering that some 95–98 percent of white Southerners never owned a single slave, it is a very small percentage of the population. By 1860, many of these same families, along with a few others such as the Ingrahams, Freelings, and Robbins, were among the citizens of north McNairy County who employed slave labor in their farming operations.[2]

One observation, which was made in the earlier history of the Finger area, *Fingerprints*, should be made again. The stereotypical slave/master relationship portrayed in popular culture is not valid concerning the facts of north McNairy County's history. From a purely economic standpoint, the purchase of a slave was a great and serious investment for the typical farmer in this part of West Tennessee. Therefore, the slave, as an asset and investment, would be cared for and treated fairly well, for an individual of such status.

However, it is apparent that masters in north McNairy County viewed their slaves from a standpoint which was not at all economic, but rather personal and familial. A number of facts and anecdotes exist to substantiate the fact that most slaveholders in north McNairy County viewed their slaves not as property, but rather as members of an extended family. For example, former slaves are buried very near to their earthly masters in the old Mount Carmel Cemetery just east of Finger. Also east of

1. 1840 United States Census (McNairy County, Tennessee).
2. 1860 United States Census (McNairy County, Tennessee).

Finger, in the small family graveyard of the Ingraham family, a prominent slaveholding family of planters, slaves are buried within the fences and only feet from John S. and Rebecca Ingraham, whom they served.[3] According to family members, some of the slaves who had belonged to John Quincy Ingraham remained with his widow following the War Between the States. Again, it is very important to remember the daily lives of slaves and masters did not vary greatly, as both worked, side by side, in the fields together to make a crop and maintain a farm.

However, any harmony in north McNairy County could not be sustained and remain untouched in the face of the havoc and uncertainty facing the rest of the nation over the issues of states' rights and slavery. Following the secession of South Carolina from the Union in 1861, other Southern states quickly followed suit. Tennessee was the last Southern state to secede and the vote in north McNairy County did not follow the pattern in the rest of the county or the rest of the state.[4] The referendum on secession in the old Eighth Civil District, the north McNairy County area of present-day Finger and surrounding communities, resulted in a 96 to 39 vote against secession. The eligible white male, landowning voters of the Eight Civil District voted to preserve the Union and repudiate the concept of the new Confederate States of America. Unfortunately, it could never be so simple as a vote on an issue and the war would soon make its way to this area.

Although the county and the state went the way of South Carolina and soon comprised a portion of the new nation, the people of north McNairy County did not give up so easily. Whether they strongly desired to preserve the Union or simply lacked sufficient sympathy for the Confederate cause, droves of men sought to enlist in the Union war effort.[5] Some joined the Union Army after traveling elsewhere to enlist, but most waited for the war to come to them.

---

3. In the Ingraham Cemetery are the graves of John S. and Rebecca Ingraham and their infant children, and four or five of their faithful slaves. See the article on the Ingraham family by Irene Ingram Hardin (1972).

4. Interestingly, Tennessee would also be the first state to be restored to the Union in 1866.

5. It is an irony that so many young men in the northern part of McNairy County today speak so fondly of the "Rebel" cause, when in fact their ancestors not only failed to rebel, they fought the Confederacy on the battlefield.

Some families and individuals exercised every option in order to serve the Union. Robert Thompson McIntyre, a member of the McNairy County Quarterly Court during the first years of the War and a staunch Republican, made use of every opportunity to serve the cause of the preservation of the Union.[6] McIntyre, a leader in the northern part of the county at the time, no doubt helped to marshal the forces opposing secession.[7] Following Tennessee's secession from the Union, McIntyre's oldest son, Isaac T. McIntyre, gave his life in the service of the United States Sixth Tennessee Cavalry in April of 1864. Young Isaac served in a regiment in which so many of the boys of north McNairy County served. It was a unit that would find itself derided and villianized over the years. General Thomas Jordan and J.F. Pryor described the unit as so many would, accurate or otherwise, in their work, *The Campaigns of Lieut.-Gen. N.B. Forrest and of Forrest's Cavalry:*

> …[A] Federal force under the notorious Hurst, that—leader and men—had become as conspicuous for their craven conduct in the presence of armed enemies, as for rapacity and brutal, cruel outrages toward the defenseless citizens of the country which they desolated. This band of merciless marauders, trusting to their supposed superior numbers, boldly approached Bolivar, with a confidence that was speedily dissipated when it became apparent that the Confederates intended to fight, and Hurst attempted to withdraw; but Neely, pursuing promptly and hotly, killed about twenty and captured some thirty, and their wagon train, (five wagons and teams) and two ambulances, with their contents, including 50,000 rounds of ammunition, much needed, as it happened, by the Confederates, at the moment. The main part of these miscreants, however, effected their escape by way of Somerville, to Memphis, from the lines of which, we are told they did not emerge for the rest of the war as a band.[8]

6. McIntyre was a member of the McNairy County Quarterly Court as early as 1858 and as late as 1885.

7. The author's rationale for this supposition will be discussed later in this chapter.

8. General Thomas Jordan and J.F. Pryor, *The Campaigns of Lieut.-Gen. N.B. Forrest and of Forrest's Cavalry, with Portraits, Maps and Illustrations* (Dayton, OH: Morningside House, Inc., 1995), 418–419.

Sergeant R.R. Hancock, of Company C of the Second Tennessee Cavalry, C.S.A., recorded the same events in his *Diary* and called Hurst "notorious."[9] The opinion regarding Hurst seemed uniform among Confederates and among Southern sympathizers. Regarding the same battle at Bolivar, General James R. Chalmers stated that Colonel J.J. Neely's cavalry "met the traitor Hurst at Bolivar, after a short conflict, in which we killed and captured 75 prisoners of the enemy, drove Hurst hatless into Memphis."[10]

Fielding Hurst

Given the notoriety attributed to Colonel Fielding Hurst and his U.S. Sixth Tennessee Cavalry, it is important to present the other perspective. Naturally, a reader should be provided a balanced picture of a historical figure. However, in Hurst's case, it is more important that the readers of this volume be provided a balanced portrait of Hurst and his regiment. After all, a majority of the men who served from this section of the county fought under Colonel Hurst. The author finds it very difficult to believe that so many good men would serve under such a character. Further, it is more difficult to believe that such men, who were considered honorable men otherwise, could constitute such band of "merciless marauders." Perhaps the answer lies in the fact that Southern sentiment has survived with vigor in the South, even in sections and areas that were, in fact, Union strongholds. Somehow, the cause that won does not mystify like the "Lost Cause."

However, there's no question that Hurst was a staunch Unionist and a hard-fighting partisan. However, there appears to have been a reason for Hurst's vitriolic actions, however exaggerated they may be. According

---

9. R.R. Hancock, *Hancock's Diary: A History of the Second Tennessee Confederate Cavalry with Sketches of First and Seventh Battalions Also Portraits and Biographical Sketches.* (Dayton, OH: Morningside Press, Inc., 1999), 303.

10. Brian Steel Wills, *A Battle from the Start: The Life of Nathan Bedford Forrest* (New York: HarperCollins Publishers, 1992), 177.

to James Washington Purviance, a Purdy (and later Selmer) newspaperman, Hurst spoke out against secession and in favor of a strong spirit of Unionism and received a harsh rebuff for this exercise in freedom of speech. According to W.V. Barry in a 1924 article in the *McNairy County Independent*, Purviance recalled:

> The treatment (Hurst) received from some of the citizens of Purdy, who had him arrested, put in chains and taken to Nashville, and for six weeks laid on the cold stone floors of the penitentiary, all because he had made a speech in Purdy opposing secession was enough to cause him....to vent some of his vengeance on those who drove him to the fighting lines.

Hurst himself, in a deposition for the Southern Claims Commission, explained his circumstances. He wrote of his circumstances as follows:

> [I] lay in prison with [Williams C. Hughes] at Nashville, Tennessee, where I had been lodged on account of a Union Speech I made in this town [Purdy] on the first Monday of [blank] 1861.[11]

Unfortunately, time and emotions have a way of enhancing reputations. Today, whether right or wrong, Hurst's character and traits have been largely characterized as villainous. Historian Stephen Z. Starr addresses Hurst's reputation and that of other Tennessee Unionists in his 1985 work, *The Union Cavalry in the Civil War*. Starr pointed out that these Tennessee Unionists, who were labeled by Nathan Bedford Forrest as "renegade Tennesseans," were not merciful toward the Confederate guerillas and bushwhackers. According to Starr, the Sixth Tennessee Cavalry was ordered to march to Purdy and was ordered to destroy all armed enemies of the United State Government.[12] It appears the Sixth Tennessee Cavalry obeyed these orders literally.[13] Upon the actions

---

11. Kevin D. McCann, *Hurst's Wurst: Colonel Fielding Hurst and the Sixth Tennessee Cavalry, U.S.A.* (Dickson, TN: McCann Publishing, 2007).

12. Stephen Z. Starr, *The Union Cavalry in the Civil War, Volume III: The War in the West, 1861–1865* (Baton Rouge: Louisiana State University Press, 1985), 403.

13. *Id.*

of Hurst's regiment, Nathan Bedford Forrest "declared Colonel Fielding Hurst, his officers, and men 'outlaws and not entitled to be treated as prisoners of war' if they fell into his hands, citing as his justification the fact that the regiment had been 'guilty of house burning, [and] guilty of murders, both of citizens and soldiers of the Confederate States."[14]

Regardless, there appears no question that Hurst's inequitable and indeed inhuman treatment over words and ideals likely resulted in an urge for vengeance against those with such disrespect for a man's freedom of thought and speech. One must wonder what history would have held in store for us had the leaders of Hurst's hometown of Purdy been accepting of opposing points of views. Why else would man burn portions of his hometown during a war in which so damage could occur without adding more to it? Why else would an elected leader such as Robert Thompson McIntyre cast his lot with such a character? Why would so many families cast their lots with Hurst?

Robert T. McIntyre tombstone

Although McIntyre's actions constituted a great sacrifice in itself, it was not unlike any other made by any other father or mother at that time in American history. However, he went a step further than some. His next son, John Absalom McIntyre, was just shy of his fourteenth birthday when the hostilities flared in the region around north McNairy County. Too young to legally enlist and likely fearful of conscript by the Confederate government, according to family oral history and lore, McIntyre sent his young son John to Illinois to enter the employment of an arms factory, either contracted or controlled by the United States government. It was there in a "Union gun factory" that young John A. McIntyre was said to have spent the war years.[15]

In 2008, it was learned that John's future mother-in-law, Isabella J. Coleman, the wife and later widow of Corporal John Coleman of the U.S. Sixth Tennessee Cavalry, made her way to Nashville, Washington

14. *Id.*

15. This portion of family history was passed down by John A. McIntyre's children including his son John Robert McIntyre (1893–1989).

County, Illinois, with her daughters to live out the rest of the war. While there, Isabella employed the services of a local attorney, Amos Watts, and made application for her widow's pension, which she received. Following the war, she returned. Although it was often a matter of speculation as to why Robert Thompson McIntyre would send his young son to Illinois where he had no contacts, he may have indeed gone there with Isabella and her family. As it turns out, Nashville, Illinois was the site of a powder magazine and plant which provided materiel for the Union war effort and may have been the source of employment for young John A. McIntyre. Further, the Colemans and the McIntyres lived near each other in north McNairy County.

Corp. John Coleman tombstone

The Plunk family saw fourteen of its sons serve during this great and destructive war. Of these fourteen, eleven fought on behalf of the Union cause. There must surely have been an overwhelming desire present in this good family to preserve the country as such a large number was involved. Of these eleven individuals, five had initially enlisted in the Confederate Army and thereafter deserted "across the lines" to serve in the Union Army. Three of these fourteen sons were killed in action, never to return to the firesides of home.

The War Between the States still seemed only a distant event as Fort Sumter was fired upon in waters off South Carolina and as troops fought at the first battle of Manassas (Bull Run). Then the distant roar of battle began to take on the identity of a great and tragic conflagration which might flare at the front door of McNairy countians. The Union and Confederate armies fought on the Kentucky and Tennessee border at Forts Henry and Donelson as the Union Navy moved down the Cumberland and Tennessee Rivers, invading the very heart of Tennessee.

The war came home on April 6, 1862, when the guns began to fire at Shiloh (Pittsburg Landing). As the sixty-two cannon, comprising

Confederate General Daniel Ruggles' assault on the Union position in the Hornet's Nest, fired, the impact could be felt far from Shiloh. James Simpson "Simp" Lain stood behind his barn and listened to the cannons' distant roar.[16] It has been said the waters of Tar Creek shimmered and became a "tad unsettled" as the vibrations of the distant artillery could be felt. Following the battle of Shiloh, citizens in McNairy County decided to become actively involved in the war effort.

Fielding Hurst, discussed previously above, was an early advocate of active military service and took the steps needed to raise a regiment of Union soldiers from the citizens of McNairy County. Upon receiving a colonel's commission, Hurst began the work of raising a regiment in August of 1862.[17] The first company, Company A, of the new First West Tennessee Cavalry was organized near Bethel Station on August 11, 1862, its captain being Robert M. Thompson.[18] Between August 25 and September 21, 1862, Company B, C, D, E, and F were organized at Bethel Station in northern McNairy County, primarily from natives of McNairy County.[19] Upon their formation, these companies were led by the following captains: Horry Hodges (Company B), Nathan Kemp (Company C), Levi Hurst (Company D), Elijah Roberts (Company E), and Daniel J. Dickerson (F).[20]

A thorough account of the activities of the United States First West Tennessee Cavalry, later renamed the United States Sixth Tennessee Cavalry, will not be given here. Far better accounts can be found of those who have researched that subject with greater particularity.[21] Rather this work endeavors to record the names and personalities from northern McNairy County (from Montezuma to the areas directly east, north and south of Finger) who were involved in the War. The lists and biographical sketches included in this work are not exhaustive, but do cover a great majority of those for whom we are concerned.

---

16. Lloyd Harris interview, February 25, 1995. Mr. Harris stated that his source for this information was the late Dr. Henry Hodges, who stated that Mr. Lain related it directly to him.

17. McCann, *Hurst's Wurst*.

18. *Id.*

19. *Id.*

20. Wright, Talbott, McCann, *Reminiscences 130th Anniversary Edition*.

21. For detailed accounts of this regiment, please refer to the following sources: McCann, *Hurst's Wurst*; *Tennesseans in the Civil War*; and Gary Blankenship, *Fielding Hurst: Tennessee Tory*.

THE WAR BETWEEN THE STATES

The following local men soldiered with the United States Sixth Tennessee Cavalry under Colonels Fielding Hurst and William J. Smith. These men lived in what was then known as the Anderson Store area and its outlying areas. Those who died during the course of the War are appropriately noted.

Fredrick J. Floyd, private, Co. B, 18 years old, son of Harmon Floyd

John F. Putman, sergeant, Co. B, 21 years old, son of Martin Putman, buried at Mount Carmel Cemetery

Elijah J. Hodges, captain, Co. B, 31 years old, son of Elisha Hodges, buried at Mount Carmel Cemetery

Horry Hodges, captain, Co. B, 29 years old, son of Elisha Hodges, died of smallpox on May 5, 1864, buried at the National Cemetery in Memphis, Tennessee, Section B-1240

Samuel Vires, private, Co. B, 49 years old

John Vires, private, Co. B, 20 years old, son of Samuel Vires, buried at Plunk Cemetery

William Vires, private, Co. B, 18 years old, son of Samuel Vires, buried at Plunk Cemetery

John L. Dickey, private, Co. B, 20 years old, son of John A. Dickey, captured at Montezuma on February 14, 1864

William W. Kerby, second lieutenant, Co. B, 22 years old, son of John Kerby, neighbor to William T. Anderson, whose son died in service to the Confederate Army

Andrew Grisson (Grisham), private, Co. A, 45 years old, died on August 4, 1864

Seaborn L. Whitman, private, 49 years old, died on May 30, 1864, buried in the National Cemetery in Memphis, Tennessee, Section B-1249 (his name was possible listed in references also as Leberen L. Whitman, a wagoner.

Fiddler S. Whitman, private, Co. B, 21 years old, son of Seaborn L. Whitman

Anderson Mozier (Mosier), private, Co. G, 28 years old, died on April 7, 1863, buried at Plunk Cemetery

Jacob Mozier (Mosier), private, Co. G, 34 years old

Peter Plunk, private, Co. G, 25 years old, died on October 27, 1864, son of Jacob Plunk Jr., buried in the National Cemetery in Memphis, Tennessee, Section B-1111

Abraham (Abram) Plunk, private, Co. B, 20 years old, son of David and Annie Plunk

Jacob S. Plunk, private, Co. B, 22 years old

John Wesley Plunk, corporal, Co. C, 19 years old, son of David and Nancy Plunk, buried in Liberty Cemetery

John W. McClure, Commissary Sergeant, Co. B, 27 years old, died on April 7, 1864

James P. Blakely[22], first sergeant, 29 years old

Elias J. Highsmith, private, Co. B, 19 years old, son of D.H. Highsmith, buried at Malone Cemetery

Franklin A. Young, Teamster, Co. A, buried Rocky Knob Cemetery

William J. Horn, sergeant, Co. D, buried at Rocky Knob Cemetery

George D. Maness[23], corporal, Co. B, buried at Rocky Knob Cemetery

Samuel C. Plunk, private, Co. B, 18 years old, son of George and Fanny Plunk, buried at Mount Carmel Cemetery

Henry C. Harris, private, Co. B. 21 years old, buried at Mount Carmel Cemetery

William F. Smith, private, Co. B, 25 years old, buried at Malone Cemetery (also known as William E. Smith)

Madison Smith, private, Co. B, about 45 years old, buried at Malone Cemetery

John L. Smith, private Co. B, 24 years old, son of Madison Smith, buried at Malone Cemetery

Henry Harrison Brickens (Burkeens), private, Co. A, 21 years old, son of James Brickens (Burkeens), died on October 25, 1862

Calvin Ozment, private, Co. G, 26 years old

George N. Bullman, private, Co. B, 35 years old, buried at Hopewell Cemetery

---

22. James P. Blakely cannot be found in the Union rosters, but he is mentioned in the Cotton Ridge letter discussed in Chapter Ten of this work.

23. Gustavus W. Dyer and John Trotwood Moore, *The Tennessee Civil War Veterans Questionnaires, Volume One* (Easley, SC: Southern Historical Press, Inc., 1985), 144. As of 1914–1915, George D. Maness was still living, according to James T. Wolverton.

THE WAR BETWEEN THE STATES

Veterans of the Sixth Tennessee Cavalry (U.S.A.)

Thomas Ellen Pegram[24], private, Co. G, 18 years old
George M. Plunk, private, Co. B, 27 years old
Abraham Sipes, private, Co. B, 52 years old, buried at Plunk Cemetery
John Sipes, corporal, Co. B, son of Abraham Sipes, died on April 4, 1864, buried in the National Cemetery in Memphis, Tennessee, Section B-1192
Charles Curtis, Commissary Sergeant, Co. B, 35 years old, died on August 25, 1864
Samuel L. Walker, private, Co. B, 18 years old, discharged on February 1, 1863, buried at Mount Carmel Cemetery
Isaac T. McIntyre, private, 18 years old, son of Robert Thompson McIntyre, died on April 23, 1864, buried at the National Cemetery in Memphis, Tennessee, Section B-1175

---

24. Dyer and Moore, *Tennessee Civil War Veterans Questionnaires, Volume One*, 144. In 1914 and 1915, Tennessee state archivist Dr. Gus Dyer sent questionnaires to all known living veterans of the Blue and the Gray. In a transcript of the questionnaire completed by seventy-seven year old veteran James T. Wolverton, a veteran of Company G of the U.S. Sixth Tennessee Cavalry, it mentions a soldier by the transcribed name of "W.G. Tegrum" of Company G of Finger, Tennessee. As no such name appears otherwise in the rosters of this regiment, it is assumed this is a transcription error and the name should read "T.E. Pegram." According to Mr. Wolverton, Pegram was still living in 1914.

William W. Russell, private, 21 years old, son of William Russell, Company B, U.S. Sixth Tennessee Cavalry.

John Coleman, corporal, 44 years old, died on June 28, 1864, buried at the National Cemetery in Memphis, Tennessee, Section B-1123

Rufus M. Coleman, sergeant, 21 years old, mustered into Co. A, U.S. Sixth Tennessee Cavalry on November 10, 1862

Francis M. Rankin, quartermaster sergeant, Co. B, 26 years old, buried at Mount Carmel Cemetery

Charles B. Covey, sergeant, Co. B, 38 years old, son-in-law of Jacob Lowrance, buried at Mount Carmel Cemetery

Grear (Greene) Blakely, sergeant, Co. B, 25 years old

David C. Lee, private, Co. B, 18 years old, son of David and Elizabeth Lee

William S. Lee, private, 30 years old, buried at Sweetlips Cemetery

William C. Walker, private, Co. B, 21 years old, buried at Mount Carmel Cemetery

John W. Highsmith, private, Co. B, died on January 9, 1863, buried at Malone Cemetery

Alfred Swain, private, Co. E, 18 years old, deserted on August 5, 1864

William (Jefferson) Swaim, private, 19 years old, deserted on August 5, 1864

George W. Tucker, private/blacksmith, Co. B, 31 years old

Jacob J. Weaver, private, Co. H, 20 years old

Benjamin L. Allen, private, Co. H, 21 years old, died April 14, 1864, buried in the National Cemetery in Memphis, Tennessee, Section B-1258

Henry Wolf[25], Company G, Sixth Tennessee Cavalry, buried at Chapel Hill Cemetery

John M. Dunn, corporal, Company B, 33 years old, buried at Sweetlips Cemetery

Mark Manual, sergeant, Company D, buried at Beaty Cemetery

William Jasper Newton Rose, Company A, buried at Liberty Cemetery

Joseph A. Plunk, Company B, buried in Liberty Cemetery

Miles Plunk, Company B, buried in Liberty Cemetery

---

25. As of 1914–1915, Henry Wolf was already dead, according to James T. Wolverton. Dyer and Moore, *The Tennessee Civil War Veterans Questionnaires, Volume One*, 144.

THE WAR BETWEEN THE STATES   61

The following men fought in other Union units during the four-year conflict.

Calvin Plunk, Private, Co. F, Tenth Tennessee Infantry, U.S.A., buried at Plunk Cemetery

John A. Fry, Company F of the 49th Illinois Infantry

Finis E. Miller, Company M of the Seventh Tennessee Cavalry, U.S.A., private, captured and sent to Andersonville Prison.[26] Buried at Sweetlips Cemetery.

J.W. Moore, Company C, Seventh Tennessee Cavalry, U.S.A., buried at Plunk Cemetery

Jesse F. Plunk, killed after being captured in Adamsville on November 6, 1863, Co. G, U.S. Sixth Tennessee Cavalry

W.M. Jeter, Company I of the 11th Illinois Cavalry, buried at Sweetlips Cemetery

Andrew J. Garner, Company I, 136th Illinois Infantry, buried at Chapel Hill Cemetery

Matthew P. Henry, Company B, 4th Tennessee Mounted Infantry, buried in Liberty Cemetery

Of course, there were a few young men in northern McNairy County who cast their lot with the cause of the Confederacy. Although there were not quite so many, they served their cause and country with great valor and grit. The list of young Confederates is as varied as that of the Unionists. It must be kept in mind the current information on these young men is not thorough. The list includes the following:

Francis C. Robinson, possibly served in Co. C of the 22nd Tennessee Infantry, C.S.A., which was made up of men from Hardeman County, Tennessee, the neighboring county to McNairy County, Tennessee

Francis (France) C. Clayton[27], Private, Company F, Thirteenth Tennessee Infantry, buried at Mount Carmel Cemetery

26. A reproduction of Miller's harrowing account of life in the infamous Andersonville Prison is found in the present chapter.

27. According to local resident Mancel Kirk, Francis (France) C. Clayton lost a leg at the Battle of Shiloh (Pittsburg Landing) in April, 1862.

John R. Cone, private, Co. D, Twenty-first Tennessee Cavalry, a.k.a. Wilson's Cavalry

G.J. Cook, private, Co. B, Twenty-first Tennessee Cavalry, a.k.a. Wilson's Cavalry

William H. Harris, private, Co. C, Twenty-first Tennessee Cavalry, a.k.a. Wilson's Cavalry, buried at Finger Cemetery

Richard Ivy Hendrix, served most likely in the 51st Tennessee Infantry, also known as the 51st Consolidated Tennessee Infantry, buried at Hendrix Cemetery

James C. Hodges, Thirty-First Tennessee Infantry, C.S.A.

William Barney Malone[28], Lieutenant, served in Company F, Thirteenth Tennessee Infantry, C.S.A., present at the battles of Belmont, Missouri, and Shiloh; later re-enlisted in the Second Tennessee Cavalry and was present in the battles of Jacks Creek, Tennessee, and Okalona, West Point, Bailey's Cross Roads and Harrisburg, Mississippi, the raids at Memphis, Tennessee and Paducah, Kentucky, the capture of Fort Pillow on the Mississippi River, the battle of Sulphur Trestle, Alabama, the battle of Pulaski, Tennessee and with Hood in Nashville and with Forrest when he surrendered at Gainsville, Alabama; buried at Malone Cemetery. (See Chapter Seven of this work for further biographical information.)

Moses M. Matlock, most likely served in Company F, 51st Tennessee Infantry regiment, where a M.M. Matlock is found to have served. Company F was mustered in service on December 17, 1861, and composed of men in and near Henderson Station, Tennessee; buried at Mars Hill Cemetery

Sydney Plunk (March 18, 1828–October 1, 1914), private, Company E, 22nd Tennessee Cavalry, buried at Sweetlips Cemetery

George Sargent Anderson, 154th Senior Infantry, Co. H, also known as Co. I, but called Co. H when in state service; also known as "The McNairy Guards" and composed of men from McNairy County, Tennessee. Marcus J. Wright began as Lt. Colonel,

---

28. W.B. Malone is remembered by William Edward Beard in his questionnaire in 1914–1915. Beard was born in Purdy, Tennessee, the son of William B. Beard and the grandson of Frank Beard, an early Trustee of McNairy County, Tennessee. He attended school at Kerby Schoolhouse, probably in the Liberty community near Purdy.

then Brigadier General in this regiment. They were present at the Battle of Murfreesboro on December 31, 1862, during which battle Anderson was killed.

Absalom W. Weaver, Jr., Thirty-First Tennessee Infantry, C.S.A.

John G. Weaver, Thirty-First Tennessee Infantry, C.S.A.

Thomas B. Weatherington (1843-1911), private, Second Mississippi Infantry, buried at Sweetlips Cemetery

Calvin M. Davis, Company K, 43rd North Carolina Infantry

I.J. Massengill (January 19, 1842–May 8, 1920), private, Company B, 21st Tennessee Cavalry and Company C, 51st Tennessee Infantry, buried at Sweetlips Cemetery

Daniel David Plunk, son of George Plunk, Company C, 51st Tennessee Confederate Infantry; died of smallpox in Henderson, Tennessee.

George Irwin Cook, private, Company B, 16th Tennessee Cavalry Regiment

Alfred Monroe Plunk, son of George Plunk, Co. C, 51st Consolidated Infantry, was a brother and comrade of Daniel David Plunk.

John Milford Hendrix, Private, Company I, 154th Senior Tennessee Infantry Regiment, buried at Hendrix Cemetery

John Richard Barham, Private, Company C, 51st Tennessee Infantry

Lee H. Ingraham, Company C, 51st Tennessee Infantry

Again, there is very little information regarding each of these men. However, a brief examination of the names given above reveals that a number of fathers and sons served together in the same units and companies. Certainly such a situation leads to great speculation in our collective mind. For instance, we find ourselves traveling cerebrally back into time. What it must have been to be a father of boys of fighting age. How many nights were spent with middle-aged mothers and fathers sitting upright in the bed discussing the plight of their brave, but inexperienced sons. These sons, full of fire and fury, ready to defend their respective causes, had never known war and its horrors. Now here are the fathers, minds already weary from the worries of raising crops as well as sons, now burdened with the thought of losing sons to the battle cries of long-winded politicians in far off capitols. What could be done? Apparently many fathers and mothers determined that it would be best if the sons were properly watched over by their fathers. Thus, a good number of middle-aged men traded plow stock for gunstock.

As both young and old settled in for a long and bloody war, the realizations soon came that soldier and citizen alike would face similar hardships. There would soon be heard more than the cries of the States' Rights man and the Abolition man, there would be heard the cries of mourning mothers, sweethearts and orphans. No one was particularly immune from the plagues of rebellion and war.

Particular instances of action in this part of north McNairy County during the years between 1861 and 1865 were fairly rare. The lack of heated skirmishes and battle does not mean the area was isolated from contact. After all, one must keep in mind that the Purdy-Lexington Road, an important thoroughfare, ran through the north end of McNairy County. As a result of this and other roads, troop movements were fairly routine at varying intervals of the war. Of course, with these troop movements came a fair amount of incidents and stories.

The John Quincy Ingraham farm and home were located on that vital Purdy-Lexington Road (presently Clarence Barham Road). Certainly, both local enlisted men and other marching regiments moved up and down this important road, especially in 1862. At this time, various campaigns were underway in an effort to gain control of West Tennessee and North Mississippi. The Ingraham home, described in chapter one of *Fingerprints*, has been identified as a location for a make-shift hospital. Certainly the home's large size and convenient location on a prosperous plantation near a major road would serve either side well in the housing of sick and injured troops. A number of sources have alleged the home's use as a type of "field hospital" including a former occupant of the home, Fayette "Fate" Carter. Carter informed Hayes Hayre that a number of Confederate "uniforms" and clothing were stored in the home when he, Carter, moved into it in the 1930s. Carter recalled he could not live in the same house with "dead men's clothes," so he carried them out behind the house and torched them near the spring. Howard Beene, the home's last owner, demolished the structure in the late 1950s.

A few other areas have been identified as encampments during the War. Union soldiers were said to have camped for a few days on Mt. Carmel hill in the old cemetery. Another encampment was said to have existed on what is known today as the Hubanks Road on property formerly owned by D.C. Hester. Finally, on the old Buren Bullman farm in the Bullman Store Community, near Hopewell, a relay station was located.

The *Official Records of the War of the Rebellion* record only one incident in and around the area now known as Finger. The activity took place near Brown's Station, the name given to the railroad crossing near present-day Finger. At the time, the area was sparsely inhabited, although there was some population and activity along the new Mobile and Ohio Railroad. The name Brown's Station or Brown's Crossing was apparently a label from the Federal government or the Union Army and was possibly named for the mulatto carriage maker and miller, Ichabod Brown, who lived and owned property nearby. At ten o'clock in the morning, on March 13, 1862, the Fifth Ohio Cavalry, under the command of Major Charles S. Hayes, destroyed the bridge across Beech Creek, located on the Mobile and Ohio Railroad between Bethel Springs and Brown's Station, three-quarters of a mile south of present-day Finger. The bridge was a 150-foot trestle, that portion of the railroad known to many as the "double trestle." Hayes' soldiers tore up the tracks, bent the rails, and threw them into the creek. Further down, these soldiers destroyed another smaller trestle. This resulted in the crippling of the railroad so that trains could not pass unless the trestle was rebuilt. During their mission, Major Hayes and his men spotted a Confederate Cavalry unit known as Robinson's Cavalry. After a pursuit, two Confederates were captured.[29]

A bevy of activity swirled around Bethel Station, now Bethel Springs. Again, it was here the United States First West Tennessee Cavalry, later renamed the U.S. Sixth Tennessee Cavalry, mustered into service. It was also here that breastworks were constructed, which have been viewed by some over the years as mysterious as had they been built by some long extinct tribe of Native Americans. However, there is nothing mysterious or ambiguous about them. This fort or breastwork was called Fort Sallie.[30] It was constructed by the Forty-eighth and Forty-ninth Illinois

---

29. These events were reported in the *Official Records of the War of the Rebellion*, Series I, Volume 10, Part One. Here it is reported that Hayes and the Fifth Ohio Cavalry destroyed a total of about one-half mile of trestle "over the swamp" north of Purdy. At this time, the Confederacy was still in control of West Tennessee and such an action could prevent the movement of supplies and troops from Jackson south to Corinth, the Confederate base of operations during the campaign at Shiloh or Pittsburg Landing

30. All of the information concerning Fort Sallie was contained in an October 23, 1923, letter to Prof. Cordie L. Majors from R.H. Croskery.

Regiments, no earlier than April 1862, and probably sometime shortly after the battle of Shiloh. Colonel Fielding Hurst and his cavalry used the fort for a while. It still exists today, but in 1923 was described as being located near "Kiser's." According to A.W. Stovall, who it is alleged assisted General Wright in gathering information for the writing of his work on McNairy County, the forts in McNairy County were built under the direction of Colonels Harvey and Sanford.[31]

Like so many other great wars of principle, those on the home front kept up with the events of the day. No detail was too small for the folks back home to consume. They were interested in all aspects and every event of the conflagration. They watched the few newspapers and all lists of wounded, missing, and killed. One example of the interest shown to detail by those at home is the following entry found in the Bible of David P. Massey:

Battle of Shiloh, McNairy County, Tennessee, April 6–7, 1862
Battle of Manassas, Virginia fought July 21, 1861
Battle of Belmont, Missouri fought November 6, 1861
Battle of Corinth fought October 3–4, 1862
Richmond, Virginia taken by the Federal troops on April 3, 1865

Such types of records suffice to show the interests of local residents during such a difficult time.[32]

Over the years, local residents' sentiments for one of the particular causes and their hatred for the other often died slow and hard. Perhaps this was a result of the difficulties and deprivations endured during the period between 1861 and the Reconstruction Period. Many anecdotal accounts persist as to the hard times and harrowing adventures experienced by locals during the devastating conflagration.

Often the farms located near the main roads were looted for stock and feed. Farmers saw their hogs, cattle, sheep, and chickens commandeered for meat. This, along with life's everyday deprivations of the times,

---

31. Nancy Wardlow Kennedy (Transcriber), *Notes of Ancil Walker Stovall: Including the Original Works of A.W. Stovall, Poetry and Speeches* (Selmer, TN: Self-published, 2001), 10, 15.

32. At one time, certain records were on deposit in the Jack McConnico Library in Selmer, Tennessee which were identified as the Massey Family Papers. Since the author researched these materials in the 1990s, they have been removed from the library by persons unknown.

left many families with little other than cowpeas, sorghum molasses, and cornbread. It was not an easy time, even for a people already accustomed to subsisting on a minimum. There were no luxuries and those commodities which today are taken for granted were not to be found in those darkest days of civil war in America. Had farmers possessed meat, they could not have so easily preserved it, as there was little salt to be enjoyed. The scarcity of salt led residents to dig up the floors of old smokehouses in the hopes of obtaining some amount of salty brine from the soil. The process entailed boiling the soil which had absorbed salt during the preservation of meat during earlier pre-war years. Mr. Guy Brown related that his great-grandfather, perhaps Pleasant A. Brown on the paternal side, lived in the area known as the "Sandhills" and had to store his goods in a hollow log.[33]

There were many stories regarding the visits paid to farms and homes by both sides in the great conflict. Often, search parties visited the home places of north McNairy County seeking soldiers who had deserted or who were wanted by the opposing side for various and sundry reasons. According to family tradition, brothers Alfred Monroe Plunk and Daniel David Plunk went to the county seat, Purdy, and were more or less coerced into joining the Confederate Army. Concerned about their plight, the two brothers went to seek advice from an elderly gentleman by the name of Lane. Mister Lane told them, "Boys, join and then desert." Therefore, in September of 1861, the two joined the Confederate Army. However, they were put off a train at Henderson Station in February of 1862 as both of them were suffering from smallpox. Daniel passed away and Alfred's clothes were laid out for his burial, but surprisingly he survived. In July of 1862, Alfred was declared a deserter.

Kizzie and Alfred Monroe Plunk

---

33. In a 1995 interview with the author, Guy Brown described the Sandhills as being near the old Poney Gibson farm.

The Confederates came looking for Alfred at his parents' place on Tar Creek on at least two occasions. On one occasion, Alfred ran toward the woods "with Confederate bullets kicking up the dirt behind him and all around him."[34] On another occasion, the local Confederate authorities came riding up to the Plunk homestead and the commander of the group called out, "Strike a light!" This meant "who's in the house?" Alfred was hiding out in the loft of the house and sleeping on cottonseed which was stored there. The family could distinctly hear Alfred moving around in the loft to a suitable hiding place. Alfred quickly made his way to the dark corner where the chimney stood and there he hid. A Confederate stuck his head up in the loft and looked around before calling to the others, "Nobody here."

It was during these times that many in north McNairy County, a hotbed of Union loyalty and activity, tired of any Confederate presence. There was occasional harassment by Confederates of the Unionist populace in north McNairy County and according to one source, there was some conflict along Tar Creek. According to this story, the local Unionists in desperation decided to lay an ambush for the marauding and harassing Rebels. About a dozen Unionists were lying low along the run of Tar Creek when they waylaid the unsuspecting Rebels, injuring at least one. Another Confederate had his horse shot out from under him and as he chased after the others on foot, the amused and satisfied Unionists laughingly called out, "Look at him run! Look at him run!" Alfred Monroe Plunk was present for this event and followed after the now-afoot Rebel with the others and eventually captured him. Needing a wagon to transport the wounded man, they sought and received help from Calloway Robison, a local blacksmith.

One wartime incident regards John Quincy Ingraham, mentioned above.[35] Ingraham was a patriotic man and considered a Union sympathizer.[36] His granddaughter recorded that he went to Purdy three different times for the drawing and three times pulled a blank meaning he

---

34. These stories were related to the author by the late Marvin Hand of Hesperia, California.

35. All of these stories regarding Mr. and Mrs. John Quincy Ingraham came from *Reminiscences of Childhood* by Irene Ingram Hardin written on January 12, 1972.

36. The author does find this story interesting in that if it is given the veracity for which he has no other reason to doubt, then and in that event, the Ingraham family is representative of so many torn families. After all, another member of the family was Lee H. Ingraham, who would serve the Confederate cause.

had to return home each time. Therefore, Ingraham never served in either army. Probably aware of what was to come following a war quickly approaching its end, Ingraham decided to move his family to his late father-in-law's farm near Henderson Station, Tennessee. His reasons were fairly simple and understandable. He and his family lived on the Purdy-Lexington Highway and being a highly traveled road, it was certain to be full of plundering Confederates and Unionists returning home. The father-in-law, John M. Johnson, a Whig member of the Tennessee State House of Representatives from 1835 to 1837 and from 1839 until 1841, had died shortly before the War. Ingraham's plan was to stay there until the tremors of war had calmed.

A Barrett man, apparently less than a gentleman, lived on an adjoining farm. He allowed his livestock to roam free in Ingraham's cornfields and was notified to keep his stock out of others' fields. Barrett apparently did not take the warning well and choose to cause the ultimate injury. When Ingraham moved his family and belongings to the Johnson farm, a faithful slave who had remained with the Ingrahams went along to assist. They spent the night and planned to return the next morning to retrieve what was left of their goods and their stock.

Early in the morning after feeding and harnessing the horses, Ingraham sent the black man to the spring to water the horses. After the time it would have taken to water the animals had passed, he did not return and thus Ingraham went after him. When Ingraham reached the servant, he was standing still and holding the horses, and when called upon, he did not answer. Just about the time Ingraham reached him, Barrett shot Ingraham in the back. Barrett had been hidden behind a forked tree with his gun resting in the fork waiting on Ingraham. He had warned the black man he would kill him if he moved or warned Ingraham.

After being shot, Ingraham sat down against a tree and sent the black man to fetch Mrs. Ingraham. She reached him in time for him to inform her as to the location of his papers and money. He died within an hour of being shot. He was buried in the Johnson family cemetery and then the family moved back home. Unfortunately, no mercy was shown to the black man, who was tied to tree and shot after telling who the murderer was. Apparently he was shot for not warning Ingraham.

Things were not easy for Mrs. Ingraham and her children. Again it was a time of difficulty and hardship when feelings over the war and all of its accompanying tragedy were still raw for everyone. The Ingrahams had their smokehouse raided in an unusual manner. A gang of looters tunneled under the back side of the smokehouse and stole their lard and meat. At the time, there was great uncertainty as to whether one would even have a place to sleep. On one occasion raiders rode up to the front of the house and ordered Mrs. Ingraham and the children outside as they were going to burn their home to the ground. Mrs. Ingraham, showing the steel that was many a Southern woman, yelled to the raiders, "Burn it, damn you, I am not coming one step!" With that, Mrs. Ingraham slammed the door shut. The raiders chose to leave her and her home alone.

Due to these types of events, it is difficult to utter the words "after the war." Anyone who ever presumed the end of the military maneuvers meant the end of the hostilities had made a great and erroneous presumption. The war, as such, would not end for many years to come. The hostilities of the summer of 1861 and all summers that followed only grew and inflamed and the summers of 1865 and those following during the Reconstruction years were only more contentious. Stories abound of the difficulties confronting the Southern people as a whole following Appomattox. The surrender of Lee did not mean the surrender of the Southern people. Their will had been severely bent, but certainly not broken. Now came the birth of new hostilities. Retaliation against former Confederate soldiers by local Unionists and carpetbaggers began. Thus also began the reprehensible violence against Unionists and their sympathizers by the former Rebels. Activity by the newly formed Ku Klux Klan began to mount and new problems faced a South struggling to hold onto the old in what would become the "New South."

Interestingly, there was no government and thus no stability in McNairy County between 1863 and 1865. No substantial activity was evidently conducted at the courthouse in Purdy during this period. However, when the war ended, Tennessee's newly installed Unionist governor, William "Parson" Brownlow, began the process of installing interim officers in the counties. Robert Thompson McIntyre took office in July 1865 as the Chief Presiding Justice of the McNairy County Quarterly Court. Thereafter, one of McIntyre's north McNairy County neighbors, Jacob Lowrance, was installed as County Trustee. Later, Elijah J. Hodges would be elected as the region's state representative on the Unionist ticket. The region began to become more stable under the leadership of these men.

With leadership and the strong will of the people of north McNairy County, the region would survive the struggles of rebirth to thrive again and its people would heal. By the end of the century, former Confederates and ever-believing Unionists could and would meet on the old battlegrounds and embrace rather than engage. Local men, with their sons and daughters, began to attend the reunions and retrace both in their mind and on the old fields and roads, their steps of so many years gone by.

Over the years, a number of reports and accounts appeared in the local newspapers regarding the festive reunions, including the following examples. In 1904, the reunion of the U.S. Sixth Tennessee Cavalry took place. Horry Hodges was the Master of Ceremonies and Captain E.J. Hodges delivered the welcome address in "his quaint and stirring manner."[37] In April of 1906, "Dan Gooch and Horry Hodges left Tuesday morning to take in the Confederate Reunion at New Orleans."[38] At the 1908 Reunion of the Sixth Tennessee Cavalry, U.S.A., Horry Hodges, son of Captain Elijah J. Hodges, delivered the response to J.W. Purviance's welcome address in "his usual felicitous manner."[39] Professor Horry Hodges took a great interest and active role in local and regional reunions of Civil War veterans, regardless of side. His great interest in and love of history contributed to this activity. His family's active role in the leadership of Company B of the U.S. Sixth Tennessee Cavalry also made a great contribution.

Today we may learn much of the War and its effect on local residents through old letters, journals, and other records and accounts. The following letter from Joe Wilshire to Captain Elijah J. Hodges gives some hint as to the friendships formed and the issues confronted during this time of great conflagration.

Office of Wilshire & Co.
Bankers and Exchange Brokers
No. 7 Madison Street

---

37. *McNairy County Independent Appeal*, September 6, 1935. Originally printed in the September 2, 1904 edition.

38. *McNairy County Independent Appeal*, April 27, 1906.

39. *McNairy County Independent Appeal*, August 28, 1908.

Memphis, Tenn., March 4th, 1865

Friend Hodges,

Your favor of the 24th is just received and I am much pleased to hear from you and the Regiment as I hear from it but seldom. I am pleased to hear that you are getting along so well and have such an easy time. In regard to your claim, it is O.K., please sign and swear to it and return it to me; it can be done in Nashville as well as here.

In regard to the vouchers of the boys, I have such a man in Washington to get them, though it is going to be difficult to do it, but he writes me that he will get them sometime sure. I received the rolls sent by Thorington but don't understand why he don't write me; give him hell for me. Tell him I got George R. West a position as paying teller in the National Bank here. I have not seen Colonel Hurst to speak to him since his return. I wish to know the P.O. address of Mary C. Dyson, widow of Hezekiah, of your regiment; also of William Bassham, father of Richard A., formerly of your company. Also of John W. Inman, father of James A., formerly of Capt. Chandler's Company as I have certificates for the money due them for arrears of pay and bounty due them from the Government and can send them the money when I hear where they are.

Write soon and oblige,
Your old friend,
Joe Wilshire

This letter from Wilshire, who was apparently a banker contracted or working for the United States government, shows the types of bonds which formed during the long struggle from 1861 to 1865. There is also the mention of a number of young men who perished in the War and their survivors. The money mentioned by Wilshire was certainly a form of relief for some whose working son or husband was taken from them, although it could hardly have been a consolation.

Wilshire mentioned John H. Thorington, OFC Adjutant of the U.S. Sixth Tennessee Cavalry, as well as a fellow by the name of George R. West. Nothing at all is known of West or his connection to the regiment.

Private Hezekiah Dyson, aged 24 of Company D, died on November 22, 1863. Private Richard A. Bassham of Company B, who was about 18 or 19, died on February 14, 1863, after less than six months in the Union Army. No record was found pertaining to a James A. Inman serving in Captain William Chandler's Company G.

Prison Experiences of Finis E. Miller

Finis E. Miller was raised around the most northern fringes of the Anderson's Store area not far from what is now considered the Sweet Lips area. He would eventually relocate to Finger and become involved in the business affairs of that town. He built a stately home on the corner of Mill Street (Talbott Street) and Apple Street. Here he and his wife and daughters lived for many years. However, long before those years, he, like many of his generation, served in the War Between the States. He served the Union cause in Company M of the United States Seventh Tennessee Cavalry.

During his service, he was captured by the Confederate Army and transported to the infamous Andersonville Prison in Georgia where he remained a prisoner for more than a year. Andersonville was a Confederate prisoner-of-war camp located in southwest Macon County, Georgia. The camp held more than 45,000 prisoners and of that number, more than 13,000 died of malnutrition, starvation and dysentery.

He wrote an account of his experiences in Andersonville in his later years which is reprinted below.[40]

> I was captured at Union City, Tennessee, on March 24, 1864, after five hours of fighting. I was one of the first men to fire upon the enemy from the fort. Our Lieutenant commanded us to cease firing until we could see the white of their eyes, so that we could hear them groan when they were dying. We got out of ammunition and had to surrender about eleven o'clock. Then we marched, day after day, from Union City, Tennessee,

---

40. The exact publication in which Miller's account was originally published is not currently known, but it was in the first years of the twentieth century. However, this version was purportedly published as originally published in a work by Bill Wagoner called *Stories About Shilon and the Tennessee Valley Area*, published by Banner Publishing Company in 1994.

to West Point, Mississippi, where we boarded the train for Mobile, Alabama. We stayed there two or three days, then we boarded a steamboat at Mobile and were taken to the railroad some twenty miles from Mobile, where we took cars for Pollard, where we stayed all night.

We boarded the train the next morning for Montgomery, Alabama. Here we camped for the night. Next morning, we had an opportunity to see Winder. We soon after boarded the train for Columbus, Georgia, changed cars and went from there via Macon, Georgia, to Andersonville. Here we landed April 21, 1864. Andersonville is located in Sumter County, Georgia; is 62 miles from Macon and 45 miles from Albany, Georgia. There were only a few hundred prisoners there when we got there. They had been there but a short time. They, most of them, had wintered on Bell Isle and in Richmond. Perhaps there were a few from Salisbury, North Carolina. They were a motley set of fellows. They were smoked as black as fine smoke would make them. The mortality at that time was about thirty a day.

About this time, new prisoners began to come in almost everyday. We could hear all kinds of rumors about the fighting in the front. The Rebs claimed great victories, while the new prisoners would tell who won the battles and how the Rebels were falling back. These stories were of daily occurrence. About the first of May, the prisoners had accumulated to several thousand and the boys began to fall sick and die. Two of our healthiest, stoutest boys died. This was a surprise to think our ablest and best men should succumb to the hardships of prison life before they had been there over one month. The names of these two boys were G.W. Pickens and James Evans. The weakliest man of our company, John Ables, lived through the thirteen months of hardships of prison life and returned home and then died.

A few things I observed while I was at Andersonville that are difficult to believe, but all who were there will testify to their truth. Our 'dead house' was inside of the outer stockade and in the last of July and first of August, it was said that 200 dead soldiers were carried out there daily for two weeks. I do not doubt the statement, I have seen two large Confederate Army wagons driven to the dead house by our own men who were out on detail or had volunteered to the work in order to get something to eat, perhaps thinking they might get an opportunity to escape. They would drive near the dead house, turn the wagon into position and two men would take hold of the dead by the arms and legs, give them a swing or two and pitch them into the wagon, like so many dressed hogs, until they got all that four horses could pull, then drive off to the place for burial. They would repeat this performance until all were buried. The next day the same performance was repeated continuously.

Oh, the untold suffering of the men inside the stockade. I have seen hundreds of poor fellows who were not able to get upon their feet that had been in that condition for several days, no nurse nor anyone to care for them, that had chronic diarrhea, had become so filthy that the flies had blown them, full grown maggots working all over them before they were dead. Sometimes one of these poor fellows would ask a favor of someone that was passing by. If he did not comply with his request he would make threats of some kind and tell him what he would do when he got back to 'God's country' not realizing that he could not possibly ever get three feet from where he then lay unless someone moved him. I have seen hundreds of just such cases. I could mention many circumstances like this.

One can only imagine the sights, sounds, smells, and experiences that Finis Miller encountered while a prisoner in this hellish place. Although most veterans of this awful and tragic conflagration faced many difficult situations and times, very few could have known the difficulties faced by those who were in Miller's place, as prisoners of war in the Confederate prison camps.

Miller mentions three members of his regiment by name. G.W. Pickens is most likely Sergeant George W. Pickens, who served with

Miller in Company M of the U.S. Seventh Tennessee Cavalry.[41] James Evans was a private in the same Company M.[42] John Ables is more likely John C. Ables, a private in Company C of the U.S. Seventh Tennessee Cavalry.[43]

Upon returning from the War, Miller married Margania E. Robbins on January 12, 1869. The couple had a number of children including Mattie, Edward Luther, James, Ella, and Callie. He was the owner of a cotton gin at Finger and a former postmaster of the Sweet Lips Post Office. Finis lived into the second decade of the twentieth century, dying on April 15, 1916. Margania passed away on February 16, 1933, and was buried in the Sweet Lips Cemetery next to Finis. Such was the life of an old soldier.

Biographical Sketches

There are a number of north McNairy countians who made contributions to the cause of the war on both sides. Men on both sides of the conflagration made their contributions out of complete loyalty to their respective causes. These few biographical sketches are representative of just a few of the region's military leaders and soldiers.

Elijah James Hodges (1831-1913)

A biographical sketch concerning Elijah James Hodges could be placed in about any chapter in this work, considering Hodges was a farmer, state representative, preacher, and supporter of academic and literary pursuits. However, the author sees fit to include Hodges' biography in the present chapter as the politics and experiences of the War Between the States greatly affected Hodges' life and view of the political realm.

Elijah James Hodges was born to Elisha Hodges and Millie (Ward) Hodges on the family farm near present-day Finger on May 18, 1831. Whether he was educated at home or obtained some formal schooling is not presently known, but Hodges was a well-read man of literary pursuits.

---

41. *Tennesseans in the Civil War: A Military History of Confederate and Union Units with Available Rosters of Personnel* (Nashville, TN: The Civil War Centennial Commission, 1965), 567.

42. *Id*, 506

43. *Id*, 453

THE WAR BETWEEN THE STATES

Elijah James Hodges and wife Nancy Jane (Dodd) Hodges

He has been described as such, "the Captain was an intellect and a great literary and Bible reader."[44]

Elijah and brother Horry enlisted in Company B of the First West Tennessee Cavalry, later known as the Sixth Tennessee Cavalry, on August 25, 1862, at Bethel Station.[45] On November 17, 1862, Hodges received a promotion to sergeant. Upon the death of William K.M. Breckinridge on October 15, 1863, Hodges received a promotion to adjutant.[46] Hodges made the rank of first lieutenant on February 29, 1864. On May 5, 1864, Elijah's brother, Horry Hodges, the captain of Company B since muster on August 25, 1862, died of smallpox in Helena, Arkansas. Upon his brother's death, Elijah James Hodges was elevated to captain, a rank he would hold until the war's end. Hodges was discharged at Pulaski, Tennessee on July 26, 1865. It should be noted that Captain Elijah Hodges made an impressive sight leading his troops on the battlefield, as he stood six feet, six inches tall an unusual height for a man in the nineteenth century.

44. Taken from Hodges' obituary in the *McNairy County Independent Appeal*, April 25, 1913.
45. McCann, *Hurst's Wurst*.
46. *Id.*

Capt. Elijah J. Hodges

Following the war, Hodges pursued a career as a politician, farmer, and preacher. Hodges was elected to the Tennessee State House of Representatives on the Unionist ticket in 1867 and represented McNairy County in the Thirty-fifth General Assembly until 1869. He was also a well-known Primitive Baptist preacher, leading among others the congregation at Mount Carmel, near his home.

Elijah married Nancy Jane Dodd on December 29, 1852, and to this union were born eleven children: Tabitha F. Hodges (December 28, 1854–August 29, 1855), Sarah Ann Hodges (August 24, 1857–July 27, 1858), John Hodges (January 27, 1862–April 18, 1862), Elizabeth Ellen Hodges Peeples (1860–1939), Mary Hodges Robertson (1866–1941), Horry Hodges (March 19, 1868–September 23, 1940), William Henry Hodges (September 19, 1869–November 16, 1941), Harmon E. Hodges (December 3, 1871–November 17, 1957), Rozetta Jane "Jennye" Hodges Scott (June 12, 1873–September 14, 1956), Maggie Hodges (March 27, 1876–October 30, 1955) and Harvey G. Hodges (March 17, 1878–September 1, 1922).[47]

Elijah often spoke at Union Army reunions and other events in his later years. More than a year prior to his death, he lost his eyesight, but according to his obituary, "everyday he was read to by some member of the family."[48] Elijah James Hodges died on April 21, 1913, at his home just east of the town of Finger and was buried in the Mount Carmel Cemetery nearby. Following the Captain's death, the remaining single Hodges' children, Horry, Henry, Harmon, Maggie, and Harvey,

---

47. Of these eleven siblings, several will be featured in biographical sketches in other portions of this work.

48. *McNairy County Independent Appeal*, April 25, 1913.

allegedly signed a pact requiring each of them to remain single and to provide for their widowed mother and the family estate.[49]

Horry Hodges (1833–1864)

Horry Hodges was born on September 25, 1833, to Elisha and Millie (Ward) Hodges, on the family farm in north McNairy County. Horry married Sarah Elizabeth Dodd in Madison County, Tennessee, on January 18, 1855. The couple had two children, Rozetta (born October 23, 1855) and James Wright Hodges (August 28, 1857–November 8, 1916). Sarah Hodges died on August 7, 1858, in McNairy County. Horry remarried on September 29, 1859, to Mary E. Lain and to this union were born three children: Virginia P. (Hodges) Cude (born November 6, 1860) and infant twins (January 8, 1863–January 11, 1863).

On July 7, 1862, Horry, having been elected Constable of the Eighth Civil District, appeared before the McNairy County Quarterly Court to have his bond approved. His bondsmen were Fielding Hurst, N.G. Ward and D.N. Huddleston.[50] However, war interrupted and cut short his service in the constabulary. The harsh storm of war came to McNairy County and Horry enlisted in Company B of the United States First West Tennessee Cavalry on August 25, 1862, at Bethel Station.[51] Upon enlistment, Horry made the rank of captain. He served in this capacity throughout his service and was involved in actions and skirmishes throughout West Tennessee, portions of Middle Tennessee, and north Mississippi.

Certainly serving with Colonel Fielding Hurst meant a number of interesting predicaments and circumstances, but a particular incident is preserved regarding Hodges. Kevin D. McCann details an incident in which Hodges was involved on July 25, 1863. Colonel Fielding Hurst allowed himself to become captured by two Confederate soldiers, a story

---

49. This has been passed down over the years by members of the family, family friends, and neighbors in the community.

50. *McNairy County Quarterly Court Records, 1858–1865,* McNairy County, Tennessee Records and Archives Room.

51. A number of transcribed records and references list the name as "Harry" but this is an incorrect rendering. His name was actually "Horry." Brother E.J. Hodges named his son Horry, the celebrated orator and educator, after him.

which was related as well by seventy-three year old former Confederate soldier, Dr. Christopher Wood Robertson in 1922. Dr. Robertson opens the story:

> [A]t one time, [Fielding] Hurst was passing south of Somerville and stopped to talk with Mrs. Lewis a widow and her daughter standing at their front gate. His command passed on and were met by C.A.S. Shaw and Hugh Nelson of my company [Company H, Fourteenth Tennessee Cavalry, C.S.A.], who were coming home to Somerville to get new horses, clothes, etc....they saw the Yankees first and dodged into the bushes until they passed and then coming on saw Hurst talking to the ladies...[Shaw and Nelson] dismounted and slipped up behind Hurst...he (Hurst) laughed and said no two rebels could take him...just as he said it Shaw and Nelson said surrender and Shaw took Hurst's pistols and buckled them on...made Hurst mount and started off with him...[52]

Kevin D. McCann picks up the story in his well-researched *Hurst's Wurst: Colonel Fielding Hurst and the Sixth Tennessee Cavalry, U.S.A.*:

> Hurst knew his men would try and find him and he rode slowly between his captors to give them more time to catch up. When they objected to his pace, he told them they could shoot him if they did not like it.
> Meanwhile Captain Harry Hodges of Company B and a group of eight soldiers from the regiment had pursued them for seven miles. When they were found, Lieutenant Risden D. Deford and an African-American servant belonging to Captain Robert M. Thompson of Company A ran ahead and began firing at them. In the confusion, Hurst 'drew rein and turned his quick grey mare' into the woods as one of his captors shot at him with one of his own pistols. Hodges gave him a revolver and the 1st West Tennessee chased the Confederate soldiers to within a few hundred feet of [Confederate Colonel Richard V.] Richardson's encampment. Outnumbered, Hurst

---

52. Dyer and Moore, *The Tennessee Civil War Veterans Questionnaires, Volume One*, 1865.

and his men turned back a short distance to the top of a hill where they were joined by the rest of the squad. They "cheered lustily, making so much noise that the Rebels thought the whole regiment was coming to avenge their Colonel's wrongs." Richardson's command was tempted but grudgingly decided to give up their trophy without a fight.[53]

What other interesting accounts of Horry Hodges' activities during the war, we do not know. Perhaps accounts exist and will one day served as part of a greater work on the great conflict in this area. Regardless, on May 5, 1864, Horry Hodges died of smallpox in Helena, Arkansas. He was buried in the National Cemetery in Memphis, Tennessee (Section B, Grave 1240). A record from the *Office of the Auditor for the War Department* regarding a claim by Hodges' son for pay and allowances discloses the pay scale for a Union Army captain during that period. His pay and allowances in full for the period of November 1, 1863 to May 4, 1864 was $821.34. Mary E. (Lain) Hodges, the widow of Horry Hodges, would outlive him by more than sixty-five years, dying in 1930. She was buried in the Oak Hill Cemetery in Selmer, Tennessee.

Frederick J. Floyd (1845–1932)[54]

One of the last surviving members of the U.S. Sixth Tennessee Cavalry was a Finger gentleman by the name of Frederick J. Floyd. He was of an old north McNairy County family. He was born in March of 1845. After the outbreak of the War Between the States, he cast his fortunes with the Union cause. He enlisted in Company B of the Sixth Tennessee Cavalry on August 25, 1862. He was mustered into service on November 13, 1862. He served under Captain Elijah J. Hodges. His obituary would state: "He was a gallant soldier in the war of the sixties, and belonged to the 6th Tennessee Cavalry, a member of Company B, his captain being

---

53. McCann, *Hurst's Wurst*, 32. A thorough account of this incident may be found in McCann's well-researched and well-written history of the U.S. Sixth Tennessee Cavalry and its controversial commanding officer, Fielding Hurst. The original sources for the information quoted on these ages may further be found in McCann's footnotes on page 32 of his work.

54. The information regarding Frederick J. Floyd was taken from his obituary in the *McNairy County Independent Appeal*, interviews with the late Hayes Hayre and the late Robert Beene, muster rolls for the U.S. Sixth Tennessee Cavalry, and McNairy County, Tennessee Marriage Records.

Frederick J. Floyd

the late Capt. E.J. Hodges." As a member of the Sixth Tennessee Cavalry, Floyd also served under the renowned Colonel Fielding Hurst. After the war, Floyd was married to Lydia E. Naylor on February 15, 1866. The wedding was presided over by Justice of the Peace Robert T. McIntyre. His bond was posted by William Mason. By the time of his death, he and Lydia would have twelve children, 54 grandchildren, 63 great-grandchildren and 5 great-great-grandchildren.

Floyd was very active in the community. For a number of years, he was an elected Justice of the Peace in his district. He was active in Freemasonry having been a Mason for sixty-three years at his death. According to his obituary, Floyd only missed two regular meetings in 54 years and that he "was of that old type of Master Masons who religiously regarded his oath and obligation." Floyd was also involved in local business affairs. He was a founding director of both Home Banking Company and its predecessor, The Bank of Finger. At his death, the McNairy County Independent Appeal said of Floyd, "Esq. Floyd was a splendid citizen, and his life has been one of service to his community and the county. He was a loyal and steadfast friend, and no one was ever deceived by him; his position was made plain on men and measures, and he had the courage of his convictions." According to the editor of the *Independent*, Floyd was a longtime friend of "those connected with its publication" meaning most likely J.W. Purviance, also a Union veteran, and the Abernathy family of Selmer.

Floyd died at his home on Sunday afternoon, April 27, 1932, in Finger, at the age of 87. His funeral was held on the porch of his home with a great crowd present. In their later years, both the late Hayes Hayre and the late Robert Beene recalled attending the funeral. At age eleven, Hayre attended with his grandfather, Lee A. Weaver, and recalled the Masonic presence at the funeral. He recalled the Masons in their Masonic funeral attire and the solemnness of the event. Beene recalled the event with even more alacrity having been a grown man already married at the time. Beene also recalled the sight of a large number of Masons present to perform the Masonic funeral service. A Reverend Lafferty conducted the funeral and W.K. Abernathy, the former Speaker of the Tennessee State Senate, spoke on the life and character of Floyd at the request of Floyd's family. Floyd's obituary recorded that "after the funeral services at the home, the Masons took charge, and about fifty of them marched to the cemetery where Masonic services were held, A.O. Wooten, of the Selmer lodge, in charge." The body was interred in the Finger Cemetery.[55]

George Sargent Anderson (1842–1862)

George Sargent Anderson was born on November 25, 1842, in the Anderson Store community of north McNairy County. The son of William Taylor Anderson and Mahala (Wisdom) Anderson, George was reared in north McNairy County, one of thirteen children born to that union. Further, as such he was a son of two prominent families. Following the outbreak of the War Between the States, George joined the Confederate Army, enlisting in Company H (also known as Company I) of the 154th Senior Tennessee Infantry Regiment, C.S.A., also called the 1st Tennessee Volunteer Regiment. Company H, as it was known in State service and Company I otherwise, it was consisting of men and boys from McNairy County and was commonly known as "The McNairy Guards." The company commanders were men most likely known to Anderson's father: Alphonso Cross, C.R. Wharton and Christopher Sherwin. There is no question that William T. Anderson and Anderson's uncle, William S. Wisdom, knew the regiment's young lieutenant colonel, none other than Marcus Joseph Wright. Young Anderson enlisted sometime between May 14, 1861 and August 13, 1861.

The regiment and young Anderson saw action at the great Battle of Shiloh. It was at this great western battle in which both the commanding Colonel, Preston Smith, and Lieutenant Colonel Marcus J. Wright were seriously injured. The regiment afterward saw service at Richmond, Kentucky.

He died in service to the Southern cause on December 31, 1862, at the battle of Murfreesboro. Several of his brothers distinguished themselves in private and public life, including his brother Hu C. Anderson, a lawyer and mayor of Jackson, Tennessee.

55. Interestingly, the Floyd home, on whose front porch the funeral was held, was the earliest boyhood home of the author which the author remembers.

William H. "Uncle Billy" Harris (1848–1933)

William H. Harris was born in Greensboro, Gilford County, North Carolina, to Arthur and Lucy (Barnes) Harris on May 19, 1848. He and his family came to Tennessee shortly thereafter, following the death of his mother while still in North Carolina. Harris enlisted in the Confederate Army in McNairy County in February of 1863. He would eventually serve in Company I of the Twenty-first Tennessee Cavalry under the command of the brother of General Nathan Bedford Forrest, Lieutenant Colonel Jesse A. Forrest. Following his first battle at Adamsville, Tennessee in the summer of 1863, Harris saw action in a number of locations including Paducah, Kentucky, Memphis, Fort Pillow, Hooker's Bend, and Como, Tennessee, and Okolona, Brice's Crossroads, and Harrisburg, Mississippi. Harris claimed to have been present when General Forrest's brother, Colonel Jeffrey Forrest, was killed. The younger Colonel Forrest was shot through the neck and killed near Okolona, Mississippi. Harris' story, which was comparatively similar to the official version recorded in modern historical works, was that General Forrest rode up, jumped down from his horse, knelt down, held his dead brother, kissed him, and quickly remounted and rode away.

Harris said in an interview in the early twentieth century that as a Confederate soldier, his clothing was poor, he got little sleep, ate corn bread and limited amounts of fat meat, and was often exposed to the cold. To his credit, he did state that he was never in a prisoner of war camp. However, Harris was captured. He was in middle Tennessee when his horse "gave out" on him. He walked into camp and requested a horse from his colonel, but his commanding officer informed him that the war was over. Harris made his way to Oxford, Mississippi, where he was captured by Union authorities. He took the oath of loyalty and began his long walk of one hundred miles home, arriving in July of 1865.

On December 19, 1872, Harris took Eliza (Paralee) Tedford to be his wife. They had at least two children: John R. Harris, local merchant and banker, and Beulah (Harris) Tucker, the wife of Dr. Nathaniel A. Tucker. Following the war, Harris pursued farming, in which he was engaged until 1897, when he moved to Selmer to operate a livery stable. Afterward, Harris moved to Finger to establish the Harris General Merchandise Store in 1900, which he operated until 1910, when his son

John R. Harris took the reins of the business. Following 1910, Harris was the depot agent in Finger. He died on September 10, 1933, and was buried in the Finger Cemetery. Mrs. Harris died on April 19, 1943.

George Irvin Cook (1842-1922)[56]

George Irvin Cook was the son of John Cook and wife Mary (Beard) Cook. John Cook had lived in Middle Tennessee, possibly Putnam County. He was married prior to his marriage to Mary Beard and had children. He afterward married Mary Beard, the daughter of Franklin Beard Jr. and wife Margaret (Brown) Beard. According to family history, John Cook was thrown from a horse and died from the resulting fall. Afterward, Mary (Beard) Cook was reputed to have ridden a horse back to her father's place while pregnant and thereafter gave birth to George Irvin Cook upon her return to McNairy County in 1842. George entered the War Between the States in 1863 on the side of the Southern Confederacy. He did not enter the war during the first year of the campaign in West Tennessee but rather stayed home to to assist his grandfather, Franklin Beard Jr., cultivate his old farm. The elder Mr. Beard was quite old, was not well and could not work much in the fields. Margaret (Brown) Beard was bedfast and Mary Cook needed George at home. George's grandmother died after he went to war and he was unable to attend her funeral.

When the War Between the States broke out, George asked his grandfather for advice as to allegiances. In other words, George wanted his grandfather's advice as to which side he should join. Accordingly, his grandfather replied that if he lived in the North, he guessed he would fight for the North but if he lived in the South, then he would fight for the South. Therefore, he joined the Confederate Army under General Nathan Bedford Forrest serving as a private in Company B of the Sixteenth Regiment of Tennessee Cavalry. Company B was organized at Oakland in Fayette County, Tennessee, on July 15, 1863. According to Nelia Cook, George had an interesting career as a soldier. He was on a furlough and missed the action at the battle of Shiloh but he could hear the cannons'

---

56. All of the information regarding George Irvin Cook was taken from a family history written by the late Nelia Cook during her later years and later found in the possession of Mary (Bell) Wilkerson of Humboldt, Tennessee.

roar at Shiloh some thirty-five miles away.[57] George fought at Gettysburg and had a horse shot from under him. Further, she stated that the bullet went through the side of the horse just behind his leg, but George never got a scratch. Supposedly he mounted another horse and went back into battle. However, there is a major problem with this story. First, it appears that George did not enlist until after July 1863. The battle of Shiloh (Pittsburg Landing) occurred on April 6–7, 1862. Second, the Sixteenth Tennessee Cavalry never fought at the battle of Gettysburg. The regiments fighting under the command of Forrest fought in the Western Theater of the War which included Tennessee, Alabama, Mississippi, Kentucky and north Georgia. Perhaps his horse was shot from under him at another battle. There were plenty of other battles including the battles of Pulaski, Johnsonville, Spring Hill, Franklin and Selma.

According to Ms. Nelia Cook:

> He was never excited, as he said he was never alone, God was with him and took care of him, bringing him safely home where he needed to take care of his mother and grandfather as he did.

George was paroled at Gainesville, Alabama, at the war's end. He returned to north McNairy County and married Louisa Caroline Walker in April 1867, although no marriage record can be found in the records of the McNairy County Court Clerk's Office. The couple had one son, Benjamin Franklin Cook (December 10, 1868–August 4, 1964).

Francis C. "France" Clayton (1841–1925)[58]

Francis C. "France" Clayton is the lone Confederate grave in the Mount Carmel Cemetery. Frankly, little is known about Clayton. It is believed that Francis C. Clayton was a brother to Robert M. Clayton. The two are buried within feet of one another and in the 1860 U.S. Census, there is a male identified as Franklin Clayton living with Robert

---

57. This account telling of the cannons' roar is in keeping with other accounts including that of Simp Lain and others that told of the waters of Tar Creek shimmering during the battle.

58. This sketch was originally published in John E. Talbott, J.D., *A Sacred High Place: A History of Mount Carmel Cemetery & Meetinghouse* (Dickson, TN: BrayBree Publishing, 2013).

M. Clayton and wife Mary C. Clayton.[59] The individual whose name was later transcribed as Franklin was born in the same period of time as France Clayton.

It is known that Francis C. "France" Clayton enlisted in the Confederate Thirteenth Tennessee Infantry. According to that regiment's commander, Colonel A.J. Vaughan, in his work, *Personal Record of the Thirteenth Regiment, Tennessee Infantry, C.S.A.*, Francis Clayton was a soldier in Company F and was living around Montezuma, Tennessee after the war.[60] In fact, Clayton probably received his mail at the Montezuma Post Office in 1897 when the book was published.

Clayton's unit, Company F, was known as "The Wright Boys." The company was originally commanded by a couple of Purdy, Tennessee's finest young men—John V. Wright (also its recent U.S. Congressman), Dew Moore Wisdom, and G.W. Churchwell.[61] As far as can be ascertained, France Clayton was engaged in the following battles during the War Between the States: the battle of Belmont, Missouri, the battle of Pittsburg Landing (Shiloh), the battle of Richmond, Kentucky, the battle of Perryville, Kentucky, the battle of Murfreesboro, Tennessee, the battle of Chickamauga, and the retreat from Atlanta, Georgia after its fall. Clayton had the opportunity to travel all over the South during his time in the Thirteenth Infantry. He and his colleagues were involved in a number of actions and activities short of battle and their activities were constant.

Francis M. Clayton tombstone Mount Carmel Cemetery

---

59. The 1860 U.S. Census spelled the name Clayton as "Claton."

60. A.J. Vaughan, *Personal Record of the Thirteenth Regiment, Tennessee Infantry, C.S.A.* (Memphis, TN: S.C. Toof & Co. Press, 1897; reprint, Memphis, TN: Frank & Gennie Myers and Burke's Book Store, 1970).

61. *Tennesseans in the Civil War, Part 1.*

Dr. Lee H. Ingraham[62]

Dr. Lee H. Ingraham was born in north McNairy County, Tennessee, in 1844, to one of the oldest families in the region. His parents were James M. Ingraham and wife Elizabeth Spencer and his grandparents were John S. Ingraham and Rebecca Ingrahm. According to Goodspeed, Lee Ingraham was the fifth of nine children. He received his early education in McNairy County, possibly at the Purdy Academy in nearby Purdy, the center of learning in the region at that time. In 1861, at the age of seventeen years, while still young and likely tempestuous, Lee Ingraham heeded the call of the day and threw his youthful passions toward the Confederate cause. He enlisted in Company C of the Fifty-Second Tennessee Infantry. By April of 1862, young Ingraham was fighting in one of the greatest battles fought on American soil and only a few miles distant from his family home and plantation. He was present for the opening shots and the resulting Confederate loss at the Battle of Shiloh.

Afterward, the Fifty-Second Tennessee Infantry consolidated with the Fifty-first Tennessee Infantry, where he served for the remainder of his fourteen month enlistment period. During his service in the Confederate Army, Ingraham saw action in the battles of Shiloh, Perryville, Kentucky, and Stone's River near Murfreesboro, Tennessee. After the war's conclusion, Ingraham returned home to north McNairy County and began the study of medicine in 1867. In 1869–1870, Ingraham attended the medical school in Louisville, Kentucky, and returned home and practiced in McNairy County for one year. The 1870 United States Census confirms Ingraham's status as a practicing physician in north McNairy County during that year.[63] Afterward, Ingraham migrated to Sebastian County, Arkansas, and thereupon became a prominent citizen, physician and farmer. As of 1889, Dr. Lee H. Ingraham and his wife, Mary E. (Arbuckle) Carroll Ingraham, were the owners of approximately 1,600 acres including land on Arbuckle Island, Arkansas. They were members of the Cumberland Presbyterian Church and Dr. Ingraham was a Democrat and a Freemason.

---

62. The information regarding Dr. Lee H. Ingraham was taken from Goodspeed's *History of Arkansas* and the 1870 United States Census.

63. 1870 United States Census.

The Life and War Experiences of Mark Perrin Lowrey

When many scholars of Civil War history think of preachers who served the cause of the Confederacy, they may immediately recall the "Bishop-Militant" Leonidas Polk, but only one could be known as the "Fighting Parson." He was Brigadier General Mark Perrin Lowrey. General Lowrey was born near present-day Finger, Tennessee, on December 30, 1828, the son of Adam and Margaret (Doss) Lowrey. Adam, an Irishman, and Margaret, an Englishwoman, immigrated to the United States and eventually found their way to north McNairy County settling somewhere around the Bob and Mary Cone homeplace. One of seven children, three of which are buried in Mount Carmel Cemetery, Mark was the youngest of the boys. Adam Lowrey along with a group of neighbors struck out for New Orleans to market their produce. Unfortunately, Adam took ill with cholera and passed away on a raft going down the river.[64] He was buried in an unmarked grave along the banks of the Mississippi River near Natchez, Mississippi.[65]

Now with a houseful of orphans, Margaret struggled to raise and feed them. After a few years, perhaps five or six, the family moved to Tishomingo County, Mississippi.[66] During his youth, he also served as an apprentice to a brick mason.[67] In 1846, General Lowrey enlisted in the Second Mississippi volunteers as a private in order to serve in the Mexican War.[68] After the War, the General had a thirst for knowledge and learning. He first apprenticed himself to a brick

Mark Perrin Lowrey

---

64. David E. Guyton, *Mother Berry of Blue Mountain* (Nashville, TN: Broadman Press, 1942).

65. Robbie Neal Sumrall, *The Fighting Parson: General Mark Perrin Lowrey, C.S.A.* Edited by Joe Gillis. (Adamsville, TN: 1994). Guyton, *Mother Berry of Blue Mountain*.

66. Ezra J. Warner, *Generals in Gray: Lives of the Confederate Commanders*. (Baton Rouge: Louisiana State University Press, 1959).

67. Guyton, *Mother Berry of Blue Mountain*.

68. *Id.*

mason for a period of three years.⁶⁹ In order to learn and gain some form of education, he boarded with the "village schoolteacher" who taught him at night when his work was done. The General's love of knowledge would eventually lead him to accomplish great deeds in the academic world, but it was his love of the Lord that led him to greater things immediately.

The General entered the ministry in 1853. Long before his entry into the ministry, he had determined he wanted to do it right. With the support of his wife, Sarah (Holmes) Lowrey, whom he married in 1849, the General built a study out in the yard and devoted part of his day to his studies.⁷⁰ He remained dedicated to his ministry until the outbreak of war in 1861.

Following the outbreak of war after Fort Sumter in 1861, Mark Perrin Lowrey, the preacher, was elected captain of a company of his neighbors. The enlistment was for a period of sixty days. Convinced to go to Corinth with the company for the formation of a regiment, he was elected unanimously to the rank of colonel.⁷¹ The group was then sent to Bowling Green, Kentucky, where in the midst of winter, many became sick and a good number of his men died.⁷² When the sixty day enlistment expired, he and his men were discharged and went home.⁷³ However, after the fall of Fort Donelson and the loss of a company of Tishomingo County men, the General was elected to the position of colonel of the Thirty-Second Mississippi Regiment which he raised and organized.

During his service, he fought with great distinction in the Kentucky campaign and at the battle of Chickamauga. Lowrey was wounded at Perryville, Kentucky and according to the General's daughter, Modena (Lowrey) Berry, who was known affectionately as "Mother Berry" to generations of students at Blue Mountain students, his recovery at home was memorable. According to Mrs. Berry:

> My father was wounded in the elbow in the first battle in which he was engaged, at Perryville, Kentucky. He was sent home during convalescence, but could not come to Kossuth

69. *Id.* Sumrall, *The Fighting Parson.*
70. *Id.*
71. *Id.*
72. *Id.*
73. *Id.*

where Mother and her nine children were, right in a nest of Yankees with pickets in sight of our home. Father went to the home of his brother, then living near what is now Blue Mountain, and sent his brother in an ox wagon all the way to Kossuth after his wife and children. We knew nothing of all this until one night about ten o'clock we heard a man drive up into the lot back of our house. Coming around to the front, Uncle delivered Father's message to Mother. We had a horse and buggy, the horse being hidden out by day and brought home at night. Mother and Uncle and a white woman whom my father had left to help Mother look after her household duties, slipped around quietly through the house, gathering up the clothes to be packed in the wagon and buggy. Maggie and I were up helping. By three in the morning we were ready to move the children from the beds to the wagons and buggy. We put down a mattress in the wagon bed with a feather bed on it, then sheets, blankets, and quilts—and on top of all, seven children, most of them sound asleep, never waking during the hurried transfer.

My mother and I climbed into the buggy, my mother the driver, and I holding close in my arms one twin-baby, and Maggie, sitting on the bed in the wagon, holding the other twin with the other five children lying on the bed, sound asleep. The Lord surely must have been helping, for there was not a single whimper from a child.

It was about three-thirty A.M. when we drove off, my uncle driving the ox wagon ahead of the buggy. Though we did not realize it then, we were leaving this home for good. Father later traded it and the eighty-acre farm for a pony and a barrel of molasses.

It took us till the late afternoon of the second day to reach the home of my uncle. Just south of Ripley, we spied my father coming to meet us. He was on his big war horse with his arm in a sling. Uncle stopped his team and we younger children piled out and ran to meet him. He alighted from his horse and gave each of us a hearty hug with his well arm, cautioning us not to press on the wounded arm. Mother remained in the buggy with one of the twins till Father made his way to her. As we had done on the night before where we found hospitality in a farm home north of Ripley, we made down the beds in Uncle's little home and after a hearty supper, the seven smaller children were soon sound asleep. This was early in November, 1862.

The next morning Father and Uncle having located for us a two-room log dwelling with a little kitchen in the back yard, we moved in, remaining there, two miles south of Blue Mountain, till the end of the war.

As soon as his arm had healed, Father returned to the army. I well remember his good-by [sic] to us when he left us to resume his military duties. He arranged for a cousin of mine, a boy of sixteen, to live with us and to help look after us and protect us. This cousin slept in one of our two rooms and Mother and the nine children in the other.

But back to Father's farewell. All of us children and mother were seated around in a semicircle. The two pairs of twins were in boxes about one and one-half feet square. The other small children were seated on the floor and the older ones of us were sitting on boxes. The cousin sat on the doorstep, holding Father's horse, already saddled for his departure. Father opened the Bible and read his favorite Scripture, Psalm 121, then knelt and prayed that the Lord would take care of the health and lives of everyone and would bring us together again in health at the close of this dreadful war. The prayer ended, he rose from his knees and went around the semicircle, kissing every child without saying a word, for he was too full of emotion to speak. Last, he kissed Mother, then stepped out the door and mounted his horse and rode away. Mother and every child that could walk ran out into the yard and watched him till he rode out of sight.[74]

Mrs. Berry also recounted other experiences regarding her family and her father during the course of the war and the harrowing times faced by

---

74. *Id*, 19–22.

them, which was no different from that faced by many active families. Again, according to Mrs. Berry:

> A company of Yankees from Corinth had been located in Kossuth to forage for food for the invaders. One night when we children were all asleep, my father came to the window by my mother's bed and called to her to open the door for him. Thinking that he was in or near Tupelo and knowing that the enemy was then in sight of our home, Mother was both confused and frightened; but she got up and let him in and carried him upstairs where he stayed for two days and two nights. He would not risk letting any of us children know that he was at home. Mother told us after the close of the war that Father came downstairs and looked at us all in bed asleep and kissed the babies, but was afraid to touch us older ones for fear we might awake.
>
> The second day, while we children were playing in front of the house, three or four Yankees soldiers came dashing up to us and said to me, the oldest, "Sissie, where is your father?" I said, "He's in the army killing Yankees." He said, "No, he's not, he's right up yonder in that house," pointing to our residence. I said, "He's not there." He said, "When did you see him?" and I told him truthfully just when I had seen him last. He saw from my countenance that I was telling the truth, so they all turned their horses and rode away, thinking they had been misinformed about my father's being at home, seeing the truth in my eyes and tone. I thought I was telling the truth, but I was not. I did not know that he was nearer than Tupelo.
>
> After the close of the war, Father and Mother told me all this and how they trembled as those Yankees talked to me, fearing they would come into the house and capture Father. Father slipped away that night as soon as it was dark and went back to his army in Tupelo.[75]

His rank of brigadier general was confirmed on October 4, 1863. After his promotion, he saw action in some of the most heated and deadly

75. *Id*, 18–19.

battles of the War. His men fought under Lieutenant General William Joseph "Old Reliable" Hardee and Major General Patrick Cleburne during the costly and devastating Atlanta campaign. When he came with Hood into Tennessee, he was present at the heated battles of Franklin, where the South lost six general officers, and Nashville. With the War quickly approaching an end, General Mark Perrin Lowrey resigned from the Confederate Army on March 14, 1865. Following his resignation, the General went back to Mississippi to be with his family who had fled to Tippah County.[76]

It was after the War that General Lowrey founded his beloved Blue Mountain Female Institute (later Blue Mountain College). After much planning and hard work, the school opened on September 12, 1873. The General passed his thirst for knowledge and dedication for service to his children. Each and every one of his children accomplished great goals and made names for themselves in the world of education and religion. The following account of his children's careers comes from a story regarding a celebration to be held at Blue Mountain College in 1940 in honor of Modena (Lowrey) Berry.[77] It also included a collage of photographs of the General and his family.

> Blue Mountain to Hold Celebration
>
> Blue Mountain, Miss., October 30—Mother Berry, whose 90th birthday will be celebrated November 16 at Blue Mountain College, belongs to a family that has well served Baptistry in Mississippi and the South.[78]
>
> This family, the Lowreys of Mississippi, has served the South in many ways. General M.P. Lowrey, the stalk from which the family sprung, was a minister of the gospel, a warrior, and an educator. He founded Blue Mountain College in 1873. Modena Lowrey Berry and her sister, Maggie Lowrey Anderson were members of the first faculty of the college.

---

76. Most of the military information from this sketch came from Warner, *Generals in Gray*.

77. *McNairy County Independent Appeal*, November 1, 1940.

78. Following this sentence was the following: "[T]he picture shows Mother Berry, her parents, and her brothers and sisters. With the exception of those of Mrs. Berry's parents, the pictures were made about 1908." This referred to a collage of photographs of the Lowrey family, not included in this work.

General Lowrey served in the Mexican War as a private, and in the War between the States he rose to the rank of General and was known along the battle fronts as 'The Fighting Parson of the Army of Tennessee." About 1872 while General Lowrey was holding a revival meeting in Jackson, the Mississippi Legislature offered him the Senatorship from Mississippi.[79] His acceptance was all that was necessary. In declining the proffered honor, Lowrey expressed his appreciation, but added: "I cannot sacrifice the commission I hold as minister of the gospel even for a commission as a U.S. Senator."

About this time also, General Lowrey was offered the executive secretaryship of the foreign Mission Board of the Southern Baptist Convention. He declined this honor for the reason in his own words, "...that a country home in Mississippi is a safer place to rear my six boys." His wife said: "...what would I do in a city like Richmond, Virginia, with my children?"

W.T. Lowrey, minister and educator, served as president of three other colleges. He has been chairman of the board of Trustees of the Baptist Hospital in Memphis since its beginning.

Janie Lowrey Sanford Graves was a missionary to the Chinese for 52 years. She founded Pooi To Academy, Canton, China, a school for Chinese girls, and was its principal. Later she found the Mo Kwong Home for blind girls in Canton and served as its superintendent until failing eyesight and ill health caused her retirement. She now lives at Mobile, Alabama, with her sister.

B.G. Lowrey, educator and statesman, served in the Congress of the United States as representative from the Second District of Mississippi. While of Blue Mountain College, he was largely instrumental in establishing the Baptist Hospital in Memphis, Tennessee. T.C. Lowrey was business manager of the college for more than twenty years.

Booth Lowrey, father of the present President of Blue Mountain College, Lawrence T. Lowrey, was an author,

---

79. This was in the time before the popular election of United States Senators. For many years, senators were chosen by state legislatures.

poet, teacher, and nationally famed humorous lyceum lecturer. P.H. Lowrey was Circuit Judge of his Judicial District in Mississippi and lives at Marks.

Sara Holmes Lowrey was the wife of General Lowrey and the mother of Mrs. Berry. Joseph Johnston Lowrey was for many years a prominent cotton man in New Orleans, and now, retired, lives in Memphis, Tennessee. Linnie Lowrey Ray was dietitian of the college for many years. Sallie Lowrey Potter is now matron at Hillman College, Clinton, Mississippi, of which Mrs. Berry's son, M.P.L. Berry is president.

All brothers and sisters are living except T.C. and Booth.

General Lowrey was born in McNairy County, Tennessee, not far from Finger and pastored several Tennessee churches before the War Between The States.

General Lowrey continued with his work as a preacher and as an administrator. As the years passed by, many improvements were made at the school, which became a college in 1877. Many vital additions and improvements were made to the grounds and buildings. He also taught history and moral science. While on a trip, General Lowrey stopped over in Middleton, Tennessee, where purchased train tickets and turned from the ticket window falling dead immediately. He was only fifty-six years old.

CHAPTER FOUR

THE EDUCATION OF NORTH McNAIRY COUNTY

Early education in north McNairy County—Subscription schools and self-education—The founding of the one teacher schools—From Fairview to Finger School—Biographical sketches of north McNairy County's prominent educators.

Education, though today an open door for virtually every youth in the United States, has been often considered in years past not as a privilege, but rather a luxury. This was often the case for youths and adults in north McNairy County during its early development. Education has always been a difficult term to define. One man's idea of an education is replete with formal training and advanced collegiate degrees. Still other men, including the famed western writer Louis L'Amour, view education as a life-long process of constant learning, most of which does not take place in the confines of a school building. Yet, that is how we most often define education, as the time spent in our youth under the direction of a teacher. Thus we must discuss the school days of yesterday.

The modern school of the 21st century consists of comfortable settings in an advanced physical plant staffed with a professional academic faculty and adequate support staff. However, this is a recent development.

The schools in and around north McNairy County in the late 19th century and early to mid- to 20th century were much different than that to which students are accustomed today. Together we will take a mental tour, however limited, through the schools of yesteryear as described by the students who experienced them.

Let us begin with the generalities surrounding the educational system of those days. During the period of the 1870s and 1880s, the teachers in the area did not have to possess a bachelor's degree or any special training. Most did not have to be licensed, although some were. The majority of area educators were men, either preachers or farmers who were literate and chose to hold school sessions during the periods they were not required in the fields. These were not well-founded ventures, but rather make-shift affairs. Students were the children of the teacher's neighbors, who paid the teacher a fee for their teaching services. These subscription schools lasted only a couple of months and emphasized the basics of reading, writing, and the ancient skill of ciphering.

Schoolmasters were stern and discipline was a certainty. Often youngsters sat on backless benches and worked on slate practicing their letters and working mathematical problems. There were a few educators who received some portion of formal training and chose to take a state administered examination. In the period following the War Between the States, such examinations consisted of areas such as the Bible, language, history, mental and written arithmetic, orthography, grammar, geography, and theory and practice of teaching.[1]

As the years passed and states began to encourage their counties to hire better qualified teachers and improve standards, teacher training schools known as normal colleges began to appear across West Tennessee and the South. Some of the new centers for learning included such venerable old institutions as Purdy University, West Tennessee Business and Normal College, Georgie Robertson Christian College, and Freed-Hardeman College.[2] These schools trained both young men and women

---

1. Certificates of teaching belonging to James Simpson Lain, founder of Lain's Academy, along with transcripts of former teachers who attended Freed-Hardeman College, contained proficiencies in these areas. Orthography was a method of spelling.

2. Purdy University was also referred to as Purdy College or Purdy Academy. Both West Tennessee Business and Normal College and Georgie Robertson Christian College were forerunners to the present-day Freed-Hardeman University.

in a variety of courses and fields in order to provide them with a vast reservoir of knowledge with which to work.

Purdy Academy or Purdy College was an early seat of learning and was actually named Purdy Institute when it was formally established in 1859. Certainly, there was some form of academy in Purdy prior to 1859 but Purdy Institute was meant to be a seat of higher learning upon its establishment. The Institute was established in August of 1859 by the leaders of Purdy. William S. Wisdom served as the President of the Board of Trustees. The institution was being established at a time when the country and indeed the state of Tennessee were in a state of turmoil. Politicians had thus failed to save the Union from disintegration with their powers of oratory and persuasion. The nation was hurriedly speeding toward war and certain of the citizens of McNairy County were continuing with progress despite the news out of distant capitals.

On August 20, 1859, *The Whig Banner*, the Purdy newspaper, announced the formation of the Purdy Collegiate Institute. The faculty included the Reverend A.M. Johnson, President and Professor of Physical, Mental and Moral Sciences, Political Economy and Belles Letters; the Reverend B.H. Malone, A.M., Professor of Ancient Languages; and Mr. J.P. Baldridge, A.M., Professor of Mathematics.[3] These gentlemen were typical of those professors and teachers of the day. The Reverend Johnson had been a teacher and "governor of youth" for more than ten years in 1859, who "has proved himself to the satisfaction of his most enlightened patrons.[4] The Reverend Malone was a local Methodist Episcopal Church South minister, who had graduated from Wesleyan University in Florence, Alabama in 1856, and his services came with the highest recommendations of the Reverend R.H. Rivers, D.L., President of Wesleyan University.[5] Professor Baldridge, it was said, "unites the manly dignity of the scholar with the urbanity of the perfect gentleman.[6]

In the same issue of *The Whig Banner*, nothing less than a prospectus appeared. What follows is a description of the campus and its amenities in 1859:

3. *The Whig Banner* (Purdy, TN), August 20, 1859.
4. *Id.*
5. *Id.*
6. *Id.*

> We have a large and beautiful brick edifice handsomely finished; well-furnished, lighted and ventilated, with all the windows curtained so as to temper the light to the comfort of the laboring eye. It stands in the centre of a large, delightful campus where the students take healthful exercise in the hours of recreation.
>
> We have lately purchased an extensive and complete Philosophical, Astronomical, Chemical and Electrical Apparatus in Boston, Mass., at a cost of Two Thousand Dollars. Our Congressional Library is worth Fifteen Hundred Dollars, and will be enlarged by the addition of other works when the interest of the students demands it.[7]

The War Between the States would wreck the dreams and hopes of the Purdy Collegiate Institute. The War would help nail the proverbial coffin shut for Purdy and its institution for higher learning. Again, education in north McNairy County entered into a period of uncertainty and again a matter of irregularity. Then again, for the child of the common farmer and laborer, it had never been any other way.

Such courses of study in the 1920s and 1930s included many which might surprise today's educator-in-training. To meet English grammar and literature requirements, many future pedagogues sat through courses such as American Poetry, English composition, Grammar, Sentences and Words, Spelling, Children's Literature, and Prose.[8] Credits in social studies were likewise diverse with such courses as European History, American History Survey, Political Science, Problems of Democracy, Economic Geography, Human Geography, Geography of Europe, and Tennessee History. Courses in mathematics and science were equally diverse: college algebra, chemistry, biology, psychology, arithmetic, human physiology, plane geometry, nature study, elementary statistics, and general science.

Finally, for the sake of being well-versed and knowledgeable, these young new teachers had to be exposed to numerous miscellaneous fields

---

7. *Id.* It is interesting that the Institute possessed a Congressional Library because one of Purdy's sons, John Vines Wright, was the 10th District's incumbent Congressman in Washington City in 1859.

8. These course offerings and those which follow were available at Freed-Hardeman College during the period of the 1920s and 1930s.

of study, while also being trained to handle a classroom. These other courses ranged from modern drama to the Elizabethan Drama to Drama, Law, and Technique, from Beginners Greek to the Life of Christ, from Child Study to the Psychology of Adolescence to Psychology and Morals. One could learn of such vital domestic topics as textiles and methods in table serving. Any new educator could benefit from Rural School Methods or Public School Music. Such courses of study and preparation were a great improvement over past practices as the state strove for educational advancement.

As for the students of these little citadels of learning, their scholastic life may not have been easy, but it was a learning and character building experience. It again was not the modern facility of today with a modern cafeteria and other such conveniences. Students, along with help from their parents, took care of themselves. The following quote illustrates the daily life of an average student in north McNairy County in the 1920s and 1930s:

> They brought their lunch in a lard bucket with holes punched in the top or rolled in newspaper or any paper they had. Several children in the same family would have their lunch packed together in a large eight pound lard bucket. The lunches consisted of fried meat and biscuits, boiled eggs, egg in a biscuit, fried potatoes in a biscuit, peanut butter & crackers. In the summer, we had ripe tomatoes and corn on the cob, fried pies and tea cakes which we sometimes stuck together with chocolate filling. The water supply came from a spring under a long hill on the south side of the school. The older students had the privilege of keeping fresh water in the one water bucket for each room and all students drank from the same dipper!

In the afternoons, two students were allowed to take the blackboard erasers outside to dust out the chalk. The heat for one school was the same as all the other country schools, an iron wood burning stove, which may have contributed to the burning of so many schools. The teacher would usually hire one of the older male students to build the first fire in the morning and the older students would keep the fire going through the day."⁹

Now let us examine the particulars of education in north McNairy County. There were a number of schools and academies in the area from the decade of the 1870s through the 1940s. Most of these institutions were one or two teacher affairs. Lain's Academy, Iola, Oak Ridge, Fairview, Hodges' Beauty, Pegram Beauty, and Mackey are just a few of the names once so familiar to the children of north McNairy County. Now they are only memories of a bygone era and their students, those who remain, are frail and aged. However, one is called to wonder "what" these places were and "who" they were. Here on these pages an attempt will be made.

Lain's (Lane's) Academy

Lain's (Lane's) Academy was established by James Simpson "Simp" Lain, a farmer and teacher, in the 1870s.[10] There were apparently two locations for Lain's Academy, the first being located on the old road running behind the place currently owned by David Ross across the highway from the Lane's Chapel Church house. Apparently this structure was destroyed and a second schoolhouse was constructed on the road running beside the D.C. Hester place.[11]

Like most schools of the time, it was a one teacher school offering grades one through eight. A number of widely recognized and reputable educators conducted their affairs in this little school including William Kendal Abernathy (1880s), Dr. Henry Hodges, Harmon Hodges, Professors Horry Hodges and Harvey Hodges, J.K. Murry (1910), Henry Carothers (1915), Mary Harris (1924–1925), Alma Davidson (1925–1926), Myrtle Reed (1926–1927), and John Robert Moore.

Although it difficult to obtain a comprehensive account of the history of Lain's Academy, one can glean strands of information from the newspapers of the early 20th century. In 1902, the Teacher's Institute was

---

9. Gracie (Plunk) Webster, e-mail message to author, February 2001. She described the situation at Mackey, which was typical of most schools at the time.

10. A biographical sketch of James Simpson Lain appears at the end of the present chapter.

11. Revealed to the author in January of 2002 by Richard Leath, the great-grandson of James Simpson Lain.

THE EDUCATION OF NORTH McNAIRY COUNTY 103

An early photograph of students and teachers at Lain's (Lane's) Academy, date unknown.

Another early photograph of Lain's (Lane's) Academy. The date and identities of most of the students is unknown. The only known students are Maggie Hodges (top row, ninth from the left) and Harvey Garfield Hodges (top row, sixth from the left).

Lane Academy students, summer 1915. Left to right: (Top row) Berth Barnes, Eubert Plunk, Martie Barnes, Lester Plunk, Parlee Barham, Hobert Patterson, Era Young, Simon Plunk, Margie Baucom, McKinley Patterson. (Middle row) Beatrice Plunk, Bertha Beyre Plunk, Minnie Baucom, Vaudie Patterson, Cora Barton, John Calvin Amerson, Louisa Plunk, Grady Robbins, Ethel Barton, Foy Patterson, teacher Henry Carothers. (Front row) Gladys Hysmith, Gossie Plunk, Alta Patterson, Pearl Barham, and two unknown students.

held at Lain's Academy. The accounts tell us that Hugh L. Hodges, later a merchant and produce dealer in Finger, delivered the welcome address and Harvey Hodges delivered the response. Major A. James was identified as the "public relations person" and Miss Maggie Hodges kept the journal for the Institute.[12] A 1932 article in the Independent spoke of a visit to its offices by Miss Maggie Hodges who bore news from her sister, Mrs. Jennie Scott of Tupelo, Mississippi. The editor wrote:

> We are glad to state that both these Hodges sisters went to the old Lane Academy when the editor [W.K. Abernathy] of this paper was teaching school there. It was a one-teacher school, and about eighty happy boys and girls attended. But that was a long time ago. We are so glad that the many friendships formed then have lasted throughout the years, and it is a pleasure to meet and greet these old pupils, and take a little time in talking of the happenings back yonder.[13]

12. *McNairy County Independent Appeal*, November 28, 1902.
13. *McNairy County Independent Appeal*, May 6, 1932.

Lain's Academy served many young people and gave them a solid start to life. Many of the county's brightest talents taught here and carried fond memories of those days with them. However, like all things physical, the school could not last forever and closed forever sometime around 1927.

Oak Ridge School

The old Oak Ridge school was established in the old Eighth Civil District in 1879. Mr. Moses Kirkpatrick made application for the school and the charter was signed by Moses Kirkpatrick, I.H. Plunk, W.L. Malone, W.F. Kirkpatrick, T.B. Malone, J.H. Malone, and David Williams.[14] The schoolhouse was located on the Crowe Road about 200 yards north of the Lee Loftin place. Crowe Road ran from the Finger-Enville Road (Center Hill Road) to the Hutcherson-Sweetlips Road. Today the Crowe Road is the Bailey Road.[15]

The Oak Ridge school remained in operation for many years, from 1879 until at least 1945. Some of the teachers there included Effie Plunk (1910), Mildred Finger, Leona Higginbottom (1922-1923), Ruby Bishop (1924-1925 and 1925-1926), Mamie Carothers (1926-1927), Burlene Orr (1927-1928 and 1928-1929), George Moore (1929-1930, 1930-1931 and 1931-1932), Myrtle Ward (1932-1933), Vivian Plunk (1934-1935 and 1935-1936), and Leonard Ward (1936-1937). Vivian Plunk boarded with the Howell Mitchell family and Leonard Ward with the Lee Loftin family.

Some of the students attending there in 1934–35 were John Howard Hutcherson, Georgia Hutcherson, Hershel Loftin, Elmo Loftin, Neil Loftin, Adele Dickey, S.D. Dickey, James Dickey, Billy Frank Mitchell, Maudie Jean Mitchell, F.C. "Ted" Mitchell, James Goff, Ruth Goff, Ora Lee Kelly, Rachel Kelly, Mary Kelly, Joe Kelly, James Kelly, Raymond Naylor, Harmon Arthur Naylor, Johnnie Naylor, Buford Naylor, and T.V. Young.

Oak Ridge schoolhouse was a one-room structure. The room in which much learning took place was 25 feet wide and about 50 feet long. The entry was a double door on the long end nearest the road, with a cloak

---

14. Gracie Webster and Mary Martin, "Elijah Kirkpatrick and Related Families," a small paper written about the genealogy of the family and families of Elijah Kirkpatrick.

15. F.C. "Ted" Mitchell to the author, February 22, 2001.

room to one side of the entry where students hung their overcoats, slickers, and store their overshoes, if any. In the cloak room the coats were hung on nails or wooden pegs. The students could store their lunch on a shelf near their hanging coats.[16] Oak Ridge schoolhouse was laid out like most other such schools. The teacher sat at his or her desk on a stage elevated about one foot above the students' desks. The stage extended the width of the room and there was a bench called "The Recitation Bench" facing the teacher's desk. Usually six to ten students would occupy the bench during the time that a particular class was being recited. There the teacher would question the students about the lesson of the day for that particular class. The late F.C. "Ted" Mitchell made the observation, "of course, one of the problems with that system was that the rest of the students were not in that class and were at their desks and listening at the class recitation. An occasional 'flub' by a member of the reciting class would cause an outburst of guffaws at the 'flub' from the entire student body."

Both at Oak Ridge and Iola, blackboards were located behind the teacher's desk and at the end of the room opposite the entry way. Much like today, where chalk boards are still in use, the blackboards were used for arithmetic, English grammar, sentence parsing, and lecture topics.

Pegram Beauty School[17]

Pegram Beauty was located about three to four miles east of Finger on the Finger-Enville Road (Centerhill Road), across from the turnoff to the road leading to the Melzer Plunk and John Brooks residences.[18] The school was located on the north side of the Finger-Enville Road, about 50 to 75 feet off of the road, and consisted of two rather large rooms with a measurement of approximately 24 feet by 48 feet. The two rooms were separated by an entry way and cloak room. The schoolhouse had a lapboard exterior painted white. The room on the east side of the building

---

16. All of the information regarding the daily activities of the teachers and students of the old one-room schoolhouses was taken from the personal reminiscences of F.C. "Ted" Mitchell as contained in an e-mail to the author on February 26, 2001.

17. This school was identified as "Pilgrim Beauty" in B.J. Naylor, Ed.D. and John E. Talbott, *Fingerprints: An Unofficial and Incomplete History of Finger, Tennessee*. This was in error, as the school was named for the nearby Pegram family. However, it was often pronounced "*Pigram* Beauty."

18. The information regarding Pegram Beauty was again drawn from the memory of F.C. "Ted" Mitchell and contained in an e-mail to the author on February 21, 2001.

Pegram Beauty School (1928–1929) taught by Miss Elsie Basham. Notice the young boy on the front row!

housed the first few grades and here these young scholars went about their lessons. The north and east walls were covered with blackboards, while the south wall contained approximately ten windows which faced the road. These windows were mounted approximately four feet off of the floor and were each three feet in width and six feet in length. These windows, which had roll down shades, provided light on sunny days.[19] The room on the west side was similarly designed and was used for the higher grades, up to seventh and eighth grades.[20]

The floors always smelled of oil due to an oil and sawdust mixture applied to the floors daily. The building's heat source was a couple of pot-bellied wood burning stoves, one in each room. The water supply came from the well of Mrs. Nancy Pegram. As with most small schools of the day, there was only one bucket and a solitary "communal" dipper for all students and the teacher.

---

19. One must remember this was largely before the days of instant light through the magic of electricity.

20. Mitchell noted that his orientation as to the directions of the two room schoolhouse might be off, in that instead of east and west rooms, they might have been north and south rooms.

The first educator to work at Pegram Beauty was J.R. Moore from 1922 to 1923.[21] Exia (Exie) Jackson taught there during the 1924–1925 school year and Foy Patterson during the 1925–1926 school year. George W. Moore and Loree Perry taught at Pegram Beauty during the 1926–1927 school year. Other teachers included Mrs. J.C. Hodges (Grades One through Four in 1930–1931) and Mr. J.C. Hodges (Grades Five through Eight in 1930–1931), Zilphah Jopling (1931–1932), W. Lloyd Smith (1932–1933), Thelma Cude (1933–1934), Adrian (Gage) Hunt (1934–1935), and Cecil Clayton (1935–1936). According to former students at Pegram Beauty, the following taught there as well: Elsie (Basham) Simpson, Pearl (Massey) Gage, Clyde Davidson, and Elvie (Lott) Loving. Many of the teachers who taught at Pegram Beauty over the years boarded with the John and Alice Brooks family, including Joplin, Gage, and Cude.

Some of the students attending Pegram Beauty in 1933 and 1934 were Atlas Plunk, Oneida Plunk, Coolidge Plunk, Gracie Plunk, Weldon Milford, Mary Ruth Milford, Ollye Brooks, Martha Brooks, Roberta Brooks, Ira Hysmith, Ebert Hysmith, Robert Favre, F.C. "Ted" Mitchell, R.B. Barham, and Marcus Barham.

The following article appeared in the *McNairy County School Journal of 1927*:

> The Pegram Beauty School opened in October 1926 for the winter session, after a splendid summer session under Mr. George Moore, as teacher. The winter session is progressing nicely, but all students have not enrolled. There are fifty students enrolled to date, and we expect a large number to enter in a few weeks. Then our building will be crowded. Miss Loree Perry is now assistant teacher here. A society has been organized and divided into two parts known as the Jacksonian and Sevier, and we expect great work out of them. We also expect our school to attend the Field Meet at Selmer this year and expect to carry away first prize on part of the contests anyway. The pupils are all doing splendid work."

Although there are probably many great memories of the days spent at Pegram Beauty, many will unfortunately go unrecorded. However, a

21. This was most likely John Robert Moore.

few have been shared with the author. During the 1934 school year when Miss Elvie Lott (later Loving) was the teacher, her brother, Warren Lott, often drove her to work and assisted her during the school day. It has been recalled that Warren assisted his sister in keeping the "books" and doing other tasks to help her get through the day. However, the young men at Pegram Beauty were more impressed by Warren's 1931 four door Chevrolet sedan. The schoolhouse at Pegram Beauty burned in 1936 and afterward many students began attending Mackey Schoolhouse (also known as Mackeyfield).

Iola Schoolhouse

The Iola schoolhouse was located at the junction of the Hutcherson-Sweetlips Road and the "Floyd" Road.[22] The schoolhouse itself was located near the Glen Smith and Willard Smith farmhouses. The description of the Pegram Beauty schoolhouse will serve as a reference for the description of Iola, as the two structures were very similar in design. The teachers who served at Iola included Blanche Plunk (1922–1923), Dovie Jopling (1923–1924), John Robert Moore (1924–1925), Ruby Dee Vinson (1926–1927), Hubert Plunk (1927–1928 and 1928–1929), Elvie (Lott) Loving (1929–1930 and 1930–1931), Hobert Young (1932–1933), Howard Mitchell (1933–1934), Myrtle Ward (1934–1935 and 1935–1936), Prince Plunk (1936–1937 and 1937–1938), Leonard Ward (1938–1939, 1946–1947, and 1947–1948), Haven Garner (1939–1940), Irene Smith (1941–1942 and 1942–1943), Ora Bullman (1944–1945 and 1945–1946), and T.V. Young Jr. (1948–1949). According to some sources, B.O. Weeks and Lula (Plunk) Younger also taught at Iola.[23] Weeks boarded with the William Plunk family. The reader may have noticed that many of the aforementioned educators boarded with families in the community. This was a common practice during the time of one-room schoolhouses, bad county roads, and unreliable transportation.

---

22. This may not have been the official name of the road, but has been referred to as such due to the fact that a certain Widow Floyd lived on the road at the time. Today this road is known as the Hillard Gann Road.

23. Most of this information was researched by Mrs. Gracie Webster based on McNairy County school records. However, the mention of B.O. Weeks comes from Mr. Marvin Hand of Hesperia, California, who was a "visiting" student at Iola in the 1920s.

Among the students attending Iola in the period around 1932 were Sam Robison, Hayse Robison, Irene Robison, Harlan Floyd, Susie Floyd, G.T. Smith, F.C. "Ted" Mitchell, John Howard Hutcherson, Belver Hutcherson, Juanita Hutcherson, and James Ward Hutcherson.[24] The Iola school was closed around 1950 and the schoolhouse was torn down and the materials used to build the old Manley Wright home in Finger, located on the corner of Litt Wilson Road and State Highway 199.

Centerhill Academy[25]

Centerhill Academy was established in 1891 in the old Sixteenth Civil District, not far from the O'Neal Cemetery, on the Leapwood-Enville Road.[26] The land on which the schoolhouse was built was donated by Mr. James M. Bishop. In the period of the early 1900s, the number of students at Centerhill Academy numbered around seventy to eighty. The early teachers at Centerhill included Terry Abernathy, Sr., Horry Hodges, Kelly Wade, Lavera (Thompson) Sewell, Ida (O'Neal) Lee, Richard "Dick" Rankin, George Poole, Fielding Maness, Leonard Owen (1910), and Homer O'Neal. The later teachers at Centerhill included Grady Droke (1922–1923), Eura (Carothers) Robison (1923–1924), Cola Davidson (1924–1925), John E. Malone (1925–1926), H.U. Prather (1926–1927), D.R. Finger (1927–1928), Parker Ellis (1928–1929 and 1929–1930), Clyde Davidson (1930–1931), Vera Plunk (1931–1932, 1932–1933, and 1933–1934), George W. Moore (1934–1935 and 1936–1937), Willard Smith (1937–1938 and 1938–1939), Arlis Plunk (1939–1940 and 1940–1941), Elmer Lee Phillips (1941–1942 and 1942–1943), Mary Nelle Smith (1943–1944), O. Cletus Harris (1948–1949 and 1949–1950), and Lester Causby (1951–1952). According to one source, a teacher named Eber Henry also taught here. Like many teachers in that day, teachers at Centerhill were paid less than fifty dollars per month. Centerhill

---

24. F.C. "Ted" Mitchell to the author, February 28, 2001.

25. A large portion of the information contained in this sketch was compiled by the late Roy O'Neal and originally printed in *Reflections: A History of McNairy County, Tennessee, 1823-1996*. A much fuller sketch can be found by Mr. O'Neal in that work.

26. Although it has been stated that Centerhill Academy was established in 1891, the school was not mentioned in the list of schools in 1902.

Academy, along with four other small nearby schools, was closed and moved to Leapwood in 1952.

Poplar Springs

Poplar Springs School was located in the Bullman Store area near Hopewell Baptist Church in north McNairy County. It is not known when the school was established, but its last known school year was 1945. Some of Poplar Springs' teachers included Vivian Henry (1925), Dovie Jopling (1927), and Ora Bullman. Nothing more is currently known regarding this little country school.

Fairview

Fairview at one time was a two-teacher school and was located on what is now the Sol Colston Road. The school was operating as early as 1910. Teachers at Fairview included Lillie Cude (1910), Samuel Henry (1922–1923), W.E. Plunk (1923–1924), Clyde Davidson (1924–1925, 1925–1926, and 1926–1927), Mary Higginbottom (1927–1928), Mrs. H.L. Young (grades 1–3 in 1930–1931), Hubert Plunk (grades 4–7 in 1930–1931), Mrs. J.C. Hodges (grades 1–4 in 1932–1933 and 1934–1935), J.C. "Clifford" Hodges (grades 5–8 in 1932–1933 and 1934–1935), Mrs. B.O. Weeks (grades 1–4 in 1933–1934), Hobert Young (grades 5–8 in 1933–1934), Geneva Davidson (grades 1–4 in 1935–1936), Raymond Hodges (grades 5–8 in 1935–1936), Ina McNeil (grades 1-4 in 1936-1937), Haven Garner (grades 5–8 in 1936–1937, grades 1–7 in 1937–1938, and grades 1–8 in 1938–1939), Leonard Ward (grades 1–8 in both 1939–1940 and 1941–1942), Clarence Hooper (grades 1–8 in 1942–1943), Mary Smith (grades 1–8), Mary Martin (grades 1–8), and Arlus (Bratcher) Plunk (grades 1–8).

One of the problems at Fairview was a common problem in many little country schools: the plight of the sharecropper's child. In other words, many of the students were the children of sharecroppers and renters who went to school the first half of the year and then dropped out the second half when their parents picked up and moved on. Such migrations were common and a great disruption to small schools and their teachers.

Arlis Plunk was the last teacher at Fairview before it closed and the students were moved to Finger.

Old Friendship

The old Friendship School was located just off of U.S. Highway 45, within sight of the highway. The students played ball and conducted recess at one far end of the cemetery, in an area that became the newer section of the cemetery. John R. Swaim taught two summers here in the early part of the twentieth century. Among the other teachers at Friendship were Georgia Hunter and Varnell Rankin. Mrs. Hunter taught there from about 1942 until it closed in 1962, a span of twenty years. Haven Garner recalled a basketball game between the students at Friendship and McNairy. The students at Friendship had not been used to a gymnasium such as McNairy had and never really learned all the rules of the game. When the game began at McNairy, the students from Friendship never dribbled or bounced the basketball. Instead, they carried the ball like a football and started running to the other end of the gym toward the goal. The spectators couldn't follow the game, due to the most part from their amusement at what they were seeing. Certainly no one remembers the score, but those present at McNairy that afternoon won't soon forget the spectacle.

Refuge

The Church of Christ at Refuge was established in 1851. During most of the years from its founding until the late 1940s, the church building also doubled as the Refuge Schoolhouse. It is not currently known when the school was actually established, but the 1851 deed refers to the use of a schoolhouse. Therefore it is very possible that Refuge had a school for almost 100 years. Teachers there included Miss Rachel Booth (1910), Eber Henry (1925), Samuel Henry (1927), Haven Garner (1940–1944), and Hazel Amerson (1945). Mr. Laney Archer had a job at Refuge School doing such small, but important jobs as keeping water accessible to the students, making fires and maintaining them in the heater, and sweeping and cleaning the schoolhouse. The old meetinghouse and schoolhouse was located exactly where the older section of the current one stands today. Among the many families whose children attended school at Refuge were, among others, the Archers, the children of Dewey Gee and Olis Robinson and the Owens children.

Clover Hill/Hodges' Beauty

Clover Hill school was located off of McCormick Road on Weeks Road about one-half mile south of the old Hodges' Beauty site. The exact date for that school's establishment is currently unknown. Teachers at Clover Hill included a Miss Massengill (1910) and Cletus Harris (1913). The Clover Hill schoolhouse burned in 1922. Upon that event, J.C. Hodges offered land on his farm, located about one-half mile north, on which to rebuild the school. However, there was one catch. The new school had to bear the name Hodges' Beauty, not Clover Hill. In fact, the new school was built on the Hodges' property. However, many parents of the children who attended Clover Hill refused to refer to the new school as Hodges' Beauty and continued to call it "Clover Hill." This had a curious result. The records existing after Hodges' Beauty was built (and, of course, after Clover Hill had burned) continue to refer to Clover Hill, with no mention whatsoever of Hodges' Beauty. This result came from the fact the McNairy County superintendent of schools refused to enter into the argument. Therefore, for a number of years the school officially retained the old name of Clover Hill.[27]

Hodges' Beauty was built in 1923 to replace the Clover Hill schoolhouse. As mentioned earlier, it was built on property donated by J.C. Hodges. Between 1922 and 1949, when the school closed, there were sixteen different teachers at Hodges' Beauty, which was still recognized as the Clover Hill school by the local superintendent's office. Regardless, teachers at Clover Hill or Hodges' Beauty included Alma Higginbottom (1922–1923), Leora Higginbottom (1924–1925), Pearl Hair (1926–1927 and 1927–1928), Mildred Finger (1928–1929), Bertha Cobb (1929–1930), Wilma Surratt (1930–1931, 1931–1932, and 1932–1933), Cola Davidson (1933–1934), Arlus Plunk (1934–1935), Howard Clifton (1937–1938 for two months), May Tucker (1937–1938 for six months), Raymond A. Stout (1940–1941), _____ Neal Shelton (1941–1942),

---

27. The information regarding the naming controversy was relayed to the author by Mrs. Merle (Gibson) Weatherford in the spring of 2001.

Fay Marie Sewell (1942–1943 and 1943–1944), Jannice Rogers (1944–1945, 1945–1946, and 1946–1947), Juanita Massengill (1947–1948), and Dorothy English (1948–1949).

According to some sources (including Mr. Mancel Kirk), other teachers included Noah Allen Robinson, Howard Davidson, and Daisy (Barham) Reed. The same sources state that Mary Higginbottom taught at Clover Hill/Hodges' Beauty and that Raymond A. Stout taught there as well as from 1939 until 1940.

Some of the families whose children attended Hodges' Beauty included those of Elbert Kirk, Pony Gibson, Bob Milford, John Surratt, John Massengill, Fayette Massengill, Hubert Barnes, Ed Clayton, Tom Barham, Charlie Barham, Elmer Clemmons, Jessie Robinson, Roma Helton, Rube Treece, Ovie Young, and Russell Plunk.

Like many small schools of the time, the water supply came from a spring near the schoolhouse. The older students often walked across the road and down the hill to the spring to procure water for the rest of the class. The spring is today just as it was seventy years ago. Like many young students at small country schools, those at Hodges' Beauty never missed an opportunity to have a little fun and play. In 1940, the students put on a play entitled, "Aaron Slick from Pumpkin Creek."[28] The school's last known date of operation was 1949.

Elm Ridge

The name for this schoolhouse was pronounced much like rural people in this area pronounced the tree name. It was pronounced as if it were spelled, "Elam" or "Elum." It probably received its name for the abundance of elm trees located on the ridge where the structure stood. The schoolhouse was said to have stood on ground bordering the Pony Gibson farm. According to Mancel Kirk of Finger, the late Clarence Barham, son of Justice of the Peace Charlie Barham, attended school here. Nothing further is known of this little house of learning.

---

28. Interview with Mancel Kirk in 2001.

Cool Springs

The exact location of this school is unknown. It is known that it operated from 1922 until 1927. According to some sources, Arlus Bratcher Plunk taught here in the mid-1930s. Regardless, those teachers known from the county school records included H.K. Maness (1922–1923), Blanche Plunk (1923–1924), Vena Davidson (1924–1925), Samuel Henry (1925–1926), and Effie Cunningham (1926–1927).

Kerby

This old school was located near the old Beaty Cemetery, east of the old Purdy and Denmark Road. According to one source, Jack and Sarah Kerby had the school built by Dick Tucker.[29] The couple had eleven children and was very interested in the children having a school to which they could attend. G.W. Bullinger was the manager or principal of Kerby. Lloyd Harris also taught at a Kirby schoolhouse in 1939.

Kerby, Third District

The second Kerby schoolhouse was located near the Chester county line near Masseyville. Among the teachers at the Third District Kerby School were Hadley Maxwell and Lloyd Smith.

Liberty

The first school session was held at old Liberty in and around the year 1835. As the years passed, many boys and girls walked through the doors at Liberty in the quest for knowledge and preparation. As expected, many of the same types of incidents and schoolyard occurrences existed at Liberty as did elsewhere. However, there were also a few very serious happenings at Liberty which have been recorded first in the minds of the young students growing up near Liberty and which were later recorded on paper with the succeeding years. Let us now examine what we know concerning the Liberty School.

---

29. This was recorded by Anna Lou (Kerby) Phillips of Memphis, Tennessee.

Liberty School students and teacher Effie Sheets (top row, second from left) circa 1919

The school was located approximately where the current Liberty meetinghouse is situated. There is no way to conclusively list all of the educators who labored at Liberty between 1835 and its closing in the 1950s. A few of the teachers during this long period included the following: Alfred Monroe Plunk (during the 1860s, following the War), Dick Pickett (1880), Charlie Plunk (1895), Harvey Hodges (1913), Horry Hodges (summer 1913), and Lorraine (Gage) Cothran (1931). According to Jose Plunk (1856–1954), there was no school in session during the War Between the States[30]

There were a number of incidents of violence which occurred at Liberty over the years. Sometime around 1861, Jim Simons stabbed Frank Morrison at Liberty School. The wound was fatal and thus Simons was taken into custody and transported to nearby Purdy, the county seat at the time, and jailed. While in jail, Simons was taken with sickness and released to go home, where he died. In the later years, it was told that Simons contracted tuberculosis. Regardless of Simons' illness, there was never a trial.[31]

---

30. Marvin Hand interview with Jose Plunk.
31. *Id.*

Rocky Knob School

According to the records of the McNairy County School System, there was a school at Rocky Knob during the 1930–1931 school year. According to the said records, the teacher at the Rocky Knob School was Ms. Bonnie Ellis.

Mackey (Mackeyfield) School[32]

Mackey School was located about seven miles east of Finger on the Finger-Leapwood Road, now State Highway 199. Mackey School was

Mackey School. Left to right: (Front row) Yancey Whorton, R.B. Burkeen, J.R. Walker, Kemit Tacker, Grady Walker, Herman Vires, Dewayne Vires, J.T. Vires, Hurley Amerson, Camran Davis. (Second row) Maurine Carpenter, unknown, Faye Carpenter, Flossie Bivins, Hazel Amerson, Muerl Amerson, Euma Vires, Junell Plunk, Louise Cloud, Oma Vires, Jimmie Nash, Newana Davis, Willodean Whorton, Dorothy Plunk, Lafonne Whorton, Faydell Clemons. (Third row) James Cloud, teacher Bertie Martin, Paul Clemons, Aleane Clemons, Albert Ray (or Cecil) Carpenter, Willie May Patterson, Beulah Chandler, Collis Burkeen, Raymond Amerson, Louise Clemons, Helen Walker, Raymond Davis, Harrell Robison, Hurley Nash, teacher Hubert Plunk. (Fourth row) Petway Plunk, Leanear Walker, Orphus Patterson, R.J. Moore, Nevil Plunk, Charles Cloud, James "Bob" Plunk, R.A. Vires, Leonard Patterson, Ray Moore, Kermit Davis, Frank Robison.

32. The information in this sketch was furnished by Gracie (Plunk) Webster in February 2001.

established in 1922, but in what exact location or building is not currently known.[33] Regardless, a permanent school building was constructed in 1926.[34] During the period of construction, classes were held in the Maggie Jones United Methodist Church building. Teachers at that time were Mr. and Mrs. Lester Moore. They were both still teaching there in the 1927. Others who taught the little ones at Mackey in those old days were Jonah A. Sipes (July 1929 to April 1930), his daughter Hermie Sipes, Hubert Plunk (1938), Bertie (Martin) Garrett (1938), Lula (Plunk) Younger, Howard Davidson, Arlus Plunk, Elvie (Lott) Loving, Irene (Smith) Fry (1942–1943), John Robert Moore, and Evelyn (Clayton) Barham.[35]

After Pegram Beauty School burned in 1936, some of those students remained at home for two years and then were sent to Mackey School. In case the question arises as to why these students were kept at home, that question can be answered in a simple manner, some students were too small to walk that far. According to Gracie (Plunk) Webster, there were "a lot of students and they came walking from all directions." Although most did walk to school, there was an alternative form of transportation. Albert Owens and Homer Carpenter drove students to school at Mackey in covered wagons in the early 1940s and Tom Phillips drove a bus sometime between 1938 and 1942.

In the early 1940s the teachers at Mackey School were Howard Davidson and Lula (Plunk) Younger. According to former students, both were good teachers and promoted basketball. Mackey School had several good players on both its girls' and boys' teams. Mr. Davidson had a pickup truck and would load the children in the truck and take them to play other local small country schools. Again Gracie (Plunk) Webster remembered that Davidson took the students to his house for refreshments consisting of good coconut cake baked by his sisters. The school burned while Davidson and Younger were teaching there and classes were again held at Maggie Jones Methodist church until the school could be rebuilt.

The school closed in 1950 and the school building was torn down by Allen M. Amerson. The lumber from the structure was used to build a house which still stands on the lot next to the Orval Amerson home.

33. Date of organization and closing can be found in the *McNairy County School Reports*.

34. *McNairy County School Journal*, October 25, 1926.

35. The 1942–1943 McNairy County School Report shows that Noah Allen Robinson was to teach at Mackey, but apparently never did.

Students of Finger School and teacher John R. Swaim in 1911. The man to the far right is Robert McMillan Weaver.

Finger[36]

School days at Finger began sometime before the year 1910. Although the exact date is currently unknown, it is possible that it was as early as 1902. In 1906, the following were listed as Finger teachers who were licensed: Allie James, Julia Hodges, Harvey Hodges, Fielding Maness, H.K. Maness, and Harmon E. Hodges.[37] It is not known whether these people actually taught at the Finger school or if they taught in some of the other local schools nearby. At any rate, at some period before 1910, young people in and around the community began attending an actual school in the village of Finger, which also carried the name of the town.[38] That schoolhouse was a two-story wood frame structure painted white. The top floor of the building was used by the local Masonic Lodge. In those days, a number of students who attended the school at Finger came

---

36. Early teachers in the present-day Finger area in the mid-nineteenth century included such individuals as William C. Beard, Robert F. Beard, and William Burns.

37. *McNairy County School Directory*, 1906.

38. Prior to the establishment of the Finger School, students in and around the village of Finger attended Possum Trot Schoolhouse, also known as Naylor's Schoolhouse.

from other towns and so a number of them boarded with local families there in town. Among the early educators at Finger School in 1910 was the future county clerk of McNairy County, John R. Swaim, and John V. Etheridge.[39] Other early educators at Finger included Major A. James, Daisy E. Curry, and E.L. Briggance. From 1921 until 1924, Miss Florence English served as principal of the Finger School.[40] English, who had a distinguished career in education, had previously served as assistant principal and instructor of mathematics and history at Selmer High School in 1911–1912 and later taught at Bethel Springs High School. In English's final year as principal of the Finger School, she was assisted by Loraine Houston, who taught, among other things, music in the high school, Clara B. Lain, and Ethel Plunk in the primary grades.[41]

From 1922 until the summer of 1927, no less than six teachers plied their vocation at the Finger School. Those teachers included: Ethel Plunk (grades 1–3 in 1922-1927), Clara B. Lain (grades 4-5 in 1922-1923, grades 4-6 in 1923-1924 and grades 7–8 in 1924-1925 and 1925-1926), Sula Bishop (grades 4-6 in 1924-1925), Mrs. Jewell (Massey) Carter (grades 4-6 in 1925-1926), A.E. Smith (grades 9-11 in 1925-1926 and grades 9-10 in 1926-1927), and Mary Cox (grades 4-6 in 1926-1927).

In July of 1927, the Finger school burned. The following article appeared in the *McNairy County Independent Appeal* regarding the incident:

> The Finger school building was burned last Thursday night, the origin of the fire unknown. It was valued at about $4000 and there was very little insurance. Besides the loss of the building, there was also that of a piano, library, and laboratory equipment. The enterprising people there will soon erect another school building.

The reader will note the article states the origin of the fire as unknown. However, a number of years ago, Clifford Young, a former resident of Finger from that time, informed the author that he had been invited to a meeting at the home of his uncle, Freelin Dickey. According to Young, who was in his twenties in 1927, the purpose of the meeting

39. *McNairy County Annual School Report*, 1910.
40. Naylor and Talbott, *Fingerprints*.
41. *McNairy County School Directory*, 1924.

was to discuss a plan to destroy the present school building. According to Young, the town fathers felt the town was quickly outgrowing the current facility and were having trouble convincing the county that a new facility was needed. Therefore, following the destruction of the current school building by a fire of unknown origin, the plan was to then procure assistance from the county in building a new modern brick structure. It must be remembered that Finger was not a municipality, but a village in the county, thereby eligible for county funds and county relief.[42] Indeed, in 1927, a new and modern brick structure was erected to house the Finger High School and Elementary School. During the period of construction, high school students attended classes on the second floor of the Home Banking Company building, while elementary students attended classes at the Finger Methodist Church building.

By the time the new facility opened for the 1927–1928 school year, the three above mentioned teachers, Houston, Lain, Plunk, plus Gretchen Harris, taught the elementary grades and the school's principal, Professor A.E. Smith, taught the majority of the high school classes.[43] During the 1928–1929 school year, the instructors included Mrs. J.B. Teague (grades 1–2), Irma Hamilton (grades 3–4), Loraine Houston (grades 5–6), J.B. Teague (grades 7–8), and Professor A.E. Smith (grades 9–10).

After the 1928–1929 school year, the records are scant. According to the surviving records, during the 1929–1930 school year, Florence English taught grades one through eight and J.R. London taught grades nine and ten. If these records are correct, then it would appear the school budget was severely cut to allow for savings. However, this is only speculation. During the 1930–1931 school year, Florence English again taught grades one through eight and J.H. "Jim" Beck taught grades nine through eleven. The only records found for school year 1931–1932 showed Aline Tucker, daughter of Dr. N.A. Tucker, teaching grades seven and eight.

By 1932–1933, the records reflect three teachers at Finger School. Those teachers were Burlene Orr (grades 1–3), Mildred Bassham (grades

---

42. In 1994, shortly before his death, Clifford Young of Cairo, Illinois, shared with the author the existence of the plan to rid the town of the old school building. Young stated the names of a number of prominent men who were involved and further stated that upon learning of the plan, he informed these gentlemen that he had no desire to participate. At the time of the fire, Young was around 25 years old or older.

43. *McNairy County School Journal*, 1927.

Finger School in 1913. A few students that can be identified include Minnie and Lucy Plunk (top row, third & fourth from the left); Lillie (Plunk) Boyd (second row from top, fifth from the left); J.O. Massey (seventh from left), Ben Floyd (second young man from left with necktie); and Hubert Plunk (standing beside Ben).

Finger School students, date unknown

Students at Finger School in the early 1930s. This and the photograph below were taken on the same day. A few individuals who can be identified include Vonnie Mae (Talbott) Garner (second row) and Faye D. (McIntyre) Talbott (third row). The teacher was Miss Bulene Orr.

Two students known in this photograph are Luther E. "Junior" Talbott (front row, fifth from the left) and Quentin Hayes Hayre (front row, sixth from the left).

The new Finger School, built in 1927

Finger School students from the early to mid 1920s. Some of the students pictured were children of W.P. Massey.

The boys and girls basketball teams for Finger School with coach Hugh Allen Basham in the 1930s.

An early photograph of the Finger School girls basketball team.

Coach Lloyd Harris and the Finger School girls basketball team

Lloyd Harris, teacher and principal at Finger School, as well as mayor of Finger.

Hugh Allen Basham, teacher and coach at Finger School and later a veterinarian.

3–5), and Aline Tucker (grades 6–8). During the 1933–1934 school year, teachers included Sula Bishop (grades 1–2), Aline Tucker (grades 3–5), and J.C. "Clifford" Hodges (grades 6–8). By the 1934–1935 school year, there were four teachers at Finger School. These were Ruby L. Gray (grades 1–2), Inetha Bishop (grades 2–5), Marguerite Harris (grades 4–5), and Edna Barham (grades 6–8). From 1935 to 1936, instructors included Ruby L. Gray (grades 1–2), Inetha Bishop (grades 3–5), Cecil Clayton (grades 5–6), Edna Barham (grades 6–8), and Hugh Allen Bassham (high school grades).

During the 1936–1937 school year, Ruby L. Gray taught grades one and two and Edna Barham taught grades seven and eight. Although there appear to be no records to reflect otherwise or to serve as confirmation, it is believed that Hugh Allen Bassham served as principal that year. The identity of the other teachers is not known. During the 1937–1938 school year, it is known that Will Clark Tucker, another daughter of Dr. N.A. Tucker, taught second and third grades. During the same year, other teachers included: Loraine Bishop (grades 4–5), Edna Barham (grade 6), Cletus E. Kiser (grades 7 and 8), and J.H. "Jim" Beck (grades 9 and 10).

For the 1938–1939 school year, there were at least six teachers at the school. There were Will Clark Tucker (grade 2), May Tucker (3 months teaching sixth grade and the remainder of the year teaching third grade), Loraine Bishop (grades 4–5), Noah Allen Robison (five months teaching sixth grade), and Cletus E. Kiser (grades 9 and 10). During the 1939–1940 school year, teachers included Will Clark Tucker (grades 2–3), Ava McBride (grades 4–5), and Noah Allen Robison (grade 6). The exact identities of the remaining teachers are not currently known. By 1940–1941, the school was going strong and teachers included Mattie Lou Ward (grade 1), Will Clark Tucker (grades 2–3), Loraine Bishop and Bertie Martin (grades 4–5), Hermie Sipes (grade 6), and Noah Allen Robison (grades 8).

Sometime during the 1930s, Hugh Allen Basham was the school administrator. Other teachers and administrators at the junior high and high school at Finger from 1937 until 1941 who have been identified by former students include Buel T. Kiser, Hubert Plunk, and Julius Hurst.

From 1941 forward, school personnel included principals Lyman Goodwin, Haven Garner, Donald Wood, Lloyd Harris, Joe Robert Henry, and Leonard Ward. Teachers included Jim Beck, Myrtle Ward Smith, Cecil Clayton, Edna Barham, Evelyn (Clayton) Barham, Arlus Plunk, Robert Nash, Mary Elam, Will Clark Tucker, Howard Mitchell, Mildred Basham, Noah Allen Robinson, Clifford Hodges, Mildred Ashe, Thelma Naylor, E.G. Sanders, Lula Bishop, Burleen Orr, Ruby Lee Wilkerson, Bertie Martin, Bobby Burgess, Helena McCloud, Howard Leath, Icie Ingle, Jimmy Gean, Reba Holt, Hugh Rogers, Janice Rogers, Jewel Massey Carter, J.B. Teague, Mary Smith Martin, and Prince Plunk.

Like many other schools, in country and town alike, both past and present, the students at Finger never passed up an opportunity to show their skills on the stage. Furthermore, it was an opportunity to have a little fun in a life of hard work. The following are announcements regarding plays which the students produced and directed at the Finger school:

- -The Finger School presents "The Southern Cinderella" on Friday night, April 29, 1921 at 7:45 P.M.
- -Friday night, May 3, 1924, the senior class at Finger will present the four act comedy, "The Wren."
- -The eighth grade girls at Finger are practicing for their play later in the term called "The Old Fireside." (April 4, 1924)

Of course, there were activities of interest other than the arts which caught the interest of students for years. Athletics was, of course, a focus of interest for many children decades ago and included, most of the time, baseball and basketball. In September of 1924, an athletic association was formed at Finger. The officers were George Naylor, president; Arthur Plunk, vice-president; and Sue Walker, secretary. As to parental involvement in academics, the Parent Teacher Association was also formed at the Finger School in September of 1924. Mrs. W.M. Barnes served as president, Mrs. Maude Mitchell served as vice-president, and Mrs. A.G. Bishop was the group's secretary.

A number of photographs exist from the old school days at the Finger School. Indeed, there are too many to print in this work. However, a few in the possession of the author are presented in this section.

Possum Trot (Naylor's) Schoolhouse[44]

The Possum Trot schoolhouse was a one-room schoolhouse constructed of logs and located approximately one mile west of "downtown" Finger in the vicinity of the present First Baptist Church and cemetery. This school was established as early as 1877, if not earlier.[45] This building was also used for worship services during the 1880s and began to be used by the Church of Christ in 1905. The land belonged to James Robert McIntyre. Among the teachers at Possum Trot were Levi Benton McIntyre, son of the landowner, and Tobe Walker. Families whose children attended the school included among others: Naylor, Jones, McIntyre, McCann, James, Brown, Floyd, Dickey, Stancil, Plunk, Young, Walker, Patterson, and Rouse.

Plunk's Schoolhouse

Plunk's Schoolhouse was mentioned in a 1902 list of schools found among the papers of the late Cordie L. Majors, former McNairy County superintendent of schools. No other record has yet turned up and it is believed this school was located around the Plunk Cemetery area.

Aimwell School

Relatively nothing is known about this school. It may have been called "Aimwell." A photograph of a large school group at this school was taken around 1897 to 1900, which included some Plunks and Miss Arky Barnes. It is believed the school was located somewhere around the area east of Finger known as Plunktown. Melzer Plunk mentioned this school to his children. No official school record has been found.

---

44. An 1896 photograph, perhaps the only existing one, of the Possum Trot school group was published in Naylor and Talbott, *Fingerprints*.

45. Neimann, *Glory of the Common Man*.

This photograph of Aimwell School was found in a trunk owned by Miss Arky Barnes. No names were found on it, but it is known that Arky is the fourth little girl from the left. She is standing directly behind another child and wearing a black collar on her dress. The teacher and other students are unknown.

Huggins Creek Schoolhouse

In the 1870s, this school was operating under the direction of a teacher by the name of Tom Bell.[46]

Sagebrush Schoolhouse

William Mason, the son of early settler James Mason and the father of John Mason, the late poet laureate of Oklahoma, taught a subscription school here during the summer months when farm work slowed down. The classes were held in an old abandoned log residence located in a field overgrown in broom sage. It was most likely located somewhere on the Floyd farm, also known as the old Eli H. Tisdale plantation and sometimes referred to the "Old Slave Plantation."

McNairy Male and Female Institute

McNairy Male and Female Institute was established in 1879 by David J. Franklin and R.D. Jennings. The men who made application for the school's charter were S.A. Norwood, T.M. Patterson, J.J. Bradley,

46. *Id.*

J.P. Rogers, E.W. Sheffield, J.H. Blakely, J.W. Conger, J.W. Fielding, L.J. Anderson, R.D. Jennings, J.S. Rogers, and R.P. Kirby. There is no known surviving anecdotal history and no records exist to give us any further glimpse of this early academy.

Montezuma Male and Female Academy[47]

Although Montezuma is now part of Chester County, this was not so until its formation in 1882 from the counties of Hardeman, McNairy, Henderson, and Madison. Until that time, Montezuma was located in northwestern McNairy County. The Montezuma Male and Female Academy was chartered around 1860. Its board of trustees was composed of John L. Rogers, John W. Estes, W.T. Weaver, R.Z. Henderson, E.Q. Farrell, Dr. L.M. Fry, G.G. Bankhead, J.G. Randolph, Martin Stewart, A. Wade, T.O. Bankhead, C.W. O'Neil (O'Neal), C.H. Steed, John Sanford, James Fry, Sr., J.J. Johnson, W. Carson, J.N. Hunter, and U. Gillespie.

The academy was a joint stock company divided into shares worth twenty-five dollars each. Trustees were to be elected annually on the first Monday in July, beginning in 1860. The charter spoke of the employment of not only teachers, but also lecturers.[48] The goal of the school was to separate males and females with the erection of separate buildings suitable for that purpose. The charter further stated the school was to be conducted on "republican principals and equity, free from the inculcation, influence, bias, or preference of any particular religious denomination."

Hepsidam

Hepsidam was chartered in 1880 by I.A. Mitchell, J.A. Maness, J.E. Mitchell, W.W. Massey, Frances Kerby, Isaac Russom, James Kerby, and W.C. Worsham.[49] The academy was located in the old Third District.

---

47. This information was taken from Chapter 78 of the *Acts of the General Assembly of Tennessee, 1860*.

48. At this point in American educational history, lecturers and lyceums were popular forms of educating both the general public and academy students on any variety of subjects and topics.

49. The first named individual may have actually been named I.H. Mitchell as the document off which this information was taken was that written by hand and recorded in the McNairy County Clerk's office.

The application was made on January 5, 1880. Hepsidam's purpose as an academy was to build up and sustain "the work of education and literary improvement of the people."

Unidentified Black School

There was an unidentified black school just east of Finger near the old W.W. Peeples farm. The schoolhouse had a small stage and was later turned into a house which was occupied by E.C. Peeples. It is believed that some of the children of Paul Vassar, a local black preacher, attended school at this location.

Biographical Sketches

Although there were many who claimed the profession of educator in north McNairy County over the last one hundred and fifty or so years, it would be difficult to write a biographical sketch on all. Rather there have been a fair number whose influence has been far reaching in a number of positive ways, whose influence remains today for the good. Here an attempt will be made to document just a small portion of the lives of just a few of these men and women of education.

Horry Hodges (1868-1940)

It is almost impossible to know where to begin in the quest to write a brief biographical sketch of the late Professor Horry Hodges. Although his name is all but lost to the present generation, his was a name well-known and almost synonymous with higher learning, scholarship and oratory. He was indeed a true Renaissance Man. Few men ever graced the county with such a presence as Horry and yet, as with all mortal men, he has gone from the world. What may have sealed his fate in near certain anonymity was the fact that Horry, like all of his brothers and one of his sisters, never married and brought children into this world. Therefore, it was all but impossible for his great legacy to continue unfettered.

Perhaps the most effective way in which to present the life of this famed educator is to do so chronologically. Even this will be challenging, as Horry was quite active and often on the go, leaving little in the way

A true Renaissance Man of Finger and north McNairy County, Herry Hodges (1868–1940) was a respected educator, public servant, eloquent speaker, and historian of McNairy County.

of records. Most of the record of his professional and even personal activity comes to the present generation in the way of correspondence and newspaper accounts. To the average member of 21st century American society examining the newspapers of yesteryear, Horry Hodges seems the greatest of oddities. Here in the early years of the twentieth century, we find a newspaper and hence an entire county keeping up with the wild and interesting life of an itinerant genius and scholar as he travels the country and the county teaching and enlightening the young. With the aid of many wonderful sources, now let us look in on an interesting and fully lived life from long ago.

Horry Hodges began his life in the type of environment he could only have wished. The son of the very literate and highly intelligent Captain Elijah J. Hodges, Horry's exact birthplace is currently in question. Although originally thought to have been born on the family farm near present-day Finger, recent discoveries reveal funeral home records that list Horry's birthplace as Morgan County, Alabama.[50] How could this be? Captain Hodges was serving in the Tennessee House of Representatives from 1867 until 1869 in the state capitol city of Nashville. Family members have speculated that Mrs. Nancy Jane (Dodd) Hodges, Horry's mother, may have gone to Alabama to reside with relatives. However, this cannot be confirmed.

Regardless of the place, Horry was born on March 19, 1868. He received his primary education in the Jackson District High School in Henderson, Tennessee.[51] Horry continued his studies there in Henderson at West Tennessee Christian College graduating with his A.B. in 1891 and his A.M. in 1893. Here he studied under such men as Arvy Glenn Freed and with such great minds as Nicholas Brodie Hardeman. Early in his life, Horry was involved with the Primitive Baptist Church, with which his father was associated for so long. On May 12–14, 1886, at the Sunday School Convention in Adamsville, convention president J.W. Purviance "stressed the fact that the present convention was a business meeting in which God-fearing men and women came together to do a great work"

---

50. Funeral records from the old Gooch Funeral Home in Selmer, Tennessee, list both Horry's and Dr. Henry Hodges' birthplaces as Morgan County, Alabama, with the source of the information being their sister, Maggie Hodges.

51. Judge John Allison, *Notable Men of Tennessee: Personal and Genealogical with Portraits* (Atlanta: Southern Historical Association, 1905).

and appointed "a resolutions committee composed of Horry Hodges, Dr. G.W. Morris, and J.H. Scott."[52] According to the report, "Horry Hodges addressed the children's department, and was most successful in his efforts to arouse interest. He loved the children and they loved him as well."[53] This testifies to Horry's interest in church affairs and in the welfare of children, for at this time Horry was only eighteen years old.

Horry began teaching school in 1887, long before earning his degree, no impediment at that time. Teaching would forever remain first in his heart and ever-present on his mind. However, politics would always lurk in the background and occasionally lurch forward to the forefront of his life. In 1894, Horry was elected to the office of circuit court clerk of McNairy County and served in that position until 1898. During this term, Horry studied law and successfully sat for the bar, being admitted to the local bar in January 1901. In 1898, Horry was elected to another countywide office, that of superintendent of schools, defeating the incumbent superintendent Calvin Hamm. After two years in the office, Horry taught two years at Shiloh National Military Park.[54] In 1902, Horry was again an official of McNairy County, this time serving as county trustee. In this position, Horry served as the county's chief financial officer until 1908.

During this extensive period of public service, Horry apparently remained active in the field of education. According to *The Selmer Post*, Horry presented a paper at the Teachers' Institute at Gravel Hill entitled "The Student, What Is He?"[55] An article from *The Weekly Post* speaks of H. Hodges' intent to deliver a lecture at the night session of The Teachers' Institute at Gravel Hill in November 1903, entitled "A True Education."[56] After he stepped down as county trustee, Horry took a teaching position at Bethel Springs High School in September of 1908.

During this period of his career, Horry became active in the area as a public speaker, which would eventually establish him as the greatest orator McNairy County ever produced. The records establish that he was active in the organization and activities of several local Civil War

52. J.C. Taylor, *Historical Articles*. This work was compiled and privately published in 1992.
53. *Id.*
54. *Id.*
55. *The Selmer Post*, April 24, 1903.
56. *The Weekly Post*, November 13, 1903.

reunions and groups. In 1909, Horry accepted a job as the organizer of the Improved Order of Red Men in Tupelo, Mississippi, a job for which he received a "handsome salary."[57]

In June of 1911, Horry was appointed principal of the McNairy County High School. Sometime after this time, he moved west. However, before leaving, Horry taught a term of summer school for brother Harvey at Liberty in the summer of 1913. Afterward, Horry made his way to Paul's Valley, Oklahoma, to seek a teaching position. He did better. By September, Horry was employed as both a teacher and an administrator. A 1913 letter to Colonel J.W. Purviance stated, "I am pleased here because I have a good position. We have 12 teachers and opened with 314 students. We now have more than 340. I teach 3½ hours each day and get out at 2:30 P.M."[58] Most probably Horry also taught in Oklahoma the following year. By 1915, Horry was back in McNairy County. From 1915 to 1916, he taught at Selmer High School. However, sometime in this period, he also taught in Cash, Arkansas, Lindsey, Oklahoma, and New Mexico. In this county, Horry taught at the Center Hill Academy and Acton at some point.

In 1920, politics again entered into Horry's mind and occupied his energies. Apparently the Republican party nomination for the United States House of Representatives was offered to Horry, but he declined the offer and instead favored Lon Allen Scott of Savannah, Tennessee. That fall, Scott was elected and Horry went to Washington, D.C., to serve as Scott's personal secretary. After beginning his new work, Horry wrote back home that he was "well pleased with his position as secretary for Congressman Lon A. Scott" and while gone was "known throughout Washington for his great knowledge of history."[59] While in the nation's capitol, Horry had opportunities unlike any. He had access to one of the greatest and voluminous collections of works in the country, the Library of Congress. It was reputed that he spent much of his time researching and reading in the great library. In fact, when he prepared to return to Tennessee in 1922, he was quoted as saying, "You know, Lon,

---

57. *The McNairy County Independent Appeal*, August 13, 1939. This item for 1909 was found in the "Thirty Years Ago" column.

58. *The McNairy County Independent Appeal*, September 12, 1913.

59. *The McNairy County Independent Appeal*, March 25, 1921, and September 27, 1940.

I hate to leave Washington, there are still a few books in that building that I haven't read."

Another event of great interest to Horry was the hearing of a case before the United States Supreme Court. The states of Texas and Oklahoma were involved in a boundary dispute, a dispute that eventually made its way to the highest court in the land. The state attorney general of Oklahoma happened to be Sargent Prentiss Freeling, who was originally from McNairy Station, Tennessee. He was a personal friend of Horry's and invited Horry to witness the specter of a Supreme Court case. Whether Horry, a licensed attorney, was asked to sit in as assistant counsel or in some other official capacity that would justify his presence as required by Supreme Court rules is not known. Freeling grew up in McNairy Station, attended Southwest Baptist University (now Union University) and later Harvard Law School. Freeling won the case for Oklahoma, defeating Texas and its two attorneys, one a former United States Attorney General.

In 1922, Lon Scott was defeated after just one term by Captain Gordon Browning of Huntington. After Horry came home to McNairy County, he was in great demand as a speaker. He traveled throughout the area speaking on matters of politics, religion and history. On many occasions, Horry, as the invited guest, would entertain and inform crowds of hundreds and even thousands at festivals, barbecues, reunions, decoration days and meetings. Often Horry was called upon to speak at the opening or closing of schools and when called upon to make an impromptu speech, he would deliver wonderful talks due to his well-informed nature. In regards to Horry's depth and capacity of mind, it is said that upon hearing a verse of Scripture, he is said to have had the ability to quote the verse before it and the verse that followed.

After his stint as personal secretary to Congressman Scott ended, Horry did not abstain from politics for very long. On Saturday, April 19, 1924, the Seventh District Congressional Convention met in Jackson and nominated Horry for the U.S. House of Representatives. After an apparently quiet campaign, Horry was defeated in the general election by the incumbent Congressman Gordon Browning. It has been stated by family members that Horry was a very reluctant candidate, agreeing to run only out of loyalty to his party.

Horry continued to teach school after 1924 and spent some of his time and energy researching and writing history. He wrote many articles for various newspapers on the subject of history. Many of his writings dealt with state and local politics and history. As a historian, Horry was known throughout the state and considered one of Tennessee's foremost historians.[60] At the time of his death, Horry had been working on a book-length history of McNairy County, but died before he could complete the task.[61] Horry's notes and research have apparently disappeared. Due to Horry's persistence and dedication, his account of the naming of the town of Finger is the only recorded contemporary account of the event.

Following the 1924 general election, Horry returned immediately to his beloved labor, that of teaching. In August of 1924, he had been present for the opening of the Selmer school, but in September he officially returned. Taking the position of principal at Adamsville High School, the newspaper reported:

> Horry has gone back to his first love, in teaching lines. He assumes the principalship of the Adamsville school, a school with which he was identified in the years that are gone. The kind of teachers of which Mr. Hodges is a splendid example has always done a wonderful lot of good in this and other counties in the state, and we predict that the Adamsville under his management and leadership will take a prominent part in the educational affairs of the county. He knows every angle of the great profession, and is thoroughly grounded and prepared in all things that belong to the life of the teacher.[62]

In 1926, Horry again heeded "the call of the wild and returned to the ranks of the pedagogues" when he was named the principal of the Enville High School.[63] Horry continued to teach in the schools of the county for the next decade as well as engage in other activities and events of an educational or cultural nature. In 1934, Horry was invited to speak at Freed-Hardeman College, the successor to West Tennessee Christian

60. *McNairy County Independent Appeal*, September 27, 1940.
61. Taylor, *Historical Articles*.
62. *McNairy County Independent Appeal*, September 12, 1924.
63. *Id.*, February 12, 1926.

College. This was certainly at the invitation of the president of the school, Professor Nicholas Brodie Hardeman, an old and warm friend of Horry's. The following was a report of that speech:

> NOTED EDUCATOR HIGHLY HONORED: Prof. Horry Hodges, one of the foremost educators in the state, accepted an invitation to deliver a lecture at the summer school of the Freed-Hardeman College on the evening of Tuesday, June 26, 1934. He responded in a way that captivated the large attendance of students and visitors. His subject was 'American History,' with which none is more familiar.[64]

Such events and invitations were common in the life of Horry Hodges, as he enjoyed a widespread reputation for his oratory and his status as a Renaissance man.

Horry was also involved in a number of other activities besides teaching and speaking. He was involved in the Annual Singers General Assembly, a singing convention whose name is owed to the imagination and mind of Horry Hodges himself.[65] Until 1940, Horry never missed a meeting of the association, and upon his death, special songs were dedicated by the estimated 21,000 in attendance at the 22nd annual convention in observance of his death.

At the time of his death, Horry was an instructor in history and foreign languages at the Michie High School. His health was beginning to fail two months before his death and some have stated they believe he may have suffered from cancer. Horry had made either a religious conversion in his life or he finally just settled on his own religious path. Although the son of a well-known Primitive Baptist preacher, Horry was a member of the Christian Church as early as 1905. This was about the time of the great decisive split in the churches of Christ over the use of instrumental music in worship. Regardless, Horry's old friends, Judge J.C. Houston and Nicholas B. Hardeman, conducted the services. Horry was buried in Mount Carmel Cemetery. Horry was an active member of the Republican Party, a member of the Royal Arch Masons and had

---

64. *Id.*, dated from 1934 and contained in a scrapbook belonging to Elizabeth "Bessie" Abernathy Bigger (1875–1941).

65. *McNairy County Independent Appeal*, September 27, 1940.

been chancellor commander of the local lodge of the Knights of Pythias, and a member of Woodmen of the World.

Harvey G. Hodges (1878–1922)

The various members of the talented Hodges' family can be described by distinct adjectives and terms. Horry was the political one, the talker. Henry was the quiet medical genius. Harmon was the industrious and thrifty farmer. What about Harvey? How could he be described? Honestly, Harvey G. Hodges could be described in so many adjectives.

Harvey G. Hodges

Harvey the amusing one might be appropriate after a quick perusal of his letters. Perhaps Harvey the passionate educator or Harvey the musical one could be utilized. Unfortunately, it seems that a most fitting term for Harvey is tragic and this is most unfortunate. However, let us examine the life and times of Harvey G. Hodges.

Harvey was born on the family farm near present-day Finger on March 17, 1878. He was the youngest child of Captain Elijah James and Nancy Jane (Dodd) Hodges. As such he was petted greatly by his older and adoring sisters, especially Maggie, his spinster sister.[66] As his brothers and sisters all did at some point in their lives, Harvey followed the path of the educators and sought his rewards in the field of teaching. According to the available accounts and records, Harvey taught in the county's public schools for over twenty years. Some of the schools where Harvey taught include Stantonville (1910) and Liberty Schoolhouse (1913). Certainly there were plenty of others, but due to the lack of adequate recordation, it is difficult to obtain a complete picture of

---

66. This has long been told by members of the family and their neighbors and close friends.

Harvey's teaching career. It is known that in late 1920, Harvey became the principal of the Gravel Hill School, where he served until his death.

Harvey, like his brothers and sisters, was a man of immense talents and varying interests. A highly literate man of letters, he and his family possessed some of the great works of history and literature in their private home library. Yet one of his great loves was music. Instrumental in the success of the annual Singers' General Assembly, a large gathering of up to 20,000 attendees, Harvey found great spiritual solace and enjoyment in putting his strong religious beliefs into verse. He put to pen a wonderful gospel song, which he labeled "a sacred song," entitled *Traveling Home*. A verse from that song would eventually serve as Harvey's tombstone epitaph.

Harvey's surviving letters and newspaper contributions revealed that he had a comical touch and amusing side. He was a true wordsmith possessing the ability to turn a phrase. However, the great point of his life that was most discussed by those who recalled him was, most unfortunately, his death. Harvey's death has been cloaked in a shroud of mystery since its occurrence in 1922. Harvey and brother Henry both had been sickly off and on through the years. Many have stated the two suffered from tuberculosis, but this cannot be conclusively known. Regardless, according to the surviving newspaper accounts, Harvey was sick at the end of his life. According to his obituary, Harvey had to return home from his teaching at Gravel Hill School because of ill health brought on by an attack of influenza. The same account stated that Harvey "went home and while he rallied many times, he gradually grew worse until the end."[67]

The next line of Harvey's obituary is interesting and shows the close relationship between the older sister and the younger brother. Maggie Hodges was present "being constantly with him, her fidelity and gentleness soothing his last hours, during all of which he showed that masterful cheerfulness which was a part of his nature, and endured with the same patient nobility to the end."[68] However, what was the nature of Harvey's sickness and death? That may be hard to ever determine, for many different stories are told. It is known that Harvey was engaged to a fellow teacher by the name of Ethel Plunk. Apparently the couple was very adamant in their desire to marry as both were past the average age

67. *McNairy County Independent Appeal*, September 8, 1922.

68. *Id.*

of marriage with Harvey at the age of forty-four. Those who have any knowledge of the relationship have stated that Maggie was firm in her opposition to the proposed marriage. It was this disagreement between Maggie and her beloved younger brother that caused events to spiral out of control and lead to Harvey's physical demise.

According to local lore and even some members of the Hodges' family, all remaining Hodges' siblings signed a pact upon the death of their father, Captain Hodges, to remain unmarried and tend to their mother and the family home and estate until their respective deaths. Apparently Harvey intended to breach this agreement and Maggie held firm to her conviction that Harvey should abide by his word as per the agreement. It was additionally stated that Maggie was also opposed on political and familial grounds. The stories then hold that Harvey, in anger and pride, moved out of the family home and camped in a fallen treetop in the woods on the Hodges' farm. It was here that he was said to have developed either influenza or pneumonia. Regardless, Harvey died on September 1, 1922, and was buried next to his parents in Mount Carmel Cemetery with the Reverend Dewberry preaching and John R. Swaim and W.H. Wilson singing. As was earlier stated, Harvey wrote his own epitaph, a line from a song he had written earlier in life:

> *We're traveling on and seeking our own,*
> *To rest after toil, to know and be known,*
> *To scenes of delight, to peace and reward,*
> *To dwell with the saints who trusted the Lord.*

Maggie and Harvey shared an especially close relationship, probably much closer than between any other of the siblings. Harvey's obituary reveals a little about their closeness as it speaks of Maggie presence with Harvey near the end and certainly to the very tragic and sad end.

What truly became of Harvey Hodges may never be conclusively known. Perhaps he simply became sick and came home to die of natural causes as was reported in 1922. Perhaps his own pride and independence caused his eventual demise. Many tales have been told including some which were not very noble, but the truth remains that we may never truly know. Still, there has long been tale of a more ignoble end, which the first edition of this work did not mention. According to some of the older citizens, it was accepted that Harvey had actually committed suicide over the emotional conflicts with his siblings regarding his unpopular marital engagement. According to L.E. Talbott, his father-in-law, John Robert McIntyre, a neighbor to the Hodges, was among the party called upon to look for Hodges in the woods around his house because he went missing. According to Talbott, McIntyre related that Hodges was found leaning against a tree and that he was found to have actually shot himself. Further, according to the late Clifford Young, he recalled the incident well and stated in a 1994 interview that Hodges indeed committed suicide. Interestingly, the mortality records for the county show that he died of tuberculosis.

James Simpson "Simp" Lain (1845-1932)

James Simpson "Simp" Lain was born on December 2, 1845, to Thomas and Jane A. Lain. Little is known regarding his early life. When the battle of Shiloh broke out on April 6, 1862, Simp was a young single man living and working on the farm. One man who remembered Lain as an old man recalled the old man saying he stood behind his barn on a hill and listened to the guns at Shiloh. The great battery of General Daniel Ruggles of the Confederacy was sixty-two guns strong and readily heard so far from the Tennessee River. Others remembered being down on Tar Creek in north McNairy County and seeing the water shimmer from the vibrations of the distant guns.

Following the war, Lain chose a career as a schoolteacher. He was teaching as early as the 1870s and was the founder of Lain's Academy. Lain taught for several years and served as a member of the McNairy County Quarterly Court for a number of decades. It was on that body that he made many important votes, including voting to remove the county seat of McNairy County from Purdy.

Lain married Nancy E. Kirby (Kerby) on September 16, 1866, with Justice of the Peace W.M. Crow officiating. They had four daughters and one son. Hugh M. Lain was born on October 29, 1867, and died on June 30, 1868. Arminta Lain was born on January 27, 1878, and died on August 6, 1889. Maudie Lain was born on August 10, 1886, and died on March 23, 1911. Jennie Lain was born on June 19, 1869, and married A. Kennel Tedford on November 24, 1885, with William Barney Malone officiating. Jennie died on September 27, 1919. These four were buried in Mount Carmel Cemetery close to Simp and Nancy Lain. Finally, Minta Pauline Lain was married to J.H. Leath.

On May 29, 1932, James Simpson Lain passed away and was buried in Mount Carmel Cemetery. Nancy E. Kirby Lain died on November 10, 1935, and was buried next to Simp.

John R. Swaim (1875-1965)

John R. Swaim is another of those characters who could be included in any number of categories of professionals and occupations. However, he is included here because of his early work in the field. Like many then and now, John Swaim chose as his first professional career, that of teaching. Like so many other young men, it gave him a base and constituency with which to work and cooperate throughout his long career.[69]

John was born in 1875 to Joseph John Swaim and wife Jane (Croskery) Swaim. The mother was a native of Ireland and the father a North Carolinian. John was raised on a farm near the New Salem community near Bethel Springs, but went to college in Henderson at one of the predecessors of Freed-Hardeman College, probably the old Georgie Robertson Christian College. On March 21, 1901, John married Miss Laura Etta Mitchell, the daughter of Jim Mitchell. At some point around 1907, he moved his family to Finger where he engaged in the hotel and livery business. The hotel in Finger, with its livery stable, was located on the hill above town across the street from the home of Orby Massey.

At some point around this same period, John taught school at the Old

John R. Swaim

---

[69]. Most of the information in this sketch comes from the county newspapers, an interview with John Swaim's son, J.R. Swaim Jr., and a family history published in *Reflections: A History of McNairy County, Tennessee, 1823-1996*.

Friendship School for about two summers. Then in 1911 he became the principal of the Finger School. How long he served in this position is not currently known. In 1918, John was elected to the office of McNairy County court clerk. He would serve four terms in this position retiring in 1934. Besides these activities, John was actively involved in a number of other activities, including fox hunting and singing. He was involved in the establishment of a fox hunting club in McNairy County and served as president of the McNairy County Singing Convention, also called the Annual Singers' General Assembly, for nearly thirty years. Following his retirement from the county clerk's office, John served in various capacities in city government in Selmer, including city judge and magistrate. John R. Swaim, Sr., died in 1965.

Leonard Ward[70] (1909–1989)

James Leonard Ward was born on April 18, 1909, the son of John G. Ward and wife Dona Ward. He attended school at Finger and Bethel Springs before attending both Freed-Hardeman College and Bethel College. Like many young teachers, he made the rounds teaching on assignment at the small one and two room schools in north McNairy County. The author had the honor to know Mr. Leonard as a youth after Mr. Leonard was an older gentleman. The sketch below was written by Ward's friend and colleague, Cecil Clayton.

"Leonard Ward, was born near Finger on April 18, 1909, the son of John and Donna Ward and was the oldest of two sons among ten sisters. He attended grade school at Finger and graduated from Bethel Springs High School in 1929. Ward spent two years at Freed-Hardeman College and later graduated from Bethel College in McKenzie, Tennessee.

He was married to Florence Melton on November 23, 1938, and they had two children, Judy and Dennis Ward. Dennis has now been a teacher in McNairy County for several years. Leonard and Florence were members of Sweet Lips Baptist Church near Finger. They celebrated their golden wedding anniversary in 1988.

---

70. This sketch was written by the late Mr. Cecil Clayton, a long-time friend and colleague of Leonard Ward. It was written shortly after Ward's death and was loaned to the author by Ward's widow, Mrs. Florence (Melton) Ward, in 2001.

Leonard Ward

He started teaching during the mid-1930s and taught at Oak Ridge, Iola, Fairview, McNairy, Finger, and Bethel Springs. His entire teaching career was spent in the grade school area. He was considered an excellent English teacher. Many of his students have expressed to me what a wonderful English teacher he was. He retired in 1974 with thirty-six years experience. He passed away on November 10, 1989, at the age of eighty.

During my boyhood days we lived near the Wards. There wasn't a week that went by that we weren't together hunting, fishing, going to parties, dances, and playing basketball. I would like to say in bringing these remarks to a close, Leonard Ward was a first class gentleman in every way, never smoked, never drank, or used drugs. I am sure all those who knew Leonard including his students learned to love, admire, and above all cherish the fond memories we have had together."

Members of the Ward family were educators in north McNairy County

Haven Garner

One of the enduring names in north McNairy County's educational history has become that of Mr. Haven Garner. Haven attended schools at Masseyville, McNairy, and Chester County High School. One afternoon in Coach Dick Stewart's classroom, another student kept working to get Haven's attention. Finally Haven turned around to see what the other young man wanted and Coach Stewart said to Haven, "Haven, you're talking, aren't you?" Due to this tiny infraction, he was given a discipline charge and had to remain for thirty minutes after school. This small detainment turned out to be a true blessing in disguise. Miss Annie Davidson was watching the students after school and told Haven, "What are you going to do? You're smart enough to go to college." That got Haven to thinking about the prospects.

Haven Garner

Later, Haven and his uncle, Varnell Rankin, himself a teacher, went down to Freed-Hardeman College to see the renowned Gospel preacher and professor Nicholas Brodie Hardeman. Haven told Hardeman he could pay for the first semester in cash, but he would have to put the next two semesters on credit. Hardeman said that would be okay. To get to college each day, Haven walked to Masseyville which was one mile and a half from his home, then caught a bus and rode five miles south to pick others up and then rode directly back the way they had came and then on to Henderson, a total of twenty-six miles. Each day he would walk into the Administration Building and warm up by an old radiator heater against the wall. In chapel one day, Hardeman told the students he had noticed a young man who stood each day by the heater, the same young man everyday. He told those assembled that he checked to see who this young man was who had gone so far each day to attend Freed-Hardeman and then announced Haven's name to all present. Apparently Hardeman was impressed with the young man's determination.

In proper time, Haven finished his studies at the college and prepared to graduate and begin his work as an educator. However, there was the item of paying off his loan note for school. He went down to the bank to see about the note and no one could find it. Finally, it was discovered that a former professor at Freed-Hardeman held the note and that the professor was now in Texas. Therefore, Haven sent the check to Texas and was ready to begin work. Haven's first teaching assignment was at the Center Ridge School, which was located at the edge of the Little Hatchie bottom, from 1932 to 1934. After two years at Center Ridge, Haven moved on to the Johnson Schoolhouse, which was located on the Buena Vista Road, near the Frank Wilson place. He taught there from 1934 to 1935 and his students included John Lee Powers and Harris Johnson.

From 1935 until 1938, Haven taught at the Fairview School. One of the problems he faced at Fairview was that of sharecroppers' children moving in the middle of the year, leaving the school short on students. After his duties at Fairview, Haven moved on to the Iola schoolhouse. He taught at Iola in 1939. Then in 1940, he moved on to Refuge, where he taught until 1944. He left in the middle of his last year and Hazel Amerson filled in for him the rest of the school year.

Haven then began teaching at Finger in 1945. When he came to Finger, the teachers there included Thelma Naylor, Lloyd Harris, and Mary Martin. It was not long until students began to be bused in from all over the countryside and it was soon apparent that an addition to the school must be made. Fielding Maness went to work building three new classrooms and a lunchroom. While the building process was ongoing, Maness asked Haven, who was also principal of the Finger School, where the kids played. Haven told Maness the children played out in front of the school. After being told the school owned more property there near the school, Maness brought in his bulldozer and began clearing off a spot to build a playground. Haven was able to make many improvements in the Finger school during his tenure. With help from local businessmen, money was raised and items donated. A large two-door freezer was donated by Grover Sibley of Selmer and Haven and Albert Weaver went to Selmer to pick it up.

When Haven began his work at Finger in 1945, the old gymnasium had a leaky tin roof. He had a student climb up the tall structure to nail the tin down. The old gym had been built by workers from the Works Progress Administration (WPA) during the mid-1930s. The old structure was built high off the ground in the back of the gym. In the mid-1950s, this structure was torn down and construction of a new gym began. After the new improvements at Finger, more teachers were added and things improved. By the time Haven left Finger in 1954 or 1955, Myrtle (Ward) Smith and Irene Smith Frye were teaching the young at Finger.

Haven next moved to McNairy, where he was also a principal and taught for thirteen years. Other teachers at McNairy when Haven started were Cletus Kiser, Susie (Walker) Kiser, Ruby (Bishop) Hodges, and Jim Beck. After his many years of service at McNairy, Haven spent his last year of teaching at Bethel Springs.

Edna Barham

Edna Barham, the daughter of local Republican magistrate Charles L. Barham and wife Flora Jane (Hysmith) Barham, was born on April 18, 1913. She was a longtime schoolteacher in north McNairy County. Miss Edna taught several years at Finger and was a serious educator. The story has been related by two former students at Finger School from the 1930s about an incident in one of her classes. One of the students, James L. Massey, was half-asleep with his chin resting in his hand when Miss Edna called out the student's name and asked, "What is the major economic activity of Spain?" The student's buddy sitting behind him, Quentin Hayes Hayre, whispered to the called upon and startled Massey, "Bull fighting. Bull fighting." The young Massey called out, "Bull fighting," and Miss Edna was not amused giving the student a good whack on the head.

Edna Barham

Miss Edna left Finger and went to Bethel Springs High School serving as the senior class sponsor for many years. She was well-known for her ability to inspire learning and creativity in her students and was extremely dedicated to the noble profession of education. She taught both elementary and high school grades. She was known as an excellent English teacher who enjoyed teaching literature and poetry. According to the memory of former students, Miss Edna was a fan of the writings of Robert Frost and Carl Sandburg. Following her retirement, she served as secretary of the McNairy County Retired Teachers Association. She lived next door to her brother and sister-in-law, Clarence and Evelyn Barham until her death on December 10, 1992, at the age of 79.

Evelyn Barham

Evelyn Christine (Clayton) Barham was born in 1918 in Finger, Tennessee. She was the daughter of Frank and Allie James Clayton. She attended Freed-Hardeman College and Bethel College and taught school in McNairy County for thirty-nine years. She taught for many years at the Finger School. She was active in civic affairs and in the McNairy County Retired Teachers' Association. Education was very important to her and she taught her students the importance of writing effectively and fluently. She believed that people could only communicate as well as they could write well.[71] The sister-in-law of Edna Barham, both of her daughters—Mrs. Janette Ray and Mrs. Jo Ann Hendrix—became school teachers. Her brother, Cecil Clayton, was a teacher as well.

She was married to Clarence Barham on December 25, 1937. He was born on August

Evelyn Barham

---

71. Mrs. Evelyn Barham taught the author's father in elementary school, and the author had the honor of having her as a teacher himself during a portion of his fifth grade year. From that first day in class until her death years later when the author was in college, Mrs. Barham never failed to remind the author that he could only communicate his ideas if he wrote well and in an effective manner. The author continues to thank Mrs. Barham for this well-taught lesson.

29, 1917, to local magistrate Charles L. "Charlie" Barham and Flora Jane (Hysmith) Barham. Clarence was a farmer and school bus driver for the McNairy County School System. He was also actively involved in civic affairs and served for many years on the McNairy County Republican Executive Committee. He had a good sense of humor. Mrs. Barham remained active until her death from cancer on June 29, 1993. Clarence Barham died on December 13, 1993. They were buried in Lake Hill Memory Gardens in Bethel Springs, Tennessee.

Florence English

Miss Florence English was born in McNairy County on December 17, 1879, to John Thomas and Virginia (Peery) English. She never married and thus did not leave any descendants to carry on any significant knowledge of her. There was a marriage license issued to Dr. H. Abernathy and Miss Florence English on June 6, 1911. It appears this union did not occur as Dr. Hayes Abernathy later married someone else.[72]

Miss English taught or served as an administrator at schools such as Leapwood, Finger, Selmer High School, and Bethel Springs High School. She served as principal of the Finger School from 1921 to 1924. In her later career, she was teaching at Bethel Springs. In 1940, she was still living in Bethel Springs as a boarder with Noah Kirby and wife Cassie Kirby. She was remembered for her sternness and rigidity. Near grown men, large and strong young men, were extremely afraid of Miss English. Of Miss English, former student Robert Beene stated that "she was a tall, stern woman, another old maid." He stated that Miss English, who was then the principal of the Finger School, intended to whip Vaudie Patterson, but he wouldn't let her as he quit school and never came back. Such was the fear of students toward Miss English. She died on March 8, 1959, and is buried at Mud Creek Cemetery.

Florence English

---

72. Miss Florence English is not to be confused with Florence (Walker) Abernathy Hockaday.

Hubert Plunk

Hubert Plunk was the son of Lawson and Mary Plunk. Early in his life, he chose the field of education as a profession. He was best known for teaching at the Finger School and the Mackey School and was known for his kindness to students at a time when teachers were often stern and extremely no-nonsense. After several years of teaching in north McNairy County, Hubert left the Finger area and moved to Alabama. There he worked for the Tennessee Valley Authority and remained in that state until his death.

The Davidsons

A number of the Davidson family spent several years in the field of education teaching at a number of small rural schools. Five of the Davidson siblings, the children of Martin Van Buren Davidson Jr., and Pearlie (Reeves) Davidson, grew up attending school at the Fairview Schoolhouse. Several of these brothers and sisters attended Freed-Hardeman College and five taught school. Among the siblings to teach were Howard Davidson, Clyde Davidson, Cola Davidson, Vena Davidson, and Geneva Davidson. These five siblings taught at various times at Pegram Beauty, Centerhill Academy, Fairview, Hodges' Beauty/Cloverhill, Cool Springs and Mackey School.

CHAPTER FIVE

THE BIRTH OF BUSINESS: BLACKSMITHS TO MERCHANTS

Early businesses and businessmen prior to the War Between the States—Development of a town and business base—The cotton gin and sawmill businesses—Importance of transportation and communication to the growth of business—The telegraph and the railroad depot—Road and highway improvements—The telephone in Finger—Business expands between 1920 and 1940—Post–World War II business life—Brief sketches of the area's prominent businessmen and businesswomen.

From the opening of the county to whites shortly after the 1818 Treaty until the outbreak of the War Between the States (the American Civil War), there were few entities that could claim the title of a business as we envision the concept and term in the present day. A man might practice a trade or particular skill for which he charged patrons, but seldom did he consider or label himself a businessman. All who did not farm, and many of those who did, practiced some type of skilled trade, for which he earned his "living." These skilled craftsmen who worked from their homes and barns would eventually give way to the "professional" businessman with an established locale of activity in the nearest town. In this chapter, an attempt will be made to record those who worked from their homes, as well as those who worked in what we now consider the traditional business role.

One of the first known businesses in such form was that of Anderson's Store, which is more specifically examined and discussed in another chapter. Anderson's Store was a business before it was a community. The community took its name from that of the business founded by William Taylor Anderson, one of McNairy County's early settlers. The exact date of the store's establishment is not known, however, it is estimated that it existed sometime around the late 1850s. The business consisted of a store, presumably dealing in general merchandise and, of course, for that time and place, a distillery.

The history of business and professional activities in north McNairy County and the Finger community can be documented fairly well. A number of informative sources exist to establish a fairly clear picture of the business life of this end of the county. Census records, memoirs, newspaper advertisements, news, and oral tradition, as well as old business ledgers and records, paint a picture of diversity and success. Many fortunes were made and lost in a few short years. This area experienced all of the economic shifts and changes of the country during its development and downfall. The great prosperity which dawned at the turn of the century and flourished throughout the 1920s was experienced by the merchants and professionals of north McNairy County. The sudden economic crash of 1929 and the crushing depression of the 1930s hit many local businessmen with a vengeance. The natural economic ebbs and flows took their course until the downturn was apparently permanent. The following chapter examines the economic and business history of the north McNairy County area from the beginning until the present.

The Early Businesses and Crafts

In the early decades of McNairy County's existence, the presence of discernible towns, villages and business bases of the county were rare. Purdy was the major village and county seat of the county and outside of Purdy many areas were still widely primitive and the population sparse. Most of the population were farmers but some practiced trades and skills which required high degrees of competency and skill. Many of these craftsmen were farmers also. The first well-documented list of businessmen, craftsmen, and professionals was for the year 1850. Those who were engaged in a business other than farmer were:

William T. Anderson (born 1804), merchant
Francis Beard (born 1791), preacher
John Beaty (born 1812), mechanic
Ichabod Brown (born 1801), carriage maker
William Brown (born 1825), mechanic
William Burns (born 1825), school teacher
Archibald Burten (born 1831), clerk, probably in Walsh's store
Alexander Greer (born 1815), shoemaker
Lafayette Ingraham (born 1828), grocer
Miles Lowrance (born 1827), blacksmith
James Maxwell (born 1820), blacksmith
Wilson McHolstead (born 1807), Methodist preacher
Robert T. McIntyre, miller
James McKary (born 1823), Methodist clergy
William Orric (born 1823), miller
James Perry (born 1817), Methodist clergy
Elisha Plunk (born 1824), miller
W.W. Ramsey (born 1810), carpenter
Andrew Reynolds (born 1804), wagon maker
Calloway Robison (born 1814), blacksmith
William Rogers (born 1812), miller
Joseph Rushing (born 1818), merchant
Robert Tisdale (born 1803), Methodist preacher
Edwin Walsh (born 1831), clerk
Madison Walsh (born 1820), merchant
William Walsh (born 1810), merchant
John Watkins (born 1824), Methodist clergy
John Wharton (born 1820), blacksmith
Moses Woods (born 1798), lawyer
Absolom Young (born 1804), cabinet maker
Thomas Young (born 1829), carpenter.

A few notes may be added regarding the above list. These people lived in the area of north McNairy County, many of them within a short distance of present-day Finger. One obvious trend is the amazingly large number of Methodist ministers in such a rural area. There were five such preachers present here in 1850. There were probably three distinct grocery and general merchandise businesses in this area in 1850, those of the Andersons, the Ingrahams, and the Walsh family. Joseph Rushing, another merchant, was the son-in-law of William T. Anderson and was thought to have worked with Anderson in the same business and same premises. By 1860, a few more craftsmen and professionals could be added to the list including the following.

Thomas Anderson, clerk in Anderson's Store
J.S. Barrett, carriage maker
J.B. Blakely, saddler
Charles Curtis, wheelwright
Samuel Farnsworth, teacher
C.L. Freeling, physician
W.L. Gattis, clergyman
Joseph Johnson, clergyman
W.G. McCoy, physician
Jesse McKinney, physician
James McMurry, shoemaker
Gehu Peeples, carriage maker
David Tillmon, grocer
Newton Wright, carriage maker

The interesting factor here is the large concentration of physicians in the northern section of the county.

The author wishes to note that from the period of 1865 until the turn of the twentieth century, McNairy County issued many merchants bonds and liquor licenses. In the northern section of the county, a number of individuals were issued such licenses. In the Montezuma area, C.M. Cason (August 1865) was issued a merchant's license for the firm of Cason & Company and W.C. Cason (February 1869) was issued a merchant's license for the firm of Cason & Skinner.[1] In April of 1870, C.M. Cason also obtained a merchant's license for the firm of Skinner & Company.[2] B.T. Peeples obtained a merchant's license from the firm of Lain &

---

1. Nancy Wardlow Kennedy, *Merchants Bonds & Liquor License, 1865–1898* (Selmer, TN, Self-published).

2. *Id.*

Peeples in October of 1866.³ Further, between October 1865 and July 1869, M.V. Peeples and B.T. Peeples obtained merchant's licenses and liquor licenses for the firms of Peeples and Peeples & James.⁴ In September of 1865, Alfred Sipes obtained a merchant's license for the firm of Sipes & Vires and the next month Sipes also obtained a liquor license. Around the time Finger was being properly established in 1895, Ike Dickey was busy obtaining a liquor license for the purpose of selling liquor.⁵

Around the area of the White Plains Cemetery on Tar Creek in the vicinity of what was known as Cotton Ridge, the Walsh brothers operated a general merchandise and cotton gin. Marcus Joseph Wright, before becoming a Confederate general and historian, spent time as a clerk for the Walsh brothers and recounted his experiences while serving as a clerk.⁶ That account is as follows:

> After leaving school, I engaged as bookkeeper and general clerk with Messengers C. and J.J. Walsh who established a store and cotton gin about 10 miles south of Purdy at a place called Cotton Ridge.⁷ The work here was rather hard. I had to be up very early in the morning and work late. My work was some distance away and I had to walk from my residence to the store for breakfast when I was selling goods and receiving and weighing cotton. Very often I worked until 12 o'clock at night. There was a large stream called Tar Creek between the residence and the storehouse which I crossed by a fallen log. I had been having chills for sometime which were very prevalent in that region and I took quinine and a solution of arsenic as a remedy but without much result. One morning when the creek was sheeted with ice and the cross

3. *Id.*

4. *Id.*

5. *Id.*

6. Wright, Talbott, McCann, *Reminiscences of McNairy County, Tennessee, 130th Anniversary Edition.*

7. It is apparent that General Wright commits either a mistake in direction or a grammatical error of sorts. He states in his narrative that Cotton Ridge was approximately ten miles south of Purdy. It is certain that General Wright meant "ten miles north of Purdy" in that Cotton Ridge was located several miles north of Purdy, Tennessee in the area near the communities of White Plains, Anderson's Store, McIntyre's Crossing and Tinsley. Today it is just east of Finger, near Tar Creek.

log covered with frost, I started to cross but slipped and fell in the creek where there were many branches of fallen trees. I struggled for sometime and extricated myself and got out of the water and when I succeeded I was thoroughly chilled, indeed, almost frozen, but from that time on I did not have any return of ague.[8]

Wright's account of his clerkship gives one an idea of the typical rural antebellum business firm. One can only wish Wright had given even more detail.

Marcus J. Wright

As far as the actual Finger area is concerned, the first businesses were established around the same period of time as the construction of the Mobile and Ohio Railroad in the 1850s. The Mobile and Ohio Railroad Company was incorporated in the state of Alabama in the 1840s and received a charter, one which exempted it from taxation, from the state of Tennessee in 1848. According to contemporary sources, it was, at the time, the "greatest railroad enterprise ever inaugurated."[9] The state of Tennessee issued 1,296 bonds amounting to nearly $1.3 million at six percent interest. The railroad was officially completed in 1858, running north to south through the county, dividing the county into near equal halves. The line was built by Irish laborers and probably some blacks.[10]

---

8. Given the time in which General Wright was educated and writing, he often used words learned in a classical education and which we do not often see today. Ague is such an example. According to Webster's Encyclopedic Unabridged Dictionary of the English Language, ague is a "malarial fever characterized by regularly paroxysms (sudden violent outbursts or attacks), marked by successive cold, hot and sweating fits; a fit of fever or shivering or shaking chills, accompanied by malaise, ains in the bones and joints." *Webster's Encyclopedic Unabridged Dictionary of the English Language* (New York: Portland House, 1989).

9. Notes on Internal Improvements in McNairy County taken from the Cordie L. Majors Collection at the University of Memphis Ned Ray McWherter Library, Special Collections Department, MSS 312, Box 6, Folder 8.

10. Neimann, *The Glory of the Common Man.*

The building and development of the railroad and modern transportation systems and infrastructure caused a number of problems in McNairy County, most notably the divisions in Purdy. Many there were opposed the building of the railroad through their village. As a result of the heated and adamant opposition, Purdy was unable to raise the required $100,000 in tax and subscriptions. Due to this failure, it would not be a point on the railroad, consequently sealing their own fate. On the other hand, new towns would spring up on the railroad as the years passed by, including Finger. Interestingly, during the War Between the States, sixty-five percent of the original cost of the construction of the line was lost as the result of demolition of the line by the rivaling factions traveling through and fighting in and around the county. According to Professor Majors' notes, "by skillful manipulation the debt to the State was paid and in 1870 resumed payment of interest on bonds."[11] In the fall of 1885, the line changed its gauge to four feet and nine inches.

Again, it was during this period that businesses and a town began to spring up around the rail line. Perhaps the earliest known business near what is today known as the town of Finger was the grist mill of Robert Thompson McIntyre (1814–1902). In fact, that business would lend the community a name for a number of years. This grist mill was operating as early as the 1850s. McIntyre's Switch or McIntyre's Crossing would be the name of the immediate area of present-day Finger at least until 1895 when a post office was finally approved for the village. McIntyre built the first known grist mill in the area on the east side of Huggins Creek. McIntyre's Mill was operating as early as the 1850s, but probably much earlier.

There was also a tavern located on the railroad, near a stretch of houses.[12] The tavern may have been built around the same time as the railroad in order to give the railroad hands a place to stay. Apparently the tavern operated for quite some time. There was also a log structure located north of the Finger crossing which was used by the workers. It was built in 1857 at the time that the railroad was under construction. It was a small structure and remained on the same site until probably sometime in the 1930's when Albert Weaver moved the structure and began using

11. *Id.*
12. Hayse Hayre, personal conversation with the author, 1994.

it for a hog shed. Other than this, there is no knowledge of the business history of this immediate area until the late 1890s.

The Development of a Modern Town and Business Base

As late as the 1890s, much of what is now the town of Finger was still woods and farmland and much of it was owned by one man, James Robert McIntyre. McIntyre was the son of Robert Thompson McIntyre and a farmer and large landowner in northern McNairy County. As he grew older and his sons left home, the maintenance of a large amount of farmland grew more taxing. At some point around the turn of the century, McIntyre decided to sell some of his land off in lots. Such decision must have been made with the view that a town proper could be formed. Finger already existed by the name. The post office had been established under that name in 1895 and the name McIntyre's Crossing ceased to exist. Yet still little existed to verify the existence of a town and the selling of these lots began the building process that would yield Finger a true village to go with the name.

The list of buyers was originally compiled and included in Naylor and Talbott's *Fingerprints*. The list gives some indication of the businesses present and those interested in locating in Finger in the first two decades of the twentieth century. The first few names are familiar for their occupations and businesses: J.S. Ball, Thomas J. Womble, C.V. Brown, I.N. Brown, I.C.B. Naylor, Major A. James, Pete E. Wharton, Dan C. Griswell, John R. Harris, Joshua Columbus Naylor, H.D. Woodward, J.B. Weaver, Andrew J. Maness, Robert McMillan Weaver, William Sherman Young, William Pinkney Massey, and H.P. Horner.

Some of these men were well-known in their day. Thomas J. Womble was a merchant and farmer who lived east of town of the Finger-Leapwood Road. I.C.B. Naylor was a farmer and popular justice of the peace. Major A. James was a schoolteacher and merchant and son-in-law of James Robert McIntyre. Pete E. Wharton was a farmer and storekeeper. John R. Harris was a banker, merchant, and cotton ginner and buyer. Andrew J. Maness was a banker and cotton buyer and William Pinkney Massey was a merchant and postmaster. Many of these men will be sketched at the conclusion of the chapter.

THE BIRTH OF BUSINESS

From 1914 and on into the early 1920s, the development of modern-day Finger took clear form. Lots were sold for the building and development of such entities and groups as the Finger Church of Christ (1915), the Finger Cemetery (1921), and the Finger School. Many businessmen bought their lots for the purpose of building their store buildings and their own personal homes. Buyers of lots in 1914 included Dr. W.M. Barnes and Rube Young. Business picked up in 1915 with the purchase of property by John G. Ward, Jess F. Mitchell, Mt. Pleasant Fertilizer Company, and Robert L. Carter. It was probably around this time that Jess Mitchell and Rube Young established their mercantile businesses in Finger.

In 1916, the Mobile and Ohio Railroad purchased one and a half acres of ground from McIntyre for the purpose of building the Finger Depot. This action would aid the small town in unimaginable ways, allowing merchants quicker access to stock goods and information. In the same year, John R. Harris, William H. "Billy" Harris, Albert Pickett, W.P. Massey, Hugh L. Hodges, C.M. Barr, and Pete Wharton all bought property. No further transactions took place until 1918 when W.P. Massey, Lee A. Weaver, Adrian McIntyre, E.D. Mitchell, C.M. Barr, W.H. "Tobe" Walker, Pete Wharton, and Zannie Brown bought lots. With these purchases came new businesses such as Hodges' Produce and Commission Company. Many others had already been established such W.P. Massey General Merchandise and Harris' General Merchandise.

In 1919, new businesses and residences came to town with the purchase of property by Robert L. Carter, F.E. Naylor, E.O. Parrish, John R. Harris, F.W. Clayton, I.C. Weaver, M.E. Bishop and Company, Isham P. Womble, and R.J. Bass. It was during this year that M.E. Bishop branched out his Enville business and sent his sons to Finger to manage the new store. The year was also significant in that Robert J. Bass, a black man, bought property near McIntyre and built his own home, a structure which stands today.[13] In 1920 and following, W.F. Clayton, J.W. Stansell, George T. Naylor, J.O. Massey, Robert M. Smith, Finger Graveyard, J.G. Young, and W.H. Harris bought lots on which most built new houses.

---

13. This house still stands today and is the home of Pete Lemons. Robert J. Bass was a well-respected gentleman who regularly did business with Finger's merchants and bankers. He was relatively comfortable in his day, a time when most blacks were impoverished and had little contact with whites unless in their employment.

The years 1900 to 1920 were marked by great prosperity in the United States and a spirit of progressive social reform in business and commerce. Such prosperity was equally present in west Tennessee. These years saw many businesses firmly established the Finger area and many local businessmen find personal and financial success. Early merchants in Finger included John A. McIntyre, William P. Massey, William H. Harris, and James R. McIntyre. Three of these men were closely related, two being brothers and Massey their nephew. John A. McIntyre, the elder McIntyre brother, was said to have originally opened a general merchandise store in a building located on present-day Apple Street, a structure which later served as the Hartle Hayre home.[14] Whether he was partnered with anyone or not during the duration of the business may never be conclusively known, but some sources have stated that McIntyre and his nephew W.P. Massey were partners at one time. Others have stated that McIntyre sold the entire business to Massey when his health began to fail. The date reputed for the establishment of W.P. Massey General Merchandise is 1892. Therefore, it is difficult to know when McIntyre's interest in the business was sold. John A. McIntyre died of skin cancer on November 6, 1897.

The firm of W.P. Massey General Merchandise was nonetheless a great success. The business was first located on the north side of Main Street very close to the old Bank of Finger/Home Banking Company building. The store building was a wooden frame structure with a very narrow alley between it and the bank building. This building burned in 1916 damaging the west wall of the bank building. Following this incident, Massey built a new brick store building on the corner of Main Street. The building is now the offices of Home Banking Company. Massey's business was a full-line general merchandise store carrying all of the necessities of any early twentieth century store. The Finger Post Office was located in the front west-side of the building. Between the new building and the bank was later another wooden frame building located on the back of the lot. Massey stored cotton, cotton seed, tools, and farm equipment in the building, which no longer stands.

Another early merchant in Finger was William H. Harris.[15] Prior to the turn of the twentieth century, Harris lived in Selmer and operated

14. This property is now the site of Joyner's Upholstery Shop.
15. Harris has already been sketched in Chapter Three of this work.

The original W.P. Massey store building (above) was located within feet of the old Bank of Finger or Home Banking Company building. It burned in 1916 and was replaced by a new building (below). Though damaged in a tornado in 1917, its survives today as the offices for the Home Banking Company.

a livery stable in that town. However, in 1900 he moved to Finger and established the Harris General Merchandise store, which he operated from 1900 until 1910. Harris' son, John R. Harris, served as the establishment's bookkeeper until 1910 when Harris retired from the store business and became the local depot agent. In that year, John R. Harris took the reins of the business and he soon established himself as one of Finger's major business figures. J.R. Harris General Merchandise carried a larger line of goods that any store in town. On each of the building's interior walls there were two long balconies on which merchandise and various kinds of stock were stored and displayed. One of these balconies can still be seen in the old building.

Harris sold the usual array of goods including groceries, dry goods, hardware, wagons, plows, harrows, cultivators, gear for horses and mules, saddles, and other essentials on the farm. Many of these larger items could be found in a large wood frame storage building which at one time was located next to the main building. Deciding to concentrate on the cotton and banking businesses, Harris sold the business to a cousin, Thee Harris (1879–1948) some years before his death. In later years,

The John R. Harris General Merchandise storefront with the window signage visable. To the left of the store is the office of Dr. N.A. Tucker, who was Harris' brother-in-law.

Willie A. Dillion (1909–1974) and Dallas Wilson bought the store from Thee Harris. Today the building houses a garage and wrecker service.

Another of the very earliest stores in Finger belonged to another of the McIntyre family. James Robert "Jim" McIntyre, the son of Robert Thompson McIntyre, the brother of John A. McIntyre, and hence the uncle of W.P. Massey, owned the lion's share of the stock in McIntyre, James, and Company General Merchandise. This store was operating as early as 1905. Jim McIntyre (1849–1921), his son Robert A. McIntyre, and his son-in-law Major A. James were all partners in the operation. The store sold the usual line of general merchandise and fresh produce.

Thee and Lela Harris, with children Mary (Harris) Gardner and Prince Harris

In 1907, Finger got into the banking business. For several years financial, commercial, and residential growth had been almost phenomenal. The need for such a financial institution was now evident. A group of local businessmen met and committed their resources and talents in order to form the Bank of Finger. These men were F.J. Floyd, W.P. Massey, James R. McIntyre, R.B. Moore Jr., and Lee A. Weaver. The first order of business was building a building in which to house the new bank. A brick kiln was set up behind a field behind the location of what would later be the Farmers' Union building. The bricks fired at this kiln were made by John T. Naylor and Fate Naylor. When this building went up it was the first brick structure in Finger. The bank was officially chartered on July 25, 1907, and opened its doors for business on October 21, 1907. Moore served as the first cashier of the new bank. In 1908, Andrew J. Maness became the bank's second cashier. The officers of the new bank were Lee Andrew Weaver, president, and W.P. Massey, vice-president. The bank's directors were Lee A. Weaver, W.P. Massey, Sherman Young, and R.H. Hill.

The continued and thrived under the management of Maness and the board and officers. However, Maness was killed in a horse racing accident in 1913. By 1915, the bank was no more. A new bank was charter on February 24, 1915. The Home Banking Company made its home at the old Bank of Finger building, after buying the building, fixtures, and assets of the old bank. The first investors and thus the first directors were Hugh L. Hodges, John R. Harris, W.P. Massey, F.J. Floyd, and Lee A. Weaver. Other early directors included C.M. Barr, Thomas J. Womble, J.S. Lain, and James R. McIntyre. The first officers included John R. Harris, president; W.P. Massey and Hugh L. Hodges, vice-presidents; and Lee A. Weaver, cashier.

Between 1900 and 1910, the businesses mentioned above and those following were to be found along the streets of Finger. Some of the names will be familiar to the reader and others will not. Former Union veteran and cotton ginner Finis E. Miller was the proprietor of Finis E. Miller and Company General Merchandise. This business most probably lasted no longer than 1916, the year Miller passed away. The general merchandise store owned by Mr. T.B. Ross lasted for a little while. However, the exact number of years that this store operated is unknown as is its location.

Weaver, Harris, and Company was another store which dealt in general merchandise and was prosperous for a while. The exact identities of the principal partners are unknown, but they were thought to be Lee Andrew Weaver and John R. Harris. Although both of these men owned sole interests in other stores, they often owned other similar businesses in order to maximize the competition scheme and the profits they could gather from it. Yet it should also be remembered many of these men during this ten year period partnered up with one another before striking out on their own. Thomas J. Womble, a half-brother to Lee Weaver, owned a general merchandise store. Tom Womble also partnered up with George Ball, another merchant, in the firm of Ball and Womble. At some point, Womble also partnered with merchant John Weaver in the firm of Womble and Weaver.

Dorsey "Dossie" Bishop owned a general store in Finger during this period. He and his brother had been sent from Enville by their father, M.E. Bishop, to establish a branch of the business. Certainly there was the Harris General Merchandise store owned by William H. Harris

THE BIRTH OF BUSINESS

This wood frame building on south Main Street housed a store owned by brothers Dorsey "Dossie" Bishop and Guy Bishop on the first floor and the Bishop and O'Neal Funeral Home on the second.

and, in 1910, John R. Harris. Finally one could find good old D.C. "Pa" Holder in the store business.

Were we to have walked the dusty streets of Finger between 1900 and 1910, we would have seen other businesses as well. Mills of various sorts, as discussed in greater detail later, abounded. The grist mills of I.W. Brown, Miller and Dickey, and Naylor and Miller Company ground corn into meal for the local residents and those in nearby communities. There was also the McCaskill Sawmill where lumber could be hauled to sale or could be procured for building purposes. If one had need of a blacksmith, luck and numbers abounded. Robert McMillan Weaver, Sherman Young, Rob Carter, James F. Young, and Basil Starks all had good names as blacksmiths.

However, there were other more specialized businesses and trades in town. If you wanted to board a dog or buy a fine top-notch well-bred hunting dog, you needed to stop by the offices of Tedford Kennels. In this day when fox hunting was a sport all gentlemen of any class could appreciate, a sure bet for a good pack of hounds was most probably

Mr. Tedford. On the other hand, if you were perhaps a jobber or traveling salesman and needed a place to stay for the night while traveling through Finger, your best bet would have been the Finger Hotel. Depending upon the year, Misters William Wharton, John R. Swaim, or Roscoe Brown would be more than willing to get you checked in and your horse in the livery stables out back.

If you wanted to sell your cotton or cotton seed, the best man to see would have been Mr. Andrew J. Maness, Cotton and Seed Buyer. Upon receiving your cash or check from Mr. Maness, you could deposit at the Bank of Finger right there on Main Street. If you were in need of crop insurance, life insurance or any form of financial protection, you had your choice of either Mr. Lee A. Weaver or Mr. F.M. Segerson. Finally, if you had been feeling under the weather and need a little tonic or tablet to make you feel better, the local druggist, Mr. John S. Scott, whose office was located just off of Main Street on Mill Street would be a welcome sight to you.

Now as the years came and went, many of these businesses and men remained, but others passed and new ones drifted into town. Rube Young opened a general merchandise store on the northwest corner of Main Street in a white wooden framed building, where he operated for many years. Young eventually moved to Henderson and opened a store there. Immediately west of Young, in an identical building, was the store belonging to Dolf C. and Annie (Davis) Holder, more affectionately known as "Pa and Ma" Holder. They were known for their generosity to children and were humble and meek people. Ma Holder once told someone that it didn't cost her and Pa anything to eat, because they got all their supplies right out of their own store. Immediately west of Pa Holder was another identical building which housed the general merchandise store of Mr. Jess Mitchell. Mitchell, who carried a pretty sufficient line of goods, lived in the stately home on the hill immediate above the store building. The home still stands. Mitchell was another merchant who eventually left Finger for Henderson.

The north side of Main Street was the first side to be developed in a modern mode. After it filled up, the south side began to develop. The firm of Bishop and O'Neal was located in a large two-level wooden building just across the street from J.R. Harris General Merchandise. As previously mentioned, this store was originally established as a branch of M.E.

Bishop's business in Enville. The store was operated by Dorsey "Dossie" Bishop and brother Guy Bishop. Over the years, the firm dealt in groceries, fertilizer, feeds and seeds, cotton and cotton seed, and eventually appliances. Above the store, on the second floor, was the Bishop and O'Neal Funeral Home and the offices of the Finger Burial Association. This was the only such business ever in Finger and it eventually was sold to the Morgan Funeral Home in Henderson. The building, pictured above, no longer stands.

Lee Weaver's Dry Goods Store was operating as early as 1900. Sometime later in that decade, Weaver expanded into the general merchandise business. He continued to operate his store sometime through the 1920s and maybe until the early 1930s. Later his son Albert Weaver would be successful in this business. Lee continued other activities such as the insurance and banking businesses. At some point in the first decade of the twentieth century, Lee did relocate in Kenton, Tennessee, where he was an officer in a local bank.

Sometime around 1920, a local company was organized for the purpose of building a store building and acquiring a tenant/merchant. The company was called Farmers' Union and that is indeed what it was, a union of farmers. The group's founders were Pete Wharton, Asa G. Plunk, R.N. Barham, H.E. Kirkpatrick, E.H. Plunk, W.L. Plunk, and M. Arthur Barham. This building was located across the street from the Home Banking Company. The first tenant in the new Farmers' Union building was Hugh L. Hodges, produce dealer and cotton broker. After a few years, Hodges' built a new building next to the Farmers' Union building, which will be discussed shortly. Following Hodges' tenancy, Lucian Patterson operated a general store in the building. This may have been the Finger Merchandise Company, which was operated by Patterson. If so, it moved from another location as that business was operating as early as 1914.

However, in 1927, Newton Perry Talbott, a Leapwood merchant, bought out Patterson and the building gained a long term resident. Talbott had operated his store on the main street through Leapwood since about 1916. However, it was often difficult for goods to get to Leapwood because the roads were bad in the winter. After all, merchandise had to be hauled in from the larger towns and from the railroad depot. The closest such depot was the Mobile and Ohio Railroad Depot in Finger.

Newton Talbott and his wife Varham (Matlock) Talbott inside their Finger store in the 1930s. The old Farmer's Union building in which the store was located lacked electricity or other modern day appliances and conveniences.

Therefore after many years, Talbott chose to move his operation there. This proved a smart move. The trouble of transporting goods to his store was eliminated as the depot was within sight of the front of his new store on Main Street in Finger.

Talbott's store in 1927 and following into the depression years contained much the same type of stock as other such stores of the time including: fatback, dry salt middling, lard, summer sausages, sugar, coffee, flour, canned tomatoes, salmon, potted meats, peaches, soda powders, and baking powders. These items were then considered basic items. He also sold plenty of tobacco items including snuff, chewing tobacco, pipe tobacco, and cigarettes. Hardware was also a necessity in those days of hard manual labor in the field and all about the farm. Such items included axes, saws, hoes, rakes, nails, staples, harnesses, pick sacks, and, in the springtime, good old straw hats for the field. In the 1930s, Talbott began selling shoes, work clothes, bolts of cloth to make dresses and other garments, machine thread, embroidery thread, quilt thread, and other such necessities. Still the children could find some occasional fruit and candy in Mister Newt's store.

Luther and his wife Faye (McIntyre) Talbott with customers Harrison Brown (left) and Rudolf Barber (at the counter) in 1957. Small grocery stores such as this one in Finger were commonplace during the period. The Talbotts operated the store until 1978.

Despite speculation and prediction from many unqualified and less than ambitious bystanders and loafers, this store lasted longer than any other business in Finger before or since, with the exception of Home Banking Company. Opened in Finger in 1927, it remained until 1988. Following Newton Perry Talbott's death in 1947, Luther E. "Junior" Talbott took the reins of the business and expanded it greatly. He operated a rolling store service, most often called a peddling truck. Customers out in the countryside would call in their orders on the telephone and Junior would fill the order, place it on the truck and deliver it. Often times he carried plenty of what the average farm wife needed and would stop by the remote farms and see if they had a need. Most times, they did. Such stops by Junior were a welcome interruption to a life of daily grind. Many adults today recall with great joy the days of their childhood when they came running barefoot to meet the peddling truck. Faye (McIntyre) Talbott, the wife of Junior Talbott, worked hard in the store every day without fail. She was kind to the children of Finger, but often firm with the adults and not afraid to take a stand in her community. The store was struck by lightening and burned in 1973. They rebuilt and expanded the building, opening a modernized store later in the year. Their customer base remained faithful. They operated the store until 1978.

In 1978, their son and daughter-in-law, Ronald and Diane Talbott, took over the reins of the grocery store. Like their predecessors, they remained faithful to the principle of hard work, innovation and honesty. They closed the business on Sundays and saw their business grow. People came from miles around to buy fresh beef and pork and it became almost a trademark of the store: "good meat." The store sponsored local tee-ball teams for the children at the Finger Ballpark and was involved, as always, in assisting people in the community. As the 1980s wore on and most businesses had closed or failed over the years, one site in town continued to swirl with activity, Talbott's Grocery. Trucks and deliveries came in at all hours of the day. Three major grocery wholesalers, three large meat plants, two major produce companies, the larger milk and bread companies, and dozens and dozens of various wholesalers dealing in health and beauty aids, tobacco, frozen foods, desserts and sweets, and hardware did business with the Talbott family. In 1988, desiring to spend more time on the farm with his family, Ronald Talbott sold the business and became the last merchant of the Talbott family.

Ike Dickey opened a store on Main Street in Rube Young's old store building. Elizabeth (Stovall) Droke, Dickey's niece, assisted him there. Dickey, who had owned a bar in Jackson in the late 1890s and early 1900s, had moved back to Finger. His store had an unusual array of goods. All three of these neighboring wooden buildings had alleys between them just wide enough for a man to walk through.

While we are concentrating on the businesses in the town of Finger, there were still other businesses out and about in the countryside. For example, John Barton Jr. and wife Dora operated a store on the Finger-Leapwood Road west of Tar Creek for several years between 1900 and 1925. Of course, there was also Bullman's Store out near the community that bore its name and close to the old Hopewell Baptist Church and graveyard.

In 1920, Hugh L. Hodges began the task of building for himself a new and modernized office, store, and warehouse for his produce and brokerage firm. He began the structure sometime in September of 1920 and it was completed by the first part of the year 1921. He bought a good deal of the cement through the Hinton-Bigger Concrete Company. He

Hugh L. Hodges (left) with his wife, son Raymond, and "Mammy" James on their front porch.

bought most of his mortar from John A. Johnson Lumber Company in Henderson as well as his lumber, plate glass windows, frames, and iron beams and works. The brick was not made locally, but rather purchased from the Corinth Brick Company. Records show a minimum of 32,000 bricks purchased for the project at a price of $765.00. One freight bill on the project for two cast iron plates, two steel channels, and one bag of separator bolts shipped from Evansville, Indiana, showed freight charges of $14.16. A number of local carpenters and laborers worked on the project. Those men were C.B. Steadman, J.C. Dickey, J.C. Hodges, Frank Walker, J.C. Dees, Carroll Walker, Sam Dickey, W.A. McIntyre, Fate Carter, Arthur Stansell, J. Kirk, C. Young, and Simp Plunk.

Hugh L. Hodges was extremely active in the commodities trading business and produce business. His business contacts extended to cities far and wide. He remained in Finger until the events of the Stock Market Crash of 1929 took their toll on his business affairs. He then moved

Murray Walker and wife

to Selmer where he continued to be active in civic and business affairs. After he closed his office in Finger, brothers Leroy and Baxter Gardner opened a Chrysler and Dodge dealership at the location. The photograph above is the H.L. Hodges' family around the time of Hodges' days in the produce business in Finger.

In 1929, of all years, a new bank came to town. For more than fourteen years Home Banking Company was the town's sole lender and banking institution. Then Lee Andrew Weaver and John R. Harris had an argument regarding personnel, management, and the mixing of the two with Harris' personal business. It was then that Lee Weaver chose to strike out on his own in the banking business. He went about the business of attracting investors, creating an organization, buying the appropriate materials, and erecting a building. On May 15, 1929, in the height of prosperity, the Union Savings Bank of Finger was chartered. The directors of the new bank were Jess F. Mitchell, Lee A. Weaver, Murry F. Walker, J. Ed Stephens, and W.H. "Tobe" Walker. The bank's building was erected on the site of Pa Holder's old store, property belonging to Jess Mitchell.

The bank opened its doors to business on September 9, 1929, which was, unfortunately, just about a month shy of that year's famous stock market crash. Despite the economic downturn of the 1930s the Union

The south side of Main Street in Finger (above) shows the railroad depot (far background) and moving forward are the Bishop and O'Neal building, Farmer's Union, Hugh L. Hodges' building, and Lee Weaver's building. Below is a view looking west of town showing the Weaver and Hodges buildings. Another building that housed such merchants as the Holders, Youngs, Dickeys, and Mitchells can also be seen.

The old Farmers' Union building that became the Talbott store in 1927. It is connected to Hugh L. Hodges' produce and commodity store. Primitive gas pumps can be seen on the street in front of the buildings.

Savings Bank went on with its business under the shrewd management of its president, Murry F. Walker, and its cashier, Lee A. Weaver. The bank's catchy slogan was: *"The world gives you credit for saving; we give you Interest."* After several years of struggling to gain a foothold in the banking business in south Chester county and north McNairy County, the Union Savings Bank was voluntarily liquidated on April 29, 1936. According to state banking records, depositors in the failed bank lost no money, but were fully protected from losses.

Yet, by 1930, the Union Savings Bank and other businesses could be patronized as one walked the streets and sidewalks of Finger. Interestingly enough, by the 1930s, sidewalks abounded in the town. A wooden sidewalk ran down Mill Street. A concrete sidewalk was located in front of the Gardner Motor Company and N.P. Talbott, Staple Groceries and Produce on Main Street. Between Talbott and Bishop & O'Neal General Merchandise, Undertakers, and Cotton Buyers was another wooden sidewalk.

Other fine business establishments could be reached from the sidewalks and little streets of Finger. If you were a gentleman coming to town by yourself for a little treatment that all gentlemen can appreciate, you

THE BIRTH OF BUSINESS

This building was located on the corner of Mill Street and the Finger-Leapwood Road in Finger. It housed businesses belonging to Logan McCaskill, L.A. Weaver, and Chili Davis.

could walk into Stephens' Barber Shop for "first-class work and shower baths." Ed Stephens could go to work giving you a first-rate haircut and shave for a nickel or for a dime at the most. After you had received the amount of pampering that respectable men could afford, you could go on your way to check about your insurance at the office of Logan McCaskill's insurance agency. Perhaps you would stop by either of the banks to check on your loans, accounts, and the contents of the safety deposit box. Finally, with a hunger pang in the stomach, you could stop by Henry's Place, the local café, and see the owner, C.H. Kirkpatrick, and have a bite to eat. If you had brought along a shopping list lovingly provided by the wife, you had your choice of the following: W.O. Mitchell and Son General Merchandise, J.R. Harris General Merchandise, N.P. Talbott Staple Groceries and Produce, W.P. Massey, Dealer in General Merchandise and Brown-Built Shoes, Bishop and O'Neal, and Weaver's Grocery and Café.

If you needed to sell some old butter or had a dried up old milk cow and a litter of pigs that you needed off of the feed bill, you could stop by and deal with Mr. Tom M. Stewart, Produce Buyer and Trader of Cattle and Hogs. Tom was well-known to many of the little ladies who were looking for a market for their old butter. For those who aren't old enough to remember the distinction between old and new butter, the following will serve as an explanation.

In the early years and decades of the twentieth century, everyone around Finger, and most rural areas, had an old milk cow. The people would churn their own fresh butter. No one locally bought fresh butter, they didn't have to. Now a person might have to buy new butter if their milk cow went dry, but usually even then their neighbor would help them out. A family might churn a pound or so of fresh butter and proceed to use that butter. If they didn't use it fast enough and it started to get an old taste to it, they would take it to town and sell it for usually about 10 cents a pound. This butter was referred to as "old butter."

Tom Stewart had his fair share of mishaps with the butter business. On one occasion, a lady came into Tom's shop and told him that she had some old butter to sell. He took the package from her and sat it under his counter. She then made the following statement: "To be honest with you, Mr. Tom, I got a mouse in my churn. But what folks don't know won't hurt them." Tom, after pretending to change out her butter for new butter, handed the woman her own old butter back and stated, "you know, you're right, what folks don't know won't hurt them." Another humorous story involves the son of a local depot agent. The young man wanted some money to purchase some candy and thus devised a plan which he executed. The boy put some horse manure in a paper bag and walked in Tom's shop. He placed it on the counter and told Tom he wanted to sell some old butter. Tom immediately placed it on the scale, figured the price and paid the young man. After a few moments, Tom opened up the bag and discovered the manure. Needless to say, the depot agent was no more amused than Tom.

In the years following the mass production of the automobile, it must be remembered that blacksmiths were just as active and in demand as ever. One reason for this was economic. Many people could not afford a vehicle. Therefore, the necessity of blacksmiths was not diminished. In fact there were many blacksmiths in the Finger area in the twentieth century. Sherman and

Sherman Young

Jim Young, who were brothers, were among the first blacksmiths in Finger. Others included Basil Starks, Rob Carter, Robert McMillan Weaver, and Henry Kirkpatrick. In the waning days of the horse or mule drawn wagon, when the pickup truck and automobile became prevalent, often the blacksmith became a mechanic and machinist using more modern equipment and tools such as welders. Yet during the days before "horseless carriages" the blacksmith was a vital part of the community as he played a vital role in both transportation and agriculture.

Other types of businesses which were more optional to citizens than blacksmiths were those of cafés and barbers. A number of individuals operated a café in Finger over the years. Henry's Place, owned by C.H. Kirkpatrick, has already been mentioned. Other operators included Hooper Massey, Jim Floyd, Floyd Naylor, Gordon Kirk, Johnny Whorton, Albert Weaver, and Evie and Buel Tacker. The first barber in Finger was Tom Grissom. The town's other barbers included Ed Stephens, Zanie Brown, Pete Whorton, Logan McCaskill, Colonel Patterson, and Tony Holmes. Many of the older men of today hold fond memories from their youth of sitting in the barber chair for the first time and receiving

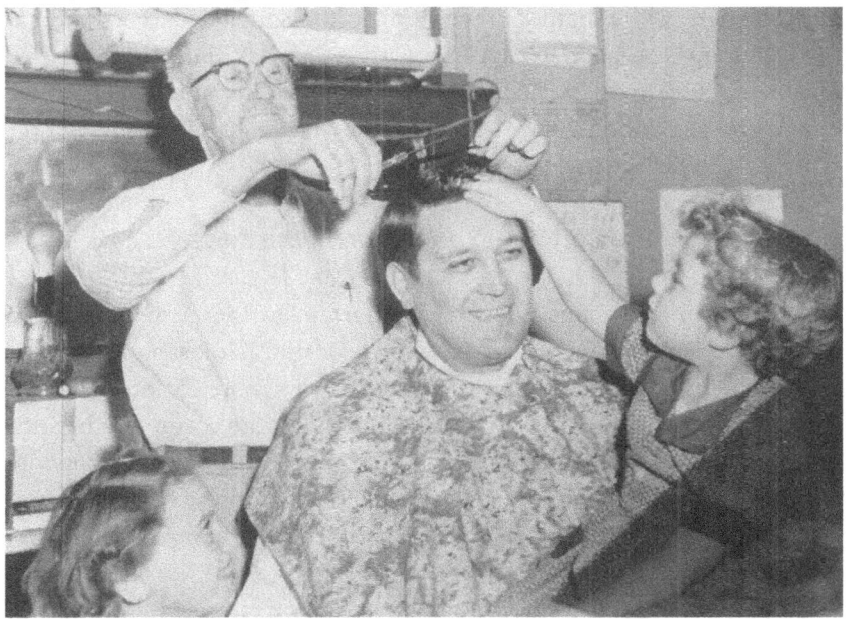

Colonel Patterson cutting Lloyd Harris's hair in his Finger barbershop. Cheryl and Shelia Clayton look on.

a haircut for anywhere from a nickel to a quarter. A few beauty shops were operated over the years by Eva Plunk, Brenda (Malone) Shelby, and Diane Talbott.

In regards to the businesses of the 1930s, most grocery stores and general merchandise firms were required to belong to the National Recovery Administration (NRA). This was a New Deal agency created by President Franklin D. Roosevelt during the 1930s to relieve the effects of the Great Depression. Most local merchants voluntarily signed up without any coercion. N.P. Talbott was not so enthusiastic. An ardent Republican, he opposed such programs. Interestingly enough, the National Recovery Administration was eventually ruled unconstitutional by the United States Supreme Court.

In the late 1940s and throughout the 1950s, new businesses came into being. Some faded and others grew. Prior to America's involvement in the Second World War, there were a few new businesses to spring up in Finger. Caudle's Store, Chili Davis' Pool Hall, Pete and Lizzie Whorton's grist mill and grocery were among a few. In the late forties, others such as Lee Brooks, Albert Weaver, and Robert Beene were in the appliance business. Other names in the store business included Tedford, Cratus Clayton, Deaton, Cagle, Albert Owens, and Willard Smith. Local mechanics during this period included Herman Vires and longtime mechanic and gas station owner Mancel Kirk. Mancel Kirk and son Lonnie Kirk ran the service station until 2012.

The Cotton Gin and Sawmill Business

The cotton crop was extremely important to the farmers of north McNairy County, whether it was lucrative or not. Almost as a tradition, farmers believed fervently that they had to grow more cotton than anything else during the growing season. Therefore, the cotton gin became a staple of business and commerce in the county. Although a number of cotton gins existed outside of the village of Finger in the outlying countryside long before the village itself existed, our discussion will primarily focus on Finger.

The first cotton gin which utilized mule power was built and operated by brothers Isom Christopher Buchanan Naylor and Joshua Columbus Naylor. The mule-powered gin was operated by George Dickey in a location across the road from the old Dickey homeplace on present-day Brown Street.¹⁶ For those who know little about such operations, a mule or mules, usually no more than two, were hooked to an apparatus which required the mules to walk in circles to provide "power" to the gin. George Dickey also established a sawmill down by the Mobile and Ohio Railroad in the old section of Finger. This site was later the site of the first steam powered cotton gin.

Another early animal-powered cotton gin was that of the Floyds. Theirs was operated by horsepower. The following description of the gin process was given by John Mason, a relative of the Floyds.

Isom C.B. Naylor and Joshua C. Naylor

> Two gin-stands of forty or fifty saws each were stationed in the upstairs of the building and connected by large cogwheels and a tumbling shaft with a big upright pillar that reached from a firmly fixed socket or "duck's nest" on the ground to the gin floor overhead and which was rotated by four horses hitched to levers ten or twelve feet long. Before my time there had been a few treadwheel gins in use.¹⁷

Mason went on to say the following regarding his grandfather Floyd's cotton gin:

> I remember seeing, when I was a lad, Grandfather Floyd's old gin. It hadn't been in use since the Civil War. When my mother was a girl, she fed the cotton into the stands. As long as she lived she carried scars on her hand which had caught in the saws. Luckily she drew her hand out in time to save her arm and possibly her life. One of her brothers, at the age of

---

16. Interview with Mr. Clifford Young, son of James and Sarah "Sally" Young, of Cairo, Illinois, on August 6, 1994. Mr. Young was then 90 years old.

17. Neimann, *The Glory of a Common Man*.

Saw mill in Finger, date unknown

ten or twelve, was killed in this gin. He got caught between the two large cog-wheels—passed between them and was cut almost in two. The only words he spoke when Granddad ran to him were, "Pap, I'm killed."

Little else is known regarding the Floyds' cotton gin.

The old cotton gin which was located down by the Mobile and Ohio Railroad behind the Finis Miller house and very near to the Cornelius Brown home just off of Mill Street (now Talbott Street) was built by Isom P. Womble, brother of Thomas J. Womble. Later he sold the gin to Finis E. Miller. Records from the Ball and Womble General Merchandise Store for 1902 show purchases by the Miller and Dickey Mill Company and by the Naylor Mill Company. Whether these partnerships were in the cotton or sawmill business or both is difficult to determine. Regardless, following Miller's ownership of the cotton gin, it passed to Albert Pickett. According to many sources, Albert Pickett operated the first steam-operated gin in Finger. Yet the gin's long and prosperous existence in Finger up this point makes one think it was already converted to steam power before Pickett's ownership.

Again, Pickett adhered to the two-fold philosophy of the business: cotton ginning in the fall and sawmilling during the rest of the year. Pickett bought white oak logs and would either cut the logs to length for staves and ship them to stave mills or go ahead and cut staves from the logs. The boiler for the operation was fed with slabs which were a ready by-product of the sawmill business. The only known workers from that old gin are Eddy Peeples and Hartle Hayre. When the new gin was built by John R. Harris, the old one served solely as a sawmill. The old gin was torn down sometime around 1930 or a little afterward.

The new gin was built on the north side of Main Street on the railroad, within a few yards of J.R. Harris General Merchandise. This new gin was incorporated as the Finger Gin Company. John R. Harris was the principal stockholder, but others including local merchants W.P. Massey, Newton Perry Talbott, Alsworth Guy Bishop, and Jess Mitchell, along with many country farmers, owned stock in the affair. During these years, Lawrence Robison and John Rouse were long-time gin workers.[18]

Following Harris' death, the gin was eventually sold to David Hodges of McNairy, the son of businessman John E. Hodges. Among Hodges' employees at the gin were Robison and Rouse as well as Robert Beene and Taft Walker.[19] According to Robert Beene, the gin was sold the next year and came under the ownership and management of local businessman Logan McCaskill.[20] During McCaskill's management, Robert Beene and Robert Harris were among the gin hands and were paid wages of five dollars per day.[21]

Eventually the gin was taken over by new owner Rudolph Barber, who ran the operation for many years. The last owner and operator was farmer and schoolteacher Robert Nash. The gin building was torn down in the early 1980s, but the old office building remains.

With the exception of the gins doubling as sawmills during ginning season, there is little else regarding the sawmill business in north McNairy County. However, there is one note of interest. In 1904, a contract was executed between H.H. Kirkpatrick, Lee Hendrix, and an enterprise known as Johnson Brothers. What is printed below is most likely a draft of the proposed contract with an official, notarized final draft

18. Robert Beene, letter to the author, October 23, 2003.
19. *Id.*
20. *Id.*
21. *Id.*

recorded elsewhere. This draft of the contract was found among the papers of the H.H. Kirkpatrick.[22]

> This is to make known to all men that Johnson Brothers, parties of the first party, and Lee Hendrix and H.H. Kirkpatrick and other undersigned parties have this day, September 23, 1904, entered into the following contract. To witness, Johnson Brothers, first party, agree to locate a sawmill on Lee Hendrix' land on or by October 15, 1904, and have free use of the mill as long as they, the first party, want it. The first party (Johnson Brothers) is to saw twos at ten cents a two, for all twos that leave the saw and edge all the lumber in good shape. The amount of logs is to be as many as 100,000. The logs are to be scaled by a 2/3 rule and sawed into such lumber as the second party desires. They are to be $4.50 per thousand for oak, $3.50 per thousand for gum, and $4.00 per thousand feet for poplar. All saw bills are to be paid within thirty days after the sawing or as soon (as the lumber is) sold, if earlier than the named date. The first party agrees to use all care in order to prevent any damages, but is not responsible for any, should any occur. The two parties agree to abide by the above contract and further agree to put on the mill yard, of the first party's request, the undersigned and [...] [This draft of the contract ends here.]

The Importance of Transportation and Communication to the Growth of Business in Finger and North McNairy County

All things commercial depend upon a modern infrastructure and efficient communication. This means that people and goods must arrive at their respective destinations on time as well as consumer orders, messages, and news. During the early twentieth century, such technology included the telegraph wire, the telephone system, the railway system and better and improved highways and roads. Yet these vital improvements did not occur overnight. The landscape of north McNairy County

22. The original draft contained phonetic spelling and improper grammar, but the author has taken the liberty of cleaning up the draft for purposes of ease of reading and understanding.

looked vastly different in 1920 than it did in 1880. An 1880 landscape, whether economic or physical in nature, would have been graced with a railroad line, a string of telegraph lines, and many narrow winding dirt roads deeply rutted by years of use during all sorts of weather. Most of the area was still wooded, yet untouched by logging crews and those seeking larger segments of land for cultivation.

Yet by 1920, great internal improvements had taken place bringing the area into a new era. The new era brought great prosperity for some, but little change for most, whose daily burden was heavy and toilsome. The telephone now made possible quick, clear and orderly business transactions.[23] Clearer instructions and communication could be had through this avenue, which were not possible through the telegraph wires. Such messages over the telegraph were short and choppy as the customer paid for each message by the letter. The development of the telephone system in Finger and surrounding areas will be discussed here. Finally the development of better roads and highways led to better transportation for all.

The Telegraph and The Railroad Depot

There is no call for a detailed history of the Mobile and Ohio Railroad, as a sufficient one for our purposes has already been outlined above. Yet with the construction of the town's railroad depot, great new opportunities and resources lay at the hands of the local merchants and businessmen. Therefore, a detailed sketch of the depot and complex, along with other vital facts as to the enterprise, are required.

The railroad's importance to towns like Finger cannot be underscored. The old run of tracks split off into two sets of tracks at the cotton gin and the two sets then ran parallel to one another until they reached a seed warehouse. Upon reaching this point, the tracks then merged again and ran southward to McNairy Station. On the south side of the crossing at Finger was the depot building. Both sides, east and west, of the depot were covered by porches and loading docks. The depot had a room which ran from one end to the other, north to south, and the agent worked in this room and could see out the bay window north toward Henderson.

23. Although the telephone was invented in 1876 by Alexander Graham Bell, it had yet to become an everyday household tool until much later in the twentieth century for most rural households.

An early photograph of the railroad depot at Finger

In this room, the telegraph operation was set up and it was here that the agent operated the signals and flags. On one side of the depot were two passenger waiting rooms, one for whites and one for blacks. On the other side of the agent's office was the freight room. At the south end of the building was a door.

If the agent had a letter or mail for the train to pick up and it appeared or was certainly known the train was not going to stop, the agent would attach the mail to a device outside of the building. He would proceed to hang the mailbag out and toward the tracks. There was a spot for the engineer or conductor to run his hand and arm through and snatch the mail without ever having to stop the train.

In and around the area of the depot were a number of buildings which served a number of purposes. Next to the depot itself was a packing shed, where farmers brought and sold their tomatoes and packed them into shipping crates. There was also a fertilizer storage warehouse down by the railroad tracks, which was owned by the late Logan McCaskill at one time.

Often a section of railroad hands was lodged nearby or in town. As the rail lines had to be constantly under maintenance for them to operate safely and efficiently, the necessity of having a steady crew of hands was ever present. In 1900, the section bosses were G.C. McCullar and

J.S. Abernathy. Both men were white, but their section crews were almost entirely black.

The telegraph service was conducted by the station agent in Finger and there were several station agents here through the years. They included William H. Harris, C.M. Barr, a Mr. Sanders, E.O. Parrish, Van Young, and Harrison Naylor. It was at the depot that merchandise, goods, and supplies for the different stores and businesses were delivered. It was also the destination for all incoming local mail including letters and packages. Passengers got on and off the train here. It was an all-purpose railway station and depot.

There were at least four different train times in Finger's heyday. First was the 8 A.M. train. Then at 10 A.M., there was a train bound for Corinth, Mississippi, a train known to countless passengers and others as the "Doodlebug" or the "Dinkie." It was the best known of the trains to run through Finger. The "Doodlebug" carried packages as well and was southbound in the morning hours and northbound during the evening hours. At 4 P.M., there was a train bound for Jackson, Tennessee. The last train to stop each in Finger was the 6 P.M. train. This train carried passengers and when it stopped in the evening, the town's folk often came out in great numbers to meet it. Perhaps they were meeting someone there who had come for a visit or sometimes they just wanted to see who was traveling through and maybe catch a glimpse of some long lost friend. The actual names of these trains were the *City of Miami* and the *Spirit of St. Louis*.

Since the beginning of rail travel, passengers have been fearful of train derailments and wrecks, which were much reinforced when images of twisted and mangled wreckage appeared in newspapers and some magazines reporting such accidents. Less worrisome for passengers in these latter days of railroad glory were holdups and robberies. Yet Finger experienced both directly. In May of 1944, the Illinois Central Engine 1332 collided with the Gulf, Mobile and Ohio Engine 481. One engineer was killed in this head-on collision.

As discussed previously in *Fingerprints*, Finger experienced its own train robbery. Unfortunately, the events of that day took on greater glory and legend than warranted. Like all such events, it was romanticized and elaborated upon to the point of exaggeration. Again to clear the record, it will be discussed here on these pages. In September of 1917, on

(Above) Harrison Naylor, agent for the Gulf, Mobile & Ohio Railroad, stands with an unidentified passenger beside the Finger Depot as a steam locomotive pulls into the station behind him. (Below) Naylor chats with someone on a GM&O caboose beside the depot.

a Thursday night, three masked men held up the northbound train near Finger. They exercised the usual plan of holding up the engineer and fireman, then cut the express car and pulled it away for some distance. Once the robbers reached their desired distance, they dynamited the safe, to find no money whatsoever. They fled in their car and were apparently never caught. In reporting the incident, the *McNairy County Independent Appeal* stated on September 28, 1917, "it is the first time a train was ever held up in the county."

Therefore, what about the infamous 1913 train robbery? Simply put, it never happened. There was no train robbery in 1913 and no long lost gold hidden in the woods of Chester County. There was no old age attempt by Frank James to recapture his glory days and it is most possible that Jesse was in no shape to assist as some have speculated, for the grave has a way of hampering such efforts. What most likely happened is most commonplace. Sometime in the 1960s and 1970s, men became interested in the events of old, especially if they were somewhat spectacular. Certainly train robberies fit that bill. Most likely someone talking to these men reported the fact that they remembered a train robbery and told of the small town speculation surrounding it plus forty or fifty years of embellishment. Sadly, this is a common situation and one often expected, to romanticize our history into fiction.

Road and Highway Improvements

Probably the greatest road improvement in north McNairy County's history was the building of the Finger-Leapwood Road in 1929. Road workers used teams of mules and breaking plows along with other tools and types of equipment in the construction process. The crews ran the breaking plow through the topsoil and ground surface and then scooped the loose soil up in order to pile it on layer by layer. The canal bridge was wooden and the lumber soaked in creosote. There were few bridges of concrete and steel in that period in this area of the state. When heavy rains came, parts of the levee would be submerged in water, so loads of gravel had to be hauled in and spread on top of the levee. In the early 1950's, the levee was built higher and blacktopped and this time the wooden bridge was replaced with a modern concrete structure. At the same time, the various hills and ridges along the path of the highway were cut into and cut down.

In regards to the original road building project of 1929 and following, the *Bushel Creek* correspondent for a local newspaper gave the progress reports on the construction project.

> March 27, 1930—"The Finger and Enville highway is in good condition at present."
> April 10, 1930—"The Finger and Enville highway is ready for the gravel. The trucks and men are ready to begin work, but the gravel hasn't arrived yet."
> April 24, 1930—"The Finger and Enville highway is being graveled rapidly."

As such roads were improved and made travel more efficient, opportunities abounded for merchants, farmers and consumers.

J. Orby Massey, son of William Pinkney Massey, sitting in his automobile

The Telephone in Finger and North McNairy County

The telephone was a great improvement which aided merchants and all businessmen in conducting their affairs. Certainly it made life more convenient for many in town. But like electricity, most who lived "out in the country" did not enjoy this new convenience. Here an attempt, however feeble it might be, will be made to chronicle the history of the telephone in the town of Finger and surrounding countryside.

When the telephone came to Finger is unknown, but it is known that its introduction was slow and steady. Like most small towns, one had to go through the switchboard and local operator before engaging in any discussion, business or otherwise. In those early days, most telephone discussions were limited to business and emergencies. If one wanted to talk to a friend, neighbor or relative, usually a personal visit sufficed and was preferred. Perhaps we will never all of the switchboard operators, but we can know a good number of them. Spinster sisters Callie and Mattie Miller ran the switchboard for a long period time out of their home on Mill Street, now Talbott Street. After they quit, Mrs. Mayhall served as switchboard operator. At some point, it was moved to Ernest Clayton's dry goods store and George Henry Davis took the operation over. However, his daughter Thelma Floyd ran it most of the time, with George Henry doing all electrical work and upkeep of the lines. Most likely the last switchboard operator was Jewel Durbin.

The switchboard was owned by the Finger Telephone Company which in turned was owned by a group of investors who bought stock which covered the expense of the equipment plus the agreement with the parent company who owned the lines. Among those believed to be stockholders were John R. Harris, Conrad Frye, Guy Bishop, W.P. Massey, Dr. Tucker, Dr. Barnes, and Jess Mitchell. The group sold the business to South Central Bell or its predecessor company during the Second World War.

One businessman, Hugh L. Hodges, had a telephone bill in May of 1914 that amounted to a whopping $1.60. A breakdown of a September 1914 telephone bill showed calls to from Hodges' office, located in downtown Finger, to Tupelo, Mississippi for forty cents, to Corinth, Mississippi for twenty cents, to Humboldt, Tennessee for twenty cents, and Jackson, Tennessee for twenty cents. Even 65 years after its development, the 1940 Finger listing, shown on the next page, gives the reader an idea of the rarity of having a telephone during that period of history in rural America.

FINGER TELEPHONE CO.

All Local Messages to and from Finger limited to five minutes.

For the Telephone Number or Address of the Nearest
Federal Bureau of Investigation Office.................Call Operator

Bank Home	81	Caudle's Store	222
Barber Shop	17	Clayton Albert r	1613
Barham Edd r	4712	Clayton Cratus r	4922
Beene Robert r	9510	Clayton Earnest r	3101
Beene Sam r	9501	Clayton Elmo r	343
Bishop A G r	273	Clayton Frank r	482
Bishop's Store	272	Clayton Jno r	29
Clayton Robert r	132	Naylor Harrison	342
Colston Sol r	162	Patterson Hobert r	33011
Davidson Clyde r	163	Plunk Hubert r	11101
Depot G M & O ofc	21	Plunk Lester r	3322
Dickey Ophelia r	3512	Plunk William r	1112
Dixie Swimming Pool	44	Rankin Lenard r	20
Frye C W r	192	Robinson Lawrence r	1101
Gage Liman	33121	Scott Will	4201
Gardner E B r	463	Smith Glen r	113
Gardner Motor Co	462	Smith Oliver	4722
Gibson Poney r	3313	Stevens Edd r	221
Hampton Harrison r	133	Stewart Tom r	25
Harris Bliss r	4713	Tedford Barney r	32
Harris Jno r	12	Tucker N A Dr ofc	102
Harris U T r	45	Tucker N C Dr r	103
Harris's Store	31	Vires Vodie r	473
Hayre Hartle r	2101	Walker C A	48121
Hendrick Bob r	313	Walker J C	143
High School	142	Walker M F r	921
Hodge Maggie	211	Walker Tobe r	50
Hunter Roy r	4222	Wamble Joe r	423
Hutcherson Jerd r	1113	Wamble M A r	422
Kirk Henry r	47121	Ward Jno r	4810
Kirk Nona r	4813	Weaver A E r	223
Massey Aubry	153	Woods Jim r	49121
Massey W P Store	152	Woodward Nolas	4221
McCaskell J R r	422	Young Calvin r	493
McCaskell W L r	193	Young F V r	4902
Mitchell Howell r	492	Young Robert r	38
Naylor Fayette r	312		

The original phone directory for Finger was placed on two pages of the old 1940 Henderson City phone directory, which also included other small towns. The reader will note that the listings are out of order.

Biographical Sketches of Prominent Businessmen

William Pinkney Massey (1868–1948)

William Pinkney Massey was born in 1868 to David Peeples Massey and Sarah E. McIntyre Massey. He was one of the many grandchildren of Robert Thompson McIntyre. In 1868, the Massey family was living in a log cabin on present-day Centerhill Road on property now belonging to Danny Beachy and located across the road from the sawmill. David Peeples Massey was born on March 15, 1834, and although old enough to have served during the War Between the States, it does not appear that Massey served in either army. He married Sarah E. McIntyre, the daughter of Robert Thompson McIntyre and wife Sarah Jane (Weaver) McIntyre, on September 22, 1861, with William Mason acting as bondsman and Justice of the Peace R.M. Clayton officiating. David and Sarah had at least two children other than William Pinkney Massey. Cyrathia A. Massey was born on October 6, 1862.

William Pinkney Massey

She lived for little more than a year before dying on December 11, 1863. Sarah J. Massey was born on August 4, 1865 and died on December 23, 1870. On March 28, 1869, Sarah E. (McIntyre) Massey died at the young age of twenty-five years. David did not long survive Sarah as he died on September 25, 1870, and was buried with his wife and daughter at Mount Carmel Cemetery.

William Pinkney Massey was raised by his grandparents, Robert Thompson McIntyre and Sarah Jane McIntyre, as well as his uncle and aunt, George and Amanda (McIntyre) Dickey. Little is known regarding Massey's early years, but it is assumed he was a fairly industrious and ambitious young man, as he accomplished a great deal in his lifetime. He was married twice. His first wife's name was C.E. Massey.[24] She was born on September 17, 1866. They had no children and in fact they were probably married no longer than just a few months. She died on February 2, 1890, and was buried in Mount Carmel Cemetery. He then married Saphronia Floyd on March 27, 1892. The couple had several children including: J. Orby Massey, Hooper Massey, Harrell Massey, Beulah O. Massey, Helen Massey, Jewell (Massey) Carter, and Pearl (Massey) Gage.

Massey was the owner of the W.P. Massey General Merchandise Store, a director and vice-president of the Bank of Finger, and a director

---

24. The author believes W.P. Massey's first wife was Cora L. Haynie (Haynes) and that the couple was married on October 15, 1889.

and vice-president of Home Banking Company. He was active in business and civic affairs in Finger for many years, even until his death. For several years, the Finger Post Office was located in the front of the Massey Store. Massey is best remembered for his large general merchandise business and was remembered by most as a good humored and gentlemanly fellow. A member of the Finger church of Christ, he died in 1948 and was buried in the Finger Cemetery. Saphronia Floyd Massey died in 1963.

John R. Harris (1874-1948)

John R. Harris

John R. Harris was born on July 1, 1874, to William H. and Eliza (Paralee) Tedford Harris. His sister was Beulah Harris Tucker. John married Miss Ora Brown on May 3, 1903 with justice of the peace Nathan R. Ward presiding. The couple had three children: Doris Harris, Anna Lee Harris, and Gretchen Harris. Doris was born on October 28, 1905, and died on January 15, 1906. She was buried in Mount Carmel Cemetery. Anna Lee, who was blind, married a gentleman from the town of Adamsville, Tennessee. Sadly enough, he too became blind as the result of exposure to fruit poison. He was spraying fruit trees and the wind blew the chemical back in his eyes and blinded him. The couple had at least one child, who died as an infant. Gretchen married Willie Arter Dillion and they had two children. Both she and her husband lived and died in Finger and are buried in the Finger Cemetery.

John, Ora and their family originally lived in the white frame home behind John's store. This would later become the John Clayton home and the Coy Russom home. He slowly climbed the ladder of success and made a fortune in the store, cotton and banking businesses. A shrewd investor and extremely frugal man, he acquired vast sums of money and property. He also had no pity on poor farmers and their families, foreclosing on farms near and far for the slightest delays in payment. It has been said that Harris himself held title to sixty such farms at one time during the 1930s.

However, his personal life did not yield such success. Sometime around 1930, John and Ora divorced. He soon married Zaida L. McCaskill, the bookkeeper and assistant cashier at Home Banking Company, who had worked for him for some time. While Ora moved to Adamsville, John built Zaida a new brick home just up the road from town. It was a spacious and well-built house, one of the few new homes built in Finger during the depression years. John and Zaida continued to work at the bank and run the financial operations of Finger Gin Company. At home, Mr. and Mrs. Lon Wynn attended to the housekeeping and gardening and other such functions for the Harris household.

John's frugal ways and business ethic were legendary. A number of stories exist to attest to his frugality. John once told a young lady he could have anything in the world, if he wanted it. Yet as he explained to her, he would rather have the money than whatever "it" is. Another time, he was having a concrete block grain bin built on a farm in the Sweetlips community. He asked one of the laborers, "Do you reckon those blocks are costing me a nickel apiece?" John redefined frugality.

John R. Harris with wife Zaida (McCaskill) Harris and Alice Floyd

Another story evidences his savvy and wily business ethic. A farmer came to the Finger Gin Company one afternoon to have a sample of cotton graded. He inquired about Mr. Harris and the gin manager told one of his hands to take the farmer to Home Banking Company to see John. Upon arriving at the bank, the bank's cashier and vice-president Leonard Rankin told the farmer, who was seeking a loan to plant his crop, the loan amount was above his limit and that if the farmer wanted to speak to John, he would have to go to the house. Up the hill, the farmer and the gin worker walked. They were shown into John's office and the request for a loan was made by the farmer. After a few moments of deliberation, John told the man he could have the loan. However, John quickly replied, "But now I remember an unpaid balance at my store from a few years ago. I guess we can add that in, with interest of course." After doing a little figuring, he told the farmer what the final sum owed would be. The farmer accepted and the two men were on their way again. Returning to the gin, the gin worker asked the farmer how he could accept such exorbitant interest on his old grocery bill. The farmer responded, "In these times, you do what you have to do to get your crop in."

John remained active in both the bank business and the cotton industry. A wealthy cotton buyer, John often attended the cotton buyers conventions and meetings. It was on his way to such a convention, when he was stricken with a heart attack. He and Zaida had just arrived in Bolivar while on their way to Memphis on November 26, 1948, when he died suddenly. He was buried in Old Friendship Cemetery. Zaida continued on in her official capacities at the bank in addition to now serving on the board of directors. She was born on November 28, 1889, and died on August 15, 1973. She was buried next to John.

Lee Andrew Weaver (1869–1952)

Lee Andrew Weaver was born on March 24, 1869, to Robert McMillan Weaver and Mary A. (Highfield) Womble Weaver. Lee was the grandson of early settler John Weaver and great-grandson of the blacksmith Adam Weaver, the first of the Weavers in this area. He was also the half-brother of Thomas J. Womble, William E. "Bill" Womble, and Isom Womble, all of whom were prominent men in north McNairy County. Lee received his education in the district schools and at one of the predecessor schools of Freed-Hardeman College.

With justice of the peace James Simpson "Simp" Lain officiating, Lee married Dovie Kerby on September 5, 1897. Dovie was the daughter of "Hickory Jim" Kerby, the niece of Hugh Kerby, and the granddaughter of Francis Kerby, the second landowner of record in McNairy County. Both Lee and Dovie could lay claim to a great heritage of brave and ambitious ancestors who blazed trails in west Tennessee as early settlers of

McNairy County. The couple had three children: Albert Weaver, Mary Young, and Alma Hayre.

Business was Lee's first interest. It preceded most other interests and his record was almost matchless in scope and intensity. His career before 1900 is not one of which we have any record. However, we do know that by 1900, Lee was a dry goods merchant in Finger. Between 1900 and 1910, most probably between 1904 and 1909, Lee and his family lived in Kenton, Tennessee, where he worked as an officer for a bank. Yet, by 1910, Lee was back in Finger running a general merchandise store. He operated this store throughout much of the 1920s.

Weaver's influence, knowledge of business, and superior ability to calculate was an asset in a spectacular trial. In 1904, McNairy County was riveted by the murder trial of Boss Perkins. Weaver, who was serving as a juror, was called upon to calculate the different numbers of years that jurors felt appropriate for Perkins and to arrive at a fair number on which to base the sentence. Of course, sentencing is an entirely different process in the current legal world. Weaver was also asked to calculate the daily cost of the Perkins trial. His calculation of the trial's cost was thirty-seven dollars per day. Finally, Weaver was chosen to write the verdict which would be given to Judge Levi S. Woods.

At some point, he became more interested in the banking and insurance businesses than the mercantile profession. As mentioned earlier, Lee served as president and director of the Bank of Finger, cashier and director of Home Banking Company, and cashier and director of the Union Savings Bank. He was also heavily involved in the insurance business. Many old documents from north McNairy County possess Lee Weaver's signature as he was a longtime notary public. Lee was also a member of the temperance movement, believing it vital that man abstain from strong drink. He died on May 8, 1952, and was buried in the Finger Cemetery.

Andrew J. Maness (1881-1913)

Andrew J. Maness is one of those characters in local history that begs us to question what his life would have brought had it not been cut so short. However, we are not at liberty to give way to our imaginations and presumptions. He may have acquired great riches and fame or, had he lived, he may have been doomed to fail and lose everything during the Great Depression or on some wildcat scheme. In short, we will never know, nor should we. Therefore, let us examine his life as it was and as far as we can know it.

Maness was born on June 18, 1881. Nothing is known of his early life. He was named the cashier of the Bank of Finger in 1908. He succeeded R.B. Moore, Jr. Maness was a very enterprising fellow and once called the "moving spirit of Finger."[25] He had a flair for business and financial handiwork. The local newspaper often served as a testimony to his financial success. In 1911, the following was reported: "It is said that A.J. Maness at Finger on an investment in the Dr. Rogers land a few months ago of $4,500 has closed a profit of $13,000."[26]

Like many businessmen during those early years, Maness was involved in more than one venture at a time. By 1909, he was a cotton buyer for the firm of Steele, Miller, and Company of Corinth, Mississippi, and a representative of the Richmond Bond Company of Hickman, Kentucky. He was an active young man with many prospects. He had married Pearl Swaim, the sister of John R. Swaim, on February 14, 1904. They had one son, Guy Maness. Unfortunately, financial success and a happy family could not sustain and save his life from an accident.

On Tuesday, October 14, 1913, Maness was taking part in what must have been a wonderful pastime, if not a passion, when his life was tragically cut short. The pastime was horse racing. Selmer, the county seat, had a racetrack as such activities were perfectly legal and commonplace in Tennessee in those days. In fact, racehorses were a favorite of men of wealth during those times. The local newspaper recorded the events surrounding Maness' injury and death.

"In a two ring dash when near the second round at the three-quarter turn, Andrew J. Maness, riding the Kirkpatrick horse, tried to pass a black horse on the inside and the best opinion is that the front feet of his horse struck the hind feet of the black horse, and the two horses and riders went down. The rider of the black horse was not hurt but Maness was so seriously injured that it was thought he would die at once."[27]

Maness did not die immediately, but neither would he tarry long. Doctors Ernest and John Smith, of Selmer, took charge of the case

25. *McNairy County Independent Appeal*, October 17, 1913.
26. *Id*, November 24, 1911.
27. *Id*, October 17, 1913.

immediately, taking Maness to Dr. Smith's house. Dr. Jere Crook of Jackson came down on the night train to Selmer to examine Maness. Following this examination, Maness was transported to the Jackson hospital aboard the ten o'clock train.

Although Maness' circulation and respiration were good, he never regained consciousness. As it happened, he had no skull fracture or other severe wounds to the body, but he suffered a severe shock to the brain. Doctors in Jackson believed that only a readjusting of the shocked parts, whatever that entailed, would save his life. Unfortunately, there was no hope in the end, as Maness died on Wednesday night, October 15, 1913, at eleven o'clock. On that fateful day, "the accident cast a gloom over the large crowd, and strong men could be seen to weep."[28]

Maness' funeral was held on the front porch of the Willie P. Massey home with Brother Nicholas Brodie Hardeman officiating. Maness became the first person buried in the Finger Cemetery, which was still at the time part of the James R. McIntyre farm. Zanie Brown and Harmon

28. *Id.*

Mourners at the funeral of businessman Andrew J. Maness held at the home of Willie P. Massey in Finger.

Hodges had to clear away wild blackberry vines in order to dig the grave. Maness' accident cut short the life of one of Finger's true entrepreneurs.

Newton Perry Talbott (1878–1947)

Newton Perry Talbott

Newton Perry Talbott was born on October 4, 1878, the oldest child of William Alexander and Angie Nora (Wright) Talbott. He was raised up on a farm near the Chester-McNairy County line. He was married first to Nancy Jane Jackson on November 7, 1900. They bought a house and sixty-eight acre farm from Haywood Hair on or about November 26, 1908. Here they lived, farmed and raised two daughters, Annie and Nona. In between the two girls was an infant son who was born and died in 1905, being buried at Hopewell Cemetery. Nancy died on December 21, 1915.

With two young daughters, Newt looked to marry once again. The second marriage was to Mary (Gilbert) Martin, already the mother of two, and the daughter of Dr. Thomas A. Gilbert and Ellen (Presley) Gilbert. Dr. Tom Abb, as he was called, was a brother of champion fiddler, John Gilbert, and was a medical doctor in Scotts Hill. With everything appearing to be well with Newt and his family, life went on. The couple bought a store building and lot in Leapwood from J. Matthew Wharton in 1916. Here they established N.P. Talbott General Merchandise. The couple had a son, William Perry Talbott, born in October 1917. But, happiness was not to be theirs. The child died in April of 1918. Then in the fall, Newt and Mary contracted influenza and both became desperately ill. Mary died on October 21, 1918, and was buried in Cedar Grove Cemetery near Scotts Hill, Tennessee. Newt was so ill he didn't know Mary was dead until she had been in the ground for nearly two weeks. Newt continued to look after Mary's two children by sending money when it was needed and the children would often come to see Newt.

Newt married the third time to Miss Beulah Varham Matlock, the daughter of local Democratic magistrate Henry Thomas Matlock and

Sarah Albertine Moore. Newt was a strong Republican in belief and practice and thus the dinner conversations between in-laws must have been lively. Newt and Varham had two children, Luther Edward Talbott and Vonnie Mae (Talbott) Garner. Newt continued to operate his store while farming and ginning cotton on occasion. Newt would himself admit that he could grow great corn, but awful cotton. A gentleman by the name of Barksdale, who worked as a jobber for the Garrett Tobacco Company, would make his rounds in a carriage or by horseback throughout the countryside filling orders. He once said he went to the fields where Newt was working in order to get his tobacco order and had to sit on the plow stock while taking the order.

Newt moved his business to Finger around 1927 in order that his business might be closer to the railroad and depot. He was an active and kindhearted merchant there for nearly twenty-one years. Unfortunately, in his later years, he was plagued with persistent heart problems and near-blindness. He passed away in 1947 and was buried in Hopewell Cemetery.

Logan McCaskill (1896–1960)

Logan McCaskill can successfully be termed as one of this area's great entrepreneurs in a career that spanned from the 1920s until his death in 1960. Logan was born in 1896 to Thomas K. and Josephine Wilson McCaskill. His early years were spent with his parents in Chester county where his father farmed and raised Logan and his siblings, Mary, Dennie, and Scott. Apparently the family had moved to McNairy County by 1920, as they were not listed in 1920 Federal Census for Chester County. Logan's interests were diverse and his talents many. He built the lake resort on U.S. Highway 45 known as Logan's Lake. Here was located a large number of cabins, a large cavernous resort lodge, and a swimming pool. All of this could

Logan McCaskill

be enjoyed just a few short yards from the large lake. Logan was also a barber and an insurance agent.

Logan was a large man with large appetites and large ambitions. He was also known for having a nervous trigger finger. The story has persisted that on one late evening while investigating a break-in and as he passed a mirror and caught a glimpse of his own image and fired his revolver at the mirror. His financial and business interests were far flung. His insurance agency was eventually ran by his wife, Alice (McIntyre) McCaskill, the daughter of James Robert McIntyre. He and Alice had no children. He died in 1960 and was buried in the Finger Cemetery.

Jess Mitchell (1884-1963)

Jesse F. "Jess" Mitchell was born to William O. and Margaret L. Mitchell of the Twelfth District of Chester county on August 7, 1884. He married Miss Maud Venada. Jess and his brothers were all men of the professional grain. One of his brothers was an attorney and another was a dentist. Jess opened a general merchandise store in Finger in the early years of the twentieth century on Main Street and operated here for many years. He later moved his operation to Henderson where he continued until his retirement. He died on December 8, 1963, and Miss Maud on June 12, 1968. Both are buried in the Henderson City Cemetery.

Guy Bishop (1892-1967)

Guy Bishop

Alsworth Guy Bishop was born to a merchant family on August 25, 1892, around Enville, Tennessee. His father was the Enville merchant M.E. Bishop (1856–1920), the founder of the firm of Bishop and O'Neal. These two families were moving forces in the small town of Enville and were interrelated. It was M.E. Bishop who sent his two sons, Guy and Dossie, to Finger to establish a second branch of the family business during the second decade of the twentieth century. Guy and Dossie were engaged in the mercantile business together and were involved in many local affairs until Dossie's tragic death in a train-car collision in 1922. Following Dossie's death, Guy carried on alone and engaged in other pursuits as well. He established the Finger Burial Association and worked as an undertaker. He also engaged in the commodities and trade business and the appliance business in his later years. He was married to Minnie Mae Tedford (1893-1971) and had one daughter, Lorraine (Bishop) Meadows, a schoolteacher. He and Mrs. Bishop are buried in the Finger Cemetery.

Hugh L. Hodges

Hugh L. Hodges was born into a family with many branches, all of whom were enlightened and adventurous. He was more business-minded than most of the family and probably less literary and lofty than the others. He was, in fact, a man of varied interests and abilities making him one of the more interesting and enterprising businessmen of north McNairy County. According to his records, he must have been quite the man of the town whom everyone sought out for various reasons. These records indeed show that Hugh must have been busy with so many activities and business ventures. Hugh was a produce dealer and commodities dealer. However, like most of the Hodges' family, he was a teacher first. He taught at Cave Springs among other places.

Hugh L. Hodges

Yet it was the produce business and cotton business that put Finger on the map and made Hodges a man of some considerable wealth and substance. His business dealings extended from Alabama to New York, from South Carolina to Missouri to Illinois. Brokerage houses, large and small alike, dealt with Hodges' office in downtown Finger. Their names included Shatz Brothers, Gallagher Brothers, and T.A. Thompson. Yet other businesses and establishments dealt with also, such as The Paris Café, Tar Creek Kennels, and Ike Dickey Commission Company. Hugh kept up with the markets in Liverpool, England, Wall Street in New York City, and the markets in Chicago. Perhaps his downfall was due to investing in stocks, commodities, and grain and cotton futures. In fact, the stock market crash of 1929 and the subsequent economic depression almost completely devastated Hugh.

Following these misfortunes, Hugh moved to Selmer. There, like in Finger, he quickly made himself a fixture in town and a man upon whom dependence was often placed. He was elected to the Selmer board of aldermen in November of 1931. After many years in McNairy County's county seat, Hugh moved to Milan where he died in the 1960s. His widow lived on until sometime in the 1990s.

Major A. James

Major A. James is not a figure well-remembered today in north McNairy County, unless the memories belong to distant relatives. He was very active here in the early years of the twentieth century, but then left the state and went west to Oklahoma where he remained for the rest of his life. He was, in fact, a local school teacher and merchant. Nothing is known of his early years. He married Callie McIntyre on February 22, 1903. She was the daughter of James Robert and Margaret Rebecca (Beene) McIntyre. At the turn of the century and shortly afterward, Major was teaching school. He was a partner in the firm of McIntyre, James, and Company General Merchandise, with his father-in-law, James R. McIntyre and his brother-in-law, Robert Allen McIntyre. Interestingly enough, in 1902, Major bought a subscription to the *McNairy County Independent Appeal* newspaper, making him one of the very paper's first subscribers ever in the northern part of the county. He and Callie had at least four children: Lessie James, Irene James Bagwell, Brode James, and Maye James.

CHAPTER SIX

THE HEALING ARTS: FROM MIDWIVES AND "DOCTORS BY EXPERIENCE" TO PROFESSIONAL PHYSICIANS

The healing arts during the earliest years—The life and duties of the midwife—The neighboring "doctor by experience"—The move from primitive cures to professional physicians—Brief sketches of the area's healers and physicians.

Like so many other regions and areas, McNairy County's earliest years were years of hardship and often suffering for its pioneers. One has only to consider the factors innate with the settlement of a wild area to understand that physical maladies were common and professional treatment a rarity. In other words, the early years of settlement were years of sickness and physical stress and trained doctors were often nowhere to be found. This chapter traces the path from primitive methods and untrained amateurs to perfected procedures and trained licensed professionals.[1]

In the days before modern medicine and high-tech research methods, when doctors were few and extremely far between, people were forced to

---

1. The reader must remember that when terms such as "perfected," "trained," or others are used, the author is referring to such standards of the day when doctors still lived and practiced in north McNairy County. This would be no later than 1950.

resort to less sophisticated methods to cure their ailments. This was often the case for the early settlers of north McNairy County. Yet the question arises as to how they knew a certain plant or extract cured a certain ailment. They simply experimented and learned from others, including most often their elders, what cures were and what cures weren't. A few of the cures which were often employed in north McNairy County will be included, as well as a few found elsewhere in other nearby regions.

Early Cures and Home Remedies[2]

Often children get earaches, as do adults, and the experience can be quite painful and cause little ones to be miserable. In the days before pediatricians were commonplace, a common cure for the earache included heating a sprout of permission and catching the sprout's sap. Once the sap cooled, it was to be dropped into the ear. This was said to work on both adults and children. Another common problem was the cough, still a common trouble in the winter and during allergy season. In olden days, cough syrup was made from cherry bark and sugar. The bark was boiled and the juice mixed with sugar and then further boiled to thickening. The resulting concoction was to be drunk.

Another treatment for winter colds and sicknesses was mullein tea. The mullein leaf is a fuzzy broadleaf which when boiled makes a tea which must be drunk while hot for best effect. For children who are teething, have hives, trouble sleeping or who are sick with influenza, catnip was the best answer to the problem.[3] For those who are a tad bit fuzzy on their botany, catnip is a strongly scented plant which has a white appearance due to the presence of fine white hairs on the stems and underside of its heart-shaped leafs. The plant grows to about two or three feet. Its leaves and purple-dotted flowers are gathered in the spring and summer time. The tea is made in a simple process of pouring one pint of boiling water

---

2. These homemade medicines were described to the author by many of the older generation, all of whom were the recipients of such concoctions.

3. The following information regarding the plant catnip is taken from Kaye (Carver) Collins, Lacy Hunter, and Foxfire Students, eds. *Foxfire 11: The Old Homeplace, Wild Plant Uses, Preserving and Cooking Food, Hunting Stories, Fishing, and More Affairs of Plain Living* (New York: Anchor Books, 1999).

over a half cup of broken catnip stems and leaves. After this is complete, the mixture is left to stand for a few minutes and then strained.

Other cures did not require any more than common items which could be found around the house. If you had a corn, you could melt an aspirin and pour it on the corn. If a joint, such as an ankle or elbow, was sprung, a person could soak a brown paper sack in apple cider vinegar and wrap it around the injured area. To bring a boil to head, an individual could either put a piece of fat meat on the boil or place the membrane of an egg on it for the desired purpose. Finally it was often told that cigarette papers were beneficial in healing spots and sores of the mouth.

Another common problem was dropsy. Dropsy is a medical problem that would probably go by another name today, that of edema. It was an excess accumulation of fluid caused by chronic heart failure.[4] This was apparently a common problem for many people, old and young alike, just as today, only the names change. This has been common as many medical conditions are researched and better diagnosed and defined.

Robert McMillan Weaver, the father of Lee Andrew Weaver, was a man with intent interest in cures and medicine. Interestingly enough, Weaver was a blacksmith, not a doctor. Among his several papers were recipes for tempering steel and other such procedures, but there were also recipes for various cures to various ailments. One was apparently given to Weaver by Mr. Roll Deaton and was an alleged cure for dropsy. That recipe, probably not accepted by pharmaceutical researchers and pharmacists today due to simplicity and lack of effectiveness, is as follows.

Robert McMillan Weaver

Recipe for Dropsy
Three roots of Seneca Snake roots
Three roots of Black Snake roots
Three roots of Star roots
Cherry tree bark, five inches long as much as you can hold between the thumb and fore-finger

4. *Id.*

Dogwood—the same dried and powdered up and put in one quart of whiskey

Direction for use: take a drank [*sic*] 3 times per day

Many of the older generations were experienced with the effects of herbs on minor medical problems. This meant going into the fields and woods to search for hard-to-find herbs and plants which had alleged medicinal qualities. Many families gathered such herbs and sent them through the mail to herbal medicine manufacturers who in turn returned to those families certain amounts of medicine manufactured from those herbs.

Other medicinal treatments came from patent medicines. One has only to dig around the dumping grounds of old home sites to see the dependence placed on such medicines and tonics. Many names were common in households of the mid to late 1800s and early 1900s. Many contained more parts of whiskey than herbs and medicine. Yet people would swear by them. Dr. Bull's Medicine, Lydia Pinkham's, Scalf's Indian River Tonic, "5-Drops" Salve, and Swanson Pills are just a few of among thousands of wonder drugs an ailing individual could buy in the years gone by.

There were many personalities in north McNairy County who held reputations as healers and "doctors." Some of them had a certain amount of practical experience by which they earned the title "doctor." Some of them were titled "herb doctors." John Plunk, sketched earlier in Chapter Two of this work, was an herb doctor, a doctor by experience, like his father, Dr. Peter Plunk. Some mystery lies behind the identity of another "country doctor." According to writer Gloria Jeter, two brothers moved into the area that was south Madison and north McNairy, now probably Chester county, from South Carolina by the names of James Franklin Jeter and Joseph Ceef Jeter. According to Ms. Jeter, James was a farmer, country dentist, and fine musician. The other brother, Ceef, was said to be doctor who practiced in what would be Chester County and McNairy County. Accordingly, his wife was a midwife and she traveled with Ceef in his horse and buggy to make house calls. There was a Ceef Jeter who lived east of Finger in the late 1800s and early to mid-1900s, but as far as anyone knows, he was a farmer. This man was Jocephus Jeter. Perhaps the country doctor was his father. Perhaps we will never know.

There were several "healers" who plied their talent as late as the twentieth century. Ivy Barton and Harrison Vires were said to have been able to remove warts without the use of a knife or any surgical instrument. The mother of Mr. Jim Dees was said to be able to stop bleeding and prevent the tragic effects of burns.[5] Finally Ms. Ludie (Griffin) Clayton was said to have been able to cure the thrash in a child. Some of these healers' methods included touching the patient while chanting certain phrases and others required other actions. Perhaps circumstance contributed to the reputation of these healers, but as years and people passed and medicine advanced, such practices were eventually abandoned.

The midwife was and still is, in some areas of the world, an integral part of the local community. Before obstetricians and even general practitioners, the local midwife was the vital link to knowledge, skill, and assistance when a newborn was expected. Mothers-to-be and their husbands placed great confidence in midwives and were often dependent upon her knowledge and experience to deliver them and the infant through the painful and often uncertain process. Such experience was vital to a safe delivery and many midwives continued their work well into their old age. The midwife's knowledge extended to all matters of the process of birth, from the preparation preceding the actual moment to the care of the mother and child immediately upon birth. Many harmful effects can occur following the birth, both to mother and child, and the midwife was peculiarly qualified to notice such problems and to correct them.

There were also doctors who traveled through the region and set up shop for a couple of days to provide services in a time when most potential patients did not venture far for such assistance. The newspapers of old are rich with notices advertising the upcoming visit of some type of physician to the area, complete with dates, times, and places. One such notice went as follows:

> Dental Notice: I will be at Finger, May 3 & 4, 1921, to do dental work. On this trip I will extract teeth free. Dr. G.W. North.

---

5. At some time around 1910, if not a little earlier, the author's own great-grandfather, John Robert McIntyre, was hit in the head by a large rock causing a deep cut and excessive bleeding. He was immediately taken to Mrs. Dees for treatment, in order that the bleeding could be stopped.

However primitive times may have been in the early years of the area, it is interesting to note that qualified and educated physicians have been present here since almost the beginning. Therefore, it should be noted that such healers, midwives, and others previously mentioned served to fill in the gaps and provide help when people couldn't afford the services of a doctor. More than a dozen doctors practiced medicine in north McNairy County over the years. Brief sketches of each of these physicians are included in this chapter. Some of the sketches are longer than others due to the level of knowledge we have about each one. Some of the doctors were much better qualified and better educated than others in the practice. They are presented in near chronological order.

Of the first few physicians in northern McNairy County, we know very little. Due to the fact that present-day southern Chester county was a part of McNairy County from 1823 until 1882, those who practiced in the area around Montezuma will be discussed. One of the first doctors was Dr. J.D. Smith, of whom we still know relatively nothing. General Wright recorded one of our few sources of information about this man:

> Dr. Smith settled at an early day near W.T. Anderson in the northern part of the county. He had several sons and two daughters. The eldest daughter, Mary, resides now in Jackson, Tennessee, having married twice. The second daughter, Sallie, married _____ Robbins. She is now a widow residing in Henderson County.[6]

In December of 1859, Dr. Smith was practicing in the area and was a customer of the Hollis and Cason General Merchandise Store in Montezuma, Tennessee. Other than this, we know no more concerning this early pioneer.

Dr. Wilson McKissick was an early doctor at Montezuma, then a part of McNairy County. Of Dr. McKissick, General Wright stated that he "was an early settler near Montezuma, in the northern part of the county. He was a very learned man, and fine physician. His eldest son, Colonel Lewis D. McKissick, has been for a number of years a distinguished lawyer in Memphis, Tennessee, but is now a citizen of San Jose, California."[7]

6. Wright, Talbott, McCann, *Reminiscences of McNairy County 130th Anniversary Edition.*
7. *Id.*

Dr. McKissick's name appears on the McNairy County Early Settlers Monument, erected in 1904 on the grounds of the courthouse in Selmer.

By 1860, three gentlemen were practicing medicine in the north McNairy County community of Anderson's Store. Dr. Jesse McKinney, Dr. C.L. Freeling, and Dr. W.G. McCoy were all living within a short distance of each other. Dr. Jesse McKinney was born in North Carolina in 1818 and his wife Elizabeth was born in Tennessee. The couple had at least seven children: Joseph (born 1841), Jesse (born 1843), Eliza (born 1847), Samuel (born 1851), John R. (born 1854), Edmond (born 1858), and George (born 1860). It is not known if Dr. Jesse McKinney was a member of the McKinney family of Purdy or not. This old Purdy family included Dr. Charles McKinney and sons, Judge James F. McKinney and Dr. William D. McKinney. It is known that Dr. Jesse McKinney received his mail from the Purdy post office, leading one to think of a connection.

Dr. C.L. Freeling was born in Tennessee around the year 1830. Mary E. Freeling, his wife, was born around 1829. Dr. Freeling, also a farmer, practiced around Anderson's Store. What became of Dr. Freeling is currently unknown. There was a Dr. Freeling practicing medicine in McNairy Station in 1884. This was recorded by William Kendal Abernathy, whose father moved their family to McNairy Station that year. However, it is known that Mary E. Freeling, the doctor's wife, sold their 163½ acre farm to Robert Thompson McIntyre on November 28, 1865, for the sum of $1400.00. Whether Freeling died during the war as a participant or not is not currently known. However, assuming something did not happen to Dr. Freeling and that he was practicing medicine in 1884, it would have been strange for his wife to have had the ability to sell their farm in 1865.

Dr. W.G. McCoy was born in 1815 in South Carolina. His wife Martha was born in Tennessee in 1825. The couple had at least eight children, all of whom were born in Tennessee. The couple's children were: Leonidus McCoy (born 1844), Mary A. McCoy (born 1846), Martha F. McCoy (born 1848), Benjamin F. McCoy (born 1850), Adaline McCoy (born 1852), Luiza J. McCoy (born 1855), Sarah McCoy (born 1857), and Emma (born 1860). Dr. McCoy practiced in and around the Anderson's Store community where he also farmed. What became of Dr. W.G. McCoy and his family is not known.

Dr. Lee H. Ingraham was living in the north McNairy County area around present-day Finger in 1870. In fact, he a member of the prominent Ingraham family of north McNairy County's old days. In 1870, Ingraham was living with Mr. James Roberts and his wife, Martha. Dr. Ingraham, who was born in 1844, was not married at the time. His life was discussed further earlier in Chapter Three of this work.

Another forgotten physician from north McNairy County's past is Dr. Robert E. Miller. He was born in 1853 in the Bullman Store-Sweetlips area, the son of Robert S. and Elizabeth J. (Willett) Miller. He was a brother of John A. Miller and Finis E. Miller, both profiled in other chapters of this work. In 1880, Dr. Miller was practicing and living in the north McNairy County area near present-day Finger. He probably married sometime after the enumeration of the 1880 Federal Census. His wife's name was Susan and they had at least one child, born on August 2, 1882, who died as an infant. Nothing further is known of Dr. Miller.

In the area around McNairy Station, a doctor by the name of J.J. Lovelace practiced medicine. However, very little is known concerning Dr. Lovelace. He was married to Sarah B. Scott, the daughter of George R. and Hester Ann (Haltom) Scott.[8] The couple had at least one son, Johnnie Lovelace.

Dr. James H. Curry Jr. lived and practiced medicine in north McNairy County and in the Finger community in the early years of the twentieth century. He married Daisy E. Sanders, the daughter of another physician, Dr. W.M. Sanders, on December 15, 1897.[9] It has been said of Mrs. Curry: "Perhaps no woman that ever lived was a better neighbor and friend than was Mrs. Daisy Curry."[10] Her sister Alma Sanders married yet another physician, Dr. Lillian Rogers and they resided in Amarillo, Texas.[11] Doctor Curry was born in August of 1870 and Mrs. Curry in August of 1877. In 1900, the couple was living in Finger where Doctor Curry practiced medicine and Mrs. Curry worked as a music teacher.[12] How many children the couple had is unknown, but in July of 1899, they

---

8. The information on Dr. Lovelace was contained in Genevieve (Scott) Bell, e-mail message to author, February 1, 2001.

9. Taylor, *Historical Articles*.

10. *Id.*

11. *Id.*

12. 1900 Federal Census for McNairy County, Tennessee.

had a daughter, Anna M. Curry. One note of interest is that in 1900, a thirteen year old black girl by the name of Daisy O'Neal was living with Curry family employed as a servant. As late as 1903, Dr. Curry resided in Finger.[13] Dr. and Mrs. Curry moved to Adamsville sometime after 1903 and remained there for the rest of their lives where he practiced medicine and she taught school. Daisy Curry died in 1948 and Dr. Curry died in 1951. The couple was buried in the Adamsville Cemetery.

Some note should be made of the various druggists who operated drug stores in Finger during the early part of the twentieth century. According to most sources the first drugstore in town was operated by either Seril Brown or John W. Scott. An early newspaper blurb stated the following: "C.V. Brown, of Finger, was among our people Monday. He has recently purchased his father's interest in the drug store at Finger, and will now conduct the business himself. He is a graduated chemist."[14] Besides these, Dr. Tucker owned a drugstore in which he sold various sundries and Dr. Barnes was the proprietor of a drugstore which sold, among other things, *Victor* records and toilet preparations. Both gentlemen are discussed in detail below.

Having dispensed with the earlier and lesser known doctors from north McNairy County's history, we concentrate on those who are more recent in memory. Many patients of these men are still living, though their numbers are diminishing with each passing year. Each of these men had a different personality and a different approach to the practice of medicine. If one had to rank these men in ability and knowledge of the body and medicine, such rank would be Hodges, Tucker, and Barnes. If such rank were to extend to the spectrum of patients and their compassion to those patients, such rank would probably be Tucker, Hodges, and Barnes. Despite their individual differences and oddities, all have their place in north McNairy County's history.

William Henry Hodges, M.D.

Dr. William Henry Hodges was born into a family of high intelligence, boundless ingenuity, and a level of curiosity which if satisfied could

13. In January of 1903, Dr. Curry was still conducting business with Thomas J. Womble's General Merchandise store. He was probably in Finger longer, but this is not known for certain.

14. *McNairy County Independent Appeal,* December 5, 1902.

Dr. William Henry Hodges

very well be quite voluminous. The son of Captain Elijah James Hodges, a farmer, politician, preacher, and soldier, and Nancy Jane (Dodd) Hodges, he was born on September 19, 1869. According to his sister Maggie Hodges, he and brother Horry were born in Morgan county, Alabama. Regardless of his birthplace, Henry was raised on the Hodges' family farm outside of present-day Finger. Like his brothers and sisters, he was surrounded by books and the love of learning was instilled in him by his father, a man of literary pursuits. After attending the district schools in Henderson, Henry taught school for a period before deciding to follow a career in medicine.[15]

In 1898, Henry graduated from the University of Nashville Medical School.[16] Henry immediately began practicing medicine actively and was soon recognized for his ability and skill as a medical professional. A newspaper quote previously cited again evidences Henry's professional reputation:

> Dr. Henry Hodges, of McNairy, has come to be a frequent professional visitor in Selmer and sometimes talks of locating here. Dr. Hodges is a physician of more than ordinary attainments for his age, and, with close application, he is destined to rank high in his profession.[17]

His expertise in the field of anatomy, physiology and medicine was such that he was consulted by his peers, by patients from all over the

---

15. It is not currently known when Doctor Hodges attended college and pursued his undergraduate degree, but he probably attended West Tennessee Christian College where Horry attended.

16. This school is now the Vanderbilt University Medical School in Nashville, Tennessee.

17. *The Weekly Post*, November 13, 1903.

countryside, and even by the court in special cases where expert opinion testimony was required.

Henry was a quiet man whose nature was reserved and contemplative. He was remembered by many for sitting in his library, quietly reading and studying works of literature, history, science, religion and medicine. However, there was another side to the good doctor, much like there is to any individual. He had a light and humorous side like anyone else and most likely a playful side. The following letter from W.H. Mills, the president of the National Association of Railway Agents of Norwalk, Ohio, illustrates the more colorful self which Henry apparently possessed.[18]

> Norwalk, Ohio
> Dec. 11th, 1902.
>
> Friend Doc,
> I think I wrote to you last and as yet I have never read any reply, what has become of you? Have you got married to that little girl with the straw hat you told me about, or have you joined the Church and quit drinking? How is everyone at McNairy and what has become of my side partner "Gould?" He said he was going to write to me but I have never received his letter yet. How is our friend Mrs. Franklin, and John and the Miss Franklin; also the good looking Station Agent? How is Mrs. Sheffield? Give them all my regards. How is the quail crop this year, are you going to have many of them? I am going to St. Louis next month on business but hardly think I will be able to get down that far this winter. I would like very much to come down and have a time with you and the other boys. How is Joe Rouse? Is he still on the turf?

---

18. The letter has a type of earthy character to it and suggests that Dr. Henry Hodges, like many younger men, knew how to have a good time. The letter discusses what many such letters among men of that period did, weather, hunting, dogs, and women, and not in that particular order. Certainly we can see that Dr. Hodges was more than just a bookworm with an insatiable appetite for books and academic pursuits. One interesting note regards Mills' tongue-in-cheek mention of joining the church. When speaking with members of the family and those who were well-acquainted with them, no one seems to have known Dr. Hodges' religious preference. No reference was made in his obituary as to his religious beliefs, but only that his services were held at the Finger Church of Christ.

You had better meet me in St. Louis and I will give you a time that you will never forget. How many puppies have you sold for me? I am going to raise a car load or two and would like to get you to act as agent for me in selling them. "That little old dog" of mine is still on the turf and can beat the "ASS" off of any of the rest around here finding quail. I have been troubled with falling of the Womb and can't walk so far as I could. Can you send me a remedy for the trouble? Let me hear from you and all about McNairy and what has been going on down there since I was there last winter; also how the quail are and if there is any good hunting there this year. Something might turn up that we might run down and make you a call. What kind of weather are you having? It has been very cold here but is some warmer now but I do not think it will last long. Ask Gould if he wants us to come down and if he will go hunting with me if I will come. Tell him I will shoot him some more rabbits. Herb was hanged for horse stealing and White is in jail for robbing chicken roosts and I have joined the Salvation Army. So you will have to be careful how you act if I come. Let me hear from you at once.

With kind regards to all of the McNairy friends, I am,

Yours Truly,

W.H. Mills

p.s. I know some good stories which I will tell you when I see you, and soon.

Henry's range of interests went far beyond that of science or medicine. He was a true lover of history. Many were the times that Horry and Henry made the short trip to Squire James Simpson "Simp" Lain's humble home to discuss the great events of old and their many implications. History was a favorite subject. One young man was granted permission to use the Hodges' private library to research a historical debate. The debate pitted this young man as Ulysses S. Grant and a classmate as Robert E. Lee and thus "Grant" was permitted to use the family library for research purposes. Henry looked up from his own studies and instructed the young man, "Tell them Grant commanded more men that Napoleon or Caesar and was never driven from the field."[19]

Many of the older residents of north McNairy County do not remember Henry practicing medicine actively, but rather remember him for the advisory role he appeared to play when consulting with other physicians. In fact, many local doctors in the area called upon Henry's expertise and seemingly boundless knowledge of the body and medicine to supplement their own reservoir and to assist them in making crucial medical determinations. However, he was actively engaged in the practice from 1898 until 1937 or 1938. According to one member of the family, Henry was employed full-time as doctor at Western State Mental Asylum from 1922 until 1938. This has been confirmed by others.[20]

Off and on through the years, Henry was afflicted with pain and sickness. The exact problem or cause remains a mystery. Again, some have stated that his problem, as with Harvey, was tuberculosis, but this cannot be proven. Regardless, ill health forced him to retire in the late 1930's. His physical health weakened, but not his mind. His drive to learn and share with others continued. One gentleman stated that an afternoon ride with "old Doc Hodges" could teach you more than you had ever learned in your life otherwise.[21] The author of the *Cyclone Bill* column wrote about all four Hodges' brothers when commenting upon Henry's death: "I never met any one of these four boys and talked with them any length of time that I didn't learn something that I didn't know before."[22] On November 16, 1941, a Sunday afternoon, Dr. William Henry Hodges died at his family home after a prolonged illness. Henry's funeral services were held at the Finger Church of Christ on Monday afternoon, November 17, 1941, with a Brother Cox and Judge J.C. Houston officiating. Henry

---

19. The young "Grant" was future teacher and politician Lloyd Harris, and the student "Lee" was Crolin Plunk, a classmate and future attorney.

20. Jerry Wilson Smith, a grandson of Mary Hodges Robertson, sister to Dr. William Henry Hodges, stated in a July 1996 interview at his home in Friendship, Tennessee, that when he spent summers there in the 1920s and 1930s, Henry was employed at the asylum. He stated that Henry caught the train to Bolivar on Monday mornings and came back to Finger on Friday afternoons. Ben Davidson, great-grandson of Bettie (Hodges) Peeples, also a sister of Dr. Hodges, says he believes he has heard the same.

21. Guy Brown of Finger, Tennessee, interview with the author, 1995.

22. *McNairy County Independent Appeal*, November 21, 1941.

was laid to rest beside his brother Horry in the old burying grounds of Mount Carmel Cemetery.

W.M. "Mark" Barnes, M.D.

Dr. W.M. "Mark" Barnes was born on January 7, 1883, in the Mud Creek area of north McNairy County. He was the son of Thomas L. Barnes and wife Nora (Hughes) Barnes.[23] Exactly when Dr. Barnes commenced his medical practice in unknown, but the local newspaper reported on December 6, 1907, that "W.M. Barnes had gone to Memphis to attend the lectures at the medical college there."[24] One writer noted the following regarding the path of Dr. Barnes' medical career:

> Mark Barnes, still another Mud Creek boy, got out of medical school about 1906. Between terms, he came to Adamsville and worked with Dr. Martin. Later he opened an office at Finger, but it seems that he moved to Henderson before his death.[25]

During his years in Memphis studying medicine, Dr. Barnes worked as a street car operator to support himself. Dr. Barnes married Estelee Bishop, the daughter of M.E. Bishop of Enville and the sister of Dorsey and Guy Bishop. Estelee was born on July 4, 1880.

Dr. and Mrs. Barnes first resided in the old Lee A. Weaver home on Apple Street in Finger. At that time, the house was a two room structure, which was added to and renovated by Mr. Weaver and later by current owners, Mrs. Arlie Smith and her late husband Richard. Later, Dr. Barnes moved across the meadow to his new home, a stately house with a large front porch and two levels of large rooms. This house is located next to the church of Christ meetinghouse in Finger.[26] Doctor Barnes was a man who enjoyed his leisure, probably more so than other doctors in the area. He had a shooting range located on land that now belongs

---

23. Glenda Parchman, *Henderson City Cemetery* (Privately published, 2011).

24. *McNairy County Independent Appeal*, December 6, 1907.

25. Taylor, *Historical Articles*. This particular article was written by Mr. Taylor on December 11, 1959.

26. The home is now owned and occupied by the Laws Rushing Sr. family.

Dr. W.M. Barnes built this home on the Finger-Leapwood Road around 1914. He and his wife lived here until they moved to Henderson in 1940. Today it is occupied by the Laws Rushing family and remains a beautiful and stately residence.

to the Smith family. He shot skeet and entertained his fellow gentlemen on many afternoons.

Dr. Barnes also had the distinction of owning the first automobile in Finger. For years, he made his rounds in a horse and buggy outfit driven by his black servant, a man some believe was named Scott.[27] His horse, named Judge, found the new automobile to be somewhat disturbing and was frightened by the strange contraption. Therefore, to facilitate the relationship between beast and horseless carriage, he tied the poor animal to the rear of the vehicle and drove down the street with him. Whether or not the animal's affections for the machine grew is not known.

Dr. Barnes was not known for patient and good bedside manners, nor was he known for being a "top-knotch" physician. Many believe his formula for successful healing was one part luck and the other part prayer, the latter part being the patient's responsibility. The recurring quote as to Dr. Barnes is "he would either cure you or kill you." He was known as one who liked to experiment with his patients. When James L.

---

27. According to several individuals, Doctor Barnes' black servant lived in a small structure behind the home. Three small outbuilding-type structures remain from those days, not including the barns. However, many of the older residents have stated the black man lived in a structure with a large tree growing through it. Such a structure no longer exists.

Hubanks became seriously ill, Dr. Barnes administered Hubanks a shot and told the old gentleman's daughter, "that shot will either cure him or kill him, we'll just have to wait and see." He lived. Another such case was that of Audrey Roberta McIntyre, the daughter of Hubert and Maggie McIntyre. Little Audrey was suffering from diphtheria and now had what appeared to be indigestion. As Dr. Barnes prepared to give her a shot, the little girl excitedly exclaimed, "If you give me that shot, I'll roll over and die." Following the dosage, the little girl died almost immediately. Many other such stories abound in the verbal chronicles of Finger's history.

As far as sympathy for other's pain, that is near legendary. One elderly gentleman shared the following story. While at McNairy Station one day, he was attempting to crank his Model A Ford. The crank kicked back on him and he cut his hand on his license plate. The cut was deep and bleeding profusely. It just happened that Dr. Barnes was nearby in the tie yard and upon examining the young man, he reached for his medical bag. Without any medicine to deaden the wound, he proceeded to stitch up the wound and then sent the young man on his way.[28] Such stories are numerous.[29]

Another story regards Mr. Robert Beene's son Arlen. This story was originally published in *Fingerprints*, but there were a number of inaccuracies and thus it is retold here on these pages as relayed by the child's father. When Arlen Beene was only two years old, Robert was working down at the barn and Arlen wanted to go down there to see him. Bessie, Robert's wife, took Arlen down to the barnyard to see his father. The little boy got behind a 26-year old horse—in fact, much too close—and the horse kicked Arlen in the head. The blow crushed the bone at the front of Arlen's skull on his forehead. Robert rushed the boy to Dr. Barnes' office for assistance. The doctor took out a round hole saw and sawed out a hole the size of a quarter in the boy's forehead. Barnes then removed the crushed skull pieces and sewed a flap of skin back over the injured place. There was no apparent side effect and the boy healed up

---

28. Robert Beene of Finger, Tennessee, interview with the author, September 17, 2002. Mr. Beene was 92 years old at the time.

29. Readers of *Fingerprints* may remember the story relayed by Luther Talbott of Finger regarding his fall on the brick sidewalk in front of the Finger School, which resulted in a deep cut on his head. Dr. Barnes sewed up the gash without any medicine to deaden the wound. At the time of his death in 2007, Talbott experienced pain whenever he combed that area of his head.

well. However, experiences such as these convinced most residents that Dr. Barnes was the type of doctor who would "cut your head off just to see if you would live or die."

Dr. Barnes' office and drugstore were located in the Bishop General Merchandise Store building. His office was on the side of the building that faced the depot. His drugstore had a wrought iron type of furniture, chairs and tables for customers to sit and drink a soda from the soda fountain. He also sold radios and car accessories there. It has been said that Miss Callie Miller worked for Dr. Barnes in the drugstore.

Another interesting sidenote to the life of Dr. Mark Barnes is that of his days collecting livestock out and around the countryside. In those days, it was not uncommon for patients and their families to have the charges which were accrued placed on the doctor's charge books. Then as the patient or the family could pay, they did so. Sometimes, a barter system was used. Most doctors were extremely patient as they waited for payment; Dr. Barnes was not. He was less patient when it came to the debts owed to him. In later days, he even acquired a livestock trailer that he hitched to his large business coupe and took to the countryside collecting on his debts. If someone couldn't pay but had a good milk cow, even if it was their only milk cow, it became Dr. Barnes' milk cow. There are many such instances of his collecting on medical debts by seizing livestock. One young man remarked as he watched Dr. Barnes cross the railroad tracks with his trailer hitched, "It took Dr. Tucker to make a cowboy out of Dr. Barnes."[30]

In 1940, Dr. Barnes and Estelee moved to 128 Crook Avenue in Henderson, where he continued to practice on East Main Street. He died on January 11, 1943, and was buried in the Henderson City Cemetery. His obituary appeared in the *Chester County Independent* newspaper on January 15, 1943:

PROMINENT LOCAL PHYSICIAN DIED IN MEMPHIS HOSPITAL
OF DOUBLE PNEUMONIA

Dr. W.M. Barnes, 60 years of age, prominent and beloved physician of Chester County, died Monday morning at the

30. Taped dialogue of Marvin Hand of Hesperia, California. Mr. Hand was a former resident of Finger and north McNairy County.

Baptist Hospital in Memphis, after an illness of only a few days. Death resulted from pneumonia which was brought on by monia which was brought on by exposure and overwork by the good doctor among his many patients and friends. There exists an acute shortage of physicians in this county at this time and Dr. Barnes, without thought of himself, gave his all to his noble profession.

Dr. Barnes was born at Morris Chapel, Tennessee, and had lived 30 years in Finger. He moved to this city about three years ago to better serve his large practice, the result of 36 years of conscientious and skillful work as a physician and surgeon in Chester and McNairy Counties.

Dr. Barnes was highly regarded by his colleagues in the medical profession and beloved by the citizens of the city and county for his rugged honesty, his friendly and charitable disposition. He will be sorely missed by the large number who had benefited from his ever helping hand, and by his multitude of friends throughout the county.[31]

He and Estelee never had any children of their own. However, they raised Inetha and Roy, the children of Estelee's late brother, Dorsey "Dossie" Bishop who was killed in 1922 in a train-car collision. Estelee lived on for a number of years before dying on February 11, 1968.

Nathaniel A. Tucker, M.D.

Nathaniel A. Tucker was born in what is now Chester County to Dr. W.C. and Lucy D. (Buckley) Tucker on April 3, 1879. Just where he received his education, medical or otherwise, is unknown. Dr. Tucker married Miss Beulah Harris, the daughter of William H. and Eliza (Paralee) Tedford Harris, on January 3, 1909. The couple lived in a large house just east of the railroad tracks that was demolished in 2002. The couple had two daughters, Will Clark Tucker and Aileen (Tucker) Lowrance. Both daughters were schoolteachers and while Will Clark never married, Aileen married Richard Alex Lowrance.

---

31. *Chester County Independent*, January 15, 1943.

Dr. Nathaniel A. "Al" Tucker and his wife Beulah (Harris) Tucker

Dr. Tucker's office building still stands. The office was located between the Home Banking Company building and the Harris General Merchandise building on the north side of Main Street. Dr. Tucker's drug store was also located here. During the days of his practice, times were difficult and money was scarce. Therefore, many people were able to pick up a little extra money by boiling out old medicine bottles and selling them to Dr. Tucker for a penny apiece. It has been stated that Callie Miller also worked for him in his drug store.

Dr. Tucker was known for being a straight talker. He didn't mince his words and he got straight to the point. Yet he was a compassionate doctor who understood the problems and heartaches that people faced. One story which has passed in the author's family regards Dr. Tucker's professional and personal fidelity. In 1947, Faye (McIntyre) Talbott gave birth to a little boy who unfortunately would not live long. The birth was a difficult one, but Dr. Tucker remained. In fact, the good doctor tarried long after the event, sitting out in the front yard with Luther Talbott, John Robert McIntyre, and Dave Alexander until two o'clock in the morning.

As for his professional reputation, he was widely known as a diligent and dedicated doctor. The late Dr. Webb, founder of Webb-Williamson Hospital of Jackson, Tennessee, stated that Dr. Tucker was one of the best diagnostic doctors in the area. In other words, Doctor Tucker had great ability to diagnose medical conditions and problems.

As to his straightforwardness, the following story serves as an example. During his term of service in the United States Navy, Luther Talbott had been exposed to malaria and occasionally needed a strong dose of a certain type of medicine to treat his recurring symptoms. He walked into Dr. Tucker's office and requested the medicine. Dr. Tucker responded somewhat suspiciously, "What do you need with that?" Talbott explained that he had taken them regularly while in the Navy and needed some now. The old doctor told him to wait a moment and shortly he returned to his work desk with a small white envelope. He proceeded to pour white tablets from a two gallon glass bottle. When he finished, he handed the envelope containing about twenty-five tablets to his young patient. Talbott asked what he owed Dr. Tucker and the old doctor gruffly replied, "Oh, about 25 cents."

Before Dr. Tucker retired from his practice, he was beginning to have problems with his memory. Perhaps a patient would pay his bill and Dr. Tucker would forget to make the proper notation, resulting in the expectation that such debt would be paid again. Most of his life, he was a cigar smoker. One Sunday morning he came walking up through town and stopped in at N.P. Talbott's house and asked if Luther could help him out. The young Talbott responded that he could and the old doctor said, "I was heading out east to see a patient and I ran off the levee out there just past the bridge about 100 feet before you get to Centerhill Road and on the left." Because there was concern that the car, a business coupe, might turn over, Luther rounded up some plow lines to tie to the vehicle. With the help of a group of young men, the two managed to get the car out. Dr. Tucker denied it, but what is believed to have happened is that while he was driving across the levee, he lit up an unwrapped cigar and the cellophane wrapping flashed up in smoke causing him to become distracted.

The Tuckers moved to Henderson around 1950. Doctor Tucker died on September 3, 1951, and was laid to rest in the Finger Cemetery. His wife Beulah lingered on until October 5, 1955. Apparently they were living with the Lowrances after they moved, for Dr. Tucker's mind was already deteriorating.

CHAPTER SEVEN

MEN AND WOMEN OF DETERMINATION

Brief sketches of some of the men led the rural community through the virtue of hard work—Brief sketches of the women who helped guide the early families—Farmers who built a community in a wilderness.

In the early history and past chronicles of any region or area are the most important elements, the characters and families who forged the communities. These characters possessed qualities which are still present in many today, but with apparently less visibility and presence. The years of the pioneers were the years of building and development, years which may seem passed, but are part of a continuous cycle of life. Yet there is a difference. These early pioneers were building upon a fresh landscape, largely unaltered by the human hand of the Native American during their long occupation. These men and women engaged in a struggle that seems so unromantic so as to appear mundane, rugged, and primitive. Yet there is an aspect to those struggles that possess their own romantic and epic qualities.

Many, if not most, of these men and women were not among the first of the early settlers. In fact, most were the children, if not even grandchildren, of the early settlers of McNairy County. These individuals were not set apart by their circumstances, but rather by the grain of their character, which was most often ruggedly individualistic. These were quiet men and women who accomplished great feats in a quiet manner in otherwise quiet times. There are many whose names are all but lost to the pages of history, but through diligence and great effort, some have survived. Many of them will be sketched on these pages.

There was, at one time in our country's history, a class of individuals whose talents and abilities gave them the distinction of serving their community in a variety of ways. For many a man in the nineteenth century McNairy County the following could be written, "farmer, public servant, gentleman." In the same manner, there could be said about many women the following words, "strong, determined, steadfast, and long-suffering." In the pages that follow, such could be written about each individual sketched.[1]

However, we must first explore the types and personalities of these earlier people. Who were they? Of what were they made? Were they always a serious type? So many questions come to mind as we probe into the past and into the lives of people almost all but lost to us in the twenty-first century. Let us endeavor to bring their qualities, if not also their personalities and struggles, back to life.

On the whole, these were individuals with qualities much like many today. The same emotions ruled the life of men and women in the 1800's as do even today, with some stronger than others. Jealousy, envy, anger, sorrow, joy, and a host of other emotions were deeply rooted in the minds and hearts of our forefathers just as in us. Yet there were differences. It must be remembered that many of these were the children of settlers who came here with very little, who had left a region where they possessed little. Therefore, there was perhaps a level of ambition that might not otherwise exist in today's world.

These determined men and women were constantly challenged by the forces of nature and circumstance to overcome any number of troubles and situations. Although existence was a daily adventure for all, the future was never far from the minds of these people. Ever-present with them was a realization that their works and those of their ancestors were

---

1. Some of these individuals have been profiled in the author's earlier work, *Fingerprints*, but corrections and additions are made on these pages.

of critical importance in the development of their new communities. Perhaps the best manner in which to examine and explain these rugged individuals is to proceed with the sketches of some of them.

Farmers, merchants, politicians, craftsmen, doctors, lawyers, teachers, and others of trade and profession populated the countryside and villages of north McNairy County in the days of yesteryear. Now we seek to explore the names, faces, and persons of those various occupations. Chronology will be followed as closely as possible.

Many of the individuals discussed in this chapter were residents of the old Eighth Civil District of McNairy County. Due to the destruction of the 1890 Federal Census, it is difficult to get a picture of the area during that period. However, we are aided by a variety of documents made during the period. Such documents as a list of heads of households and white male voters for 1891 fill in the gaps left by the destruction of records, the passing of souls, and the fading of memories.

The Citizen Politicians

The local politician has always been the subject of interest, entreaties, influence, ridicule, and disgust, often all at the same time. Many gentlemen who served in public office did so with the will of the majority solidly behind them throughout their entire term and tenure. Most men elected to offices of trust and responsibility were true gentlemen of character. The following is a partial list of those who served the north McNairy County area as magistrates or justices of the peace from the 1850s through the early 1900s.

Robert Thompson McIntyre	(Republican 1858–1880s)
William Taylor Anderson	(old line Whig; also a constable)
Robert M. Clayton	(1861)
John Kirby	(1865–1880)
Francis Beard	(served eighteen years)
E.W. Peeples	(1867)
Tinsley Weaver	(1865–1870)
Harmon Purdy Floyd	(two or three terms, 1870s)
B.T. Peeples	(1871–1878)
Jacob Lowrance	(1870–1876)

J.J. Franklin	(1876–1880)
Henry Barham	(1881–1882) (perhaps longer)
William Barney Malone	(1882–1888)
John Aldridge	(1882–1897) (perhaps longer)
James Simpson Lain	(1882–1910) (at least)
Arthur Harris	(1882–1889)
William Washington Peeples	(1888–1894) (at least)
F.J. Floyd	(1891–1910) (at least)
Nathan R. Ward	(1899–1903)
Major W. Ferrell	(1903–1905) (at least)
J.E. "Ed" Barham	(1906–1930s) (at least)
France M. Clayton	(1908–1910) (perhaps longer)
W.H. Hodges	(1910) (at least)
C.L. "Charlie Barham	(1924–1930s) (perhaps longer)
M.C. Patterson	(1924–?)

All of these local magistrates performed weddings in the community. Some were more requested than others. Among the most requested at marriage ceremonies during their respective times were Robert Thompson McIntyre, who performed 26 marriages, Jacob Lowrance, who united 44 couples, and James Simpson "Simp" Lain, who presided over 74 weddings.[2] Many of these men are sketched below.

Robert Thompson McIntyre (1814–1902)

Robert Thompson McIntyre was born in Mecklenburg County, North Carolina, near Charlotte, on May 28, 1814. The son of Isaac and Elizabeth (Thompson) McIntyre, he was not far removed from the generations of the glorious days of the American Revolutionary War. His grandfather, John McIntyre Jr., was a soldier in the Continental Army, serving in South Carolina. His father was present as a boy when his own grandfather, John McIntyre Sr., and a group of neighbors and friends defeated a group of scavenging British troops under the command of Lord Charles Cornwallis. With the help of a colony of bees, the troops were successfully routed and the story of the "bees and the bullets" grew into

---

2. These numbers are based on the McNairy County Marriage Records for 1861 to 1911. Therefore, it is possible for any of the three to have conducted more ceremonies.

MEN AND WOMEN OF DETERMINATION

the legend of the hornet's nest surrounding Charlotte.

Robert's father, Isaac, died while the children were young. After his burial in the old Hopewell Presbyterian Cemetery with so many ancestors, his widow Elizabeth struggled to continue. After some years, Elizabeth and her four sons moved to north McNairy County in 1833. Surely the experience must have been daunting for a poor widow with five children making such a move completely on her own. Once in the present-day area of Finger, Robert and his mother remained while his brothers moved on to other areas.

Like many of his generation in a relatively newly settled region, Robert was dependent upon himself to make life a success. He was married to Sarah Jane Weaver, the daughter of Absolom Weaver, an early settler. To this union were born seven children: Antione Jane Stewart, Sarah Elizabeth Massey, Isaac T. McIntyre, Amanda Dickey, James Robert McIntyre, John Absalom McIntyre, and Nancy Caroline McIntyre. A number of prominent and hardworking people would descend from these various lines. Some of Robert's grandchildren included W.P. Massey, Freelin Dickey, Doll Dickey, Ophelia Dickey, Sally Young, John Robert "Johnny" McIntyre, Adrian McIntyre, and Zelphia Whitt.

Robert T. McIntyre tombstone

As early as 1840, Robert was identified as a manufacturer and tradesman, namely a grist miller. He established and operated the first grist mill on Elisha's Branch, which breaks off from Huggins' Creek in the area that is now Finger. Robert's own operation was actually in all probability located in more than one location over the years. Sometime in 1854, Robert bought forty acres from the mulatto Ichabod Brown and located his mill there. The water powered mill was now located on the east side of the creek. However, in less than a year, Robert resold the property to

Brown. According to the deed dated April 21, 1855, Robert sold Brown land "containing by estimation forty acres more or less, being the same tract of land you conveyed to me on the 8th of June 1854 and upon which I have Grist Mill now in operation together with the Mill Rocks and all other mill apparatus now in use on said premises." Apparently Robert bought the mill again later, for he was said to have been in the milling business in the latter portion of the nineteenth century.

When there was no milling to do, Robert fished off the back of the porch of the mill building. However, when a customer came by to have their corn ground, they rang a bell so Robert could put his fishing aside and tend to business. After the milling was done and the visiting complete, Robert would go back to his fishing.[3] Besides the milling business, Robert speculated in land and farmed, finding success in both enterprises.

With the formation of the new Republican party in 1854, Robert found a political party to which he and most of his descendents would be loyal for generations to come. In 1858, Robert was elected to the McNairy County Quarterly Court to represent part of north McNairy County. As is mentioned in Chapter Three on the War Between the States, Robert took a strong stance in favor of the Union and its preservation. Therefore he opposed any efforts at secession. McIntyre had an opportunity to be involved in the post-war government that occupied the county seat in Purdy, Tennessee. As it happened, there was no effective operating county government in McNairy County between 1863 and May of 1865. In July of 1865, the new carpetbagger governor of Tennessee, William G. "Parson" Brownlow appointed various north McNairy countians who had been ardent supporters of the Union to positions of responsibility. McIntyre became Chief Presiding Justice over the McNairy County Quarterly Court and Jacob Lowrance became County Trustee. Within months, McIntyre became Associate Presiding Justice of the Court and remained on the Court until the 1880s.

Robert's wife, Sarah Jane, died on January 12, 1875. He remained active yet unmarried until his remarriage to the widow Ellen Hubanks on November 19, 1876. Whether Ellen died or the marriage was unsuccessful is not known. Apparently the marriage was over by the end of the nineteenth century. It is believed she died and is buried next to Robert

3. These stories were passed to Robert Thompson McIntyre's grandchildren by him and to other descendents by those grandchildren.

in Mount Carmel Cemetery. In his last years, Robert spent time visiting with his grandchildren. Robert was a member of the Church of Christ and a member of the International Order of Odd Fellows. He died on November 7, 1902.

Ichabod Brown

Ichabod Brown is one of those little known characters in north McNairy County's history that fascinates the author and could excite the interests of anyone who possesses a sense of history. He was apparently a man of mixed blood. General Marcus J. Wright wrote of him and another north McNairy countian: "Ichabod Brown and Hartwell Keter settled early in the northern part of the county. They came from North Carolina and were a mongrel creed of people. They were quiet, honest farmers, who had the respect of their neighbors."[4] Ichabod and his wife Charlotte had at least seven children. Their only son was William Brown, who was a mechanic by trade.

Ichabod was a farmer and miller. Brown owned a forty acre farm on Elisha's Branch near present-day Finger. In 1854, he sold the farm to Robert Thompson McIntyre, who erected a grist mill on the property. In 1855, Brown bought the property back from McIntyre, who apparently continued to operate the mill for years thereafter. As of January of 1859, Ichabod Brown, also often referred to as Achabod Brown, was doing business with the well-known establishment of Hollis & Cason in Montezuma, Tennessee. He remained active in the community until the outbreak of the War Between the States.

Around the time that the War Between the States was breaking out, it appears that Mr. Brown's mental health may have begun to break. In November of 1860, Ichabod Brown was charged with arson. Among the witnesses listed in this matter were neighbors of Brown's including Eli Tisdale, M.G. Ward and R.T. McIntyre. A few months later in February of 1861, James F. McKinney filed in McNairy County Chancery Court a *Petition to Sell Land of a Lunatic* against Achabod Brown, also known as Ichabod Brown.

It is unknown if his health began to suffer further or if some other issue arose because of his racial status in a divided and war-torn region,

---

4. Wright, Talbott, McCann, *Reminiscences 130th Anniversary Edition*.

but suddenly he appointed another in the community to act as his attorney in fact. He also began to see his property and assets being burdened by liens from pro-Confederate merchants. By 1863, Ichabod Brown was dead and his estate was in turmoil. The author believes it possible that Ichabod Brown was the victim of political and racial discrimination. At that time, pro-Confederate businessmen in the area were placing liens on the property of pro-Union citizens as evidenced in the records of the McNairy County Register of Deeds. One of the most notorious was C.M. Cason, a Montezuma merchant and businessman.

A.M. Worthington

A.M. Worthington was a prominent gentleman who lived in the old Anderson's Store area. Worthington was born on March 18, 1833, in Tennessee. He served as postmaster of the Anderson's Store area for a short time in 1860. Little is known regarding either Worthington or his wife. His wife's full name is not even known, only her initials. It is known that L.M. Worthington was born in North Carolina around the year 1836. By 1860, the Worthingtons had two children. Most probably they had others afterward, but that is not currently known. The two children who are known were sons by the names John W. Worthington and Findley D. Worthington. John was born around 1856 and Findley in 1860. In 1861, Worthington held an account with Hollis & Cason General Merchandise in Montezuma, Tennessee.

A.M. Worthington enlisted in Company G of the Nineteenth (19th) Tennessee Cavalry Regiment (also known as the Eighteenth Tennessee Cavalry Regiment or Newsome's Cavalry). Worthington most likely mustered into the service at Rose Creek, McNairy County, Tennessee, on or about April 10, 1864. Worthington fought at the battles of Brice's Crossroads, Harrisburg, Mississippi, and Tuscumbia Creek. Following the War Between the States, A.M. Worthington moved to the state of Arkansas where he became a dentist. He was still living in 1882. There is no information available as to what became of Worthington after 1882.

The Kirkpatrick Family

Elijah Kirkpatrick (1800-?)

One of north McNairy County's oldest families was the Kirkpatrick family. The first of this family to settle in McNairy County was Elijah Kirkpatrick. He was a native of North Carolina and married Patsey Harris on July 22, 1822, in Guilford County, North Carolina. The couple had at least three sons: James Moses Kirpatrick, Charles Hugh Kirkpatrick, and William Elijah Kirkpatrick. They migrated to West Tennessee and McNairy County in the mid-1840s. All three sons married into respectable and good families. Patsey Kirkpatrick appears to have died before Elijah left Guilford County, North Carolina, to migrate to McNairy County, Tennessee. Elijah himself died sometime during the period of 1850 to 1860. He is likely buried in either the Mount Carmel Cemetery or the Malone Cemetery.

James Moses Kirkpatrick (1824-1909)

Moses Kirkpatrick was born in North Carolina on April 8, 1824, the year after McNairy County was established. He came to north McNairy County on January 12, 1844. He was first married to Miss Margaret Young on March 11, 1851. At some point, it appears that Margaret died. Thereafter, Moses would eventually marry Miss Mary Smith, the daughter of Madison and Elizabeth Smith of the Anderson's Store area, on March 15, 1857. This family would eventually spawn a long line of physicians and businessmen in the Selmer area. In fact, Mary Kirkpatrick was the older sister of the original Dr. Smith, James Louis Smith of Selmer, Tennessee. Moses and Mary were united in marriage in 1857 and started a large family.

Kirkpatrick's obituary had the following to say regarding Kirkpatrick, "Mr. Kirkpatrick was one of the most prominent figures in this section for a number of years. He possessed a remarkable memory, being able to recall incidents happening fifty or sixty years ago, giving exact dates. He knew personally many of the great politicians before and after the war, and it was a treat to hear him discuss their speeches and the issues of the campaigns." Although Kirkpatrick never himself sought public office, he was a well-informed gentleman who was very active in his community and interested in the important events and issues of the times. He was an old line Whig and "could tell how every man in his district would vote."[5] Kirkpatrick remained in good health throughout most of his life. It was only in the last two years of his life, after a bout with congestive chill, that his health began to fail. He passed away on August 12, 1909, and was buried in Malone Cemetery.

Charlie Hugh Kirkpatrick (1830–1907)

Charlie Hugh Kirkpatrick

Charlie Hugh Kirkpatrick was born to Elijah and Patsey Kirkpatrick on August 8, 1830, in North Carolina. Mr. Kirkpatrick married Mary A. Elizabeth "Betsy" Young. Betsy was born in 1841. The couple had six children: Louisa B. Kirkpatrick, Mattie Kirkpatrick, Charles Steve Kirkpatrick, Margaret Kirkpatrick, Susannah Kirkpatrick, and Henry Hugh Kirkpatrick. Charles Steve Kirkpatrick married Trudy Rowland October 27, 1890, with Squire J.S. Lain officiating. Henry Hugh Kirkpatrick married Lizzie Carpenter on February 18, 1906, with W.H. Morgan officiating. Louisa B. Kirkpatrick married John R. Case on October 24, 1900, with Squire C.C. Plunk officiating. Charlie Hugh Kirkpatrick died on February 6, 1907, and Besty Kirkpatrick lived a long life dying at age 90 or 91 in 1932. Both were buried in Mount Carmel Cemetery.

William Elijah Kirkpatrick (1832–1913)

William Elijah Kirkpatrick was born on August 7, 1832, to Elijah and Patsey Kirkpatrick in North Carolina. Kirkpatrick married Martha Ann Barham on January 8, 1874, with Squire Jacob Lowrance officiating. Martha Ann was born on December 19, 1837. They had two children: Mollie Bell Kirkpatrick (1874–1949) and John T. Kirkpatrick (1877–1953).

5. *McNairy County Independent Appeal*, August 20, 1909.

Mollie Bell never married and remained a spinster throughout her life. She was buried in the Mount Carmel Cemetery. Her brother, John T. Kirkpatrick, also known as Jack, married Catherine A. Weaver (1888–1970). They are buried at Mount Carmel Cemetery as well. William Elijah was a farmer like his brothers. He died January 4, 1913. Martha Ann died on August 23, 1915, surviving her husband by a little more than two years. Both were buried in Mount Carmel Cemetery.

Francis Beard (1795-1867)

Many families that have possessed great political or social prominence in a community over the years eventually find their numbers dwindling and their stars fade. McNairy County has had many such families over the years including the Beard family. This family possessed many prominent members in north McNairy County who assisted in the building up of the area. Perhaps the best known member of this old family was the late Francis Beard.

Francis Beard was born in 1795 in the old state of South Carolina. After living in Giles County, Tennessee, for a few years he moved to northern McNairy County in 1827, making him one of the very early settlers of McNairy County. Beard married the former Margaret Brown and to this union were born ten children, four boys and six girls. The names of his sons are known. George Beard married Isabel O'Nail (O'Neil), William Beard married Harriet Onsley, Allen Beard married Rebecca Maxwell, and John Beard married E.J. Dunn.

Beard was a man of many occupations and interests much like the mold of men during his era. He was a popular Primitive Baptist preacher, having served a number of congregations and communities in McNairy County. Beard established the first church near Rosehill and served such congregations as Gravelhill, Pleasant Ridge, Winding Ridge, Chapel Hill, and Liberty. However, in 1850, Beard got in trouble with the Primitive Baptists which earned him an expulsion from the church. His offense was joining the Free and Accepted Masons, a secret fraternal organization. Regardless of the actions of the church, Beard did not stop preaching, he continued on with his spiritual work preaching to large congregations.

His political career was certainly worthy of mention. He served on the McNairy County Quarterly Court for eighteen years, two years as state and county revenue collector, and two or three years as the Superintendent of Weights and Measures. Beard passed away in 1867 and was buried in the old Beaty graveyard.

David Peebles Massey (1834–1870)

David Peebles Massey was born on March 15, 1834.[6] Not much is known of David. It is known he was a schoolteacher and had "excellent penmanship." He married the daughter of Robert Thompson McIntyre, Sarah Elizabeth McIntyre, on September 5, 1861. They had three children. Cyrathia Ann Massey was born on October 6, 1862, near present-day Finger. Unfortunately, in a time of little medical advancement and relatively primitive medicines, the little girl died on December 11, 1863. She was buried in Mount Carmel Cemetery in the McIntyre family plot. Their second child was Sarah Jane Massey, who was born on August 4, 1865. Although this child lived longer than the first daughter, again, this child did not live too long. Sarah Jane died on October 23, 1870, in an apparent epidemic of sickness and was buried next to her father. The last child was a son, William Pinkney Massey, who was born on January 6, 1868.

David was perhaps the son of Thomas P. Massey, who once gave him a Bible with the following inscription:

> D.P. Massey
> Dear Sir: I send you this Bible and I wish you to study and keep it free from dust. Thomas P. Massey.

---

6. This information comes from a February 11, 1956, letter from Frances Bowles to Mrs. Romus Massey. The two ladies were researching the history of the Massey family. They transcribed the inscriptions and records located in David P. Massey's Bible, which had later belonged to his son William P. Massey. Frances Bowles speculated and believed that the Peebles name should actually have been Peeples or Peoples. However, there is a family by the name of Peebles and since the name was acquired in a place other than McNairy County, Tennessee. According to the correspondence between Bowles and Mrs. Massey, David P. Massey was the son of Thomas and Mary (Peebles) Massey. However, this Thomas Massey would have had to be very aged when David was born. It is more likely that Thomas and Mary were the grandparents of David.

Thomas P. Massey was himself the son of Thomas Massey and Mary (Peebles)Massey. The elder Thomas Massey was born in Virginia in 1740 and died in Rockingham, North Carolina.

The Masseys lived in a log home on the Robert Thompson McIntyre farm, land now owned by Danny Beachy located on Centerhill Road. Unfortunately, sickness and death would visit the Massey family on too many occasions. On November 28, 1869, Sarah Elizabeth (McIntyre) Massey passed away at the young age of 26, leaving David to raise the surviving two children, Sarah Jane and William Pinkney. However, that was not to be. On September 25, 1870, David passed away, followed shortly by the daughter Sarah Jane. By the first of November, William Pinkney Massey was the only surviving member of the Massey family, left to be raised by his grandparents, Mr. and Mrs. Robert Thompson McIntyre with some help from Mr. and Mrs. George Dickey.

William Washington Peeples (1850-1904)

Squire William Washington "Wash" Peeples was born on November 29, 1850, in Savannah, Hardin County, Tennessee, the son of Henry Calvin Peeples and Susan Elizabeth "Cynthieana" (Malugen) Peeples. The elder Peeples was a law officer in Savannah during that period. During his earlier years, Wash lived in Kentucky with some of his relatives, the Blakelys.[7] Following Henry Calvin's death sometime around 1858, Susan married William Martin Major Hendrix (1820–1879). Susan died in Columbus, Hickman County, Kentucky, around 1861.

At some point, while he was a young adult, Wash left and went to Arkansas for a while, but upon his return he promised his sweetheart, Bettie Hodges, that he would never leave her again, meaning he would not cross the Mississippi River again. Wash married Elizabeth Ellen "Bettie" Hodges, the daughter of Captain Elijah James Hodges,

William Washington Peeples

---

7. For further reference, see the Cotton Ridge article in Chapter Ten of this work.

on November 26, 1882. Wash was a farmer and member of the McNairy County Quarterly Court and was one of nine members of the Court who voted against removal of the McNairy County seat from Purdy. Little is known about Wash directly. He, his wife, and their son, Eddy, lived near Finger. They resided in close proximity to the Hodges' farm. Bettie "was a very interesting character and a great student, reading much of her time, history being the subject that she liked above others."[8] Wash Peeples died on February 16, 1904, and was buried in the Mount Carmel Cemetery. Bettie Peeples passed away on July 29, 1939, and was buried next to her husband.

The Masons

One family whose influence was exerted primarily through the talent of one of its members was the Mason family. Though this was a noble family it is familiar today by virtue of the fact that one member, John Mason, became known as a writer and thinker in the mid-twentieth century after most of his life had passed. The first of the Masons to settle in north McNairy County was James Mason. James was born on July 1, 1804, in central North Carolina, near Fayetteville. He remained there until he was thirty-eight years old. He became involved in a quarrel with his father, Foster Mason, and traveled to West Tennessee on horseback. Unfortunately, the father and son never reconciled. According to Mason's grandson, John, he rambled across West Tennessee a year or two before buying 127 acres in north McNairy County from his brother Rufe Mason. According to John Mason, "there were a few acres cleared and a one-room cabin on the place Grandfather bought; maybe a side-room also, I remember seeing the skeleton walls of this old primitive building where my father and two or three of his brothers and sisters were born. Some years later my grandfather built a story and half house of heavy hews of logs on higher ground a hundred yards to the west."[9]

James Mason married Margaret Priscilla Patterson in 1834. She was the daughter of Wilson and Charity Patterson, who came from the Greensboro, North Carolina area. The couple had at least six children. John Mason described his grandparents' physical features and personality

8. *McNairy County Independent Appeal*, August 4, 1939.
9. Neimann, *The Glory of a Common Man*.

traits. James Mason was a tall man for the times, six foot-two inches tall. He was "big-boned, lean and muscular; mentally alert; out-spoken, a square-shooter; jovial, witty and at times sarcastic." Priscilla was rather short with a "dumpy build, brown eyes, and a great talker." According to the grandson, she was an excellent storyteller. James passed away on June 14, 1880, and was interred in the Mount Carmel Cemetery. Priscilla, who was born on January 13, 1814, died on July 20, 1888, and was buried next to her husband at Mount Carmel.

William Mason was born in 1835, the oldest of the children of James and Priscilla Mason. He married Sarah C. Floyd on July 15, 1866. The couple was married by the Reverend Wilson A. McHolstead, who is buried next to Mason's parents at Mount Carmel. William and Sarah were quiet natured people. According to their son, John Mason, Sarah could read and write and knew the fundamental operations of arithmetic, but she usually read only for an hour or so each Sunday. William was an intelligent man with an inquiring mind and an interest in certain types of literature. He was a farmer and occasional school teacher.

Their son, John, was born on August 9, 1867, in an old two-room frame house in the "southwest corner" of present-day Finger. According to John, the family moved one mile southwest to a farm known as the "Branch Place." According to John, the family's house was located close to a branch which drained several farms from both east and west before emptying its contents into Huggins Creek. John later migrated to the Indian Territory, which now comprises the state of Oklahoma. It was here that John married Etta Darrow on October 13, 1895. Over the years, John spent much time in reading, writing, and reflecting. He eventually published two books of poems, *Traditional Poems* and *Down to Earth Poems*. Following his death, his daughter completed and published his autobiography, *The Glory of a Common Man*. Shortly before his death, Oklahoma Governor Dewey Bartlett bestowed upon John the title of Honorary Oklahoma Ambassador because of his cultural contributions to Oklahoma. John Mason died on March 21, 1968, at more than 100 years of age.

Harmon Purdy Floyd

Harmon Purdy Floyd was born in the "northeast corner" of South Carolina in 1818 or 1819, the son of Frederick and Sarah (Bullock) Floyd. When Harmon was about 20 years of age, he made the "long trip over the mountains" to western Tennessee.[10] Coming to the area Harmon brought with him his father and mother, Mr. and Mrs. Frederick Floyd, and his maternal grandmother Bullock. Mrs. Bullock brought with her a few slaves. Frederick passed away on October 19, 1840, at the age of 52. Sarah passed away on September 17, 1855. Both were buried in the old Floyd Cemetery.

Harmon married shortly after arriving in north McNairy County. At some point in the 1870's and probably earlier, Harmon served two or three terms as a member of the McNairy County Quarterly Court. The date of his death and the location of his burial site are currently unknown.

Robert M. Clayton (1827-1863)

Robert M. Clayton was born on February 17, 1827, in Tennessee. Clayton and his wife, Mary C. Clayton, had at least two children. William Clayton was born around 1857 and Permelia J. Clayton was born on January 31, 1860. Whatever became of Mary is unknown, but there is a sunken grave next to his grave and it is presumed that she died after he did and was buried here with no marker of her own. Robert served on the McNairy County Quarterly Court as earlier as 1861. Robert died on January 14, 1863, and was buried in Mount Carmel Cemetery. The daughter Permelia died in 1866 and was buried on one side of her father.

John Aldridge (1823-1903)

Another north McNairy countian who would eventually find a life in public affairs was John Aldridge. Aldridge was born sometime around the year 1823 in North Carolina and when he arrived in Tennessee is not known. He was twice married. He and his first wife, Mary Ann,

---

10. The majority of the information in this sketch comes from the writings of John Mason in a book about his life, *The Glory of a Common Man: A Biography*, written by Mason's daughter, Ruth Mason Neimann, which has been referenced frequently.

had five children: Sarah, Susan, Kiza "Kizzie," William, and Martha. He and his second wife Martha had at least two children: Mary and Nancy E. Aldridge.

Following the War Between the States, Aldridge served in the Thirty-fourth (Reconstruction) and Thirty-fifth General Assemblies. This was during the Reconstruction period and he was originally elected to fill the vacancy caused by the resignation of the infamous Colonel Fielding Hurst. His first term spanned from October 2, 1865, to October 6, 1867. He was reelected to the state Senate in 1867 and served until 1869 representing McNairy, Henderson, and Hardin counties. He later served on the McNairy County Quarterly Court in the 1880s and 1890s. Aldridge was another of the nine members of the Court who voted to keep the McNairy County seat in Purdy. A farmer in the old Eighth District, Aldridge served a census enumerator for McNairy County in 1870 and at one time served as Assistant United States Marshal. Aldridge moved to Missouri to live with his daughter and died in Pascola, Pemiscot County, Missouri, in 1903. He was buried in Refuge Cemetery not far from his old home.

Jacob Lowrance (1803-1882)

The simple slab of limestone marking the silent earthen tomb of Jacob Lowrance says so little about the life its occupant lived. To stand before this thin slab one can learn only the name and dates, but there is so much more to know about this man. Jacob Lowrance began this life on April 20, 1803, twenty years before the formation of McNairy County. He was the son of Abram Lorance, one of the earliest settlers in the county, who settled in the north end of the county in 1824. Jacob married Susana Gage, the daughter of Aaron Gage. Gage was himself a veteran of the Revolutionary War who also had settled in the county around 1824. Susana was born on October 14, 1814. She and Jacob had at least three children: Elizabeth Lowrance, David Marion Lowrance, and John M. Lowrance.[11] Elizabeth was born between 1830 and 1840 and married a Tedford. David Marion Lowrance was born in February of 1834. John M. Lowrance, born in 1836, married Harriet E. Putman on January 27,

11. The information regarding these three children comes from *The History of the Lowrance Family* compiled by Marie F. Whitehead.

1867. John and Harriet had three children by 1870: David M. Lowrance, born in 1868 or 1869, and twins, William S. Lowrance and Martin E. Lowrance, born in 1869 or 1870. Susana died on April 19, 1837.

As to the identity of a fourth child of Jacob and Susana, there is some disagreement and controversy. Buried next to Jacob in Mount Carmel Cemetery is Mary Covey.[12] Some sources have said Mary is the daughter of Jacob and Susana. Others have said she was the second wife of Jacob. Regardless, this is what we know of her. Mary, who was born on January 6, 1833, and died on January 24, 1893, was married Charles B. Covey (1824–1862), who served in Company B of the U.S. Sixth Tennessee Cavalry during the War Between the States. Covey died on November 22, 1862, and was buried in Mount Carmel Cemetery. The couple had four children: Fineti Covey, born in 1849; Henry H. Covey, born in 1856; Martha A. Covey, born in 1858; and Susan L. Covey, born in 1860. From there nothing is really definitely known about Mary's activities or relationships. The rest may be purely speculation at this point.

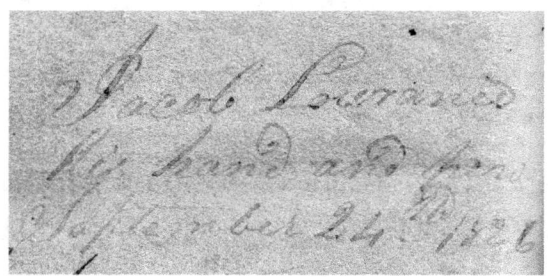
Autograph of Jacob Lowrance

In 1870, the Federal Census records that Mary was living with Jacob Lowrance and his son David M. Lowrance, along with her children. However, this should not be taken as evidence that Mary and Jacob were unrelated and had gotten married, for there is no marriage record of such a union in existence. It is therefore more likely that Mary was indeed the child of Jacob and Susana Lowrance and that she moved back into the house with her father upon the death of her husband in 1862. There is a child buried next to Jacob and Mary in Mount Carmel Cemetery by the name of John L. Lowrance (March 28, 1872–November 9, 1873) but this may very well be the child of either John or David Lowrance, the sons of Jacob.

---

12. It is the opinion of the author that Mary Covey was indeed the daughter of Jacob Lowrance, and that all available evidence supports this conclusion.

Jacob Lowrance served in a number of capacities in county and local government during his years. He served on the McNairy County Quarterly Court a number of years including 1870 to 1876. He also served as McNairy County Trustee, only the fifth man in the county's history to hold that position. In regards to occupations, Jacob was also a grocer and merchant. He was also a member of the Freemasons. Jacob died on August 11, 1882.

If one were to visit the graves of this family at Mount Carmel they would find a seemingly peculiar sight, in that the graves are located in different parts of the cemetery. There is a simple explanation for this. When Susana died early in 1837, the cemetery at Mount Carmel was still relatively small and concentrated in the center portion of the present cemetery. As the years passed the circle of graves grew wider and larger. Eventually there was little or no room for some relatives to be buried next to those who were now long dead. The dates of the graves of Susana in 1837 and Jacob in 1882 give some idea of the years that passed and the graves that were established.

It is very unfortunate that a better documented trail cannot be obtained regarding this very early family. Certainly Abram and Jacob Lowrance were interesting men in an interesting time, but possessing a clearer image of this family's genealogy would also provide a clearer picture of north McNairy County's history. Perhaps with time and effort this will be possible.

John A. Miller (1847–1928)[13]

John A. Miller was born on April 24, 1847, the son of Robert S. and Elizabeth J. (Willett) Miller. He was the grandson of Francis and Margaret (Skinner) Miller. Miller's father, Robert S. Miller, was born in 1816 in South Carolina, but Francis and Margaret Miller came to north McNairy County when Robert was a young man and settled around the Tar Creek area, not far from Sweetlips. Robert was a farmer and a tanner by trade. His wife, Elizabeth J. Willett, was known as "Eliza."

---

13. This information from this sketch was largely taken from a biographical sketch included in *Goodspeed's History of Tennessee: Chester County, Illustrated*. Other information regarding this man was researched by the author and taken from public records, tombstone inscriptions, and other sources.

She was born on May 22, 1822, in McNairy County, making her one of the first white children born in this territory. Her parents were Edward and Polly (Tedford) Willett. Mr. Willett was born in Virginia around the year 1790, but moved to Lincoln County, Tennessee when he was a young man. He was a farmer and served for a short period of time in the "Jackson War." Mr. Willett was twice married. His wife, Polly Tedford, was born around the year 1800 in the old region of East Tennessee. She died in 1836.

As for John A. Miller, he was one of ten children who received his education in the district schools at Purdy. Around 1879, he was elected a magistrate of McNairy County's Eighth Civil District. However, the next year, he was elected to the position of county trustee. Miller served in this position until the area of his residence was ceded to form the new county, Chester County. Following the formation of Chester County in 1882, Miller was elected magistrate of his new district in Chester County. He was a farmer by occupation and in 1886 was still operating the cotton gin his father had built in 1838. John A. Miller was a staunch Republican and a member of the Grange Order. He died on November 16, 1928, and was buried with the many generations of his family in Sweetlips Cemetery.

George W. Dickey (1846–1918)

More is known about the children of George Dickey than is known of the man himself, yet we know some things. George W. Dickey was born on February 12, 1846, in Mississippi. He was the son of John A. and Sarah Dickey and the grandson of William Dickey. During a part of his childhood, Dickey grew up in the Anderson's Store area. He married Amanda McIntyre, the daughter of Robert Thompson and Sarah Jane (Weaver) McIntyre, on December 28, 1870. Amanda was born on January 30, 1847. Their children included Ike Dickey, Sarah E. "Sally"

George W. Dickey

(Dickey) Young, Frances E. "Doll" Dickey, Amanda Ophelia Dickey, William "Bill" Dickey, James Rufe Dickey, Lillie U. (Dickey) Sergerson, Lela (Dickey) DuBerry, and George Freelin Dickey. Dickey was a farmer and a cotton gin operator, as mentioned in Chapter Five of this work. He and his family lived on the old Dickey homeplace which is in the crossroads on Brown Street in Finger. He and his wife kept her father in his last years. Dickey died on March 2, 1918, and was buried in the recently established Finger Cemetery next to Amanda who had died on August 9, 1916.

Robert McMillan Weaver (1833-1918)

Robert McMillan Weaver was born March 9, 1833, to John and Mary (McMillan) Weaver. His grandfather was the early settler Adam Weaver, a blacksmith. He farmed and learned his trade, one which was practiced by several in his family. At the age of thirty-four, Robert was married to Mary A. (Highfield) Womble on September 11, 1867. She was previously married to Manley Womble, by whom she had two sons, William E. Womble and Thomas J. Womble. Following his apparent death and her marriage to Robert, they had one son, Lee Andrew Weaver, in 1869.

Robert McMillan Weaver

Robert farmed and worked as a blacksmith in north McNairy County throughout his life. He had a great interest in medicine and the effects of herbs on the human body. In Chapter Six of this work, his recipe for dropsy is given. His papers reveal many receipts for mail-order catalogs and books and pamphlets on medicine and home remedies. Perhaps, in other circumstances, he would have become a medical doctor. In his old age, he developed many peculiarities and his descendants have speculated that his mind went bad. Always one who loved children and had a great affection for them, he seemed to have entered a second childhood himself. When the schoolchildren had their group picture made at the

Finger school, he was often present. When the pictures came back, there was kindly, smiling Robert McMillan Weaver standing on the edge of the group.

He also believed in the medicinal purposes of whiskey, but for medicinal purposes strictly. Although he lived with his son, a strict teetotaler, in his home on Apple Street, he took his "medicine" every night before retiring. One grandchild remembered the son speaking about the ill effects of alcohol and praying about it and then hearing from the grandfather's room, "Ahhh, that's good."[14] Robert's wife, Mary, died on August 13, 1900, and was buried in the Old Friendship Cemetery. He lived on until August 9, 1918. He was buried next to Mary at Old Friendship.

William Barney Malone (1842–1911)

William Barney Malone

One of the more accomplished yet forgotten families was that of William Barney Malone. Malone was born on June 13, 1842, in the vicinity of the north McNairy County communities of Anderson's Store and White Plains. His father was Jesse Malone, a native of North Carolina, but currently his mother's identity is unknown. Malone attended the common schools and the rest of his education would consist of experience and attempts at self-education.

During the War Between the States, Malone served the Confederate cause. He served first with the Thirteenth Tennessee Infantry, being a member of Company F. With this company, he saw action at the battles of Belmont, Missouri, and Shiloh, one of the bloodiest battles of the war. After Shiloh, Malone took sick leave and upon returning, he reenlisted in the Confederate Army at Jack's Creek with the Second Tennessee Cavalry. This regiment later became the Twenty-first Tennessee Cavalry, also known as Wilson's Cavalry. As a member of this regiment, he served under Generals Nathan Bedford Forrest and John Bell Hood. Under General Hood,

---

14. This information was taken from a conversation with Hayse Hayre, a great-grandson of Robert McMillan Weaver, prior to Hayre's death in 2000.

he fought at Okalona, West Point, Bailey's Cross Roads, and Harrisburg in Mississippi. He was wounded at Harrisburg, but was present during Forrest's raids on Memphis and Paducah, Kentucky. Malone took part in the capture of Fort Pillow and the battles of Athens and Sulphur Trestle, Alabama. He also took part in the battle of Pulaski, Tennessee, and was with General Hood in Nashville. Malone was with Forrest's command at Gainesville, Alabama, when it surrendered on May 10, 1865.

After the War, he farmed 750 acres east of Finger. Malone was a Democrat in politics and was elected in 1899 to the Tennessee State House of Representatives on their ticket. From 1899 until 1901, he represented McNairy County in the 51st General Assembly. He was also a member of the Presbyterian Church and the Free and Accepted Masons. In 1910, in the last year of his life, Malone moved to Nashville to live with some of his children, most probably sons Littleton or Dee. He died in Nashville on June 8, 1911. He was brought back to north McNairy County and buried in the Malone Cemetery.

He was first married to Eliza White, born on November 6, 1839, by whom he had two children, Frances C. Malone and Lula Malone. Unfortunately, Eliza died on August 10, 1869, and was buried in Malone Cemetery. After Eliza's death, Malone married Margaret Jane Tedford on February 7, 1871. Margaret was born on June 22, 1844, and passed away on June 25, 1920, and was buried in the Malone Cemetery. They had five children: Littleton Malone, Robert Malone, Nora Malone, Eliza Malone, and Marcus Dee Malone.

John Absalom McIntyre (1848–1897)

John Absalom McIntyre came from a long line of hardy people and was made much from the same grain as his forefathers, being very interested in both advancing the community and gaining a substantial estate through the virtues of hard work and thrift. He was born to Robert Thompson and Sarah Jane (Weaver) McIntyre on April 27, 1848. During the War Between the States, he saw his brother go off to war and never return. Perhaps he thought the same fate might befall him, as he was put on a train bound northward to a Union gun factory in Illinois. It was here he spent the war. Most assuredly, his mother and father knew someone in that northern state before sending their young son so far away.

John Absalom McIntyre

In fact, many local Unionists fled to southern Illinois and that included several families who were neighbors to the McIntyres. The Bulliner family, who lived close to the McIntyres, eventually settled in Williamson County, Illinois. However, another neighbor also ended up in southern Illinois. That was Isabel J. Coleman, a neighbor of the McIntyres and the future mother-in-law of John A. McIntyre. She and her small daughters, Malissa America Coleman and Mary Roberta Coleman, fled to southern Illinois after their husband and father, John Coleman, enlisted in the U.S. Sixth Tennessee Cavalry. Perhaps John stayed with one or more of these neighbors. Interestingly, Mrs. Coleman resided in Nashville, Washington County, Illinois, and there was located there a Federal installation for the storage and manufacture of gun powder. It may have been that young John A. McIntyre labored.

After the war, he farmed with his father and family in and around present-day Finger. Apparently he was a very ambitious young man as his personal holdings grew rapidly during the years 1880 to 1897. He acquired over a thousand acres in north McNairy County on just one farm. He also had other land holdings including a farm at Mount Peter and other lots and properties near his farm. It has been passed down that at one time, McIntyre's thousand acre-plus farm was completely enclosed by a split-rail chestnut fence. The late Hayes Hayre remembered the existence of an old split-rail fence running near an old road on his father's place, which actually would have been a boundary for McIntyre's farm.

McIntyre married Mary Roberta "Robertie" Coleman, the daughter of John and Isabel Jane Coleman, on March 18, 1880. The couple had a number of children including Zenar McIntyre, W. Adrian McIntyre, Zelphia Roberta (McIntyre) Sanders Whitt, Sarah (McIntyre) Whitt Fowler, John Robert McIntyre, and Ulysses Hubert McIntyre.

Like his father, he was a strong Republican in his politics, a member of the Church of Christ and a brother of the Free and Accepted Masons. He became sick with skin cancer after a spot appeared on his arm. In those early days when no significant treatment existed but major surgery, he soon withered. On the evening of November 6, 1897, lying in his bed, McIntyre told his eldest son, Adrian, to go feed the horses and tend to the barn chores. Shortly after sending him along, John Absalom McIntyre, breathed his last and expired leaving a wife and six children, one of whom was only a few months old. McIntyre was buried in Mount Carmel Cemetery.

Mary Roberta McIntyre (1860-1907)

Mary Roberta Coleman McIntyre is sketched on these pages for the purposes of giving the reader an example of the determination which flowed through the veins of women as well as men. Society has a habit of stereotyping the "settler" as usually a man. Yet there were countless women of strength and courage who helped mold our county and it sons and daughters. One of those was a lady often referred to as "Robertie."

She was born on February 28, 1860, to John and Isabela Jane Coleman. Just a few weeks shy of Robertie's third birthday, her father enlisted in the United States Sixth Tennessee Cavalry. Most likely she never remembered much regarding her father, as he died in the summer of 1864 in service to the cause of the Union. Her mother was left to raise her and at least one sister three years her senior. Her marriage to John Absalom McIntyre and their family is mentioned immediately above, therefore no further such factual information is required. Their

Mary Roberta McIntyre

life, personally and financially, was a good one. By 1896, sixteen years after their marriage, John was the owner of a general store in Finger, a substantial farmer and a large-scale landowner. He owned farms on the edge of present-day Finger stretching from the Mobile and Ohio Railroad to Mount Carmel Cemetery and a large farm at Mount Peter. However, John's untimely and premature death from cancer in 1897 forced Robertie into a role not often assumed by women in that time, that of breadwinner and head of the family.

From 1897 until her death in 1907, Robertie carried on as few women did, given her circumstances and responsibilities. She did not take to the rocking chair and she did not sell off family lands in order to make her way. Instead, she continued farming her husband's grounds and apparently cleared new grounds with the help of two brothers who often worked for her, Lark and Steve Burkeens. Two of the old fields located on her farm were referred to for generations afterward as the "Lark newground" and the "Steve newground." Old business records from the first decade of the 1900s contain mentions of Robertie's hands and oldest son, Adrian, bringing loads of cross-ties to town to sell and there are cotton transactions between Robertie and whoever controlled the gin at any given time. Certainly, Robertie did not resign herself to the role of a passive and inactive widow. Her son, John Robert McIntyre, said often that she was the best farm manager he had ever seen.

Sometime between 1900 and 1907, Robertie moved her family to the village of Finger so that her children would be closer to a school. Her children attended the Possum Trot Schoolhouse, also known as Naylor's Schoolhouse. The family moved into a home which still stands today, the current J.L. Joyner house. It was here the family lived as Robertie continued to own and operate the old farm east of town where her husband lived, worked, and died.

In the winter of 1907, an outbreak of typhoid fever struck the area carrying away lives and hopes and plans for the future. In this house, an entire family was stricken by this ravenous fever and its winds blew strong against this family, eventually carrying away three of its beloved members. Grady Sanders, the husband of Zelphia McIntyre and son-in-law of Robertie, took ill and his family and took him with them because the McIntyres had enough ill to tend. Grady died shortly thereafter. Robertie herself became too ill to continue and passed away on November 8, 1907.

Her oldest daughter, Zenar, followed her home on December 6, 1907. According to family history, Zenar was engaged to Bedford Cone, who was apparently away at the time, and when the letter reached him regarding Zenar's death, his tears smeared the ink on the unfortunate letter. Robertie had seen and suffered much. Yet despite the sorrows of this life, despite losing her father in the War Between the States, despite losing her husband in the full flush of life and success, she carried on. She was buried with her family and her husband in Mount Carmel Cemetery.

James Robert McIntyre (1849–1921)

James "Jim" Robert McIntyre was the son of Robert Thompson McIntyre and Sarah Jane (Weaver) McIntyre and the brother of John Absalom McIntyre. He was born on November 29, 1849, in north McNairy County near present-day Finger. He married Margaret Rebecca Beene, the daughter of Allen Louis Beene and Mary Jane (Fuller) Beene, on December 28, 1870, at Poplar Corners, Madison County, Tennessee.[15] Jim and Rebecca had eleven children and gained much prosperity during their marriage. Rebecca was born on November 7, 1851, in Alcorn County, Mississippi. Their children were Robert Allen McIntyre, B.A. McIntyre, Levi Benton McIntyre, Virgie McIntyre, Isaac T. McIntyre, John J. McIntyre, Callie (McIntyre) James, William Samuel McIntyre, Mary (McIntyre) Smith, an unnamed infant, and Henry McIntyre.

Margaret (Beene) McIntyre, first wife of James R. McIntyre

As the years passed, Jim prospered in his land dealings and was involved in a number of ventures and businesses. He was part owner of McIntyre, James, and Company, a general merchandise company. He was on the board of directors of the Bank of Finger and on the first board of directors of Home Banking Company. As mentioned earlier, he sold the

---

15. Bettye Sitton Reed, *My Three Sons: Volume III, Beene-McIntyre and Allied Lines* (Self-published, 1984).

lots there in town to those who would eventually build homes and businesses. All of the lots there in Finger originally belonged to Jim McIntyre. He was also actively involved in the Finger Church of Christ. The original meeting place of the congregation was the old Possum Trot Schoolhouse, which Jim provided, and he served as one of the first elders. The congregation eventually moved to a building built in large part by Jim on land he donated. The church continues to meet on that site today.

James Robert McIntyre and second wife Fannie E. (Carroll) McIntyre

Rebecca passed away on November 16, 1904, and was buried in the Mount Carmel Cemetery. Following Rebecca's death, Jim eventually married Miss Fannie E. Carroll on March 24, 1907. Five children were born to this union: Ruth (McIntyre) Moore, Alice (McIntyre) McCaskill, Wilma (McIntyre) Sharpe, Rachel McIntyre, and Carroll McIntyre. In his old age, Jim remained active in civic and social affairs. He was member of the International Order of the Odd Fellows and the Free and Accepted Masons. Jim also donated the land for the Finger School and the Finger Cemetery. He first donated land for the cemetery in 1913 and then donated additional property in 1921 just two weeks before his death. Jim McIntyre died December 30, 1921, and was buried in the Mount Carmel Cemetery with Brother N.B. Hardeman officiating.

The Beene Family

One family who eventually made its way to McNairy County was the Beene family. Although this was not one of the earliest families in northern McNairy County, it became, after just a few years, one of the most populous. From this family came several prosperous and prominent people. The family stems from one of Tennessee's oldest families, the Beans of East Tennessee. Allen Louis Beene married Mary Jane

Fuller in 1848. The couple eventually made their way to the present-day Finger area from Mississippi. The couple had seven children: William Moses Beene, Margaret Rebecca (Beene) McIntyre, Henrietta Beene, John Samuel Beene, Levi Benton Beene, Martha Ann (Beene) Cobb Schrink, and Malinda Jane (Beene) Walker.

The Beenes are known for their longevity and, in times past, for their abundance. William Moses Beene had ten children, John Samuel Beene had nine children, and Levi Benton Beene had four children. In all, Allen Louis and Mary Jane had twenty-eight grandchildren. Allen Louis was born on September 11, 1826, and passed away on June 24, 1890. He was buried in the Mount Carmel Cemetery. Mary Jane lived on until March 2, 1909.

Allen Louis and Mary Jane's children were, on the whole, successful and productive citizens whose own children and grandchildren were also successful. Their oldest son, William Moses Beene, married twice, first to Amanda Dickey and second to Melissa America Coleman. His children included Samuel Beene, Gussie (Beene) Tedford, Myrtle (Beene) English, Walter G. Beene, Carrie (Beene) Wheatley, Maggie (Beene) Patterson, Euda (Beene) Jones, S.G.B. Beene, E.H. Beene, and Zenar Beene.

Allen Louis Beene and family

Levi Benton Beene, the second son, married M.L. Cherry and had four children: Allen Beene, Francis Beene, Ida Beene, and J.H. Beene. The third child, Martha Ann Beene, married first to a Cobb and had a son named Charlie Cobb. She married next to a Schrink and moved to Texas. The fourth child, Margaret Rebecca (Beene) McIntyre, and her family are discussed above.

John Samuel Beene, the fifth child, married Sarah E. Floyd and had nine children: James Samuel "Sam" Allen Beene, Robert Beene, Soucelia Ann (Beene) Patterson, Mary E. (Beene) Stovall, Nora I. (Beene) Walters, Johnie (Beene) Nix, Rebecca (Beene) Murchison, Laura (Beene) Holder and Edda (Beene) Meeks. John Samuel and Sarah Beene are pictured with part of their children and his mother, Mary Jane (Fuller) Beene.

The sixth child, Malinda Jane Beene, married Curt Walker and had two son, Hershel and Frank Walker. The Beenes' final child, Henrietta Beene, was mentally retarded and never married. However, further tragedy tainted her sad and short lifetime. While traveling from her home to that of relatives, she was raped by a group of young men. In due time, she gave birth to a son named Charlie. Sadly enough, Henrietta passed away in October of 1899, and Charlie passed away the next spring, in April of 1900.

The Naylor Family

Another of the old families who made strides in the north McNairy County community over the years was the Naylor family. However, it appears that the Naylor family migrated to McNairy County somewhat later than most of the families previously discussed in this work. In fact, General Marcus J. Wright did not mention the Naylor (also spelled earlier as Nailor) family at all in his 1882 work on McNairy County.

Probably the first Naylors to settle in north McNairy County were Joshua Naylor (1813–1868) and his wife Charity Naylor (1814–1903). Little is known about this couple. The next generation of Naylors were better known and of a higher profile. George Thomas Naylor (1860–1942) was a well-known craftsman, a woodworker. He was known in the community as a first-rate maker of caskets. Many local citizens were ushered into their grave in one of Naylor's coffins. J.C. Naylor (August 31, 1837–October 29, 1927) married Mary Estes (July 30, 1863–?)

on September 3, 1902. Both J.C. and his wife were well-known in the Finger community. Isom Christopher Buchanan "Buck" Naylor was a well-known justice of the peace, farmer, and ginner. It was he, along with his brother J.C. Naylor, that operated the first mule-powered cotton gin in north McNairy County. It was I.C.B. Naylor's son, Harrison, who would serve as the depot agent in Finger.

Other members of the Naylor family who were highly respected and well-liked included John T. Naylor, Fate Naylor, Everett Naylor, and Hubert Naylor. Two of the Naylor women who were well-beloved by local children included two ladies known as "Aunt Mary Lum" and "Aunt Mary Tom." Both ladies were playful with the small children and extremely kind to others in the community.

The Men of North McNairy County in the 1890s[16]

To give the reader an idea and a view of the local community and its social and political landscape on the 1890s, the following list will be of great assistance. Most of what we have concerned ourselves with thus far has been the old Eighth Civil District of McNairy County. Other names are added to the end of this list to give as complete as possible an overview of the citizenry of the time. Many of these men were profiled above.

Eighth District[17]

Alexander, Tom	Case, James	Gallagher, Charles
Ash, J. Quincy	Cock, F.	Halstead, _____
Ash, J.W.	Combs, P.T.	Harris, Charles B.
Baker, Rufe	Cook, Ben	Harris, J.J.
Barham, C.N.	Cook, J.T.	Harris, N.A.
Barham, H.C.	Davis, Bill	Harris, W.H.
Barham, H.	Davis, J.N.	Harris, Bill
Barham, John	Deaton, Mathew	Hendrix, Alex
Barham, Nath	Deaton, Will	Hendrix, W.B.

16. This list was originally published in Nancy Kennedy, *The 1890s: A Documentation of McNairy County, Tennessee, 1890-1891, Volume I.*

17. This enumeration was made by William Barney Malone, himself the subject of a sketch in this chapter.

Barham, R.N.
Barnes, Henry
Barnes, W.H.
Beard, R.T.
Boyd, H.C.
Bradshaw, B.
Brooks, J.R.
Browder, Tom
Brown, Henry
Carroll, Hugh
Carroll, J.
Kirkpatrick, E.
Kirkpatrick, H.
Kirkpatrick, J.W.
Kirkpatrick, M.
Kirkpatrick, S.
Kirkpatrick, W.C.
Lain, James Simpson
Lee, Sid
Long, Frank
Long, Joe
Laughton, _____
Laughton, Joe
Malone, F.C.
Malone, William B.
Massey, A.M.
Matthews, M.
McCann, W.
McDaniel, _____
McIntyre, James R.
Miller, Finis E.
Miller, Will
Mills, H.
Moore, B.B.
Moore, E.E.
Morgan, W.A.
Morris, T.

Dickey, A.
Dickey, Dolph
Dickey, George
Dickey, Ike
Draper, Bill
Draper, F.
Eddings, John
Foulkes, Cass
Foulkes, Jim
Foulkes, John
Fowler, R.
Roberson, B.
Roberson, G.
Robbins, William A.
Roland, Alex
Ross, D.
Ross, J.E.
Ross, Tobe
Starks, Elijah
Stancel, John W.
Tedford, A.K.
Tedford, A.W.
Tedford, J.V.
Tedford, Tom
Walker, J.S.
Walker, Murry F.
Walker, W.C.
Warsham, F.J.
Warsham, U.J.
Wharton, Bill
Wilkerson, H.
Wilkerson, John
Williams, D.
Williams, Robert
Williams, Tom
Womble, Thomas J.
Young, F.

Hill, M.C.
Hill, R.H.
Hodges, Elijah J.
Hodges, Dr. Henry
Hodges, Prof. Horry
Hodges, James Wright
Hill, Rufe
Hubanks, W.B.
Hysmith, D.T.
Ingraham, John Quincy
King, Bill
Davis, G.S.
Etheridge, D.
Etheridge, J.H.
Etheridge, N.C.
Estes, G.W.
Floyd, Frank
Floyd, Samuel Sr.
Floyd, G.W.
Floyd, Sam
Floyd, F.G.
Griswell, E.H.
Griswell, Dan C.
Henry, Samuel
Henry, W.M.
Harris, G.W.
Henry, John
Henry, G.
Hubanks, J.L.
Henry, W.H.
Helton, J.H.
Hurst, D.H.
Hodges, W.J.
Harris, W.M.
Harris, P.G.
Johnson, M.
Jackson, W.F.

Mosier, A.
Naylor, G.
Naylor, Tom
Overman, Jake
Owens, J.T.
Owens, R.W.
Owens, Rube
Ozment, Tom
Peeples, William W.
Plunk, A.M.
Plunk, C.W.
Plunk, David
Plunk, I.H.
Plunk, J.N.
Plunk, Mike
Plunk, Nath
Plunk, Sam
Putman, Bill
Putman, M.
Rankin, R.D.

Young, Jimmy
Young, R.W.
Young, Sherman
Aldridge, John
Aldridge, W.B.
Archer, H.C.
Archer, P.M.
Archer, W.J.
Archer, V.J.
Brown, J.C.
Bryant, M.C.
Covey, H.
Clayton, W.F.
Clayton, R.M.
Clayton, G.W.
Clayton, R.F.
Deaton, R.S.
Draper, Gabe, Sr.
Draper, Gabe, Jr.
Draper, Bob

James, Jake
Jackson, Lewis
James, William
Kerby, M.F.
Kerby, J.W.
Kerby, H.
Lovelace, J.J.
Lowry, G.
McCaskill, J.A.
McIntyre, John A.
Mitchell, J.E.
Massey, W.W.

CHAPTER EIGHT

RELIGION AND THE PURSUIT OF FAITH

The religion and morals of the working man—Life's lessons learned in the home—Established religion in north McNairy County—Brief sketches of the area's prominent preachers and congregations.

Who are the faithful? That is dependent on the party which is questioned. In fact, it is almost a doctrinal question and since it is not the purpose of this work, we will now leave that question behind us. It is the writer's wish to expose the reader to the vast variety of religious views held by the area's early settlers and citizens. Therefore the faithful will be defined as those who held a belief in the Almighty God and feared the finality of His wrath.

As with all needs or desires, the needs of the religious must be met in some form or another. One must be mindful of the lack of general establishment suffered, if you will, by the area's earliest settlers. Although some were perfectly content to leave such established institutions behind in an attempt to practice their own rugged individualism, others lamented the lack of a structured religious institution or religious community. Just prior to the founding of McNairy County in 1823, the region known as "the west" included West Tennessee, Arkansas, Missouri, Mississippi, and Alabama. Due to their recent settlement, many early settlers were isolated and established towns and governments were absent or very young. Religious and educational institutions would have to follow man's government on the time line of local history.

This did not mean that faith or reverence for God was not present. Rather the pioneers of old could not have sustained and survived, perhaps were it not for a strong sense of faith and mission. It is granted that many did seek financial gain and reward as their primary goal for beginning anew. However, under the circumstances, it took great confidence and assurance in God that they would survive in such an isolated environment. After all, faith, as according to the eleventh chapter of Paul's Epistle to the Hebrews, is "the substance of things hoped for, the evidence of things not seen." The early citizens often had no choice but to experience the spiritual in their homes, fields, or wherever convenient. As a result, worship was not always viewed as a weekly event in which one dressed their best to see the neighbors "down the way" at church services. Rather, the spiritual was experienced as some thought it should be, daily through hard work, virtue, and adherence to an inherent code of morality, passed down from generation to generation. Faith was an everyday occurrence in the heart and mind.

As a man plowed, there was hope and faith that he would reach his goal before the sun went down or before the next heavy rains descended. As that same farmer planted he might silently, or verbally, pray for sufficient rain to give life to the seed so recently buried. As his crops grew, he constantly kept his eye on the weather and God and his mind on the bounty of harvest. When harvest came and that portion of his labor was finished, there was thankfulness for what had been provided and hope for continued blessings.

The woman was not absent from such events. Like her husband's, it was many times a silent reverence for her Maker and Sustainer. Her work was done with a realization that no one would record her efforts for the chronicles of history. Rather it was completed daily, realizing that her goal as a wife, mother, or faithful daughter, was being met and that generations of her family would thrive, due in part to her great efforts. The hardships that women faced in this time will not be particularly addressed in this work. However, it is extremely important to remember that the wife and mother molded her children and her household after many of the same ideals and virtues which she held. John Mason, in his memoir, *The Glory of a Common Man*, recalled the fact that his mother had only one day of the week to read and she choose the Bible as her text. Although her husband was an occasional teacher and a man with literary interests, she chose to spend her few precious spare moments reading and studying the book of faith.

It was this kind of influence that made for a "good upbringing." Most frontier children experienced a positive home life and though filled with hard work and strenuous activities, even these were a valuable influence. Parents taught children life's lessons through everyday experiences. Values were taught through the medium of the ax, plow or other work implement. They were lessons which would not be forgotten in the next instance, for they were lessons which found application in all walks of life. The ideas of justice would not be exposed to these young ones by way of the state or federal courts, but rather through Biblical stories, the occasional sermon, and, most prevalently, through parental influence. The father's dealings with a neighbor, merchant, or even a complete stranger served as an example to the son or daughter. The undying dedication of the mother to her husband and children set forth an example of fidelity which would not be forgotten by her descendants. Such conditions as existed made for stronger individuals with greater character and respected families with strong ties to community and spirituality.

None of this is to imply that all were spiritual or that no organized religious groups existed in the county. In fact, neither of these assumptions would be correct. There were surely, in the early existence of the county, those individuals who exhibited little positive character, but they were few and far between. There was organized worship at some early point in the county's history, but for some time after the settlement of the area, even "a church in the wildwood" was rare. However, as the wheels of progress began to turn, church buildings were constructed and congregations established as the faithful began to assemble. Here begins our study of the organized religion of north McNairy County.

Organized religion in Tennessee began in the far reaches of East Tennessee. According to many historians, Tidence Lane holds the distinction of being the first pastor to lead an organized body of believers.[1] The Baptist preacher founded the first Baptist Association in Tennessee in Washington County in 1786.[2] However, Lane was not the first Baptist preacher in Tennessee. That distinction possibly belongs to one of two men, Jonathan Mulkey or Matthew Talbot. Lane's distinction is in regards to organization, whereas the other two ministers' claim regards residency and work. In those days it was certainly possible for a preacher to work in the mission fields of the frontier without accomplishing the task of organizing any physical religious institution. The only institution with which he might be associated is that which he preaches, the Lord's church, which is a spiritual entity. Mulkey resided in Carter's Valley as early as 1775 and Talbot on the Watauga River before 1776.[3]

In regards to West Tennessee, the Baptist and Methodist faiths were the predominant beliefs during the early years of settlement, according to historian Samuel Cole Williams.[4] Williams wrote that the first attempts to spread religion in the Jackson Purchase Treaty Territory was in 1820, when the Tennessee Annual Conference sent a missionary to labor and report of the opportunities in West Tennessee. The first two missionaries sent into the territory were Lewis Garrett Jr. and Benjamin Peebles. By 1821, the first two permanent circuits, the Big Hatchie and the Forked Deer Circuits, were formed.[5] The Regular Baptist Association was formed in 1835 in Hardeman and McNairy counties. The organization was a split from the Big Hatchie Circuit and was opposed to the Masonic movement.[6]

We most likely have no way of knowing the identities of the first "faithful" to actively practice and worship in McNairy County, but it very well could have been the Methodists. Most certainly, there was some active practice of faith in McNairy County before 1835, as the county was officially formed in 1823. There were definitely more of the Methodist

1. Samuel C. Williams, "Tidence Lane–Tennessee's First Pastor," *Tennessee, Old and New, Volume I* (Kingsport, TN: Kingsport Press, 1946).

2. *Id.*

3. *Id.*

4. Samuel C. Williams, *Beginnings of West Tennessee: In the Land of the Chickasaws, 1541–1841.* (Johnson City, TN: Watauga Press, 1930).

5. *Id.*

6. *Id.*

faith in north McNairy County during the first few decades. In 1850, five Methodist ministers were residing in northern McNairy in the area around Anderson's Store. These men, who most probably rode the circuit, included Robert Tisdale, John Watkins, James McKary (McKay), and James Perry. The fifth, Wilson A. McHolstead, was a Wesleyan Methodist. By 1860, Joseph Johnson and W.L. Gattis had joined the ranks of the ministers in north McNairy County. It was during this period that Elijah J. Hodges, home fresh from the War, began preaching, a career that would continue until his retirement in 1905. Moses Robbins also preached during this period. In the 1870s and 1880s, David J. Franklin began preaching in the McNairy Station area and S.A. Norwood was preaching in and around north McNairy County.

As far as established Methodist congregations are concerned, it cannot be firmly established whether there was a particular meetinghouse established where these good people met. However, it is known that one of the few meetinghouses that served the Methodists at some point or another was Mount Carmel. As explained further in Chapter Eleven of this work, this meetinghouse served both the Baptists and the Methodists. As for the Baptists, their major advocate in 1850 was Francis Beard, who was a man of many interests and is profiled in Chapter Seven of this work. It is most unfortunate that a more complete portrait of the history of organized religion in north McNairy County cannot be painted. However, we may get a glimpse of this rich history by discussing a few local churches and some of the old time preachers.

Finger Church of Christ

Brethren of the church of Christ first assembled for the purpose of worship in Finger in 1905. About twenty people met in the Possum Trot Schoolhouse and the congregation continued to hold meetings in that structure until 1915, when the present location was procured. The land belonged to James Robert McIntyre as did the property on which the schoolhouse was located. McIntyre's contribution of land came with several important provisions which are interesting and give some indications of his own personal religious views. In donating the property, McIntyre was "promoting the cause of Christ" and more particularly establishing

Finger Church of Christ

a Church of Christ meetinghouse in Finger "where the Gospel of Jesus Christ may be preached in its simplicity and purity."

The McIntyre gift was given as a trust and the covenant in the deed made it clear that "no instruments of music such as organs, violins, cornets, horns, or any other instruments are to be used in Sunday or Bible School, regular services, or church worship." There were also to be no suppers or plans for raising money for amusements. The trusteeship of the church property was to consist of five members of the Church and if a death or resignation occurred, the remaining trustees were to elect a new trustee. The original five trustees were George W. Dickey, W.H. "Tobe" Walker, M.A. Womble, Murry F. Walker, and Clarence M. Barr. Should the plan and wishes of McIntyre not be followed, the property would revert back to McIntyre or his heirs. There was no financial consideration for the transaction, but rather "for the purpose of advancing and promoting the cause of Christ."

After 1915, the congregation met in its new meetinghouse, pictured above. Shortly after the completion of the meetinghouse, the structure was struck by a tornado in 1917. According to newspaper accounts, the building was "wrecked." However, the building was salvaged and repaired. This particular building was used for the next forty years as the congregation's meetinghouse.

The first elders to serve the spiritual needs of the Christians at the Finger church of Christ were James Robert McIntyre, W.H. Walker, and Clarence M. Barr. Since that time, many able and good men have served as elders leading this congregation. Among the early Gospel preachers to serve or assist the Finger brethren were Arvy Glenn Freed, Nicholas Brodie Hardeman, W.H. Owen, A.H. Lannom, L.L. Briggance, E.R. Harper, and C.A. Wheeler. Most of these names are well-known to members of the church of Christ. Freed and Hardeman were renowned scholars, preachers of the Gospel, leaders and namesakes of nearby Freed-Hardeman University. Brother Biggance was a well-known preacher of the Gospel and educator at Freed-Hardeman. Brother Harper was well-known to many in the South as a dynamic Christian preacher who was said to have baptized hundreds of people. In more recent years, the congregation has been served by such preachers as Professors Everett Huffard, B.J. Naylor, and Earl Edwards.

The present meetinghouse was built in 1958 and a number of additions and renovations have been made to this structure in the last twenty years. Besides a large auditorium, the building also houses a church library, an office, a nursery, and a training room. In the late 1990s, a new fellowship hall was constructed which included classrooms on the upper level of the structure.

Finger Methodist Church

The exact date of the establishment of the Finger United Methodist Church is somewhat in question. According to some members of that congregation, the Methodist Church in Finger was established in 1914. However, the property on which the old structure is situated was not purchased for the use of the church until November 6, 1916. According to the deed, the lot was purchased from James Robert McIntyre at a date prior to the above date by "C.E. Pickett and of C.H. Pickett by Bishop and O'Neal." From that time until November 6, 1916, the lot was owned by the business firm of Bishop and O'Neal, which consisted of M.E. and Mag Bishop, H.B. and Minnie O'Neal, J.A. and Erie Parker, A.G. and Minnie Bishop, and D.E. and Lela Bishop. On the above date, the firm sold the lot to W.H. Harris, J.B. Weaver, R.A. Freeman,

Finger Methodist Church

A.G. Bishop, and Ila Brown, the trustees of the Methodist Episcopal Church South in Finger.

It was after the above transaction that the actual structure was built in 1917, rather than 1914. It is apparent, however, that the congregation was already meeting in Finger prior to that time, most likely as early as 1914. According to the provisions of the deed, the trustees were to hold the property in trust "that said premises shall be used, kept, maintained, and disposed of, as a place of divine worship for the use of the ministry and membership of the Methodist Episcopal Church South subject to the discipline, usage, and ministerial appointments of said church as from time authorized and declared by the General Conference of said Church, and by the annual conference within whose bounds the said premises are situated."

It is interesting to note the name of the original church, the Methodist Episcopal Church South. At some point, either its affiliation, or simply the name, changed to the Finger United Methodist Church. The first pastor of the congregation was R.A. Morgan, who served for the first twelve years of the congregation's existence. The first Sunday School Superintendent was Willie Martin. Upon Martin's death, A.G. Bishop served as Superintendent until his death in 1957. Other men to have served as pastor included W.W. Henley, U.H. Lafforty, Warner Pafford, W.H. Smith, H.T. Sanson, John H. Horton, Tommy Peel,

Zolan Clayton, Fred Tucker, Eugene Barnes, Ronald Allen, Mike Deal, Harry Burkhead, John Hitz, Tony Moss, and Keith Brown.

Finger First Baptist Church

The First Baptist Church of Finger was organized on June 29, 1952, at Logan McCaskill's dining hall at Logan's Lake. There were nine individuals present at the first meeting. Three Baptist ministers were present for the event including Bro. Wayne Cox, Bro. W.C. Nevil, and Bro. Charles Joe Baker. Nevil served as the new congregation's first pastor on an interim basis. On August 19, 1952, Nevil baptized four more individuals who placed membership with the congregation, bringing its total of charter members to twelve. On November 30, 1952, the members of the church elected as their first permanent minister, Charles Joe Baker. Baker was paid ten dollars a week. On April 26, 1953, the membership of Finger First Baptist Church elected to move their services from Logan's Lake to the Finger School building where they met beginning on May 10, 1952.

On September 6, 1953, the congregation first began conducting Sunday School and were looking forward to the process of building a meetinghouse, a process which actually began that month. On February 14, 1954, M.D. Kemp and L.L. Dallas were elected to serve as deacons. On April 11, the congregation held all-day services in their new building. Sixty people were present for the ten o'clock Sunday School and Charles Joe Baker brought the message to the congregation that day. After a noon lunch, Wayne Cox brought the 1:30 P.M. message which was a dedication of the building.

All decisions regarding the activities and missions of the First Baptist Church at Finger were made by the members in a business meeting. Those decisions included those of spending money, electing teachers, and determining what literature would be used for Sunday School classes. Among the leadership positions were Sunday School Superintendent, Sunday School Secretary, Church Treasurer, Church Clerk, Adult Teacher, Junior's Teacher, Primary Teacher, and Young People's Teacher. Among the earliest pastors were W.C. Nevil, Charles Joe Baker, Douglas Brewer, Hawthorne Hurst, H.R. Coleman, A.B. Russom, and Joe Joe Baker. Among the earliest families to attend the First Baptist Church of Finger from 1952 to 1960 were: Dallas, Rouse, Harris, Kemp, Connor, Bulliner, Young, Burross, Woodward, Jones, Russom, Joyner, Smith, Vickery, Bevil, Rankin, Milford, Vinson, Lipford, Baker, Julian, Brown, Melton, Dickey, Clayton, Hysmith, Garner, Moore, Strain, Frye, Lofton, Coleman, and Wharton.

Finger Christian Fellowship Church

Beginning in the early 1970s, there was a migration of peoples to the north McNairy County-Finger area. These good folks were commonly referred to as the Mennonites. It is generally assumed among the general populace that they came down from the more strict Amish religious community. However, they refer to themselves as simply "Christians." On the whole, they are an industrious lot and have been involved in business activities such as logging and sawmilling, farming, the production of food products such as baked goods and sorghum molasses, construction, and the mechanic trade.

They have congregated and been schooled at two locations locally. Many years ago, several used the old Mount Carmel meetinghouse as a meetinghouse and school. In the early to mid-1980s, they constructed a meetinghouse of their own west of town just off of State Highway 199. The Finger Christian Fellowship Church also serves as a school for the children and a private cemetery is located on site. Among the families to locate here were the Stoll, Beachy, Raber, Mast, Stoltzfus, Martin, and Hostetler families. Some members of these families later migrated to Perry county, Tennessee, where they have returned to more traditional ways of living and working.

Mount Carmel Church

Much will be said regarding Mount Carmel in Chapter Eleven of this work, but a little should be stated in this chapter regarding its mission as a meetinghouse and place of worship. Exactly when the first meetinghouse was constructed is not currently known, but it has been written that the cemetery was established in 1826 or 1827. The first meetinghouse was originally constructed about where the Leroy Smith and John R. McIntyre lots are currently located just in view of Mount Carmel Road.

Mount Carmel Church

The size and construction of this structure is unknown. At some point, a second structure was built on the site of the current meeting-house. This structure was a large frame building with an open ceiling that showed exposed rafters and the walls were constructed of beaded board material. Several wooden pews provided a place for members to sit and worship.

The meetinghouse served both the Primitive Baptists and the Wesleyan Methodists at varying times. Two of the better-known preachers of the mid to late nineteenth century preached at the Mount Carmel meetinghouse, Wilson A. McHolstead and Elijah J. Hodges. McHolstead, a Wesleyan Methodist, was a renowned circuit-rider and highly respected among the Wesleyans. He preached a number of meetings and funerals at Mount Carmel as well as presiding over a number of weddings. Hodges, who has previously been sketched in Chapter Three of this work, was a celebrated Primitive Baptist minister. Living near Mount Carmel, he preached there for several years. Other ministers at Mount Carmel included Wesleyan ministers J.J. Crumly (1876), E.M. Garrett (1882), J.W. Robinson (1887), and Primitive Baptist minister Francis Beard.

The second meetinghouse at Mount Carmel was used primarily by the Primitive Baptists. This old building was also used by the local black community for singings, preachings, and the occasional funeral when the black section of the cemetery was still in use and in good repair.

However, the structure eventually began to deteriorate. At some point, some bandit made off with the windows and the doors. When the decision was made to build a new meetinghouse, the old one was leaning badly and in great need of being razed. Henry Kirkpatrick bought the old flooring and Zanie Brown bought the building itself, dismantling it and carting off the materials. The present block building was then constructed in the late 1940s. Pete Wharton spearheaded the construction efforts with financial help from some local families and businesses. A number of interested residents gave their time to assist in the actual construction of the building.

Among the members of this congregation in the 1920s through the 1940's were Pete and Lizzie Brown Wharton, Lula Womble McIntyre, and Newton Perry Talbott. Brother Hallie Stanfill of Chester County served as the pastor of the Mount Carmel church from 1946 until 1961. Unfortunately, no permanent records of the activities of this church exist to give a more detailed history of this good place. A current list of those buried at Mount Carmel Cemetery can be found in Chapter Eleven of this work.

Lane's Chapel Nondenominational Church[7]

The members of Lane's Chapel Church first congregated together in a brush arbor meeting between the site of the present meetinghouse and the old Jess Helton home site. Following this brush arbor meeting, the brothers and sisters of this congregation attended services at Maggie Jones Memorial United Methodist Church for a short period of time. Dissatisfied, however, with this experience, they chose to build a meetinghouse in which to worship. The gentlemen who came together to build the Lane's Chapel meetinghouse were Orby Plunk, R.B. Barham, Fate Barham, Howard Cone, Floyd Cone, Snooks Hysmith, Albin Carpenter, Cecil Carpenter, and Melzer Plunk.

The building was constructed 1955 and the first worship service was held there on March 18, 1955. The first preacher was W.E. Sharp of Booneville, Mississippi. He was followed by such men as R.C. Spencer,

---

7. The information for this sketch was provided to the author by the late Mrs. Ivy Cone, who was a member of Lane's Chapel Nondenominational Church since the very beginning of the congregation.

Justin Ivy, David Massengill, Joseph Massengill, Hollis Reaves, and Leo McDaniel, who served the congregation for ten years. More recent preachers have included Don Lipford, Kenneth Crowe, and W.O. Bullman. The first person to be buried in the Lane's Chapel Cemetery was Howard Cone in 1965.

Maggie Jones Memorial Methodist Church (New Church)

When this congregation of Methodists was organized in 1915, the pastor was Mr. E.H. Jones. He and his wife had one child, a daughter named Maggie. She was born to the couple on July 22, 1900. Little is known of her life except that it was not to be long. Little Maggie died on May 18, 1914, and was laid to rest in the Plunk Cemetery. The new church tended by Brother Jones was quickly named Maggie Jones Memorial Methodist Church from the outset. Due to the fact the church was indeed new, the term "new Church" began to be commonly used. The original structure had no bathrooms and no running water, very much the primitive meeting house of the period. It served simply for the worship of God. After serving the congregation for more than 35 years, the old structure had deteriorated to the point that a new building was definitely needed. Therefore, in 1951, the current structure was completed just above the site of the original one.

Among the early pastors at Maggie Jones Memorial were E.H. Jones, E.F. Deaton, a Mr. Ramsey, and Albert A. Plunk. As it happened, Plunk would preach for the congregation longer than any other. Among the pastors to serve since the late 1940s were Harold Montgomery, Jerry Smith, Allen Wolf, Zolon Clayton, Tommy Peal, Fred Tucker, George Archer, J.G. Gilbert, Neal Henson, Bob Beck, Mike Deal, Paul Mulroy, Harry Burkhead, John Hitz, Mark Kennedy, Tony Moss, Tommy Phillips, and Keith Brown.[8]

The cemetery at Maggie Jones Memorial was donated by the two local landowners of the land on which it sits today. The first person to be buried there was a child of Harrison and Hester Vires. Homecoming at Maggie Jones Memorial is much like homecoming at many places, but like all such places, it is a special event. People come from near and far

---

8. These are not presented in any particular order. The information from this sketch was provided by Gracie (Plunk) Webster.

The original meetinghouse for the congregation of Maggie Jones Memorial Methodist Church in 1915.

The current Maggie Jones Memorial Methodist Church, which is located across the road from the cemetery.

to remember their loved ones and place a memorial of flowers on their earthen tombs. A person traveling on State Highway 199 will see immediately as he approaches the "New Church" area the great crowd of good people on the fourth Sunday in May as they visit in the cemetery after lunch on the grounds and a wonderful singing of those great old Gospel songs.

The cemetery at Maggie Jones Memorial United Methodist church has grown greatly over the last several decades. Many of north McNairy County's better-known citizens of the twentieth century were buried here as older family and community cemeteries began to fill to capacity. Although the cemetery is easily accessible, a list of those buried at Maggie Jones is included in Chapter Eleven of this work.

The senses are soon aroused upon arriving at the ever-thriving "Decoration Day" at Maggie Jones. The smells of country cooking, fresh flowers, and fresh-cut grass delight the nose and the sound of beautiful singing soothes the ears. May is a month long anticipated by many good people in McNairy County and the Finger area.

Pine Hill Assembly

The Pine Hill Assembly church has been located in north McNairy County on Centerhill Road for many years. Instrumental in the church and school there for many years has been Don Lipford. The school began around 1980 in a one room structure. Over the years it grew to provide a private education to young men and women from the elementary level through senior high school. The curriculum was like any other state approved school, but with a strong concentration on religious values. This church and school played a vital role in the lives of many in north McNairy County for many years. The school no longer exists.

Hopewell Baptist Church

Hopewell Baptist Church has long been a fixture in north McNairy County. Among the most active in this congregation over the years has been the Bullman family. Many have served the congregation in a number of capacities. Among the Sunday school teachers has been Elvis Bullman, Orce (Ora) Bullman, and Leonard Gately. Preachers have included

W.P. Littlefield. This is an old congregation having been around since the middle of the nineteenth century. It is located in the most northern reaches of the county in a heavily wooded area. It is a serene and beautiful location where many of the county's oldest pioneers are buried.

These various congregations have served the people of north McNairy County for many years and for many purposes. Such congregations have offered many an extended family and a gathering of friends. Many souls have passed through the doors of these meeting-houses and have made their impact on these congregations.

A number of men chose to preach the gospel of Christ in north McNairy County. Some were Primitive Baptist, some Methodist, some Presbyterian. It was indeed the day of "the church in the wildwood." These men, of course, farmed or plied some other trade during the week and performed their ministerial duties on Sundays and special occasions. However, there were those who made a career of preaching and invested considerable time traveling to spread the message. Many of those are remembered by those of their number who remain faithful today.

Wilson Alfred McHolstead (1806–1891)

Wilson Alfred McHolstead was born in North Carolina on November 11, 1806. According to one family member, McHolstead married Elizabeth S. (Taylor) Lane on November 1, 1826, in Guilford County, North Carolina.[9] According to the same source, they had eight children in a span of twenty-six years. In 1830, he and his wife were living with a young daughter in Rockingham, North Carolina. In 1840, he and his wife and four children were living in McNairy County, Tennessee, along with McHolstead's brother, Smith McHolstead. In 1850, Brother McHolstead was living in the Eighth District and his mother, Nancy McHolstead, and brother, Smith, were living with the family. By 1860, Brother McHolstead was living in Strawberry, Arkansas. His mother had moved there as well and was living next door with her grandson, Jordan. As it turned out, Nancy McHolstead was born in Pennsylvania in and around the year 1777. Interestingly enough, by 1870, Nancy McHolstead was living still, although her age could have been anywhere from 88 to 93 years of age. The McHolsteads were back in McNairy County,

9. Information provided by Diane Taylor, a descendant of Wilson A. McHolstead.

Tennessee, in 1870. Further, Nancy McHolstead's birth state was this time listed as Maryland. Smith McHolstead was still single in 1870. By 1880, McHolstead was becoming elderly. Now, interestingly, the birthplace of McHolstead's mother is listed as Virginia.

At what point he decided to turn his energies toward the ministry is unknown, but he became one of the most influential preachers of the Tennessee Conference of the Wesleyan Church. He eventually served as president and secretary of the conference. In 1879, McHolstead was the pastor assigned to Mount Carmel Wesleyan Methodist Church east of present-day Finger. In 1880, his other charges included the congregations at Purdy, Pleasant Hill, Combs Chapel, Washington Valley, Mill Creek, Liberty, Hardeman, Sulphur Springs, Winding Ridge, and the North Alabama Mission.[10] According to historical sources available, McHolstead was an active and well-traveled minister.

In 1882, McHolstead served as secretary for the conference, the same year that another prominent McNairy County minister, F.M. Cude, served as president. An article from the *American Wesleyan* stated the following regarding McHolstead, "Brother McHolstead is a veteran in this Conference. He is seventy-five years of age, and he made a report which should fire the hearts of younger men to accomplish great things for Christ. He reported the largest salary of any man in the Conference, which was nineteen dollars and thirty cents. Part of this amount was actually paid over to him during the year, and the rest had been subscribed, and the account was thought to be good. This aged soldier of the cross living on 'borrowed time' said: 'I have preached seventy-one sermons and traveled seven hundred miles this year.' A good many miles on a small amount of money."[11]

Following her death in 1886, McHolstead married again, this time to Mary M. Yarbrough. The marriage ceremony took place on August 9, 1887, with Elijah J. Hodges officiating. What became of Mary

---

10. Donna Watson, Assistant Director of the Archives and Historical Library, International Center, The Wesleyan Church, Indianapolis, Indiana, correspondence to the author, June 30, 1994.

11. *American Wesleyan*, November 8, 1881. This excerpt was sent to the author in a letter from Donna Watson, Assistant Director of the Archives and Historical Library, International Center, The Wesleyan Church, Indianapolis, Indiana, on June 30, 1994.

McHolstead is unknown. McHolstead passed away on March 23, 1891, at the age of eighty-four.[12]

John Wesley Plunk (1842-1920)[13]

John Wesley Plunk was born in McNairy County on December 3, 1842, the son of Daniel and Nancy (Inman) Plunk. At 19 years old, he enlisted in Company G of the United States Sixth Tennessee Cavalry during the War Between the States. While stationed at the Federal post at Bolivar, Tennessee, he contracted what he described as "sore eyes" from winter exposure in January 1863, which resulted in the loss of sight in his left eye. He was promoted to the rank of corporal before the war ended, and was honorable discharged at Pulaski, Tennessee, on July 26, 1865. Afterward, he married Elizabeth Jane Tacker, daughter of Joseph Orkerson and Elizabeth (Page) Tacker, in McNairy County on January 25, 1866, and settled down to a life of farming.

Rev. John Wesley Plunk

Plunk was a member of Liberty Church, where his faith and speaking skills were noticed by the Reverend Wilson A. McHolstead, president of the Quarterly Conference of liberty Circuit in the Tennessee Conference, which belonged to the Wesleyan Methodist denomination. On August

---

12. To the author, there remains some question about McHolstead's personal life. His wife Elizabeth S. McHolstead is buried next to him in Mount Carmel Cemetery. However, in McNairy County's marriage records is a record of a marriage between a W.A. McHolstead and an E.S. Henderson on January 12, 1871. Following Elizabeth's death in 1886, McHolstead married again, this time to Mary M. Yarbrough. The marriage ceremony took place on August 9, 1887, with Elijah J. Hodges officiating. Whether or not McHolstead had any children is not currently known. McHolstead passed away on March 23, 1891, at the age of eighty-four.

13. Biographical sketch of John Wesley Plunk taken from Kevin D. McCann, *History of Liberty Church and School, McNairy County, Tennessee* (Ashland City, TN: Self-published, 1995), 47–48.

13, 1883, he was authorized "to hold public meetings for the promotion of the Cause of God" as an exhorter in the Wesleyan Methodist Church. An exhorter was considered an assistant to the preacher and often accompanied him on his circuit rounds. At times, an exhorter's "gifts of persuasion" were used after the preacher had delivered his sermon.

Plunk received his preacher's license on September 27, 1884. For thirty-five years, he preached the Gospel and once served as pastor of four churches at the same time. He died at his home in McNairy County on March 10, 1920, at the age of 77 and was buried at Liberty Church Cemetery. An obituary written by Ophelia Henry was published in the Wesleyan Methodist on April 7, 1920:

> **Plunk** – J.W. Plunk was born in December, 1842, and died March 10, 1920. Brother Plunk leaves a wife and seven children to mourn their loss, four boys and three girls, all grown to manhood and womanhood, and a host of friends. He was a Wesleyan Methodist preacher and had been for about thirty-five years. He lived in McNairy County, Tennessee, and was the last white preacher in the West Tennessee conference. He was laid to rest in Liberty Cemetery, March 11. Brother L.E. Jones held the services. Text, "And if the dead rise not, then is Christ not risen."

CHAPTER NINE

THE MYSTERIOUS, THE UNEXPLAINABLE, AND THE DOWNRIGHT TRAGIC

Mysterious Murder of Sol Thomason—Mystery of Quincy Ash—Tragic Deaths of the Alexanders, the Bishops, and others—The Tornados of 1909, 1917, and 1942—The disappearance of Spy Jack—The shootings of William Whitt and Jim Rufe Dickey—The death of young Troy Clayton—The horrible death of Quinn Ingram—The "wanderings" of Lee Tacker.

The Mysterious Murder of Sol Thomason

Somewhere in north McNairy County, Mr. Sol G. Thomason lost his life in 1864.[1] Thomason was born on May 13, 1805, and apparently lived near the present-day Enville area in the vicinity of Shady Hill or Old Bishop Store. A couple of different tales exist as to the facts surrounding this foul deed. Thomason was traveling through the area with a yoke of oxen and his wagon. The stories conflict as to whether Thomason was coming from Memphis or Saltillo at the time. In fact, two locations have been given for the location of the actual killing and there are even disputes as to the *modus operandi* of the killer or killers.

---

1. The various facts and theories behind this story come from a personal conversation with Gracie (Plunk) Webster on August 20, 2002, and from the work *Cemeteries in Chester County* by Lewis P. Jones, copyrighted 1982.

One account has Thomason shot first while traveling through Leapwood, apparently proceed with his journey in an injured state, only to be hanged upon his return from Saltillo. A second account has Thomason carrying cotton to market in Memphis and then shot on his return trip while traveling through the area now known as New Church, east of present-day Finger. According to this variation of the tale, Thomason was then robbed of his valuables and money and placed in his wagon with his team of oxen carrying his corpse home.

The motive behind Thomason's murder is unknown, other than robbery. Perhaps it was for money alone, the usual motive for robbery. Then again, perhaps it was a mix of greed and politics. According to Lewis P. Jones, Thomason was mentioned in the Battle of Henderson Station trial as one of the Rebels fined for damages which were due to Union property owners.

Over the years, the legend of Sol Thomason grew in the New Church area. Many, young and old alike, had seen and heard a number of strange and frightening events, sights and sounds. Most have attributed them to the presence of Sol Thomason. Whether superstitious or not, the dead man's legacy has taken root since his untimely demise.

The Mystery of Quincy Ash

In almost every small community, there are small mysteries that linger long after the big events that gave life to the mystery. Those mysteries long outlive the participants and span for generations. Usually those mysteries are the result of some tragic and unexplainable disappearance or death, whose occurrence is shrouded in a cloak of uncertainty. The purpose of the following sketch is only to render a permanent record of such events, or at least a record of the theories which have been tossed about for generations in oral form.

Whatever else could have been remembered about Quincy Ash has long been forgotten lest it deal with his disappearance and presumed death. Therefore, other than the theories regarding his disappearance, there are few facts we do indeed know of Quincy Ash. Quincy was the son of James W. and Sarah M. Ash, both of whom are buried in Mount Carmel Cemetery. Quincy was born around 1861 and had, at least, one older sister, Mary Virginia Ash Surratt, who is buried next to her parents.

On November 17, 1881, Quincy married Miss Mollie J. Moore.[2] At some point, the couple settled on the Frank Tedford place near the Bailey Crossroads, on what is now Knuckles Road.[3] This is confirmed by the 1910 United States Census which shows Mollie J. Ash, now a widow, and son Albert M. Ash, living next to the Hubert F. Tedford household.[4] According to local residents who were youths around the first decade of the twentieth century, Quincy, Mollie, and Albert Ash lived in Frank Tedford's rent house.[5] There is not much else known concerning Quincy Ash's life, except that which also concerns his disappearance.

The general consensus of those who were contemporary to Quincy Ash and those who heard of him from their parents was that he was a "mean-spirited" man and downright deplorable.[6] That his presence in the community was detested made for wild speculation and numerous theories when he vanished. So, what happened to Quincy Ash? Maybe no one knows, but here the writer will attempt to outline the reports and theories of this man's demise.

Apparently the year was 1909, for, as has already been mentioned, the 1910 United States Census reported that Mollie J. Ash was a widow of one year. Therefore, if this information is correct, Quincy Ash was about forty-eight years old at the time of his disappearance. One of the first reports concerning Quincy's demise was from a neighbor who said they "passed the Ash homestead at or near midnight and Mollie was at the stable with a kerosene lamp or lantern."[7] Keeping with the nature of this account, Ms. Moline Robison once related that when she, a little girl at the time, and the older members of her family returned home from working in the fields at the end of the workday, they would pass by the Ash place.[8] Often Mollie would be sitting in the doorway of the stable,

---

2. McNairy County, Tennessee Marriage Records, 1861–1911.

3. Marvin Hand, letter to Judy Hammons, April 13, 1996.

4. 1910 United States Census for McNairy County, Tennessee, edited by R. Harold Cox.

5. Hand, letter to Hammons.

6. This has been the general description of this man by at least two women and one man who lived in the community at the time of the disappearance, all of whom are now dead. The same description was passed to innumerable descendants of Ash's contemporaries.

7. Hand, letter to Hammons.

8. *Id.*

crying.[9] There was speculation that Quincy was buried in the stable. At the time, the disappearance of Quincy Ash was the main topic of conversation in the neighborhood, so it is no wonder the story or stories have remained.

A couple of other interesting accounts include one regarding Quincy's son Albert and one concerning an Ammie Robbins. One person, at the time, stated that Albert made the comment, "Didn't I get rich quick?"[10] One can only speculate what Albert meant by this. Another source said that Ammie Robbins lost his mind in his older years, following the disappearance, and would jump out of his bed and shout, "There's Quincy Ash! I killed him years ago!"[11] Whether or not these reports are true may never be known. The story concerning Robbins could possibly confirm the story that a group of men, who viewed Quincy as a menace, had, in fact, conspired and acted upon a plan to kill Quincy.[12]

If one were to visit the Sweetlips Cemetery, he would find the clues to the rest of the story, but not the mystery. It is here, however, that Mollie and Albert were buried. Albert died relatively young and apparently unmarried. Albert was born on July 20, 1889, and died on January 21, 1918. Mollie J. (Moore) Ash was later married to a Gage. She died on January 25, 1931. Apparently there were no descendents left from this direct line. Regardless of when and who killed Quincy Ash, his character, his life, and the circumstances surrounding his disappearance and death will most likely remain a mystery and a question mark upon the pages of north McNairy County's history.

The Alexander Tragedies

In late 1926, the late Dave Alexander suffered two extremely tragic and almost unimaginable losses. Mr. Alexander, then living between Finger and Leapwood in the Hodges' Beauty area, first lost his only child, a son, J.P. Alexander. On October 17, 1926, J.P. and at least one other

9. Id.

10. Id.

11. Id.

12. This theory that a group of men conspired together to kill Ash and then did so, perhaps throwing him down into an abandoned well and then filling it has, in fact, been passed to a number of local residents over the years.

Dave and Daisy Alexander   *Daisy Alexander*

young man, Vannie Loftin, were driving down what is now Finger-Leapwood Road or State Route 199.[13] The car, a new 1926 Ford, belonged to one of the boys and they had been out all evening celebrating the event by taking an extended drive.[14] As they rode along, the driver lost control and wrecked in the edge of what was then the Floyd yard (approximately the corner of William Branson "Jim" Garner's property and the large white house next door, the Floyd home in 1926).[15] The car flipped over and trapped J.P. The Loftin boy ran for help, but it arrived too late. J.P.'s chest was crushed by the weight of the car, thus causing his death at the young age of nineteen.[15] Interestingly enough, years later Mr. Dave Alexander would relocate to Finger and live in the Floyd home.

Certainly, Mr. Alexander was left reeling over this tragic event when another equally devastating event occurred. On November 3, 1926, J.P.'s

13. Luther E. Talbott, interview with the author, December 31, 2000. In 1926, the road ran parallel and south of where it runs today. To give the reader a better understanding of its location at the time, the tree line running through Luther Talbott's front yard was the path of the old road.

14. *Id.*

15. *Id.*

16. Robert Beene states that only two boys were in the car, Vannie Loftin and J.P. Alexander. Other sources claim that a Plunk boy accompanied them on their ill-fated joy ride.

mother, Daisy Alexander, fell into an open fire and "was so badly burned, she died within a short time."[17] Both J.P. and Daisy Alexander were laid to rest in the Finger Cemetery. In only a matter of two and a half weeks, Mr. Dave Alexander lost his family in unexpected and sudden ways, thereby once again affirming the brevity and fragility of this life.

The Swift Deaths of the Dossie Bishops and Scott McCaskill

Dorsey "Dossie" Bishop, a native of nearby Enville, came to Finger in the earliest years of the twentieth century to engage in the mercantile business with his brother Alsworth Guy Bishop.[18] Bishop built the home which once occupied the corner of Finger Leapwood Road and Brown Street, next door to brother Guy and across the street from brother-in-law, Dr. W.M. Barnes. This home burned in 1998. Dossie and his wife were actively involved in the business and social life of Finger and north McNairy County in the early 1900s. Their tragic deaths were a great blow to many of their friends and associates in the area. Many ways could utilized to tell the story of the tragedy which cut short the life of Bishop, his wife, and their companion, but perhaps it is best to reproduce the article written about the accident at the time.

PROMINENT PEOPLE KILLED
Dorsey Bishop and Wife and Scott McCaskill Meet
Death In A Horrible Manner.

On Sunday afternoon Dorsey Bishop and wife and Scott McCaskill, while driving in an automobile from Jackson, Tennessee, to Finger, were struck on the public road crossing two miles south of Pinson by a north bound M. & O. passenger train and all of them instantly killed. With the party was a little girl of Mr. and Mrs. Bishop, aged about 6 years. She was frightfully injured and is not expected to recover, her skull being fractured, besides suffering from other injuries. The party was returning home from a visit and no one seems to know the cause of the awful and deplorable accident. The

17. *McNairy County Independent Appeal*, November 5, 1926.
18. *McNairy County Independent Appeal*, June 30, 1922.

THE MYSTERIOUS, THE UNEXPLAINABLE

theory is advanced that the dusty condition of the roads kept the driver of the car from seeing the approaching train. Others state that the engine of the automobile went dead on the railroad track, making it impossible for the automobile to be moved. This terrible accident has cast a gloom over the county where all of the parties were reared and by whom they were so well and favorably known by so many people

Mr. Bishop was a prominent merchant of this county and had with his brother, Guy Bishop, been in the mercantile business several years in Finger, while his wife was loved and admired by her neighbors and friends. Mr. McCaskill was a valued employee of the firm and was a most exemplary young man. The funeral of Mr. McCaskill[19] was held at Finger, early Tuesday morning, and that of Mr. Bishop and wife at the old burying ground, the O'Neal graveyard in the northeast part of the county, in the early afternoon.

A large number of the friends from Selmer and other places in the county attended the funeral.

Mr. Dorsey Elihu Bishop of Finger, Tennessee, was born January 26, 1884, and Miss Lela Woodward, March 2, 1885. They were happily married on Easter Sunday, 1907. To this union, four children were born, but two of them died in infancy.

On Sunday, June 25, 1922, Mr. and Mrs. Bishop were instantly killed at the Johnson crossing, two miles south of Pinson, when the automobile in which they were riding was struck by a north bound Mobile and Ohio passenger train. Mr. Bishop's watch stopped eight minutes after five o'clock, which probably marks the exact time the train struck them.

Scott McCaskill

---

19. Scott McCaskill, brother of the late Logan McCaskill, was laid to rest in the Finger Cemetery.

The driver, Scott McCaskill, who was also instantly killed, had the reputation of being an unusually careful driver. Perhaps we shall never whether he failed to see the train in time to stop the car, or whether he tried to stop and the brakes failed to work. We are almost certain that he did not see the train at a distance, then tried to beat it to the crossing. Scott McCaskill was born February 21, 1893. He did not belong to any church, but professed faith in Christ in 1918, while serving with the Army of Occupation in Germany.

Inetha, age seven, daughter of Mr. and Mrs. Bishop, was the only occupant of the car that escaped instant death. She is now in the Civic League hospital in Jackson in a semi-conscious condition, with only a "fighting chance" for recovery.[20] The only member of the Bishop family left is Roy, age 13, who preferred to remain at home and play rather than make the trip to his uncle's.

Mr. Bishop is survived by his mother, Mrs. Maggie Bishop; one brother, Guy Bishop; and three sisters, Mesdames Minnie O'Neal, Estelee Barnes,[21] and Earl Parker; and Mrs. Bishop, by two brothers, Joe and Charles Woodward; and six sisters, Mesdames Sallie O'Neal, Dora Mullins, Lorenza Gaddy, Estella McCaskill, Jennie Nolen, and Caroline Mills. Both also leave a great number of near relatives and a host of friends.

When only a child, Mrs. Bishop gave her life to God and united with the Methodist church. She was a faithful and active member until death. Mr. Bishop was not a member of the church, but was interested in it and one of its most liberal supporters. He was always ready to do his part, and more in whatever promised to build up the community, and in caring for the sick and needy he could always be depended on. Both will be missed in the community life, the school life, and the church life. He was a successful businessman, being

---

20. As it happened, Inetha recovered, with the exception of some crippling effects, to attend and graduate college, become a schoolteacher, and later marry.

21. Estelee (Bishop) Barnes was the wife of Dr. W.M. Barnes of Finger. Their home was located across the road from the Dorsey Bishop home. Dr. and Mrs. Barnes would take charge of the raising of Roy and Inetha Bishop following their parents' deaths.

a member of the firm of Bishop and O'Neal. They had two stores, one at Finger and another at Enville.

The tragic deaths gave the greatest shock this whole country ever had. We read about similar accidents almost every day, but this is the first one to occur in this community.

The funeral services were conducted at the O'Neal cemetery, the old family burying place, by the writer and Rev. V.E. Banks, their pastor. It was estimated that some 1,500 to 2,000 people came to pay the last tribute of respect to the deceased ones, who now sleep side by side in the same grave, awaiting the resurrection at the last day.

J.D. CANADAY

The Destructive Winds of Nature[22]

The Tornado of 1909

Little is known as to the level of destruction reached in the now almost forgotten storm of 1909. If the particular cyclone which struck the north McNairy area was of the same storm system that ripped apart lower McNairy County and western Hardin County that year, then it is almost completely certain the destruction was momentous. However, as to our current knowledge of this storm, there is very little, so let us proceed. It is not known if one storm or more struck that season. A letter written by Professor Harvey Hodges to John E. Hodges on November 3, 1909, refers to the storm that "wrecked" the Liberty church house. In his letter, Professor Hodges states:

> I went to Liberty Sunday to see the wreck and by the way, that Liberty Church is torn, eminently, preeminently, absolutely, entirely, literally, everlastingly, completely, bodily, surely, actually, really and body snatchingly all to thunderation, scattered to the forewinds, scattered from the rivers to the ends of the earth, scattered from Maine's Dark Pines and Craigs of snow,

---

22. The text of the newspaper account for the 1917 tornado, taken from the *McNairy County Independent Appeal* of Friday, June 1, 1917, also appeared in Naylor and Talbott, *Fingerprints*. It is here expounded upon with new material and commentary.

to where magnolia breezes blow, scattered on the highland, scattered in the valley, scattered on the lowland, on the plain, scattered in the forests, on the highseas, snatched up by the roots and scattered from Jerusalem to Jerricho, scattered from on the landscape, on the farstretching prairies, on undulating hills, on sunny slopes, scattered on towering mountains, on queenly oceans, on laughing streams, scattered on sparkling cascades, in gigantic trees, scattered to every state in the Union, to every possession of the U.S., scattered into every dark recess of every remote corner of every foot of civilized and uncivilized dirt on the face of God Almighty's mundane sphere. The Elysian fields of classic fable, the floral plains of Eden were not more cloudless, calm, and purely beautiful than the [...] [*illegible*] of this structure which was protected by a No. 18 burglar lock, sublime as the Stars and Stripes, important as a mule's daddy, gentle as the deathless silence of the dreamless dust, fruitful as a 30 acre orchard rife with the vintage of harvest. Within her sacred walls many sinners have been called to repent and sanctification and the second before it was auctioned off to the highest bidder, with a 10 cent preacher crying the sale, but in all this the Lord said... she is coming down...and she came.[23]

A few short observations should be made. It is quite apparent that Professor Hodges was a master of overstatement. But in all fairness, according to his surviving writings, he was masterful at turning a phrase. It seems apparent from this letter that the storm came on quickly and caught local residents by surprise.

The Tornado of 1917

The tornado of 1917 may not have been the first storm of size to hit the small town or its outlying areas, but it was certainly the first to be greatly remembered by the citizens. It was, more than likely, the first to strike since the establishment of Finger, in its proper form. Surely a great

---

23. Letter from Harvey Hodges to cousin John E. Hodges, November 3, 1909. The letter was provided to the author by Harvey Hodges' descendant, Ben Davidson of Bingham, Illinois.

number of stories and accounts grew out of this harrowing experience, but only two are greatly remembered and recounted today by those who witnessed it and are still surviving (a relatively and understandable small number) and by the children of Finger's residents from 1917. The first story regards a small child who survived an occurrence which could have proved fatal. Ralph Young, the son of Rube Young, was only an infant in 1917. As the story goes, little Ralph was lying in his crib near the hearth with his grandparents keeping guard over him when the storm struck. It has been passed down that he was found after the storm, under the house, unharmed, and hanging from a floor joist with his crib clothes caught on a nail.[24] Some have told that Ralph was found in a barrel, unharmed and unscratched.

The second story regards the W.P. Massey General Merchandise store building.[25] After W.P. Massey's wooden store building burned in 1916, he came back stronger than ever with a new larger and more modern brick building in 1917.[26] Massey surely never anticipated the strength of nature's forces when the winds blew on that fateful day in May of 1917. When the winds and the dust settled, Massey saw the west wall of his beautiful new store building lying in the adjacent street. Though the brick and mortar lay in rubble, the shelves along the now fallen wall remained intact with their inventory in place, including a few lamps which stood tall and untouched. Afterward, Massey put into place a long iron rod which ran from the west wall to the east wall, and held in place with two iron plates which were screwed onto the ends of the rod. The plates can still be viewed from the outside of the building.

So what did the "storm at Finger" look like? How was it described? The following account from the local newspaper is put as well as it could be.

> McNairy County did not escape Sunday's tornado. About 5 o'clock Sunday a cyclone struck Finger, doing great damage.

---

24. This account was confirmed in a conversation between the author and Ralph Young, when the now elderly Mr. Young visited Finger some eighty years later in 1997. He had made his home for many years in Gastonia, North Carolina.

25. This is now the Home Banking Company building. It was a store building from the time of its construction in 1916 until about the late 1980s. Beginning in 1994, the building underwent massive renovations and became the offices of Home Banking Company in 1995.

26. Naylor and Talbott, *Fingerprints*.

Among the most seriously hurt were: John Young, arm and ribs broken, and daughter badly hurt. They were blown 75 yards from their home, which was demolished. The houses of D.E. Bishop, J.W. Mitchell, Mrs. Ash, Frank Tedford, Rube Young, Frank Clayton, John Young, John Fry, James P. Halstead, John Rouse, and Lem Naylor were totally demolished. The Christian church was wrecked.[27] The brick store of W.P. Massey was seriously damaged, one wall being blown out. Many other buildings were unroofed and damaged. The property loss will reach $25,000 about half covered by tornado insurance. L.A. Beaty was on the spot Monday, and took most excellent photographs of the ruined buildings, which give a vivid idea of the storm's rage. Damage was done in the country along the line of the storm, which was about 300 feet wide. It did no damage on the south side of Main Street in Finger.

The Deadly Storm of 1942

Despite the great structural damage and even personal injury resulting from the storm of 1917, it could at least be said of that storm that no one was killed. The same would not be true of the storm brewing in the clouds above McNairy County in March of 1942. This time the toll would be greater and the misery intent. On that early spring day in 1942, it is certain that few Finger and McNairy County residents were concerned with the weather, unless it regarded their schedule for "getting their garden out." Perhaps they thought about how wet or dry the year might be, or how the bugs would be. It is more likely that in Finger, the minds were occupied with the death of one of their own, Mr. Thomas Naylor, who was to be buried in the Finger Cemetery that afternoon. Naylor, who had long been known for his ability to build a sufficient and strongly built coffin, would now himself be committed to his earthen tomb. It is probably certain that most of the men and women in town and in the surrounding countryside were more aware and therefore more concerned

---

27. This is referring to the meeting house of the Church of Christ which was newly built on land donated James R. McIntyre, an early elder, in 1915. The building, though damaged, was used for worship services continually until the present building was built on that site in 1958.

about the boiling winds of war sweeping over Europe and the Pacific than the clouds of destruction preparing to sweep over north McNairy County. The thoughts were on who would provide for the family if a son or a father was called to action rather than who and what would be left standing when the winds calmed.

Yes, it is certain, as with most events in history, that everyone, for the most part, was carrying on with their normal, day-to-day activities on March 16, 1942. On that Monday, businesses were open, farmers and their families were working in the fields, and many were preparing to travel to the cemetery to say their goodbyes to one of the town's oldest and most respected citizens. Little did they know that soon their grief would be multiplied.

In town, things were bustling as always. Young Luther Talbott was putting up a partition in his father's store, when he hit his thumb with his hammer.[28] Getting down from his ladder and commenting on this unfortunate occurrence with less than flattering words, he went out into the street. There he and other of the gentlemen in town saw the great natural force of a tornado at work to their south. Talbott grabbed his father, Newton P. Talbott, then almost blind, and told him to go up the street with him to Albert Weaver's store building. As they were preparing to jump into a culvert behind Weaver's store, they saw the tornado was not going to strike the heart of town after all and thus returned to speculate with others as to what the damage might be. This was representative of what the reaction in town was on that day.

Out in the countryside, the reaction was much more tense, as it was the countryside which received the full force and brunt of the cyclone. Many did not have storm houses and were forced to sit the storm out by crouching low in a ditch or lying under a bed, though it certain that a good number of folks spend the afternoon in their fruit cellars. Those with actual storm houses crowded into them, along with several neighbors, to await the uncertainty to follow. One such storm house was that of Mr. Hartle Hayre. The Hayre storm house was and is located in the hillside across the road from the John Robert McIntyre homeplace. On March 16, 1942, a number of people sought refuge here. Hartle and Alma Hayre and their two sons, Hayes and Bill, were there as were two other

28. Luther E. Talbott, interview with the author, 1997. The events written about in this paragraph were all taken from this oral interview.

The aftermath of the devasting tornado that struck north McNairy County on March 16, 1942

families. John and Ollie McIntyre and five of their six children, Helen, Lessie, Vivian, Faye, and J.R., along with Fonzo and Ella Young, were also present. Mrs. Young was fearful to go into the shelter with all of the others, saying she would "smother." John McIntyre stood at the doorway of the shelter, keeping an eye on its path, finally turning to his wife to say, "It got your papa's place."[29]

The storm had begun it path, as far as McNairy County was concerned, in the Rose Creek area and traveled to a point near Enville, in the Bullman Store Community.[30] As it traveled northeast, it left a great path of death and destruction in its wake.[31] A good number of people were severely injured in north McNairy County. In the Refuge community, three women were so severely injured, they required hospitalization. Those were Mrs. Mandy Kernodle, Ms. Virgie Kernodle and Mrs. Ada Archer.[32] Located within the Refuge community was what was referred to as the Archer and Harris community. In that community, the homes of Misters Delmas Archer, Dick Harris, and Harmon Harris were destroyed completely, with one of the young Harris men left injured. The homes of two black families were also destroyed in the vicinity, those of Paul Vasser and Ada Brantom.

The Austin Gee place, also known then as the Ben Archer old place, and his barn received a considerable amount of damage. Among those places destroyed that day in that area were the Mandy Kernodle residence and the Lois Moore place, then the home of a Mr. Broadway. Unfortunately, all members of Ms. Kernodle's household were seriously injured, thus requiring hospitalization. Two of the houses located on the Hodges' farm, west of McNairy Station, were badly damaged. The houses were occupied at the time by Dan Horn and Gib Hickman. Fortunately, no one received any injuries at these places. The storm then crossed Highway

29. The events of this account recounted above were taken from 1997 oral histories taken of Hayes Hayre, Faye (McIntyre) Talbott, Vivian McIntyre, and Lessie McIntyre. In referring to "your papa's place," John McIntyre was referring to the old Arthur Marion Douglas "Whig" McCann homeplace (now the Dell McCann place) where Ollie Pearl (McCann) McIntyre's stepmother, Celia (Weaver) McCann, continued to live. In fact that home was completely destroyed and large trees around it were completely pulled from the ground and dragged several yards, plowing up the ground.

30. *McNairy County Independent Appeal*, March 20, 1942.

31. The actual storm path was about a quarter mile wide.

32. *McNairy County Independent Appeal*, March 20, 1942.

45 damaging the Walter Miller place and destroying the old Putman house. There around McNairy Station, the old Henry settlement received a good deal of damage. The house where Frank Rouse was residing, on the Samuel Henry farm, was demolished. The houses of Charlie Henry and Jack Kirkpatrick were completely destroyed.

East of McNairy Station, in the old Griswell community, Virgil and Arnelia Smith's house was demolished. This was the old Dan Griswell place. The M.C. Patterson place was also damaged. Other damage done in the old Griswell community included the places of Ephe Griswell, Andrew McCann, and Celia McCann, the widow of Whig McCann. The old Whig McCann place was the one referred to by John McIntyre above.

The storm and its destructive winds continued to travel further northeast hitting the places of Walter Smith, George Calvin Holmes, and Bud Smith. Nelius Young's residence, owned by John Tedford, was badly damaged. Newell and Lexie Cone's residence was completely destroyed. They survived by taking refuge in a nearby culvert. Ervin Deaton's place, also called the old Carroll place, was completely demolished. It was then occupied by Major McCaskill.

As the tornado continued to travel, it's wrath became all the more furious, rather than letting up. The places of Robert Bailey and Herman Naylor were demolished. When the storm hit Millard Moore's place, true tragedy struck. Millard and his wife, Inez, the daughter of Murray F. Walker of Finger, were in their home along with their daughter, Sandra Kay. When the tornado swept through, Millard was left with a broken pelvis, Inez had been killed, and Sandra Kay was severely injured. Millard, with his broken pelvis, loaded Inez and Sandra Kay into a wheel barrow and pushed them up and down the hills to the nearest neighbor's place for help. This was on the Center Hill Road near where the Bullman Road crosses. They were eventually taken in an ambulance, probably Guy Bishop's funeral ambulance, to Finger to see Dr. Tucker. The ambulance stopped in front of Bishop's Store, where a number of men attempted to get Millard's boots off of his feet. Millard was in great pain and the men continuously jerking at his boots in an attempt to remove them did not help. Finally, one young man who was accustomed to wearing the same type of boots, removed them for Millard.

As the storm continued to move in both a fast and furious manner, the destruction did not subside. In the old Bullman Store community, a number of structures and other property were damaged and destroyed. Many houses and barns owned by the various members of the Bullman family were destroyed or badly damaged. The houses and barns of Bud Bullman, Elvis Bullman, George Bullman, and Otis Bullman were destroyed. In addition, Bud Bullman's store was destroyed and Elvis Bullman was injured.

Although much has been said regarding the destruction of barns, houses and sheds, nothing can compare to the destruction of the natural resources in north McNairy County and everywhere the storm traveled. Incalculable amounts of timber were downed, knarled, twisted and completely destroyed. Livestock of all types was completely wiped out on many farms. The newspaper reported that in some places so many chickens were destroyed that not one live bird could be found. Of course, automobiles and farm equipment were thrown and twisted beyond use.

From start to finish, throughout the South, the tornado claimed 156 lives and injured 1105 individuals. The breakdown of casualties was as such: Mississippi, 82 dead and 650 injured; Tennessee, 28 dead and 150 injured; Kentucky, 24 dead and 75 injured; Alabama, 2 dead and 10 injured; Illinois, 18 dead and 170 injured; and Indiana, 2 dead and 50 injured. This was the most deadly tornado to rip through McNairy County in the 20th century.

One Last Storm

The date of the last significant storm was believed to be around 1962, but this date is not certain. This storm consisted of two funnel clouds moving closely together. Where exactly it began is unknown, but it soon struck the Arthur Vires farmhouse, causing some structural damage. The storm traveled on completely destroying the house where the Reeves lived. The house actually exploded in the pressure of the funnel clouds. In an instant, it had taken the roof off of John and Ollie McIntyre's house across the road. As the storms gained strength it moved across the farmland and eventually destroyed Pink Cone's house. Other houses were destroyed and damaged, but these were still in the memory of many.

The Disappearance of Spy Jack

Over the years stories are told that often are revisited leaving behind additions, new drama, and other aspects of the story that were not exposed until recently. One such story may be that of Spy Jack. The story told was that a black man by the name of Spy Jack, evidently a nickname, was a member of the road crew engaged in building the Finger-Leapwood Road (present-day State Route 199). That road, built in 1929, was constructed in a comparatively primitive manner. Mules pulled breaking plows and most of the work was completed through sheer brute force. The road crew, whose foreman was a temperamental Floridian by the name of Morris, maintained a camp near Finger.[33] The road hands struck out from camp each day with a full day's work ahead of them.

On this particular crew was Spy Jack. Jack had a negative attitude and scornful disposition as it regarded others. For these attributes he made enemies more quickly than he made lasting friends. The story continues that Jack disappeared and was never heard from again. Most believed he was buried in one of the new road's levees. Yet time and research bring us new clues. The following story was recently revealed to the author. A black man by the name of Jack Spivey was employed as a road hand on the new Finger-Leapwood Road project in 1929. He and another black man were apparently owed money either in the form of back pay or a loan. Supposedly the two black men made an argument regarding the money owed them. In the heat of argument, the foreman shot both men fatally. Accordingly the two men were buried in one of the new levees then being constructed.

This account was passed down by individuals who lived near the highway and near the alleged location of the killings. At the time of the event, many of the ladies in the community watched the buzzards for clues as to Jack's disappearance. Certainly, such an event, if not well concealed, would be fodder for anyone with a tendency for gossip and intrigue.

---

33. Another source states the foreman to have been a fellow by the name of Fletcher, who did not hesitate to use the "black snake" and who was, as they say, a "rough customer."

William Whitt's Last Act

William Whitt's death could have been prevented, but in his haste to kill Grover McDaniel, he accidentally put the nails in his own coffin. For whatever reason, on late Friday afternoon, June 11, 1926, Whitt and McDaniel, while in the course of arguing got rough and tumble. Whitt, a man of some height and size, grabbed McDaniel, a much smaller and shorter individual, and held McDaniel against himself with McDaniel's back pressed against his own chest and then shot McDaniel.[34] According to one source, Whitt pointed the muzzle of the pistol at the top of McDaniel's head and the bullet traveled through McDaniel's body downwards before striking Whitt in the chest.[35] The 1926 newspaper report on the shooting stated that McDaniel died instantly and that "Whitt received a wound in the abdomen, and was hurried to a hospital in Corinth." The report went on to say that a warrant charging Whitt with first degree murder was sworn out.[36] Of course, the warrant wouldn't matter for Whitt died shortly thereafter.

The Killing of Jim Rufe Dickey[37]

William "Bill" Duberry, also spelled often as Dewberry, had been hard at work. He had a stash of beer that he was preparing to convert into whiskey. Be it understood, that this author has no idea how this is done, but trust that those telling the story are indeed qualified, or at least informed. However, something was dreadfully wrong with Bill Duberry's batch. Someone had salted the brew and it was passed around that the culprit was Jim Rufe Dickey. Regardless of Dickey's guilt or innocence, Duberry met Dickey in the road at the "foot" of Massey Hill, in the vicinity of the driveway entrances of Johnny and Murray Cook. On that

---

34. Passed through various members of the John A. McIntyre family, whose daughter was William Whitt's wife.

35. Roy R. McIntyre shared this account of Whitt's fatal actions with the author on May 18, 2002, while standing at Whitt's grave in Mt. Carmel Cemetery. Whitt was married to Roy McIntyre's aunt, Zelphia Roberta (McIntyre) Whitt.

36. *McNairy County Independent Appeal*, June 18, 1926.

37. The text of the original newspaper article regarding this story appeared previously in Naylor and Talbott, *Fingerprints*, but here the story is relived through the words of those who remembered the tragic event. The young man in the photograph is a young Jim Rufe Dickey.

Jim Rufe Dickey as a child

Monday night in May of 1921, Duberry put five shots in Dickey with his pistol, following an argument. Dickey died three hours later. Bill Duberry was taken to Selmer, the county seat, and jailed. He was later indicted for murder by the McNairy County Grand Jury. He was later tried by the circuit court and the issue of his imprisonment is subject to debate. Some sources state that Duberry went to prison while others state that he managed to avoid a prison sentence. Regardless, no further research has been conducted on the matter. As it happened that night, Jim Rufe Dickey's sister, Ophelia Dickey, was on her way to Bill Duberry's house with her granddaughter, Elizabeth Stovall Droke. Interestingly, Duberry later learned that Dickey had nothing to do with the incident. Unfortunately, Duberry had picked a fatal fight with the wrong man.

A Hunting Trip Turns Fatal

Jack Dickey and Troy Clayton, like many young men, decided early one September morning to try a little rabbit hunting. Like many before and since, they walked down the tracks of the Mobile and Ohio Railroad to try their luck at swamp rabbits. After spotting a rabbit, Troy jumped up to shoot it at the same time Jack was sighting the rabbit with his shotgun. Unfortunately, Troy jumped in the path of Jack's fire and was fatally wounded. Jack ran up the tracks toward town to get help for his downed friend. Several remembered the townsmen running south down the tracks to reach Troy.[38]

Following the publication of this work in 2003, Mr. Robert Beene memorialized in writing his own recollections of that sad day. Mr. Beene wrote as follows:

> I was one of the first ones out there when he [Clayton] was killed a short distance in front of the depot in the bottom.

---

38. Clifford Young and L.E. Talbott both remembered the event and the sight of the men running down the tracks to lend assistance to the dying boy.

There were 3 boys in the rabbit hunt: Troy Clayton, Jack Dickey and Raymond Patterson, Lucian's boy. They had only one gun, Troy's gun, a 20 gauge. It was said his [Troy's] Dad bought it [for] Christmas. The top of his head was blown off, his brains was on the ground when his dad got there. He picked up his brains with both his hands and put them back in his head. That was an awful sight to see. The section hands was working close to the depot. They came out and carried him on a tarp to Guy Bishop's, he was the undertaker at that time…I doubt if anyone is living now that was out there but me.

Robert Beene[39]

Troy was the only son of John Clayton. These events transpired on September 17, 1927, and Troy was laid to rest in the Finger Cemetery.

Death By Train

In late March 1907, one of the sons of Quinn Ingram, of the well-known and affluent Ingraham family, met a frightful demise. The eighteen year old boy was apparently thrown from the "local train" by a passing "express wagon near the track." According to the local newspaper of the time, he was instantly killed and his body badly mutilated.

Another local boy met his end on the mighty steel rails of progress. Allen R. Womble was born on July 4, 1885, the son of William B. Womble and wife Mary E. (Beene) Womble. Surviving photographs reveal that he was a handsome young man. He married Miss Bettie Naylor on July 23, 1905, with Horry Hodges acting as his bondman and Justice of the Peace of C.C. Plunk officiating. It appears that they had at least two children, Carl Womble and Mary Womble. Mary died in 1910 at less than one year of age. At some point after 1905, Allen and his wife moved to Memphis, Tennessee, where Allen worked as a streetcar conductor. He conducted Streetcar No. 533 and it was during this profession that Allen would lose his life while still a very young man. According to a newspaper at the time, Allen became a "first class conductor." On Friday, July 30, 1909, when the car he was driving was struck by a switch engine as it crossed the railroad tracks, Allen was killed instantly and a number of

---

39. Letter from Robert Beene to John E. Talbott dated May 15, 2004.

his passengers were seriously hurt. His body was sent to Finger and he was buried in Mount Carmel Cemetery.

The Clash of Wills

Will Plunk and Will Browder crossed paths one day in the road near where the Rudolph Barber home was built, present-day State Highway 199. It was told that Will Browder approached Will Plunk from behind while driving his Ford Model T. It was also told that Browder did so in a harassing manner. Regardless, when the fracas ended, Will Browder was shot and killed by the hand of one Will Plunk.[40]

The Wanderings of Lee Tacker

The morning was much like any other in West Tennessee as Lee Tacker approached the gate of Johnny McIntyre. Lee stopped his horse at the foot of the hill, hitched him to the fence, entered the gate, and lumbered up the incline. He had gifts in hand and prepared himself to say goodbye to his kinfolk. Life in Tennessee had not been easy for Lee, but he had found kindness among his cousin, her husband, and family. Lee was a first cousin to Ollie Pearl (McCann) McIntyre, the wife of John Robert "Johnny" McIntyre. Lee visited with the children and gave homemade dolls to two of McIntyre's daughters. He then informed his cousins that he planned to leave immediately to seek his fortunes in the west. Lee Tacker was never heard from again.

Certainly life had not been charmed for Lee Tacker. He was a good-hearted man given to vice. Among his most damaging was that of drinking. He spent the bulk of his wages on this vice. Yet, though a man with a drinking habit, he was not one to shun old fashioned manual labor. Lee often performed work such as cutting and splitting firewood and chopping cotton. Still his vices controlled. He was often jailed for excessive public drinking, also called "tippling." One afternoon while in Selmer, Johnny McIntyre passed by the county jail and heard someone calling his name. Looking up toward a cell window, McIntyre saw Lee Tacker, who quickly stated, "Johnny, do me a favor and go get me some chewing tobacco."

40. Marvin Hand of Hesperia, California, telephone interview with the author, 2001.

What is tragic about such stories as this is that such men often have great amounts of talent and intelligence. Lee was an extraordinary musician, his pastime being the fiddle. He came from a musically inclined family, many of whom could play a variety of stringed instruments. Lee planned to go to Arkansas or Missouri. Whether he reached his destination or not cannot be known. Perhaps he died on the way, due to his drinking or an accident. Then again, perhaps he made it, safe and secure. He could not read or write and therefore had no way of communicating with his family. Whatever became of Lee Tacker will forever be overshadowed by the mystery surrounding his disappearance.

CHAPTER TEN

WRITINGS OF SPECIAL HISTORICAL NOTE TO NORTH McNAIRY COUNTY

Journal writings—Personal letters—Published articles and accounts—Informative and humorous accounts of note—Business notes and accounts—Public records.

In this chapter are found a good number of accounts, notes, letters, and other writings which give one a special and personal look into life in the nineteenth and twentieth centuries. Some of them are humorous and others are laced with a touch of sadness. Some are simple and others are written in an ornate and descriptive manner. All are interesting and add further volume to our reservoir of local historical knowledge.

Keeping Up Those Old Roads

In these days of high gasoline taxes and every other tax imaginable, it is hard for most citizens to fathom the idea of pitching in to help keep up the roads. Despite the fact that potholes continue to occur and always will, now someone employed with the state department of transportation, county highway department, or city street department is quickly dispatched to fix the problem. However, at the turn of the twentieth century, it was not that simple. McNairy County, not a particularly wealthy county, had fairly bad roads and no strong tax system to support their maintenance. There was, however, an alternative to paying taxes for road upkeep. An individual could opt to perform manual labor or loan equipment and time to maintenance. The particular methods of election and record keeping for this system are currently unknown, but often various businessmen in the town were responsible for keeping up with who contributed to the upkeep of the various roads. Likely the county court appointed supervisors to assist in the upkeeping of the roads. Various records have been previously published in *Fingerprints: An Unofficial and Incomplete History of Finger, Tennessee*, and the first edition of *Let's Call It Finger: A History of North McNairy County and Finger, Tennessee and Its Surrounding Communities*. Those records were taken from the pages of Hugh L. Hodges' business ledgers for the years 1915 through 1922, and the records of H.H. Kirkpatrick.

Levi Benton McIntyre and the Problem of Temperance

During the early days of the twentieth century and prior to Prohibition, there were many groups and societies committed to the concept of temperance. Many community leaders advocated temperance or the refraining from drinking intoxicating liquors and beer. Those men who were members of fraternal organizations and societies were often forbidden by the rules of their organizations from drinking or advocating drinking of spirits, beers and liquors. It was just such rules and bylaws that caused Levi Benton McIntyre problems with his fellow brothers in the local lodge of the Independent Order of the Odd Fellows (I.O.O.F), No. 257, headquartered in Henderson, Tennessee, before moving to Finger, Tennessee in later years. Levi Benton "Ben" McIntyre had been a school teacher at Possum Trot Schoolhouse in the late 1890's, but had taken to tending bar for his relative, Ike Dickey. In 1907, Ike owned a saloon in Jackson, Tennessee. As temperance and refraining from encouraging others from partaking in such habit was integral to the beliefs of the Odd Fellows, McIntyre's barkeeping activities caused a serious problem.

Although, McIntyre was indeed dismissed from the fellowship of the Odd Fellows, the author chooses to let the letters tell the rest of the story.[1]

Henderson, Tenn.
May 3rd, 1907

Mr. L.B. McIntyre
Jackson, Tenn.
Dear Sir & Brother: —

By order of Forked Deer Lodge #257, I.O.O.F. I write you. It has come to the ears of the Lodge that you are engaged in "Bartending," "Saloon Keeping" or in the sale of whiskey or other intoxicating liquors for Ike Dickey at Jackson, Tenn. I cite you to Article XI, Section 17 of the Constitution of Subordinate lodges for Tennessee, in regard to members engaging in the sale of liquors.

Brother McIntyre, please answer at once and let the Lodge know whether you are engaged or not in the business of selling liquors.

Should you be engaged in this business and will quit it, the order will be only too glad to continue you as a member and brother in good standing but should you persist in it or pay no attention to these inquiries, the constitution as you see makes the lodge's duty very clear to them, which is to prefer charges against you and if upon investigation, the charges are proven true, to expel you from the order.

This the Lodge regrets very much to do, as they want you as a brother so long as you abide by the laws, constitution and by-laws of this order.

Brother McIntyre, you will see it is not a personal matter but a question of the Lodge's doing its duty and for your good and for the good of the order.

So please respond at once about this matter.

Yours Fraternally,
B.S. Smith, N.G.

---

1. The original letters between Levi Benton McIntyre and the Forked Deer Lodge of the Independent Order of the Odd Fellows from 1907 are in the private collection of the author.

Jackson, Tenn.
May 14 – 07

Mr. B.S. Smith, N.G.
Henderson, Tenn.
Dear Brother: —

Your inquiry of May 3rd, just to hand and contents duly noted and will confess that I am working for Ike Dickey and am all the time looking for something else to do and will quit here first as soon as I can get something else to do and I would rather withdraw from the order than to be expelled for I must confess my ignorance as to the constitutional by-laws and will get out of this business just as soon as I can.

Your Brother
L.B. McIntyre

∞

Henderson, Tenn.
June 28, 1907

Mr. L.B. McIntyre
Jackson, Tenn.
Dear Sir & Friend

Forked Deer Lodge # 257 met last night and ordered me to cite you to appear before said lodge at its next regular meeting night, Thursday, July 11, 1907, at 8 o'clock P.M. and answer the charges preferred against you of being engaged in bar-tending or selling liqors [*sic*].

Bro. McIntyre, it is your privilege to appear and explain the matters if wish to do so.

The Lodge does not wish to be hasty & is willing to grant you all your privileges & rights.

Yours Fraternally,
W.A. Davis, Sec'y.

∞

Jackson, Tenn.

July 3 – 07
Mr. B.S. Smith, N.G.
Henderson, Tenn.
Dear Sir and Friend: —
    This is to notify you that I can't be at the meeting next Thursday night so anything you all may do will have to satisfy me.
    I am sorry such is the case but never-the-less it is true.

Your friend,
L.B. McIntyre

McIntyre was expelled from the Lodge on July 13, 1907, by a vote of the Lodge's members. Interestingly, during the same period and at one of the same meetings at which his conduct was discussed, a decision was also made to visit the grave of his long dead grandfather, Robert Thompson McIntyre, as well as that of a Brother Clayton, at Mount Carmel Cemetery.

Lula (Womble) McIntyre's Little Business Ledger[2]

The following list almost reads like one which could be expected to be found in someone's family Bible, but this particular item was found in Lula McIntyre's little business ledger. Here she has recorded local deaths and like most Americans during the Second World War, it is apparent that Lula McIntyre had great interest in the boys from her small town who were doing their part, as a few of them are also mentioned. Certainly the list of servicemen as contained in her little journal is not complete, but contains a couple from the early years of American participation.

Kermit Davis left January 10, 1942.
William More (Moore's) boy got killed January 9 and brought back
    the 15th of January 1942.
Roy McIntyre come home January 13, 1942.
March 14 (1942), Thomas Naylor died.
March 16 (1942), Inez More (Moore) killed by Storm.

---

2. This tiny ledger was given to the author by the descendents of Lula McIntyre in 1993. It contains only a few pages with both business and personal notes.

Kermit Davis left March 17th, 1942.
Kermit Davis left July 14, 1942.
Mrs. Mary O'Neal died March 6, 1942.
Mr. Joe Weaver passed away March 6, 1942.
Roy McIntyre left August 16, 1942.
Roy McIntyre left January 25, 1943.
Kermit Davis left October 24, 1942.
Kermit Davis left January 21, 1943.

McIntyre also kept a number of other interesting records for primarily business purposes, including the dividends enjoyed from the ownership of her father's, Thomas J. Wemble, bank stocks, lists of farmhands and others sharing in the profits of the crops, and numerous other expenses and revenues. The following record regards the baling of hay and the pay given to those who helped.

Paid out in September—Worked in Hay
- Hatton Williams $2.25
- Guy Brown $2.25
- Oscar Joyner $0.75
- Hayse Hayre & Howard Young $0.75
- Lester Weaver $0.75
- W.A. McIntyre $1.00 (not paid)
- Roy McIntyre $1.00
- Ila Brown $1.00 (not paid)

Other entries regard the amounts paid for certain necessities. These range from firewood to household goods and certain grocery items. Ms. McIntyre also recorded the amounts she was paid for certain items as eggs, chickens, and cotton.

July 30, 1942
- 1¼ cord of stove wood $7.50
- 1 cord of stove wood $6.00

January 1943
- Sack flour $2.00
- Matches $0.25

Soda	$0.05
Baking powders	$0.10
Apples	$0.20
Oranges	$0.10
Bread	$0.10
Aspirin tablets	$0.10
Sugar (5 pounds)	$0.35
Onion plants	$0.15

January 13, 1943
  Sold chickens for $22.12.

January 12, 1943	Eggs, 7 dozen at 30 cents— $2.10
January 19, 1943	Eggs, 4 dozen at 31 cents
January 24, 1943	Eggs, 2½ dozen at 31 cents
February 15, 1943	Eggs, 8 dozen at 32 cents $2.56
February 15, 1943	Eggs, 5 dozen at 32 cents $1.60
February 15, 1943	Eggs, 7 dozen at 30 cents $2.10

As one will notice, the cost of many items which are often used today are certainly less than in the 1940s than today. So often was the costs of labor and materials for building. The entry below dealt with the cost of upkeep on the Tom Womble place, the house now occupied by Georgia and Jerry Russom.

House Covering	$190.00
Work on Barn and garden	$9.00
Car note	$7.85
Grass seeds	$8.00
Fertilizer	$7.00

One very interesting record found in the pages of this tiny book was the doctor bills incurred by Thomas J. Womble shortly before his death, which were paid out by his administrator in the settlement of his estate. These prices provide some idea of the cost of medical care prior to the Second World War, just as the nation was coming out of the worst economic disaster in history, the Great Depression of the 1930s. Womble's medical bills for 1939, the year of his death, were as follows: Dr. Nathaniel A. Tucker is due the amount of $13.50 and Dr. William Henry

Hodges is due the amount of $10.00. The total amount of Womble's funeral expenses in 1939 was $378.50, due to Rowsey and Morgan Funeral Home. Another interesting small entry showed a cord of firewood to cost $6 in 1942.

Personal Letters of T.J. Womble

In the days prior to the widespread use of the telephone, texting, the Internet, the various versions of e-mail, and now social media, an individual was almost entirely dependent upon either telegraphs, letters or personal visits. Certainly this fostered a greater appreciation for one's acquaintances, friends, and family. Old letters are often difficult to acquire and when they are, they provide a wonderful source of personal and community history as glimpsed through the eyes of the writer. The following three letters were written by Thomas J. Womble, pictured above, a longtime merchant and farmer in the Finger area. The person to whom two of these are written is currently unknown. One is written to Womble's half-brother, Lee Andrew Weaver, then living in Kenton, Tennessee. These letters have been edited in order that their grammar and spelling would be better understood.[3] These letters allow the writer to talk about many of the same subjects he would talk about in person to the individual: the weather, the crops, local government and action, people's health, and, of course, business, always on the mind of many men in the early twentieth century. It appears these letters were first written in a rough draft form in Womble's ledger and then

T.J. Womble

---

3. If one is curious as to how these letters originally appeared, please see the Womble-Weaver letter reprinted in original form in Naylor and Talbott, *Fingerprints*.

he, it can be surmised, mailed a final version to its recipient, retaining a copy for Womble's records.[4]

Letter One
T.J. Womble to L.A. Weaver[5]

Finger, Tennessee

Brother and family,

After hearing from you I have neglected to answer your letter I received from you, but was glad to hear from you all. This has been the hardest time to try to make a crop that I ever saw. Crops are small and sorry. You can bet cotton is small. You can bet I ain't got any planted. I have commenced to laying by my corn. We had a fine rain Friday evening and it was needed bad. It has been so cold stuff won't grow, but it will come on now. I guess your crop is fine. Well, L.A., we have a tick law now and are under a warrantee law and you can bet the people don't like it much.[6] We have got some night riders here.[7] They are giving some others to turn out their corn and if not turned out, they will go up in ashes. But I think it is more for revenge than anything else. Well, Lee, Sam McIntyre came up and Lula went back with him. Lucy has been sick, but is better now. I will close by saying "come and see us all."

---

4. All three of these letters were found in Thomas J. Womble's *1904 Cash and Barter Book*.

5. Taken from page 55 of Womble's *1904 Cash and Barter Book*.

6. Some mention or record regarding McNairy County's tick and warrantee laws were at one time found in the McNairy County Register of Deeds office.

7. Womble mentions night riders in McNairy County, which is interesting because in the period that this letter was written—between 1904 and 1909—night riders plagued the Reelfoot area and the area around which Lee Weaver was then living.

WRITINGS OF SPECIAL HISTORICAL NOTE

Thomas J. Womble and wife Lucy in front of their house.

Letter Two

T.J. Womble to Unknown Friend[8]

Finger, Tennessee
This April the 5th 1908
Dear old friend,
After so long a time I will answer your letter and was sure glad to hear from you all. We are all well at this time, hope you are the same. Well, W.B. and family are all okay.[9] Well, I have now much to write. I now have corn planted yet it rains every week so the people's (crops) will be late this year. Me and Lucy was aiming to start to see you and Lucy last Sunday, but I told Lucy that we would have to stop on the way, for old Fanny would have a mule on the way. She has got the best mule from your jack that she ever had. It will be just the color of old Fanny. I believe that Major James will come by out in your country.[10] Everything is on the drag here now. I

---

8. This letter was found on page 288 of Womble's *1904 Cash and Barter Book*.

9. This is probably referring to Womble's brother, William "Bill" Womble, who lived several miles outside of Finger.

10. Major James was a merchant in Finger and former schoolteacher. This may be referring to his move out west with his wife, Callie (McIntyre) James, the daughter of his business partner James Robert McIntyre, of McIntyre, James, and Company General Merchandise. James' move to the western states was made around this period.

do not know what I will do by fall, but I think now I will sell out and go somewhere. I will not farm next year. I can beat farming and do nothing here.

Letter Three

T.J. Womble to N.R. _____[11]

Hello N.R.,

After so long a time, I will answer your letter and was glad to hear from you all. We are all well, hope these few lines will find you all the same. My crop is very good. Cotton is not as good as people thought it was. It will be about as good as it was last year. Corn is better than it was last year. I am building a house for Lula and Sam where old Bill Draper lived on the road.[12] I will turn old Uncle Bill off and also Gabe.[13] Well, Finger is very dull now. Cotton opened up at nine cents and will be cheaper soon. This is Billy Bryan's year, but I don't think he will come in.[14] We are having less sickness here now than we have had in a long time, so Dr. Hodges says.[15] Old McNairy is almost dead as it can be now. Cross has bought the Dayton Sawmill and Gin outfit and I guess they will leave there soon and go to Martin, Tennessee. That is their talk now.

---

11. This particular letter was found on page 383 of the same ledger, Womble's *1904 Cash and Barter Book*.

12. This house stood until around the year 2007; it was the house known as the old Oscar Joyner place, on Payne Road, just east of Finger.

13. Bill Draper and Gabe Draper were black men who lived in the community.

14. This letter was most certainly written in 1908, as the Billy Bryan referred to is the Great Commoner William Jennings Bryan. Bryan, a Progressive Democrat, was running for President on the Democratic ticket in 1908, just as he had in 1896 and in 1900. Three times the Democratic nominee for President, three times Bryan was defeated. He would later be known for his role as a prosecutor, opposite Clarence Darrow, in the sensational trial of Rhea County High School teacher John T. Scopes, the evolution trial also known as the Scopes Monkey Trial in 1925. Bryan died in Dayton, Tennessee, shortly after the close of the trial.

15. Dr. William Henry Hodges (1869–1941) of Finger.

The Old Hodges Oak Tree[16]
by Horry Hodges

Not long ago the announcement was made early one morning by a member of the family that the Old Oak had been blown down in the night. This brought to mind memories of the past, tinged with feelings of sadness. Though the old tree had been dead several years, yet it was held in the highest esteem by members of the family for the good it had done in the past, for the hopes it had inspired, and for the silent lessons it had taught from its youth to the day of its death.

Through tradition handed down by the pioneers, settlers, and relatives of ours in this section, we have learned the natural history of this old tree.

And here it is: Our people settled here in 1818, when the nearest neighbors lived four miles away, at what is now called the Red House.[17] In 1826, just a few years after West Tennessee was opened for settlement, they felled a giant oak as they worked in the unbroken forests. As this 'Patriarch of Trees,' as the English poet Dryden called the oak, came crashing to the ground, and breaking and smashing saplings, trunks of trees, limbs and branches, it brought down and pinned under its ponderous body a slender post oak sapling about four inches in diameter.

Horry Hodges

The little oak, thus bowed down by the ponderous weight of the mighty monarch, was released from its miserable attitude by a settler who chopped off its top. The humble little tree then changed its position

---

16. This reflective discourse was originally published by Professor Horry Hodges' friends the Abernathy's of Selmer, Tennessee, in their newspaper, the *McNairy County Independent Appeal* on September 7, 1934.

17. The Red House was the home built by John S. Ingraham, actually sometime in the early 1820's. It is probably safe to assume that to be the period in which Professor Horry Hodges' family settled, as 1818 was the year of the treaty with the Chickasaw. This treaty as mentioned in chapter two of this work gave the area including north McNairy County to the white settlers.

from a 'dead level to a perpendicular,' and thus stood a truncated sapling in the midst of the stately trees of the forest. The necessities and demands of the times caused the destruction of all the trees on that immediate premises except the little oak.

It was about twenty-five feet high and a cluster of branches grew near the top, extending in all directions except downward. It grew and waxed strong in beauty and symmetry.

Viewed from any point on the compass, this tree had the appearance of a hemisphere, balanced on a column more than four feet in diameter. It was the largest tree in all the section round about. When it reached its majority, its maturity, and its prime, it was a thing of beauty and a joy for more than one century. At high noon the shadow of this unique tree was almost circular and more than 100 feet in diameter. No ray of light ever touched the ground under this tree except early in the morning and late in the afternoon.

The oak, ash, and elm, and various other trees have been held as sacred by numerous tribes and nationalities of the human race from the beginning to the present time.

The oak was the sacred tree, and object of worship of the Celtic race in Gaul on the Continent, and in Britain, across the Channel. The representatives of the old Druidical priesthood assembled in the sacred groves, composed of sacred oaks, made their articles of religion, studied the origin and destiny of man, prayed and meditated upon the immortality of the soul.

This race was one of the seven divisions of the Aryan or Indo-European race, and the oak tree was the symbol of its religion. This old Druidical religion has been a veritable fountain of spiritual knowledge and history, from which streams have poured in all the succeeding centuries.

The "oldest historical tree in the world" is on the island of Borneo. It is a cutting from the famous tree in India, 'under whose contemplative shade' Buddha (Gotama) sat and received the inspiration of a religion at whose shrines and fanes and alters more than 180 million devotees bow at this day. This sacred tree is a kind of fig and is 2179 years old.

Trees are not only used for ceremonial rites and religious purposes, but are held in high esteem for the endurance of the timber value in them.

The shrine of Edward the Confessor, the last of the Saxon kings, was built nearly nine centuries ago. It is in good condition today. This shrine is in Westminster Abbey.

The Charter of Connecticut was concealed in the body of an oak in 1687. That tree became famous and was blown down by a storm in 1886.

Washington took charge of the Continental Army under the branches of an elm and in the following seven years so demeaned himself that he passed on to 'Fame's Eternal Camping Ground' and the elms passed into history.

In 1900 a giant California redwood was felled that was 1763 years old when Columbus discovered America. Scientists figured out the age of that tree.

But I must leave these famous trees and go in imagination back to the cooling breezes and refreshing shades of my old oak. This tree, about which I write, was not, is not, and will not be very historical. It spent its life "far from the maddening crowd's ignoble strife." So did the great German philosopher Kant, who changed the current of history and revolutionized the thought of the world. In writing his history, it was found that he was never more than twelve miles from home.

My tree was the Brave Old, though it withstood the droughts, floods, storms, tempests, heat, and cold for one and one-half centuries. It was not the oak that furnished the staves that formed and shaped the well-known old bucket that hung in the proverbial old well. No eccentric and erudite personage, with lofty and poetic imagination, 'in fiery, frenzy rolling,' has ever stopped to make this old tree the subject of its immortal song.

No painter with his brush, no sculptor with his chisel, has left a reminder of this old tree. No scientist, no naturalist, has made any postmortem examination of this old tree's body to throw light on some dubious theory or hypothesis of forestry or botany.

No philosopher, no dreamer, has used its spirit to represent the soul, or to demonstrate man's place in nature.

And yet, this tree is not unwept, nor is it unsung, and I should note that it is not unhonored.

We regretted to see this old tree perish, for its shade was the delectable scene of many lofty conversations on various subjects in the long ago.

If the old tree could speak today, 'from the lips of the unreplying dead,' it "could a tale unfold" that would be entertaining, instructive, and helpful.

It could tell the captivating stories that it heard upon the return of the seasoned and patriotic veterans from the Mexican War, as they told of their triumphant march from Palo Alto via Buena Vista, Monterey, Vera Cruz, and on to the City of Mexico.[18]

It could tell of countless theological discussions, dating from the county's pioneer days, in which the Trinitarian was against the Unitarian, and the Arminian was against the Calvinist.

The tree, in its prime, heard the neighbors, as they waxed warm in their discussions of the Dred Scott decision, handed down by Chief Justice Roger B. Taney, on March 6, 1857.

It could tell the complete history of the County, State, and Nation, for it has heard it all.

Many distinguished men and women have enjoyed the hospitality of this tree of scared memory. Many Primitive Baptist preachers in the long ago were in our home and enjoyed the shade of the old tree, and among these preachers were T.S. Dalton of Baltimore, Md., S.F. Cayce of Kentucky, Claude Cayce of Arkansas, Ben Casey of Mississippi, J.E.W. Jenkins, Nicholas Gooch and many others.[19]

Gen. W.J. Smith, the Hon. James Warren, State Senator Manley Tillman and Prof. M.R. Abernathy were among the strong characters who saw and admired this unique tree.[20]

In 1885, Prof. M.R. Abernathy was a welcome guest in our home for a few days while he was conducting a Teacher's Institute at Lain's Academy.

As he stood near this tree, he told us of the famous trees of history. He talked to a small group just as of he were addressing a convocation of the brightest minds of the earth. So here endeth my 'didactic disquisition' on the Old Oak.

---

18. Many family friends of the Hodges' were adventuresome and seasoned military men who when traveling by the old family farm were glad to stop and share tales of battlefield triumphs and glories.

19. It must be remembered that Captain Elijah J. Hodges was also a Primitive Baptist minister.

20. These men were gentlemen with whom Captain Hodges had served in his many capacities as soldier, legislator, and preacher.

Sargent Prentiss "Prince" Freeling
A Legal Giant from North McNairy County

One of north McNairy County's unsung success stories was a young man named Sargent Prentiss "Prince" Freeling. He was born on January 25, 1874, in north McNairy County and grew up there, the son of John Freeling. He graduated from Southwest Baptist University in Jackson, Tennessee, in 1893. He later attended Harvard University Law School in Boston, Massachusetts and graduated from that prestigious law school in their 1899 class.[21] He was admitted to the Oklahoma bar in 1900 after locating in Pottawatomie, Oklahoma.[22] He served as Deputy Attorney for Pottawatomie County from 1901 until 1907.[23] He was gifted and outstanding orator and was elected to the office of Oklahoma State Attorney General in 1914 and served in that position until 1922.

Sargent Prentiss Freeling

During Freeling's tenure as Attorney General, he had the opportunity and talent to handle a number of high profile cases. These cases had important consequences in the legal history of the early twentieth century. He was the Attorney General of the state at the time of the tragic Tulsa race riots in 1917. In 1920, the duties of his office intersected with Presidential politics. The year 1920 saw the rejection of Wilsonian principles at the polls and the election of an amiable but wholly ineffective United States Senator from Ohio, Warren G. Harding. One of the appointments which Harding would be forced to make was that of Secretary of the Interior. The Department of Interior handled, then and now, such matters at the management of

---

21. Secretary's Report, Harvard Law School, 1899.
22. www.oklahoma heritage.com/portals/0/PDF's/HOF%20bios/Freeling,%20 Prince pdf
23. *Id.*

federally owned lands, relations with Native Americans and the native of leasing and management of federally owned natural resources.

In 1920, President-elect Harding's first choice to lead the Interior Department was Ardmore, Oklahoma oilman and in-law of Florence Harding, Jake Hamon. Hamon was preparing to move his wife to the capitol city of Washington, D.C. However, Hamon's longtime mistress, Clara (Smith) Hamon—who adopted his surname—preferred not to be left behind in Oklahoma while her lover and his usually estranged wife settled in the hustle, bustle and excitement of the nation's capitol. On November 21, 1920, after having told Clara to clear out and fade out of his life after ten years of devotion, Jake Hamon lay down in his Armore, Oklahoma hotel room. Clara emerged from the shadows and stroked his forehead with her left hand and shot him in the chest with her right hand. The bullet tore through his ribs and lodged in his liver. He lived five days and died. Thereafter, Clara was charged with murder and her trial began on March 10, 1921, lasting a week. The prosecutor was none other than the state's Attorney General, Sargent Prentiss Freeling. The trial was sensational and the jury returned a verdict of "not guilty" surprising everyone including Freeling and Clara Smith Hamon.[24]

In 1921, Prince Freeling argued the case for which he is best known. As the Attorney General for Oklahoma, he argued the case of the state of Oklahoma in its Red River boundary line dispute with the state of Texas. The case of *State of Oklahoma v. State of Texas (United States, Intervener)*, 258 U.S. 574, 42 S.Ct. 406 (1921) was the next step in an already long history of the boundary dispute between the states. That controversy has continued until even recently. However, in 1921, the dispute again revolved around the ownership of the river bed of the Red River. Oklahoma and the United States claimed the boundary ran along the south bank of the river but Texas claimed the medial line of the river as the boundary. In this case, the Court's concern was with proprietary claims to the bed of the river and to the proceeds of oil and gas taken from a 43-mile section of the southerly half of the river.

After the high Court acquired jurisdiction in the matter, the state of Oklahoma asserted that it held title to the entire river bed and the state of Texas claimed title to the southerly half. The United States disputed

---

24. Laton McCartney, *The Teapot Dome Scandal: How Big Oil Bought the Harding White House and Tried to Steal the Country* (New York: Random House, 2008), 57–59. All information regarding the Jake Hamon murder is found in this particular work.

both claims and asserted full proprietorship of the southerly half and an interest in portions of the northerly half due to its relation to Indian allottees. There were also a number of disputes, even armed conflicts, regarding possession of the river bed and surrounding area due to the exploitation of oil and gas in the region. The case is complicated and the Court's findings were too complicated to expound upon in this article; what matters is how Freeling handled the case.

The Oklahoma-Texas boundary dispute was not Freeling's first appearance before the United States Supreme Court. He has argued cases before the nation's highest court on previous occasions including the case of *Shaffer v. Howard*, 249 U.S. 200 (1919). Freeling was quoted as saying, "I would rather be mistaken than to fail to be friendly to someone who needs it worse than I." Freeling continued with his legal career and was regarded highly as a statesman and orator. He authored an interesting and provocative little volume entitled, *The Trial of Jesus Christ from a Lawyer's Standpoint*. Such projects demonstrate the breadth of Freeling's mind and intellect. He died suddenly of a heart attack in 1937 in his hotel room. He was buried in Rose Hill Burial Park in Oklahoma City, Oklahoma.

The Tinsley Settlement

In the course of researching, examining, and writing the history of an area or location, the researcher/author usually has a ready knowledge of the names and geographic subdivisions of the area in question. In other words, it is seldom that he finds a new name or new political or geographic subdivision following his initial research. However, the author of the present work did make an interesting discovery in the preparation and research for this work.

After more than ten years of intense research into the colorful history of north McNairy County and its many different communities, a new community or community name surfaced during a survey of antique maps conducted by the author. The map in question included a number of counties, but was labeled, *Chester and McNairy Counties, Tennessee, ca. 1875*.[25] Due south of the Sweetlips community was an apparent community called "Tinsley."

25. Frank A. Gray, *Gray's New Map of Kentucky and Tennessee*. The original was undated and should thus remain, for the 1875 date cannot be authentic as Chester County was not formed until 1882.

Certainly this was an exciting find, if not also a mysterious one. For weeks, people were consulted, books referenced and re-referenced, and maps of all types and categories consulted, to no avail. The only "proof" that Tinsley ever existed was confined solely to this one random map discovery. Unlike the story of Anderson's Store, which had been passed down through successive generations and had endured, no one held any recollection or tradition regarding the lost community of Tinsley.

Then luck, and no more, struck. Bits and pieces of information just began to surface in the search for other facts. The initial discovery of this local community disclosed that Tinsley was located in north McNairy County, even following the formation of Chester County, just a short distance, probably no more than an eighth of a mile, east of Tar Creek. That which follows is a short discourse on what has been discovered regarding Tinsley.

A post office was established at this location on November 1, 1875, and on the approved application was the name "Tinsley."[26] Next comes the question of why that particular name was used. The first, and only, postmaster of Tinsley was a man by the name of Tinsley Weaver.[27] Exactly who this man was, and from which set of Weavers he came, is not currently known. It is known, however, that Tinsley Weaver served on the McNairy County Quarterly Court from 1865 until 1870, at the least.[28] Weaver also performed a total of nineteen weddings in his capacity as a justice of the peace during that period.[29] Tinsley Weaver was born in or around the year 1799 in North Carolina. His wife, Martha, was born there also in or around the year 1798. The number and names of their children, if any, is currently unknown. In 1860, the couple was living in the Anderson Store area.[30] According to available records, Tinsley Weaver served as postmaster of Tinsley until October 20, 1884, when the post office was discontinued and merged with the Sweetlips Post Office, now in Chester County.[31] Interestingly enough, that would put Tinsley Weaver

---

26. Reflections Committee, *Reflections: A History of McNairy County, Tennessee.*
27. *Id.*
28. McNairy County Marriage Records, 1861–1911.
29. *Id.*
30. This information in addition to their birth years comes from 1860 U.S. Census.
31. Reflections Committee, *Reflections: A History of McNairy County, Tennessee.*

at age 85 when he stepped down as postmaster. When Weaver and his wife passed away is currently unknown, as is the location of their burials.

Our Small Communities in North McNairy County

As with any rural area, the region of north McNairy County possesses small communities within communities. In the Finger area, a number of communities grew around the concentration of settlers and most often families in one particular area. A number of names have come and gone into the dusty leaves of history in the last 190 years. Some we have come to know because of the records left behind in the form of deeds and vintage newspapers. To others we have become accustomed through stories and tales of days long since passed. Where were these now extinct communities and who resided there? These questions are answered in some cases and remain a mystery in others.

Some we may identify through the use of geographic, geologic, or natural occurrences and others by familial name. Certainly some physical concrete reason lies behind the naming of Red Hill, Black Jack Ridge, Willow Lane, Cotton Ridge, Rabbit Ridge, Carroll Branch, Tar Creek, Rock Hill, and Rocky Knob. These names were not chosen at random. Black Jack Ridge was a ridge very close to the town of Finger. The names of its long deceased residents mark its location. The McIntyres, Wombles, and Hodges resided along this ridge or in close proximity. Rabbit Ridge was said to be abundant with the small furry creature. It runs near the old Purdy-Lexington Highway on the old William Taylor Anderson plantation.

Others took their name from the families who occupied their hills, ridges, and hollows. The names Plunktown and Wilsontown come to mind. It is most assured the good and humble residents of these small communities did not abide by these names. These names were applied by others for the purposes of identifying such areas with such high concentrations of a particular family. The best way to gather a notion of the population of Plunktown is to take a leisurely stroll through old Plunk Cemetery. The sketch of the Plunk family provided in Chapter Two of this work discusses in some detail the early history of this family and therefore suffices for purposes of this chapter. Many of the children of Jacob Plunk, son of Dr. Peter Plunk, remained in this community to raise their children and farm the land. Still many descendants of the Plunks remain on nearby farms and within minutes of the old burying ground.

The area referred to by some as Wilsontown was located just off of present-day Litt Wilson Road. A number of houses once lined the old ridge over which the road travels. None of the old houses remain, but many of the Litt Wilson family still reside along this stretch. In the days that are gone, the father and brothers of Justice of the Peace Litt Wilson lived along this ridge. They included William Wilson, Emitt Wilson, Tom Whitt and wife (herself a Wilson), and others of the family. Another brother, Jess Wilson, lived in a small house located on the Mount Carmel Road. This house stood until about twenty-five years ago.

An area around present-day Hopewell Baptist Church and Cemetery was known as Bullman's Store. As could be quite easily determined, the community took its name from a business. George N. Bullman, a Union veteran of the War Between the States, established a small store on his farm in the years following the war. Apparently this enterprise was continued by succeeding members of the family. A large family, the Bullmans were known for their kindness and decency to others. It is thought the store was also a voting precinct was located at the store. It was also in this community that the Poplar Springs School was located.

Close to the actual Bullman store building was the Bailey farm. Here, Edgar W. Bailey and family lived. Edgar and Bud Bullman operated a cotton gin and sawmill on Bailey's farm. In the operation of the gin, the gentlemen dumped the cotton into the hopper from large baskets which was then processed through the power of a steam engine. When ginning season ended, the apparatus was put to work as a sawmill. The depression left behind from the old mill pond can still be found just yards from the west side of the old Bailey house. Edgar and his wife raised a young man by the name of Arl Keel.[32] He was the son of Martha (Plunk) Keel, who died in 1908 and was buried in Mount Carmel Cemetery. Apparently, Arl was a young man with a mischievous streak. It was once told that Edgar went to begin work ginning one day and found Arl asleep in the area of the hopper, dangerously close to the mechanisms which could have injured a person the most.

---

32. Keel's name may have been spelled "Irel." This is a possibility in that Edgar's grandson was named Irel, pronounced Arl.

It must be remembered that a community does not have to possess businesses, a post office or any official governmental charter to claim the title of community. Such status may be liberally granted by virtue of a number of characteristics including its inhabitants, features and economic activity. However, in the rural areas comprising McNairy and Chester counties, a community could claim such status by the number of one particular family and its branches and their involvement in the area's development and control.

Some communities took their names from churches and schools. Iola and Fairview took their names from community schoolhouses, although it is entirely possible that both schools came along after the community name, but such determinations are now difficult to make. New Church took its name from Maggie Jones Memorial Methodist Church. Following the construction of the church building in 1915, local residents began to referring to the community in general as "New Church" referencing the fact that a new church had just been built. Some of the names known to this area included the Vires, Nash, Plunk, and Amerson families, just to name a few.

Indeed our smaller communities were vital to both their residents and to the rest of us. Their history and ideas as individuals, families, and communities have made the rest of us the richer. Unfortunately, most have ceased to exist physically and demographically. For the most part, they are now relegated to the past with its fading memories and aging papers.

Was There Really a Cotton Ridge, and Where Was It?

Much like the Tinsley community, there is mystery surrounding the existence of a community or area known by the name "Cotton Ridge." In many years of researching the history of the area, never did the name appear. Then one day it did. The late Hayse Hayre, an avowed student of history and fine Christian gentleman, called the author one evening and asked the question, "Have you ever heard anyone talk of a place called Cotton Ridge?" This was quickly followed by the question, "Was it the name of the Finger area once?" Someone had appeared at the McNairy County Courthouse researching their family and produced an old letter discussing the "history" of Cotton Ridge. After some discussion, the decision was made that no such place existed in this area. But perhaps somewhere in the span of the years, some early settlers did call some portion of north McNairy County by that particular name. Perhaps such a possibility cannot be summarily dismissed. Since then, two other references have surfaced regarding Cotton Ridge. The evidence, scant as it may be and questionable as it may be, is presented on these pages.

The letter in its entirety will be reproduced on these pages for the investigation and perusal of the reader and the student of history. However, the other two pieces of a questionable and perhaps somewhat confusing puzzle will be presented first. Among the papers of the late Cordie L. Majors, former McNairy County superintendent of schools, was a typed page purporting to be the transcription of an old newspaper clipping, although no evidence of the actual clipping surfaced. The following is the only explanation of the "clipping."

> Albert Lott, of the 17th District, was in to see us on the 25th of January 1936. While here he gave us a clipping from an old paper, which he found among the effects of the father, D.H. Lott. It was found in the old family Bible.

The "clipping" was entitled *Good Springs* and included the following line: "Tom Beurey settled at Cotton Ridge in 1800." Another reference to this place called Cotton Ridge was found in the McNairy County Deed Books. On page 307 of deed book H was found a description including the phrase "for cash in Hand at Cotton Ridge in McNairy County, Aug. 2, 1860, J.P. Blakely sold to J.P. Peeples a two year old bay filly and two head of cattle."

The most interesting item regarding Cotton Ridge was a letter from a grandfather to his grandson. In 1931, a gentleman by the name of Thomas Benton Blakely wrote to his grandson Thomas Blakely Wilhite about his own youthful experiences and some of the people he knew in his youth. The letter mentions a number of prominent north McNairy countians. Just a very few minor corrections have been made in order to improve the flow and grammar of the letter.

Coal Hill, Arkansas
January 10th, 1931
Mr. Thomas Blakely Wilhite
Nashville, Arkansas

My Dear Thomas, sparing partner and grandson:

When I was just your age, 4 years old, I went to Memphis, Tennessee. My father was in the war and was stationed at Memphis, and my mother, little sister Dorah and Aunt Pagan Barham went to see my father. My aunt went to see her son Leander Barham who was afterwards killed in the corner of a fence, he and a young man, George Manus, while they were asleep killed by bushwhackers. I remember very little about the trip, however, I can remember my aunt lost her pocket book. We camped and she walked back several miles to look for it. I do not know if whither she found it or not. I can remember the soldiers and the little tents and going down on the bank of the Mississippi River. I thought it was a very large river. I was born March 25, 1859, in a little log house chinked in the suburbs of Cotton Ridge, Tennessee, a little town of about 29 inhabitants.

During the war, my mother moved to town on a small farm where we lived until I was 9 years old; my grandfather owned a water mill about 200 yards from his home, a big two-story log house. It was in the millpond I leaned to swim when I was about 7 years old.

My father came home in June of 1865, brother Pink [Dr. Pinkney Blakely] and I was at school when we heard my father was at home. We ran all the way home, a distance of about 2 miles. I was not very well acquainted with my father as I had never seen him but once as I remember. That was in Memphis in 1863. You see, he left home when I was 2 years old, hence my limited acquaintance. It was in this millpond that my father would let us boys go swimming as often as we wanted to, if we would go in before breakfast. We went in between daylight and sun up beginning about the first of

March and continuing through the spring, summer and fall and about the 15th of November we would go into winter quarters. I became an expert in the water, could swim like a duck and dive like a fish.

The first school I ever attended was the summer of 1865. The teacher's name was John Canterbury, a cripple caused from infantile paralysis. I did not know then what was the cause, but I know now. Well, I continued to attend the Cotton Ridge School every summer until I was 9 years old when we moved to Graves County, Kentucky, 15 miles from Mayfield, the county seat. By the way, it was in Mayfield that I saw my first man hanged. I can well remember how he was dressed. He said he did not do the actual killing. The man he was with was a very bad man. He told his pal to come away and let the woman alone, but instead his pal killed her but the real killer was never caught as I understand.

Well, I can remember the move from Cotton Ridge, McNairy County, Tennessee, to Viola Station, Kentucky. We moved by way of trucks pulled by a yoke of steers, one red and a black one. The red steer was named after me, "Tom", and the black one's name was "Dick." It was about 1868 and the roads were very bad and muddy, so we made very slow progress. I remember we got within about 10 miles of our goal, Wash Peeples [William Washington Peeples], a cousin of mine, who had been with us, left us one morning and walked ahead of the moving van to tell the news. It sure did make us sore as when we got there we had no strange news to tell as Wash had told it all. My grandfather and some uncles and aunts lived in Kentucky at that time, so when we arrived my father looked around and bought a farm from old man Taylor. The house on the farm was a two-story house, a big room and a kitchen, a hall between so we was well fixed for room and shelter. Us boys worked on the farm, made and gathered crops, going to school about three months each year after crops was made. We lived on this farm 5 years, Mother died on the 23rd day of November 1872 and was buried the next day in a country graveyard on Brother Pink's birthday. In

March 1873, my father married a Mrs. McCalister who had 4 children. We did not get along, so in December 1873, we broke up housekeeping and moved back to Tennessee, leaving my stepmother and half-brother in Kentucky.

Lest I forget, my mother (Mary E. (Peeples) Blakely) died three days after my little brother Ira was born. It was my mother's request that her sister, Aunt Eunice [Eunice (Peeples) Cantrell], take Dora [Dora (Blakely) Crook] and the baby and keep them, so she did. Taking them to Tennessee where Ira died at the age of 9 months. I remember what we were doing the day we received the letter that Ira was dead. We were cleaning up a turnip patch and Uncle Ned Peeples [Edward D. Peeples] brought the letter down to the field to my father.

After going back to Tennessee, brother Jim and I worked for my grandfather on a farm at $8.00 per month. We made and gathered a crop for which we received 4 cents each. I went to school that summer 2 months to a teacher by the name of Henry Wamble. He taught school in a log dwelling house. He was a fine man and teacher. He could read, write, cipher and spell real well. I had only 2 books to lug to and from school, a blue back speller and a McGuffies Reader. This was 1874, so the next year I worked for my Uncle Ben Peeples and wages had gone sky high. We, Jim Pink and I, all got $12.50 per month; worked eight months for over $100. Nothing much to buy, we all saved about 95 cents a piece and spent it at going to school.

The next year, 1875, all of us brothers and sister started in housekeeping. Rented what was called the Covy farm one mile from McNairy Station. We lived on this farm two years. We moved to another place and brother Will and I got a job on a section. I worked at this job 2 years never losing a day. Saved all the money I could and went to school as much as possible. I had made such great progress that I was employed as a teacher in a grade school in the country. One of my students finally made a doctor out of himself and it was he that attended Mr. J.J. Bradley in his last illness.

Well, after working on the railroad and teaching school, I entered school again. I went to the Southwest Baptist University of Jackson, Tennessee. I went back home and during the winter of 1879, went to Dr. J.W. Conger. It was while attending this school that I first met a little blue-eyed girl that afterwards became your Mama.

In or on the 26th day of February, I landed in Knoxville, Arkansas, and bought a carload of stuff through my uncle Bent Peeples [Benton Tatum Peeples]. I made a sharecrop with him that year and made 9 bales of cotton and 150 bushels of corn. I picked all the cotton and gathered all the corn and went back to Tennessee. I landed there on the 9th day of November 1882, attended my sister's wedding that night and went to my grandmother's funeral the next day and was married myself on the 18th of November 1882. I came back to Arkansas and made 2 crops and went to work for Cozort Brothers on the day Grover Cleveland was elected President.

Back to my first year in Arkansas, after crops were laid by, a friend of mine by the name of Sam Evans took a notion to go west, so we rigged up a one horse wagon and pulled out for Indian territory. We went as far west as Weber Falls and in order to make expenses, we rigged up a small slight of hand show. I was Houdini, so I had some bills struck which read like this: "Thomas B. Blakely, the great slight of hand performer, Legerdemain and Ventriloquist will perform tonight at the schoolhouse, admission 10 and 25 cents." And strange to say, we made expenses and then some.

Well, Thomas, with the help of your grandmother keeping boarders and helping to save money, I was able to attend the medical college at Little Rock, Arkansas, during the year 1892 and 1893, graduating. Ten years later I took a postgraduate course in Chicago, Illinois, and I am sure you have heard your mother say what a famous doctor I am. Cure cancers, relieve ear ache, stop the colic in a three month old kid. You see, I finally made what my father wanted me to be. Now if I could live to see you become a great doctor, I certainly would be happy.

Tell your mother I will tell her what the wonderful salve is made of after she is cured but I am afraid to tell her now as the remedy is so simple she wouldn't have any confidence in it. Now you know if I was to tell her this is what the salve is made of, she would quit using it. I sure hope her ears will get well and stay well as I can't think of anything I would rather see than to see her ear well when she comes up to see us next spring and eat vegetables and fried chickens. Don't you know it will soon be time to garden, not quite a month, the 17th day of February is the time to start.

Thomas, I hope you enjoy this letter and I will write you some more one of these days. I will write you before gardening time as I will be so busy then I won't have time. When you see your grandmother, look on her finger and you will see a ring that I put there years ago, one Sunday evening while we were hunting huckleberries.

Love to you all,
Your grandfather
Thomas Benton Blakely

Now let us examine the contents of this interesting letter. First, we shall take a look at the individuals mentioned by the elder Mr. Blakely. Dr. Thomas Benton Blakely was the son of J.B. and Mary E. Blakely, residents of the Anderson's Store area. In 1860, the Blakely family consisted of four sons: William (born circa 1854), James H. (born circa 1856), Pinkney (born circa 1858), and Thomas (born in 1859). The father, J.B. Blakely, was by profession a saddler, and on August 25, 1862, he enlisted in Company B of the U.S. Sixth Tennessee Cavalry. The Blakely family resided next door to the parents of Mary Blakely, C.W. and Thursday Peoples (Peeples).

Blakely mentions his cousin, Leander Barham. The records mention a Corporal Charles L. Barham of Company B of the Sixth Tennessee Cavalry. This Barham, probably the same, was killed in action on March 21, 1864. One history mentions that the Sixth Tennessee Cavalry was carrying on operations against Nathan Bedford Forrest in West Tennessee between March 16 and April 14, 1864.[33] There are also two individuals by the name of George Maness, but one of those survived until the end of the war. The fate of the other is unknown.

Blakely mentions his paralyzed schoolteacher John Canterbury. Indeed a gentleman by the name of John Canterbury lived in Anderson Store in 1860 with the T.M. Roberson family. Also living in the Anderson's Store community in 1860 was Benton T. Peoples, the uncle of Thomas Blakely.

Having mentioned all of this, we are left with the question of the location of Cotton Ridge. Some have speculated that Cotton Ridge lay around the area which has long been known as Rabbit Ridge. A portion of the old Purdy-Lexington Highway ran along the ridge known as Rabbit Ridge and it was on this highway that Anderson's Store, the actual business which gave the name to the community, was located. With no other reasonable explanations, the author is left with the following conclusions. There was probably no official Cotton Ridge, in that no post office was ever established under that name and no census included any community by that name. Most probably it was the name used by a few of the residents of Anderson's Store for a particular area in that community. Perhaps we can never know with great assurance of anything more.

Go West, Young Man! To Tulia, Texas!

One of the common patterns to be noticed in history is the correlation between Tennesseans eventually making their way westward to Texas. So many early settlers of western Tennessee found their journey far from finished once they reached McNairy, Henderson, or Hardeman county. After a few years in this area, many often trudged on to Texas where they completed their long and arduous journey. Yet as the years passed, there were individuals who traveled only temporarily to the various sections of Texas to find work and then return.

Interestingly, one of most common destinations was the town of Tulia in Swisher County, Texas. For those who haven't brushed up on their Texas geography lately, Swisher county is located in the Panhandle region of Texas. It is located relatively near to the towns of Amarillo, Miama, Silverton, and Pampa. It was known for its wheat farming and

33. McCann, *Hurst's Wurst*.

cattle ranching. It was also the stomping grounds for a large number of McNairy countians who migrated there in the period between the late 1890's and the early decades of the twentieth century. A thorough accounting of all individuals who left McNairy County to seek a fresh start or temporary employment in Tulia is probably not possible. However, we can glimpse a little of this migration through the eyes and experiences of a few.

Among the first to leave McNairy County for Swisher county was Blaine Barnes. Barnes operated the livery stables between Silverton and Tulia, before moving to 402 North Maxwell Street in Tulia. He served as a town commissioner, nightwatchman, and deputy under legendary Texas sheriff Hugh White. He also served under sheriffs Tom Walters and Mosely. Barnes' service wasn't confined only to the arena of public safety, but also extended to service on the local rationing board during World War II. An avid horseman, Barnes was also a member of the American Quarter Horse Association and the National Quarter Horse Association. He married Ida Clayton, daughter of James Madison and Mary Elizabeth Clayton, in 1910, and thirteen children were born to the union. Following her death, he courted a Miss Townsend who ran a boarding house in Tulia.

Other early migrants to Tulia from north McNairy County were Earl and Ulyss (Eulis) Kerby and their mother. The boys' uncle, John Wesley Kerby (1851–1922) lived in Tulia and most likely they migrated there to be near him. The boys were actually Naylors, but apparently their mother, Rosaline (Kerby) Naylor, left their father, Frank Naylor, when the boys were small and went to Texas. She settled in Tulia, never to return, dying on June 2, 1924. Both sons became successful farmers and owners of large tracts of land. One of the brothers married, but the other did not. Photographs taken in the early 1930s show a fleet of dozen or more combines to be utilized in the harvest of wheat. Both were good gentlemen whose first love was farming. Earl had bought a new Chevrolet business coupe and while driving across the farm he came across a newborn calf in need of assistance. He picked up the calf and put it in the backseat and proceeded on his way. The Kerby brothers' father made an attempt late in his own life to become reacquainted with his sons, who were taken away from him so early in their lives. He offered both brothers a new rifle as gifts upon their meeting. However, both brothers refused a meeting and showed no interest in getting to know their elderly father.[34]

Many of the individuals who went to Texas did so during the period of the Great Depression for the purpose of procuring steady employment and decent wages. Sometimes just the men went and sometimes a husband and wife team made the trip. One couple who made their way to Tulia was Hobert and Cora Patterson.[35] This couple did not let grass grow under their feet, for they were always on the move or so it seemed. At various points, Hobert and Cora could be found working in Tulia. One of their native Texas friends was Murphy Myers, ranch foreman for William Charlie "Judge" Dinwiddie. Hobert first took his family to Tulia in 1927, where he worked on a dairy farm for his half-brother, Blaine Barnes. In 1929, Hobert left Texas and returned to McNairy County where he purchased a farm at the head of Tar Creek near Mount Peter in 1933 and farmed here until 1945. At that point, Hobert moved to Grayson, California. He remained there until 1948, when he returned to Tulia to farm. In 1950, Hobert moved back to McNairy County and farmed until 1958. At that point, the couple again felt the urge to relocate. This time, Hobert and Cora moved to the Los Angeles area and were employed at the Knots Berry Farm and Ghost Town amusement park. Hobert worked in the grist mill grinding corn and waiting on customers. Cora was a greeter in the Little Red Church. In 1965, the couple moved again, this time back to Bethel Springs in McNairy County,

Hobert and Cora Patterson

---

34. These stories regarding the Kerby brothers were passed on the author by the late Hayse Hayre, who visited the Kerby brothers and family in Texas in the 1930s with his grandfather, Lee Andrew Weaver, whose wife was Dovie (Kerby) Weaver.

35. The information regarding Hobert and Cora Patterson was furnished by Luther E. Talbott and from a sketch published in Reflections Committee, *Reflections: A History of McNairy County, Tennessee.*

but ill health forced them to move for a final time to Memphis in 1973. Hobert died in 1975 and Cora in 1987.

Another north McNairy countian hard at work in Texas was Emanuel "Manley" Chandler. It was said by many in and around Tulia that Chandler, called "Chan" by the locals in Tulia, could outwork two men in a day's time. Exactly how long he spent in Tulia is unknown, but he made a name for himself in that far-away little Texas town. Some members of the Hodges' family of Chester and north McNairy counties also settled eventually in the towns of Tulia and Silverton, Texas.

Members of the Plunk and Womble families eventually found their way to Tulia also. Brothers Orby and Orville Plunk both wound up in the small Texas town working first in the wheat harvest as so many other immigrants from Tennessee and then they found other work and other enterprises. The Wombles, which was eventually changed to Wamble, had a number of their family settle permanently in Swisher County, Texas. A brother of Marcus A. "Mark" Wamble lived out his life as a farmer in Tulia. One amusing story demonstrates an answer to the adage that everything is bigger in Texas. One year, before harvesting a wheat or cotton crop in a field just off of current Highway 45 near the junction of Friendship Road, Mark Wamble walked out in the middle of the field and got on his knees to have his picture taken. According to contemporary sources, Wamble then sent the picture to his brother in Tulia with a caption regarding the success of his crop for that particular year.

In 1941, a young man of twenty years by the name of Luther E. "Junior" Talbott decided for himself to strike out for Tulia, Texas. He and Horry Young decided to go and find for themselves work in Texas. Horry had been before, as he was many years older than Junior. Upon arriving in Tulia, the duo stayed the evening in a boarding house owned by Ms. Townsend. As Horry and Junior ambled down the stairs the following morning and into the establishment's restaurant, they saw a gentleman sitting there waiting on them to arrive. The gentleman introduced himself as Judge W.C. Dinwiddie, a cattleman and farmer. He told the two that he heard they were looking for work and that he had plenty for them if they were interested. It was apparent that news traveled just as quickly in small Texas towns as it did in small Tennessee towns.

After hiring the two, Mr. Dinwiddie inquired as to a friend of the two. He asked, "Do you know a fellow by the name of "Chan?" They

Luther E. "Junior" Talbott

two asked if he was referring to Manley Chandler and he said he was. After a little conversation, the two made their way out to the Judge's spread. Horry's employment with Judge Dinwiddie proved to be short-lived. After sustaining a cut on his chin, he determined that he should return to town to seek treatment. After a few days, Junior and the Judge received word from Horry that he was back in Finger. Junior's employment and time in Texas proved of much longer duration. He remained in the Judge's employment for more than a year before to returning to answer the call to arms in Europe and the Pacific.

Others in north McNairy County migrated to other parts of Texas and the American West. Several individuals who lived in and around north McNairy County eventually made their way to the state of Oklahoma. Two young men, who were raised in McNairy County prior to the War Between the States and later moved to Oklahoma, were brothers John and Daniel W. Webster, the sons of William and Nancy Webster. John Webster married Rebecca Caroline (Plunk) Mosier on March 28, 1865, the daughter of Joseph and Nancy (Haley) Plunk.

Daniel Webster served in Company H of the United States Seventh Tennessee Volunteer Cavalry and later served thirteen months in the infamous Andersonville Prison in Georgia. Following the War, Daniel married Martha L. Greer on December 7, 1866. The couple had three sons: William M. Webster, Marcus W. Webster, and Eber T. "E.T." Webster. Following Martha's death, he married his sister-in-law's daughter, Eliza Adline (Mosier) Powers, a widow with six children, in 1892. Following their marriage, they moved west, apparently following the path of John and Rebecca Webster, who had moved to Rocky, Oklahoma. The couple settled first in Marlow, Indian Territory. They also eventually made their way to Rocky, Oklahoma, where they remained for the rest of their lives. Other members of the Webster family remained in the McNairy-Chester county area, where their descendants remain.

The Lost Art of Satirical Letter Writing

One of the greatest of lost art forms is that of satirical letter writing. Many great satirists have thrived over the centuries including Jonathan Swift of *Gulliver's Travels* fame. In earlier years, it was a common sight and an amusing read for the involved newspaper reader to find a satirical letter to the editor. In fact, although addressed to the editor, the letter was meant for the general public to consume and analyze. Before we proceed any further, if it has been too long since your days in English and Literature class, allow me to refresh your memory as to satire. *Webster's Encyclopedic Unabridged Dictionary of the English Language* defines satire as "the use of irony, sarcasm, ridicule, or the like, in exposing, denouncing, or deriding vice, folly, etc." and as "a literary composition, in verse or prose, in which human folly and vice are held up to scorn, derision, or ridicule. Now you know what the probable mindset of the author was in writing this letter. Let us now examine the old letter.

> Hiram Bridges' Letter
> Possum Trot, Tenn.
> Nov. 22, 1915
>
> Editor Independent:
> I went ter mill las Saterday and while was waterin mi nag and a waitin fer mi tern to be ground, I seed a lot of fellers squatted down on the sunny side o' the hous and they was 1 feller a reading of a paper to em—they se dot was mr Jim pervinzes peper and they was still as they cud be and finely one feller sed ef they was one he was a goin to it, I sed, ef they hav one what & he sed a mask meetin er a mass meetin ersum kind of a meetin and as I doant go round much ceptin to our monthly preachin and to mill as I sta purty clos to home as it takes me & Sally and all the children a kickin all the time to maik a liven, I ast who was a goin to preach at this mast meetin and they sed no sertin one'ud preach, jest anibody cud talk that wanted to, and I ast what they was gointer talk about and they sed about our taxes bein so hi, about so many iron briges and a few fellers a buyin em and a hole lot of other things and the moari talked the moar I found out and they

sed we ode about $15000 on the fust lot of briges and that the fellers who sold em to our county officers was pade with county warents andthat them warents is now a drawin 6 per cent intrust, I found out too that these saim fellers, I mean them fellers what go to Selmer ever Jinnerary, Aprile July and Octoaber, them squirs desided to by us 5 er six thousen $ wuth moar iron briges when they had there last meetin. The thing got to interstin me a hole lot cause ive ben wunerin whar our tax money gos. Si I axed the feller what was a doin of the reading a hole lot moar about things and he larnt me lots for he peared to be the best posted man in the crowd. He sed they dident by the briges like we wood by a hoss. That is get the best one we cud from the feller that wood sel it the cheepist, and sed he herd that the last lot of briges what was bought and what aint been put up yit he sed was bought by 4 or 5 fellers what got up sum writins to show who they was and tuck the trane fer sum place away up clos to Shicoger and they was gone for severl days but dident go to see but 1 feller that made iron briges & this feller pade all the expenses of them 4 fellers so I herd, that is I herd the Boss of the crowd, who is the boss of the squares ever time they come to Selmer, got a check for $75 frum this brige feller afore they all started and I shore bet them fellers had sum big time a ridin on the tranes, eatin on the eatin coach, a ridin autermobeels amd eatin and sleepin in them big hotels. Sum feller sed that aint nun of our biznes as the brige feller was a payin fur them fellers and I se def they wuz, ide bet they added it all onto the bridge. I guess this is one thing we lern at the mast meetin who these fellers was what went up thar and bought all tem briges and who pade thare way thar and back and who tuck keer of them while they was up thar. It looks like that feller up thar, as they is just one of him, cud have come to Selmer cheapern em 4 fellers cud a went up thar, besides it looks like cud hav put a notis in the paper about them briges and had a hole lot of fellers a biddin agin each other, like I seed a road comissoner a way back when I was a young feller. He put up a notis about a brige over tar creek and giv how long it was and all about it & a feller bid it off about $25 cheapern anuther feller sed hed bild it and they want no money pade lo nobody for coming ater this brige, but the deestrict saved about $25 on this bridge. Haint our squares got a rite to hav our briges bilt this way? Pleas put in yore Paper when they air gointer hav this here mast meetin for I shore am a comin to it.

Yores Trooly,
  Hiram Bridges

The reader most certainly recognizes the difficulty in reading the letter as it was originally printed. The letter was written in this manner for a variety of reasons. First, it is written in the manner of an uneducated man writing a letter, but demonstrates toward the end of the letter that even the uneducated can understand the present situation and see what the most sensible and honest answer would be. It is written under a pseudonym, i.e. a pen name or fictitious name used by the author to conceal his identity. The name "Hiram Bridges" symbolizes the solution suggested by the author of the satirical letter. In other words, the county should bid out the hiring of bridge construction. The residence or location of the letter writer is identified as Possum Trot, Tennessee. In McNairy County, there were three places called Possum Trot, all the names of school houses. However, this was probably the one located around Finger, due to the mention of Tar Creek.

Before we proceed any further let examine the letter again, in an edited form as we would write a letter today. This will help us to gain an understanding of the situation that was present as to the political and patronage systems in McNairy County in 1915. Though such situations seem foreign to us today, such political activity still thrives in certain regions and systems.

  Hiram Bridges' Letter
   Possum Trot, Tenn.,
    Nov. 22, 1915
Editor Independent:
I went to the mill last Saturday and while I was watering my nag and waiting for my turn to be ground, I saw a lot of fellows squatted down by the sunny side of the house and there

was a fellow reading a paper to them. They said it was Mr. Jim Purviance's paper and they were still as they could be and finally one fellow said if there was one he was going to it.[36] I said, "if they have one what" and he said, "a mask meeting or a mass meeting or some kind of a meeting." As I don't go around much except to our monthly preaching and to mill as I stay pretty close to home, as it takes me and Sally and all of the children a kicking all the time to make a living, I asked who was going to preach at this mass meeting.[37] They said no certain one would preach, just anybody could talk that wanted to. I asked what they were going to talk about and they said, "about our taxes being so high, about so many iron bridges and a few fellows buying them and a whole lot of other things." And the more I talked, the more I found out. They said we owed about $15,000 on the first lot of bridges and that the fellows who sold them to our county officers was paid with county warrants and those warrants are now drawing six percent interest. I found out too that these same fellows, I mean those fellows who go to Selmer every January, April, July, and October, those Squires decided to buy us five or six thousand dollars worth more of iron bridges when they had their last meeting.[38]

The thing got to interesting me a whole lot because I've been wondering where out tax money goes. So I asked the fellow who was doing the reading a whole lot more about things and he taught me lots for he appeared to be the best posted man in the crowd. He said they didn't buy the bridges like we would by a horse, that is get the best one we could from the fellow that would sell it the cheapest.[39] He said he heard

---

36. Colonel J.W. Purviance (1842–1936) was the longtime publisher of the *McNairy County Independent Appeal* newspaper. Colonel Purviance was a lawyer and a well-known orator.

37. Here the letter writer is advocating the use of the mass meeting or public gathering as a way to address the issue and to give the readers an idea of how to ideally handle such a situation.

38. The group of men being discussed is the McNairy County Quarterly Court, members of which were referred to as "squires" in those earlier days.

39. The writer here is referring to the bidding process, an old and effective system for attaining county business.

that the last lot of bridges that were bought and which haven't been put up yet were bought by four or five fellows who got up some writings to show who they were and took the train for some place away up close to Chicago. They were gone for several days but didn't go to see but one fellow that made iron bridges and this fellow paid all the expenses of those four fellows, so I heard.[40] That is I heard the Boss of the crowd, who is the boss of the squires every time they come to Selmer.[41] They got a check for $75 from this bridge fellow before they all started and I sure bet those fellows had some big time riding on those trains, eating on the eating coach, riding automobiles, and eating and sleeping in those big hotels.[42] Some fellow said that is none of our business as the bridge fellow was paying for those fellows. I said if they were, I'd bet they added it all onto the bridge.[43]

I guess this is one thing we learned at the mass meeting; who these fellows were that went up there and bought all those bridges and who paid their way there and back and who took care of them while they were up there. It looks like that fellow up there, as there is just one of him, could have come to Selmer cheaper than those four fellows could have went up there.[44] Besides it looks like they could have put a notice in the papers about those bridges and had a whole lot of fellows bidding against each other, like I have seen a road commissioner back when I was a young fellow.[45] He put up a notice

---

40. Here may be the first allegations of wrongdoing by at least some members of the county court. It would not be generally accepted for a potential supplier of the county to pay the expenses of county court members who could and most possibly would, in turn, do business with that firm.

41. This "Boss" is actually the chairman of the county court.

42. Here the letter writer is referring to potential bribery of members of the county court.

43. The writer is keenly aware of the "pass it on" theory of business.

44. The writer knows full well that such a way of doing business would never entice any person or account like a good, old fashioned trip away from home and the constituents would do a group of politicians in the old days.

45. Here another function proper and often legally necessary in the purchase or sale of property and equipment by a government entity is the issuance of a notice in a newspaper of record. The letter writer mentions all of these things as helpful to the county court with full knowledge that each is already required.

about a bridge over Tar Creek and gave how long it was and all about it and a fellow bid it off about $25 cheaper than another fellow said he could build it and there wasn't any money paid anybody for coming after this bridge, but the district saved about $25 on this bridge. Haven't our Squires a right to have our bridges built this way?[46] Please put in your paper when they are going to have this mass meeting for I sure am coming to it.[47]

Yours truly,
Hiram Bridges

The Fading Businesses of the Grist Miller and Blacksmith

During the mechanization of the world and its occupations during and following the Second World War, many old ways of life began to give way to others. The blacksmith was slowly becoming a relic of the past with increased use of tractors and automobiles. Old barn-like structures replete with anvil, tongs, furnace, and a bevy of iron working equipment gave way to garages complete with oil pit, air hose and gasoline pump.

Henry H. Kirkpatrick

The grist miller of old was already gone in that kerosene and steam engines turned the machinery that ground corn into meal. No longer were the days of the mill located on the local run whose wheel turned all day in the water. People now began to go to the grocery store and buy meal in 10, 25, and 50 pound bags turned out by the large mills at Jackson and other larger cities. Gone were the days of whiling away a little time at the mill talking to friends. Model Mills and other large corporations held the business. Yet a few held on in the ever changing tide that swept the country and the countryside. One gentleman who continued in both businesses was Henry H. Kirkpatrick of Finger. Located in the old Union Savings Bank

---

46. Of course, the answer here is that they have an obligation to build bridges that way.
47. As the writer well knows, no such meeting is planned.

building, he continued to ply both the trade of miller and blacksmith. Below is a sampling from his 1952 account book.

> Irons to fasten back gate—$1.15 to A.J. Young in January 1950
> Posthole digger handles—$1.00
> Lee Brooks—2 pairs of horseshoes, No. 5—$1.60 on June 18, 1952.
> Fred Helton—work on harrow on March 29, 1950—$3.60
> Dewitt Clouse—plow stock—$6.00 on June 21, 1947.
> Jewell Durbin—Irons to hang harness, 50 cents on March 20, 1948.
>   Six bushel of corn—$14.40 on June 8, 1948.
> Will Baggett—handsaw filed—50 cents on August 14, 1951.
> Hard Leath—plow point ground- 30 cents on April 21, 1949 joe
>   blade handle—$1.05 on October 17, 1951
> Coolidge Plunk—one wagon—$82.50 on February 10, 1949.
>   156 feet of lumber—$9.36 on February 10, 1949.
> Ervin Plunk—two sets of stove flu irons—$3.00 on February 28, 1950.
> Andrew & A.D. McCann—one sorghum mill—$40.00 on
>   August 15, 1950.
> Elbert Kirkpatrick—four pair of mule shoes with nails—$2.60 on
>   August 15, 1950.
> Emanuel Chandler—200 pound of corn- $7.05 on February 10, 1951.
> J. Crow—fertilizer drill—$5.00 on May 1, 1951.

The Early Post Offices and the Founding of the Finger Post Office

One of the vital components of the communities of old, if not in fact the centerpiece of these communities, was the local post office. Indeed the community often took its name from the post office and vice versa. Many post offices sprang up in north McNairy County between the founding of the county in 1823 and the establishment of the Finger post office in 1895. Some of these have been discussed already in this work, but many others will be discussed here.

During the period prior to the War Between the States, a number of post offices were established to link the residents of north McNairy County to each other and the outside world via the United States mail. The reader must remember the world of the early settlers was much bigger than today. To live in West Tennessee was to live in a largely wild place

Children standing in front of the Finger Post Office

with no great established urban areas offering education and culture to the willing student. Rather it was a rough hewn place and the general merchandise store, blacksmith shop and post office offered a window to the current news and the outside world from which it emanated. Therefore, one cannot sufficiently demonstrate the importance of the post office in early McNairy County or West Tennessee.

Apparently the first known post office in north McNairy County was Montezuma. The first postmaster was an early settler in north McNairy County, Josiah R. Wamble. Wamble served from February 26, 1839, until November 1, 1845. Wamble was then succeeded by several men bearing family names familiar to many residents of Montezuma over the years. Those postmasters following Wamble were Elliot Burkhead (November 1, 1845 to January 14, 1848), John L. Rodgers (January 14, 1848 to November 10, 1848), Samuel M. Fry (November 10, 1848 to December 27, 1850), A.H. McKinnon (December 27, 1850 to March 20, 1860), and John L. Rodgers (March 20, 1860 to September 22, 1866). The post office at Montezuma was discontinued as of September 22, 1866. The reason for the discontinuance is unknown. However, the post office was reopened on April 30, 1868, with Aquilla Q. Simmons serving as postmaster. Simmons served until April 26, 1870. Following Simmons were John B. McKinnon (April 26, 1870 to November 22, 1878), Absalom W. Skinner (November 22, 1878 to January 13, 1880), George W. Brown (January 13, 1880 to February 3, 1880), John P. Hollis (February 3, 1880 to December 21, 1880), and William W. Senter (December 21, 1880 to April 1882). The post office at Montezuma continued on following April 1882. However, it was by then located in the newly formed Chester County.

Another old post office in north McNairy County was Anderson's Store. This area and the business which gave the community a name have already been discussed. However, the post office itself will be discussed here. The post office itself was located in William Taylor Anderson's store on the old Purdy-Lexington Highway. The post office began operations on October 19, 1846, with William Taylor Anderson serving as postmaster. He served in this capacity until May 1, 1857, when William C. Robbins assumed the position. Robbins served until July 18, 1860, when A.M. Worthington became postmaster. This gentleman's name has appeared as A. McWorthington, but this is in error, apparently the product of an error in transcription. Worthington served less than a month as postmaster and on August 10, 1860, was replaced by Charles W. Peeples. Peeples served as postmaster until the post office was discontinued on July 18, 1866.

Huggins Creek is one of the oldest named physical or geographical landmarks of north McNairy County. It was originally referred to Hugganses Creek. It flows more or less southwest to northeast from the area around McNairy Station to Finger. Sheffield Branch, Billies Creek, Hogwallow Creek, and Bushel Creek flow into Huggins Creek, which eventually empties into the Forked Deer River. Huggins Creek originally possessed a crooked and often shallow flow until work commenced in the early twentieth century straightened the creek and increased its flow and depth. It can only be surmised that Huggins Creek was at the least a significant landmark for residents of north McNairy County in the nineteenth century. Somewhere along this creek was located a post office named appropriately the Huggins Creek Post Office. This particular office was established as of December 23, 1847. The first postmaster was James Wilson. He was succeeded by Hugh Kerby, the county's firstborn white child, on June 7, 1854. The post office was discontinued on October 24, 1854.

Another early and little-known post office was Ridgeway. The exact location cannot be known for certainty at this writing. It can only assumed that it was located on the farm of the only postmaster to serve this location. Still that would be foggy speculation at its best. Eli H. Tisdale became the postmaster of the newly created Ridgeway Post Office on April 3, 1855. Tisdale lived in the vicinity of what is now referred to as Floyd's Crossing. In those days, it was not a far trip to Mount Carmel or farther west toward the Floyd Cemetery. Tisdale and his wife Hannah had a daughter, Sarah J. Tisdale, buried in Floyd Cemetery on October 22, 1849. Tisdale owned a large farm which included that area now known as Floyd's Crossing. Therefore, it is possible that Ridgeway was located in that area. After a little more than two years in operation, the Ridgeway post office was discontinued on August 18, 1857.

The post office and possible community at Tinsley was discussed in great detail above, but for purposes of discussing the existence of post offices in north McNairy County, the date of its operation will be discussed here. The Tinsley Post Office was established on November 1, 1875. The first and only postmaster was Tinsley Weaver, who was seventy-six years old at the time the post office began operations. He continued in this post until the office was discontinued on October 20, 1884, and moved to Sweet Lips.

The Sweet Lips Post Office began operations on April 22, 1878, with William P. Miller serving as the first postmaster. On December 16, 1879, Finis E. Miller, a Union Army veteran and survivor of Andersonville Prison, became postmaster. He served until December 13, 1880, when John M. Hodges took over. On February 24, 1881, Finis E. Miller took charge of the post office once again and the office was moved to Chester county upon its formation.

In late 1894 or early 1895, the decision was made to establish a post office in the fledgling village of McIntyre's Crossing. Robert Allen McIntyre, the son of James Robert McIntyre and grandson of Robert Thompson McIntyre, officially made the application. Originally, the name "Cash" was chosen for the new post office, which, of course, would mean a name change for the small hamlet. For whatever reason, that name was not chosen. For years, a number of theories have existed as to why the name Finger was finally chosen. Over the years, many new theories have arisen which have absolutely no supporting evidence from the time period which would be most helpful in solving this mystery, the year 1895. Many stories have been passed down through the years, but this in no way establishes them as historical fact. Such stories are no more than interesting or funny oral traditions.

The only contemporary written account of the event was composed by Professor Horry Hodges. Hodges, a prominent historian, educator, and politician, was very active in the affairs of McNairy County. In 1895, Hodges was serving as McNairy County circuit court clerk. The professor chronicled much of McNairy County's history and wrote many articles during his career in an effort to further the knowledge of the area's history. In regards to the naming of Finger, Professor Hodges recorded that "the town was named by the Reverend J.J. Franklin as a joke and in derision." It is believed that this same gentleman was one John J. Franklin, who also served as the postmaster of McNairy Station.

For those who seem fascinated with the theory of Finger getting its name following the shaking of many fingers at a heated meeting, the following may provide some acceptable explanation for the validity of that theory. Most likely it would seem that during the discussions regarding the name for the post office, Franklin may have jokingly suggested the name after observing the situation. This could have been Franklin's suggestion after observing the alleged finger-pointing and arguing. Regardless of what occurred at the meeting or meetings, the author chooses to abide by the only recorded account written by Professor Hodges.

Regardless of the origins of the name, the Finger post office became operational on June 13, 1895, with William Pinkney Massey serving as the town's first postmaster. The exact building in which the Finger post office was first located in currently unknown. It is known that it was located in Massey's wooden store building directly next to the Bank of Finger during the first few years of the twentieth century. Following the destruction of this building by fire on April 1, 1916, the post office was then moved to Massey's new store building, a brick structure, still on Main Street. Here the post office was housed for more than thirty years.

Ward W. Maness succeeded Massey as postmaster on August 21, 1914. Maness served in the position for a little more than four years before advancing in the United States Postal Department. Upon his advancement, James Orby Massey succeeded to the postmaster's position by appointment of President Woodrow Wilson on February 11, 1919. The

Murray Walker and his mail wagon

son of W.P. Massey, he held the position longer than anyone else, serving for the next forty-three years. During his tenure as postmaster, the office was moved from the Massey store building to a red brick building which once stood across the street, which was also used by Ed Stephens as a barber shop. After a while the post office was moved to the old Dr. N.A. Tucker office.

For many years, the mail was delivered by train, being brought in on the morning passenger train. As the train passed through the town, the mail bags were thrown from the train onto the porch of the depot. It was at the depot that Mr. Tom McCaskill picked up the mail, placed it into his wheelbarrow and then pushed it up to the post office to be placed in the mailboxes. Following Tom's death, the postmaster, Massey, would drive the very short distance down to the depot, pick it up and drive it back to the office. Orby Massey was known for putting the mail up in the evening after it arrived rather than waiting until the next morning to sort and place it in the boxes. Massey was also known for opening the post office on Sundays, which is absolutely unheard of today.

In the earlier days of the Finger post office, much of the mail went out on the rural mail routes, where most people lived. Therefore, rural mail carriers played an important role in keeping rural dwellers in touch with the outside world. There were three routes which operated from the Finger post office, the Star Route, the Rural Route East, and the Rural Route West. The Star Route ran from Finger to Leapwood and back. The Rural Route East made a large circle covering a territory which now includes Hutcherson Road, Rocky Knob Road, Bailey Road, and back down Center Hill Road to the Finger-Leapwood Road. The Rural Route West went south on U.S. Highway 45, then proceeded down the present Sol Colston Road (old Fairview Road), came out on the present Garner Road and then out by Logan's Lake. From there, the route continued south on Highway 45 and then proceeded towards Masseyville. It eventually came out near the present-day Chester County Memory Gardens and then down the Old Finger Road. This route included all of the little roads which branched off from Old Finger Road.

W.H. "Tobe" Walker (left) and his son Carroll Walker were mail carriers in and around Finger.

A number of good gentlemen carried the mail on these old country routes. The Walker brothers, Murray and Tobe, carried the mail on the two Rural Routes. Murray Walker carried the mail on the western route.[48] Eddy Peeples was a substitute mail carrier for Murray. Tobe Walker delivered mail on the eastern route. Both brothers originally delivered the mail using a horse and mail wagon. Sometime prior to Tobe's retirement, his son Carroll drove him as he delivered the mail. After one of the brother's retirement, the routes were combined and others delivered the mail on the larger combined route. Among those early deliverymen

---

48. One source, Robert Beene, stated that Murray Walker carried the mail on Route Two, which would have been the Rural Route East. He stated that Tobe Walker delivered the mail on Route One or Rural Route West.

who carried the mail on this combined route were Fate Boyd, Willard Smith, and a Mr. Thompson. The Star Route was carried by such gentlemen as Thomas Martin, who carried the mail from 1925 to 1933, Tom Phillips, Jack Loving, and John Wharton. Loving drove Phillips on the route before taking it over himself and Wharton was the last person to run the Star Route. Around the turn of the century, Bob Carter was carrying the mail around the Finger area.

James Orby Massey served as postmaster until he was succeeded by Christine (Brown) Harris on June 22, 1962. She served as postmaster until 1988. Around the time of her retirement, the post office again found a new home. The current post office building was opened in 1988 and continues in operation there today (2013). On December 31, 1988, Carolyn Hurst was appointed to the position of postmaster. She remained in that position until Yoga R. Carroll was appointed on October 3, 1990. Shortly thereafter, on January 12, 1991, Favil Allen Meek was appointed as Finger's postmaster. Meek was extremely well-liked in the community and was truly a gentleman to all who encountered him. He served well and continued in his duties even after being stricken with cancer. He fought a hard battle with the disease and continued to work until shortly before his death in 1999. A number of individuals have held the position since 1999.

The Finger Barbecue
"The Daddy of All Barbecues"

One of the great social events which Finger residents most anticipate and have for years is the Finger Barbecue and Picnic. It is an event with a great and distinguished history steeped in proud tradition. It is an event that has survived several changes of venue, many events in the world and many successive generations of north McNairy countians. The events and attractions at the barbecue were varied and interesting. The crowds were large and came from states all over the country. The barbecue was first held in 1895 on the John A. McIntyre farm east of town in the bottom near Bushel Creek. That location is to the right of Centerhill Road just across from the entrance to the Stoltfuz sawmill. It is believed that it was held here for only a year or two, but no more.

WRITINGS OF SPECIAL HISTORICAL NOTE

Thousands gather at the Finger Barbecue.

Hardy "Hard" Leath (in apron) and an unknown female fiddler at the Finger Barbecue

The second location for the barbecue was in the grove where Dr. W.M. Barnes' home was later built. It was held here probably for several years including the first several years of the twentieth century. Arthur "A" Williams, a businessman from Bethel Springs, attended the barbecue from 1901 to 1910. In 1901, he estimated the crowd to be anywhere from six to ten thousand. Williams stated that in 1901, a Ferris wheel was erected for the enjoyment of the crowd. Another interesting attraction on that first Saturday in August of 1901 was Professor Nicholas B. Hardeman preaching one of his great sermons.

According to the old *Memphis News-Scimitar* newspaper, six to eight thousand people heard Mr. T.B. Whitehurst, a leading attorney of the Selmer bar, speak on the subject of "Railroad Domination and Its Evil Effects" at the August 1905 Finger Barbecue.

Many of these interesting speeches and people were featured at the barbecue because of the diligence and planning of one man. He was G.F. Dickey and was often referred to as the "Barbecue King." The late Jackson businessman and columnist Bob Parker wrote, "it seemed that 'old G.F.' had been to the folks of Finger what Barnum was to the circus world." Dickey was the son of George and Amanda McIntyre Dickey and yet another grandson of Robert Thompson McIntyre. He was the head of "The Committee." He coordinated the appearance of talent, political figures, the roasting of dinner, the availability of deserts and drinks, and any other activity vital to make the barbecue a genuine and memorable success. He was, for his day and his town, a true master showman and he ran this show from 1900 until 1943.

A young man enjoys an ice cream cone at the Finger Barbecue around 1908.

WRITINGS OF SPECIAL HISTORICAL NOTE

(Above) A scene from the Finger Barbecue, year unknown

(Left) Members of the McIntyre family attending the Finger Barbecue. Left to right: Hubert McIntyre, John McIntyre, Sarah (McIntyre) Fowler, and Adrian McIntyre.

Among the other great speakers to entertain, inform, and hold the crowd were such mighty and colossal figures as Captain Gordon Browning, a United States Congressman and future Tennessee Governor, Professor Horry Hodges, a well-known historian, political figure, and beloved educator, Senator W.W. Craig, and Senator William Kendal Abernathy. These men were renowned in their day and played a great role in the governance of affairs in Tennessee. The entertainment was equally impressive. Such legendary acts as the famous Carter Family, Buck Turner, Speedy McNatt, Slim and Speck Rhodes, the Golden West Cowboys, Little Texas Daisy, Sarie and Sally, Pee Wee King, the Delmore Brothers, and the Snuff Variety Gang put on shows that made the trip to the picnic grounds truly worth the effort and time.

Sometime in the 1920s, the barbecue changed venue again. It was moved to a spot not far from the Finger Cemetery on land owned by the family of the late James Robert McIntyre. It flourished here until 1963. Although some have stated the barbecue was postponed during World War II, an advertisement from 1944, the year following G.F. Dickey's death, announces the annual Finger barbecue. According to the late Robert M. Smith, it was not until 1964 that a barbecue was not held. Unfortunately, that would continue for several years. Regardless of these later events, the barbecue was a great success under Dickey's leadership.

Dickey had great help in the barbecue pit. Hard Leath, Robert M. Smith, and John Rouse all practiced the art of the barbecue while working the many Finger barbecues and barbecue they did. The advertisement for the 1924 barbecue states, "We will barbecue forty big fat hogs, this year, with 15 nice fat sheep thrown in for a snack." It may have been a barbecue, but there were plenty of good cold snacks for youngsters and adults alike to enjoy. The same flyer boasts the availability of 5,000 cases of cold drinks, six thousand gallons of ice cold lemonade, and 2,000 gallons of cold ice cream, a great treat on a hot August day in Tennessee.

As county politicians, and those who sought to become one, walked around visiting with the men and women of north McNairy County and smiling at the playful little children, there were people who had called Finger and the surrounding area home many years before. These people had moved away and now came back from more than twenty-five states, with some years seeing visitors from about thirty states. These people, who now lived here and there afar, looked forward to the first Saturday in August every year as they prepared to amble back down the paths of their own yesteryear.

At some point, the barbecue was moved for one year to a spot on U.S. Highway 45 near the old W.A. Dillion homesite. After the barbecue faded from its former glory and passed into memory alone, a few years of inactivity passed. Sometime around 1970, a new festival was established by the name of the "Finger Friendly Festival." However, this festival was not for the purpose of providing a homecoming or moment of respite for the residents of and visitors to north McNairy County. Rather, it was held for the personal gain of a few. Like such activities where there was no feeling of common interest, it faded after just a couple of years.

Then, like the mythical phoenix arising from the ashes, the barbecue was resurrected. The final and present location for the Finger Barbecue was the area in front of the old Finger School and Gymnasium. It was here the barbecue began again in 1984 to aid in the fundraising efforts of the Finger Volunteer Fire Department. Since that year, good crowds have come back home to visit, eat barbecue sandwiches and homemade ice cream, and meet plenty of local and state politicians. Although nowhere near the scale of G.F. Dickey's "Daddy of All Barbecues," it has taken on some of the spirit of the barbecues of bygone times. Perhaps one day it will ascend to the ranks of greatness, like that greatness that characterized it as a fine festival in the early years of the twentieth century.

CHAPTER ELEVEN

THE BURYING GROUNDS OF NORTH McNAIRY COUNTY

Alexander—Anderson Family—Baucum—Beaty—Finger—Finger Christian Fellowship—Floyd—Griswell—Hendrix—Hopewell—Ingraham—Ingraham/Smith—John Plunk—Jones—Kerby- Lane's Chapel—Liberty Church—Maggie Jones Memorial—Malone—Mount Carmel—Old Oak Grove—Plunk—Rocky Knob—Wharton—White Plains.

Often there is no more fascinating afternoon walk than a walk through an old cemetery. Like the craters of the moon, the widely varying tombstones of an old country cemetery or family plot make that tiny portion of the earth's surface so different from any other. A cemetery can tell anyone a number of important facts and clues as to the lives that once were led and the ordeals that were faced and met during those lives. Though the occupying tenant of an earthen tomb is now dust and no more physically, we may know that each life was one full of tragedy, joy, a wealth of experience and the usual range of emotions that belongs to man. But yet, we often learn no more of the man or woman who lies beneath the sod than what is engraved on the marble, limestone, or granite slab. Therein lies the great tragedy of man today. We are foreclosed from learning any more about our forebears than what we can desperately scratch out of fading memories and dusty old books and records.

Therefore, we often find our first and sometimes only information regarding an ancestor on the cold, stone memorial to his life. These old stones, so often worn, weathered, and crumbling, give us vital, poetic, and occasionally historical information regarding one so vital themselves in our own lineage and existence today. They, our ancestors, led lives that would be often viewed as dull by today's standards and yet sometimes often very exciting and adventurous. They were laid to rest in small cemeteries that have grown in size and in small cemeteries that have simply grown up in weeds, saplings, and other undergrowth. Others went to their eternal slumber in small family plots now forgotten by all but relatives of the family and some even forgotten by families.

Some cemeteries were not originally included in the first edition of this work because they were easily accessible, in good repair, and information from them could be easily obtained. The majority of those discussed in the first edition were smaller, harder to access, and some were on private property that was hard to reach or on which the casual visitor might not be allowed. In this edition, the reader will note that Maggie Jones (New Church), Finger, Finger Christian Fellowship, Hopewell, Lane's Chapel, Beaty, Liberty, and Rocky Knob have been added. These additions were made to document them more thoroughly than had been done previously despite their easy accessibility. What follows are cemeteries that are easily accessible, those that may be reached only by a long and arduous walk through undergrowth and brush, and a few of the oldest and most historical of our cemeteries.

All causes of death listed with the decedents are taken from the records contained in the *McNairy County, Tennessee Death Books (1914-1939)* and are marked with an asterisk (*) and a reference the *Death Book* in which the decedent's death may be found.[1] These records show the types of illnesses which plagued men, women and children during the early part of the twentieth century at a time when medicine was still primitive and physicians were rare in numbers.

---

1. Nancy Kennedy and Marie Mills, compilers. *McNairy County, Tennessee Death Book B.C,D, Ca. 1914-1915* (Selmer, TN: Privately published, 2013).

Alexander (Leath) Cemetery

Alexander Cemetery was located on the old Ingraham plantation east of present-day Finger, just off of Clarence Barham Road, just off Weeks Road on Hollens Road. Buried here are members of the Ingraham, Alexander, and Leath families. There are a few unmarked graves in this cemetery which, in recent years, was covered by small saplings, brush and sage grass.

1. Albertine, wife of Alexander H. Ingraham Born 1821 Died 1856
    Alexander H. Ingraham was buried in the Ingraham-Smith portion of the New Oak Grove Cemetery.
2. John A. Alexander (February 15, 1821–April 10, 1893)
3. Catherine Alexander (October 15, 1828–December 23, 1903)
4. Nancy A. Hendrix Bassinger (August 29, 1828–December 5, 1852)
    Unmarked grave
5. Julius Leath, son of J.B. & N.E. Leath (March 10, 1894–July 23, 1897)
6. Jane Alexander (February 14, 1868–December 4, 1892)

Anderson Cemetery

A cemetery located on the side of the old Purdy-Lexington Road, which can be most easily reached by traveling to the end of Hilliard Gann Road, also referred to as Bishop Loop Road, has been identified as the Anderson Family Cemetery. It is located on the edge of the Millard Moore farm and the David Earl Plunk farm just on the edge of the traces of the old Purdy-Lexington Highway. This would have been in close proximity to the location of the old William Taylor Anderson home and store. There are two discernible graves and both are located in an area covered with a creeping vine of sorts and are marked by sandstones. One stone has the initials W.H.A. carved into it and the other stone has no identifying markings.

Research has uncovered a son of William Taylor Anderson who died in infancy. The child's name was William Harrison Anderson (W.H.A.). The child was born between sons Thomas Bryant Anderson and George Sergent Anderson. Most likely his birth date was 1840 or 1841. This was the same time period that William Henry Harrison was elected President of the United States. Anderson, a staunch Whig, most likely named his infant son after the widely popular Whig President. The other grave is most likely that of Annette Anderson (August 8, 1852–May 24, 1860), the youngest child of William Taylor Anderson. William Taylor and Mahala Anderson moved to Jackson, Tennessee, after the War Between the States and were buried there.

Baucum Cemetery

The Baucum Cemetery is a long-forgotten family cemetery located east of Finger on the Albert Owens Road. According to one source, the burying ground lies north of the road. No directions can be given as to its exact location as the author has never personally visited the site, but has had to rely upon existing sources and conversations to provide this small amount of information. There appear to be only five marked and identified graves in this small cemetery. There is the possibility that some unmarked or unknown graves do exist as in so many other small graveyards.

1. Annetta P. Baucum (April 15, 1870–December 13, 1874) Daughter of W. & M.E. Baucum
2. Susan B. Baucum (June 10, 1877–April 14, 1879)
3. Willie B. Baucum (June 25, 1880–December 2, 1884)
4. W.F. (William Fielding) Beard (July 23, 1861–August 23, 1937) 76 years and one month *Died of senility (Death Book B, page 6).*
5. George Irvin Cook (February 14, 1842–June 8, 1922) *Private, Company B, 16th Regiment, Tennessee Cavalry, Confederate States of America.* *Died of chronic nephritis (McNairy County Death Book D, page 15).*

Beaty Cemetery

According to a monument placed in the cemetery, the Beaty Cemetery was a part of the homestead entered by William Beaty in about 1827. The cemetery is located on the Bob Kirk Road in north McNairy County. This cemetery is located on a small knob surrounded by woods. There are approximately 63 graves located in the cemetery, of which approximately thirteen are marked by sandstones. Two additional sandstone markers are carved with the decedent's names and dates.

1. Beard, Frank (1839–1922)
2. Beard, John T., son of R.F. & M.M. Beard (September 6, 1872–September 11, 1873)
3. Beard, Linn (1846–1933)
4. Beaty, Bettie, wife of William H. Beaty
5. Beaty, Bill
6. Beaty, Bob
7. Beaty, Elizabeth, wife of John Beaty
8. Beaty, Elizabeth, wife of William Beaty
9. Beaty, George W. (May 22, 1851 – June 12, 1929) *Dropped dead (Death Book D, page 111)*
10. Beaty, John
11. Beaty, Mollie E., daughter of G.W. & Sarah Beaty (November 30, 1883–May 8, 1894)
12. Beaty, Otis H. (October 12, 1889–August 22, 1963)
13. Beaty, Sarah (October 29, 1853–May 30, 1942)
14. Beaty, V. Etter, Infant daughter of G.W. & Sarah Beaty (October 1, 1896–October 17, 1896)
15. Beaty, William "Early Emigrant"
16. Beaty, William Hugh
17. Burceen, Jennie C., daughter of W.L. & M.L.C. Burceen (February 10, 1912–February 15, 1912)
18. Harris, Charlie (1852–1932) *Died of mitral regurgitation (Death Book B, page 21)*
19. Harris, Emily (August 22, 1817–October 17, 1892) *Carved sandstone*
20. Harris, J.B. (March 21, 1840–August 17, 1872) *Carved sandstone*
21. Harris, Willie (1891–1901)
22. Hendrix, Elizabeth, wife of W.B. Hendrix (June 23, 1851–June 3, 1906)
23. Hendrix, Sarah E., wife of W.B. Hendrix (October 7, 1850–October 27, 1884)
24. Hendrix, William B., Private, 21st Tennessee Cavalry, Confederate States Army (May 7, 1840–October 1, 1912)
25. Hill, Mary J., wife of R.H. Hill (August 10, 1848–January 14, 1902)
26. Hill, R.H.
27. Kerby, Ben F., son of W.W. & Mary Kerby (Died 1868, Aged 5 days)
28. Kerby, Deborah (1857–1940)
29. Kerby, Hugh, son of W.W. & Mary Kerby (Died 1874, age 2 years)

30. Kerby, James F. (May 27, 1838–January 2, 1870)
31. Kerby, John (January 31, 1816–October 18, 1881)
32. Kerby, John E. (1852–1927)
33. Kerby, Mary (May 1845–March 28, 1882)
34. Kerby, Nancy L., daughter of John & Sarah Kerby (August 16, 1842–September 12, 1843)
35. Kerby, Sallie, wife of John Kerby (March 11, 1817–November 28, 1883)
36. Kerby, W.W. (February 14, 1840–October 18, 1919)
37. Morris, Catherine
38. Manual, Mark, Serg't, Co. C, 6th Tennessee Cavalry, Union Army Manual actually served in Company D of the regiment. He was born in Lafayette, Alabama circa 1821, and was recorded as an enumerated male voter in McNairy County in 1891.
39. Morris, Jennie H. (1870–1894)
40. Morris, Thornie
41. Needham, Elizabeth Kerby (1844–1924) *Died of the influenza (Death Book D, page 237)
42. Roland, Alex (November 15, 1847–February 11, 1929) *Born in Canada, died of the influenza (Death Book B, page 46)
43. Roland, Allie (Died 1905)
44. Roland, Johnny (Died December 31, 1904)
45. Roland, Saphronia (May 15, 1846–July 11, 1928)
46. Wharton, John (Born & Died July 28, 1890)
47. Wharton, Susan B. (January 21, 1860–January 3, 1891)
48. Williams, Infant Daughter of Dave & Errett Williams (February 8, 1933–March 3, 1933)
49. Williams, Infant Son of Dave & Errett Williams (August 19, 1920)
50. Williams, Infant Son of Dave & Errett Williams (October 25, 1931)
51.–63. Unknown graves marked by sandstones

Finger Cemetery

The Finger Cemetery is, in the span of events, a relatively young cemetery. It does not date back to the founding of the area but rather closer to the founding of the modern town itself. The cemetery is not yet a century old. It began, like relatively all cemeteries, with a single burial. When one of the young town's enterprising spirits died in a horse racing accident in 1913, he became appropriately the first burial in a new cemetery in a relatively new town in which the man was a leading force. That man was Andrew J. Maness.[2] The site chosen for Maness' burial was on the farm of another leading spirit in the young town, that of James Robert McIntyre. A spot was chosen on a small rise or knob covered in wild blackberry vines. Zanie Brown and Harmon Hodges cut a clearing in the vines and dug the grave that would serve as an earthen tomb for the very first grave in the new Finger Cemetery. In 1913, the new cemetery sat on the outskirts of the residential area of the town. All of the property donated for the cemetery was donated by James Robert McIntyre of an interval between 1913 and 1921. Today, this cemetery is home to many of Finger's past leading citizens and sponsors and more than 450 graves.

1. Adams, Estilee (1874–1951)
2. Adams, Joseph P., Tennessee, Pvt., Coast Artillery Corps, World War II (September 17, 1918–May 6, 1947)
3. Alexander, Daisy, wife of D.E. (February 18, 1884–November 3, 1926) *Fell into a fire*
4. Alexander, David E. (June 7, 1882–March 12, 1963)
5. Alexander, Evelyn (June 1, 1907–February 5, 2001)
6. Alexander, Ima Gean, daughter of D.E. & Evelyn (August 25, 1928–August 26, 1928)
7. Alexander, J.P., son of D.E. & Daisy (May 12, 1907–October 17, 1926) *Killed in an automobile wreck (Death Book D, page 70)*
8. Armour, Jeanette Redmon (January 18, 1935–September 22, 1991)
9. Baker, F. Jewell Sanders (November 30, 1915–March 10, 1979)
10. Baker, Ray A., Jr. (Dec. 27, 1950–October 18, 2010)
11. Bark, Elizabeth Ann (March 1, 1923–May 30, 2002)
12. Barton, Bobby Earl, Sr. (April 10, 1947–June 26, 2013)
13. Barton, Edna E. Bell (October 31, 1910–February 10, 1985)
14. Barton, Kinzy Sam (October 19, 1917–June 3, 1964)
15. Barton, Sarah (February 13, 1866–December 17, 1956)
16. Baucom, Mary Jane, wife of Levi Baucom (1853–1937) *Died of pneumonia (Death Book B, page 6)*
17. Beene, J.S. (October 22, 1863–February 20, 1946)

2. For more information on Andrew J. Maness, see Chapter Five: The Birth of Business: Blacksmiths to Merchants.

THE BURYING GROUNDS OF NORTH McNAIRY

18. Beene, Sarah E. (March 24, 1869–January 8, 1924)
19. Bell, John M. (1868–1935) *Died of apoplexy (Death Book B, page 4)*
20. Bell, Mary "Doch" (1871–1940)
21. Birmingham, Verble L. (1921–1966)
22. Bishop, Minnie May (November 27, 1893–December 26, 1971)
23. Bishop, Alworth Guy (August 25, 1892–November 27, 1967)
24. Brock, Mollie Eva (November 14, 1899–April 7, 1989)
25. Brown, B. Lillian (February 2, 1895–July 7, 1973)
26. Brown, Henry Harrison, Tennessee, PFC, 11th Infantry, World War I (August 11, 1888–December 30, 1969)
27. Brown, Hilda Jane (November 24, 1927–July 19, 2009)
28. Brown, James Guy, S2, U.S. Navy, World War II (September 5, 1912–November 6, 1997)
29. Brown, Margaret C. (January 26, 1887–January 14, 1964)
30. Brown, Zanie W. (December 30, 1885–September 27, 1983)
31. Bryant, M.C. (February 24, 1872–?)
32. Bryant, M.L. [Marcus] (March 14, 1873–October 11, 1922) *Died of cancer of the lip (Death Book B, page 4)*
33. Bryant, Roger Wade (1958–2010)
34. Buchanan, George Lee, CMSgt., U.S. Air Force Ret., Korea & Vietnam (September 23, 1934–September 20, 2006)
35. Buchanan, Sadie Ruth Kennamore (April 23, 1938–April 4, 2011)
36. Burgett, John W. (Died May 11, 1956, aged about 75 years)
37. Burke, Carol Ann (September 4, 1950–January 5, 2007)
38. Carter, Eugene Lafayette "Fate" (1899–1984)
39. Carter, Jewell Massey (1903–1965)
40. Cherry, Florine Massey (September 3, 1917–October 25, 2011)
41. Cherry, William B. "Bill" (October 27, 1917–August 25, 2005)
42. Clayton, Ada D. (October 31, 1889–August 30, 1957)
43. Clayton, Albert H., Tennessee, Private, Co. C, 117 Infantry, 30th Division, World War I (August 31, 1894–March 26, 1970)
44. Clayton, Cora Nello (March 23, 1911–May 27, 1957)
45. Clayton, Craig L. (January 26, 1961–August 18, 1992)
46. Clayton, Ernest L. (July 16, 1889–September 7, 1975)
47. Clayton, Gayle M., U.S. Army, Korea (January 16, 1934–May 4, 2006)
48. Clayton, Hugh Leonard, Private, U.S. Army (September 20, 1892–April 28, 1974)

49. Clayton, James B., son of J.P. & Ada Clayton (August 30, 1914–June 25, 1918)
50. Clayton, John P. (September 23, 1887–April 8, 1975)
51. Clayton, Johnnie T., Jr., Infant Son of J.T. & Earlene Clayton (1946)
52. Clayton, Johnnie Tillman, Tennessee PFC, Co. C, 7th Infantry, World War II, SS-BSM-PH & Oak Leaf Cluster (September 7, 1923–October 24, 1959)
53. Clayton, Lucy A. (September 9, 1863–August 19, 1944)
54. Clayton, Mary Earlene (September 16, 1924–August 17, 2010)
55. Clayton, Mattie S. (August 6, 1892–March 19, 1964)
56. Clayton, May H. (1899–1975)
57. Clayton, Murry P., Tennessee, S. Sgt., 1495 Svc. Comd. Unit, World War II, BSM-PH (April 28, 1920–December 12, 1963)
58. Clayton, Nora Pitts (July 23, 1899–September 1, 1987)
59. Clayton, Robert A. (July 10, 1884–October 26, 1970)
60. Clayton, Sula D. (May 30, 1892–January 5, 1965)
61. Clayton, Troy L., son of J.P. & A.D. Clayton (May 15, 1917–December 17, 1927) *Died of a gunshot wound (Death Book D, page 87)*
62. Clayton, William Brandon (September 24, 1976–May 17, 2013)
63. Clayton, William F. (March 14, 1858–July 15, 1937) *Died of chronic nephritis (Death Book B, page 9)*
64. Connor, Ralph Ray, TSGT, U.S. Air Force, Korea & Vietnam (February 10, 1930–December 7, 2012)
65. Cook, Fauntella Brock (January 22, 1927–June 9, 2009)
66. Cupples, Bonnie Marie Ward (April 25, 1919–July 11, 2004)
67. Dallas, Amy A. (November 16, 1907–June 5, 2007)
68. Dallas, Lonnie L. (April 12, 1903–November 29, 1987)
69. Davidson, Charles M., SM3, U.S. Navy, World War II (November 24, 1925–August 25, 1990)
70. Davidson, Clyde (November 27, 1903–August 21, 1982)
71. Davidson, J.V., son of M.V. & Pearlie Davidson (June 3, 1917–January 24, 1918) *Died of pneumonia (Death Book B, page 11)*
72. Davidson, Lucy (November 23, 1921–April 22, 1998)
73. Davidson, M.V. (December 22, 1881–November 1, 1934) *Died of a hemmorage (Death Book B, page 12)*
74. Davidson, Pearlie (December 7, 1885–May 2, 1954)
75. Davidson, Sara Ann (July 16, 1940–August 2, 1940)

76. Davidson, Vera (July 18, 1908–February 10, 1965)
77. Davis, Exie Horton (1915–1935)
78. Davis, Feelian A. (September 21, 1886–January 30, 1960)
79. Davis, George Henry (1886–1953)
80. Davis, Hattie C. (1886–1950)
81. Davis, John R. (May 5, 1883–January 2, 1968)
82. Davis, Leonard C., Tennessee, Corporal, Battery B, 1st Coast Battery Artillery, World War II (July 13, 1919–January 14, 1968)
83. Davis, Mattie Ann, Wife of W.G. Davis, Mother of M.E., A.E., & W.M. Davis (October 6, 1881–March 29, 1945)
84. Davis, Murry Dwayne (October 18, 1969–October 19, 1970)
85. Davis, Myrtle (April 1, 1889–November 3, 1950)
86. Davis, Wm. G., Husband of M.L. & M.A. Davis, Father of F.A., M.E., A.E., & W.M. Davis (June 8, 1857–April 1, 1940)
87. Davis, William Marvin, PFC, U.S. Army, World War II (January 30, 1918–March 14, 2001)
88. Dees, Allie E. (October 20, 1909–September 28, 1933)[3] *Died of a suicide (Death Book B, page 11)*
89. Dees, Ernest B., son of J.C. & M.E. Dees (March 25, 1900–September 18, 1917)
90. Dees, James C. (January 10, 1879–April 15, 1969)
91. Dees, Mattie E. (March 24, 1882–September 7, 1953)
92. Dickey, A. Ophelia (March 14, 1881–February 1, 1954)
93. Dickey, Amanda, wife of G.W. Dickey (January 30, 1847–August 9, 1916) *Died of asthma (Death Book B, page 11)*
94. Dickey, Brother Bill
95. Dickey, Charles Hays (1924–1926)
96. Dickey, "Uncle" Dolph
97. Dickey, Eliza (1868–1941)
98. Dickey, Frances "Doll" (June 24, 1878–November 18, 1956)
99. Dickey, G. Freelin (1882–1943)
100. Dickey, G.W. [George] (February 12, 1846–March 2, 1918) *Died of pellagra (Death Book B, page 11)*
101. Dickey, "Brother" Ike

3. According to sisters Lessie McIntyre, Vivian McIntyre and Faye McIntyre Talbott, Allie Dees committed suicide by drinking bluing. According to these sisters, Ms. Dees put on a very nice dress, fixed herself, drank the bluing and lay down and crossed her hands and died shortly thereafter.

102. Dickey, James R. (June 11, 1884–May 16, 1921) * *Died of a homicide/gunshot (Death Book D, page 14)*
103. Dickey, Mary Jones (1877–1929) *Died of tuberculosis and a hemorrhage (Death Book D, page 116)*
104. Dillon, Gretchen Harris (August 7, 1909–July 11, 1985)
105. Dillon, Willie Arter (February 5, 1909–December 2, 1974)
106. Droke, Elizabeth (1916–1992)
107. Droke, Jim, Corporal, U.S. Army, World War II (1914–1982)
108. Droke, Minnie B. (1877–1953)
109. Droke, Samuel F. (1876–1952)
110. Findley, Lou (1888–1930)
111. Floyd, Alice Ross (August 28, 1889–) *No Death Date Engraved Upon Stone*
112. Floyd, F.J. (March 3, 1845–April 17, 1932) *Died of chronic bronchitis (Death Book D, page 164)*
113. Floyd, James Ervin (September 13, 1885–January 15, 1920)
114. Floyd, James S. (1905 – 1973)
115. Floyd, L.E. [Lydia] (November 9, 1847–January 11, 1939) *Died of chronic nephritis (Death Book B, page 16)*
116. Floyd, Thelma D. (1916–1992)
117. Frix, Carroll (1914–1935)
118. Frix, Jim (July 15, 1884–January 30, 1965)
119. Frix, Ova (July 9, 1893–April 25, 1983)
120. Fry, John A., Co. F, 49th Illinois Infantry, Union Army *Fry was an Illinois native born July 17, 1844. He died on or about November 17, 1919, at the age of 75 from mitral insufficiency. (Death Book B, page 15)*
121. Fry, Martha, wife of John A. Fry (July 28, 1864–January 1, 1936) *Like her husband, she was also an Illinois native. She died from apoplexy (Death Book B, page 16)*
122. Fry, Willie (April 15, 1901–November 29, 1916) *Died of malaria (Death Book B, page 15)*
123. Frye, Conrad W. (April 9, 1894–May 12, 1969)
124. Frye, Doris Louise (August 12, 1918–July 16, 1989)
125. Frye, Infant son (1920)
126. Frye, Infant son of A.D. & Lela (June 2, 1942)
127. Frye, Lela (May 22, 1896–March 10, 1920)
128. Frye, Mary (December 8, 1891–November 19, 1955)

129. Gaddy, Amburs J. (1903–1975)
130. Gaddy, E.L. (April 8, 1866–June 6, 1923) *Born in North Carolina and died of an unknown complication (Death Book B, page 17)*
131. Gaddy, Joyce Virginia, Infant of Ray & Johnie Gaddy (August 1, 1929)
132. Gaddy, Lou (July 5, 1878–November 21, 1969)
133. Gaddy, Paul E. (July 19, 1910–October 26, 1938)
134. Gaddy, Quay Leory (January 16, 1927–June 12, 2010)
135. Gaddy, Ruby M. (1906–1991)
136. Gage, Infant Daughter of L.J. & Pearl (August 1, 1934) *Died stillborn (Death Book D, page 235)*
137. Gage, Lyman (1907–1985)
138. Gage, Pearl (1908–2003)
139. Gage, Ronald H. (May 26, 1945–December 20, 2009)
140. Garner, Barry Lynn, son of Jim & Vonnie Garner (July 29, 1956)
141. Garner, Terry Branson (February 11, 1959–September 10, 2007)
142. Garner, Vonnie Talbott (August 21, 1924–February 15, 2011)
143. Garner, William Branson (August 14, 1921–October 25, 2012)
144. Gowan, Elizabeth Criswell (April 1, 1913–July 6, 2006)
145. Gowan, William Andrew, U.S. Navy, World War II (November 17, 1908–July 24, 1997)
146. Griffin, J.A. (April 3, 1860–February 2, 1941) A Mason
147. Griffin, N.E. [Nancy Ellen], wife of J.A. Griffin (July 16, 1864–December 6, 1930) *Died of a carcinoma of the colon (Death Book D, page 122)*
148. Grimes, Bennett L. [Lee] (1867–1937) *Died from cancer of the bowels (Death Book B, page 18)*
149. Grimes, Tennie N. (1880–1962)
150. Griswell, E.T. (March 8, 1877–December 7, 1948)
151. Griswell, Ollie (July 13, 1890–May 16, 1983)
152. Hair, A.B. [Annie Bell] (May 19, 1868–February 21, 1918) *Died from mitral regurgitation (Death Book B, page 20)*
153. Hair, W.M. (January 12, 1865–November 12, 1934) *Died of meningitis (Death Book B, page 21)*
154. Hampton, G.W.H. (January 28, 1876–August 29, 1950)
155. Hampton, August 24, 1874–August 7, 1957)
156. Hand, Amanda Ann (September 22, 1880–May 6, 1958)
157. Hand, Martha E. (1922–2004)

158. Hand, Raymon E. (1921–1963)
159. Hand, W.Z. (June 19, 1891–April 4, 1937)
160. Harmon, Elsie Y. (1910–1976)
161. Harmon, Francis, S Sgt., U.S. Army, World War II (May 15, 1916–November 23, 1987)
162. Harris, Eliza Paralee Tedford, wife of W.H. Harris (May 4, 1852–April 19, 1943)
163. Harris, John Lloyd (October 11, 1918–February 2, 2000)
164. Harris, Lela (1880–1958)
165. Harris, Thee (1879–1948)
166. Harris, William H. [Hamilton] (May 19, 1848–September 10, 1933) *Died of nephritis and a brain concussion (Death Book D, page 213)*
167. Haynes, Maxine Long (September 11, 1931–March 15, 2009)
168. Hayre, Alma W. (May 17, 1901–December 3, 1950)
169. Hayre, Hartle (December 26, 1898–January 7, 1991)
170. Hayre, Hayes, Sgt., U.S. Army Air Force, World War II (June 3, 1921–July 16, 2000)
171. Hayre, Stella (March 16, 1925–June 15, 1996)
172. Hickman, Betty June (1933–1935) *Scalded to death (Death Book B, page 21)*
173. Hoagland, Lula Mae Gibson (February 6, 1921–October 10, 1994)
174. Holder, Annie Davis
175. Holder, D.C. [Dolph Calvin] *Born November 6, 1856. *Died on or about March 25, 1928, at the age of 71 from pneumonia (Death Book D, page 105)*
176. Holder, Laura A. (1902–1939)
177. Holder, Marie (1920–1923)
178. Holder, Mary Lee (1928–1947)
179. Hollingsworth, Everett (1909–1957)
180. Hollingsworth, Girtha (1908–1973)
181. Horn, Infant of Dan & Eliza
182. Horton, Infant daughter of Lester & Jo Lee Horton (March 17, 1929)
183. Horton, Joe Lee Dickey (August 12, 1911–April 3, 1931)
184. Hubbard, Luther B. (August 16, 1902–August 27, 1955)
185. Hubbard, Nellie Ailene (February 19, 1908–November 10, 1937)
186. Hurt, Elester [Martha E.], daughter of H.L. & R.E. Hurt (November 6, 1906–June 20, 1925) *Died of mastoriditis (Death Book D, page 27)*

187. Hurt, Hugh L. (September 1, 1876–May 24, 1940)
188. Hurt, Rettie E. (November 30, 1883–October 25, 1944)
189. Ingle, Billy L. (October 1, 1931–December 15, 1977)
190. Ingle, Fate (1871–1963)
191. Ingle, Sarah (1871–1926) *Her death date is given as August 26, 1925 at the age of 54 and that she died of tuberculosis (Death Book B, page 24)*
192. Ingle, Sarah Ellen (December 12, 1888–March 27, 1955)
193. Jones, Rose Marie Meadows (February 26, 1953–May 6, 2006)
194. Joyner, Charles R. (September 13, 1932–March 21, 2009)
195. Joyner, Eula M. (September 18, 1929–May 25, 2010)
196. Joyner, Infants, Triplets of G.L. & Lottie Joyner (Born & Died June 25, 1931)
197. Joyner, James L. (June 6, 1929–January 9, 2000)
198. Joyner, Joyce Ann (October 13, 1953–January 15, 1954)
199. Joyner, Lottie Ward, wife of G.L. Joyner (1901–1945)
200. Joyner, Lueela (February 4, 1911–March 4, 2006)
201. Joyner, Oscar (October 10, 1909–July 3, 1994)
202. Joyner, Rachel G (May 11, 1935–March 19, 2008)
203. Kail, Erchel Lewis, son of Earl & Beulah Kail (1932)
204. Kirkpatrick, C.S."Steve" [Charles] (July 19, 1866–November 20, 1938) *Died of "labor pneumonia" (Death Book B, page 28)*
205. Kirkpatrick, Charles H. (1893–1955)
206. Kirkpatrick, Cora B. (1911–2001)
207. Kirkpatrick, Eula A. (1896–1983)
208. Kirkpatrick, Fuller (1858–1935)
209. Kirkpatrick, H.H. (1882–1962)
210. Kirkpatrick, Hardy (1897–1981)
211. Kirkpatrick, Homer M. (1910–1982)
212. Kirkpatrick, Infant Daughter of Perry & Lillie Mae (December 3, 1936)
213. Kirkpatrick, Jim (April 11, 1874–December 29, 1957)
214. Kirkpatrick, Lizzie C. (1890–1959)
215. Kirkpatrick, Parlee (1902–1983)
216. Kirkpatrick, Trudie E. (July 27, 1872–April 22, 1963)
217. Kirkpatrick, Will (April 26, 1864–March 27, 1948)
218. Kiser, Don Carlos, Infant Son of Mr. & Mrs. C.E. Kiser (Born & Died October 12, 1934)

219. Lay, Calvin Fay, SP4, U.S. Army (February 28, 1935–September 19, 1990)
220. Leath, Elzetta E. (April 16, 1860–July 12, 1945)
221. Leath, James B. (November 28, 1856–November 11, 1944)
222. Leath, John Hardy (September 15, 1891–March 22, 1967)
223. Leath, Mollie (1893–1973)
224. Leath, Pauline T. (May 23, 1896–November 9, 1979)
225. Leath, Reva Mae, daughter of J. J. & Pauline (July 22, 1913–June 3, 1921)
226. Leath, Mrs. Sallie, mother of J.B. Leath (August 15, 1833–November 27, 1923)
227. Leath, W.H. (1889–1920)
228. Leath, William Howard (1915–1970)
229. Leath, Willie Hugh [William H.] (March 6, 1924–January 25, 1927) *Died of diphtheria (Death Book B, page 30)*
230. Leathers, Ruby Walker (January 14, 1915–January 30, 1998)
231. Lemons, Albert Edward "Pete", U.S. Army, World War II (April 21, 1927–August 3, 2005)
232. Lofton, Charles Ray (November 13, 1935–April 19, 1997)
233. Lofton, Lettie Ward (February 13, 1908–January 17, 1997)
234. Lofton, Vannie L. (December 16, 1907–May 19, 1971)
235. Long, Albert R. "Bob", TEC 5, U.S. Army, World War II, Bronze Star Medal, Purple Heart & Oak Leaf Cluster (March 31, 1921–October 16, 2005)
236. Long, Chester
237. Long, Dalton (1888–1962)
238. Long, Hester
239. Long, James
240. Long, Johnny
241. Long, Nannie May (1892–1976)
242. Malone, Marcus D. (1879–1938) *Died on or about March 16, 1938 of myocarditis angina (Death Book B, page 36)*
243. Maness, A.J., Husband of Pearl Maness (June 18, 1881–October 15, 1913)
244. Maness, Flossie G. (August 4, 1909–December 3, 1990)
245. Maness, Guy D. (April 17, 1910–April 3, 1999)
246. Maness, Pearl, wife of A.J. Maness (May 22, 1884–June 10, 1952)

247. Massey, Helen R. (September 22, 1905–October 27, 2001)
248. Massey, James Orby (July 29, 1895–August 4, 1990)
249. Massey, William P. (1868–1948)
250. Massey, Sophronia (1873–1963)
251. Massey, Vivian P. (September 2, 1898–December 15, 1987)
252. McCaskill, Alice (1909–2008)
253. McCaskill, B. Scott, Member of 38th Infantry, 3rd Division M.G.C., Allied Expeditionary Force (February 21, 1893–June 25, 1922)
254. McCaskill, Josephine (October 11, 1864–July 15, 1946)
255. McCaskill, Logan (1896–1960)
256. McCaskill, Thomas K. (August 2, 1856–June 8, 1941)
257. McIntyre, Ella (September 14, 1877–June 5, 1935)[4]
258. McIntyre, Ethel M. (1908–2005)
259. McIntyre, James T. (1943–1962)
260. McIntyre, William Adrian (1881–1979)
261. McKenzie, James R., S. Sgt., U.S. Army, World War II (April 15, 1921–December 22, 1997)
262. McKenzie, Loraine B. (December 15, 1921–October 12, 1999)
263. Meadows, Loraine Bishop (February 2, 1915–January 11, 2000)
264. Meadows, Doyle Bland, SKD2, U.S. Navy, World War II (April 14, 1915–January 16, 1996)
265. Middleton, James Grady, U.S. Navy, World War II (December 19, 1921–November 1, 2001)
266. Middleton, Mary Lynn (August 23, 1930–February 11, 2013) *Wife of James Grady Middleton*
267. Miller, Earnest Ray (September 14, 1946–November 2, 1999)
268. Miller, Essie M. (July 21, 1916–August 24, 2004)
269. Miller, Johnny Ray, son of Ray & Sandra Miller (September 26, 1967–November 8, 1967)
270. Miller, Leland R. (May 9, 1916–March 2, 1995)
271. Mitchell, Allison, son of J.W. & Hattie Mitchell (December 18, 1915–March 13, 1917)
272. Mitchell, Edna (February 21, 1898–February 26, 1988)
273. Mitchell, Ernest D. (January 18, 1887–July 18, 1971)

---

4. Ella McIntyre was the daughter of Finis Miller, the sister of Callie Miller and Mattie Miller. She was married to Adrian McIntyre and the couple had one daughter Cecil McIntyre Parrish. She died after falling on a cut stalk or "stob" which punctured her abdomen.

274. Mitchell, F.C. "Ted", Major, U.S. Air Force, Korea & Vietnam (September 30, 1925–April 17, 2009)
275. Mitchell, Frankie M. (1908–1997)
276. Mitchell, Hal D. (1908–1988)
277. Mitchell, James N. (1937–1937)
278. Mitchell, James Ovid (1906–1965)
279. Mitchell, John L., Sgt., U.S. Army, World War II (August 3, 1911–May 29, 2001)
280. Mitchell, Mary Lou (1916–2013) *Wife of James Ovid Mitchell*
281. Mitchell, Son of E.D. & Edna Mitchell (Born & Died June 22, 1921)
282. Moore, Elaine S. "Pudge" (July 28, 1948–August 2, 2000)
283. Moore, Inez Walker, wife of Millard Moore (May 10, 1910–March 16, 1942)
284. Moore, John Robert (June 29, 1899–December 11, 1967)
285. Moore, Ruth McIntyre (February 26, 1908–November 8, 1978)
286. Morgan, Emma Fowler (July 31, 1905–August 1, 1985)
287. Morgan, William A., Tennessee, PFC, U.S. Army, World War I (January 14, 1897–July 11, 1972)
288. Naylor, Betty (April 15, 1870–January 15, 1947)
289. Naylor, Charlie H. (October 20, 1931–September 26, 1974)
290. Naylor, Cora B. Clayton (August 29, 1882–September 1, 1937)
291. Naylor, George Thomas (February 1, 1860–March 14, 1942)
292. Naylor, Hubert H. (1891–1965)
293. Naylor, Infant sons of Bill & Sue Naylor (September 19, 1951)
294. Naylor, Jimmie C. (August 1, 1929–June 23, 2007)
295. Naylor, John T. (July 14, 1887–November 3, 1979)
296. Naylor, Lena R. (1905–1989)
297. Naylor, Mary Ellen (July 28, 1862–July 12, 1954)
298. Naylor, Mattie Lou (April 6, 1936–February 6, 1937) *Died of double pneumonia (Death Book B, page 39)*
299. Naylor, Willie Earl "Bill," U.S. Army, World War II (September 13, 1916–January 27, 2008)
300. Nix, Willis, son of Glover & Johnie Nix (August 25, 1918–December 27, 1918)
301. Noel, Ivan Homer, Tennessee, TEC5, 2nd Coast Artillery, World War II (November 8, 1920–April 26, 1956)
302. Noel, Ottie Faye (June 29, 1926–April 1, 1981)

303. Patterson, Bernice (1910–1999)
304. Patterson, Colonel (1899–1979)
305. Patterson, Kenton (February 17, 1936–March 4, 2006)
306. Patterson, Nora Beene (October 3, 1895–August 3, 1939) *Wife of Allen Patterson, who is buried at Mount Carmel Cemetery.*
307. Peeples, E.C. "Eddie" (1884–1964)
308. Peeples, Oma K. (1891–1965)
309. Petty, J.H. (1849–1925) **Died of nephritis on or about August 16, 1925 (Death Book B, page 41)*
310. Phillips, Allie Sue (May 26, 1927–March 20, 1982)
311. Phillips, Edward L., Sgt., U.S. Marine Corps, World War II (June 15, 1921–April 29, 1998)
312. Plunk, Callie Albia (July 28, 1904–January 27, 1937) **Died in childbirth (Death Book B, page 43)*
313. Plunk, Frank (December 28, 1909–March 10, 2000)
314. Plunk, Luda J. (October 19, 1911–January 5, 2001)
315. Randall, Cooper (1888–1961)
316. Randall, Ina (1896–1967)
317. Redmon, Colonel R. (January 30, 1913–May 17, 1983)
318. Redmon, Crystal Ward (October 10, 1913–June 9, 1993)
319. Reed, Kimberly Dawn Tignor (January 22, 1978–October 23, 2009)
320. Reed, Wyatt Landon, son of Ricahrd & Kim Reed (December 5, 2003)
321. Reeves, Flossie (August 11, 1917–September 21, 1977)
322. Roberson, Infant Daughter of F.C. & Annie (December 15, 1939)
323. Roberson, Infant Son of F.C. & Annie (August 2, 1941)
324. Robertson, Jim (1867–1934) **Transcribed as "Jim Robinson" on death records but is in fact Jim Robertson who died on or about January 27, 1934 at the age of 67 of apoplexy and asthma. (Death Book B, page 46)*
325. Robertson, Lemma (1879–1934) **Died on or about December 29, 1934 of pneumonia (Death Book B, page 46)*
326. Robison, Emma Melene (1902–1995)
327. Robison, Infant daughter of Mr. & Mrs. W.H. Robison (August 30, 1945)
328. Robison, Jerry Lee (October 13, 1945–April 11, 1970)
329. Robison, Larry W. (February 24, 1941–July 27, 1989)
330. Robison, Lawrence W. (October 17, 1902–January 19, 1982)
331. Robison, Sue A. (November 27, 1911–January 3, 2008)

332. Robison, Wm. Harrison (1888–1967)
333. Ross, Betty A. Boyd (October 25, 1870–?)
334. Ross, T.B. [Tobe B.] (August 29, 1861–November 15, 1930) *Died of cancer of the jaw (Death Book B, page 46)*
335. Russom, Buford (January 22, 1908–September 13, 1994)
336. Russom, Georgia (April 27, 1912–October 8, 2003)
337. Scott, Gladys Dorothy (November 12, 1922–August 31, 2005)
338. Scott, Mickey Thos., son of T.A. & Gladys Scott (November 27, 1949–April 30, 1950)
339. Segerson, F.M. (1878–1945)
340. Segerson, Lillie (1886–1976)
341. Simpson, Ada Dora (1905–1968)
342. Simpson, Kinney A., Corporal, Army Service Corps, World War I (November 18, 1892–May 29, 1968)
343. Sims, Joseph P., Jr., (December 10, 1964–February 2, 1997)
344. Smith, Doris Annette (September 19, 1938–November 26, 1939)
345. Smith, Frank P. (1905–1970)
346. Smith, G.C., Jr. (August 4, 1946–August 4, 1946)
347. Smith, Louise, daughter of Bob & Luelar Stovall (May 25, 1925–March 12, 1943)
348. Smith, Mary Beatrice (1901–1955)
349. Smith, Mary R. (November 17, 1888–February 24, 1920) *Died of tuberculosis (Death Book B, page 51)*
350. Smith, Robert M. (1887–1976)
351. Smith, Russell Ray (January 15, 1944–March 20, 2007)
352. Smith, Virginia M., daughter of Arthur & Emma Stovall (September 28, 1926–November 7, 1988)
353. Smith, Willie H. (1910–1999)
354. Stansell, John W. (June 27, 1855–?)
355. Staton, Tom (July 8, 1880–July 24, 1962)
356. Stewart, Infant Son of Lester & Margie (November 20, 1936)
357. Stovall, "Little" Arthur (1908–1927) *Died on or about November 26, 1927 of pneumonia (Death Book D, page 87)*
358. Stovall, Beulah F. (July 30, 1898–August 5, 1984)
359. Stovall, Charlie W. (1879–1964)
360. Stovall, Edith, daughter of R.L. & Beulah Stovall (February 19, 1913–October 21, 1913) *Died of dysentery (Death Book B, page 51)*

361. Stovall, Emma Lee (July 1, 1897–August 30, 1976)
362. Stovall, James *Could be James F. Stovall (February 17, 1848–May 19, 1925)*
363. Stovall, James A. (July 2, 1895–October 23, 1980)
364. Stovall, Janie R. (1883–1968)
365. Stovall, Jesse C. (September 15, 1893–January 19, 1966)
366. Stovall, Mary (August 29, 1893–May 7, 1917)
367. Stovall, Mary F.
368. Stovall, Louella M. (1885–1953)
369. Stovall, Nannie, wife of R.L. Stovall (March 23, 1901–September 6, 1917)
370. Stovall, Riley L. (November 7, 1897–April 17, 1974)
371. Stovall, Robert T. (1886–1963)
372. Sutton, Era M., daughter of J.G. Young (December 12, 1902–March 17, 1929)
373. Talbott, Faye McIntyre (March 10, 1924–October 16, 2011)
374. Talbott, Luther Edward "Junior," U.S. Navy, World War II (July 23, 1921–January 2, 2007)
375. Talbott, Michael E., son of L.E. & Faye Talbott (July 13, 1947–July 22, 1947)
376. Taylor, Georgia A. (September 28, 1910–March 17, 1997)
377. Taylor, Walter L. (August 18, 1913–April 21, 1997)
378. Tedford, Earl Willie, Tennessee, QM3, U.S. Navy, World War II (May 13, 1922–February 8, 1949)
379. Tedford, Ernest S. (March 22, 1890–January 1, 1976)
380. Tedford, Gussie Beene (September 10, 1895–August 29, 1978)
381. Tedford, Infant son of E.S. & Lucy (1929)
382. Tedford, J.V. [John] (1857–1930) *Died on or about July 17, 1930, of senility (Death Book B, page 54)*
383. Tedford, Lucy Clara, wife of E.S. Tedford (September 22, 1893–April 29, 1952)
384. Tedford, Lula (1867–1942)
385. Tedford, Mary Birtie (1893–1980)
386. Tedford, Nora M. (April 4, 1898–August 21, 1973)
387. Tedford, Sarah Ada, wife of E.S. Tedford (February 1, 1896–October 22, 1925)
388. Tedford, Vaudie Lee (1891–1946)
389. Tedford, William Barney (February 4, 1897–December 24, 1952)

390. Tilley, infant triplets of L.D. & Orell (Born & Died October 1949)
391. Tucker, Beulah Harris (July 9, 1883–October 5, 1955)
392. Tucker, Nathaniel A., M.D. (April 3, 1879–September 3, 1951)
393. Tucker, Will Clark (January 22, 1912–December 3, 1976)
394. Vickery, I. Dellar (May 22, 1888–December 28, 1968)
395. Vickery, James Yullis (September 2, 1879–February 12, 1947)
396. Vires, Alvia M. (1908–1993)
397. Vires, Arthur W. (1908–1984)
398. Virgin, Dorothy Imogene (February 25, 1929–August 14, 2002)
399. Walker, Charles F., Private, U.S. Army, World War II (September 17, 1904–June 26, 1980)
400. Walker, Edna (1876–1955)
401. Walker, Hildred W. (1910–1994)
402. Walker, Ida F. (1873–1954)
403. Walker, Infant daughter of J.C. & Hildred (April 13, 1933)
404. Walker, J.C. (1902–1971)
405. Walker, Murry F. (1866–1950)
406. Walker, Penny Lynn Williams (1965–1998)
407. Walker, W.H. "Tobe" (October 21, 1872–February 20, 1948)
408. Ward, Dona (1879–1955)
409. Ward, James Leonard (April 18, 1909–November 10, 1989)
410. Ward, John G. (1872–1967)
411. Ward, John Gilbert, son of J.G. & Dona Ward (September 4, 1924–April 28, 1937)[5] *Died of sarcoma of the hip (Death Book B, page 59)*
412. Weaver, Dovie K. (December 11, 1873–March 8, 1962)
413. Weaver, John B. (January 12, 1872–May 30, 1959)
414. Weaver, Lee A. (March 24, 1869–May 8, 1952)
415. Weaver, Lester L. (1900–1979)
416. Weaver, Lue J. (1907–1994)
417. Weaver, Lydia M. (November 13, 1879–September 29, 1963)
418. Webb, Mary Orell Ward (March 22, 1921–February 7, 2007)
419. Webster, Mary C. (January 1874–June 19, 1944)

5. John Gilbert Ward's classmate and childhood friend, Faye D. McIntyre Talbott (1924–2011), recalled Ward's illness in her dotage. She recalled that he was a sweet child and easygoing in his youthful demeanor. He began to hurt in his hip and was suddenly unable to run and play and withered away quickly. She remembered his death vividly because he was the second of her childhood friends to die during their children, the first being her first cousin, Audrey Roberta McIntyre (1928–1935).

THE BURYING GROUNDS OF NORTH McNAIRY 373

420. Wharton, Hassie Pyron (October 6, 1896–November 10, 1954)
421. Wharton, Johnnie H. (September 27, 1885–January 10, 1963)
422. Wharton, Lottie Marie (May 16, 1926–February 23, 1927)
423. Wicker, Arbon (1905–1978)
424. Wicker, Nancy Inetha, daughter of Arbon & Sudie Wicker (June 7, 1936) *Died of prenatal trauma (Death Book B, page 59)*
425. Wicker, Nina Olivia, daughter of Arbon & Sudie Wicker (April 10, 1941)
426. Wicker, Sudie (1912–1971)
427. Williams, Barbara Ann (1957–1976)
428. Williams, Bernice (1919–2012), wife of Ward Williams
429. Williams, Euda (November 23, 1887–September 26, 1972)
430. Williams, Hatton (March 10, 1885–March 16, 1972)
431. Williams, Raymond Hayes, son of Bernice & Ward Williams (September 3, 1939–November 18, 1939)
432. Williams, Ward (1916–1986)
433. Williams, Warren W. (1919–2010)
434. Wilson, A.J. (1922–1975)
435. Wilson, Alfe M., son of A.J. & Frances (June 22, 1949–June 16, 1950)
436. Wilson, Harold Joe (August 27, 1947–January 22, 2014)
437. Wilson, Jo Ellen, daughter of J.V. & Mavoureen (January 6, 1941–January 11, 1942)
438. Wilson, Regina Ann, daughter of Harold & Brenda Wilson (Born & Died April 29, 1973)
439. Womble, Fannie (October 24, 1874–June 17, 1933) *Died of an organic heart disease or heart lesion (Death Book B, page 58)*
440. Womble, I.P.(August 11, 1861–May 13, 1954)
441. Young, Cora E. (1897–1974)
442. Young, Ella (1878–1962)
443. Young, Frank, U.S. Army, World War II (August 21, 1911–April 29, 1986)
444. Young, Hillard Hazel (1906–1965)
445. Young, Horry, Private, U.S. Army, World War II (December 14, 1906–May 5, 1986)
446. Young, Infant Son of R.G. & C.B. (June 7, 1925)
447. Young, James A. (1869–1955)
448. Young, James F. (August 27, 1868–September 4, 1939)

449. Young, John G. (1876–1948)
450. Young, Lessie (1901–1981)
451. Young, Martin Hampton (January 1, 1878–September 9, 1931) *Died of carcinoma cancer of the stomach (Death Book B, page 61)*
452. Young, Ollie Floss (October 7, 1911–January 6, 1998)
453. Young, Robert (1906–1990)
454. Young, Sarah L. (November 18, 1876–November 23, 1948)
455. Young, Winnie May (May 26, 1884–October 29, 1955)
456–458. Three unknown graves marked by rusty metal markers

Finger Christian Fellowship Cemetery

The Finger Christian Fellowship Cemetery is located behind the church of the same name. It is located on Mockingbird Lane in Finger just off Highway 199/Finger-Leapwood Road. The cemetery was established to allow for the burial of members of this church and members and associates of the greater population of the community known commonly (and mistakenly) around Finger as the Mennonites.

1. Hostetler, Ada (August 27, 1962–September 27, 2004)
2. Koehn, Alma (January 16, 1919–August 26, 2000)
3. Koehn, Curtis (October 13, 1921–November 10, 1988)
4. Mast, Colton Walker (January 27, 2012–June 22, 2013) Son of William Mast, Jr. & Carolyn Weaver Mast. *Currently marked only by a wooden board with initials C.W.M.*
5. Mast, Weston Avery (December 28, 2010–December 30, 2010) *Infant Son of Junior & Carolyn Mast*
6. Shipman, Tabitha Joy, Daughter of Terry & Cindy Shipman (August 8, 1989–August 10, 1989)
7. Stoll, Victor (November 17, 1931–November 23, 2010) Pastor of Finger Fellowship Christian Church for 22 years and founder of the Purple Martin Festival. *Grave is currently unmarked.*
8. Stoltzfus, Emanuel S. (April 18, 1934–December 17, 1992)
9. Stoltzfus, Paul Wayne (August 17, 1972–August 14, 2000)

Floyd (Mickens) Cemetery

The Floyd Cemetery is located on the old Curt Walker farm just off of Clayton Road between McNairy and Finger. It is the burying ground of many of the Floyd family, one of the oldest families in the county. Today it is in great disrepair and covered in undergrowth. Because the author could better discern the rows of graves in this cemetery, it will be listed as to rows. However, keep in mind that early settlers were not overly concerned with a cemetery that was symmetrical, but rather functional.

Row One
1. Ulyssus J., son of U.J. and M.E. Warsham (June 25, 1895–March 21, 1896)
2. U.J. Warsham, husband of M.E. Warsham (October 24, 1867–March 5, 1895)
3. Susie, daughter of U.J. and M.E. Warsham (September 1, 1888–October 1, 1889)
4. William J., son of U.J. and M.E. Warsham (February 12, 1892–March 15, 1896)
5. Joel Harris (headstone completely worn and cannot be read)
6. Avy M., daughter of Joel mad Temperance Harris (dates are illegible due to damage)

Row Two
7. T.J. Warsham, Company B, U.S. Sixth Tennessee Cavalry
   Thomas J. Warsham, born in Rome, North Carolina circa 1837, date of death unknown.
8. Susan T., wife of T.J. Warsham, (died August 13, 1887, aged 52 years)
9. Sophronia U., daughter of T.J. and S.T. Warsham (April 28, 1863–March 19, 1884)
10. S.L. Warsham
11. Sarah J., daughter of E.H. and Hannah Tisdale (died October 22, 1849, aged 12 days)
12. Frederick, son of Francis and Eliza Floyd (died March 25, 1841, aged 3 months)
13. Avy J.G., daughter of F. Floyd (died August 15, 1840, aged 27 years, 8 months, and 7 days)

14. Elizabeth H.M., daughter of F. Floyd (died May 20, 1839, aged 12 years, 5 days)
15. Sarah Floyd (July 22, 1792–September 17, 1855)
16. Frederick Floyd (died October 19, 1840; 52 years, 3 mo., 16 days)

Row Three
17. Unknown—Cedar
18. Unknown—Sandstone
19. Unknown—Sandstone
20. Unknown—Sandstone
21. Unknown—Sandstone
22. Unknown—Cedar
23. Unknown—Cedar and sandstone
24. Unknown—Cedar and sandstone
25. Unknown—Cedar
26. Unknown—Cedar stump
27. Unknown
28. Unknown—Sandstone
29. Unknown—Cedar
30. Unknown—Cedar
31. Unknown—Cedar
32. Unknown—Sandstone
33. Unknown—Sandstone
34. Unknown—Cedar stump and sandstone
35. Unknown—Cedar stump
36. Unknown—Cedar stump

Row Four
37. Unknown—Cedar and sandstone
38. Unknown—Sandstone
39. Unknown—Sandstone
40. Unknown—Sandstone
41. Josephene, wife of S.W. James (March 26, 1851—September 22, 1875)
42. Infant daughter of S.W. and J. James (born 1871)

There are a few notes on Floyd Cemetery which should be addressed. First, M.E. Warsham, the wife of U.J. Warsham is probably buried in one of the "unknown" graves, as well as perhaps Temperance Harris and S.W. James. Second, why this has been called Mickens Cemetery is not exactly known. There are no marked Mickens' graves. Perhaps they are buried in some of the unmarked graves, but there seems to be no way to know. Because many of the tombstones in this old cemetery are badly damaged, much care was taken to correctly read these markers.

Griswell Cemetery

Griswell Cemetery is located on the old Virgil Smith farm just off of present-day Payne Road. At best count there are 22 individuals buried in this old graveyard. Most of these graves are probably Griswells. Some of the unmarked graves are known and can be identified, even though the exact grave cannot be matched with the name. In other words, they are out there but one cannot say with particularity which grave is which.

1. Matilda G. Plunk, wife of J.A. Plunk (August 1827–March 11, 1852). *It is quite possible that J.A. Plunk is buried here also in an unmarked grave. However, there is a J.A. Plunk (January 25, 1825–November 11, 1918) buried in Liberty Cemetery.*
2. Sarah Phillips, wife of Isaac Phillips (February 10, 1803–April 10, 1863). *It is quite possible that Isaac Phillips is buried here also in an unmarked grave.*
3. Daniel C. "Dan" Griswell (August 1865–September 20, 1938)[6] *Died of "traumatic pneumonia" (Death Book B, page 18)*
4. E.R. Griswell, father of Dan Griswell (born 1821, died before 1900)
5. Margaret S. Griswell, wife of E.R. Griswell (born 1833, died after 1900)
6. Daniel Harwood Barham (November 11, 1811–1860)
7. Mary Penina Shelton Barham, wife of Daniel H. Barham (1816–1873)
8.–22. Unknown

Hendrix Cemetery

Hendrix Cemetery is located on the Clarence Barham Road east of Finger, about a mile and a half off of the Finger-Leapwood Road. The cemetery was established in 1839 by William Hendrix and his son Richard

---

6. The Federal Census for McNairy County stated Dan Griswell's birth year as 1865, but according to Gooch Funeral Home Records, he was seventy-eight years old at the time of his death, making his birth year 1860.

Ivy Hendrix. There are approximately 49 graves in this small cemetery. A census of this cemetery appears in the book *Fingerprints* in the form of a grave by grave track, complete with grave identifiers. Here, however, a simple list will be presented with additions which have been marked and identified since the publication of that prior work and have been discovered to have been unmarked graves otherwise documented elsewhere and the works themselves only recently discovered and enjoyed by the author.

1. Robert Lee Hendrix (April 5, 1869–April 28, 1947) *Freemason*
2. Thomas Edgar Hendrix (December 28, 1877–September 10, 1879)
3. Richard Ivy Hendrix (1804–1888) *Although this is a marked grave, the same individual appears to be enumerated as an unmarked grave in an index of unmarked graves in McNairy County and is listed as Richard Ivy Hendrix (December 31, 1804–July 14, 1888).*[7]
4. Rebecca Cherry Hendrix (1808–1839) wife of Richard Ivy Hendrix.[8] *Although this is a marked grave, the same individual appears to be enumerated as an unmarked grave in an index of unmarked graves in McNairy County and is still listed as Rebecca Cherry Hendrix (March 19, 1808–February 1, 1839).*[9]
5. John Milford Hendrix (March 10, 1823–March 7, 1865) first child of R.I. and R.C. Hendrix; husband of Mary Brown; father of eight; Private, Co. I, 154th Senior Tennessee Infantry Regiment, Confederate States of America. Footstone reads: "Widow of J.M. Hendrix, Mary B. Hendrix, buried at Pontotoc, Mississippi."[10]
6. Zillah, daughter of A.H. and Joca Hendrix (January 2, 1880–August 27, 1906)
7. Susie Pauline, daughter of Mr. and Mrs. A.H. Hendrix (August 5, 1908–August 22, 1908)
8. A.H. Hendrix (January 1, 1856–July 21, 1941)
9. Sidney Ann Hendrix (September 9, 1866–March 22, 1909) wife of A.H. Hendrix
10. Joceophen, wife of A.H. Hendrix (June 30, 1856–January 5, 1887)

7. Kennedy, *Unmarked Graves in McNairy County, Tennessee.*
8. Apparently this was the first grave in the cemetery.
9. *Id.*
10. John Milford Hendrix was killed, perhaps murdered, during the hostilities of the War Between the States. See Chapter Three of this work for greater detail.

THE BURYING GROUNDS OF NORTH McNAIRY

11. W.C., son of W.R. and M.O. Hendrix (December 17, 1908–July 5, 1910) *Although this is a marked grave, the same individual appears to be enumerated as an unmarked grave in an index of unmarked graves in McNairy County and is listed as William Claude Hendrix, the son of William Richard Hendrix and Mary Hendrix.*[11]
12. Nancy Beard, wife of Richard Ivy Hendrix (1818–1856) *Although this is a marked grave, the same individual appears to be enumerated as an unmarked grave in an index of unmarked graves in McNairy County and is listed as Nancy Beard Hendrix (1818–January 11, 1856).*[12]
13. Nicy Hendrix Cocke (1847–1893) *Although this is a marked grave, the same individual appears to be enumerated as an unmarked grave in an index of unmarked graves in McNairy County and is listed as Nicy Cansady Hendrix Cocke (May 12, 1841–September 13, 1893).*[13]
14. Juda A., wife of E.W. Starks (June 6, 1840–September 3, 1876)
15. G.G. Vires (February 10, 1877–February 20, 1919) *Died of influenza and pneumonia (Death Book D, page 10)*
16. Mahala Francis Hendrix Davis (Barton), wife of Jasper Davis (April 29, 1844–April 28, 1908)
17. Davis A. Barton, died January 28, 1943 *Metal marker located next to Ivy Barton*
18. William Ivy Barton (February 21, 1870–February 1, 1945)
19. Nancy Ann Barton (March 21, 1889–November 1, 1958) wife of Ivy Barton
20. Ellen Francis Barton, Child of Ivy & Nancy Barton
21. Nicie Lee Barton, Child of Ivy & Nancy Barton
22. Ivy Allen Barton, Child of Ivy & Nancy Barton
23. Johnny Hubert Barton, Child of Ivy & Nancy Barton
24. Jim Barham Barton, Child of Ivy & Nancy Barton
25. Moses Aaron Barton, Child of Ivy & Nancy Barton, (April 10, 1926–January 27, 1943)
26. David Barton, Child of Ivy & Nancy Barton
27. Daniel Barton, Child of Ivy & Nancy Barton
28. Moses Barton, Child of Ivy & Nancy Barton
29. Francis Massengill (July 18, 1859–March 18, 1864)

11. *Id.*
12. *Id.*
13. *Id.*

30. Drury Goss Hendrix (December 29, 1825–June 1, 1853) *Unmarked grave*[14]
31. Nancy Ann Bratcher Hendrix (1763–1849)
32. Sarah Malinda Hendrix, Daughter of Ivy and Nancy Hendrix (April 10, 1849–November 23, 1858) *Unmarked grave*[15]
33. William Hendrix (1760–1843)
34. John Allen Barton (March 10, 1846–November 20, 1878)
35. Unknown

Hopewell Cemetery

Hopewell Cemetery lies in the far northern section of McNairy County near the Chester County line. It is located in the vicinity of the Bullman Store community. Within the confines of this old burying ground are the families who long ago settled and inhabited that area: the Bullmans, Baileys, Talbotts, Loftins, and Stewarts. A church has existed there for generations, prior to the War Between the States. Although the author does not currently have any information regarding the original deed or gift of conveyance to the old cemetery and church, it is known that U.N. Bullman and family and neighbors did donate two and one-half acres of land in 1914. The deed of conveyance was from U.N. Bullman, Mollie Bullman, S.H. Bullman, G.C. Bullman, E.S. Bullman, S.V. Loftin, M.T. Stewart and Florence Lee. It was dated January 9, 1914, and conveyed the following tract of land to the church:

> **BEGINNING** south east of Hope Well Church on a red oak Runs north 11 poles to a red oak; then west 13 poles to a hickory; then north west 8 poles to a hickory same being the north east corner of Grave Yard lot; then west 18 poles to a hickory; then south 11 poles to a post oak; then east 18 poles to a post oak; then south east 8 poles to a red oak; then east 13 poles to the beginning, containing two & one half acres more or less.

14. *Id.*
15. *Id.*

Today, there are approximately 132 graves in the cemetery including approximately 47 unknown graves; some eighty-five graves are marked and identified.

1. Bailey, A. Irel (June 6, 1911–June 9, 1985)
2. Bailey, Florence Elsie (May 22, 1908–September 18, 1941)
3. Bailey, Ruby A. (February 13, 1922–July 29, 2011)
4. Browder, Thomas, husband of Sarah Plunk (1861–1900)
5. Bullman, Clarence D. (January 13, 1937–August 20, 2000)
6. Bullman, Clarence E. (October 7, 1919–September 10, 1938)
7. Bullman, E.S. [Betsey] (August 23, 1838–April 20, 1915) *Died of paralysis (Death Book D, page 3)*
8. Bullman, G[eorge] N[ewton], Co. B, U.S. Sixth Tennessee Cavalry (May 18, 1828–April 27, 1907) *Born in Union County, South Carolina.*
9. Bullman, George C. (1869–1938)
10. Bullman, infant son of G.C. & Lessie Bullman (1908)
11. Bullman, Jewell Ruth (January 11, 1916–December 8, 1995)
12. Bullman, Lessie Ann (1884–1980)
13. Bullman, Leon (February 2, 1928–September 10, 1998)
14. Bullman, Mary, daughter of U.N. & Luarkey Bullman (August 10, 1903–August 4, 1906)
15. Bullman, Mary M. (May 24, 1862–August 13, 1943)
16. Bullman, Mittie, daughter of S.H. & W.E. Bullman (November 27, 1906–May 20, 1909)
17. Bullman, Newton Van Buren (December 8, 1910–June 17, 1993)
18. Bullman, Ocie (March 2, 1913–February 9, 1919)
19. Bullman, Pearl Gatley (June 16, 1902–December 29, 1990)
20. Bullman, Sam H. (May 6, 1872–January 8, 1928)
21. Bullman, Tillie (June 6, 1877–December 24, 1950)
22. Bullman, William Odis (July 18, 1909–December 6, 1980)
23. Connor, Charles Ray, FN, U.S. Navy, Vietnam (June 9, 1949–October 14, 1998)
24. Cupples, Jerry Paul, A1C, U.S. Air Force (May 10, 1942–September 24, 2007)
25. Davis, Claudie T. (May 14, 1904–December 28, 1977)
26. Davis, Elizabeth, wife of H.C. Davis

27. Davis, G.W. (1854–1921)
28. Davis, H.C. (February 20, 1828–February 1, 1896)
29. Davis, J.H. (February 22, 1860–November 5, 1891)
30. Davis, Lou W. (1873–1955)
31. Fowler, Lucy, wife of O.W.Fowler (1882–May 5, 1917)
32. Goff, Linda Sue (January 30, 1949–December 5, 1997)
33. Greene, Lessie O. (November 9, 1932–September 25, 1933)
34. Greene, Marvin H. (December 14, 1908–October 8, 1931)
35. Kinchen, Royce Alton (August 27, 1910–December 24, 1989)
36. Kinchen, Ruth Mae (May 17, 1917–March 14, 2005)
37. Kizer, Joseph (March 16, 1801–March 4, 1868)
38. Kizer, Sarah (December 31, 1803–October 14, 1866)
39. Lee, Florence (1881–1973)
40. Lee, Hollis Wildon (January 12, 1943–July 13, 2013)
41. Lee, J. Edd (1884–1927) *Died of pellagra on or about January 19, 1927 (Death Book B, page 30)*
42. Loftin, Infant Son of W.A. & S.V. (April 27, 1895–May 4, 1895)
43. Lofton, James S. (1844–1920)
44. Lofton, Martha Ann (1856–1935) *Died of pneumonia on February 7, 1935 (Death Book B, page 30)*
45. Lofton Triplets
46. Lofton Twins
47. Massengill, J.F. (November 19, 1871–May 1, 1930) *Died of paralysis (Death Book B, page 34)*
48. Melton, Brodie (1903–1963)
49. Melton, Lena
50. Melton, Lutie (1906–1996)
51. Melton, Virgie [Virginia E.] *Died on July 22, 1935, at the age of 35 from a miscarriage (Death Book B, page 34)*
52. Patterson, Enoch (1846–1916) *According the death records, he died of dysentery on July 4, 1917 (Death Book B, page 41)*
53. Patterson, Piny (1850–1883)
54. Patterson, Samuel McKenley (June 15, 1897–October 3, 1921) *Died of malaria (Death Book B, page 42)*
55. Pickett, Clyde (March 27, 1909–January 13, 1992)
56. Pickett, Murna (June 12, 1916–September 22, 2005)

57. Plunk, Roberta [Frances R.], wife of O.M. Plunk (December 18, 1888–December 10, 1918) *Died of influenza (Death Book B, page 42)*
58. Ridley, Joe Lee, U.S. Navy, World War II (January 6, 1917–April 24, 2008)
59. Ridley, Lidy Mae (October 31, 1924–April 16, 1999)
60. Shannon, George W., ARM 3, U.S. Navy, World War II (September 27, 1924–April 3, 2004)
61. Smith, Brodie Hartford (1911–1927) *Died of pneumonia on either November 14 or 15, 1927 (Death Book B, page 50)*
62. Smith, Lee A. (1875–1929)
63. Smith, Rosa T. (1876–1969)
64. Stewart, infant daughter of T.M. & M.T. Stewart (July 2, 1911–July 3, 1911)
65. Stewart, Mary Elizabeth, daughter of T.M. & M.T. Stewart (July 19, 1906–July 25, 1906)
66. Talbert, Charlie H. (March 10, 1885–July 10, 1954)
67. Talbert, Sarah M. (July 8, 1881–June 26, 1955)
68. Talbert, W.C. (April 20, 1880–October 31, 1956)
69. Talbott, Alexander P., Infant son of N.P. & Nancy Talbott (1905)
70. Talbott, Angie Nora (1849–1926)
71. Talbott, Bessie Arlene "Lena" Gateley (1893–1930)[16] *Died of embolus on or about July 31, 1930 (Death Book D, page 121)*
72. Talbott, infant child of Luther & Lena (1930) *Died stillborn on or about July 19, 1930 (Death Book D, page 121)*
73. Talbott, Nancy J., wife of N.P. Talbott (1876–December 21, 1915)
74. Talbott, Newton P. (1878–1947)
75. Talbott, Varham (1889–1970)
76. Talbott, William Alexander (1844–1916)
77. Talbott, William P., son of N.P. & Mary Talbott (Spring 1918–October 30, 1918)[17]
78. Tidwell, Lula B. (1897–1977)

---

16. Family tradition and oral history had held that Lena died giving birth to her and Luther Talbott's son. However, she outlived the stillborn child by some twelve days. Certainly, it still possible if not probable that Lena's death was certainly childbirth related.

17. This child is said to have died of influenza during the great influenza pandemic of 1918-1919 that killed millions worldwide. The child's mother has died earlier in the year and was buried in Henderson County, Tennessee, near her hometown of Scotts Hill.

79. Williams, C.C. (1895–1917)
80. Williams, Dee (1863–1939)
81. Williams, Doskey Dahlia (February 21, 1900–August 14, 1976)
82. Williams, Ervin E., U.S. Army, World War II (March 26, 1906–November 20, 1985)
83. Williams, George (1865–1920)
84. Williams, M.I. (1891–1896)
85. Williams, Preasley Payton (July 1, 1903–May 9, 1979)
86. Williams, W.W. (1897–1910)

Ingraham Cemetery

The old Ingraham Family Cemetery is located on McCormick Road on the old John S. Ingraham plantation. It is located across the road from the old Tom Barham house just to the north of where the Ingraham mansion house was once located. John S. Ingraham was one of the early settlers of north McNairy County and is profiled in chapter two of this work. In this cemetery are members of John S. Ingraham's immediate family, which are marked, and five marked with cedars and one marked with a brick. These latter graves belong to the slaves of the Ingrahams, who preferred to bury these servants close to them in the family plot. The small cemetery was, in 1995, in very good condition and well-kept. However, by 2012, the cemetery was littered with fallen limbs and portions of trees.

1. John S. Ingraham (Died August 8, 1855, Aged about 65 years)
2. Rebecca Ingraham, wife of John S. Ingraham (Died February 16, 1830, Aged about 40 years)
3. Infant Son of J.S. and R. Ingraham (Died December 10, 1826)
4. Infant Daughter of J.S. and R. Ingraham (Died February 10, 1830)
5. Ingraham slave—Cedar and brick
6. Ingraham slave—Cedar
7. Ingraham slave—Cedar
8. Ingraham slave—Cedar
9. Ingraham slave—Cedar stump

It is interesting to note that Rebecca Ingraham died on February 16, 1830, just six days after giving birth to the infant daughter buried on the old plantation. Such occurrences were common during the years before modern medicine and medical facilities.

Ingraham-Smith Portion of New Oak Grove Cemetery

Although a part of Chester County in the heart of the Talleytown community and looking over Whistle Hill, this old section of New Oak Grove Cemetery was once located in north McNairy County. It is the oldest section of the present cemetery, but much older and kept in the less than satisfactory repair. Here lie some of the prominent early settlers of the county. It is easily located when a person is standing in New Oak Grove Cemetery. The names are presented in the order they are laid out, for purposes of identification if ever a need arises.

1. A.H. Ingraham (1819–1870)
2. Myrtle D., daughter of N.P. and A.B. Ingraham (July 31, 1882–June 8, 1916)
3. Nimrod Ingraham (September 22, 1843–April 24, 1925)
4. Athnair Watkins Ingraham (November 22, 1851–April 24, 1925)
5. Quinn Adams Ingraham (November 27, 1853–September 16, 1931)
6. Mary Jane Ingraham (October 14, 1866–November 12, 1938)
7. Bettie Gorrell (June 15, 1826–May 15, 1914)
8. Infant son of Q.A. and M.J. Ingraham
9. Infant daughter of Q.A. and M.J. Ingraham
10. Adam, son of Q.A. and M.J. Ingraham (April 19, 1890–January 18, 1896)
11. Lottie May, daughter of Q.A. and M.J. Ingraham (October 21, 1894–November 16, 1894)
12. Robert A. H., son of S.H. and N.G. Farnsworth (March 6, 1837–July 5, 1855) aged 18 years and 4 months
13. Margaret J.D. Smith (October 20, 1832–April 16, 1843)
14. A. Jefferson Moore (June 6, 1823–June 22, 1855)
15. James T. Smith (October 16, 1818–August 24, 1855)
16. Hugh Smith (February 26, 1779–October 27, 1855)

17. William A., son of Hugh and S.W. Smith (Died June 19, 1862, Aged 24 years, 9 months, and 2 days)
18. J.H. Robins (January 29, 1828–March 25, 1868) aged 40 years, 1 month, and 26 days
19. Mary Jeff, daughter of J.H. and S.C. Robins (Died July 25, 1858) aged 9 months and 23 days
20. B.S. Moore (1836–June 1878)

The reader will note that four of the individuals listed above passed away in 1855 between June and October. One will notice if walking through an old cemetery that a large number of people died in large numbers during long and hard winters and still others during the hot summers. Epidemics and the lack of effective medicines brought about great sadness and true feelings of loss as entire families were sometimes all but decimated in the wake of a deadly disease.

A few notes are needed regarding the occupants of this cemetery. First, the reader may have quickly noticed that Mr. and Mrs. Nimrod Ingraham have the same death date. That is exactly what is on the tombstones. Whether they died in an accident of some sorts or whether there was a serious outbreak of illness in their family or home is not known. Second, it should be noted that there are another 25–30 graves in the woods behind this section. This is apparently a black cemetery. Many of the graves are evidenced only by deep sunken spots in the ground. There are about three which are marked with sandstones and another six or seven which are marked with metal markers. There is one identified grave which belongs to Willie F. Burton (1928–1945).

John Plunk Family Cemetery

The graves of Mr. and Mrs. John Plunk, Sr., are located on the J.C. Pickett farm. The exact location is not precisely known to the author at this writing. However, it is known that John Plunk Sr., settled in the vicinity of this farm near Sweetlips Creek. It was on this farm that John Plunk Sr., born sometime around 1773 and dying sometime in the 1850s, was buried alongside his wife, Elizabeth Plunk.

Jones Family Cemetery

This tiny family cemetery is located on the old Jacob Jones farm, now a portion of the farm having belonged to the late Grady Middleton of Finger. There are apparently only two graves, those of Jacob Jones, who was born in Virginia in 1798, and his wife Agnes Jones. Both graves are marked by metal mower blades. Further information about Jacob Jones can be found in chapter two of this work.

Kerby Family Cemetery

Kerby Family Cemetery is located north of the town of Finger on the Young Road. The cemetery is on the east side of the road and is located on Westvaco land. There are a number of unmarked graves, perhaps a dozen or more. At least two of the inhabitants of this cemetery are currently known and they are among the earliest settlers and pioneers of north McNairy County. Those are Francis Kerby (1788–ca. 1839) and his wife Nancy Sparks Kerby (1790–ca. 1840s). These two individuals were the parents of the firstborn white child in the territory that would become McNairy County, Hugh Kerby, born in 1821. Another note of interest as to Francis Kerby is the fact that he was the second landowner to register land in McNairy County in 1823 after the formation of the county.

Lane's Chapel Cemetery

Lane's Chapel Church existed a full ten years before the cemetery came into existence. The building was constructed in 1955, and the first worship service was held there on March 18, 1955. For more information on the church itself, see Chapter Eight of this work. The first person to be buried in the Lane's Chapel Cemetery was Howard Cone in 1965.

1. Burcham, Jerry Wayne, Jr. (August 13, 1985–February 25, 2012)
2. Carpenter, Albin Tracey (1915–1988)
3. Carpenter, James Tracey (1939–1966)
4. Carpenter, Lola Mae (September 26, 1943–February 27, 2008)
5. Carpenter, Mary Belle (1918–2009)
6. Clark, Rebekah Kay (October 11, 2004–February 2, 2005)

7. Cone, Eunice O. (October 27, 1923–March 17, 2003)
8. Cone, Floyd (1917–1973)
9. Cone, Ivy I. (1916–2011)
10. Cone, Mary M. (April 13, 1894–October 18, 1972)
11. Cone, William H. (March 18, 1922–April 19, 1965)
12. Cone, William M. (February 5, 1893–July 31, 1967)
13. Crowe, Georgie Harold, Private, U.S. Army, World War II (July 20, 1928–February 3, 1983)
14. Crowe, Jessie Harold (November 23, 1948–July 27, 1978)
15. Delaney, Mishie L. (November 25, 1918–April 10, 2002)
16. Doyle, Alice Maxine (October 4, 1923–December 3, 1992)
17. Doyle, Frank L. (June 18, 1923–September 17, 1993)
18. Doyle, James F. (April 1, 1899–August 8, 1972)
19. Doyle, Maude Creel (March 24, 1901–January 1, 2000)
20. Haynes, Lenon (September 3, 1905–October 31, 1969)
21. Haynes, Pearlie (December 19, 1906–December 21, 1976)
22. McCormick, Willie O'Neal (October 5, 1936–December 31, 2007)
23. McNair, Betty M. (1919–1974)
24. McNair, Wylie Newton, S. Sgt., U.S. Army, World War II (June 17, 1915–May 8, 2000)
25. Plunk, Lurie M. (May 22, 1911–October 12, 1994)
26. Plunk, Thomas E., Private, U.S. Army, World War II (February 22, 1915–July 16, 1985)
27. Phillips, James Harold (February 16, 1935–May 19, 2002)
28. Smith, Elbert L., TEC 5, U.S. Army, World War II (February 27, 1924–March 17, 2004)
29. Stanley, J.C. (March 25, 1925–May 1, 1969)
30. Stanley, Lois (November 9, 1927–October 10, 2008)
31. Stanley, Roger D. (January 17, 1949–June 5, 2004)

Liberty Church Cemetery

Liberty Cemetery is located off Forty Forks Road on a small ridge adjacent to Liberty Church. The earliest marked grave is that of Mary J. Plunk, who died on July 16, 1861, at the age of three. The earliest adult is Mark M. Rose, who served as a bugler in Company A of the U.S. Sixth Tennessee Cavalry and died at the regimental hospital at Bolivar,

Tennessee on March 11, 1863. His body was brought back to McNairy County and buried here. The earliest discovered land transaction involving the present cemetery is dated November 20, 1891. Daniel A. Hill deeded William J.N. Rose, William S. Plunk, and Anderson Henry, trustees of "the Liberty Church grave yard," two acres and 49 square rods "for a burial ground." Apparently, the property was transferred to the trustees at no cost. The author was unable to trace Hill's acquisition of the cemetery land through the county deed books. An additional 0.473 acres beside the cemetery for additional burials was sold by Anna Lou (Kerby) Phillips and Gary Kerby to cemetery trustees Ward Moore, Noah Eskew, John Ross Gage, Oakley Henry, and Randy Kiestler for $10 on March 12, 1991. The following burials were transcribed by Jerry and Kevin D. McCann on March 20, 2013.

1. Abbott, Arlie Nathaniel "Pa Pa" (August 27, 1950–)
2. Alberson, Lynda McVay (August 23, 1943–April 11, 2001) Sister of A.C. McVay
3. Barham, Daisy (1881–1886)
4. Barham, Harriet Rebecca (August 13, 1880–September 29, 1964)
5. Barham, J.M. (January 9, 1884–September 22, 1926)
6. Barham, John Edgar (April 21, 1880–January 10, 1964)
7. Barham, John R. (1841–1905) Company C, 51st Tennessee Infantry CSA
8. Barham, Mary E. (1858–1902)
9. Barham, Minnie (1886–1900)
10. Barham, W.G. (May 16, 1877–August 28, 1878) Son of R.N. and Jane
11. Baucom, [Mary] Jane (August 9, 1843–April 4, 1920) *Burned to death (Death Book D, page 13)*
12. Baucom, Martha (1823–1900)
13. Baucom, Ransom (March 22, 1802–March 18, 1881)
14. Beard, Albert Kerby (1884–1948) Brother of Harriet. *Funeral home records show exact dates as (April 15, 1884–September 27, 1948)*.[18]
15. Beard, Harriet Surrat (1886–1948) Sister of Albert
16. Blagg, Anethea (June 10, 1950–May 9, 2003)
17. Blagg, Floyd Keith (April 14, 1952–February 6, 2006)

18. Albert Brown, transcriber, "McNairy County Funeral Home Records December 1927–1957" www.mcnairytnhistory.com/images/Funeral_Home_1927-1957.pdf

18. Blagg, Ivalee Henry (May 4, 1930–)
19. Blagg, Jason Keith (January 14, 1975–July 30, 2002)
20. Brock, infant of J.P. and Cynthia (September 27, 1908–September 27, 1908)
21. Brock, Cynthia (October 15, 1866–January 12, 1961) Wife of James
22. Brock, James P. (July 15, 1862–October 6, 1927) Husband of Cynthia
23. Burkeens, Harrison, Private, U.S. Army, World War II (August 11, 1895–September 19, 1972)
24. Burkeens, Lena Bell (November 30, 1890–November 13, 1891) Daughter of S.W. and M.J.
25. Burkeens, Stella (1892–1925)
26. Brewer, Allen S. Jr. (June 21, 1928–October 9, 1954) *Masonic symbol*
27. Brock, infant of J.P. and Cynthia (September 27, 1908–September 27, 1908)
28. Brock, Cynthia (October 15, 1866–January 12, 1961)
29. Brock, James P. (July 15, 1862–October 6, 1927)
30. Brock, Wanona (1901–1988) *Shackleford Funeral Home marker*
31. Camper, Barbara K. Plunk (February 24, 1935–June 23, 2007) Mother of Jeff and Greg Massengill
32. Carroll, Yvonne (August 28, 1936–January 3, 2003) *Shackleford Funeral Home marker*
33. Cartwright, Annie Rea Goodrum (August 6, 1924–September 11, 2001) Wife of Everette
34. Cartwright, Everette Eugene (July 14, 1912–October 7, 1973)
35. Cartwright, Everette Jr. (December 17, 1943–December 28, 2007)
36. Cartwright, Mary J. (November 12, 1929–December 29, 1978)
37. Cartwright, Robert Eugene (September 18, 1950-December 1950)
38. Cartwright, Ted Mack (June 4, 1956–August 17, 2011) *Rankin Funeral Home marker*
39. Cartwright, Wendell L. (October 12, 1913–January 22, 1993) PFC U.S. Army World War II
40. Case, E.A. (December 28, 1855–October 3, 1884)
41. Coleman, Judy F. (April 6, 1953–May 25, 1998)
42. Cook, Ben F. (1868–1964) *Funeral home records show his exact dates as (December 10, 1868–August 4, 1964).*[19]

---

19. Albert Brown, transcriber, "McNairy County Funeral Home Records 1958–1968." www.mcnairytnhistory.com/images/Funeral_Home_1958-1968.pdf

THE BURYING GROUNDS OF NORTH McNAIRY 391

43. Cook, Margie Lee (July 27, 1894–October 9, 1972)
44. Cox, Bertie L. (December 26, 1888–September 4, 1973)
45. Cox, Luther L. (August 30, 1915–) Husband of Zettie
46. Cox, Oliver C. (May 1, 1888–December 26, 1955)
47. Cox, Zettie H. (September 2, 1918–July 18, 1995) Wife of Luther; Married January 31, 1935
48. Davis, Connie I. (August 14, 1938–January 27, 1992)
49. Duncan, Ella E. (June 25, 1936–) Wife of James; Married September 22, 1962
50. Duncan, James L. (October 27, 1933–July 5, 2009) Husband of Ella
51. Duncan, John Frank (February 14, 1908–August 16, 1973)
52. Duncan, Mary Luisa (June 23, 1915–April 9, 2001)
53. Eskew, Hazel Mae Ross (October 24, 1922–August 19, 2006)
54. Eskew, Noah Fate (July 6, 1924–January 2, 2001)
55. Eskew, Ruth Ann (December 19, 1950–) Wife of Tim; Married March 21, 1970
56. Eskew, Tim Noel (April 25, 1951–October 31, 1982)
57. Evans, Edward A. (September 10, 1929–October 3, 1998) SFC, U.S. Army, Korea
58. Evans, Juliann (January 18, 1944–) Wife of Edward
59. Floyd, Beedie [Estella] Plunk (December 14, 1911–July 28, 2011)
60. Floyd, Holland L. (Pop) (1915–1974)
61. Floyd, Lowell Tom (1955–1973)
62. Gage, Amelia (1912–1978)
63. Gage, Arthur L. (1902–1962)
64. Gage, Aubrey E. April 5, 1907–July 29, 1980)
65. Gage, Catherine (May 2, 1875–March 30, 1921)
66. Gage, Daisy (September 22, 1889–April 29, 1912) Wife of C.C.
67. Gage, Jack (February 12, 1870–April 23, 1967)
68. Gage, Jerry Nathaniel (June 21, 1938–June 29, 2009) Married October 23, 1964
69. Gage, Oscar M. (1894–1957) 45th Tennessee Infantry World War I. *Funeral home records show exact dates as (February 8, 1894–December 11, 1957).*[20]
70. Gage, Shirley Ann Teague (July 11, 1943–) Married October 23, 1964
71. Gage, Willie I. (February 27, 1916–January 7, 2008)

20. *Id.*

72. Gould, Charles W. (June 2, 1920–May 16, 1997) Husband of Donna
73. Gould, Donna J. (October 9, 1941–) Wife of Charles
74. Graham, Emily Savannah (January 16, 2006)
75. Gullett, James Keith (May 20, 1958–)
76. Gullett, Janie Stout (January 3, 1955–August 18, 2011) Wife of James; Married September 9, 1980
77. Hall, Alieanna Raven Cheyenne (April 13, 1995–October 1, 1996)
78. Halstead, Jessie P. (June 23, 1878–April 27, 1953)
79. Halstead, Romie Hill (August 26, 1897–April 29, 1928)
80. Hamilton, Bobbie A. (September 21, 1940–) Married April 28, 1955
81. Hamilton, Donald L. (September 27, 1939–March 4, 2006) Married April 27, 1987
82. Hamilton, Doris J. (December 22, 1949–) Married April 27, 1987
83. Hamilton, J. Hershel (September 22, 1937–August 2, 1992) Married April 28, 1955
84. Hamilton, Rhonda Ann (March 31, 1959–May 23, 1962)
85. Harris, Gurley Junior [Bill] (November 2, 1926–March 1, 2011) S2, U.S. Navy, World War II
86. Harris, Hettie B. (1870–1913)
87. Harris, John L[ee] (1869–1953) *Funeral home records show exact dates as (August 28, 1869–April 27, 1953).*[21]
88. Harville, James Mason (July 15, 2005–February 9, 2013) *Shackleford Funeral Home marker*
89. Henry, infant ("Baby Boy") (May 1962)
90. Henry, infant son of Mr. and Mrs. Ray (July 18, 1949)
91. Henry, infants of C.H. And Flora (November 30, 1914–December 2 & 6, 1914)
92. Henry, infant daughter of Elton and Loran (September 27, 1947) *Funeral home records show birth/death date as September 26, 1947, in Selmer. Parents listed as Charles E. and Minnie L. (Smith) Henry.*[22]
93. Henry, Mr. & Mrs. Erected by Henry Families
94. Henry, A.C. (February 10, 1881–March 16, 1936) *Masonic symbol*
95. Henry, Ada Noraline (January 22, 1922–August 2, 1926) Daughter of R.E. and Lora

21. Brown, "McNairy County Funeral Home Records December 1927–1957."
22. *Id.*

96. Henry, Alester Dean "April 23, 1951–January 27, 2004) "Deano"; Married October 24, 1978
97. Henry, Alester Dean Jr. (February 19, 1973–February 19, 1973)
98. Henry, Almedia (1926–)
99. Henry, Alvin Lee "Big A" (September 26, 1947–)
100. Henry, Anderson (1851–1925)
101. Henry, Arnold N. (1917–1986) Private, U.S. Army, World War II (September 25, 1917–May 4, 1986)
102. Henry, Avon H. (October 1, 1938–January 31, 1943)
103. Henry, Beatrice Cox (November 27, 1922–January 25, 2006) Married September 16, 1939
104. Henry, C. Elton (November 26, 1921–April 15, 1984) SFC U.S. Navy World War II
105. Henry, Catherine (April 5, 1852–July 20, 1949) Wife of Sam
106. Henry, Charles Leonard (December 1, 1944–) Son of Jessie and Clara Mae
107. Henry, Charlie H. (October 14, 1891–January 31, 1981)
108. Henry, Christopher Michael (November 20, 1972–November 21, 1972) Infant son of Hershel and Shelia
109. Henry, Clara Mae (October 14, 1926–July 27, 2006)
110. Henry, Clarence James "Jim" (April 21, 1940–January 18, 2013) *Shackleford Funeral Home marker*
111. Henry, Cora May (1882–1909)
112. Henry, Darla Jane (August 14, 1947–January 16, 1955) Daughter of R.E.
113. Henry, Deborah Dianne (October 8, 1968–May 24, 1969) Infant daughter of Hershel and Shelia
114. Henry, Drexel (1926–1968)
115. Henry, Edgar (no dates) Brother of Willie and Son of John and June
116. Henry, Eliza (June 9, 1854–February 7, 1920)
117. Henry, Elvie Lee (September 26, 1947–) Infant daughter of Elton and Lorene
118. Henry, Evelyne (February 8, 1939–)
119. Henry, Flora A. (December 27, 1897–August 22, 1983)
120. Henry, Girtha I. (1891–1970) Wife of Joel; Married November 4, 1906
121. Henry, George W. (1877–1923)
122. Henry, Gordon Keith (August 29, 1937–June 18, 2009) SGM U.S. Army Vietnam

123. Henry, Hershal N. (April 7, 1945–) Married April 22, 1967
124. Henry, Hershel R. (December 31, 1933–January 4, 1934) Son of Mr. and Mrs. Bluford Henry
125. Henry, Izola Frye (May 24, 1907–August 14, 1989)
126. Henry, Jane (July 25, 1822–August 13, 1910)
127. Henry, Janice Marie Julian (February 14, 1951–) Wife of Alvin; Married July 3, 1969
128. Henry, Jessie Millard (August 13, 1908–June 1, 1985)
129. Henry, Joe Allen (October 22, 1963–)
130. Henry, Joe Louis (September 19, 1919–June 22, 1927) Son of J.R. and Nora
131. Henry, Joel H. (1889–1972)
132. Henry, Rev. John (February 23, 1828–August 18, 1897)
133. Henry, John Michael (October 14, 1961–January 23, 2011)
134. Henry, John Robert (June 10, 1876–August 15, 1950)
135. Henry, Julie C. (1895–1909)
136. Henry, Kimmie F. "Hank" (August 17, 1958–July 21, 1995)
137. Henry, Levi (May 7, 1883–July 29, 1955)
138. Henry, Lottie Odell (1918–1924) *Died on or about November 26, 1924, from diabetes (Death Book D, page 27)*
139. Henry, M. Emaline (1843–1910)
140. Henry, M. Lorene (October 12, 1930–) Married March 16, 1946
141. Henry, Martha Lenora (Nora) (February 10, 1891–January 18, 1964)
142. Henry, Mary (September 9, 1851–April 24, 1907) Wife of Matthew P.
143. Henry, Mary E. (June 13, 1854–November 18, 1926) Wife of Tillman
144. Henry, Matthew P[leasant] (March 7, 1846–July 4, 1914) Husband of Mary; Company B, 4th Tennessee Mounted Infantry USA, Civil War.
145. Henry, Mildred (February 8, 1914–February 9, 1914)
146. Henry, Miles A. (1884–1963) *Funeral home records show his exact dates as (February 25, 1884–June 26, 1963).*[23]
147. Henry, Minnie (January 28, 1882–February 3, 1958)
148. Henry, Nora C. (May 23, 1882–June 13, 1974)
149. Henry, Ophelia B. (1877–1964) *Funeral home records show his exact dates as (June 8, 1877–January 23, 1964).*[24]

---

23. Brown, "McNairy County Funeral Home Records 1958–1968."
24. *Id.*

150. Henry, Quinn (November 11, 1920–May 5, 1942) Killed in Coral Sea
151. Henry, R.E. (February 5, 1921–August 30, 2004) Married September 16, 1939
152. Henry, Rosie Lee (1924–2004)
153. Henry, Rosie Marie (June 16, 1966–June 18, 1966) Daughter of C.J. And D.A.
154. Henry, Sam [Samuel] (November 25, 1850–July 29, 1921) *Died of apoplexy (Death Book D, page 27)*
155. Henry, Samuel (March 1, 1875–May 9, 1965)
156. Henry, Samuel C. (February 15, 1909–February 25, 1909)
157. Henry, Samuel E. (November 20, 1900–February 21, 1993)
158. Henry, Samuel L. (1873–1947)
159. Henry, Sarah Ann (1882–1947)
160. Henry, Sard S. (1887–1909) *Died of typhoid fever while being treated by Dr. William Henry Hodges*
161. Henry, Shelia D. (May 11, 1948–) Wife of Hershell N.
162. Henry, Sherry Ann (March 27, 1960–) "Gizmo"; Married October 24, 1978
163. Henry, Tillman (January 1, 1854–September 28, 1931)
164. Henry, Warren D. (July 6, 1876–February 5, 1950)
165. Henry, William (June 13, 1852–February 28, 1939)
166. Henry, Willie (no dates) Brother of Edgar and Son of John and June
167. Hester, Ethel E. (April 26, 1889–May 29, 1976)
168. Hester, John Daniel (December 18, 1917–March 30, 2006) Married September 12, 1942
169. Hester, Ruth Smith (September 24, 1912–December 17, 2005) Married September 12, 1942
170. Hickman, Daisy L. (January 29, 1918–February 7, 1998)
171. Hill, Charles R. (December 1, 1873–December 22, 1895) Son of Mack and Caroline
172. Hill, Loyd R. (July 1, 1930–June 26, 1936) Son of S.C. and M.M.
173. Hill, Mack R. (May 24, 1843–May 22, 1906) Husband of Reda Caroline
174. Hill, Mary H. [Helen] (November 20, 1935–February 29, 1936) Daughter of S.C. and M.M. *Died of erysipelas septic (Death Book B, page 22)*
175. Hill, Margaret M. (September 7, 1906–December 31, 1984)

176. Hill, Roda Caroline (September 1, 1848–February 25, 1929) Wife of Mack R.
177. Hill, Samuel C. (November 12, 1903–March 23, 1998)
178. Hill, W.S. (born and died April 14, 1929) Son of S.C. and M.M. *Premature birth (Death Book B, page 19)
179. Holland, Arthur M. (1896–1979) U.S. Army, World War I
180. Holland, Billy Carroll (February 17, 1939–December 31, 1940) Son of Arthur and Lydian
181. Holland, Charlotte (1862–1907)
182. Holland, Dellar (1898–1928) Mother of Raymond
183. Holland, Doc Perry (1883–1970)
184. Holland, Ernest (July 18, 1893–December 6, 1964) Company B, Tennessee PFC 212 FLD Signal BN, World War I
185. Holland, Lydian (1914–1998)
186. Holland, M. Charlotte (born and died 1913) (2 months) Daughter of E.C. and Sula
187. Holland, Maude Etheridge (1895–1970) Wife of Ernest
188. Holland, Raymond (1923–1936) Son of Dellar
189. Holland, Shannon (October 27, 1988–October 27, 1988) Daughter of Glenn and Tina
190. Holland, William [Columbus] (1856–1924)
191. Houston, Glenn O'Neal (February 21, 1960–January 21, 1999)
192. Houston, Shannon M. (October 27, 1988–October 27, 1988)
193. Ingle, Annie B. Plunk (1894–1947) *Wife of Charles Preston Ingle. Funeral home records show exact dates as (February 8, 1894–October 13, 1947).*[25]
194. Ingle, Buell (November 26, 1935–September 21, 1998)
195. Ingle, Florence L. (December 7, 1940–)
196. Ingle, infant daughter of John C. and Mary H. (born and died 1923)
197. Ingle, Preston (1899–1982) *Shackleford Funeral Home marker (shows full name as Charlie Preston Ingle)*
198. Johnson, Blanche Beaty (September 11, 1887–February 15, 1980)
199. Johnson, Dora (1851–1931)
200. Johnson, Dorothy Lee "Dot" McVay (May 5, 1933–December 21, 1990) Wife of Kenneth

---

25. Brown, "McNairy County Funeral Home Records December 1927–1957."

201. Johnson, Eva (1899–1942) Wife of J.N. *Funeral home records list her full name as Mary Eva (Miller) Johnson (November 24, 1899–July 20, 1942), daughter of John & Flora (Hale) Miller.*[26]
202. Johnson, Floella (October 25, 1947–May 23, 1966)
203. Johnson, Henry Clay (April 17, 1879–August 5, 1932) *Died of a gastric carcinoma (Death Book B, page 25)*
204. Johnson, Howard B. (April 2, 1914–April 16, 1945) Tennessee TEC 5 349 Infantry, 88th Division, World War II
205. Johnson, Imogene P. (December 23, 1927–) Married December 23, 1944
206. Johnson, infant daughter of J.N. and Eva (no dates) "Little Sister"
207. Johnson, infant daughter of M.J. and Dora (September 11, 1873–September 29, 1877)
208. Johnson, Rev. James P. (December 25, 1925–August 31, 2000) PFC, U.S. Army, World War II; Married December 23, 1944
209. Johnson, Jesse D. (April 19, 1939–February 11, 1943) Son of R.D. and Julia
210. Johnson, Jimmy Dale (born and died September 28, 1945) Son of Mr. & Mrs. J.P.
211. Johnson, John N. (1887–1980)
212. Johnson, Johnny B. (1931–1959) *Funeral home records show his exact dates as (February 26 1931–December 28, 1959).*[27]
213. Johnson, Julia M. (April 1, 1911–March 9, 1976)
214. Johnson, Kenneth "Zap" (June 6, 1923–April 26, 1994) Husband of Dorothy
215. Johnson, Lieutisha (October 6, 1874–August 25, 1877) Daughter of M.J. and Dorah
216. Johnson, Mable F. (1933–)
217. Johnson, Mike (1850–1932) *Died of apoplexy on December 28, 1932 (Death Book B, page 25)*
218. Johnson, O.Q. (April 5, 1916–May 4, 1975)
219. Johnson, R.D. (May 16, 1910–March 5, 1950)
220. Johnson, Wanetta F. (February 25, 1923–December 22, 1996)
221. Johnston, infant daughter of Paul and Della (born & died March 13, 1930)

26. *Id.*
27. *Id.*

222. Johnston, infant son of Paul and Della (born & died April 30, 1938)
223. Jones, Wendell Keith (1915–1988) MSGT, U.S. Air Force, Korean War November 21, 1915–June 14, 1988
224. Julian, Brian Wayne (January 20, 1973–October 23, 2012) *Shackleford Funeral Home marker*
225. Keck, Ford Henry (March 14, 1917–January 20, 1992) BKR1, U.S. Navy, World War II
226. Keck, Inez Henry (October 16, 1915–September 9, 1997) Wife of Ford
227. Kiestler, Chester L. (September 26, 1931–February 1, 2010)
228. Kiestler, Rhonda King (December 27, 1960–March 16, 2009) Wife of Steven; Married July 25, 1981
229. Kiestler, Sandra Gage (February 3, 1936–September 19, 2011) Wife of Chester; Married August 6, 1955
230. Kiestler, Steven Wayne (August 17, 1960–)
231. Kindberg, Linda Blagg (April 21, 1948–June 10, 2002) Daughter of Anethea Blagg
232. Knight, William L. (1922–2002) Father of Denise
233. Lofton, M.H. (August 4, 1867–April 6, 1955)
234. Lofton, Minnie B. (December 20, 1879–December 30, 1969)
235. Malone, Dorsey Allen (March 10, 1937–)
236. Malone, Marcus Allen (December 19, 1905–July 21, 1969)
237. Malone, Martha Sue (January 6, 1939–)
238. Malone, Martha Verona (March 27, 1905–November 22, 1990) Wife of Marcus
239. Martin, Hazel Bendall (March 1, 1936–November 2, 1008) Wife of James
240. Martin, James F. (August 18, 1929–February 22, 2003) Husband of Hazel
241. Martin, Peggy (July 10, 1974–) Wife of Wayne
242. Martin, Terry Joe (July 4, 1959–May 30, 2012) *Shackleford Funeral Home marker*
243. Martin, Wayne (January 20, 1979–April 14, 2008) Husband of Peggy
244. Matlock, Maurine (1936–1950) *Wife of Wilson Matlock. Funeral home records show her exact dates as (April 13, 1936–June 25, 1950).*[28]
245. Matlock, Wilson (1931–)
246. McCann, Alex (no dates) Son of John & Betty

28. *Id.*

THE BURYING GROUNDS OF NORTH McNAIRY 399

247. McCann, Doctor W. "Dock" (1827–1896)
248. McCann, Dora V. (1888–1932) *Daughter of Doctor W. "Dock" McCann. Dates should be March 17, 1888–May 12, 1940.*
249. McCann, Eliza Ann (November 9, 1828–October 29, 1885) Wife of D.W.
250. McCann, Ida (1897–1910) Black servant of Thomas & Lucy. **Died on July 17, 1910 of consumption while being treated by Dr. William Henry Hodges.*
251. McCann, Lean (no dates) Child of John & Betty
252. McCann, Lucy (1872–1934) Wife of Thomas
253. McCann, Minnie May (May 25, 1881–October 30, 1882) Daughter of W.H. & Rebecca
254. McCann, Obedience (April 5, 1787–July 15, 1871) *Believed to be an unmarked grave near her son Doctor W.*
255. McCann, Thomas (1862–1917) **Died of pellagra on March 2, 1917 (Death Book B, page 37)*
256. McCann, William S[herman] (April 21, 1865–January 1, 1889)
257. McCormick, James Leon (September 3, 1944–)
258. McCormick, Margie Marie (September 20, 1949–July 30, 1999) Wife of James
259. McVay, A.C. (November 13, 1945–April 10, 2007) Brother of Lynda Alberson SSGT, U.S. Air Force
260. Miller, Bradley Austin (February 10, 1979–August 21, 1980)
261. Mills, Scotty Lane (June 7, 1964–July 11, 1964) Son of Mr. & Mrs. Bobby
262. Mitchell, Billy Frank (May 17, 1928–December 22, 1978)
263. Mitchell, Maggie Lee (January 27, 1934–August 27, 2009)
264. Monfee, Christine Stanfill (August 21, 1964–January 17, 2009)
265. Monroe, Doris (June 9, 1943–June 4, 1997)
266. Moore, Alice D. (1882–1958) *Wife of John Moore. Funeral home records show her date of death as November 21, 1958, but no date of birth is listed.*[29]
267. Moore, John W. (1831–1970)
268. Moore, Lillian Henry (October 30, 1915–September 19, 2002) *Artist's palette symbol*
269. Moore, Mackie (1877–1915) Wife of W.A.

29. Id.

270. Moore, Ruby (July 3, 1912–June 6, 1915) Daughter of J.W. & Alice
271. Mullen, infant son of W.B. and Alberta (Died June 6, 1943) (2 days) *Funeral home records show his parents as William B. & Alberta (Cartwright) Mullen.*[30]
272. Mullins, Robert Daniel "Danny" (August 31, 1968–July 18, 1994)
273. Navarro, Donna (April 1, 1954–)
274. Navarro, Nick (April 5, 1971–July 15, 2005)
275. Newton, Arnold Bradley (February 29, 1960–November 11, 2005)
276. Newton, Elbert "Bubba" (December 28, 1934–September 28, 2010) SN, U.S. Navy, Korea. Married May 23, 1959. *Full name on military marker given as Elbert Copeland Newton.*
277. Newton, Elbert Benjamin (no dates) Beside Ester Marie Newton
278. Newton, Ester Marie (August 19, 1943–) Wife of Arnold
279. Newton, Ethel I. (February 3, 1910–April 20, 1995) Wife of James Milo
280. Newton, James Milo (October 9, 1904–January 15, 1949) Husband of Ethel; "Laid to rest in Bastrop, Louisiana"
281. Newton, Maggie Faye (August 11, 1942–March 19, 2007) Married May 23, 1959
282. Plunk, Ader (June 6, 1881–March 15, 1948) Wife of George
283. Plunk, Albert T. (September 12, 1911–June 14, 1913) Son of W.B. & M.U.
284. Plunk, Amos Calvin (October 27, 1924–April 29, 1990) PFC, U.S. Army, World War II; Married September 11, 1943. *Masonic symbol*
285. Plunk, Arbie O[lea] (October 24, 1926–July 19, 2011) Married July 31, 1948
286. Plunk, Artie C. (May 20, 1918–May 25, 1918) Twin brother of Jeffie D. and son of George & Ader
287. Plunk, Austin R[ay] (1933–1952) *Funeral home records show his exact dates as (November 27, 1933–January 2, 1952. Died from injuries suffered in an automobile accident. Son of Joseph O. & Maggie (Moore) Plunk.*[31]
288. Plunk, Betty Jo (January 26, 1933–January 3, 1967) Wife of Arbie
289. Plunk, Beulah S. (January 13, 1902–March 29, 1996)
290. Plunk, Charles C. (August 3, 1860–January 17, 1924)

30. *Id.*

31. Brown, "McNairy County Funeral Home Records December 1927–1957." Austin Ray Plunk Death Certificate No. 52-01054.

THE BURYING GROUNDS OF NORTH McNAIRY 401

291. Plunk, Clifford Lee (July 20, 1913–September 18, 1987)
292. Plunk, Daniel J. (December 23, 1891–May 24, 1953)
293. Plunk, Edward (1910–1922)
294. Plunk, Elbert C. (February 29, 1897–September 10, 1899) Son of W.B. & M.U.
295. Plunk, Elizabeth (January 16, 1797–November 2, 1887)
296. Plunk, E[lizabeth] J[ane] (April 6, 1844–November 22, 1921)
297. Plunk, Emma Y. (May 30, 1872–September 6, 1934) *Died of apoplexy (Death Book B, page 42)*
298. Plunk, Edward (1910–1922)
299. Plunk, Fannie (1894–1979)
300. Plunk, Flossie L[ena] (1890–1994)
301. Plunk, Frank (1892–1985)
302. Plunk, George (November 8, 1871–January 3, 1970)
303. Plunk, George Edward (November 7, 1921–July 12, 1985)
304. Plunk, George W. [Washington] (April 10, 1862–December 9, 1934) *Died of paralysis (Death Book B, page 42)*
305. Plunk, George W. (May 23, 1907–June 24, 1981)
306. Plunk, Gregory Scott (born & died July 23, 1975) Son of George & Mara
307. Plunk, H. Porter (November 14, 1922–March 13, 2006)
308. Plunk, infants (3) of Lucy Ann and C.C. (no dates)
309. Plunk, infant daughter of Lucy Ann and C.C. (no dates)
310. Plunk, infant son of W.M. and M.A. (born & died October 2, 1869)
311. Plunk, J[efferson] David (January 12, 1921–December 31, 1944) Son of D.J. & M.L.
312. Plunk, Jane Starkey (February 18, 1923–June 11, 2006) *Wife of Leonard Plunk.*
313. Plunk, [William] Jasper (April 15, 1871–April 16, 1937) *Died of pneumonia and heart disease (Death Book B, page 43)*
314. Plunk, Jeffie D. (May 20, 1918–May 27, 1918) Twin of Artie and son of George & Ader
315. Plunk, John (May 29, 1800–May 23, 1882)
316. Plunk, Rev. J[ohn] W[esley] (December 3, 1842–March 10, 1920) Company G, 6th Tennessee Cavalry U.S.A., Civil War. *Died of apoplexy (Death Book D, page 13)*

317. Plunk, J[ohn] W[esley] [Sargent] (Sard) (1881–1960) *His exact dates are (October 19, 1881–May 19, 1960).*
318. Plunk, Joe H. [Joseph Henry] (1874–1926) *Son of John & Elizabeth Jane. *Died of apoplexy (Death Book D, page 70)*
319. Plunk, Joseph A[lex] (January 25, 1825–November 11, 1918) Company B, 6th Tennessee Cavalry U.S.A., Civil War
320. Plunk, Joseph Orkerson (April 10, 1900–January 12, 1987)
321. Plunk, Josephine [Jose] (April 2, 1856–September 2, 1951)
322. Plunk, Laura (May 18, 1854–October 17, 1920) Wife of N.B.
323. Plunk, Lena Mae (June 3, 1926–   ) *Wife of Calvin Plunk*
324. Plunk, Leonard Barber (July 16, 1921–February 6, 2009)
325. Plunk, Katie (August 25, 1875–September 19, 1925)
326. Plunk, Lessie E. (1903–1968) *Funeral home records show her exacr dates as (September 25, 1893–March 30, 1968).*[32]
327. Plunk, Lester F. (1899–1974)
328. Plunk, Lissie M. (1902–1988)
329. Plunk, Lucy Ann (August 15, 1869–December 18, 1954) *Wife of Charles C. Plunk*
330. Plunk, M[aggie] Viola (May 8, 1873–November 3, 1933) *Wife of William Bell Plunk*
331. Plunk, Mack (Died 1879) (Age about 38 years)
332. Plunk, Maggie Moore (November 22, 1906–February 11, 2000) *Wife of Joseph Orkerson Plunk*
333. Plunk, Mahaia A. (November 20, 1837–January 11, 1911) *Wife of Joseph A. Plunk*
334. Plunk, Marcus (June 17, 1854– [...] 1883) *Broken tombstone*
335. Plunk, Marcus (December 21, 1879–December 28, 1956) *Son of Lafayette & Mary C. (Shelton) Plunk.*[33]
336. Plunk, Martha A. (August 10, 1836–February 7, 1908) Wife of W.S.
337. Plunk, Martha E. (1872–1955)
338. Plunk, Martha L. (October 21, 1901–July 2, 1999)
339. Plunk, Mary (October 28, 1832–April 5, 1900) Wife of Miles
340. Plunk, Mary (June 11, 1875–June 24, 1957)
341. Plunk, Mary (February 10, 1883–May 4, 1889) Daughter of John & Elizabeth

32. *Id.*
33. *Id.*

342. Plunk, Mary E. (July 29, 1850–May 2, 1993) Wife of N.B
343. Plunk, Mary F. (1895–1974)
344. Plunk, Mary J. (July 26, 1857–July 6, 1861) Daughter of W.M. & M.A.
345. Plunk, Max Allen (January 27, 1955–July 9, 2012) PV1, U.S. Army
346. Plunk, Miles (December 27, 1829–April 25, 1900) Company B, 6th Tennessee Cavalry U.S.A., Civil War
347. Plunk, Minnie E. (1911–1979)
348. Plunk, Mollie (April 12, 1869–November 22, 1966) Wife of Henry C.
349. Plunk, Monia G. (May 10, 1919–July 7, 1999)
350. Plunk, Myrtle (1899–1977) Wife of Frank
351. Plunk, Nancy Ann Sanders (September 12, 1868–April 20, 1888) Wife of George W. and mother of Albert C.
352. Plunk, Neal B. (August 17, 1847–February 24, 1915) Masonic symbol
353. Plunk, Nellie F[rancis] (1939–1941) *Daughter of Joseph and Maggie (Moore) Plunk. Funeral home records show exact dates as (August 24, 1940–June 26, 1942. However, her death certificate gives her birth date as August 12, 1941. Nellie died from "circulatory failure" due to "toxicity and debilitation."*[34]
354. Plunk, Nellie Mae (1898–1973)
355. Plunk, O. Lafayette (September 19, 1918–June 23, 1920) Son of O.L. & Nellie
356. Plunk, Oscar (1895–1991) U.S. Army, World War I
357. Plunk, Otis (1891–1988) U.S. Army, World War I
358. Plunk, Robert Earl (February 22, 1899–December 11, 1964)
359. Plunk, Robert Floyd (June 28, 1921–November 12, 2008)
360. Plunk, Robert L[ee] (1867–1938) *Died on February 16, 1938 lobor pneumonia (Death Book B, page 43)*
361. Plunk, Robert P. (August 12, 1869–November 24, 1908)
362. Plunk, Rosette (1889–1891)
363. Plunk, Sam (September 10, 1868–August 14, 1899)
364. Plunk, Shirley Jean (October 27, 1937–March 24, 1979) Daughters Cheryl & Gina
365. Plunk, Thomas Edward (1926–1995)
366. Plunk, William B. (November 21, 1868–November 11, 1926) *Died of influenza and pneumonia (Death Book B, page 42)*

---

34. Id. Nell Plunk Tennessee Death Certificate No. 13304.

367. Plunk, William Henry (January 13, 1925–March 11, 2005) Daughters are Cheryl & Gina
368. Plunk, W[illiam] S[argent] (January 31, 1831–November 18, 1915)
369. Plunk, William Carlos (1894–1973)
370. Plunk, Winnie L. (1873–1959) *Wife of Robert L. Plunk. Funeral home records show exact dates as (November 28, 1873–December 2, 1959).*[35]
371. Plunk, Uless (1894–1960) *Funeral home records show exact dates as (September 10, 1894–February 17, 1960).*[36]
372. Pomeroy, Martha C. Plunk (January 10, 1929–December 13, 2009)
373. Porter, Andrew Phillip (April 9, 1951–December 14, 2011)
374. Porter, Ruth Mary (October 28, 1956–) Wife of Andrew
375. Porter, Vinal James Jr. (October 16, 1923–October 12, 2011)
376. Reed, Nicholas A. (2002–2002)
377. Roberts, Sallie (Died April 1881)
378. Rook, Mattie Henry (March 11, 1894–November 9, 1928) Daughter of Tillman & Mary E. Henry
379. Rose, Hannah (January 29, 1818–September 1, 1905) *Wife of Mark M. Rose*
380. Rose, Mark M. (July 21, 1816–March 11, 1863) *Buglar in Company A, 6th Tennessee Cavalry U.S.A., Civil War. Died at regimental hospital in Bolivar, Tennessee.*
381. Rose, Naomi H[annah] (June 25, 1840–August 3, 1906)
382. Rose, Roseannah (March 10, 1842–February 10, 1882)
383. Rose, W[illiam] J[asper] N[ewton] (no dates) Company A, 6th Tennessee Cavalry U.S.A., Civil War. *(June 14, 1838–January 4, 1917)*
384. Ross, Charles Elbert (May 9, 1872–December 3, 1874) Son of J.E. & R.A.
385. Ross, J.A. (May 7, 1871–October 25, 1903) Wife of J.R.
386. Ross, J.E. (March 19, 1849–April 18, 1900)
387. Ross, Rosie Ann (June 22, 1871–September 13, 1874) Daughter of J.E. & R.A.
388. Ross, Rosie J. (March 10, 1902–March 4, 1904) Daughter of J.E. & R.A.
389. Ross, Rillie Ann (August 15, 1851–January 17, 1940) Wife of John
390. Ross, Sophronia Jane (July 24, 1876–August 12, 1897) Daughter of J.E. & R.A.

35. *Id.*
36. *Id.*

391. Rosser, Dizana (Died 1916) (age about 65 years)
392. Rosser, Robert Wesley (1919–1921) *His death certificate gives the dates as (August 26, 1919–May 17, 1921) and cause of death as "cholera inflammation."*
393. Rhodes, infant daughter of W.K. and Beryl (born & died May 25, 1930)
394. Sanders, Victoria (September 14, 1891–July 22, 1906)
395. Sharpe, infant son of Mr.& Mrs. Bill Sharpe (May 8, 1954) *Funeral home records show his parents as Bill Jack & Nora F. (Henry) Sharpe.*[37]
396. Sheets, Henry Walker (born & died December 4, 1914) Son of Oscar & Effie
397. Sicilia, Charlie E. (1909–1972)
398. Sicilia, Mary F. (1915–1979)
399. Smith, Ardelia Annette (November 23, 1940–October 3, 2008) Wife of William
400. Smith, Elizabeth (June 6, 1885–November 8, 1918)
401. Smith, Ida M. (1896–1976) Daughter of E.A. & M.E.
402. Smith, Iva Dodd (1905–1993)
403. Smith, Martha E. Plunk (1872–1955) Wife of E.A. *Funeral home records show exact dates as (March 29, 1872–October 18, 1955).*[38]
404. Smith, Ralph (October 3, 1914–July 16, 1916) Son of E.A. & M.E.
405. Smith, Ruby (April 4, 1898–August 28, 1903) Daughter of E.A. & M.E.
406. Smith, Waitman F. (1901–1984)
407. Smith, William Roy (February 2, 1939–) Husband of Ardelia
408. Stanfill, Iley B. (October 2, 1925–October 6, 2010) Husband of Lorraine
409. Stanfill, Lorraine L. (May 27, 1922–)
410. Story, Mildred Johnson (July 20, 1925–April 4, 1998) Wife of Rubel
411. Story, Rubel A. (July 22, 1924–April 9, 1992) Husband of Mildred
412. Sullivan, Bertha Lee (January 5, 1921–November 17, 1994)
413. Summers, Helen Plunk (August 20, 1928–October 9, 2011)
414. Sutton, Mackie (1877–1915) Wife of W.A.
415. Sutton, Nancy E. (1850–1929) Wife of William "Bill" Sutton
416. Tacker, D[avid] A[mos] (1896–1935) *Death certificate shows he died in Memphis, Tennessee on October 1, 1935—almost seven months after his wife passed away—from "acute infections, arthritis, staphylococcus [and] septicemia."*

37. *Id.*
38. *Id.*

417. Tacker, Alpha B. [Lipford] (1903–1935) *Wife of D. Amos Tacker. Funeral home records show exact dates as (November 13, 1903–March 31, 1935). *Died from influenza and lobar pneumonia (Death Book B, page 54)*
418. Tacker, Arna (June 25, 1886–September 21, 1906) *Daughter of David and Martha (McCann) Tacker*
419. Tacker, Cora (February 28, 1884–March 7, 1886) *Daughter of David and Martha (McCann) Tacker*
420. Tacker, David J. (1847–1931) "Son of Joseph O., grandson of Seaborn buried at Rose Hill" *Died June 2, 1931 of organic heart disease (Death Book B, page 54)*
421. Tacker, Elizabeth (June 2, 1816–March 27, 1885)
422. Tacker, Joseph O[rkerson] (July 4, 1812–June 17, 1883)
423. Tacker, L[eroy] J. (1842–1896) Company G, 6th Tennessee Cavalry U.S.A., Civil War
424. Tacker, Martha (March 9, 1854–September 6, 1880) *Wife of David J. Tacker*
425. Tacker, Oliver (January 5, 1873–September 19, 1880) *Son of David & Martha (McCann) Tacker*
426. Tate, Nora B. (August 23, 1886–August 19, 1939)
427. Walker, Mary C. (July 10, 1851–October 15, 1947) *Wife of Robert M. Walker*
428. Walker, Robert M. (December 25, 1841–April 1, 1902) Private, Anderson's Cavalry CSA
429. Wells, Betty Jo (July 4, 1926–August 13, 2001) Wife of James Ted Wells; Married April 11, 1948
430. Wells, Chris Alan (April 19, 1959–June 5, 1993) Son of Van and Ruth. *Pharmacist symbol*
431. Wells, James A. (October 13, 1867–March 26, 1935)
432. Wells, James Ted (November 24, 1928–) Married April 11, 1948
433. Wells, Lillie Plunk (November 7, 1896–May 17, 1988)
434. Wells, Ted Oren (October 11, 1898–August 6, 1970) *Ted Wells oversaw the construction of the present-day Liberty Church building and laid much of the stonework.*
435. Wells, Dr. Van Henry (January 24, 1931–May 28, 2012)
436. Williams, Kathy (May 29, 1959–April 28, 2012) *Shackleford Funeral Home marker*

437. Wood, Judy E. Plunk (October 15, 1944–November 18, 2010)
438. Yarbrough, James J. (June 9, 1809–October 6, 1879)
439. Yarbrough, Minnie Mae (June 20, 1880–February 21, 1971)
440. Yarbrough, W.H. (July 18, 1874–May 10, 1904)
441. Yarbrough, William C. (February 14, 1832–December 28, 1904)
442. 1 Concrete square (beside Harriett Bachum)
443. 2 Concrete squares (beside J.M. Baucum)
444. 2 Sandstones (beside W.C. Baucum)
445. 1 Stone (beside Holland L. Floyd)
446. 1 Concrete-encased PVC markers (head and foot) (beside Ted Mack Cartwright)
447. 1 Steel pole with frayed top (beside M. Charlotte Holland)
448. 1 Concrete squares (head and foot) (beside Matthew P. Henry)
449. 1 Sandstone (broken) (head and foot) (beside Matthew P. Henry)
450. 1 Concrete square (beside Matthew P. Henry)
451. 1 Sandstone (Jenette Tacker?)
452. 1 Sandstone (flat) (Oliver Tacker?)
453. 1 Unmarked grave with flowers (beside Annie B. Ingle)
454. 1 Sandstone (in front of Rev. J.P. and Imogene Johnson)
455. 1 Sandstone (beside infant daughter of M.J & Dora Johnson)
456. 1 Sandstone (head and foot) (beside Doctor W. "Dock" McCann)
457. 1 Sandstone (head and foot) (beside Roseannah Rose)
458. 1 Gray rock (flat) (near Elbert C. Plunk)
459. 5 Sandstones (between infant daughter of M.J. & Dora Johnson and Elbert Plunk)
460. 1 Sandstone (flat) (beside Mack Plunk)
461. 1 Gray rock (beside infant son of W.M. & M.A. Plunk)
462. 4 Sandstones (flat) (beside infant son of W.M. & M.A. Plunk)
463. 1 Sandstone (flat) (beside Mary J. Plunk)
464. 1 Concrete square (head and foot) between Hannah Rose and William S. McCann
465. 2 Concrete squares to right of Victoria Sanders
466. 2 Sandstones (head and foot) beside Mark M. Rose
467. 1 Sandstone (flat) beside Mark M. Rose
468. 1 Sandstone (head and foot) beside Mackie Sutton
469. 1 Sandstone fragments beside Nancy Sutton

470. 1 Sandstone (flat) beside L.J. Tacker
471. 1 Concrete square (lying on the ground) beside D. Amos Tacker

Maggie Jones Cemetery/New Church

The Maggie Jones Cemetery is located on Tennessee State Highway 199 between Finger and Leapwood. It was established with the burial of a stillborn child in 1920. Clarnth Vires was the child of Harrison and Hester Vires.[39] The church had been previously established across the road from the new burying ground. Over the next ninety or more years, the cemetery would become the final resting place to many of the area's oldest families including the Burkeens, Davis, Moore, Nash, Plunk and Vires, among many others. These families and others are closely linked together by the bonds of having attended Maggie Jones Methodist Church, attending Mackey School or simply living near one another in the community. In many ways, there is a distinct community among these good people. Today there are almost four hundred graves in the Maggie Jones/New Church Cemetery.

1. Ada, Cpl. France Jr. (1928–1953)
2. Ada, Lillie Mae (February 12, 1903–April 18, 1983)
3. Ada, Matt France (March 15, 1893–September 1, 1976)
4. Ada, Robert F. (March 4, 1945–May 28, 2004) U.S. Navy
5. Ada, William Wiley (March 26, 1934–June 22, 2004) Pvt., U.S. Army, Korea
6. Amerson, Brenda (November 29, 1941–July 29, 1942)
7. Amerson, James E., son of Lula Perkins (February 13, 1922–March 3, 1922)
8. Amerson, John C. (1904–1941)
9. Amerson, Mandy C. (January 3, 1921–October 25, 2011)
10. Amerson, Nicy I. (1913–1977)
11. Amerson, Orval M. (September 21, 1916–July 28, 1994) Sgt. U.S. Army, World War II
12. Austin, Berry (March 14, 1890–April 28, 1958) Arkansas, PVT, 16 Co. 162 Depot Brigade, World War I

39. According to the death records of McNairy County, Tennessee, this was a male child (Death Book B, page 56).

New Church Cemetery at Maggie Jones Memorial Methodist Church

13. Austin, Edith Brooks (July 4, 1867–November 15, 1946)
14. Austin, Elsie B. (May 11, 1912–June 10, 1975)
15. Austin, Paul, son of G.P. & Elsie Austin (September 25, 1943, age 3 days)
16. Barham, H.A. (April 20, 1887–May 4, 1980)
17. Barham, Ida C. (April 21, 1887–April 26, 1961)
18. Barham, James H. (February 14, 1932–September 26, 1987)
19. Barham, James L. (July 2, 1892–April 2, 1946)
20. Barham, Kinnie H. (May 9, 1894–May 4, 1984)
21. Barham, Lessie A. (January 3, 1909–November 4, 1978)
22. Barham, Richard Ray (June 26, 1929–May 22, 1994)
23. Barham, Sarah M. (1894–1978)
24. Barham, Thomas A. (1891–1973)
25. Barnes, Arkie B. (October 3, 1892–April 8, 1992)
26. Barnes, Ida Mae (February 1, 1896–October 1, 1966)
27. Barnes, Prentis Odell (January 8, 1917–February 19, 1972) Tennessee, Pvt. U.S. Army, World War II PH
28. Barnes, R.C. (August 21, 1931–October 8, 2013)
29. Barton, Dora C. (August 6, 1881–November 27, 1971)
30. Berg, Deborah Diane Huckabee (July 11, 1956–April 19, 2010)
31. Bickings, Dave (September 26, 1916–May 10, 1983)
32. Bishop, Lecter Burkeen (November 24, 1908–January 7, 1988)

33. Bivens, Jerry
34. Bridges, James Paul (January 7, 1929–December 5, 2012)
35. Brock, Buford (June 13, 1924–January 3, 2007) TSgt., U.S. Air Force, World War II, Korea
36. Brooks, Rob (May 1880–July 1935) Husband of Ethel Corbin
37. Bullock, Exie Jackson (1902–1938)
38. Burkeens, Amandy (February 4, 1861–?)
39. Burkeens, Charlie (1901–1947)
40. Burkeens, Doris Irene (1932–1980)
41. Burkeens, Fay [Plunk] McCann (April 2, 1919–September 4, 2010)
42. Burkeens, Henry (September 15, 1887–April 5, 1973)
43. Burkeens, Johnnie G. (June 30, 1919–December 4, 1941)
44. Burkeens, Lark [Larkin W.] *Died on or about July 28, 1934 at the age of 53 from dropsy (Death Book B, page 5)*
45. Burkeens, Luther A. (January 1, 1880–October 12, 1944)
46. Burkeens, Luverna (January 25, 1894–)
47. Burkeens, Maggie J. (June 22, 1877–January 27, 1954)
48. Burkeens, Mary Morris (1877–1965)
49. Burkeens, S.W. (June 14, 1856–June 7, 1928)
50. Burkeens, Vera Lee (1906–1935) *Died on or about November 21, 1935 at age 29 of interfusion of the bowels (Death Book B, page 5)*
51. Burkeens, Willie Loys (March 27, 1921–January 3, 1935) *Died of pneumonia (Death Book B, page 5)*
52. Busby, Meleah R. (February 12, 1999–February 17, 1999)
53. Carpenter, Addie Pearl (1897–1978)
54. Carpenter, Albert Ray (October 10, 1922–November 2, 1977)
55. Carpenter, Cecil W. (March 19, 1919–December 23, 1989) S2, US Navy, World War II
56. Carpenter, Delbert (February 18, 1930–March 21, 1930)
57. Carpenter, Homer Calvin (1892–1954)
58. Carpenter, Montie E., son of C.W. & W.M. Carpenter (Born & Died April 20, 1948)
59. Carpenter, Robt. Lee, son of C.W. & W.M. Carpenter (January 8, 1939)
60. Carpenter, Wanna Mae (May 1, 1922–April 13, 1986)
61. Carpenter, W. Landon (1936–1963)
62. Case, L. Belle (1860–1938) *Died on or about April 12, 1938, at age 77 from pneumonia (Death Book B, page 9)*

THE BURYING GROUNDS OF NORTH McNAIRY   411

63. Case, John R. (1860–1938) *Died on or about August 25, 1938, at age 77 from a "strepto infection" of the leg (Death Book B, page 10)*
64. Chandler, Aubrey A. (July 13, 1943–August 6, 2013)
65. Chandler, Emanuel R. (September 28, 1905–June 11, 1988)
66. Chandler, Jammie Darrell (August 12, 1965–January 6, 1991)
67. Chandler, John Edward (July 9, 1940–December 17, 2003) U.S. Air Force
68. Chandler, Minnie S. (December 4, 1911–November 17, 1992)
69. Chandler, Robert Larry (April 26, 1948–January 6, 1969) Tennessee, PFC, Trp B, 4 Cav, 25 Inf. Div., Vietnam SS-BSM-PH
70. Chandler, T.C. (May 20, 1877–September 24, 1941)
71. Clemons, Elsie Jackson (1907–1949)
72. Clemons, Velmer (1901–1973)
73. Clemons, William Forest (March 23, 1929–March 20, 2000)
74. Clouse, Deewitt (April 25, 1911–October 18, 1974)
75. Clouse, Vionia (July 30, 1915–December 4, 2002)
76. Cone, Lexie (September 7, 1920–February 20, 2012)
77. Cone, Newal (September 8, 1918–September 18, 1990)
78. Crowe, Harold W. (March 21, 1941–October 4, 1991)
79. Dallas, Blanche Fowler (1908–1927)
80. Dallas, Ezra
81. Dallas, Inetha
82. Dallas, Sarah P. (1877–1929)
83. Dallas, Vera (ca. 1907–1928) *Died on or about January 11, 1928 of pulmonary tuberculosis (Death Book D, page 87)*
84. Davis, A.E. (March 23, 1866–April 18, 1951)
85. Davis, Angela Darline (December 7, 1969–June 17, 1970)
86. Davis, Annie (1899–1992)
87. Davis, Armour E. (1897–1978)
88. Davis, Arnold B. (July 28, 1919–October 5, 1941)
89. Davis, Charles Cranston, son of C.T. & A.F. Davis (September 8, 1925–October 18, 1927) *Died of meningitis (Death Book D, page 87)*
90. Davis, Coleen E. (September 4, 1926–April 25, 2007)
91. Davis, Dallas (1892–1970)
92. Davis, Doris M. (August 17, 1938–April 21, 2001)
93. Davis, E.B. (April 25, 1916–July 10, 1937)
94. Davis, Ernest E. (September 23, 1938–November 17, 2007)

95. Davis, Geneva V. (1915–1997)
96. Davis, James Kermit (July 12, 1919–March 17, 2008)
97. Davis, Marena (1902–2000)
98. Davis, N. Keith (May 16, 1948–August 26, 2002) SP4 U.S. Army, Vietnam
99. Davis, Raymond T. (November 20, 1917–January 19, 2010)
100. Davis, Regina L. (December 17, 1964)
101. Davis, Troy (1891–1973)
102. Davis, Virginia I. (May 31, 1868–November 8, 1943)
103. Deaton, Rev. B.F. (April 21, 1857–February 1932)
104. Droke, Aubrey Wayne, son of A.R. & V.I. Droke (October 30, 1931, Age 2 days) *Died of "capillary congestion" (Death Book D, page 138)
105. Droke, Rufus (March 19, 1908–January 3, 1992)
106. Droke, Vadie (March 12, 1911–June 26, 2005)
107. Ervin, infant daughter of G.V. (November 11, 1938)
108. Florom, Jeannie Kay (1945–1988)
109. Fowler, Mary L. (1872–1927)
110. Fowler, Tom [Thomas] M. (1880–1937) *Died of apoplexy on or about November 19, 1937 (Death Book B, page 15)
111. Gaddy, Beulah H. (1903–1986)
112. Gaddy, Camarie, daughter of O.L. & Bulah [sic] Gaddy (Born & Died May 21, 1920)
113. Gaddy, Oliver L. (1897–1975)
114. Garrard, Glenda Kay (December 5, 1954–May 5, 1991)
115. Gresham, Majorie H. (June 5, 1923–February 21, 1999)
116. Griswell, Nicole Charm (August 20, 1988–June 17, 2007)
117. Griswell, Raven LeAnn (October 4, 1991–June 16, 2007)
118. Griswold, Fred A. (1879–1944) Co. B, 52nd Regt. Ia. Inft. Vol.
119. Griswold, Myrtle (1893–1967)
120. Harris, Annie Ree, daughter of R.B. & Mollie Harris (January 25, 1912–March 18, 1924) *Died of congestive heart failure and stenosis (Death Book D, page 237)
121. Harris, Martha J. (September 17, 1860–April 16, 1937)
122. Harris, Mollie (May 19, 1878–August 20, 1951)
123. Harris, R.B. (May 11, 1876–September 26, 1963)
124. Helton, Everette R. (May 16, 1925–December 30, 2005)

125. Helton, Gerald Hardiman (October 1, 1946–January 16, 2010) SP5, U.S. Army, Vietnam
126. Helton, Maurine B. (September 21, 1925–March 4, 1991)
127. Hendrix, W. Marie (1945–1987)
128. Henley, Joshua Daniel (June 22, 1986–July 12, 2003)
129. Henley, Robert L. (February 17, 1930–March 25, 1995)
130. Henley, Sylvia L. (April 25, 1931–May 14, 2007)
131. Hill, Hassie (March 7, 1914–July 18, 2001)
132. Hill, Jeffrey Allen, infant son of Kenneth & Brenda Hill (April 13, 1965)
133. Hill, Paul Edward, son of Tab & Hassie Hill (June 25, 1936–December 3, 1936)
134. Hill, Tab (September 15, 1911–November 11, 2009)
135. Huckabee, Alvin Lee (December 27, 1925–September 25, 1983) PFC, U.S. Army, World War II
136. Hudson, Gloria P. (1941–1941)
137. Hughes, Baby of Carl
138. Hunt, Willis Bennett (March 30, 1942–April 22, 1972) Tennessee, SP4, U.S. Army, Vietnam
139. Hysmith, Eula, daughter of D.T. & Velma Hysmith (June 19, 1926)
140. Hysmith, Ebert Tony (August 26, 1918–July 9, 1983)
141. Hysmith, Fuller (1883–1971)
142. Hysmith, John D. (November 11, 1923–April 27, 2003) SM1, U.S. Navy, World War II
143. Hysmith, Mary V. (1892–1976)
144. Hysmith, Tommye Lee (October 30, 1926–November 27, 1991)
145. Jackson, E. Oliver (1878–1953)
146. Jackson, Essenia (1882–1963)
147. Jackson, James H. (December 12, 1912–March 16, 1973) Tennessee, S Sgt., U.S. Army, World War II
148. Jones, Dorothy Marie (October 21, 1929–March 2, 1931)
149. Jones, Jocie Lorene (May 23, 1922–May 30, 1923)
150. Jones, Mary Jane (born & died April 23, 1927)
151. Jones, Robert W. (November 30, 1931–January 28, 1932)
152. Joyner, Bufford M., Son of Mr. & Mrs. M.D. Joyner (1924–1924)

153. Lane, A.B. [Allie Bell] (1911–1930) *Died on or about December 18, 1930 of typhoid fever (Death Book D, page 130)*
154. Lane, Baby (1930–1930)[40]
155. Lilly, H. [Henry] (1928–1931) *Died on or about April 14, 1931 of typhoid fever (Death Book B, page 30)*
156. Lofton, Vonnie Moore (September 29, 1901–September 6, 1955)
157. Lyles, Victoria Moore (March 14, 1902–August 13, 1965) Wife of M.W. Lyles and Mother of Arnold Davis
158. Malone, Lorene Staton (September 1, 1916–December 23, 2004)
159. Malone, Robert Mack (February 28, 1902–December 19, 1979)
160. Maness, Dallas Ray (October 3, 1990–June 25, 1993)
161. Maness, Justin Ray (July 31, 1988–June 25, 1993)
162. Marsh, Ronald (February 14, 1951–August 24, 1957)
163. Massey, Freddie Martin, son of Hooper & Artie Massey (September 21, 1937–January 20, 1938)
164. McCann, infant daughter of N.E. [Noah Ernest] & B.V. [Belia Victoria] (February 1928)
165. Miller, Callie Grace (born & died January 31, 2007) Infant Daughter of Rickey & Melanie, Twin Sister of Owen Miller
166. Miller, Jimmy Lee (September 7, 1988–May 26, 2012)
167. Mohrhoff, Cynthia Mae (Cindy) Plunk (January 29, 1962–December 28, 2013)
168. Mohrhoff, John Dee, Jr., (September 5, 1985–June 7, 2002)
169. Moore, Pvt. Arlin R. (October 25, 1919–January 11, 1942), Med. Det. 115th E.A.
170. Moore, Carl (September 24, 1918–)
171. Moore, Clyde Monroe (February 7, 1945–May 11, 2005)
172. Moore, Curt (1880–1953)
173. Moore, Ebert G. (July 5, 1909–December 9, 1968)
174. Moore, George R. (1874–1926)
175. Moore, Lena P. (1881–1970)
176. Moore, Lessie B. (February 16, 1897–February 11, 1933)
177. Moore, M. Victoria (August 31, 1854–July 18, 1934) *Died of pneumonia (Death Book D, page 235)*
178. Moore, Maggie C. (December 17, 1915–February 2, 2000)

40. There is a record for an infant male child with the last name of Lane which died on December 6, 1930 in Death Book D, page 120.

179. Moore, Margie M. (February 20, 1915–May 25, 2001)
180. Moore, Marlie (1908–1952)
181. Moore, Millard G. (February 4, 1918–February 15, 1995)
182. Moore, Murray Kenneth (January 29, 1937–March 26, 1937)
183. Moore, Odie E. (March 12, 1911–April 10, 1994)
184. Moore, Ollie (1910–1993)
185. Moore, Pattie L. (1877–1956)
186. Moore, Wilburn, son of Eber & Hazel Moore (1933–1934)
187. Moore, William A. (April 17, 1893–April 1, 1959)
188. Moore, William N. (August 7, 1852–September 21, 1937)
189. Moore, Zacharia Allen Wayne (July 15, 2010)
190. Morris, Alex (1879–1957)
191. Nash, Carl Henry (March 13, 1912–June 23, 1961), Tennessee, S2, U.S.N.R., World War II
192. Nash, Charles Ira (1957–1961)
193. Nash, Christine (August 6, 1928–July 8, 1997)
194. Nash, Della (1921–1924)
195. Nash, Devon (1915)
196. Nash, infant son of Ira & Marie (1949)
197. Nash, Ira (1913–1972)
198. Nash, Jessie B. (February 11, 1885–June 4, 1946)
199. Nash, Joe N., Jr. (January 19, 1960–June 3, 1993)
200. Nash, Joe N., Sr. (July 15, 1935–February 10, 1997)
201. Nash, Lela (December 27, 1888–January 7, 1973)
202. Nash, Lula (1890–1971)
203. Nash, Maggie (1916–1986)
204. Nash, Marie (1912–1996)
205. Nash, Paul Ray (April 16, 1962–July 31, 1964)
206. Nash, Robert E. (September 28, 1925–July 14, 1987) Cpl., U.S. Army, World War II
207. Nash, Ruby (1910–1929)
208. Nash, S.V. "Sill" (1837–1946)
209. Nash, Thomas (1855–1929)
210. Naylor, A.J. (May 31, 1929–April 10, 2005)
211. Naylor, Donal Ray (1953–1962)
212. Naylor, Harriet (January 13, 1851–November 12, 1934)
213. Owen, Albert N. (1898–1990)

214. Owen, Eula V. (1897–1965)
215. Owen, Ruben, son of A.N. & E.V. Owen (September 29, 1921–November 18, 1932)
216. Owen, Velva J., wife of Albert Owen (April 15, 1912–April 15, 1979)
217. Parsons, R.L., Jr., son of Mr. & Mrs. R.L. Parsons (March 8, 1931–September 6, 1933) *Died of sarcoma of the hip (Death Book D, page 213)
218. Patterson, Cora M. (May 18, 1903–December 4, 1987)
219. Patterson, Hobert E. (April 8, 1900–April 4, 1975)
220. Perez, Richard (March 16, 1907–February 4, 1983)
221. Perkins, Lula L., wife of T.L. Perkins (January 1, 1907–April 28, 1926) *Died of influenza (Death Book D, page 71)
222. Plunk, Acie A. (1894–1969)
223. Plunk, A. Foster, son of D.S. & Nona Plunk (June 29, 1923–December 14, 1986)
224. Plunk, Rev. Albert A. (September 29, 1891–March 13, 1972)
225. Plunk, Albert C. (1912–1975)
226. Plunk, Aline, daughter of W.L. & S.M. Plunk (February 3, 1912–March 6, 1934) "She was the sunshine of our home."
227. Plunk, Allen L., son of J.M. & F.J. Plunk (June 15, 1922–December 3, 1922)
228. Plunk, Annie, wife of H.A. Plunk (March 4, 1886–December 30, 1940)
229. Plunk, Annie L. Burkeens (December 2, 1929–March 8, 1996)
230. Plunk, Arcilla Burkeen (January 6, 1907–July 7, 1937)
231. Plunk, Beulah C. (1908–2007)
232. Plunk, Billie Sue (November 21, 1932–March 18, 2013)
233. Plunk, Bobby R. (August 11, 1939–August 25, 1986)
234. Plunk, Bonnie (December 11, 1920–December 22, 2013)
235. Plunk, Charles Ervin (August 2, 1949–April 25, 2007)
236. Plunk, Charles Nathan (August 12, 1934–July 16, 2007)
237. Plunk, Curtis Albert (March 27, 1916–November 8, 1981)
238. Plunk, D.S. (February 16, 1887–June 4, 1957)
239. Plunk, David F., son of Foster & Billie Plunk (January 31, 1951–January 2, 1971)
240. Plunk, Dustin Wayne (October 30, 1986–January 31, 2008)
241. Plunk, Earnest F. (March 21, 1926–December 3, 1966) Tennessee, PFC, Co. D, 750 Tank Bn., World War II
242. Plunk, Edgar (1878–1965)

243. Plunk, Edgar L. (March 8, 1921–January 25, 1945) T/Sgt., Co. C, 410th Infantry Regiment, 103rd Infantry Division, Killed in Action in France.
244. Plunk, Ervin (1893–1967)
245. Plunk, Exie (1904–1974)
246. Plunk, Flousia (February 22, 1901–October 22, 1991)
247. Plunk, Glenda (July 15, 1937–February 8, 1999)
248. Plunk, Hercial S. (September 1, 1912–March 16, 1977)
249. Plunk, Horace A. (October 9, 1883–December 7, 1944)
250. Plunk, Howard (1908–1977)
251. Plunk, J.N. (1853–1932)
252. Plunk, James A. (November 25, 1921–October 25, 1964)
253. Plunk, James L. (April 3, 1953–February 10, 2000)
254. Plunk, Jessie B. (1910–1947)
255. Plunk, Jessie M. (1913–2002)
256. Plunk, Joshua E. (June 29, 1981–December 10, 1985)
257. Plunk, Lessie M. (February 24, 1890–January 26, 1960)
258. Plunk, Lillian L. (July 20, 1915–May 13, 1996)
259. Plunk, Louise M. (May 30, 1920–November 29, 1998)
260. Plunk, Margaret L. (May 6, 1862–April 4, 1934) *Died of influenza (Death Book B, page 42)*
261. Plunk, Mark Wm., son of Neville & Tommie Plunk (May 16, 1937–July 17, 1969)
262. Plunk, Marlie A. (October 8, 1924–November 27, 1969) Tennessee, PFC, Co. A., 121 Infantry, World War II
263. Plunk, Martha J. (July 3, 1946–January 8, 1999)
264. Plunk, Matt L. (July 10, 1901–March 20, 1964)
265. Plunk, Melzer (November 21, 1895–October 13, 1971)
266. Plunk, Mildred (1913–)
267. Plunk, Muerl (October 21, 1927–October 16, 1988)
268. Plunk, Nathan A. (September 16, 1857–April 24, 1929) *Died of pneumonia (Death Book B, page 42)*
269. Plunk, Neville Nathaniel, son of D.S. & Nona Plunk (February 28, 1917–October 21, 1982)
270. Plunk, Nona E., wife of D.S. Plunk (November 4, 1890–September 11, 1924)
271. Plunk, Nora C., wife of D.S. Plunk (August 2, 1881–August 17, 1967)

272. Plunk, Ollye P. (June 21, 1894–July 7, 1973)
273. Plunk, Oscar M. (July 28, 1883–October 1, 1933) *Died of malaria (Death Book B, page 42)*
274. Plunk, P.K. "Pete" (1923–1984)
275. Plunk, Prince A. (February 6, 1914–July 14, 1997)
276. Plunk, Rhonda (January 22, 1976–October 28, 2011)
277. Plunk, Roy N., son of H.A. & Anna Plunk (May 25, 1911–December 10, 1933)
278. Plunk, Rudell (1895–1949)
279. Plunk, Shelby Jean (1936–1938) *Died of colitis (Death Book B, page 43)*
280. Plunk, Susie M., wife of W.L. Plunk (1885–1945)
281. Plunk, Theodore (March 12, 1922–September 21, 1994) Cpl., U.S. Army World War II
282. Plunk, Tommie Corinne (July 25, 1918–June 30, 1990) Wife of Neville N. Plunk Sr. and Daughter of Thomas Guillette & Ann Corinne Pippen Moynihan
283. Plunk, Tony S. (1908–1967)
284. Plunk, W.L. (January 21, 1880–December 6, 1952)
285. Plunk, Walter A. (July 7, 1917–May 8, 1985)
286. Plunk, Wenona (August 19, 1912–March 9, 2003)
287. Plunk, Wm. Arlus (September 1, 1909–October 16, 1977)
288. Plunk, William J. (December 30, 1885–April 6, 1948)
289. Plunk, William L. (January 11, 1928–September 10, 1955) Tennessee, PFC, Battery B, 67th Armored FA BN, World War II
290. Price, Anna Lynn (September 7, 1970–September 8, 1970)
291. Randall, Dorothy B. (May 17, 1928–March 31, 2009)
292. Redmon, Thomas A. "T.A." (December 6, 1917–September 4, 2003) Son of Robert Franklin Redmon & Surilda Hatch Redmon. He married Karen Hysmith on December 12, 1970.
293. Robb, H. Marie (1918–1986)
294. Roberson, W.D. (June 2, 1914–August 25, 1956)
295. Robbins, Ruby Fay (December 17, 1942–February 8, 1962)
296. Rogers, H. Ray (September 18, 1949–December 24, 2003)
297. Rogers, Marty A. (April 21, 1947–August 22, 2009)
298. Russom, Coy Lester (March 25, 1912–June 10, 1991)
299. Russom, Florence (1883–1950)
300. Russom, Mansel (1886–1964)

THE BURYING GROUNDS OF NORTH McNAIRY 419

301. Russom, Minna Lena (November 4, 1919–November 25, 1996)
302. Sims, Baby Boy
303. Sims, Grabel Maelean
304. Sims, Immar Rachel
305. Smith, Aberdeen (January 27, 1913–June 15, 1989)
306. Smith, Billy B. (August 19, 1918–August 23, 1992)
307. Smith, Edna (1912–1953)
308. Smith, James T. (July 29, 1945–October 22, 1991)
309. Smith, Herman K., Jr. (December 21, 1949–January 2, 1950)
310. Smith, Hubert T. (December 1, 1906–May 26, 1971)
311. Smith, Kent (1907–1995)
312. Smith, Retha A. (January 28, 1917–April 23, 2006)
313. Smith, Truman L. (1925–1928)
314. Spencer, Chester A. (November 24, 1903–February 23, 1984)
315. Staton, Alean (February 15, 1914–September 30, 2001)
316. Staton, Lula (1885–1943)
317. Staton, Vroner (1873–1961)
318. Stegall, W.B. [William] (March 18, 1859–March 22, 1928) *Died of mitral regurgitation (Death Book D, page 105)*
319. Surratt, A.J., infant son of A.T. & Jewell Surratt (July 14, 1932)
320. Surratt, Ada (1889–1967)
321. Surratt, Arnold, son of F.B. & Ada Surratt (April 7, 1921–October 1, 1925)
322. Surratt, Barnell (March 17, 1924–September 2, 1988)
323. Surratt, F. Bell (1879–1930) *Died on October 14, 1930 of carcinoma of the rectum (Death Book D, page 124)*
324. Talbott, Essie Mae (January 16, 1904–July 28, 1987)
325. Talbott, Luther P. (February 1, 1888–October 9, 1964)
326. Townsend, Hugh Jennings, Jr. (July 17, 1944–November 27, 2011) Major, U.S. Army, Vietnam, Bronze Star Medal and Purple Heart
327. Trammel, Omie Vires (October 27, 1924–August 31, 2001)
328. Trammel, Robert W. (May 24, 1918–May 11, 1986)
329. Vires, Alna (1898–1952)
330. Vires, Bobby Wright (May 9, 1938–September 18, 2007)
331. Vires, Charles H. (1930–1984)
332. Vires, Clarnth (August 12, 1920–August 12, 1920)
333. Vires Cordie (February 3, 1899–July 7, 1925)

334. Vires, Dizzy L. (July 23, 1945–December 21, 1964)
335. Vires, Dorothy B. Smith (November 10, 1923–January 6, 1996)
336. Vires, E. Loraine (June 25, 1923–June 19, 2006)
337. Vires, Euma, daughter of V.V. & Reedie Vires (March 27, 1922–September 11, 1940)
338. Vires, Flora L. (October 17, 1905–January 18, 1997)
339. Vires, George A. (1879–1954)
340. Vires, Hester (1895–1971)
341. Vires, Harrison (1890–1982)
342. Vires, Herman Lee (October 4, 1922–May 20, 1985)
343. Vires, Rev. J. Asa (November 26, 1890–September 16, 1962)
344. Vires, Jerry L. (July 23, 1945)
345. Vires, Jess F. (January 14, 1868–February 29, 1952)
346. Vires, Jessie T. (May 9, 1923–July 3, 1998)
347. Vires, Margaret E., wife of J.F. Vires (November 22, 1869–September 24, 1935) *Died of cardiac dropsy and tuberculosis (Death Book B, page 56)*
348. Vires, Minnie Pearl (May 13, 1922–January 20, 1962)
349. Vires, Myrtle (Died February 5, 1929)
350. Vires, Newana C. (May 19, 1923–November 6, 2010)
351. Vires, Ophelia (1889–1957)
352. Vires, R.A. (April 27, 1918–September 26, 1947)
353. Vires, Reedie P. (December 9, 1905–December 9, 1990)
354. Vires, Robert Louis (February 6, 1940–August 12, 2010)
355. Vires, T. Dewayne (October 11, 1922–October 20, 1973)
356. Vires, Toy (1893–1975)
357. Vires, Vaudie (June 22, 1901–September 17, 1965)
358. Wagoner, Zellie Droke (April 1, 1903–December 23, 1927) *Died of pulmonary tuberculosis (Death Book D, page 87)*
359. Walker, David Ray (December 17, 1968–January 9, 1992)
360. Walker, Fate E. (January 26, 1896–December 9, 1974)
361. Walker, Grady Shelton (February 6, 1925–September 8, 1955)
362. Walker, Vennye E. (December 10, 1896–June 8, 1982)
363. Wallis, J.T. (January 30, 1918–September 28, 1992)
364. Wallis, Joy D. Plunk (November 12, 1930–September 24, 1981)
365. Ward, Mrs. Susan O. (July 18, 1872–May 3, 1947)
366. Weaver, Katherine Ann (April 6, 1946–May 29, 1963)

367. Weaver, Lula Fay (June 19, 1926–March 31, 1981)
368. Webster, Blanche Fowler (1908–1927)
369. Webster, C.D. "Sam" (1906–1971)
370. Webster, Donna, daughter of C.D. & Helen Webster (April 29, 1948)
371. Webster, infant son of C.D. & Helen Webster (August 1, 1944)
372. Webster, James Ralph (January 23, 1926–November 8, 2004)
373. Wilkerson, Cecil L. (July 12, 1926–September 16, 1993)
374. Wilkerson, Jimmie N. (January 7, 1935–July 28, 1992)
375. Williams, Era Burkeens (August 27, 1905–December 3, 1934) *Died of cancer of the bowels (Death Book B, page 59)*
376. Williams, Johnny Earl (September 28, 1959–March 11, 2012) Son of Earl Williams & Betty Williams Helton
377. Wilson, Arzo C. (1901–1946)
378. Winningham, Frankie Plunk (November 9, 1920–June 18, 2009)
379. Wright, Lessie (1885–1947)
380. Wright, Lexie C. (October 3, 1915–June 1, 1981)
381. Wright, Manley E. (November 10, 1909–January 18, 1989)
382. Wright, Willie R. (1884–1950)
383. Young, Inez (1916–1995)
384. Young, J.C. (1913–1966)
385. Young, Mary Lou (November 7, 1940–March 19, 1956)
386. Zachary, Thomas Wayne (October 9, 1924–July 28, 2013)
387. Zachary, Vinnie Plunk (August 28, 1925–May 2, 2007)

Graves 388 through 394 are unmarked graves. Fortunately, there are only seven discernible unknown graves in Maggie Jones/New Church Cemetery.

Malone Cemetery

Malone Cemetery is located east of present-day Finger on Malone Cemetery Road which is just off of Centerhill Road. The old cemetery is located on a farm which has been logged in the last few years. According to a census taken of this cemetery on July 6, 1972, by Missus Guy McMaster and Herbert May of Jackson, Tennessee, and Mrs. Sam McMaster of Toone, Tennessee, the cemetery was located on the Hopewell Road on the Asa Young farm. Of course, as the years pass, road names change and so does the ownership of land. The following names and dates come from that census, as the author has been to the site on at least two occasions, but has never transcribed the information from the stones.

1. Moses Kirkpatrick (April 8, 1824–August 12, 1909) *He was born in North Carolina and at his death was attributed to old age and he was attended by Dr. William Henry Hodges.*[41]
2. Thomas J. Tedford (January 1, 1810–October 17, 1879)
3. Thomas H. Barham, son of T.N. and M.A. Barham (March 29, 1853–June 3, 1872)
4. Annie Kirkpatrick, wife of J.W. Kirkpatrick (October 17, 1862–August 25, 1893)
5. N.P. Robertson, wife of F.R. Robertson (Died September 22, 1900, Aged 20 years, 8 months, and 16 days)
6. Bob Malone, son of W.B. and M.J. Malone (July 27, 1873–November 6, 1875)
7. Infant of Lit and Mary Malone (Died March 1913)
8. Mary L. Peeples, wife of M.V. Peeples (Died May 12, 1872, Aged 84 years and 11 days)
9. W[illiam] F. Smith, Co. B, Sixth Tennessee Cavalry, USA *Smith was born circa 1837 in Giles County, Tennessee, and died in McNairy County on April 4, 1866.*[42]
10. Madison Smith, Co. B, Sixth Tennessee Cavalry, USA *Smith was born in Lincoln County, Tennessee circa 1817.*[43]
11. J[ohn] L. Smith, Co. B, Sixth Tennessee Cavalry, USA *John L. Smith was born in Giles County, Tennessee circa 1838. Although this is a marked grave, there appears a John Loney Smith enumerated as an unmarked grave in an index of unmarked graves in McNairy County. It lists his death date as April 10, 1885.*[44]

---

41. McNairy County, Tennessee Death Book, 1908–1912. McNairy County Records Commission.

42. W.F. Smith Civil War Service Records and Pension Files of Veterans www.fold3.com

43. Madison Smith Civil War Service Records www.fold3.com

44. John L. Smith Civil War Service Records www.fold3.com. Kennedy, *Unmarked Graves in McNairy County, Tennessee.*

12. Elias J. Highsmith, Co. B, Sixth Tennessee Cavalry, USA *Born in Wayne County, Tennessee circa 1843, he died in Wilburton, Oklahoma on September 2, 1915. His Civil War Service Records spell his surname as Hysmith.*[45]

13. J[ohn] W. Hysmith, Co. B, Sixth Tennessee Cavalry, USA *Born in Henderson County, Tennessee circa 1833, he died "at his residence" in McNairy County on January 9, 1863.*[46]

Elias Highsmith tomstone Malone Cemetery

14. Infant son of J.J. and S.T. Morris
15. Infant daughter of J.B. and Fibbie Dunn
16. Nora Malone, daughter of W.B. and M.J. Malone (April 9, 1875–February 17, 1895)
17. Daniel Malone (October 25, 1828–December 19, 1880)
18. Rosa L. Malone, daughter of J. and P.T. Malone (April 9, 1864–September 6, 1873)
19. E.J. Highsmith (September 1847–December 27, 1876)
20. Mary P., daughter of J. and P.T. Malone (March 15, 1863–November 5, 1884)
21. Jesse Malone (April 15, 1820–April 5, 1873)
22. Margaret J. Malone, wife of William B. Malone (June 22, 1844–June 25, 1920)
23. William B. Malone (June 13, 1842–June 8, 1911) *Former member of the McNairy County Quarterly Court, the Tennessee State Legislature, and a former soldier of the Confederate States of America Army.*
24. Eliza Malone, consort of W.B. Malone (November 6, 1839–August 10, 1869)

45. Elias J. Highsmith (Hysmith) Civil War Service Records and Pension Index. www.fold3.com
46. John W. Highsmith (Hysmith) Civil War Service Records. www.fold3.com

25. M.C. Malone, wife of W.D. Malone (June 2, 1840–January 13, 1911)
26. Martha Smith (born July 21, 1844)[47]

Mount Carmel Cemetery

Mount Carmel Cemetery was first laid out in 1825. According to most sources, the first burial was that of Abram Lorance (Lowrance).[48] Oral tradition has it that the first man to be buried in Mount Carmel was cutting wheat not far from that hill and became very hot. Accordingly, the man drank too much water and then suffered something like a heat stroke from his exposure and overexertion.[49] The second grave was said to be that of a Mrs. Tabbie White.[50] Apparently this is Tabitha Hodges White. She was the daughter of Elisha and Amilla (Millie) Ward Hodges. She married Samuel White, who is probably buried there himself, but this cannot currently be known with certainty. However, there is a problem with these statements of fact. Tabitha did not die until the 1850s and there are old markers in the cemetery with death dates indicating death in the 1830s. Therefore, she was most probably not the second occupant of Mount Carmel Cemetery.

Regardless of the identity of the first or second individuals to be buried in the cemetery, it should be noted that Mount Carmel is one of the oldest burying grounds in the county. Three different articles have been written concerning the old cemetery, one in 1922, another in 1927 and a final article in 1934. Each of these will be reprinted here with any appropriate notes. Following these articles and some further commen-

---

47. *Id.*

48. A September 8, 1922, article in the *McNairy County Independent Appeal* concerning Mt. Carmel identified Abram Lowrance as being the first grave there "about 100 years ago." Interestingly enough, General Wright mentioned an Abram Lorance, probably this one and stated that he came to McNairy County in 1824 and lived to an old age, of about 90 to 100 years. However, there is the possibility that two Abrams existed, one the father and the other the son. However, such speculation will serve only as a possibility which the reader is free to consider and subsequently accept or reject.

49. However, if this is the same Abram Lorance as mentioned by General Marcus J. Wright, it is doubtful that Lorance, at such an advanced age, would be cutting wheat.

50. *Id.* This article mentioned that this Tabbie White was the great-grandmother of Mrs. John Tedford.

Mount Carmel Cemetery

tary is a complete and updated list of the occupants of Mount Carmel Cemetery (2012).

The following article appeared in the *McNairy County Independent Appeal* on September 8, 1922. It was probably authored by Will K. Abernathy or Orpheus Abernathy upon a visit to the cemetery during the graveside services for the late Professor Harvey G. Hodges.

> We visited this historic burying ground on the occasion of the funeral of Harvey Hodges, and within its confines rest the ashes of many of the county's oldest and most respected citizens. It is situated on an eminence overlooking the valleys surrounding it, east of the railroad, and southeast of the town of Finger. The first grave made there was that of Abram Lowrance about 100 years ago and the second was that of Mrs. Tabbie White, the great-grandmother of Mrs. John Tedford. On the weather-stained side of an old monument chiseled by the sculptor many years ago we found the inscription 'Mrs. Rebecca Bullner, born in 1789, and died in 1855." The grandfather of W.J. Clayton, Jessie Clayton, sleeps in the old cemetery, as do the father and mother of Esq. J.S. Lain, Thomas Lain, born in 1807, dying in 1886, and Jane Lain, born in 1821, dying in 1879. We found the monument of Dave Owen, showing him to have been born in 1810,

dying in 1885. There in the silent tomb sleep the remains of the grandfather of Wash Gage, Bobby McIntyre, and scores of others of the older citizens who aided in the upbuilding of the county. What a wonderful history is held in these silent and ever sacred places and what recollections of other days come upon all of us when we read these lettered monuments.

Mount Carmel in the olden times had associated with it the name of Elijah, the prophet. In this Mount Carmel there is the association of another Elijah, Elijah Hodges, father of the deceased, who in his day was a tower of strength in the Primitive Baptist Church, with which church Harvey Hodges had been identified for many years.

The following article, entitled "Mt. Carmel Memorial" is taken from the May 20, 1927, edition of the *McNairy County Independent-Appeal*. Once again it is very likely the author of this article is one of the Abernathy family, the publishers and editors of the newspaper. However, it is possible that a close friend of that family, the Honorable Horry Hodges, could have written it. However, because it is unsigned, it is more probable that one of the editors is the true author.

> A large crowd assembled at old Mt. Carmel last Sunday for an all-day memorial service. It was an ideal day. Parker preached an interesting sermon in the morning. A most sumptuous dinner, just such as the good women in that community are in the habit of spreading, was served. In the afternoon the many graves in the old cemetery were decorated. There was a song service. W.K. and Terry Abernathy delivered brief memorial addresses and Horry Hodges was master of ceremonies.
>
> Mt. Carmel is one of the oldest burying grounds in the county. It was laid out as such in 1825. It is on an eminence, with gentle slopes all around. Nature has provided perfect drainage. Nearby is the old church building in which so many of the funeral services have been held, and where the old time ministers of the Gospel preached in the years that are gone in their good, old-fashioned way.

THE BURYING GROUNDS OF NORTH McNAIRY 427

In this cemetery sleep the ashes of the early pioneers and settlers of that section. Matthew Ward, great grandfather of J.G. Ward, pitched his tent and established a habitation on these grounds in the early twenties of the last century. There he set out his orchards, and built his humble home in the then wilderness. Others joined him and a settlement was formed. Death visited the settlement and into the bosom of old Mt. Carmel were laid the remains of this first one to answer the summons; the old cemetery is almost filled with the graves of the old and the young.

The writer strolled through it; he read from the lettered monuments a history of the past one hundred years and more of McNairy County; one of toil and labor and sacrifice.

There was a plain slab and on it was the chiseled name of Rebecca Bullner, and the record, born in 1789, died in 1855.[51] And another monument to David Bullner born in 1814, died in 1898. There was one in memory of an old preacher, Rev. W.A. McHalstead, born in 1808, died in 1891; that of his companion Elizabeth, born in 1809, died in 1886. There was a monument at the grave of Jacob Lorance, a pioneer and former trustee of the county, born in 1803, died in 1882. And there was the monument in memory of Hugh and Lige Kirkpatrick, brothers who walked the uncharted way from North Carolina and settled in that section nearly a century ago. There is one in memory of the Carrolls, the Harris brothers, Henry and Pink; to the Owens, and Covey.

In the north end of the cemetery are the graves of Capt. E.J. Hodges, and his faithful companion. Monuments mark their resting places. He was born in 1831 and died in 1913, and his companion was born in 1834 and died in 1921. Capt. Hodges was another of the old-time preachers; a stalwart citizen. Then we saw the monument at the grave of their son, Harvey G. Hodges. He was born in 1876 and died in 1922. We saw the monument at the grave of Jim Wright Hodges. He was born in 1857 and died in 1916. There was a monu-

---

51. Strangely enough, both articles mention Rebecca Bulliner and both articles misspell her name.

ment at the grave of W.W. Peeples. He was once a member of the county court, born in 1850 and died in 1902.

There is double monument in memory of J.F. Putman, who was born in 1841 and died in 1921, and his wife, who was born in 1844 and died in 1922. The monument at the grave of Robert M. Clayton shows he was born in 1827 and died in 1863.

We saw the grave of Francis M. Clayton, an old citizen and at one time justice of the peace. In another part of the cemetery we saw three old graves flower-strewn and unmarked. They were of the Lowreys of the family of Gen. Mark Lowrey, who resided near this place in the early part of the last century. The Lowreys of Mississippi are of this family.

It is a beautiful custom to assemble on these annual memorial occasions, and take part in all the services. To scatter upon the graves of loved ones the sweet flowers of the springtime is a fitting and tender tribute, an expression of the love and affection we have for loved ones sleeping in these cities of the dead.

Finally, the last column was typed on a piece of stationery belonging to the St. Louis Police Veterans' Association, St. Louis, Missouri. It is dated August 9, 1958, and is entitled "Reprint of Memorial Day at Mt. Carmel, Sunday, May 20, 1934." The following statement is found at the top of the document: "I, William S. McIntyre, was at the Decoration day, Sunday, May 18, 1958, and the same usual crowd was there but only a few missing each time; a very large crowd was present." This is Sam McIntyre, son of James Robert McIntyre and grandson of Robert Thompson McIntyre.

Sunday, May 20, 1934, a great crowd assembled at Mt. Carmel in the 8th District to observe the annual memorial and Decoration Day in the old burying ground. The day was ideal and the people there assembled took a keen interest in the proceedings. Horry Hodges, whose ancestors sleep in this burying ground, was master of ceremonies, and in his usual happy manner, carried out the program. His address, historical and reminiscent, was enjoyed by all. W.K. Abernathy, who had been invited to deliver a memorial address, was present and spoke briefly.

Mt. Carmel was laid out as a country graveyard in 1826, one hundred and eight years ago. It was so named by the old pioneers, who were students of the Bible and who were familiar with these old Testament characters.

In that cemetery sleep the remains of Elijah Hodges, a celebrated Primitive Baptist Minister in the early days of the county. He received his name from parents who knew the history of Biblical Mt. Carmel and of the part that Elijah of old played on the summit of the mountain far removed from old Jerusalem. His devoted companion sleeps beside him there in the sanctuary of the tomb in Mt. Carmel, and others of the blood sleep there also. Not only do these good old people rest there, but it is the final resting place of others of these pioneers. We recall the names of the Youngs, Harris, Womble, Kirkpatrick, Barham, Naylor, Lowery, Lain, Malone, Carroll, and Cook.

When this burying ground was laid out, McNairy County had just been established a year before, in 1825.[52] Within the confines of the Mt. Carmel burying grounds are many imposing monuments. There are rough grave stones that mark the graves of many of the old settlers who found honored sepulture in old Mt. Carmel.

On the polished surface of some of these monuments are chiseled the names of those whose graves are marked by these monuments, erected by loving hands in memory of some departed loved ones. While these rough crude stones bear no inscriptions, they are none the less tokens of the love and affection of those who placed them there. We saw great cedar trees that had been set out by some loving hand a long time ago. They shade the ground and in season and out, bear mute, but eloquent testimony to the undying love of a father, mother, husband, wife or child, for someone whose remains sleep in the soil at Mt. Carmel. We have been to Mt. Carmel before

---

52. This is incorrect, as the county was formed in 1823.

on memorial occasions. But the occasion last Sunday was one of the most impressive of any.

Flowers were placed upon all the graves, and besides, there were flowers then blooming in the wildest profusion where some loving hand had planted them in the years that are gone.

It is interesting to note that the first white child born in McNairy County was Hugh Kerby. The child grew to manhood, and his remains now repose in Mt. Carmel. This old settler is the grandfather of Mrs. Mary Lain Malone, whose father was the late J.S. Lain. Another interesting bit of history is that in the graveyard are the remains of the ancestors of Gen. M.P. Lowery who served with Gen. Forrest in the Civil War. Gen. Lowery was a Brigadier General at 33 and a Major General at 35.[53]

This concludes the text of the surviving three articles which have been written concerning the old Mount Carmel Cemetery. However, there is a great deal more to discuss concerning this old hallowed ground. Today, the old cedars have been cut and long gone for many decades, probably since the late 1940s or early 1950s. There exists what appears to be great void in the center of the cemetery. But make no mistake, every bit of that ground is occupied by someone's earthen tomb. Today almost 500 graves occupy this land.

There is also an issue as to the existence of a slave and black section of the cemetery. On the west side of the present-day cemetery was at one time a separate section for slaves, former slaves, and other blacks. During a period as late as the late 1930s, this section was enclosed by a white wooden fence. The exact location of these graves is disputed. Three locations have been identified by various sources over the years. Some say it is located in the woods across the cemetery drive on the backside (west side) of the cemetery. Others say it is located, at least partially, where the cemetery drive has been constructed. In other words, the black section was disturbed in order to build the drive. Still others believe it is

---

53. Again there is some inaccuracy in this account. General Mark Perrin Lowery rose to the rank of Brigadier General at the age of 35 and that is the highest rank he attained in the Confederate Army.

located on the bare and vacant looking area around the edge of the west side of the cemetery.[54]

So what is the answer? Probably all three are correct. Most who remember the black section when it was kept remember it being well-kept and fairly large. Therefore, it is very possible that it occupies all three areas mentioned above. Regardless, it is a shame that such destruction has been done.

As to the church at Mount Carmel, its history is spotty and incomplete at its very best. It has been said the original Mount Carmel meetinghouse stood about where the graves of John Robert and Ollie Pearl McIntyre are today. In fact, members of that family once found an old square head nail while cleaning the graves of their parents. Whether or not it was from the old structure will never be known. Actually the original structure was probably a log structure which would have required wooden pegs in the construction process rather than iron nails. Whether or not that original structure burned or was just torn down is not known. Regardless, another meetinghouse was built where the current structure stands now.

The new meetinghouse was a large frame building. The interior of the building was spacious and open. There was no ceiling of the modern sense. One could look up all the way to the rafters. The walls were beaded. There were a few old wooden pews in the structure, for church services, funerals and weddings. Apparently the building was used most frequently for Baptist or Wesleyan Methodist worship services. The original building may have been the site of more of the Wesleyan meetings and the later structure for the Primitive Baptist services.

Some of the preachers who spoke at Mount Carmel include old names like Elijah J. Hodges, Wilson A. McHolstead, Hallie Stanfill, and a Rev. Stansell, among others. In the 1930s, the congregation was an older set of believers including Pete and Lizzie Wharton, Newton Perry Talbott

---

54. The cemetery drive constructed around Mount Carmel Cemetery in the 1950s was turned back to cemetery lawn space in 2008 and the driveway was covered with fill dirt and sewn with grass. It now comprises a portion of the cemetery lawn and is much more pleasing to the eye than the red gravel drive. The demolition of the drive was in keeping with long-range plans to restore the cemetery grounds to their original purpose. Further, restoration of the space on the backside of the cemetery was also in keeping with some type of recognition of that space as hallowed ground for those citizens whose graves were so crudely disturbed and desecrated when the road was built after World War II.

and Lula Womble McIntyre. Occasionally, the believers of the black community used the meetinghouse for singings and preaching.

Eventually, however, the large frame meetinghouse began to deteriorate. Someone removed the windows and doors from the structure and carried them away. Finally the time came to make a change. The decision was made to erect a new structure on roughly the same site. That meant demolishing the old structure. Henry Kirkpatrick bought the flooring from the building and Zanie Brown bought the building itself. The building was already leaning badly by the time it was actually demolished.

The present block meetinghouse was built either in the late 1940s or early 1950s. Pete Wharton was the driving force behind the construction of a new building. However, it would not have been possible without the aid of so many donors who gladly contributed to the building of a new meetinghouse. Of course, others who could do so, gave their time and expertise in the construction process. In more recent years the building had been used by the Mennonites for church services and a school.

The list which follows contains the names of some 400 individuals. Several of these graves once occupied the unmarked and unknown column. Thankfully after much research and time, more than thirty graves have been reclaimed. This list will appear alphabetically.

1. Ada, A.L., nephew of J.L. & Susan Hubanks (November 24, 1898–September 3, 1904)
2. Ash, J.W. (September 25, 1833–September 7, 1898)
3. Ash, Mary Virginia (April 19, 1854–May 27, 1941)
4. Ash, Sarah M. (1835–May 23, 1915)[55] *Died of mitral insufficiency (Death Book D, page 3)*
5. Barker, Ida Elizabeth Floyd (September 14, 1900–October 30, 1918) *Unmarked grave. *Died of influenza (Death Book D, page 11)*
6. Barnes, Emily Elizabeth Lain, wife of Henry Calvin Barnes and daughter of James Lain and Cinthia Dennis Lain (January 21, 1832–July 20, 1918) *Unmarked grave. *Died of dysentery (Death Book D, page 11)*
7. Barnes, Henry Calvin (May 5, 1822–October 20, 1898) *Unmarked grave*

---

55. Sarah M. Ash's maiden name was Floyd. *McNairy County, Tennessee Death Book, 1908–1912.* McNairy County Records Commission.

8. Barnes, Henry White, son of H.C. & E.E.L. Barnes and father of Arky and Ida Barnes (October 22, 1863–?) *Unmarked grave*
9. Barnes, J.A. (April 3, 1858–January 12, 1885)
10. Beecham, Missouri (no dates)
11. Beene, Allen Louis (September 14, 1826–June 24, 1890)
12. Beene, Charlie R., son of Henrietta L. Beene (April 1, 1897–April 4, 1900)
13. Beene, E.H., son of W.A. & M.A. Beene (August 29, 1888–May 13, 1901)
14. Beene, Henrietta L., daughter of A.L. & M.J. Beene (April 3, 1874–October 2, 1899)[56]
15. Beene, Melissa America (Coleman), wife of W.M. Beene (June 7, 1857–June 16, 1919)
16. Beene, Mary Jane, wife of A.L. Beene (December 27, 1833–March 2, 1909)
17. Beene, S.C.B., daughter of W.M. & M.A. Beene (July 27, 1879–August 29, 1897)
18. Beene, William Moses (1849–1927)
19. Boyd, George (1909–2000)
20. Boyd, Jewell Cayce (1918–1999)
21. Boyd, James Albert (July 30, 1949–May 31, 2013)
22. Boyd, Kenneth Alton (February 28, 1939–April 19, 2009)
23. Boyd, Rebecca Kay Bigham (February 10, 1953–January 16, 2014)
24. Boyd, Tommy (no dates)
25. Boyd, William Jerry (October 20, 1937–October 18, 1938) *Died of colitis (Death Book 3, page 6)*
26. Brown, Buddie (June 22, 1892–October 4, 1899)
27. Brown, Cornelius (no dates)
28. Brown, infant daughter of Z.W. & M. (August 30, 1918)
29. Brown, James G. (January 8, 1881–August 26, 1919)
30. Brown, Lydia A. (February 5, 1865–February 22, 1913)
31. Brown, Sudie Womble (June 13, 1885–October 10, 1958)
32. Brown, Virginia (no dates)
33. Bulliner, David (July 4, 1814–February 9, 1899)

---

56. Sadly, Henrietta Beene was born mentally retarded and never married. According to members of the Beene family, Henrietta was raped by a group of young men while walking from her parents' house to another relative's house. She had Charlie afterward.

34. Bulliner, David A., son of G.W. & Nancy Bulliner (died March 30, 1874, aged 25 years, 6 months, and 16 days)
35. Bulliner, Elizabeth, wife of David Bulliner (March 12, 1837–July 2, 1904)
36. Bulliner, George W. (died December 12, 1873, aged 61 years, 10 months and 9 days)
37. Bulliner, Martha A. (January 9, 1848–April 11, 1864)
38. Bulliner, Micajah, son of D. & E. Bulliner (September 25, 1879–August 26, 1902)
39. Bulliner, Nancy, wife of G.W. Bulliner (died August 10, 1880, aged 58 years, 6 months, and 4 days)
40. Bulliner, Nancy (1818–December 1, 1877)
41. Bulliner, Rebecca (1789–October 19, 1855)
42. Bulliner, Sudie, daughter of G.W. & Jennie Bulliner (August 11, 1871–April 25, 1874)
43. Burkeen, George Thomas (January 15, 1882–July 19, 1943)
44. Burkeen, Parlee Robison (February 27, 1893–August 11, 1963)
45. Burkeens, Fay Marie, daughter of G.T. & E.P. Burkeens (June 14, 1926–August 9, 1927)
46. Burkeens, Uneeda May (May 21, 1922–July 20, 1924)
47. Carroll, H.W. (October 31, 1846–September 24, 1919)[57] *Died of an appendicitis (Death Book D, page 12)*
48. Carroll, Lenora J. (1883–1966)
49. Carroll, Lucindia C. (1872–1951)
50. Carroll, M.V., daughter of H.W. & M.A. Carroll (December 29, 1878–October 28, 1879)
51. Carroll, [Rachel] Mary, wife of H.W. Carroll (March 13, 1851–April 1, 1927) *Died of pneumonia (Death Book D, page 86)*
52. Case, J.D. [James David] (1846–1934) *Died on January 24, 1934, of nephritis (Death Book B, page 8)*
53. Case, Joan, wife of J.D. Case (1853–1913)
54. Catron-Hambrick, Christopher Sean (October 14, 1989–April 4, 1999)
55. Clayton, France (1841–1925)
56. Clayton, Nicy B., wife of John B. Clayton (March 25, 1854–February 21, 1873)
57. Clayton, infant daughter of John B. & Nicy B. (February 21, 1873)

57. Carroll's first name was Hugh.

THE BURYING GROUNDS OF NORTH McNAIRY

58. Clayton, Jesse (no dates) *Unmarked grave*
59. Clayton, Permelia J., daughter of Robert M. Clayton (born January 31, 1860, aged 6 years)
60. Clayton, Robert M. (February 17, 1827–January 14, 1863)
61. Cogdell, Elmer Louis (February 3, 1923–April 8, 2012)
62. Cogdell, Nancy Virginia. wife of Elmer Cogdell (November 13, 1923– July 11, 1989)
63. Coleman, Isabella J. (May 18, 1825–August 20, 1891)
64. Covey, Mary A., wife of C.B. Covey (January 6, 1833–January 24, 1893)
65. Covy, Charles B. (December 6, 1823–November 22, 1862)
66. Covy, infant son of C.B. & M.A.
67. Crowe, C.G., son of M.T. & W.S. Crowe (August 8, 1903–November 10, 1903)
68. Crowe, William Sherman, son of W.S. & Mary T, Crowe (November 13, 1901–January 10, 1905)
69. Cude, Lydia J., wife of N.W. Cude (December 4, 1860–May 8, 1884)
70. Davis, Allie B. (1908–1968)
71. Davis, Arl E. (June 29, 1914–June 30, 2008)
72. Davis, Jessie N. (November 20, 1917–May 26, 1999)
73. Davis, Louise (December 16, 1935–February 1936)
74. Davis, Michael (January 22, 1950–September 6, 1956)
75. Deaton, James Ervin (1879–1950)
76. Deaton, Minnie Lee, wife of J.E. Deaton (1880–1967)
77. Dempsey, Malisa A. (November 4, 1876–September 19, 1904)
78. Dickey, John R., son of G.W. & A.E. Dickey (December 21, 1871–September 20, 1873)
79. Draper, Mrs. (died in 1887) *Unmarked grave*
80. English, Myrtle Beene, wife of Lee English (1890–1934)
81. Floyd, Ben A. (November 3, 1892–December 25, 1943)
82. Floyd, Effie, daughter of I.P. & S.L. Floyd *Died October 9, 1911, at age 13 of typhoid fever and was attended by Dr. Nathaniel A. Tucker of Finger, Tennessee.*[58]
83. Floyd, I.P. (December 7, 1867–April 15, 1941)
84. Floyd, Ida, daughter of I.P. & S.L. Floyd
85. Floyd, infant son of W.E. & Jewell (born & died March 3, 1930)

---

58. *McNairy County, Tennessee Death Book, 1908–1912*. McNairy County Records Commission.

86. Floyd, Lydia [Ann], daughter of I.P. & S.L. Floyd. *Died of pneumonia on February 14, 1914 at age 6 (Death Book B, page 15)*
87. Floyd, Sarah L., wife of I.P. Floyd (September 6, 1870–February 26, 1959)
88. Floyd, William E. (July 8, 1910–April 2, 1982)[59]
89. Fowler, Nancy Plunk (May 27, 1847–November 25, 1925) Daughter of George and Fannie Gorman Plunk. Unmarked grave.[60] *Died of fractured hip and joint (Death Book B, page 15)*
90. Gage, the grandfather of Wash
91. Gibson, Thomas Leonard (August 18, 1938–December 17, 2003)
92. Green, Linda Charlene (May 21, 1953–September 2, 2005)
93. Griffin, Charlie B. (March 28, 1890–December 14, 1964)
94. Griffin, [Mary] Eunice, daughter of J.W. & Ophelia Griffin (August 5, 1913–October 15, 1915) *Died of colitis (Death Book D, page 4)*
95. Griffin, J.W. (July 8, 1888–May 4, 1971)
96. Griffin, Ludie W. (July 15, 1894–February 8, 1988)
97. Griffin, M.E., wife of J.A. Griffin (September 21, 1878–October 31, 1900)
98. Griffin, Sara Ophelia, wife of J.W. Griffin (January 2, 1884–April 13, 1960)
99. Griswell, Louisa Rebecca (born in July 1860)
100. Griswell, Mary M. (L.) (April 1873–July 1, 1928)[61] *Died of chronic nephritis (Death Book D, page 105)*
101. Guinn, Cayce Allen (born & died 1996)
102. Hair, Prince E., son of J.C. & M.E. Hair (August 23, 1882–June 29, 1883)
103. Halstead, Emily F. (January 24, 1843–September 29, 1924)
104. Halstead, John W. (September 26, 1879–February 27, 1917) *Died of pneumonia (Death Book D, page 7)*
105. Halstead, Taylor (1850–1894)

59. William E. Floyd's grave lies beneath a double tombstone with his wife, Jewell B. Floyd. Following her death, Jewell B. Floyd chose to be buried in the Old Friendship Cemetery on Old Friendship Road with members of her family. She was born in 1908 and died in 2010, well past the age of 100 years.

60. Kennedy, *Unmarked Graves in McNairy County, Tennessee.*

61. The Federal Census for McNairy County listed Griswell's birth year as April 1873, but Gooch Funeral Home Records indicate that she was sixty-four years old at the time of her death, placing her birth year as 1864.

106. Hand, Minnie Irene Plunk (May 19, 1896–May 19, 1921) Daughter of Alfred Plunk and Kizzie Dunn Plunk. *Died of poison (Death Book D, page 14)
107. Harris, Allie B. (no dates)
108. Harris, Augustus (1876–1930) *Died of carcinoma of the liver on December 22, 1930 (Death Book D, page 130)
109. Harris, Doris, daughter of J.R. & Ora Harris (October 28, 1905–January 15, 1906)
110. Harris, Earnest, son of J.J. & N.C. Harris (May 21, 1884–April 16, 1885)
111. Harris, Emma, wife of T.G. Harris (April 3, 1875–March 3, 1905)
112. Harris, Fannie (1882–1971)
113. Harris, Henry C. (June 11, 1844–October 10, 1917)
114. Harris, James J. (1851–1930)
115. Harris, Jimmie (February 4, 1873–February 17, 1942)
116. Harris, Joanna, wife of N.A. Harris (February 27, 1844–March 2, 1913)
117. Harris, N.A. (April 20, 1838–February 10, 1916)
118. Harris, Nancy A., wife of Henry C. Harris (April 21, 1850–May 1, 1936) *Died of senility (Death Book B, page 21)
119. Harris, Nancy C., wife of James J. Harris (1850–)
120. Harris, Pinkney A., son of Arthur & Lucy Harris (May 31, 1853–August 11, 1890)
121. Harris, T.G. (March 27, 1866–December 9, 1954)
122. Harris, W.A., son of J.J. & N.C. Harris (September 14, 1872–February 25, 1917)
123. Heathcock, Robert L., Jr (July 15, 1946–August 28, 2005)
124. Hendrix, Mary Uda, daughter of Mr. & Mrs. A.H. Hendrix (September 10, 1894–November 19, 1894)
125. Hill, Larry C. (1949–1984)
126. Hodges, Elijah J., Captain of the Sixth Tennessee Cavalry, U.S.A. (May 18, 1831–April 21, 1913)
127. Hodges, infant of Horry & M.E. (January 8, 1863–January 11, 1863)
128. Hodges, infant of Horry & M.E. (January 8, 1863–January 11, 1863)[62]
129. Hodges, Harmon E. (December 3, 1871–November 17, 1957)
130. Hodges, Harvey G. [Garfield] (March 17, 1878–September 1, 1922)

---

62. These were indeed twin infants who were born during Captain Horry Hodges' service in the War Between the States.

131. Hodges, Horry (March 19, 1868–September 23, 1940)
132. Hodges, James Wright (August 28, 1857–November 8, 1916) *Died of cholera morbus (Death Book B, page 20)*
133. Hodges, [Nancy] Jane [Dodd], wife of E.J. Hodges (September 22, 1834–September 8, 1921) *Died of chronic nephritis (Death Book D, page 15)*
134. Hodges, John, son of E.J. & N.J. Hodges (January 27, 1862–April 18, 1862)
135. Hodges, Julia Ann (1878–1958)
136. Hodges, Maggie (March 27, 1876–October 30, 1955)
137. Hodges, Mary Elizabeth, wife of James W. Hodges (January 2, 1859–February 4, 1936) *Died of bronchial pneumonia (Death Book B, page 21)*
138. Hodges, Sarah Ann, daughter of E.J. & N.J. Hodges (August 24, 1857–July 27, 1858)
139. Hodges, Tabitha F., daughter of E.J. & N.J. Hodges (December 28, 1854–August 29, 1855)
140. Hodges, Dr. William Henry (September 19, 1869–November 16, 1941)
141. Holland, Jennie Sipes, wife of W.C. [William Columbus] Holland (1868–1924)
142. Hubanks, Annie (February 15, 1894–October 1, 1947)
143. Hubanks, Dave (February 12, 1857–August 16, 1924)
144. Hubanks, Erleana (1890–1906)
145. Hubanks, J. [James] L. (January 6, 1846–January 1, 1915) *Died of apoplexy (Death Book D, page 3)*
146. Hubanks, J.L.P., son of J.L. & Susan Hubanks (June 5, 1880–July 17, 1880)[63]
147. Hubanks, J.L. Posey, son of J.L. & Susan Hubanks (June 5, 1880–July 27, 1880)
148. Hubanks, Jennie (1864–1904)
149. Hubanks, John Shelley (September 20, 1898–October 18, 1982)
150. Hubanks, Ruffie N. (1901–1906)
151. Hubanks, Sam J. (January 19, 1893–June 18, 1979)
152. Hubanks, Susan, wife of J.L. Hubanks (January 20, 1843–June 21, 1913)
153. Hubanks, W.B. (July 19, 1847–April 24, 1938)
154. Hubanks, William Barney (October 6, 1896–March 28, 1994)

63. J.L.P. Hubanks and J.L. Posey Hubanks are most likely the same child, not twins.

155. James, Mary J., daughter of J.H. & S.I. James (September 8, 1862–July 1864)
156. James, Nancy A., wife of William R. James (November 15, 1838–September 15, 1923)
157. Johnson, John (1826–June 22, 1876)
158. Johnson, Ewin (1822–March 30, 1857)
159. Johnson, Joannah E. (April 13, 1850–February 2, 1875)
160. Johnson, Margaret E. (March 5, 1852–October 7, 1861)
161. Johnson, Mary J. (July 13, 1853–April 14, 1873)
162. Johnson, N.S.C. (1853–March 12, 1876)
163. Jones, Callie E., daughter of C.C. & M.J. Jones (September 22, 1881–March 10, 1895)
164. Jones, John R. (October 8, 1886–November 13, 1909)
165. Jones, Mary Alabama (October 30, 1855–March 19, 1903)
166. Joyner, Thomas Arley (March 6, 1912–December 12, 1959)
167. Kaufman, Ava Lee (September 1, 1931–August 26, 2004)
168. Keel, Martha Plunk (1879–1908)
169. Kerby, Alonzo (1858–1862) *Son of Hugh and Martha Kerby. Unmarked grave.*[64]
170. Kerby, Hugh (1821–1870)
171. Kerby, Martha J. Hendrix, wife of Hugh Kerby (February 11, 1830–July 3, 1864)
172. Kinney, Alice Mae (April 19, 1928–August 25, 2007)
173. Kinney, Edward D. (March 26, 1926–January 9, 2005)
174. Kinney, Thomas E. (March 15, 1953–December 6, 1991)
175. Kirkpatrick, [Mary E.] Betsy (1841–1932) *Died of chronic bronchitis (Death Book D, page 171)*
176. Kirkpatrick, Catherine A. (1888–1970)
177. Kirkpatrick, Charlie Hugh (August 8, 1830–February 6, 1907)
178. Kirkpatrick, Elbert A. (October 27, 1914–March 11, 1985)
179. Kirkpatrick, Eliza (1822–ca. 1855) *Unmarked grave*[65]
180. Kirkpatrick, John T. (1877–1953)
181. Kirkpatrick, Martha Ann Barham (December 19, 1837–August 23, 1915) *Died of dropsy (Death Book D, page 4)*
182. Kirkpatrick, Mollie Bell (1874–1949)

64. Kennedy, *Unmarked Graves in McNairy County, Tennessee.*
65. *Id.*

183. Kirkpatrick, W.E. (August 7, 1832–January 4, 1913) *Given name was William Elijah Kirkpatrick*
184. Kiser, Harlie W. (January 31, 1922–1986)
185. Kiser, Opal, wife of H.W. Kiser (February 28, 1924–August 13, 1984)
186. Lain, Amanda C., wife of A.C. Lain (April 22, 1850–September 19, 1878)
187. Lain, Araminta, daughter of J.S. & N.E. Lain, (January 27, 1878–August 6, 1889)
188. Lain, Hugh M., son of J.S. & N.E. Lain (October 29, 1867–June 30, 1868)
189. Lain, J.S. [James Simpson] (December 2, 1845–May 29, 1932) *Died of chronic bronchitis (Death Book D, page 171)*
190. Lain, Jane A., wife of Thomas Lain (March 17, 1821–August 25, 1871)
191. Lain, John H., son of Thomas & Jane Lain (July 16, 1840–November 11, 1855)
192. Lain, Lillie Amandy, daughter of A.C. & M.G. Lain (July 13, 1878–February 11, 1903)
193. Lain, Mary Ollie, daughter of A.C. & Mattie Lain (June 15, 1888–June 30, 1897)
194. Lain, Mattie, wife of A.C. Lain (1850–1942)
195. Lain, Maudie, daughter of J.S. & N.E. Lain (August 10, 1886–March 23, 1911)
196. Lain, Nancy E., wife of J.S. Lain (January 10, 1850–November 10, 1935) *Died of chronic nephritis (Death Book B, page 30)*
197. Lain, Nannie C., wife of W.M. Lain (January 21, 1858–January 29, 1889)
198. Lain, Reuben G., son of Thomas & Jane A. Lain (August 22, 1856–August 12, 1876)
199. Lain, Sarah A., wife of W.M. Lain (August 4, 1854–February 27, 1878)
200. Lain, Susan V. Rhodes, wife of W.M. Lain (November 23, 1865–July 29, 1938) *Died of apoplexy (Death Book B, page 31)*
201. Lain, Thomas (March 15, 1807–November 15, 1886)
202. Lain, W.M. (April 20, 1848–March 2, 1903)
203. Lane, A.C. (August 20, 1850–October 29, 1904)
204. Livingston, Josephine L., wife of G.W. Livingston (June 17, 1859–July 16, 1888)

THE BURYING GROUNDS OF NORTH McNAIRY   441

205. Lofton, Rosie (died 1906) *Died in childbirth*
206. Long, James (February 10, 1845–August 21, 1914) *Son of Reuben Long and Martha Jewell Long.* *Died of pellagra (Death Book B, page 30)*
207. Long, Susan A. Ferguson, wife of James Long (July 28, 1856–July 9, 1949)
208. Loudermilk, Eldridge Wayne (May 20, 1934–August 26, 1991)
209. Lowrance, Abram (died 1826) *Unmarked grave*
210. Lowrance, Jacob (April 20, 1803–August 11, 1882)
211. Lowrance, John L., son of J.M. & H.E. Lowrance (March 28, 1872–November 9, 1873)
212. Lowrance, Susana, wife of Jacob Lowrance (October 14, 1814–April 19, 1837)
213. Lowery, child of Adam and Margaret (Doss) Lowery *Unmarked grave*
214. Lowery, child of Adam and Margaret (Doss) Lowery *Unmarked grave*
215. Lowery, child of Adam and Margaret (Doss) Lowery *Unmarked grave*
216. Macon, Elijah (Died September 27, 1867, aged 57 years, 1 month, and 14 days)
217. Macon, Honor, wife of Elijah Macon (January 20, 1812–March 6, 1898)
218. Maness, Dovy Honor, daughter of R.G. & Missouri Maness (July 5, 1877–July 27, 1877)
219. Maness, George Thomas, son of R.G. & Missouri Maness (September 25, 1874–November 29, 1874)
220. Maness, Melitia, wife of George R. Maness (February 4, 1848–February 14, 1871)
221. Mason, James (July 1, 1804–June 14, 1880)
222. Mason, Priscilla, wife of James Mason (January 13, 1814–July 20, 1888)
223. Massey, Beulah O., daughter of W.P. & S.L. Massey (March 20, 1901–May 4, 1904)
224. Massey, C.E., wife of W.P. Massey (September 17, 1866–February 2, 1890)
225. Massey, Cyrathia A., daughter of D.P. & S.E. Massey (October 6, 1862–December 11, 1863)
226. Massey, D.P. (March 15, 1834–September 25, 1870)
227. Massey, Sarah E., wife of D.P. Massey (September 5, 1843–March 28, 1869)
228. Massey, Sarah J., daughter of D.P. & S.E. Massey (August 4, 1865–December 23, 1870)

229. McCann, A.D. (June 16, 1910–August 4, 1964)
230. McCann, A.M. [Arthur Marion] (April 11, 1859–August 24, 1937)
    Died of cancer of the lip & jaw (Death Book B, page 38)
231. McCann, Arthur C. [Columbus] (May 25, 1883–July 10, 1962)
232. McCann, Betty Jane (August 10, 1939–April 9, 1940)
233. McCann, Billy Joe, son of Marion H. & Dahlia McCann (born & died August 6, 1934)
234. McCann, Celia W., wife of A.M. McCann (September 20, 1892–January 22, 1968)
235. McCann, Dell (January 3, 1916–May 20, 1999)
236. McCann, Elsie, wife of W.A. [William Andrew] McCann (August 6, 1886–January 22, 1958)
237. McCann, Hazel, infant (born & died February 8, 1928) *Infant daughter of Arthur M. and Celia (Weaver) McCann.*
238. McCann, Mary A. (1909–1927)
239. McCann, Nora W., wife of A.D. McCann (December 23, 1911–May 18, 1973)
240. McCann, Ola (June 1914–June 1, 1928) *Family tradition states that Ola died as a result of bumping heads with her younger sister Beulah McCann. No death certificate could be found to obtain the official cause of death.*
241. McCann, Pearl, daughter of W.A. & E.A. McCann (September 9, 1908–July 29, 1916)
242. McCann, R.B. (born & died 1919) **Per the death records of the county, R.B. McCann died on either August 5, 1918 or August 15, 1918 of premature birth (Death Book B, page 37 and Death Book D, page 11)*
243. McCann, Rex Adell, infant son of Dell & Fay McCann (born & died August 2, 1949)
244. McCann, Truman [Pleasant] (December 30, 1880–March 5, 1948)
245. McCann, Verdie R., daughter of W.A. & Elsie McCann (October 24, 1922–May 29, 1925)
246. McCann, W.A. [William Andrew] (January 1, 1886–August 1, 1970)
247. McHolstead, Elizabeth S., wife of W.A. McHolstead (November 25, 1809–March 17, 1886)
248. McHolstead, Reverend W.A. [Wilson A.] (November 11, 1806–March 23, 1891)

THE BURYING GROUNDS OF NORTH McNAIRY 443

249. McIntyre, Audrey Roberta (November 19, 1928–September 25, 1935) *Died of nephritis and diphtheria (Death Book B, page 38)*
250. McIntyre, B.A., son of J.R. & M.R. McIntyre (December 26, 1874–January 3, 1877)
251. McIntyre, Elizabeth (died January 8, 1858, aged 78 years)
252. McIntyre, Fannie E. Carroll, wife of James R. McIntyre (December 13, 1874–August 6, 1950)
253. McIntyre, Henry, son of J.R. & M.R. McIntyre (September 8, 1891–September 10, 1891)
254. McIntyre, Hubert U. (1897–1976)
255. McIntyre, infant son of Mr. & Mrs. U.H. (born & died 1926)
256. McIntyre, infant son of J.R. & M.R. (born & died August 25, 1870)
257. McIntyre, Isac T., son of J.R. & M.R. McIntyre (December 15, 1880–December 17, 1880)
258. McIntyre, John Absalom (April 27, 1848–November 6, 1897)
259. McIntyre, James E., son of R.A. & S.F. McIntyre (May 5, 1899–October 4, 1900)
260. McIntyre, James R. (November 29, 1849–December 30, 1921)
261. McIntyre, John J., son of J.R. & M.R. McIntyre (March 28, 1882–November 7, 1883)
262. McIntyre, John Robert (July 27, 1893– September 19, 1989)
263. McIntyre, Lessie (December 25, 1914–January 2, 2005)
264. McIntyre, Lula Womble (May 23, 1890–October 9, 1966)
265. McIntyre, Maggie L., wife of H.U. McIntyre (1898–1973)
266. McIntyre, Margaret R., wife of James R. McIntyre (November 7, 1851–November 16, 1904)
267. McIntyre, Mary Helen (July 2, 1912–November 8, 1962)
268. McIntyre, Nancy Caroline, daughter of R.T. McIntyre (October 14, 1852–October 7, 1855)
269. McIntyre, Ollie Pearl, wife of John R. McIntyre (October 7, 1894–February 19, 1930)
270. McIntyre, Robert Thompson (May 28, 1814–November 7, 1902)
271. McIntyre, Rachel, daughter of J.R. & Fannie McIntyre (December 25, 1910–January 28, 1914) *Died of peritonitis (Death Book D, page 1)*
272. McIntyre, Robertie M., wife of J.A. McIntyre (February 28, 1860–November 8, 1907) *Her actual name was Mary Roberta (Coleman) McIntyre.*

273. McIntyre, Sarah F., wife of R.A. McIntyre (February 20, 1873–April 2, 1900)
274. McIntyre, Sarah Jane, wife of R.T. McIntyre (August 7, 1820- January 12, 1875)
275. McIntyre, Vergie I., daughter of J.R. & M.R. McIntyre (December 9, 1878–July 28, 1898)
276. McIntyre, Vivian (November 28, 1921–November 13, 2004)
277. McIntyre, Zenar, daughter of J.A. & M.R. McIntyre (February 15, 1883–December 6, 1907)
278. McVay, Carl T. (1909–1971)
279. McVay, Eula E., wife of Carl T. McVay (1909–2000)
280. McVay, Johnie Mildred (born & died 1928) *Died October 5, 1928 or October 15, 1928, of premature birth (Death Book B, page 37 and Death Book D, page 105)*
281. McVay, Norman (December 7, 1940–August 21, 2013) *Norman's ashes are buried between his parents, Carl and Eula (McCann) McVay.*
282. Miller, Mrs., Mother of R. Jenkins Miller
283. Miller, R. Jenkins (aged 80 years)
284. Nash, General B. *Unmarked grave*
285. Owen, David F. (March 14, 1810–June 24, 1889)
286. Owen, J.N. (1876–1952)
287. Owen, Mary E., wife W.R. Owen (October 25, 1883–July 4, 1901)
288. Owen, Mary Elizabeth (died December 1991)
289. Owen, Mary Jane, wife of J.N. Owen (1877–1955)
290. Owen, Mary S., daughter of W.R. & M.A. Owen (October 16, 1873–September 16, 1897)
291. Owen, R.H. (September 20, 1870–August 5, 1898)
292. Owen, W.R. (December 13, 1835–June 9, 1914) *Although this is a marked grave, the same individual appears to be enumerated as an unmarked grave in an index of unmarked graves in McNairy County and is listed as Robert W. Owen (December 14, 1834–June 9, 1914).*[66] *Son of David Owen. *Died of organic heart failure (Death Book B, page 40)*
293. Ozment, T.H. (1846–1913)
294. Pace, C.P. (March 5, 1881–October 12, 1958)
295. Pace, Clara Stanfill, wife of C.P. Pace (August 11, 1902–March 8, 1942)

---

66. Mary Francis Patterson Death Certificate No. 14964. *Id.*

296. Pace, Hassie Mae, daughter of C.P. Pace (August 27, 1911–March 3, 1912)
297. Pace, James Leroy (February 17, 1913–January 9, 1948)
298. Pace, Luzena, wife of C.P. Pace (July 7, 1888–January 31, 1934)
299. Patterson, infant son of Allen & Mary (born & died October 20, 1914) *Unmarked grave*[67]
300. Patterson, Allen (no dates)
301. Patterson, Mary [Frances] (no dates) *Mary Francis (Ramey) Patterson's death certificate gives here birth date as May 18, 1881 and the daughter of Bert and Elizabeth (Estes) Ramey. *Died of erysipelas on July 8, 1932, at the age of 57 (Death Book D, page 171)*
302. Peeples, Bettie, wife of W.W. Peeples (1860–1939)
303. Peeples, Charles Banner (December 19, 1868–March 17, 1951)
304. Peeples, John C. (1872–August 18, 1949)
305. Peeples, Mary Jane "Molly" (1865–March 8, 1952)
306. Peeples, Nancy C. (August 4, 1839–March 9, 1917) *Died of organic heart failure (Death Book D, page 7)*
307. Peeples, W.W. (November 29, 1850–February 16, 1904)
308. Phillips, Charles Franklin, son of Tennie Starks (February 1, 1924–April 1, 2002)
309. Plunk, Alfred Monroe (1836–1918) Son of George Plunk. *Died on August 8, 1918 of aortic stenosis (Death Book D, page 10)*
310. Plunk, David F. (1885–1976)
311. Plunk, E. Lawson (October 22, 1870–August 1, 1909)[68]
312. Plunk, Elisha L. (December 27, 1824–March 17, 1911) *Died of dysentery while being treated by Dr. Nathaniel A. Tucker.*[69]
313. Plunk, Emily Dickey (1844–1879)
314. Plunk, H.J., child of S.C. & L.A. Plunk (March 21, 1877–July 20, 1879)

---

67. Unnamed Patterson Tennessee Death Certificate No. 153. Tennessee Death Records 1914–1955. familysearch.org. The certificate indicates the premature baby was buried at Mount Carmel, Bishop & O'Neal of Finger, undertakers.

68. According to the death records of McNairy County, Tennessee. Lawson Plunk was claimed in death by typhoid fever under the treatment of Dr. William Henry Hodges. This reason for death somewhat conflicts with the oral tradition that Plunk was injured in the 1909 tornado and eventually died of his wounds. However, the author admits that it is possible that Plunk became sick with typhoid fever during his recuperation. *McNairy County, Tennessee Death Book, 1908-1912.* McNairy County Records Commission.

69. According to the death records of McNairy County, his first name was Elijah.

315. Plunk, infant of D.F. (born & died 1913)
316. Plunk, infant of J.M. & wife (no dates)
317. Plunk, infant of J.M. & wife (no dates)
318. Plunk, Kizzie Dunn (1850–1925)
319. Plunk, L.A. [Lavina], wife of S.C. Plunk (August 29, 1842–March 19, 1927) *Died of influenza (Death Book B, page 42)*
320. Plunk, M.F., child of S.C. & L.A. Plunk (August 21, 1873–August 16, 1876)
321. Plunk, Mary E., wife of E. Lawson Plunk (August 8, 1871–December 10, 1961)
322. Plunk, Moriah (1834–1915) *Although this is marked grave, one source lists Moriah as "Mariah" and shows his dates as being from March 8, 1834 to December 31, 1915 and the son of George Plunk.*[70] *Died of an ulcerated leg (Death Book D, page 5)*
323. Plunk, S.C. (January 5, 1845–February 14, 1905)
324. Plunk, Samuel, infant of W.L. & Susie Plunk (no dates)
325. Plunk, Soferia J., wife of David F. Plunk (1883–1960)
326. Putman, Alie (January 20, 1845–December 21, 1919) *Died of pulmonary tuberculosis (Death Book B, page 42)*
327. Putman, Henry E., son of J.F. & M.E. Putman (October 13, 1870–December 29, 1870)
328. Putman, J.E. (July 10, 1874–September 15, 1874)
329. Putman, John F. (August 23, 1841–July 29, 1921) *Died of colitis (Death Book B, page 42)*
330. Putman, John O., son of J.F. & M.E. Putman (April 22, 1880–November 16, 1887)
331. Putman, Martha E., wife of John F. Putman (April 29, 1844–November 8, 1922)
332. Putman, Martin (August 20, 1818–February 2, 1900)
333. Putman, Tulitha (March 25, 1843–March 8, 1900)
334. Putman, W.A. (August 1849–February 1925)
335. Rankin, Bettie E., wife of Francis M. Rankin (1834–1926)
336. Rankin, Francis M., Q.M.Sgt, Co. B, Sixth Tennessee Cavalry, U.S.A. (1836–1890)
337. Rankin, Frank M, son of F.M. & B.E. Rankin (September 15, 1871–May 20, 1894)

70. Kennedy, *Unmarked Graves in McNairy County, Tennessee.*

338. Rankin, John Dodridge (1816-1870) *Unmarked grave*
339. Rankin, Mary Kerby (1820–1880s) *Unmarked grave*
340. Robinson, David Harl, brother of Oneva Robinson (February 13, 1917–December 22, 1988)
341. Robinson, L.C. [Larkin] (July 11, 1866–August 6, 1927) **Died of pellagra (Death Book B, page 46)*
342. Robinson, Oneva, sister of David Harl Robinson (December 22, 1914–December 1991)
343. Robison, A. Tucker (August 5, 1906–October 22, 1967)
344. Robison, Charity Ann, wife of L.C. Robison (1868–1948) *Her death certificate gives her dates as (September 25, 1868–June 24, 1948). Her parents were Samuel and Lavina (Mason) Plunk.*[71]
345. Robison, J. Frank (October 20, 1918–November 14, 1992), PFC, U.S. Army, World War II
346. Robison, Gary Lynn (August 9, 1956–December 19, 1998) U.S. Army
347. Robison, J.F. (March 14, 1892–October 23, 1918)
348. Robison, L.C. (July 11, 1866–August 6, 1927) *His full name was Larkin Caloway Robison, son of Genile (?) and Margarete (Martin) Robison.*[72]
349. Robison, Martha, wife of Hayse Robison (January 11, 1922–April 20, 1999)
350. Robison, William Hayse (June 14, 1923–December 17, 1991) PFC, U.S. Army, World War II
351. Rouse, infant son of J.M. & M. (born & died May 17, 1874)
352. Rouse, J.M. (August 27, 1852–March 5, 1907)
353. Rouse, Lydia H., daughter of J.M. & M. Rouse (September 27, 1875–December 16, 1875)
354. Rouse, Mary, wife of J.M. Rouse (June 22, 1850–April 1906)
355. Smith, Bethel S. (February 28, 1947–December 20, 1988)
356. Smith, Curt James (no dates)
357. Smith, Daisy Kathleen (no dates)
358. Smith, Frances, daughter of J.W. & May Smith (December 18, 1920–September 30, 1921)
359. Smith, Fred B. (January 1, 1915–May 14, 1996)

---

71. Charity Ann (Plunk) Robison Tennessee Death Certificate No. 13266. Tennessee Death Records 1914–1955 familysearch.org

72. Larkin Caloway Robison Tennessee Death Certificate No. 20472. *Id.*

360. Smith, infant daughter of Lee Roy & Lora E. (May 7, 1934–June 3, 1934)
361. Smith, Lee Roy (September 11, 1903–September 21, 1970)
362. Smith, Leonard Riley (no dates)
363. Smith, Lora E., wife of Lee Roy Smith (January 14, 1909–January 11, 1976)
364. Stansell, John William (May 15, 1871–June 16, 1926) *Died of suicide (Death Book B, page 52)*
365. Starks, Almeda, wife of Elijah Starks (1849–1937) *Died on or about September 23, 1937, of apoplexy (Death Book B, page 53)*
366. Starks, Elijah (1845–1907)
367. Starks, John (1880–1950)
368. Starks, Tennie, wife of John Starks (1898–1987)
369. Stewart, Mary A., daughter of of J.F. & A.M.J. Stewart (April 8, 1870–January 9, 1871)
370. Stewart, Nancy A., daughter of J.F. and A.M.J. Stewart (May 27, 1866–January 12, 1871)
371. Stout, Enna Etheridge (1889–1972)
372. Stout, Evelyn, daughter of Elvis & Enna Stout (born & died July 16, 1924)
373. Stout, Hugh Elvis (1894–1973)
374. Stout, Louis A. (May 8, 1871–January 28, 1958)
375. Stout, Martha E., wife of Louis A. Stout (July 8, 1888–February 25, 1970
376. Stout, Rachel Orra Elizabeth, wife of L.A. Stout (October 18, 1870–January 3, 1911)
377. Strickland, Bertha N. (January 9, 1919–January 3, 1988)
378. Strickland, Debbie K. (September 7, 1957–October 3, 2002)
379. Strickland, Leslie "Buddy" (April 28, 1944–March 19, 1993)
380. Surratt, Eugene (September 30, 1879–March 18, 1943)
381. Tedford, A[llen] K[ennie] (November 21, 1859–April 17, 1927) *Died of Mitral Regurgitation (Death Book B, page 54)*
382. Tedford, infant daughter of E.S. & Sarah Ada (born & died 1917)
383. Tedford, Jennie Bell Lain, wife of A.K. Tedford (June 19, 1869–September 27, 1919) *Died of pulmonary tuberculosis (Death Book B, page 54)*

384. Vanwart, Beulah, wife of Lewis A. Vanwart (May 15, 1921–April 18, 1994)
385. Vanwart, Lewis A. (October 16, 1928–April 16, 1994) ATC, U.S. Navy, Korea
386. Walker, Curtis A. (July 24, 1872–February 23, 1959)
387. Walker, George R., son of W.C. & S. Walker (May 17, 1870–October 22, 1875)
388. Walker, Hubert B., son of C.A. & Melinda Walker (December 22, 1895–June 17, 1396)
389. Walker, infant son of W.C. & S. (born & died December 15, 1876)
390. Walker, James H., son of W.C. & S. Walker (November 26, 1874–March 21, 1895)
391. Walker, Melinda, wife of C.A. Walker (November 13, 1868–November 21, 1898)
392. Walker, Mary Lou, wife of C.A. Walker (February 10, 1882–April 24, 1969)
393. Walker, Susan, wife of W.C. Walker (October 10, 1841–August 16, 1904)
394. Walker, William C[arroll], Co. B, Sixth Tennessee Cavalry, U.S.A. *(December 11, 1841–October 1, 1929)*[73]
395. Walker, Winnie M., daughter of C.A. & Melinda Walker (February 3, 1898–January 7, 1899)
396. Wamble, infant son of J.M. & M.A. (born & died February 14, 1854)
397. Wamble, Mary, daughter of A.R. & Bettie Wamble (January 26, 1910–October 20, 1910)[74]
398. Ward, John B. (August 8, 1847–October 10, 1915) *Died of pulmonary tuberculosis (Death Book B, page 58)*
399. Ward, Mary Ann Louriza, wife of N.G. Ward (January 7, 1828–August 1, 1900)
400. Ward, Nathan G. (June 15, 1821–January 6, 1891)

---

73. William Carroll Walker Tennessee Death Certificate No. 25050. Id. William C. Walker card in Organization Index to Pension Files of Veterans Who Served Between 1861–1900 (Tennessee Cavalry, Regiment Sixth, Company B) fold3.com.

74. According to the death records of McNairy County, Mary Wamble died on October 26, 1910, of diphtheria with Dr. William Henry Hodges attending. *McNairy County, Tennessee Death Book, 1908-1912*. McNairy County Records Commission.

401. Ward, Thankful C., wife of John B. Ward (April 4, 1850–January 24, 1874)
402. Weaver, J.F., son of R.M. & M.A. Weaver (January 12, 1872–October 5, 1875)
403. Wells, Ernest (January 26, 1893–April 6, 1921) Son of Fred Wells and Laura Love. *Died of malaria fever (Death Book D, page 14)*
404. White, Tabitha Eunice Hodges (August 8, 1820–January 5, 1853) unmarked
405. Whitt, Adell, daughter of W.H. & Z.R. Whitt (November 1, 1918–October 31, 1919)
406. Whitt, Andrew Carroll (1849–1925)
407. Whitt, Olar Ethmy, daughter of J.W. & Sarah Whitt (September 24, 1909–August 4, 1911)[75]
408. Whitt, William Harrison (February 8, 1889–June 18, 1926)
409. Whitt, Zelphia Roberta, wife of William H. Whitt (1886–1965)
410. Whorton, Lizzie, wife of P.E. Whorton (1883–1971)
411. Whorton, P.E. (1881–1960)
412. Willis, Bert Orvil Leslie, son of Walter & Esta Willis (September 7, 1970–February 11, 1971)
413. Wilson, Myrtle Elizabeth (November 13, 1930–February 18, 2011)
414. Womble, Allen R. (July 4, 1885–July 30, 1909)
415. Womble, infant daughter of W.B. & M.E. (born & died April 16, 1897)
416. Womble, Jessie T., son of W.B. & M.E. Womble (February 14, 1896–May 14, 1896)
417. Womble, Lucy E., wife of T.J. Womble (October 10. 1860–March 25, 1926) *Died of influenza (Death Book B, page 58)*
418. Womble, Mary E. Beene, wife of W.B. Womble (April 6, 1866–July 2, 1904)
419. Womble, Mary E. Case, wife of W.B. Womble (April 23, 1877–?)
420. Womble, T.J. (December 11, 1858–September 3, 1939)
421. Womble, W.B. (July 20, 1856–July 28, 1940)
422. Young, Addie, wife of William S. Young (1878–1966)
423. Young, Catherine, wife of Johnson Young (About 1840–August 1884)
424. Young, J.R.F. (July 17, 1872–March 20, 1909)

---

75. According to the death records of McNairy County, her name was Paralee Whitt, a child who died of dysentery while attended to Dr. Nathaniel A. Tucker. *McNairy County, Tennessee Death Book, 1908-1912*. McNairy County Records Commission.

425. Young, Johnson (February 25, 1835–March 14, 1880)
426. Young, Lessie G. (November 5, 1917–February 7, 1953)
427. Young, Lottie M. (July 1913–October 1914)
428. Young, Lude (1832–1908)
429. Young, Martha, wife of Stephen Young (October 10, 1803–May 18, 1886)
430. Young, William A. (August 1905–September 1905)
431. Young, William S. (1868–1952)
431.–496. Unknown

There are, to date, about 67 discernible unmarked graves located in the cemetery. In 1991, that number was at about 100 plus. Since that time, about 34 graves have been recovered from anonymity and disregard. The above articles from the *McNairy County Independent Appeal* were the first written sources discovered which identified graves which were never marked or no longer marked. After a review of surviving funeral home records from the 1930s and 1940s, family Bible records, and other private records, a number of other names were retrieved from the unknown column. Finally, members of families and those who were decorating unmarked and unidentified graves were consulted for the names of these graves, with better than fair results.

This process to identify and recover lost graves is an ongoing process with no definite date of completion. Between 2000 and 2002, seventeen granite markers were purchased and erected at the graves of loved ones previously unmarked or whose marker was in disrepair to the point of being lost to eternity. Four were purchased and erected by family members and thirteen were purchased and erected by the Mount Carmel Monument Association. Eventually a monument will be placed in the cemetery which contains the history and bounds of the cemetery and the names of at least twenty, if not more, individuals buried in unmarked graves.

The following individuals are believed to be buried in Mount Carmel Cemetery according to family lore, tradition, records, and circumstantial evidence.

Elisha Hodges
Millie Ward Hodges
Father of Jennie Sipes Holland

Mother of Jennie Sipes Holland
C.C. Jones
M.J. Jones
Esther Ward
Matthew Ward
Samuel White (husband of Tabitha E.Hodges White)
Ellen Hubanks McIntyre
Lenora Derrick
Jesse Hodges
Sarah Elizabeth Dodd Hodges, first wife of Captain Horry Hodges
   (died August 7, 1858)

However, until further reliable and substantiating evidence can be found to support these suppositions, they will have to remain just that, suppositions.

Old Oak Grove Cemetery

The old Oak Grove Cemetery is located off Bishop Road on a dead-end lane. This was the original location of the Oak Grove Cumberland Presbyterian Church, now located on Talley Store Road in Chester county. The church burned in the early 1920s and was relocated. However, prior to its relocation, several generations of north McNairy countians found their final resting place to be this little cemetery now located in an isolated area down a narrow country lane. Several of the area's older families could find their ancestors buried here. These include the Browder, Freeman, Robbins, Robinson/Robison/Robeson Stansell and Talley families.

The cemetery contains sixty-three marked graves and approximately seventy-four unmarked graves. The cemetery is in need of some repair (as of 2012) but is otherwise fairly well-preserved otherwise. The following is a census of Old Oak Grove Cemetery taken in 1994 by the author and originally published in *Fingerprints: An Unofficial and Incomplete History of Finger, Tennessee* in 1995.

THE BURYING GROUNDS OF NORTH McNAIRY

1. Allen, infant son of J.P. & M.A. (died October 19, 1887) *John P. Allen and Mattie A. Robbins were married on December 22, 1886, with William Barney Malone officiating.*
2. Browder, B.F. (1866–1918)
3. Browder, Claude (May 5, 1903–February 6, 1923)
4. Browder, infant son of J.C. & R.J. (born & died December 16, 1894)
5. Browder, infant of Mr. and Mrs. J.N.
6. Browder, J.C. (July 19, 1862–November 3, 1895)
7. Browder, Joe L. (December 8, 1866–July 5, 1923)
8. Browder, Lulu M., wife of Joe L. (August 15, 1871–May 17, 1957)
9. Browder, Rebecca Jane, wife of J.C. (November 15, 1866–September 22, 1918) *She was Rebecca Jane Tedford. She married J.C. Browder on February 29, 1888, with James Simpson Lain, Justice of the Peace, officiating. *Died of a malignany tumor of the ovary (Death Book D, page 11)*
10. Browder, S.T., wife of W.R. (1832–1898)
11. Browder, W.R. (1832–1898)
12. Bryant, J.S. (Died March 21, 1885, age 43 years) *This was Josiah S. Bryant.*
13. Bryant, M.C., wife of J.S. (February 11, 1833–?) *This was Mary C. Clayton. She married Josiah S. Bryant on on or about December 20, 1864.*
14. Bryant, Mary P., daughter of J.S. & M.C. (August 31, 1869–March 21, 1882)
15. Corbin, F.M. (1864–1928)
16. Corbin, Martha, wife of F.M. (1866–1945)
17. Estes, A.D. (1876–1922)
18. Estes, Nellie, wife of A.D. (1873–1950)
19. Freeman, Barber S., wife of J.J. (January 14, 1834–?)
20. Freeman, Irene, daughter of Will & Mallie (1917–1918)
21. Freeman, J.J. (April 15, 1830–August 29, 1909)
22. Freeman, Polina (February 21, 1872–March 19, 1908)
23. Freeman, Sarah (December 17, 1856–May 13, 1891)
24. Griffin, Houston (February 9, 1898–July 12, 1898)
25. Griffin, Mittie (March 18, 1896–July 26, 1896)
26. Griffin, S.C., wife of J.A. (April 30, 1858–July 3, 1896)
27. Griffin, Susie (April 23, 1885–September 21, 1896)

28. Hancock, Herschel W. (November 16, 1897–April 19, 1925)
29. Lott, E.L., wife of John (October 12, 1824–September 18, 1855)
30. Moore, Stoke (1830–October 21, 1855)
31. Morris, infant son of V.C. & Vera (born & died September 27, 1923)
32. Naylor, Rosie Griffin (December 24, 1880–March 5, 1901)
33. Oliver, Ben Frank, son of B.N. & M.E. (August 19, 1893–September 9, 1900)
34. Oliver, son of H.N. & Jessie (July 31, 1915)
35. Ozier, Sallie A., wife of M.W. (December 2, 1852–October 27, 1871) *After Sallie A. Ozier's death, M.W. Ozier remarried to Kate Gillespie on August 13, 1873.*
36. Robbins, Joseph L. (July 4, 1821–March 19, 1883)
37. Robbins, Marcus J. (1846–1909)
38. Robbins, Martha F., wife of J.L. (January 30, 1823–March 5, 1900)
39. Robbins, Mary E., wife of Marcus J. (1850–1928) *Her maiden name was Mary E. Hollis and married Marcus J. Robbins on December 22, 1868 and officiated over by Justice of the Peace A.W. Skinner.*
40. Robbins, Mattie A., wife of M.M. (September 23, 1844–May 3, 1871)
41. Robbins, Mollie, daughter of M.M. & Mattie A. (April 10, 1866–August 30, 1869)
42. Robbins, Permela T., wife of William (December 13, 1804–March 12, 1873)
43. Robbins, Sarah Alice, daughter of M.M. & M.A. (October 24, 1870–July 9, 1871)
44. Robbins, William A. (December 2, 1800–April 23, 1880)
45. Robeson, Blanchie, daughter of T.M. & Alice (born & died May 5, 1903)[76]
46. Robeson, Dora, daughter of T.M. & Alice (September 21, 1868–October 27, 1897)
47. Robeson, Lula, daughter of T.M. & Alice (November 30, 1865–January 27, 1905)
48. Robins, Jasper M. (March 25, 1836–March 17, 1873)
49. Robins, Mary E., wife of W.C. (Died May 20, 1864, aged 29 years, 2 months, 3 days)

---

76. This birth/death date must be incorrect. The reader will note that it is a full thirty-eight years after the birth of Blanchie's sister, Lula, and thirty-five years after the birth of her sister, Dora.

50. Robinson, Amanda Melvina, daughter of T. & A. (Died March 28, 1864, aged 5 years, 4 months, 17 days)
51. Robinson, John Ross, son of Hugh P. & Lula (October 23, 1888–July 18, 1890)
52. Robinson, John Ross, son of T. & A. (Died April 5, 1864, aged 3 years, one month)
53. Robinson, Mary Alice, daughter of T. & A. (Died April 11, 1864, aged 8 years, 5 months, 7 days)
54. Robinson, Moore M., son of Hugh P. & Lula (January 12, 1893–April 21, 1895)
55. Robinson, T.M. (May 15, 1817–March 20, 1879) *a Freemason*
56. Stansell, A.J. (May 18, 1849–August 11, 1900)
57. Stansell, Amanda, wife of A.J. (June 20, 1833–May 9, 1913)
58. Stansell, L.C. (November 23, 1883–June 23, 1902)
59. Stansell, Martha, wife of J.W. (March 17, 1840–February 15, 1924) **Died of gastritis influenza (Death Book D, page 237)*
60. Talley, B. (June 17, 1854–August 5, 1919) *This was Bannister Talley, who migrated to this area from Hardin County, Tennessee.*
61. Talley, M.E. (August 29, 1853–July 6, 1935) *This was Melissa E. Freeman, who married Bannister Talley and came from Hardin County, Tennessee to this area.*
62. Tedford, Maggie L., wife of J.V. (July 15, 1867–August 26, 1888)
63. Tedford, Minnie May, wife of J.V. (May 1874–January 1894) *She was Minnie May Moore and married J.V. Tedford on April 17, 1890, with James Simpson Lain, Justice of the Peace, officiating. After her death, J.V. Tedford married yet again. His third marriage was to Lula Malone on December 26, 1895, again with Justice of the Peace James Simpson Lain officiating.*
64.–138. Unknown and unmarked graves

Plunk Cemetery

Plunk Cemetery is located on a hill in the remains of what used to be known far and wide as the Plunk settlement. The area held a large concentration of the Plunk family, many of which were the descendants of the sons of Jacob Plunk (1775–ca. 1828). To find the old cemetery, one must travel down Centerhill Road and then turn right on Plunk Cemetery

Road. Past the old Melzer Plunk place and the Coolidge Plunk home, the road will dead-end at the cemetery. The names and graves will be presented in a slightly different order than the usual alphabetical order of such records.

1. Millia Jane Vires (April 6, 1846–December 26, 1902) Aged 56 years, 8 months, and 20 days)
2. William Vires, Company B, Sixth Tennessee Cavalry, U.S.A. (November 27, 1842–November 28, 1914) *Son of Samuel Vires and Polly Sipes; *Died of cancer of the lip (Death Book D, page 2)*
3. Lawson Sipes (May 3, 1833–April 24, 1900)
4. Infant son of J.D. and Polly B. Plunk
5. Polly Bratcher Plunk (1857–1876) Died when 19 years old.
6. J.D. Plunk (April 14, 1853–April 3, 1919)
7. J.W. Moore, Company C, Seventh Tennessee Cavalry, U.S.A. *John W. Moore (born ca. 1834 in Carroll County, Tennessee) initially enlisted in Company M of the 7th Tennessee on August 27, 1863. He was captured on March 24, 1864, and released September 1, 1864. He was later arrested by the Federal provost marshal at Mount Sterling, Kentucky on January 3, 1865, and was imprisoned at Lexington and Louisville the remainder of the war. Apparently he was demoted from the rank of sergeant to private at that time. He may have married Mary Plunk after the war, although no marriage record could be found in McNairy County.*[77]
8. Katherine Plunk (1859–1891)
9. Calvin Plunk, Company F, Tenth Tennessee Infantry, U.S.A. *Calvin Plunk died in Adamsville, Tennessee on September 17, 1926.*[78]
10. Abeye Plunk, wife of Calvin Plunk (March 28, 1833–February 18, 1917) Aged 83 years, 10 months, and 20 days
11. Harry Crowder, son of R.H. and Cillia Crowder (January 23, 1895–January 29, 1895)
12. Betty Ozment, daughter of J.D. and M.A. Ozment (October 20, 1861–July 28, 1893)

77. John W. Moore Civil War Service Records www.fold3.com. I.H. Moore Tennessee Death Certificate No. 26481. Tennessee Death Records 1914–1955 www.familysearch.org.

78. Calvin Plunk card. Organizational Index to Pension Files of Veterans Who Served Between 1861 and 1900 www.fold3.com.

13. Bonnie May Harris (May 15, 1902–March 26, 1903)
14. Anderson Mozier, Company C, Sixth Tennessee Cavalry, U.S.A. *Anderson Mozier (ca. 1837–April 7, 1863) was born in either the town or county of Monroe in Tennessee, and enlisted in the 6th Tennessee on September 15, 1862. He died "of disease" seven months later at the Federal military hospital in Bolivar, Tennessee.*[79]
15. Maggie D. Jones (July 22, 1900–May 18, 1914)
16. John Vires, Company B, Sixth Tennessee Cavalry, U.S.A. *Born circa 1842 in McNairy County; date of death not known.*[80]
17. Anna H.R.L.T. Plunk (1816–1898)
18. Dave Plunk (1810–1886)
19. Earl Staton (March 1, 1910–October 7, 1910)
20. Ira Staton (November 12, 1905–August 16, 1906)
21. D.T. Hysmith (May 1, 1852–March 17, 1921)
22. Mary Hysmith, wife of D.T. Hysmith (October 22, 1848–January 12, 1908)
23. Annie Young, wife of J.G. Young (August 31, 1876–October 3, 1911) *Died of heart disease while being attended to by Dr. William Henry Hodges*
24. David H. Plunk (1861–1925)
25. Tina E. Plunk (1869–1952)
26. Jacob Plunk (ca. 1774–ca. 1828) *Beneath large beech tree*
27. Baby Lilly (1920)
28. W.R. Plunk
29. M.R. Plunk
30. R.E. Hicks
31. Theodore Roosevelt Plunk (1903–1972)
32. Z.M. Melton
33. S. Plunk
34. E.B. Plunk
35. J.D. Plunk
36. M.J. Plunk
37. S.P. Plunk
38. N. Plunk (1816–?)
39. D.D. Plunk (1811–?)

---

79. Anderson Mozier [Moser] Civil War Service Records www.fold3.com.
80. John Vires Civil War Service Records www.fold3.com.

40. J. Plunk
41. Abraham Sipes (April 17, 1812–February 6, 1880)
42. Joseph Plunk (1809–December 24, 1885) Son of Jacob Plunk
43. Nancy Haley Plunk, wife of Joseph Plunk
44.–172. Unknown

The approximately 130 unknown graves in Plunk Cemetery are marked by sandstones, cedar trees and stumps, and one rock formation. Probably most are members of the Plunk family. A few notes, however, are warranted. First, the Maggie Jones buried here is the daughter of the Rev. E.R. Jones, pastor at New Church also referred to as Maggie Jones Memorial Methodist Church. She was an only child. Second, the grave which lies beneath the rock "formation" there at Plunk Cemetery is the grave of a young girl whose parents were traveling through in a wagon train.

Rocky Knob Cemetery

Rocky Knob Cemetery is located on the farm northern border between Chester County and McNairy County. There are 140 people buried in Rocky Knob Cemetery. Some of the rocks were difficult to read and thus there is some small room for error regarding certain of the older more eroded tombstones.

1. Alexander, Lois G. (November 13, 1912–September 23, 1945)
2. Bargiaghi, Dolores (August 6, 1928–August 30, 1968)
3. Barton, William Odeus Leon (December 9, 1935–January 31, 1936)
4. Bradford, Jerry Wayne (194_–1998) *The rock does not contain a definite birth year*
5. Bradford, Rev. Melvin F. (September 13, 1927–November 13, 2011)
6. Bradford, Merle N. (July 19, 1925–April 5, 2002)
7. Brooks, Alice A. (September 23, 1884–August 14, 1971)
8. Brooks, Barnie Earl (January 10, 1911–September 24, 1968)
9. Brooks, Colonel D. [Dewy] (July 23, 1916–November 27, 1921)
10. Brooks, Horace Lee (November 28, 1905–December 20, 1978)
11. Brooks, John L. (September 2, 1872–April 22, 1957)
12. Brooks, Mattie Lou (December 2, 1902–October 30, 1995)

13. Brooks, Retha E. (September 21, 1915–May 18, 2000)
14. Burkeens, Drew A. (1910–1959)
15. Burkeens, Gerald J. (1936–1937)
16. Burkeens, Jesse D. (December 10, 1937–October 24, 2006) Pvt., U.S. Army
17. Burkeens, Linda Gail (February 17, 1951–January 7, 1999)
18. Burkeens, Robert D. (May 31, 1929–January 4, 1985)
19. Burkeens, Ruth F. (1912–) *No death date is engraved on tombstone*
20. Bussler, John I. (May 7, 1916–February 27, 1978)
21. Cosby, C.K. (1866–1929)
22. Cosby, Eula (1895–1917)
23. Cosby, Fannie (1873–1954)
24. Cosby, Flossie Lee (1917–1919)
25. Cosby, Lawson (1866–1936)
26. Deck, Charles E. (1931–1979)
27. Dicus, Roy (1933–1988)
28. Ethridge, Ruben D. (Died April 25, 1942)
29. Frazier, Sue N. (July 28, 1933–December 25, 2009)
30. Fuller, Luther Paul (December 12, 1960–July 28, 2007)
31. Garrett, Annie Mae (Died January 12, 1956)
32. Garrett, Ben J. (September 2, 1874–February 8, 1937)
33. Garrett, Carl B. (December 2, 1913–June 17, 1976)
34. Garrett, Fronia C. (July 24, 1913–?) *No death date is engraved on stone*
35. Garrett, Lessie, Daughter of Mr. & Mrs. W.L. Garrett
36. Garrett, Maggie (September 10, 1874–January 3, 1916)
37. Garrett, Ophelia H. (March 15, 1884–April 28, 1957)
38. Garrett, W.L. (September 29, 1876–February 5, 1965)
39. Garrett, Walter, Son of Mr. & Mrs. W.L. Garrett *Born in 1909 and died on February 1, 1909. "Tennessee Deaths and Burials, 1874–1955." familysearch.org*
40. Hampton, Edna (1908–1960)
41. Hampton, Paul (June 13, 1946–June 19, 2001)
42. Hampton, William M. (1916–2002)
43. Hellott, Linda Guynell (1931–1997)
44. Holmes, W. Royce (December 1, 1938–February 2, 1996)
45. Holmes, William "Billy" Jr. (August 8, 1960–October 27, 2006)
46. Horn, L.F., wife of William J. Horn (October 21, 1841–March 7, 1882)

47. Horn, William J., Sergeant, Company B, Sixth Tennessee Cavalry
48. Jackson, Burl (1866–1932)
49. Johnson, Lawson (July 19, 1807–April 25, 1892) a Mason
50. Johnson, M.A., Wife of W.J. Johnson (June 4, 1829–December 31, 1897)
51. Johnson, Sue S., Daughter of W.J. & M.A. Johnson (December 19, 1857–March 5, 1906), aged 48 years, 2 months & 16 days
52. Johnson, W.J. (December 3, 1829–February 28, 1906) a Mason; aged 76 years, 8 months & 17 days
53. Keen, Eurah (June 15, 1918–July 20, 1965)
54. Keen, Hillard (August 12, 1914–March 22, 1990)
55. Keen, William Justin (November 10, 1979–November 19, 1979)
56. King, Mary F. (1943–1968) Wife of Allen King
57. King, Pearl A., Jr. (May 6, 1925–October 7, 1983) PFC US Army, World War II
58. Lee, Blanch (1896–1988)
59. Lee, Hardie (1902–1962)
60. Lee, Ruby (1904–1974)
61. Lee, Sid L. (1870–1958)
62. Lee, Susie B. (1868–1933)
63. Maness, Allie M. (September 6, 1910–January 12, 2006)
64. Maness, [*Illegible*] infant of J.D. & Mattie Maness (born & died July 25, 1891)
65. Maness, Claud T. (December 18, 1909–December 21, 1997)
66. Maness, George D., Corporal, Company B, Sixth Tennessee Cavalry, U.S.A. *Born June 5, 1844, in McNairy County, died from "chronic Bright's Disease" in Adamsville, Tennessee on October 20, 1925.*[81]
67. Maness, Hugh K. (1882–1975)
68. Maness, L.E. (March 9, 1843–August 1, 1915) Age 72 years, 4 months, 22 days
69. Maness, Margie (August 26, 1892–February 1, 1972)
70. Maness, Tera R. (1883–1971)
71. Maness, W.F. (October 8, 1870–September 4, 1957)
72. Marin, Channing River Wolf (August 29, 2011)
73. Moore, Nancy (Died February 6, 1920) Wife of John Moore

---

81. George D. Maness Tennessee Death Certificate No. 249 familysearch.org. George D. Maness Civil War Service Records fold3.com.

THE BURYING GROUNDS OF NORTH McNAIRY 461

74. Nash, Buford Herman (June 1, 1926–April 27, 1997)
75. Nash, Ernest (November 16, 1895–January 5, 1947)
76. Nash, Ludie (November 15, 1900–October 31, 1955)
77. Neill, Laurah L., wife of S.B. Neill and daughter of L.H. & C.R. Johnson (January 7, 1851–May 10, 1882)
78. Neill, Mamie, Daughter of S.B. & L.L. (September 10, 1874–August 13, 1879)
79. Null, Hazel I. (May 23, 1916–October 13, 2008)
80. Null, Robert H. (July 12, 1908–June 5, 1977)
81. Plunk, Amy Eva (October 25, 1914–August 4, 1991)
82. Plunk, Atlas (December 14, 1918–July 28, 1963)
83. Plunk, Don E. (April 3, 1945–February 19, 2005)
84. Plunk, G.M., wife of J.N. Plunk, (August 30, 1857–July 15, 1900)
85. Plunk, Garrey T. "Peck" (July 3, 1943–May 1, 2006)
86. Plunk, infant son of Jacob A. & Josephine Plunk
87. Plunk, Robert (1867–1931)
88. Plunk, Robert Lewis (December 16, 1941–September 14, 1972)
89. Plunk, Roberta (June 20, 1919–November 21, 1983)
90. Plunk, Rosa May (June 10, 1900–July 19, 1968)
91. Plunk, Stanley Ike (June 10, 1955–May 10, 2004)
92. Plunk, Virgil Allen (December 22, 1886–June 30, 1947)
93. Plunk, William Arthur (November 3, 1906–February 23, 1986)
94. Pratt, Joan J. (July 10, 1931–July 23, 2003)
95. Pratt, Ronald (February 10, 1927–May 3, 1987)
96. Raburn, Tommy Leon, Sr. (March 17, 1951–September 20, 2010)
97. Rider, Beverly J. (January 13, 1946–January 18, 2006)
98. Rider, George B. Sr. (September 16, 1941–January 28, 2008)
99. Robison, Artie M. (January 7, 1915–February 17, 1942)
100. Robison, Crocia, Daughter of J.N. & M.I. (August 11, 1885–January 12, 1886)
101. Robison, Jasper N. [Newton] (April 11, 1854–August 7, 1935)
102. Robison, Jeames Tilden, Tennessee, Private, U.S. Army, July 10, 1939
    Robison was born on September 21, 1882, according to his World War I Registration Card.
103. Robison, Lillie (1882–1956)
104. Robison, Lular Sedore, Daughter of J.N. & M.I. (March 16, 1884–October 22, 1884)

105. Robison, Martha D. (March 28, 1848–May 28, 1933)
106. Robison, Martha I., wife of J.N. Robison (October 28, 1851–November 17, 1914)
107. Robison, Robert L. (1886–1962)
108. Robison, T.C. (August 29, 1849–January 2, 1927)
109. Sharp, Eula Mae (1912–2000)
110. Sharp, Nesby W. (1906–2002)
111. Simmons, Annie Birthel (April 17, 1898–December 19, 1990)
112. Simmons, Joel M. (February 6, 1926–August 5, 1984) PFC, U.S. Army, World War II
113. Simmons, Joel Mann, Jr. (March 6, 1955–March 23, 1989)
114. Simmons, Phillip Wayne (March 25, 1956–September 23, 1982)
115. Taylor, Frank Benjamin, Sr. (December 14, 1928–July 2, 1995)
116. Tyson, Gail Marie (June 8, 1956–October 30, 2009)
117. Webster, E.T. (November 6, 1871–March 23, 1918)
118. Webster, Elma (June 12, 1889–May 29, 1966)
119. Webster, Fannie (March 7, 1902–December 19, 1902)
120. Webster, Harrison (February 18, 1892–July 22, 1912)
121. Webster, Martha (June 29, 1872–June 16, 1956)
122. Young, Franklin A., Co. A, 6th Tenn. Cavalry
123. Young, Hannah, wife of R.G. Young (1843–1892)
124. Young, Infant Son of R.G. & C.B. (May 4, 1915–June 3, 1915)
125.–140. Unknown

Wharton Cemetery

Wharton Cemetery is located off of McCormick Road on the Ruth Hill farm on a mound in the pastures. Many stories have been generated throughout the years about the Wharton family and the Wharton farm. Like many individuals and families, there have been legends and lore regarding the Whartons. Because no extensive research has been conducted by the author concerning this family, none of those stories shall be discussed for fear of adding to the great mounds of inaccuracy that often accumulate through the process of speculation. One of the problems with the stories regarding this family is a problem of timeline discrepancies, i.e. the time of the events cannot match the people who are currently known.

THE BURYING GROUNDS OF NORTH McNAIRY

Wharton Cemetery is grown up and there are many trees which have rotted and fallen to the ground on and around the graves. The cemetery itself is situated on a mound built up in the middle of the flat pastures. It has the dimensions and features of almost being a Native American Indian mound, but there is no proof for that guess. There are approximately 21 graves on the mound, but that number could vary either up or down, as the graves were difficult to identify due to ground cover.

1. John Wharton (January 23, 1853–April 11, 1893)
2. Josie Wharton (1853–July 3, 1893)
3. W.K. Brown (September 20, 1848–October 23, 1920)
4. Sarah A. Brown (August 8, 1853–December 1, 1927)
5.–12. Unknown (marked with a sandstone)
13.–21. Unknown (marked with cedar trees; one marked by cedar stump)

White Plains [82]

White Plains is a little-known cemetery located on a rise or mound just east of Tar Creek. The little burying ground is located on the farm of the late Marcus Barham. Although it is small in size and largely forgotten by many today, it is the resting place of several of McNairy County's earliest and bravest settlers. It is located in a little island of trees and undergrowth north of Sweetlips Road in a field just a few hundred feet past the bridge over Tar Creek. Here the earliest settlements were made by the Wisdoms and the Andersons.[83] The cemetery

Mary Anderson tombstone at White Plains Cemetery

82. See Chapter Two for information regarding recent findings regarding the actual community of White Plains, a settlement that had existed during the nineteenth century.

83. See Chapter Two for more information on some of the individuals buried in White Plains Cemetery.

is covered in undergrowth, saplings, and a few larger trees, along with a climbing and spreading ivy of sorts so often found in old cemeteries.

1. Susannah Wisdom (Died November 1835, Aged 60 years)
2. James Wisdom (Died March 13, 1828, Aged 55 years)
3. Tebitha Ann Wisdom (April 4, 1811–December 11, 1827)
4. Mary Anderson (January 22, 1780–October 1832)
5. W.T. Brewer (January 2, 1849–October 8, 1855)
6. Unmarked (sunken grave)
7. Unmarked (sunken grave)
8. Unmarked (sunken grave)
9. Unmarked (sunken grave)

A few notes regarding the early settlers buried in this cemetery are in order. First, James and Susannah Wisdom are the parents of William Sargent Wisdom, the county's first financier and banker and upstanding citizen of Purdy. Second, Mary Anderson is the mother of William Taylor Anderson, the founder and postmaster of the Anderson's Store community and owner and operator of Anderson's Store and Distillery. Third, it is most probable that Thomas Anderson, her husband, is buried in one of the unmarked graves. Fourth, the name "Tebitha" above is not a misspelling, but an exact rendering of the tombstone. This W.T. Brewer may very well be the son of W.H. and Lucy A. Brewer of the Anderson's Store community.

White Plains was a settlement on the banks of Tar Creek. A voting precinct and places of business were located there. Some semblance of a settlement remained at White Plains from the 1820s on into the 1870s.

SOURCES CONSULTED

Books

Allison, Judge John. *Notable Men of Tennessee: Personal and Genealogical with Portraits*. Southern Historical Association, Atlanta, Georgia, 1905.

Angle, Paul M. *Bloody Williamson: A Chapter in American Lawlessness*. University of Illinois Press, Chicago, Illinois, 1992.

Collins, Kaye Carver, Lacy Hunter, and Foxfire Students. *Foxfire 11: The Old Homeplace, Wild Plant Uses, Preserving and Cooking Food, Hunting Stories, Fishing, and More Affairs of Plain Living*, Anchor Books, New York, 1999.

Corlew, Robert E. *Tennessee: A Short History*. The University of Tennessee Press, Knoxville, 1990.

Cox, R. Harold. *Marriages of McNairy County, Tennessee: 1861–1911*, G & P Printing Services, Selmer, Tennessee, 1989.

Cox, William E. *Hensley Settlement: A Mountain Community*. Eastern National Park and Monument Association, 1978.

Dyer, Gustavus W. and John Trotwood Moore, *The Tennessee Civil War Veterans Questionnaires, Volume One*. Southern Historical Press, Inc., Easley, South Carolina, 1985.

Goodspeed's History of Tennessee: Chester County, Illustrated. The Goodspeed Publishing Co., Nashville, 1886.

Goodspeed's History of Arkansas.

Guyton, David E. *Mother Berry of Blue Mountain*, Broadman Press, Nashville, Tennessee, 1942.

Hancock, R.R. *Hancock's Diary: A History of the Second Tennessee Confederate Cavalry with Sketches of First and Seventh Battalions Also Portraits and Biographical Skectches*. Morningside Press, Inc., Dayton, Ohio, 1999.

Jones, Lewis P. *Cemeteries in Chester County*. White Printing Company, Henderson, Tennessee, 1982.

Jordan, General Thomas, and J.F. Pryor. *The Campaigns of Lieut.-Gen. N.B. Forrest and of Forrest's Cavalry, with Portraits, Maps and Illustrations*. Morningside House, Inc., Dayton, Ohio, 1995.

Kennedy, Nancy Wardlow, compiler. *Merchants Bonds & Liquor Licenses, 1865–1898*, Self-published, Selmer, Tennessee, date uncertain.

Kennedy, Nancy and Marie Mills, compilers. *McNairy County, Tennessee Death Book B.C,D, Ca. 1914–1915*. Privately published, Selmer, Tennessee, 2013.

Kennedy, Nancy Wardlow (Transcriber). *Notes of Ancil Walker Stovall: Including the Original Works of A.W. Stovall, Poetry and Speeches*. Self-Published, Selmer, Tennessee, 2001.

Kennedy, Nancy Wardlow, *The 1890s: A Documentation of McNairy County, Tennessee, 1890–1891*, Volume I, Self-Published, Selmer, Tennessee, date uncertain.

Kennedy, Nancy Wardlow (Compiler). *Unmarked Graves in McNairy County, Tennessee*, Self-Published, Selmer, Tennessee, 2006.

Luther, Edward T. *Our Restless Earth: The Geologic Regions of Tennessee*. The University of Tennessee Press, Knoxville, 1977.

McCann, Kevin D. *Hurst's Wurst: Colonel Fielding Hurst and the Sixth Tennessee Cavalry, U.S.A.*, McCann Publishing, Dickson, Tennessee, 2007.

McCann, Kevin D. *History of Liberty Church and School, McNairy County, Tennessee*, Ashland City, Tennessee, Self-published, 1995.

McCann, Kevin D. *The McCanns of McNairy County, Tennessee*. Ashland City, Tennessee, Self-published, 1993.

McCartney, Laton. *The Teapot Dome Scandal: How Big Oil Bought the Harding White House and Tried to Steal the Country*, Random House, New York City, New York, 2008.

Naylor, B.J. and John E. Talbott. *Fingerprints: An Unofficial and Incomplete History of Finger, Tennessee*. White Printing Company, Henderson, Tennessee, 1995.

New Analytical Bible and Dictionary of the Bible. World Bible Publishers, Iowa Falls, Iowa, 1973.

Niemann, Ruth Helen. *The Glory of a Common Man: A Biography*. Privately published, 1976.

Official Records of the War of the Rebellion, Series I, Volume 10, Part One, Government Printing Office.

Reed, Bettye Sitton. *My Three Sons: Volume III, Beene-McIntyre and Allied Lines*. Privately published, 1985.

Reflections: A History of McNairy County, Tennessee, 1823–1996. Heritage House Publishing, Marceline, Missouri, 1996.

Satz, Ronald N. *Tennessee's Indian Peoples: From White Contact to Removal, 1540–1840*. University of Tennessee Press, Knoxville, 1979.

Starr, Stephen Z. *The Union Cavalry in the Civil War, Volume III: The War in the West, 1861–1865*, Louisiana State University Press, Baton Rouge, Louisiana, 1985.

Sumrall, Robbie Neal. *The Fighting Parson: General Mark Perrin Lowrey, C.S.A.* Joe Gillis, editor, _____.

Talbott, John E., J.D., *A Sacred High Place: A History of Mount Carmel Cemetery & Meetinghouse*, BrayBree Publishing Company, LLC, Dickson, Tennessee, 2013.

Taylor, J.C. *Historical Articles*. This work was compiled and privately published in 1992.

Tennesseans in the Civil War: A Military History of Confederate and Union Units with Available Rosters of Personnel, The Civil War Centennial Commission, Nashville, Tennessee, 1965.

Vaughan, A.J. *Personal Record of the Thirteenth Regiment, Tennessee Infantry, C.S.A.*, S.C. Toof & Co. Press, Memphis, Tennessee 1897; reprinted by Frank & Gennie Myers and Burke's Book Store, Memphis, Tennessee.

Wagoner, Bill. *Stories About Shiloh and the Tennessee Valley Area*, Banner Publishing Company, Adamsville, Tennessee, 1994.

Warner, Ezra J. *Generals in Gray: Lives of the Confederate Commanders.* Louisiana State University Press, Baton Rouge, 1959.

Webster's Encyclopedic Unabridged Dictionary of the English Language, Portland House, a division of dilithium Press, Ltd., New York, NY, 1989.

Wigginton, Eliot, editor. *Foxfire 6: Shoemaking, Gourd Banjos and Songbows, One Hundred Toys and Games, Wooden Locks, A Water-Powered Sawmills and Other Affairs of Just Plain Living.* Anchor Press/Doubleday, Garden City, New York, 1980.

Williams, Emma Inman. *Historic Madison: The Story of Jackson and Madison County, Tennessee from Mound Builders to World War I.* McCowat-Mercer Press, Inc., Jackson, Tennessee, 1972.

Williams, Helen W. *The Weavers Beginning With Adam.* Privately published, date unknown.

Samuel C. Williams, *Beginnings of West Tennessee: In the Land of the Chickasaws, 1541–1841.* Watauga Press, Johnson City, 1930.

Samuel C. Williams, "Tidence Lane- Tennessee's First Pastor." *Tennessee, Old and New, Volume I.* Tennessee Historical Society, Kingsport Press, 1946.

Wills, Brian Steel. *A Battle from the Start: The Life of Nathan Bedford Forrest.* HarperCollins Publishers, New York, NY, 1992.

Wright, Marcus J., John E. Talbott, J.D. and Kevin D. McCann, editors. *Reminiscences of the Early Settlement and Early Settlers of McNairy County, Tennessee, 130th Anniversary Edition.* BrayBree Publishing Company, LLC, Dickson, Tennessee, 2012.

Government Records

1840 United States Federal Census for McNairy County, Tennessee
1860 United States Federal Census for McNairy County, Tennessee
1870 United States Federal Census for McNairy County, Tennessee
1880 United States Federal Census for McNairy County, Tennessee

SOURCES CONSULTED

1900 United States Federal Census for McNairy County, Tennessee
1910 United States Federal Census for McNairy County, Tennessee
McNairy County, Tennessee Death Book, 1908-1912.
McNairy County Deed Book A, page 2.
McNairy County Deed Book B, page 211
McNairy County Deed Book B, pages 291 and 341-342.
McNairy County Deed Book C, page 267.
McNairy County Marriage Records for 1861 to 1911
McNairy County, Tennessee Records and Archives Room
McNairy County Quarterly Court Records, 1858-1865
McNairy County Annual School Report, 1910
McNairy County School Reports.
McNairy County School Journal, October 25, 1926
McNairy County School Directory, 1906
McNairy County School Directory, 1924.
McNairy County School Journal, 1927

Interviews/Oral Histories/Correspondence with the Author or Assistance to the Author

The late Luther E. Talbott
The late Faye D. Talbott
The late Arlie G. Harris
The late F.C. Mitchell of California
Omar DuBerry
The late Haven Garner
The late James L. Massey
Billy Frank Harris
The late Robert Beene
Glenn Naylor
Louise Murry
The late Albert Floyd
The late Leslie Floyd
Ben Davidson of Bingham, Illinois
Jerry Wilson Smith
The late Professor Jim Hodges of Virginia
Robert Hodges

Gary O'Neal
Kevin D. McCann
Florence Ward
Brian Neal Dickey, Margie Norwood, and Trish Smith
The late Vivian McIntyre
The late Lessie McIntyre
The late Lloyd Harris
The late Guy Brown
Mancel Kirk
Richard Leath
The late Merle Weatherford
The late Clifford Young
The late Vonnie Mae Garner
The late Ethel McIntyre
The late Roy McIntyre
Tanya Becker
Billy Hugh Kirkpatrick
Don Lipford
Mildred Smith
The late Ivy Cone.
The late Marvin Hand
The late Hayes Hayre
Anna Lou (Phillips) Kerby
Gracie (Plunk) Webster
Diane Taylor
The late Alice (McIntyre) McCaskill

Library Collections

Anderson Family Records File, Jack McConnico Memorial Library, Selmer, Tennessee
Cordie L. Majors Collection at the University of Memphis Ned Ray McWherter Library, Special Collections Department
Romus Massey Papers, Jack McConnico Memorial Library, Selmer, Tennessee
Memoirs of Marcus J. Wright, Tennessee State Library and Archives

Newspapers and Journals

American Wesleyan, November 8, 1881.
Chester County Independent, January 15, 1943
McNairy County Independent Appeal, November 28, 1902.
McNairy County Independent Appeal, December 5, 1902
McNairy County Independent Appeal, April 27, 1906.
McNairy County Independent Appeal, December 6, 1907
McNairy County Independent Appeal, August 28, 1908
McNairy County Independent Appeal, August 20, 1909
McNairy County Independent Appeal, November 24, 1911.
McNairy County Independent Appeal, April 25, 1913
McNairy County Independent Appeal, September 12, 1913
McNairy County Independent Appeal, October 17, 1913
McNairy County Independent Appeal, June 1, 1917,
McNairy County Independent Appeal, March 25, 1921
McNairy County Independent Appeal, June 23, 1922.
McNairy County Independent Appeal, June 30, 1922
McNairy County Independent Appeal, September 8, 1922
McNairy County Independent Appeal, September 12, 1924.
McNairy County Independent Appeal, February 12, 1926
McNairy County Independent Appeal, June 18, 1926
McNairy County Independent Appeal, November 5, 1926
McNairy County Independent Appeal, "Mount Carmel Memorial," May 20, 1927
McNairy County Independent Appeal, May 6, 1932
McNairy County Independent Appeal, 1934
McNairy County Independent Appeal, September 7, 1934
McNairy County Independent Appeal, September 6, 1935; originally printed in the September 2, 1904 edition.
McNairy County Independent Appeal, August 4, 1939
McNairy County Independent Appeal, August 13, 1939
McNairy County Independent Appeal, September 27, 1940
McNairy County Independent Appeal, November 1, 1940
McNairy County Independent Appeal, November 21, 1941.
McNairy County Independent Appeal, March 20, 1942
The Selmer Post, April 22, 1903.

The Weekly Post, November 13, 1903
The Whig Banner, August 20, 1859, Purdy, Tennessee

Papers and Unpublished Works

Hardin, Irene Ingram. *Reminiscences of Childhood* (1972)
Ward, Dennis. *Ward Family Genealogy*. Circa 1986
Webster, Gracie and Mary Martin. *Elijah Kirkpatrick and Related Families*, undated
Whitehead, Marie F. *The History of the Lowrance Family*

Private Collections

Private Collection of Ben Davidson, Ramsey, Illinois
Hodges Family Papers
Private Collections of John E. Talbott, J.D.
Samuel Perkins Talbott-Hattie Cone Bray Family Papers.
Thomas J. Womble's 1904 Cash and Barter Book.
Forked Deer Lodge of Independent Order of the Odd Fellows Papers
Lula (Womble) McIntyre Papers

Websites

www.martygrant.com
www.oklahoma heritage.com/portals/0/PDF's/HOF%20bios/Freeling,%20 Prince.pdf
Brown, Albert, transcriber. "McNairy County Funeral Home Records December 1927–1957" www.mcnairytnhistory.com/images/Funeral_Home_1927-1957.pdf
Gray, Frank A. Gray's New Map of Kentucky and Tennessee
Gooch Funeral Home Records
Secretary's Report, Harvard Law School, 1899

INDEX

This Index does not include the content in Chapter Eleven: The Burying Grounds of North McNairy County, which consists of alphabetized lists of the dead buried in some twenty-five local cemeteries as found on pages 352–464.

A

Abernathy family, 82, 311
Abernathy, Dr. Hayes, 151
Abernathy, J.S., 187
Abernathy, Professor M.R., 314
Abernathy, Terry, Sr., 110
Abernathy, William Kendall (W.K.), 83, 102, 104, 350
Ables, John C., 75, 76
Acton, 136
Adams, B.B., 35
Adams, Martha, 43
Adams, Matt., 42n, 43
Adams, T.L., 43
Adamsville, Tennessee, 61, 84, 135, 133, 194, 195
Aimwell School, 129, 130

Alabama, 152
Albany, Georgia, 74
Aldridge, Jesse B., 49
Allison, Judge John, 134n
Allen, Benjamin, 60
Allen, Elizabeth, 36
Amarillo, Texas, 328
American Quarter Horse Association, 329
Amerson, Allen, 118
Amerson family, 321
Amerson, Hazel, 112, 117, 148
Amerson, Hurley, 117
Amerson, John Calvin, 104
Amerson, Muerl, 117
Amerson, Orval, 118
Amerson, Raymond, 117
Anderson, Annette, 26

Anderson County Tennessee, 28
Anderson, E. Fay Eveline, 25
Anderson, Eleanor, 26
Anderson family, 16, 24, 26, 28, 29, 156, 464
Anderson, George Sargent, 26, 63, 83
Anderson, Hugh Crump, 26, 28, 84
Anderson, James (grandfather of William Taylor Anderson), 24
Anderson, James Wisdom, 25, 25n, 26n, 27
Anderson, J.H., 46n
Anderson, John Harrison, 26
Anderson, L.J., 131
Anderson, Maggie (Lowrey), 95
Anderson, Mahala (Wisdom), 28, 83
Anderson, Mary Caroline, 25, 465
Anderson, Neil Publis, 26, 28
Anderson, Samuel, 25
Anderson, Susan, 25
Anderson, Telitha Jane (married name Walsh), 25, 28, 36
Anderson, Thomas (father of William Taylor Anderson), 25, 465
Anderson, Thomas Bryant (son of William Taylor Anderson), 26, 27, 156
Anderson, William (grandfather of William Taylor Anderson), 24
Anderson, William Harrison (son of William Taylor Anderson), 26
Anderson, William Taylor, 24, 25, 26, 27, 28, 36, 49, 57, 83, 154, 155, 156, 210, 319, 341, 465
Anderson's Store, Tennessee, 15, 16, 27, 29, 43, 46, 57, 73, 83, 154, 157n, 318, 327, 328, 341, 465
Andersonville Prison, 61, 61n, 73, 74, 75, 332, 342
Angle, Paul M., 44, 44n, 46
Annual Singer's General Assembly, 139, 141, 145
Appomattox, Virginia, 70
Arbuckle Island, Arkansas, 89
Archer, Mrs. Laney, 112
Archer family, 113
Ardmore, Oklahoma, 316
Asaton, Tennessee, 15

Ash family, 16
Ashe, Mildred, 128
Ausment family, 17

B

Baggett, Will, 339
Bagwell, Irene James, 204
Bailey's Crossroads, 62, 246, 279
Bailey, Edgar W., 320
Bailey, Irel, 320n
Bailey, Robert, 292
Baker family, 267
Baker, Bro. Charles Joe, 266
Baker, Joe Joe, 266
Baker, Rufe, 255
Baldridge, J.P., 99
Ball and Womble General Merchandise Store, 166, 182
Ball family, 16
Ball, George, 166
Ball, J.S., 160
Bank of Finger, 343
Bankhead, G.G., 131
Bankhead, T.O., 131
Banks, Reverend V.E., 285
Baptist Hospital, 95, 96, 222
Barber, Rudolph, 171, 183, 298
Barham, Charles L. "Charlie," 114, 149, 151
Barham, Corporal Charles L., 327
Barham, Clarence, 114, 151
Barham, C.N., 255
Barham, Edna, 127, 128, 150
Barham, Evelyn Christine (Clayton), 118, 128, 150n, 150
Barham family, 16
Barham, Fate, 269
Barham, Flora Jane (Hysmith), 149, 151
Barham, Frank, 150
Barham, H., 255
Barham, H.C., 255
Barham, Henry, 228
Barham, J.E., 228
Barham, John, 255
Barham, John Richard, 63
Barham, Leander, 323, 327
Barham, M. Arthur, 169
Barham, Marcus, 28, 108, 464

INDEX

Barham, Martha Ann, 234
Barham, Nath, 255
Barham, Pagan, 323
Barham, Parlee, 104
Barham, Pearl, 104
Barham, R.B., 108, 269
Barham, R.N., 169, 255
Barham, Tony, 114
Barnes, Arky, 129, 130
Barnes, Bertha, 104
Barnes, Blaine, 329, 330
Barnes, Dr. W.M., 161, 191, 213, 218, 219, 219n, 220, 220n, 221, 222, 282, 284n, 348
Barnes, Eugene, 266
Barnes, Estelee Bishop (Mrs. W.M.), 128, 218, 221, 222, 284, 284n
Barnes family, 16
Barnes, Henry, 255
Barnes, Hubert, 114
Barnes, Martie, 104
Barnes, Nora (Hughes), 218
Barnes, Thomas L., 218
Barnes, W.H., 256
Barnett, J.S., 156
Barr, C.M., 161, 166, 187
Barr, Clarence, 263, 264
Barrett, Mr., 69
Barrett family, 16
Barton, Cora, 104
Barton, Dona, 172
Barton, Ethel, 104
Barton, Ivy, 209
Barton, John Jr., 172
Barton, Tabitha (Hodges), 19
Barry, W.V., 53
Bartlett, Dewey, 239
Basham, Elsie, 107
Basham, Hugh Allen, 125, 126
Basham, Mildred, 121, 128
Basinger, Sally, 35
Baskwell, Ruth, 43
Bass, Robert J., 161, 161n
Bassham, Hugh Allen, 127
Bassham, Richard A., 72, 73
Bassham, William, 72
Battle of Athens, 247
Battle of Belmont, Missouri, 66, 87

Battle of Chickamauga, 88, 91
Battle of Corinth, 66
Battle of Franklin, 86, 94
Battle of Henderson Station, 278
Battle of Johnsonville, 86
Battle of Manassas, Virginia, 66
Battle of Murfreesboro, Tennessee, 26, 27, 63, 84, 88
Battle of Nashville, 94
Battle of Perryville, Kentucky, 88
Battle of Pulaski, 86, 247
Battle of Richmond, Kentucky, 88
Battle of Shiloh (McNairy County, Tennessee), 66, 83, 86, 88, 143, 246
Battle of Selma, 86
Battle of Spring Hill, 86
Battle of Sulphur Trestle, Alabama, 247
Baucom, Minnie, 104
Beachy family, 267
Beachy, Danny, 192, 237
Beard family, 16, 235
Beard, Allen, 235
Beard, Francis, 155, 227, 235, 262, 268
Beard, Franklin, 62n
Beard, Franklin Jr., 85
Beard, George, 235
Beard, John, 235
Beard, Margaret (Brown), 85
Beard, Robert F., 119n
Beard, R.T., 256
Beard, William, 235, 236
Beard, William Edward, 62n
Beaty Cemetery, 60, 115, 236
Beaty, John, 155
Beaty, L.A., 288
Beck, Bob, 270
Beck, J.H. "Jim," 121, 127, 128, 149
Bedford County, Tennessee, 25, 26, 34
Beech Creek, 65
Beene family, 252, 253
Beene, Allen (son of Levi Benton Beene), 253
Beene, Allen Louis, 251, 252, 253
Beene, Bessie, 220
Beene, Charlie, 254
Beene, E.H., 253
Beene, Francis, 253

Beene, Henrietta, 252, 254
Beene, Howard, 64
Beene, Ida, 253
Beene, James Samuel "Sam" Allen, 254
Beene, J.H., 253
Beene, John Samuel, 253, 254
Beene, Levi Benton, 253
Beene, Malinda Jane, 254
Beene, Margaret Rebecca, 251
Beene, Martha Ann, 254
Beene, Mary Jane (Fuller), 251, 252, 253, 254
Beene, Robert, 81n, 82, 83, 151, 180, 183, 183n, 220n, 254, 281n, 296, 297, 297n, 345n
Beene, Samuel, 253
Beene, S.G.B., 253
Beene, Walter G., 253
Beene, William Moses, 252, 253
Beene, Zenar, 253
Bell, Alexander Graham, 185n
Bell, Genevieve (Scott), 212n
Bell Isle, 74
Bell, Mollie, 235
Bell, Tom, 130
Belmont, Missouri, 62, 246
Berry, Modena (Lowrey), 91, 93, 94, 95, 96
Berry, M.P.L., 96
Bethel College, 145, 146, 150
Bethel Springs High School, 120, 145, 146, 150, 151
Bethel Springs, Tennessee, 15, 23, 65, 144, 145, 146, 149, 151, 330, 348
Bethel Station, 56, 65, 77, 79
Beurey, Tom, 322
Big Hatchie Circuit, 261
Bigger, Elizabeth "Bessie" (Abernathy), 139n
Billies' Creek, 341
Bishop and O'Neal General Merchandise, 168, 175, 176, 177, 202, 264, 285
Bishop and O'Neal Funeral Home, 167, 169
Bishop, Alsworth Guy, 183, 202, 264, 265, 282, 283, 284, 292, 297

Bishop, Dorsey E. "Dossie," 166, 167, 169, 202, 203, 218, 222, 264, 282, 283, 284, 284n, 288
Bishop General Merchandise Store, 221
Bishop, Guy, 167, 169, 191, 203, 218
Bishop, Inetha, 127, 222, 284, 284n
Bishop, James M., 110
Bishop, Lela, 264, 284
Bishop, Lorraine, 127
Bishop, Lula, 128
Bishop, Maggie, 264, 284
Bishop, M.E., 161, 166, 168, 169, 202, 218, 264
Bishop, Minnie, 264
Bishop, Mrs. A.G., 128
Bishop, Roy, 222, 284, 284n
Bishop, Ruby, 105
Bishop, Sula, 120, 127
Bishop's Store, 292
Bivins, Flossie, 117
Black Jack Ridge, 319
Black School, 132
Blakely family, 16, 237, 327, 328
Blakely, Dorah, 323
Blakely, Grear (Greene), 60
Blakely, Ira, 325
Blakely, J.B., 156, 327
Blakely, James P., 58, 58n, 322
Blakely, James H., 131, 327
Blakely, Mary E. (Peeples), 325, 327
Blakely, Dr. Pinkney "Pink," 323, 324, 327
Blakely, Thomas Benton, 322, 326, 327, 328
Blakely, William, 327
Blankenship, Gary, 56n
Bloody Vendetta, 44
Blue Mountain, Mississippi, 91, 92
Blue Mountain College, 94, 95, 96
Blue Mountain Female Institute, 94
Bolivar, Tennessee, 51, 52, 196, 217n, 275
Bond, Helen, 26
Booneville, Mississippi, 269
Booth, Rachel, 112
Boston, Massachusetts, 315
Bowles, Frances, 236n
Bowling Green, Kentucky, 90
Boyd, Fate, 346

Boyd, H.C., 256
Boyd, Lillie (Plunk), 122
Bradley, J.J., 130, 325
Bradshaw, B., 256
Branch Place, 239
Brantom, Ada, 291
Breckinridge, William K. M., 77
Brett (Britt) family, 16
Brewer family, 16
Brewer, Douglas, 266
Brewer, Lucy A., 465
Brewer, W.H., 465
Brewer, W.T., 465
Brian, Jane, 25
Brice's Crossroads, Mississippi, 54, 232
Brickens, Henry Harrison (Burkeens), 58
Brickens, James (Burkeens), 58
Bridges, Hiram (pseudonym), 335, 338
Briggance, E.L., 120
Briggance, L.L., 264
Broadway, Mr., 291
Brooks, Alice, 108
Brooks, Lee, 339
Brooks, Martha, 108
Brooks, Ollye, 108
Brooks, John, 106, 108
Brooks, J.R., 256
Brooks, Lee, 180
Brooks, Roberta, 108
Browder family, 16
Browder, Tom, 256
Browder, Will, 298
Brower, John, 38
Brown, 129, 267
Brown family, 16
Brown, Archibald, 37
Brown-Built Shoes, 177
Brown, Charlotte, 231
Brown, Cornelius, 182
Brown, C.V., 160, 213
Brown, George W., 341
Brown, Guy, 67, 67n, 217n
Brown, Harrison, 171
Brown, Henry, 256
Brown, I.C.B., 160
Brown, Ichabod, 65, 155, 229, 230, 231, 232
Brown, Ila, 265

Brown, I.W., 167
Brown, J.C., 257
Brown, Keith, 266, 270
Brown, Margaret, 235
Brown, Ora, 194, 195
Brown, Pleasant A., 67
Brown, Roscoe, 168
Brown, Seril, 213
Brown, William, 155, 231
Brown, Zannie, 161, 179, 199, 269
Browning, Captain Gordon, 137, 350
Browning, Gordon (Congressman), 138
Brownlow, William "Parson," 71, 230
Brown's Crossing, 48, 65
Brown's Station, 65
Bryan, William Jennings, 4
Bryant family, 16
Bryant, M.C., 257
Bucklier Tavern, Virginia, 19
Buena Vista, Mexico, battle of, 314
Bulliner family, 16, 43, 44, 45, 248, 267
Bulliner, David A., 46
Bulliner, George W., 44, 45, 115
Bulliner, Monroe, 46
Bulliner, Rebecca, 45
Bullman family, 16, 272, 293, 320
Bullman, Bud, 293, 320
Bullman, Buren, 65
Bullman, Edgar, 320
Bullman, Elvis, 272, 293
Bullman, George N., 59, 293, 320
Bullman, Ora, 109, 111, 272
Bullman, Otis, 293
Bullman Store, 111, 212, 320
Bullman Store Community, 65, 291, 292
Bullman, W.O., 270
Burgess, Bobby, 128
Burkhead family, 16
Burkhead, Elliot, 340
Burkhead, Larry, 270
Burkhead, Harry, 266
Burkeen, Collis, 117
Burkeen, R.B., 117
Burkeens (Brickeens) family, 16
Burkeens, Lark, 250
Burns, William, 119n, 155
Burross, 267
Burten, Archibald, 155

Burton, A.M., 36
Burton, Permelia T., 46
Bushel Creek, 190, 341, 346
Butler, Bennett, 35
Butler, Joannah, 35
Butler, John C., 35
Butler, Margaret, 35
Butler, Martha, 35

C

Cagle family, 180
Cairo, Illinois, 121n, 181n
Calloway, Rebecca, 20
Canaday, J.D., 285
Canterbury, John, 324, 328
Canton, China, 96
Cantrell, Eunice (Peeples), 325
Carbondale, Illinois, 44, 45
Carothers, Henry, 102, 104
Carothers, Mamie, 105
Carpenter, Albert Ray "Cecil," 117
Carpenter, Albin, 269
Carpenter, Cecil, 269
Carpenter, Faye, 117
Carpenter, Homer, 118
Carpenter, Lizzie, 234
Carpenter, Maurine, 117
Carpenter, Nicholas 2, 3
Carroll Branch Community, 319
Carroll family, 292
Carroll, J., 256
Carroll, Yoga R., 346
Carson, W., 131
Carter Family (musical group), 350
Carter, Bob, 346
Carter, Fayette "Fate," 64, 173
Carter, Jewell Massey, 120, 128, 193
Carter, Rob, 167, 179
Carter, Robert F., 35n
Carter, Robert L., 161
Carter's Valley, 261
Case, James, 255
Case, John R., 234
Casey, James, 19
Cash (proposed name of Finger), 342
Cason & Company, 156
Cason & Skinner, 156
Cason, C.M., 156, 232

Cason family, 16
Cason, W.C., 156
Catawba County, North Carolina, 23
Caudle's Store, 180
Causby, Lester, 110
Cave Springs community, 203
Cave Springs Cemetery, 32
Cayce, Claude, 314
Cayce, S.F., 314
Cedar Grove Cemetery, 200
Centerhill Academy, 110, 110n, 136, 152
Center Ridge School, 148
Chalmers, Gen. James R., 52
Chandler, Beulah, 117
Chandler, Emanuel "Manley" (also "Chan"), 331, 332, 339
Chandler, Captain William, 73
Chapel Hill (McNairy County, Tennessee), 235
Chapel Hill Cemetery, 60, 61
Charlotte, North Carolina, 228, 229
Charter of Connecticut, 313
Chatham County, North Carolina, 37
Cherokee Indians, 7
Cherry, M.L., 253
Chester County, Tennessee, 5, 11, 15, 20, 33, 38, 115, 131, 176, 189, 200, 201, 202, 207, 208, 210, 221, 222, 244, 269, 317n, 318, 321, 331, 341, 342
Chester County High School, 147
Chester County Independent newspaper, 221, 222n
Chicago, Illinois, 326, 337
Chickasaw Indians, 8
Chickasaw Nation, 9, 34
Chickasaw Purchase Territory, 14, 34
Chickasaw Territory, 7
Chili Davis' Pool Hall, 180
Chism, Order Sergeant David, 18
Choctaw Indians, 7
Christian Church, 139
Church of Christ, 129, 231, 249, 288n
Church of Christ at Refuge, 112
Church of Christ Meetinghouse, 218
Churchwell, G.W., 87
City of Miami (train), 187
Clarence Barham Road, 34, 64

INDEX 479

Clark, William, 7
Clayton, Allie (James), 150
Clayton, Cratus, 180
Clayton, Cecil, 108, 127, 128, 145, 145n, 151
Clayton, Cheryl, 179
Clayton, Ed, 114
Clayton, Ernest (Dry Goods Store), 191
Clayton family, 16, 267
Clayton, Francis C. "France," 62, 62n, 87, 88
Clayton, Frank, 288
Clayton, F.W., 161
Clayton, G.W., 257
Clayton, John, 194, 297
Clayton, Ida, 329
Clayton, Justice of the Peace R.M., 193
Clayton, Ludie (Griffin), 209
Clayton, Mary C., 87, 240
Clayton, Mary Elizabeth, 329
Clayton, Permelia J., 240
Clayton, R.F., 257
Clayton, Robert M., 87, 227, 240, 257
Clayton, Shelia, 179
Clayton, Troy, 296, 297
Clayton, W.F., 161, 257
Clayton, Zolan, 266, 270
Cleburne, Major General Patrick, 94
Clemmons, Elmer, 114
Clemons family, 16
Clemons, Faydell, 117
Clemons, Louise, 117
Cleveland, Grover (U.S. President), 326
Clifton, Howard, 113
Clinton, Mississippi, 96
Cloud, Louise, 117
Clouse, Dewitt, 339
Clover Hill (McNairy County, Tennessee), 113, 114, 152
Clover Hill School, 113
Coal Hill, Arkansas, 323
Cobb, 254
Cobb, Bertha, 113
Cobb, Charlie, 254
Cobb family, 16
Cock, F., 255
Coleman family, 55, 267
Coleman, Corporal John, 55

Coleman, H.R., 266
Coleman, Isabella Jane, 248, 249
Coleman, Isabella J., 55, 248
Coleman, John, 60, 248, 249
Coleman, Malissa America, 248, 253
Coleman, Mary Roberta "Robertie," 248
Coleman, Rufus, 60
Columbus, Georgia, 74
Columbus, Kentucky, 237
Combs Chapel, 274
Combs, P.T., 255
Como, Tennessee, 84
Cone, Bedford, 251
Cone, Bob, 89
Cone, Floyd, 269
Cone, Howard, 269, 270
Cone, John R., 62
Cone, Lexie, 292
Cone, Mary, 89
Cone, Mrs. Ivy, 269n
Cone, Newell, 292
Cone, Pink, 293
Confederacy, the Southern, 27, 50n, 61, 88, 89, 143
Confederate Army (generally), 55, 57, 67, 73, 75, 84, 86, 88, 94, 246
Confederate States of America, 50, 54
Conger, Dr. J.W., 131, 326
Congress of the United States, 96
Conover, North Carolina, 23
Conner, Elexius, 23
Connor family, 267
Continental Army (Revolutionary War), 228, 313
Cook, Ben, 255
Cook, Benjamin Franklin, 86
Cook, George Irvin, 63, 85, 85n, 86
Cook, G.J., 62
Cook, John, 85, 295
Cook, J.T., 255
Cook, Mary (Beard), 85
Cook, Murray, 295
Cook, Nelia, 85n, 86
Cool Springs, 115, 152
Coon Creek, 4, 5
Corinth Brick Company, 173
Corinth, Mississippi, 43, 90, 93, 187, 191, 198

Cornwallis, Lord Charles, 228
Cothran, Lorraine (Gage), 116
Cotton Ridge School, 324
Cotton Ridge, Tennessee, 15, 16, 29, 58n, 157, 157n, 237n, 319, 321, 322, 323, 324, 328
Covey, Charles B., 60, 242
Covey, Fineti, 242
Covey, H., 257
Covey, Henry C., 242
Covey, Mary, 242, 242n
Covey, Martha, A.242
Covey, Susan L., 242
Cox, Brother, 217
Cox, Bro. Wayne, 266
Cox, Mary, 120
Cox, R. Harold, 46n, 279n
Cozort Brothers, 326
Craig, Andrew B., 49
Craig, Senator W.W., 350
Crain family, 45
Crainville, Illinois, 44
Crook Avenue, 221
Crook, Dora (Blakely), 325
Crook, Dr. Jere, 199
Croskery, Martha "Mattie," 37
Croskery, R.H., 66n
Croskery, Thomas, 37
Cross, Alphonso, 83
Crouse, Jacob Green, 30
Crow, J., 339
Crow, Justice of the Peace W.M., 144
Crowe, Kenneth, 270
Crowe Road, 105
Crumly, J.J., 268
Cude, F.M., 274
Cude, Lillie, 111
Cude, Thelma, 108
Cude, Virginia P. Hodges, 79
Cumberland Mountains, 25
Cumberland Presbyterian Church, 89
Cumberland River, 20, 56
Cunningham, Effie, 115
Curry, Anna M., 212
Curry, Daisy E., 120
Curry, Dr. James H., Jr., 212, 213, 213n
Curry family, 213
Curry, Mrs.213

Curtis, Charles, 59, 156
Curtis family, 16
Cyclone Bill (newspaper columnist), 217

D

Dallas family, 267
Dallas, L.L., 266
Dalton, T.S., 314
Darrow, Etta, 239
Darwin, Charles, 4
Davidson, Alma, 102
Davidson, Annie, 147
Davidson, Ben, 17n, 18n, 20n, 217n, 286n
Davidson, Cola, 110, 113, 152
Davidson, Clyde, 108, 110, 111, 152
Davidson County, Tennessee, 30
Davidson family, 16, 152
Davidson, Geneva, 111, 152
Davidson, Howard, 114, 118, 152
Davidson, Martin Van Buren Jr., 152
Davidson, Mary (Anderson), 24
Davidson, Pearl (Reeves), 152
Davidson, Thomas, 24
Davidson, Vena, 115, 152
Davidson family of Chestnut Street, Philadelphia, PA, 24
Davis, Bill, 255
Davis, Calvin M., 63
Davis, Camran, 117
Davis, Chili, 177
Davis family, 16
Davis, George Henry, 191
Davis, G.S., 256
Davis, J.N., 255
Davis, Kermit, 117
Davis, Newana, 117
Davis, Raymond, 117
Deal, Mike, 266, 270
Deaton(merchant), 180
Deaton, E.F., 270
Deaton, Ervin, 272
Deaton family, 16
Deaton, Mr. Roll, 207
Deaton, R.S., 257
Deaton, Will, 255
Dedford, Lieutenant Risden D., 80
Deep River, North Carolina & South Carolina, 18

Dees, J.C., 173
Dees, Jim, 209
Delmore Brothers (entertainment group), 350
Denmark Road, 115
Dennie, Mary, 201
De Soto, Hernando, 7
Dewberry, Reverend, 142
Dick, Captain William, 18
Dickerson, Daniel J., 56
Dickey family, 129, 245, 267
Dickey (merchant), 175
Dickey, A., 255
Dickey, Adele, 105
Dickey, Amanda, 229, 253
Dickey, Amanda (McIntyre), 31, 40, 193, 245, 348
Dickey, Amanda Ophelia, 229, 245, 296
Dickey, Doll, 229
Dickey, Dolph, 255
Dickey family, 16
Dickey, Frances E. "Doll," 245
Dickey, George, 181, 193, 237, 256, 348
Dickey, George Freelin, 120, 229, 245, 348, 350, 351
Dickey, George W., 263
Dickey, Ike, 157, 172, 244, 256
Dickey, Jack, 296, 297
Dickey, James, 105
Dickey, J.C., 173
Dickey, James (Jim) Rufe, 245, 277, 295, 295n, 296
Dickey, John A., 57, 244
Dickey, John L., 57
Dickey, Mrs. George, 237
Dickey, Sam, 173
Dickey, Sarah, 244
Dickey, S.D., 105
Dickey, William "Bill," 245
Dillion, Willie A. "Arter," 165, 194, 251
Dinwiddie, Judge William Charlie "W.C.," 330, 331, 332
Dodd, Mark, 49
Dodd, Sarah Elizabeth, 79
Douglas, Mary, 20
Draper, Bill, 256
Draper, Bob, 257
Draper, Buffern Y., 40

Draper, C.P., 40
Draper, Elizabeth, 39
Draper, F., 256
Draper family, 39, 40
Draper, Gabe Jr., 257
Draper, Gabe Sr., 257
Draper, Gabriel "Gabe," 40
Draper, George W., 40
Draper, Greene, 39
Draper, Henry, 39
Draper, James, 39
Draper, James B., 40
Draper, John, 39, 40, 49
Draper, John Harrison, 39, 40
Draper, Joicy "Joyce," 39, 40, 49
Draper, Mary, 39
Draper, Paralee, 39
Draper, Rufus, 39
Draper, Solomon, 39
Draper, Temperance, 39
Droke, Elizabeth (Stovall), 172, 296
Droke, Grady, 110
DuBerry, Lela (Dickey), 245
DuBerry, William "Bill," 295, 296
Duck River, 25
Duke, Bettie, 43
Dunaway, Ellen, 25
Dunn, E.J., 235
Dunn, John M., 60
Durbin, Jewel, 191, 339
Dyer and Moore, 59n, 60n, 80n
Dyer County, Tennessee, 32, 38
Dyer, Dr. Gus, 59n
Dyer, Gustavus W., 58n,
Dyson, Hezekiah, 72, 73
Dyson, Mary C., 72

E

East Tennessee, 244, 260
Eddings, John, 256
Edwards, Earl, 264
Eighth Civil District (McNairy Co., TN), 27, 29, 50, 79, 105, 227, 241, 244, 255, 273
Eightieth Regiment, Tennessee Militia, 10, 17
Elam, Mary, 128
Elisha's Branch, 229, 231

Ellis, Bonnie, 117
Ellis, Parker, 110
Elm Ridge, 114
Emmons family, 16
English, Dorothy, 114
English, Florence, 120, 121, 151
English, John Thomas, 151
English, Myrtle (Beene), 253
English, Virginia (Peery), 151
Enville High School, 139
Enville, Tennessee, 161, 166, 169, 202, 218, 277, 282, 285, 291
Erwin, Milo, 46
Estes family, 16
Estes, G.W., 256
Estes, John W., 131
Estes, Mary, 254
Ethridge family, 16
Etheridge, D., 256
Etheridge, John V., 120
Etheridge, J.H., 256
Etheridge, W., 46n
Evan, James, 73, 74, 75, 76
Evans, Sam, 326
Evansville, Indiana, 173

F

Fairview community, 97, 102, 111, 112, 146, 152, 321
Fairview School, 148, 152
Farnsworth family, 16
Farnsworth, Samuel, 156
Farrell, E.Q., 131
Farmer's Union, 165, 169, 170, 175
Favre, Robert, 108
Fayette County, Tennessee, 49, 86
Fayetteville, North Carolina, 238
Fentress, James, 10
Ferrell, Major W., 228
Fielding, J.W., 131
Fifth Ohio Cavalry, 65
Fifty-First Consolidated Tennessee Infantry, 62, 63
Fifty-First General Assembly, 247
Fifty-First Tennessee Infantry, 62, 63, 88
Fifty-Second Tennessee Infantry, 88
Finger and Enville Highway, 190
Finger Ballpark, 172

Finger Barbecue, 347, 348, 349, 351, 346
Finger Burial Association, 169, 203
Finger Cemetery, 62, 85, 161, 197, 199, 202, 203, 224, 245, 252, 282, 283n, 288, 297, 350
Finger Christian Fellowship Church, 267
Finger Church of Christ, 161, 194, 215n, 217, 252, 262, 263, 264
Finger Depot, 161, 188
Finger, D.R., 110
Finger Elementary School, 121
Finger First Baptist Church, 266
Finger Gin Company, 183, 195
Finger Graveyard, 161
Finger Hotel, 168
Finger-Enville Road, 105, 106
Finger High School, 121
Finger-Leapwood Road, 117, 160, 172, 177, 189, 219, 281, 282, 294
Finger Merchandise Company, 169
Finger Methodist Church, 121, 264, 265
Finger, Mildred, 105, 113
Finger Post Office, 162, 194, 339, 340
Finger School, 97, 119, 119n, 120, 121, 122, 123, 124, 125, 126, 127, 128, 145, 148, 149, 152, 161, 220n, 245, 252, 266, 351
Finger Telephone Company, 191, 192
Finger, Tennessee, 4, 5, 10, 11, 21, 23, 37, 46, 49, 50, 59n, 65, 73, 76, 77, 79, 81, 82, 83, 85, 89, 96, 104, 106, 110, 112, 114, 117, 119n, 120, 121, 126, 127, 128, 129, 132, 133, 134, 138, 140, 145, 146, 148, 149, 150, 151, 153, 154, 155, 157, 157n, 158, 159, 160, 161, 161n, 162, 164, 165, 166, 167, 168, 169, 170, 171, 172, 174, 175, 176, 177, 178, 179, 180, 181, 182, 184, 185, 186, 187, 189, 191, 192, 194, 197, 198, 199, 200, 201, 202, 203, 204, 207, 209, 212, 213, 213n, 214, 217n, 218, 219, 220, 220n, 221n, 222, 229, 231, 236, 238, 239, 245, 247, 248, 250, 252, 254, 255, 262, 263, 264, 265, 274, 278, 280, 282, 283, 284n, 285, 286, 287, 288, 292, 294, 298, 319, 321, 332, 335,

338, 341, 342, 343, 344, 345, 346, 348, 350
Finger United Methodist Church, 254, 265
Finger Volunteer Fire Department, 351
Fingerprints (publication), 49, 64, 120n, 160, 187, 220n, 225n, 242n, 285n, 287n, 295n
Finis E. Miller and Company General Merchandise, 166
First Baptist Church, 129
First National Bank, 25n
First Tennessee Volunteer Regiment, 83
First West Tennessee Cavalry, 55, 56, 77, 79
   See also: Sixth Tennessee U.S. Cavalry
   See also: United States First West Tennessee Cavalry
Fletcher, _____, 294n
Floyd, Alice, 195
Floyd, Avy J.G., 41
Floyd, Ben, 122
Floyd Cemetery, 41, 240
Floyd, Eliza, 41
Floyd, Elizabeth H.M., 41
Floyd, Elizabeth (Page), 40
Floyd family, 16, 40, 41, 129, 130, 181, 280
Floyd, F.G., 256
Floyd, F.J., 165, 166, 228
Floyd, Francis, 41
Floyd, Frank, 256
Floyd, Frederick, 40, 41, 240
Floyd, Frederick J., 57, 81, 81n, 82
Floyd, G.W., 256
Floyd, Harlan, 110
Floyd, Harmon, 57
Floyd, Harmon Purdy, 40, 41, 227, 240
Floyd, James, 40
Floyd, Jim, 179
Floyd Road, 109
Floyd, Sam, 256
Floyd, Samuel Sr., 256
Floyd, Saphronia, 193
Floyd, Sarah (Bullock), 40, 41, 240
Floyd, Sarah C., 239
Floyd, Sarah E., 254
Floyd, Sarah (Pitman), 41

Floyd, Thelma, 191
Floyd, Widow, 109n
Floyd's Cotton Gin, 182
Floyd's Crossing, 342
Forked Deer Circuit, 261
Forked Deer River, 341
Forrest, Col. Jeffery, 84
Forrest, Gen. Nathan Bedford, 53, 54, 62, 84, 86, 246, 247, 327
Forrest, Lt. Col. Jesse A., 84
Fort Donelson, battle of, 56, 90
Fort Henry, battle of, 56
Fort Pillow, battle of, 62, 84, 247
Fort Sallie (at Bethel Station), 66, 66n
Fort Sumter, battle of, 55, 90
Forty-Eighth Illinois Regiment, 66
Forty-Ninth Illinois Infantry, 61
Forty-Ninth Illinois Regiment, 66
Forty-Third North Carolina Infantry, 63
Foulkes, Jim, 256
Foulkes, John, 256
Fowler family, 16
Fowler, R., 256
Fourteenth Tennessee Cavalry, 80
Fourth Civil District, 43
Franklin, David J., 130, 262
Franklin, Rev. J.J., 228, 343
Franklin, John J., 343
Franklin, Mrs., 215
Franklin, Miss, 215
Free and Accepted Masons, 235, 247, 249, 252
Freed, Arvy Glenn, 134, 264
Freed-Hardeman College, 98, 98n, 100n, 139, 145, 146, 147, 148, 150, 152, 196
Freeling, Dr. C.L., 156, 211
Freeling family, 16, 49, 315
Freeling, John, 315
Freeling, Mary, 211
Freeling, Sargent Prentiss "Prince," 137, 315, 316, 317
Freeman, R.A., 264
Friendship School, 112
Friendship, Tennessee, 217n
Frost, Robert, 150
Fry, Dr. L.M., 131
Fry, Irene (Smith), 118

Fry, James Sr., 131
Fry, John, 288
Fry, John A., 61
Fry, Samuel M., 340
Frye family, 267
Frye, Conrad "Conard," 191
Frye, Irene (Smith), 149

G
Gaddy, Lorenza, 284
Gage family, 280
Gage, Pearl (Massey), 108, 193
Gage, Aaron, 241
Gage, Susana, 241
Gainesville, Alabama, 62, 86, 247
Gallagher Brothers, 203
Gallagher, Charles, 255
Gaston County, North Carolina, 22
Gastonia, North Carolina, 287n
Gardner, Baxter, 174
Gardner, Leroy, 174
Gardner, Mary (Harris), 165
Gardner Motor Company, 176
Garner family, 267
Garner, Andrew J., 61
Garner family, 16
Garner, Haven, 109, 111, 112, 127, 147, 148, 149
Garner, Vonnie Mae (Talbott), 123, 201
Garner, William Branson "Jim," 281
Garrett, Bertie (Martin), 118
Garrett, E.M., 268
Garrett, Lewis Jr., 261
Garrett Tobacco Company, 201
Gately, Leonard, 272
Gattis family, 16
Gattis, W.L. 156, 262
Gean, Jimmy, 128
Gee, Austin, 291
Gee, Dewey, 113
Georgetown District, 40, 41
Georgie Robertson Christian College, 98, 98n, 145
Gettysburg, battle of, 86
Gibson, Pony, 114
Gilbert, Dr. Thomas, 200
Gilbert, J.G., 270
Gilbert, John, 200
Giles County, Tennessee, 235
Gillespie, U., 131
Goff, James, 105
Goff, Ruth, 105
Golden West Cowboys, 350
Gooch Funeral Home, 134n
Gooch, Nicholas, 314
Good Springs, 20n, 314
Goodspeed, Westin A., 33, 88, 88n
Goodwin, Lyman, 127
Grange Order, 244
Grant, Marty, 41n
Grant, Ulysess S., 216, 217, 217n
Granville County, North Carolina, 30
Gravel Hill community, 135, 235
Gravel Hill School, 141
Graves, Janie Lowrey Sanford, 95
Gray, Frank A., 317n
Gray's New Map of Kentucky and Tennessee, 317n
Gray, Ruby L., 127
Grayson, California, 330
Great Depression, 180, 198
Greene, Gen., 18
Greer, Alexander, 155
Greer, Martha L., 332
Greensboro (Gilford County), North Carolina, 84, 238
Grissom, Tom, 179
Grisson, Andrew Grisham, 57
Griswell community/neighborhood, 292
Griswell, Dan C., 160, 256, 292
Griswell, E.H., 256
Griswell, Ephe, 292
Guilford County, North Carolina, 18, 233, 273
Guilford Court House, North Carolina, 18
Gulf Coastal Plain of West Tennessee, 5
Gulf, Mobile and Ohio Engine, 48, 187
Gulf, Mobile and Ohio Railroad, 188, 296
Guyton, David E., 89n, 90n

H
Hair, Pearl, 113
Halifax County, Virginia, 18
Halifax Old Court House, Virginia, 18

INDEX 485

Hallis family, 16
Halstead, _____, 255
Halstead, James P., 288
Haltom's Chapel Cemetery, 32
Hamilton, Irma, 121
Hamm, Calvin, 135
Hammons, Judy, 279n
Hamon, Clara (Smith), 316
Hamon, Jake, 316, 316fn
Hancock, Sergeant R.R., 52, 52n
Hand, Marvin, 22n, 68n, 109n, 116n, 221n, 279n, 298n
Hanks, James S., 49
Hardee, Lt. Gen. Joseph, 94
Hardeman family, 131, 274
Hardeman County, Tennessee, 32, 49, 61, 261, 328
Hardeman, Bro. Nicholas Brodie, 134, 139, 140, 147, 148, 199, 252, 254, 348
Hardin County, Tennessee, 9, 237, 241, 285
Hardin, Irene (Ingraham), 50n, 63n
Hardin, Nancy M., 46n
Harding, Florence, 316
Harding, President-Elect Warren G., 315, 316
Harmon family, 140
Harper, Bro. E.R., 264
Harris family, 48, 162n, 267
Harris, Anna Lee, 194
Harris, Arthur, 83, 228
Harris, Beulah, 222
Harris, Bill, 255
Harris, Charles B., 255
Harris, Christine (Brown), 346
Harris, Cletus, 113
Harris Community, 291
Harris, Dick, 291
Harris, Dora, 194
Harris, Dr. Rufus, 26
Harris, Eleanor (Anderson), 28
Harris, Eliza Paralee Tedford, 194, 222
Harris family, 16
Harris General Merchandise Store, 85, 161, 164, 166, 223
Harris, Gretchen, 121, 194
Harris, G.W., 256

Harris, Harmon, 291
Harris, Henry C., 58
Harris, J.J., 255
Harris, John, 195, 196
Harris, John R., 85, 160, 161, 164, 166, 167, 174, 183, 191, 194
Harris, Lela, 165
Harris, Lloyd, 56n, 115, 126, 127, 148, 179, 217n
Harris, Lucy (Barnes), 84
Harris, Marguerite, 127
Harris, Mary, 102
Harris, N.A., 255
Harris, O. Cletus, 110
Harris, Patsey, 233
Harris, P.G., 256
Harris, Prince, 165
Harris, Robert, 183
Harris, Thee, 164, 165
Harris, W.H., 161, 255, 264
Harris, William H. "Billy," 62, 84, 85, 161, 162, 164, 166, 187, 194
Harris, W.M., 256
Harris, Zaida L. (McCaskill), 196
Harrisburg, Mississippi, 62, 84, 232, 246, 247
Harrison, Evaline, 36
Harvard Law School, 137, 315, 315n
Harvey, Colonel, 66
Hayes, Major Charles S., 65
Haynie, Cora L. (Haynes), 193n
Hayre, Alma, 197, 289
Hayre, Bill, 289
Hayre, Hartle, 162, 183, 289
Hayre, Quentin Hayes, 64, 81n, 82, 83, 159n, 246n, 123, 149, 248, 289, 291n, 321, 330n
Helena, Arkansas, 78, 81
Helton, Fred, 339
Helton, Jess, 269
Helton, J.H., 256
Helton, Roma, 114
Henderson City Cemetery, 202, 218n
Henderson County, Tennessee, 13, 20, 131, 210, 241
Henderson family (Williamson Co., Illinois), 45
Henderson, Felix "Field," 44

Henderson, Tennessee, 63, 134, 145, 147, 168, 169, 173, 185, 192, 202, 214, 218, 219, 221, 224, 328
Henderson Station, Tennessee, 62, 68, 69
Henderson, R.Z., 131
Hendrix, Alex, 255
Hendrix Cemetery, 62, 63
Hendrix family, 16
Hendrix, Jo Ann, 151
Hendrix, John Milford, 63
Hendrix, Lee, 183, 184
Hendrix, Martha Jane, 21
Hendrix, Rebecca (Cherry), 21
Hendrix, Richard Ivy, 21, 62
Hendrix, W.B., 255
Hendrix, William, 49
Hendrix, William Martin Major, 237
Henley, W.W., 265
Henson, Neal, 270
Henson, Tilda Emeline, 32
Henry, Charlie, 292
Henry, Eber, 110, 112
Henry, G., 256
Henry, Joe Robert, 127, 128
Henry, John, 256
Henry, Matthew P., 61
Henry, Ophelia, 276
Henry, Samuel, 111, 112, 115, 256, 292
Henry, Vivian, 111
Henry, W.H., 256
Henry, W.M., 256
Henry settlement, 292
Henry's Place, 177, 179
Hepisdam, 131
Hesperia, California, 109n, 221n, 298n
Hester, D.C., 65, 102
Hickman, Gib, 291
Hickman, Kentucky, 198
Hickman County, Kentucky, 237
Higginbottom, Alma, 113
Higginbottom, Leona, 105
Higginbottom, Leora, 113
Higginbottom, Mary, 114
Highsmith, D. H., 58
Highsmith, Elias J., 58
Highsmith family, 16
Highsmith, John W., 60
Hill, M.C., 255

Hill, R.H., 165, 255
Hill, Rufe, 256
Hillard Gann Road, 109n
Hillman College, 96
Hinton-Bigger Concrete Company, 172
Historic Madison, 28n
Hitz, John, 266, 270
Hockaday, Florence (English) Abernathy, 151
Hodges family, 16, 17, 48, 140, 142, 143, 174, 203, 314n, 319, 331
Hodges, Clifford, 128
Hodges, David, 183
Hodges, Elijah, 19
Hodges, Capt. Elijah James, 17, 20, 57, 71, 76, 77, 78, 79, 79n, 82, 134, 140, 142, 214, 237, 256, 262, 268, 274, 314n
Hodges, Elisha (the younger), 19, 20, 21
Hodges, Elisha M.R., 20
Hodges, Elizabeth (Collins), 18, 19
Hodges, Elizabeth Ellen "Bettie," 237, 237
Hodges, Harmon E., 78, 79, 102, 119, 199, 200
Hodges, Harvey, 19
Hodges, Professor Harvey Garfield, 78, 79, 103, 104, 116, 119, 140, 141, 142, 143, 217, 285, 286, 286n
Hodges, Captain Horry, 17n, 20, 56, 57, 71, 77, 79, 80, 81, 297
Hodges, Horry (educator), 17n, 20, 78, 79, 79n, 102, 110, 116, 132, 133, 134, 134n, 135, 136, 137, 138, 139, 140, 214, 214n, 216, 218, 256, 311, 311n, 343, 350
Hodges, Hugh L., 104, 161, 166, 169, 172, 173, 174, 175, 176, 191, 203, 204
Hodges, James Wright, 256
Hodges, J.C., 113, 173
Hodges, J.C. "Clifford," 127
Hodges, James C., 19, 20, 62
Hodges, James G., 20
Hodges, James Wright, 79
Hodges, Jeremiah, 19
Hodges, Jesse C., 20
Hodges, Jesse Jr., 19

Hodges, Jesse Sr., 17, 18, 19, 20
Hodges, John, 78
Hodges, John E., 183, 285, 286n
Hodges, John E.C., 20
Hodges, John M., 342
Hodges, Joseph H., 20
Hodges, Josiah, 19, 20
Hodges, Maggie, 78, 79, 103, 104, 134n, 140, 141, 142, 214
Hodges, Marcus, 19
Hodges, Mary E. (Lain), 81
Hodges, Mr. J.C., 108
Hodges, Mrs. J.C., 108, 111
Hodges, Nancy Jane (Dodd), 77, 78, 124, 140, 214
Hodges, Raymond, 111, 173
Hodges, Rozetta, 79
Hodges, Ruby (Bishop), 149
Hodges, Sarah Ann, 78
Hodges White, Tabitha, 20, 78
Hodges, Tempa, 20
Hodges, Thomas Collins, 19
Hodges, William Cayson, 19, 20, 49
Hodges, William Cayson Jr., 20
Hodges, William Henry, M.D., 20, 56n, 78, 79, 102, 134n, 213, 214, 214n, 215, 215n, 216, 217, 217n, 256
Hodges, W.J., 256
Hodges' Beauty, 102, 113, 114, 152
Hodges' Beauty Area, 280
Hodges' Family Papers, 20n
Hodges' Farm, 238, 291
Hodges' Produce, 161
Hogwallow Creek, 341
Holbert, Spencer, 36
Holder, Annie (Davis), 168
Holder, Dolf C. "Pa," 167, 168, 174
Holder family, 16, 21, 175
Holder, Laura (Beene), 254
Hollis and Cason General Merchandise Store, 210, 231, 232
Hollis, France "Fanny" (Hodges), 19
Hollis, John P., 341
Hollis, Mary E., 46n
Holmes, George Calvin, 292
Holmes, Tony, 179
Holstead, Rev. Wilson A., 239
Holt, Reba, 128

Home Banking Company, 82, 121, 162, 163, 166, 169, 171, 174, 194, 195, 197, 223, 251, 287n
Hood, John Bell, 62, 94, 246, 247
Hooker's Bend, 84
Hooper, Clarence, 111
Hopewell Community, 65
Hopewell Baptist Church, 111, 172, 272, 320
Hopewell Cemetery, 59, 200, 201, 320
Hopewell Presbyterian Cemetery, 229
Horn, Dan, 291
Horn, William, J.58
Horner, H.P., 160
Hornet's Nest, 56
Horry District, South Carolina, 40
Horton, John H., 265
Hosteler family, 267
Houston, Judge J.C., 140, 217
Houston, Loraine, 120, 121
Howard, Lizzie, 26
Howard, Mitchell, 109
Howell Mitchell family, 105
Hubanks, Eubanks, 230
Hubanks, James L., 219, 220
Hubanks, J.L., 256
Hubanks Road, 65
Hubanks, W.B., 256
Huddleston, D.N., 79
Hudgers, Capt. Thomas, 19
Huffard, Professor Everett, 264
Hugganses' Creek, 9, 341
Huggins Creek, 4, 21, 37, 229, 239, 341
Huggins Creek Post Office, 21, 341
Huggins Creek Schoolhouse, 130
Hughbanks family, 16
Hughes, William C., 53
Humboldt, Tennessee, 85n, 191
Hunt, Adrian (Gage), 108
Hunter, Georgia, 112
Hunter, J.N., 131
Huntington, Tennessee, 137
Hurst, Carolyn, 346
Hurst, Col. Fielding 51, 52, 53, 54, 56, 57, 66, 72, 79, 79n, 82, 241
Hurst, D.H., 256
Hurst family, 16
Hurst, Hawthorne, 266

Hurst, Julius, 127
Hurst, Levi, 56
Hutcherson, Belver, 110
Hutcherson, Georgia, 105
Hutcherson, James Howard, 110
Hutcherson, John Howard, 105, 110
Hutcherson, Juanita, 110
Hutcherson Sweetlips Road, 105, 109, 345
Hysmith family, 267
Hysmith, D.T., 256
Hysmith, Ebert, 108
Hysmith, Gladys, 104
Hysmith, Ira, 108
Hysmith, Snooks, 269

I

Ice Ages, 4
Ike Dickey Commission Company, 204
Illinois, 44, 54, 247, 248, 293
Illinois Cavalry (136th), 61
Improved Order of Red Men, 136
Indian Territory, 239, 326, 332
Indiana, 293
Ingle, Icie, 128
Ingraham, Alexander H., 35
Ingraham, Celia L., 35
Ingraham Cemetery, 50
Ingraham, Dr. Lee H., 34, 88, 88n, 89, 212
Ingraham family, 16, 33, 49, 50, 50n, 70, 212, 297
Ingraham Family Cemetery, 34
Ingraham, Granville, 35
Ingraham, James M., 88
Ingraham, John M., 34
Ingraham, John Quincy, 50, 64, 68, 69, 70, 256
Ingraham, John S., 33, 34, 35, 36, 50, 50n, 88, 311n
Ingraham, Lee H., 63, 69n
Ingraham, Mary E., 35, 35n
Ingraham, Mary E. Arbuckle Carroll, 89
Ingraham, Ms. John Quincy, 70
Ingraham, Quinn, 277, 297
Ingraham, Rebecca Hardin, 34, 35, 50, 50n, 88
Ingram family, 33, 36

Inman family, 16
Inman, James A., 73
Inman, John A., 72
Inman, John W., 72
Interior Department (U.S.), 316
International Order of Odd Fellows, 231, 252
Iola Schoolhouse, 102, 106, 109, 110, 146, 148, 321
Ireland, 24, 144
Ivy, Justin, 270

J

Jacks Creek, Tennessee, 13, 62, 26
Jack McConnico Memorial Library, 24n, 66n
Jackson, Andrew, 8
Jackson District High School, 134
Jackson, Exia (Exie), 108
Jackson family, 16
Jackson, Lewis, 256
Jackson, Nancy Jane, 200
Jackson Purchase Treaty of 1818, 3, 8, 12, 34
Jackson Purchase Treaty Territory, 261
Jackson Savings Bank, 25n
Jackson, Mississippi, 95
Jackson, Tennessee, 27, 28, 42, 84, 137, 172, 187, 191, 199, 210, 223, 282, 315, 326
Jackson War, 244
James family, 129
James, Allie, 119
James, Brode, 204
James, Callie (McIntyre), 251
James, Frank, 189
James, Jesse, 189
James, Lake, 256
James, Leslie, 204
James, Major A., 104, 120, 160, 165, 204
James, "Mammy," 173
James, Maye, 204
James, Susan, 32
James, William, 257
Jamison, Mr., 18
Jenkins, J.E.W., 314
Jennings, R.D., 130, 131

INDEX

Jerricho, 286
Jerusalem, 286
Jesus Christ, 263
Jeter, Ceef, 208
Jeter, Gloria, 208
Jeter, James Franklin, 208
Jeter, Jocephus "Ceef," 208
Jeter, W. M., 61
John A. Johnson Lumber Company, 173
Johnson Brothers, 183, 184
Johnson Crossing, 283
Johnson family, 16
Johnson Family Cemetery, 70
Johnson, Fred, 41n
Johnson, Harris, 148
Johnson, Joseph, 156, 262
Johnson, John M., 69
Johnson, J.J., 131
Johnson, M., 256
Johnson, Martha, 36
Johnson, Rev. A.M., 99
Johnson Schoolhouse, 148
Johnson, W.F., 256
Jones family, 16, 129, 267
Jones, Euda (Beene), 253
Jones, L.E., 276
Jones, Lewis P., 43n, 277n, 278
Jones, Maggie, 270
Jones, Mr. E.H., 270
Jopling, Dovie, 109, 111
Jopling, Mrs. W.D., 36
Jopling, Zilphah, 108
Jordan, Gen. Thomas, 51, 51n
Joyner family, 267
Joyner, J.L., 250
Joyner's Upholstery Shop, 162n
J.R. Harris General Merchandise, 164, 168, 177, 183
Julian family, 267

K

Keel, Arl, 320, 320n
Keel, Martha (Plunk), 320
Keeter family, 16
Kelly, James, 105
Kelly, Joe, 105
Kelly, Mary, 105

Kelly, Ora Lee, 105
Kelly, Rachel, 105
Kemp, 267
Kemp, M.D., 266
Kemp, Nathan, 56
Kennedy, Mark, 270
Kennedy, Nancy (Wardlow), 66n, 156n, 255n
Kenton, Tennessee, 169, 197
Kentucky, 44, 55, 86, 237, 293
Kentucky campaign, 91
Kerby Schoolhouse, 115
Kerby, Alonzo, 21
Kerby Brothers (Earl & Eulis), 330n
Kerby Cemetery, 21
Kerby, Dovie, 196
Kerby, Earl, 329
Kerby, Emily, 22
Kerby, Eulis (Ulyss), 329
Kerby family, 21
Kerby, Francis, 21, 131
Kerby, H., 257
Kerby, Hugh, 21, 22, 341
Kerby, James, 131
Kerby, James "Hickory Jim," 22, 196
Kerby, Jack, 115
Kerby, John 21, 57
Kerby, John Wesley, 329
Kerby, J.W., 257
Kerby, M.F., 257
Kerby, Nancy (Sparks), 21, 49
Kerby, Sarah, 115
Kerby Third District, 115
Kerby, William W., 57
Kernodle, Mandy, 291
Kernodle, Virgie, 291
Keter, Hartwell, 231
Kincaid, Virginia, 36
King, Bill, 256
King, Pee Wee, 350
Kirby, Cassie, 151
Kirby family, 16
Kirby, John, 227
Kirby, Katherine, 36
Kirby, Nancy, 37
Kirby, Nancy E., 144
Kirby, Noah, 151
Kirby, R.B. 131

Kirby, Winaford, 36
Kirk, Elbert, 114
Kirk, Gordon, 179
Kirk, J., 173
Kirk, Lonnie, 180
Kirk, Mancel, 62n, 114n, 180
Kirk, Mrs. Mancel, 114
Kirkpatrick, 198
Kirkpatrick, Betsy, 234
Kirkpatrick, C.H., 177, 179
Kirkpatrick, Charles Hugh, 233, 234
Kirkpatrick, Charles Steve, 234
Kirkpatrick, E., 256
Kirkpatrick, Elbert, 339
Kirkpatrick, Elijah, 105n, 233, 234
Kirkpatrick family, 16, 233
Kirkpatrick, H., 256
Kirkpatrick, Henry, 179, 269
Kirkpatrick, Henry H., 338
Kirkpatrick, Henry Hugh, 234
Kirkpatrick, H.H., 169, 183, 184
Kirkpatrick, I.H., 105
Kirkpatrick, Jack, 292
Kirkpatrick, James Moses, 233, 234
Kirkpatrick, John T., 235
Kirkpatrick, Louisa B., 234
Kirkpatrick, M., 256
Kirkpatrick, Margaret, 234
Kirkpatrick, Mary, 233
Kirkpatrick, Mattie, 234
Kirkpatrick, Mollie (Bell), 234
Kirkpatrick, Moses, 105
Kirkpatrick, Patsey, 233, 234
Kirkpatrick, S., 256
Kirkpatrick, Susannah, 234
Kirkpatrick, W.C., 256
Kirkpatrick, W.F., 105
Kirkpatrick, William Elijah, 233, 234, 235
Kiser, Buel T., 127
Kiser, Cletus E., 127, 149
Kiser, Susie Walker, 149
Kiser's, 66
Knights of Pythias, 140
Knotts Berry Farms, 330
Knoxville, Tennessee, 17
Kossuth, Mississippi, 91, 93
Ku Klux Klan, 70

L

Lafferty, Reverend, 83
Lafferty, U.H., 265
Lain & Peeples, 156, 157
Lain, Arminta, 144
Lain, Clara B., 120, 121
Lain family, 37
Lain, Hugh M., 144
Lain, Jane A., 143
Lain, James Simpson, 37, 56, 56n, 86n, 98n, 102, 102n, 143, 144, 166, 196, 216, 228, 234, 256
Lain, Jennie, 144
Lain, Louisa D., 37
Lain, Martha E., 37, 42
Lain, Mary E., 79
Lain, Maudie, 144
Lain, Minta Pauline, 144
Lain, Rueben G., 37
Lain, Thomas, 143
Lain, William M., 37
Lain's Academy, 98n, 102, 103, 104, 105, 314
Lake County, Tennessee, 32, 38
Lake Hill Memory Gardens, 151
L'Amour, Louis, 97
Lane Academy, 104
Lane, Alexander C., 37
Lane, Elizabeth S. (Taylor), 273
Lane family, 16, 37
Lane, Jane A. (Holder), 37
Lane, Nancy E. (Kerby), 21
Lane, Rueben, 37
Lane, Thomas, 37
Lane, Thomas A., 37
Lane, Tidence, 260, 261, 261n
Lane's Chapel Cemetery, 270
Lane's Chapel Church, 102, 269
Lane's Chapel Nondenominational Church, 269, 269n
Lannom, A.H., 264
Larwill, Dr., 43
Laughton, _____, 256
Leapwood, 4, 111, 151, 169, 200, 278, 280, 345
Leapwood-Enville Road, 110
Leath, Hardy "Hard," 339, 347, 350
Leath, Howard, 128

Leath, J.H., 144
Leath, Richard, 102n
Lee family, 16
Lee, Ida (O'Neal), 110
Lee, Robert E., 70, 216, 217n
Lee, Sid, 256
Lee Weaver's Dry Goods Store, 169
Lee, William S., 60
Lemons, Pete, 161n
Lewis, Merriwether, 7
Liberty, 24, 115, 136, 235, 274
Liberty Cemetery, 58, 61, 276
Liberty Church, 275, 285
Liberty Meetinghouse, 116
Liberty School, 116
Liberty Schoolhouse, 115, 141
Lipford family, 267
Lipford, Don, 270, 272
Lindsey, Oklahoma, 136
Lincoln County, North Carolina, 22
Litt Wilson Road, 110, 320
Little Hatchie Bottom, 148
Little Texas Daisy, 350
Littlefield, W.P., 273
Liverpool, England, 204
Loftin, Elmo, 105
Loftin, Hershel, 105
Loftin, Lee, 105
Loftin, Neil, 105
Loftin, Vannie, 281, 281n
Lofton family, 267
Logan's Lake, 201, 266, 345
London, J.R., 121
Long Creek, 22
Long family, 16
Long, Frank, 256
Long, Joe, 256
Lorance, Abram (Abraham), 37
Lorance family, 37
Lott, Albert, 322
Lott, D.H., 20n, 322
Lott, Elvie, 109
Lott family, 16
Lott, Warren, 109
Louisville, Kentucky, 88
Lovelace, Dr. J.J., 212, 212n
Lovelace, Johnnie, 212
Lovelace, J.J., 257

Loving, Elvie (Lott), 108, 109, 118
Loving, Jack, 346
Lowrance, Abram, 241, 243
Lowrance, Aileen (Tucker), 222
Lowrance, David Marion, 241, 242
Lowrance, Elizabeth, 37, 241
Lowrance family, 16, 37
Lowrance, Jacob, 37, 38, 42, 60, 71, 227, 228, 230, 234, 241, 242, 242n, 243
Lowrance, John L., 42, 242
Lowrance, John M., 42, 241, 242
Lowrance, Martin E., 242
Lowrance, Miles, 155
Lowrance, Nicholas, 37
Lowrance, Richard Alex, 222
Lowrance, Susana, 42, 243
Lowrance, Susana (Gage), 242
Lowrance, William S., 242
Lowrances, 224
Lowrey, Adam, 89
Lowrey, B.G., 96
Lowrey, Booth, 96
Lowrey, G., 257
Lowrey, Gen. Mark Perrin "Fighting Parson," 48, 89, 90, 91, 94, 95, 96
Lowrey, Joseph Johnston, 96
Lowrey, Lawrence T., 96
Lowrey, Margaret (Doss), 89
Lowrey, P.H., 96
Lowrey, Sarah (Holmes), 90, 96
Lowrey, T.C.. 96
Lowrey, W.T., 95
Lowreys of Mississippi, 95
Lyles Creek, 23
Lynch, John, 30

M

Mackey, 102, 102n, 118, 118n
Mackeyfield, 109, 117
Mackey School, 117, 118, 152
Mackey Schoolhouse, 109
Macon County, Georgia, 73
Macon family, 16
Macon, Georgia, 74
Madison County, Tennessee, 9, 15, 23, 25, 27, 33, 34, 49, 79, 131, 207, 251
Madison, James, 329

Maggie Jones Memorial United Methodist Church, 118, 269, 270, 271, 272, 321
Maine, 285
Majors, Prof. Cordie L., 66n, 129, 158n, 159, 322
Malone Cemetery, 58, 60, 62, 233, 234, 247
Malone, Eliza, 247
Malone family, 17
Malone, F.C., 256
Malone, Frances C., 247
Malone, Jesse, 246
Malone, J.H., 105
Malone, John E., 110
Malone, Littleton, 247
Malone, Lula, 247
Malone, Marcus Dee, 247
Malone, Nora, 247
Malone, Rev. B.H., 99
Malone, Robert, 247
Malone, T.B., 105
Malone, William Barney, 62, 62n, 144, 228, 246, 247, 255n, 256
Malone, W.L., 105
Manassas (Bull Run), battle of, 55
Maness, Andrew J., 160, 165, 166, 168, 197, 198, 199, 200
Maness family, 16
Maness, Fielding, 110, 119, 148
Maness, George, 328
Maness, George D., 58, 58n
Maness, Guy, 198
Maness, H.K., 115, 119
Maness, J.A., 131
Maness, Ward W., 343
Manual, Mark, 60
Manus, George, 323
Marks, Mississippi, 96
Maryland, 274
Mars Hill Cemetery, 62
Martin family, 267
Martin, Bertie, 128
Martin, Dr. _____, 218
Martin, Mary, 105n, 148
Martin, Mary (Gilbert), 200
Martin, Mary Sue, 128
Martin, Mary, 111
Martin, Willie, 265
Martin, Thomas, 346
Mason family, 17, 238
Mason, Foster, 238
Mason, James, 130, 238, 239
Mason, John, 40, 130, 181, 238, 239, 240n, 260
Mason, Priscilla, 239
Mason, Rufe, 238
Mason, William, 82, 130, 193, 239
Masonic Lodge, 119
Masonic Movement, 261
Masons, 83, 238
Massengill, David, 270
Massengill family, 17
Massengill, Fayette, 114
Massengill, I.J., 63
Massengill, Joseph, 270
Massengill, John, 114
Massengill, Juanita, 114
Massengill, Miss., 113
Massey, A.M., 256
Massey, Beulah O., 193
Massey, C.E., 193
Massey, Cyrathia A., 193
Massey, Cyrathia Ann, 236
Massey, David, 237
Massey, David P., 66, 236n
Massey, David Peeples, 192, 193, 236
Massey, Elizabeth (McIntyre), 31
Massey family, 192, 237
Massey Family Papers, 66n
Massey, Harrell, 193
Massey, Helen, 193
Massey Hill, 295
Massey, Hooper, 179, 193
Massey, James L., 149
Massey, James Orby, 122, 145, 161, 190, 193, 343, 346
Massey, James L., 150
Massey, Mary (Peeples), 236n, 237
Massey, Mrs. Romus, 236n
Massey, Saphronia (Floyd), 194
Massey, Sarah Elizabeth (McIntyre), 192, 193, 229, 237
Massey, Sarah Jane, 236, 237
Massey Store, 194
Massey, Thomas (the elder), 237

INDEX 493

Massey, Thomas P. (the younger), 236, 237
Massey, William Pinkney (Willie P. or W.P.), 124, 161, 162, 163, 165, 166, 177, 183, 191, 193n, 199, 229, 236, 236n, 237, 287, 288, 343, 344
Massey, W.W., 131, 257
Masseyville, 115, 147, 345
Mast family, 267
Matlock, Beulah (Varham), 200
Matlock, Henry Thomas, 200
Matlock, Moses M., 2
Matthews, M., 256
Maxwell, Hadley, 115
Maxwell, James, 155
Maxwell, Rebecca, 235
Maury, Abel V., 10
Mayhall, Mrs., 191
Mayfield, Kentucky, 324
Mayo, Council, 36
M.E. Bishop and Company, 161
Meadows, Lorraine Bishop, 203
Mecklenburg County, North Carolina, 38, 39, 228
Meek, Favil Allen, 346
Meeks, Edda (Beene), 254
Melton family, 267
Memphis, Tennessee, 8, 51, 52, 62, 84, 95, 96, 115n, 196, 210, 218, 221, 222, 246, 277, 278, 297, 323, 331
Memphis News-Scimitar, 348
Mennonites, 267
Merchuson family, 16
Methodist, 155, 261, 262
Methodist Episcopal Church South, 99, 265
Mexican War, 90, 95, 314
Michie High School, 139
Middle Tennessee, 79, 85
Middleton, Tennessee, 96
Milan, Tennessee, 204
Milford family, 267
Milford, Bob, 114
Milford, Mary Ruth, 108
Milford, Weldon, 108
Mill Creek congregation, 274
Mill Street, 73, 168, 176, 177, 182, 191

Miller and Dickey, 167
Miller and Dickey Mill Company, 182
Miller, Callie, 76, 191, 221, 223
Miller, Dr. Robert E., 212
Miller, Edward Luther, 76
Miller, Elizabeth J. (Willett), 212, 243
Miller, Ella, 76
Miller family, 17
Miller, Finis E., 48, 61, 61n, 73, 73n, 76, 166, 182, 212, 256, 342
Miller, Francis, 243
Miller, James, 76
Miller, John A., 212, 243, 244
Miller, Margaret (Skinner), 243
Miller, Mattie, 76, 191
Miller, Robert S., 212, 243
Miller, Susan, 212
Miller, Walter, 292
Miller, William P., 342
Mills, Caroline, 284
Mills family, 17
Mills, W.H., 215, 216
Minton, Elizabeth A., 31
Mission Board of the Southern Baptist Convention, 95
Mississippi, 79, 86, 94, 95, 96, 247, 251, 252, 259, 293
Mississippi Legislature, 95
Mississippi River, 7, 14, 62, 89, 237, 323
Missouri, 24, 24n, 203, 241, 299
Mitchell, Billy Frank, 105
Mitchell, E.D., 161
Mitchell, F.C. "Ted," 105, 105n, 106, 106n, 107n, 108, 110, 110n
Mitchell, Howard, 128
Mitchell, I.A., 131
Mitchell, I.H., 132n
Mitchell, J.E. 131, 257
Mitchell, Jess, 191
Mitchell, Jess F., 161, 168, 174, 183, 202
Mitchell, Jim, 145
Mitchell, J.W., 238
Mitchell, Laura Etta, 145
Mitchell, Margaret L., 202
Mitchell, Maudie Jean, 105
Mitchell, Mrs. Maudie, 128
Mitchell, William, 202
Mitchells, 175

Mo Kwong Home for blind girls, 96
Mobile, Alabama, 74, 96
Mobile and Ohio Railroad, 15, 65, 158, 161, 169, 181, 182, 185, 250, 282, 283
Model Mills (Jackson, Tennessee), 338
Monterey, Mexico, 314
Montezuma Male and Female Academy, 130
Montezuma Post Office, 87
Montezuma, Tennessee, 5, 15, 30, 32, 42, 43, 57, 131, 156, 210, 231, 232, 340, 341
Montgomery, Harold, 270
Moore family, 17, 267
Moore, B.B., 256
Moore, Clinton L., 49
Moore, E.E., 256
Moore, George, 105
Moore, George W., 108, 110
Moore, Inez, 292
Moore, J.R., 107
Moore, J.W., 61
Moore, John Robert, 102, 108n, 109, 118
Moore, John Trotwood, 58n
Moore, Lois, 291
Moore, Lula, 43
Moore, Millard, 292
Moore, Mollie J., 279
Moore, Mr. Lester, 118
Moore, Mrs. Lester, 118
Moore, R.B. Jr., 165, 198
Moore, Ray, 117
Moore, R.J., 117
Moore, Ruth (McIntyre), 252
Moore, Sandra Kaye, 292
Moore, Sarah Albertine, 201
Morgan, Col. Hayne, 18
Morgan County, Alabama, 41, 134, 134n, 214
Morgan Funeral Home, 169
Morgan, R.A., 265
Morgan, W.A., 256
Morgan, W.H., 234
Morris family, 294
Morris Chapel, Tennessee, 222
Morris, Dr. G.W., 135
Morris, John, 31
Morris, T., 256
Morrison, Frank, 116
Mosasaurs, 4
Moser family, 17
Moses, 4
Mosier, A., 256
Mosier, Rebecca Caroline (Plunk), 332
Mosely, Sheriff (Swisher Co., Texas), 329
Moss, Tony, 266, 270
Mother Berry, 91, 94, 95n
Mount Carmel, 33, 65, 78, 262, 267, 269
Mount Carmel Cemetery, 20, 21, 24, 31, 33, 37, 39, 40, 42, 43, 45, 46, 49, 57, 58, 59, 60, 62, 79, 87, 89, 140, 142, 144, 193, 194, 218, 231, 233, 234, 235, 236, 239, 240, 242, 243, 249, 250, 251, 252, 253, 269, 278, 295n, 298, 320
Mount Carmel Church, 267, 268
Mount Carmel Meetinghouse, 267, 268
Mount Carmel Memorial, 33n
Mount Carmel Road, 267, 320
Mount Carmel Wesleyan Methodist Church, 274
Mount Peter, 248, 250, 330
Mount Pinson, 25
Mozier, Anderson (Mosier), 58
Mozier, Jacob (Mosier), 58
Mt. Pleasant Fertilizer Company, 161
Mud Creek, 218
Mud Creek Cemetery, 151
Mukley, Jonathan, 261
Mulroy, Paul, 270
Mullins, Dora, 284
Murchison, James, 25
Murchison, Martha, 36
Murchison, Rebecca (Beene), 254
Murchison, William, 43
Murry, J.K., 102
Muse family, 16
Muse, Susan, 32
Myers, Murphy, 330

Mc

McBride, Ava, 127
McCalister, Mrs., 325
McCallum family, 17
McCann family, 129

McCann, A.D., 339
McCann, Andrew, 292, 339
McCann, Arthur Marion Douglas "Whig," 291n, 292
McCann, Celia (Weaver), 291n, 292
McCann, Dell, 291n
McCann, Kevin D., 29n, 53n, 56n, 77n, 80, 81n
McCann, W., 256
McCartney, Laton, 316n
McCaskill, Alice McIntyre, 202, 252
McCaskill, Estella, 284
McCaskill family, 17
McCaskill, J.A., 257
McCaskill, Josephine (Wilson), 201
McCaskill, Logan, 177, 179, 183, 186, 201, 202, 266, 283n
McCaskill, Major, 292
McCaskill Sawmill, 167
McCaskill, Scott, 201, 282, 283, 283n, 284
McCaskill, Thomas K., 201
McCaskill, Tom, 344
McCaskill, Zaida, 195
McCaskill's Insurance Agency, 177
McCloud, Helena, 128
McClure, John W., 58
McCormick Road, 34, 113
McCoy, Adaline, 211
McCoy, Benjamin F., 211
McCoy, Dr. W.G., 211
McCoy, Emma, 211
McCoy family, 17
McCoy, Leonidus, 211
McCoy, Luiza J., 211
McCoy, Martha F., 211
McCoy, Mary A., 211
McCoy, Sara, 211
McCoy, W.G., 156
McCullar, G.C., 186
McDaniel, _____, 256
McDaniel, Grover, 295
McDaniel, Leo, 270
McGuffies' Reader, 325
McHolstead family, 16
McHolstead, Jordan, 273
McHolstead, Mary, 275
McHolstead, Nancy, 273, 274

McHolstead, Rev. Wilson A., 40, 155, 262, 268, 273, 273n, 274, 275
McHolstead, Smith, 273, 274
McIntyre, Adrian, 161, 229, 249, 250, 349
McIntyre, Amanda, 244
McIntyre, Audrey Roberta, 220
McIntyre, B.A., 251
McIntyre, Callie, 204
McIntyre, Carroll, 252
McIntyre, Elizabeth (Thompson), 38, 39, 228, 229
McIntyre family, 16, 38, 55, 129, 165, 236, 248, 250, 319
McIntyre, Fannie E. (Carroll), 252
McIntyre, Faye, 291
McIntyre, Helen, 291
McIntyre, Henry, 251
McIntyre, Hubert, 220, 349
McIntyre, Isaac, 38, 60, 228, 229
McIntyre, Isaac McKay, 31, 39
McIntyre, Isaac T., 51, 229, 251
McIntyre, James, 32
McIntyre, James, and Company, 251
McIntyre, James, and Company General Merchandise, 165, 204
McIntyre, James Robert, 31, 129, 160, 161, 162, 165, 166, 199, 202, 204, 229, 251, 252, 256, 262, 264, 288n, 342, 350
McIntyre, James T., 231
McIntyre, John (son of John James McIntyre), 32
McIntyre, John Absalom, 31, 54, 54n, 55, 162, 229, 247, 248, 249, 250, 251, 257, 295n, 346
McIntyre, John J., 251
McIntyre, John James, 32, 38
McIntyre, John Jr., 228
McIntyre, John R., 267
McIntyre, John Robert (Johnny), 54n, 143, 209n, 223, 229, 248, 250, 289, 291, 291n, 292, 293, 298, 349
McIntyre, John Sr., 228
McIntyre, J.R., 291
McIntyre, Lessie, 291, 291n
McIntyre, Levi Benton, 129, 251
McIntyre, Lula (Womble), 259

McIntyre, Maggie, 220
McIntyre, Margaret Rebecca (Beene), 204, 253, 254
McIntyre, Mary Roberta (Coleman), 249, 250, 251
McIntyre, Nancy Caroline, 31, 229
McIntyre, Ollie Pearl (McCann), 291, 291n, 293, 298
McIntyre, Rachel, 252
McIntyre, Rebecca, 251
McIntyre, Robert Allen, 165, 204, 251, 342
McIntyre, Robert Thompson, 31, 38, 39, 40, 51, 54, 55, 60, 71, 82, 155, 159, 160, 193, 227, 228, 229, 230, 230n, 231, 236, 237, 244, 247, 251, 342, 348
McIntyre, Roy, 295n
McIntyre, Sara C. "Sally," 38
McIntyre, Sarah E., 193
McIntyre, Sarah Elizabeth, 236
McIntyre, Sarah Jane (Weaver), 230, 244, 247, 251
McIntyre, Ulysses Hubert, 248
McIntyre, Virgie, 251
McIntyre, Vivian, 291, 291n
McIntyre, W. Adrian, 173, 248
McIntyre, William (son of John James McIntyre), 32
McIntyre, William Cogbourne, 38, 39
McIntyre, William Kendall, 211
McIntyre, Zelphia, 250
McIntyre, Zenar, 248, 250, 251
McIntyre's Crossing or Switch, 15, 16, 157n, 159, 160, 342
McKary, James, 155, 262
McKenzie, Tennessee, 146
McKinney, Dr. Charles, 211
McKinney, Dr. Jessie, 43, 211
McKinney, Dr. William, 211
McKinney, Edmond, 211
McKinney, Eliza, 211
McKinney, Elizabeth, 211
McKinney family, 211
McKinney, George, 211
McKinney, Jesse, 156
McKinney, John R., 211
McKinney, Joseph, 211

McKinney, Judge James F., 211
McKinney, Samuel, 211
McKinnon, A.H., 340
McKinnon, John B., 341
McKissick, Col. Lewis D., 210
McKissick, Dr. Wilson, 210, 211
McMillan, Mary, 30, 32
McNairy County Appeal School Report, 120n
McNairy County Chancery Court, 231
McNairy County Court Clerk's Office, 86, 132n
McNairy County Courthouse, 321
McNairy County Early Settlers/Pioneers Monument, 21, 33, 211
McNairy County-Finger Area, 267
McNairy County High School, 136
McNairy County Independent Appeal, 33n, 53, 71n, 79n, 81n, 82, 94n, 104n, 120, 138n, 139n, 141n, 189, 198n, 204, 213n, 217n, 218n, 238n, 282n, 285n, 291n, 295n, 311n, 336n
McNairy County Quarterly Court, 27, 51, 51n, 71, 79, 230, 235, 238, 240, 241, 243, 318, 336n,
McNairy County Quarterly Court Record, 79n
McNairy County Republican Executive Committee, 151
McNairy County Register of Deeds, 232
McNairy County School Directory, 120n
McNairy County School District, 119n
McNairy County School Journal, 118n, 121n
McNairy County School Journal of 1921, 108
McNairy County School Reports, 118n
McNairy County School System, 117, 151
McNairy County Singing Convention, 145
McNairy County, Tennessee, 3, 4, 5, 6, 7, 9, 10, 11, 15, 16, 17, 20, 21, 22, 23, 24, 24n, 25, 27, 28, 29, 30, 31, 32, 33, 34, 36, 37, 38, 39, 40, 41, 42, 43, 44, 45, 46, 48, 49, 50, 50n, 51, 54, 55, 56, 59, 61, 63, 64, 66,

INDEX

67, 68, 70, 71, 76, 78, 79, 81, 84,
85, 86, 88, 89, 96, 97, 98, 99, 100,
101, 102, 109n, 111, 112, 113,
120, 129, 132, 133, 135, 136, 137,
138, 143, 144, 145, 146, 147, 149,
150, 152, 154, 155, 156, 158n,
159, 160, 176, 180, 183, 184, 189,
191, 196, 197, 200, 201, 203, 204,
205, 205n, 206, 207, 208, 210,
211, 212, 212n, 213, 214, 215,
216, 217, 218, 221n, 222, 226,
227, 229, 230, 231, 232, 233, 235,
236n, 238, 240, 241, 243, 244,
245, 246, 247, 248, 251, 254, 255,
258, 260, 261, 262, 272, 273, 274,
275, 276, 277, 280, 282, 285, 288,
289, 290, 291, 293, 311n, 315,
317, 318, 319, 321, 322, 328, 329,
330, 331, 332, 335, 339, 340, 341,
342, 343, 346, 350, 351
McNairy County, Tennessee Marriage Records, 279n
McNairy, Judge John, 11
McNairy Male and Female Institute, 130
McNairy Station, Tennessee, 15, 137, 185, 211, 212, 220, 262, 291, 292, 325, 341, 343
McNatt, Speedy, 350
McNeil, Ina, 111
McWorthington, A., 341

N

Nailor, 254
Nailor family, 17
Nash family, 321
Nash, Hurley, 117
Nash, Jimmie, 117
Nash, Robert, 128, 183
Nashville, Arkansas, 323
Nashville, Tennessee, 53, 62, 134, 214n, 247
Nashville, Illinois, 55, 248
Natchez, Mississippi, 89
National Association of Railway Agents, 215
National Cemetery (Memphis, Tennessee), 57, 58, 59, 60, 81

National Quarter Horse Association, 329
National Recovery Administration, 180
Native Americans (Indians), 23, 65, 225, 316
Naylor and Miller Company, 167
Naylor, Annis, 32
Naylor, "Aunt Mary Lum," 255
Naylor, "Aunt Mary Tom," 255
Naylor, Bettie, 297
Naylor, B.J., ED.D., 106n, 120n, 264
Naylor, Buford, 105
Naylor, Charity, 254
Naylor, Everett, 255
Naylor family, 17, 129, 254, 255, 329
Naylor, Fate, 165, 255
Naylor, F.E., 161
Naylor, Floyd, 179
Naylor, Frank, 329
Naylor, G., 256
Naylor, George, 151
Naylor, George Thomas, 254
Naylor, Georgia, 128
Naylor, Harmon Arthur, 105
Naylor, Harris, 187
Naylor, Harrison, 188, 255
Naylor, Herman, 292
Naylor, Hubert, 255
Naylor, Isom Christopher Buchanan "Buck," 42, 180, 181, 254, 255
Naylor, J.C., 254, 255
Naylor, John T., 165, 255
Naylor, Johnnie, 105
Naylor, Joshua, 180, 254
Naylor, Joshua Columbus, 160, 181
Naylor, Lum, 288
Naylor, Lydia E., 82
Naylor Mill Company, 182
Naylor, Raymond, 105
Naylor, Rosaline (Kerby), 329
Naylor, Thelma, 128, 148
Naylor, Thomas, 238
Naylor, Tom, 257
Naylor's Schoolhouse, 119n, 250
Neely, 51
Neely, Col. J.J., 52
Neimann, 40n, 129n, 158n, 181n, 238n
Neimann, Ruth (Mason), 240n
Nelson, Hugh, 80

Nelson, Violet, 31
Nevil, Bro. W.C., 266
New Church, 278, 321
New Deal, 180
New Mexico, 136
New York, 203
New York City, 204
New Oak Grove Cemetery, 38
New Orleans, Louisiana, 89, 96
New Salem community, 144
Newground, "Lark" and "Steve," 250
Newsome's Cavalry, 43, 232
Nineteenth Tennessee Cavalry Regiment, 232
Ninth Surveyor's District, 9
Nix, Johnie Beene, 254
Nolen, Jennie, 284
North Alabama Mission, 274
North Carolina, 29, 30, 31, 37, 38, 39, 41, 42, 46, 84, 211, 231, 232, 233, 234, 238, 240, 246, 273, 318
North Mississippi, 64
Norfolk, Ohio, 215
Norwood, S.A., 42, 130, 262
N.P. Talbott General Merchandise, 200
N.P. Talbott Staple Groceries and Produce, 177

O

Oak Hill Cemetery, 81
Oakland, Tennessee, 86
Oak Ridge School, 102, 105, 106, 146
Ohio, 315
Okalona, Mississippi, 62, 84, 246
Oklahoma, 130, 136, 137, 204, 239, 316, 332
Old Bishop Store, 277
Old Friendship Cemetery, 196, 246
Old Friendship School, 145
Old Oak Grove Cemetery, 46, 46n
Old Montezuma Cemetery, 43n
Old Slave Plantation, 130
O'Nail, Isabel (O'Neil), 235
One Hundred Fifty-Fourth Senior Infantry, 63, 83
One Hundred Eightieth Tennessee Cavalry Regiment, 232
O'Neal, 175
O'Neal Cemetery, 110, 285
O'Neal, Daisy, 213
O'Neal family, 16
O'Neal Graveyard, 283
O'Neal H.B., 264
O'Neal, Homer, 110
O'Neal, Minnie 264, 284
O'Neal, Roy, 110n
O'Neal, Sallie, 284
O'Neil, C.W. (O'Neal), 131
Onsley, Harriet, 235
Orr, Burlene, 105, 121, 123, 128
Orric, William, 155
Overman, Jake, 257
Owen, Leonard, 110
Owen, W.H., 264
Owens, Albert, 118, 180
Owens, J.T., 257
Owens, Rube, 257
Owens, R.W., 257
Owens, 113
Oxford, Mississippi, 84
Ozment, Calvin, 58
Ozment family, 17
Ozment, Tom, 257

P

Paducah, Kentucky, 62, 84, 247
Pafford, Warner, 265
Parchman, Glenda, 218n
Parker, Bob, 348
Parker, Earl, 284
Parker, Elizabeth, 31
Parker, Erie, 264
Parker, J.A., 264
Parrish, E.O., 161, 187
Pascola, Missouri, 241
Patterson family, 16, 129
Patterson, Alta, 104
Patterson, Colonel, 179
Patterson, Cora, 330, 330n, 331
Patterson, Foy, 104, 108
Patterson, Hobart, 104, 330, 330n, 331
Patterson, Leonard, 117
Patterson, Lucian, 169, 297
Patterson, Maggie (Beene), 253
Patterson, Margaret Priscilla, 238
Patterson, M.C., 228, 292

INDEX 499

Patterson, Orphus, 117
Patterson, Raymond, 297
Patterson, Soucelia Anne (Beene), 254
Patterson, T.M., 130
Patterson, Vaudie, 104, 151
Patterson, Willie May, 117
Paul's Valley, Oklahoma, 136
Peel, Tommy, 265, 270
Peeples and Peeples & James, 157
Peeples, Benjamin, 261
Peeples, Benton "Bent" Tatum, 326
Peeples, B.T., 156, 157, 227
Peeples, Charles W., 341
Peeples, C.W., 327
Peeples, E.C., 132
Peeples, Eddy, 183, 238, 345
Peeples, Edward D. "Ned," 325
Peeples, Elizabeth Ellen "Bettie" Hodges, 78, 217n
Peeples, E.W., 227
Peeples, Gehu, 156
Peeples, Henry Calvin, 237
Peeples, J.P., 322
Peeples, M.V., 157
Peeples, Susan Elizabeth "Cynthieana" (Malugen), 237
Peeples, Thursday 237
Peeples, William Washington, 132, 228, 237, 257, 324
Pegram Beauty, 102, 106, 106n, 107, 108, 109, 118, 152
Pegram family, 17, 106n
Pegram, Nancy, 107
Pegram, T.E., 59n
Pegram, Thomas Ellen, 59
Pemiscot County, Missouri, 241
Pennsylvania, 273
Pensacola, Florida, 42
Peoples family, 17
Peoples, Benton T., 328
Perkins, Boss, 197
Perry County, Illinois, 30
Perry County, Tennessee, 267
Perry, James, 155, 262
Perry, Loree, 108
Perryville, Kentucky, 91
Person, A.B., 35
Person County, North Carolina, 39

Phillips, Anna Lou (Kerby), 115n
Phillips, Elmer Lee, 110
Phillips family, 17
Phillips, Tom, 118, 346
Phillips, Tommy, 270
Pickens, G.W., 74, 76
Pickens, Sgt. George W., 76
Pickett, Albert, 161, 182, 183
Pickett, C.E., 264
Pickett, C.H., 264
Pickett, Dick, 116
Pickett family, 17
Pigram family, 17, 106n
Pilgram Beauty, 106n
Pine Hill Assembly, 272
Pinson, Tennessee, 23, 282, 283
Pittsylvania County, Virginia, 13, 18, 19, 20
Pleasant Hill, 274
Pleasant Ridge, 235
Plunk family, 16, 22, 23, 24, 55, 129, 281n, 320, 321, 331
Plunk, Abraham (Abram), 58
Plunk, Albert A., 270
Plunk, Alfred Monroe, 63, 67, 68, 116, 257
Plunk, Anna (Gage), 23, 24
Plunk, Annie, 58
Plunk, Arlus Bratcher, 110, 111, 112, 113, 114, 118, 128
Plunk, Arthur, 128
Plunk, Asa G., 169
Plunk, Atlas, 108
Plunk, Barbara, 22, 23
Plunk, Blanche, 109, 115
Plunk, Calvin, 61
Plunk, Catherine, 23
Plunk, C.C., 234, 297
Plunk Cemetery, 23, 24, 57, 58, 59, 61, 129, 270, 319
Plunk, Charles, 117
Plunk, Charlie, 116
Plunk, Coolidge, 108, 339
Plunk, Crolin, 217n
Plunk, C.W., 257
Plunk, Daniel, 275
Plunk, Daniel David, 63, 67, 68
Plunk, Dave, 24n

Plunk, David, 23, 57, 257
Plunk, Dr. Peter, 22, 23, 207, 319
Plunk, Effie, 105
Plunk, E.H., 169
Plunk, Elisa, 24, 24n, 155
Plunk, Elizabeth, 23
Plunk, Ervin, 339
Plunk, Ethel, 120, 121, 142
Plunk, Eubert, 104
Plunk, Eva, 180
Plunk, Fanny, 58
Plunk, George, 24, 58, 63
Plunk, George M., 59
Plunk, Gossie, 104
Plunk, Gracie, 108
Plunk, Hubert, 109, 111, 117, 118, 122, 127, 152
Plunk, I.H., 256
Plunk, Jacob, 23, 24, 319
Plunk, Jacob Jr., 58
Plunk, Jacob S., 58
Plunk, James "Bob," 117
Plunk, Jesse F., 61
Plunk, John, 23, 37, 207
Plunk, John Wesley, 58, 275, 276
Plunk, Jose, 116
Plunk, Joseph, 23, 24, 332
Plunk, Joseph A., 61
Plunk, Junell, 117
Plunk, J.N., 257
Plunk, Kizzie, 67
Plunk, Lawson, 152
Plunk, Louisa, 104
Plunk, Lester, 104
Plunk, Lucy, 122
Plunk, Mary, 152
Plunk, Melzer, 106, 129, 269
Plunk, Mike, 257
Plunk, Miles, 61
Plunk, Minnie, 122
Plunk, Nancy, 275
Plunk, Nancy (Haley), 23, 24, 58, 332
Plunk, Nath, 257
Plunk, Nevil, 117
Plunk, Oneida, 108
Plunk, Orby, 269, 331
Plunk, Orville, 331
Plunk, Peter, 57

Plunk, Petway, 117
Plunk, Prince, 109, 128
Plunk, Rev. Hollie, 24
Plunk, Russell, 114
Plunk, Sam, 257
Plunk, Samuel C., 58
Plunk, Sidney, 62
Plunk, Simon, 104
Plunk, Simp, 173
Plunk, Vera, 110
Plunk, Vivian, 105
Plunk, W.E., 111
Plunk, Will, 298
Plunk, William, 109
Plunk, W.L., 169
Plunk's Schoolhouse, 129
Plunktown, 23, 129, 319
Polk, Leonidas "Bishop-Militant," 89
Pollard, 74
Poney Gibson farm, 67n
Pooi To Academy (Canton, China), 95
Poole, George, 110
Poor Barrens, 48
Pope, Carodis, 32
Pope family, 17
Pope, Joel, 32
Poplar Corners, Tennessee, 251
Poplar Springs School, 111, 320
Possum Trot, 129n, 333, 335
Possum Trot Schoolhouse, 119n, 129, 250, 252, 262
Pottawatomie County, Oklahoma, 315
Potter, Sallie Lowrey, 96
Powers, Eliza Adline (Mosier), 332
Powers, John Lee, 148
Prather, H.U., 110
Presbyterian Articles of Faith, 28
Presbyterian Church, 247
Primitive Baptists, 268, 314, 314n
Primitive Baptist Church, 135, 139
Procter, Nancy, 29, 30
Pryor, J.F., 51, 51n
Pulaski, Tennessee, 62, 78, 275
Purdy Academy, 88, 98n, 99
Purdy and Mifflin Road, 26
Purdy Collegiate Institute, 99, 100
Purdy College, 98n, 99
Purdy Institute, 99

INDEX 501

Purdy-Lexington Road, 29, 64, 69, 319, 328, 341
Purdy Post Office, 211
Purdy Road, 115
Purdy, Tennessee, 5, 14, 21, 24, 29, 53, 54, 67, 69, 70, 87, 88, 99, 99n, 100, 116, 143, 154, 157, 157n, 159, 211, 230, 238, 241, 244, 274, 465
Purdy University, 98, 98n
Purviance, Col. James Washington, 53, 71, 82, 135, 136, 336, 336n
Putman family, 292
Putman, Alie, 42
Putman, Bill, 257
Putman County, Tennessee, 85
Putman family, 16, 41
Putman, Harriet E., 42, 241, 242
Putman, John F., 37
Putman, John Franklin, 42, 57
Putman, Juda, 42
Putman, Louellen, 42
Putman, M., 257
Putman, Martin, 41, 42, 57
Putman, Martin Ernest, 42
Putman, Mary Frances, 42
Putman, Nancy E., 42
Putman, Thomas Franklin, 42
Putman, Tulitha, 42
Putman, William A., 42
Putman, William Harrison, 42

R

Raber family, 267
Rabbit Ridge, 319, 328
Ramolis Mills, battle of, 18
Ramsey, Illinois, 20n
Ramsey, Mr., 270
Ramsey, W.W., 155
Raney, R.G., 36
Randolph, Allie, 43
Randolph, Elizabeth "Lizzie," 43
Randolph family, 16, 42, 43n
Randolph, Gayle, 43
Randolph, Capt. G.W., 43
Randolph, John G., 42, 43, 131
Randolph, Lavinia, 43
Randolph, Lelia V., 43n

Randolph, Levena Ann, 43n
Randolph, Martha, 43
Randolph, Mary, 43, 43n
Randolph, Polk, 43
Randolph, Rev. George W., 43n
Randolph, Samuel, 43, 43n
Randolph, Sarah, 43
Rankin family, 16, 267
Rankin, Francis M., 60
Rankin, R.D., 257
Rankin, Richard "Dick," 110
Rankin, Varnell, 112, 147
Ray, Linnie Lowrey, 96
Ray, Mrs. Janette, 150
Reaves, Hollis, 270
Reconstruction period, 66, 70, 241
Red House (old Ingraham home), 311, 311n
Red River (Texas-Oklahoma boundary), 316
Reed, Bettye (Sitton), 31n, 251n
Reed, Daisy (Barham), 114
Reed family, 17
Reed, Myrtle, 102
Reeves family, 293
Refuge (community, church, cemetery & schoolhouse), 112, 113, 148, 291
Refuge Cemetery, 22, 241
Refuge Schoolhouse, 112
Republican, 136
Republican Party, 140
Revolutionary War, 241
Reynolds, Andrew, 155
Rhodes, Slim, 350
Rhodes, Speck, 350
Rhodes, Susan V., 37
Richardson, Col. Richard V., 81
Richmond Bonding Company, 198
Richmond, Kentucky, 84
Richmond, Virginia, 66, 74, 95
Ridgeway post office, 342
Ripley, Mississippi, 92
Rivers, Rev. R.H., 99
Riverside Cemetery, 28
Robbins family, 49
Robbins, Adeline, 46
Robbins, Ammie, 280
Robbins, Betsy, 46

Robbins, Bryant, 46
Robbins, Clayton, 46
Robbins family, 16
Robbins, Grady, 104
Robbins, John Henry, 46
Robbins, Joseph Leod, 46
Robbins, Katherine, 46
Robbins, Maclin, 46
Robbins, Margania E., 76
Robbins, Marion, 46
Robbins, Marcus J., 46, 46n
Robbins, Marion M., 46n
Robbins, Martha Jane, 46
Robbins, M.J., 46n
Robbins, Moses, 262
Robbins, Nannie C., 37
Robbins, Rebecca Anne, 46
Robbins, William A. "Big Bill," 46, 256
Robbins, William C., 341
Robbins, William Crockett, 46, 46n
Roberson, B., 256
Roberson, G., 256
Roberson, T.M., 328
Roberts, Elijah, 56
Roberts, Mr. James, 212
Robertson, Dr. Christopher Wood, 80
Robertson family, 17
Robertson, Mary (Hodges), 78, 217n
Robeson County, North Carolina, 41
Robeson family, 17
Robinson family, 16
Robinson, Francis C., 61
Robinson, Frank, 117
Robinson, Harrell, 117
Robinson, Hayse, 110
Robinson, Irene, 110
Robinson, Jessie, 114
Robinson, J.W., 268
Robinson, Noah Allen, 114, 118n, 127, 128
Robinson, Olis, 113
Robinson, Sam, 110
Robinson's Cavalry, 65
Robison, Calloway, 155
Robison, Eura (Carothers), 110
Robison, Lawrence, 183
Robison, Ms. Moline, 279
Rock Hill community, 319

Rockingham, North Carolina, 28, 237, 273
Rocky, Oklahoma, 332
Rocky Knob Cemetery, 58
Rocky Knob Community, 319
Rocky Knob Road, 345
Rocky Knob School, 117
Rodgers, John L., 340
Rogers, Dr., 198
Rogers, Dr. Lillian, 212
Rogers, Elmira, 36
Rogers family, 17
Rogers, Hugh, 128
Rogers, Janice, 114, 128
Rogers, John L., 131
Rogers, J.P., 131
Rogers, J.S. 131
Rogers, William, 155
Roland, Alex, 256
Roosevelt, President Franklin D., 180
Rose Creek, 232, 291
Rose Hill Burial Park, 317
Rosehill, 235
Rose, William Jasper Newton, 61
Ross, D., 256
Ross, David 102
Ross, J.E., 256
Ross, Mr. T.B. 166
Ross, Peter E., 38
Ross, Tobe 256
Rouse family, 129, 267
Rouse, Frank, 292
Rouse, Joe, 215
Rouse, John, 183, 288, 350
Rowan County, North Carolina, 30
Rowland, Trudy 234
Rowsey family, 16
Ruggles, Gen. Daniel 56, 143
Rupard, Elizabeth, 30, 31
Rural Route East, 345, 345n
Rural Route West, 345, 345n
Rushing, Joseph, 155, 156
Rushing, Joseph Lawton, 25
Rushing, Laws Sr., 218n, 219
Russell, Tom, 46
Russell, William, 30, 31, 60
Russell, William W., 60
Russom family, 267

Russom, A.B., 266
Russom, Coy, 194
Russom, Isaac, 131

S
Sagebrush Schoolhouse, 130
Salisbury, North Carolina, 74
Saltillo, Tennessee, 277, 278
Sandburg, Carl, 150
Sanders, Alma 212
Sanders, Daisy E., 212
Sanders, Dr. W.M., 212
Sanders, E.G., 128
Sanders, Grady, 250
Sanders, Mr., 187
Sandhills, 67, 67n
Sanford, Colonel, 66
Sanford, John, 131
San Jose, California 210
Sanson, H.T., 265
Sarie and Sally (entertainers), 350
Savannah, Tennessee, 136, 237
Schrink, Mr. _____, 254
Schrink, Martha Ann (Beene) Cobb, 253
Scott (black servant of Dr. Barnes,)219
Scott, George R., 212
Scott, Hester Ann (Haltom), 212
Scott, Jennie, 104
Scott, J.H., 135
Scott, John S., 168
Scott, John W., 213
Scott, Lon Allen, 136
Scott, Rozetta Jane Hodges "Jennye," 78
Scott, Sarah B., 212
Scotts Hill, Tennessee, 200
Sebastian County, Arkansas, 89
Second District of Mississippi, 96
Second Mississippi Infantry, 63
Second Mississippi Volunteers, 90
Second Tennessee Cavalry, C.S.A., 52, 62, 246
Second World War, 180, 191
Segerson, F.M., 168
Sells, Benjamin, 49
Sells family, 16
Selmer High School, 120, 151
Selmer School, 138

Selmer, Tennessee, 24n, 33, 34, 53, 81, 83, 85, 108, 134n, 136, 138, 145, 149, 156n, 162, 174, 198, 199, 204, 211, 214, 233, 283, 298, 334, 336, 337, 348
Senter, William W., 341
Sergerson, Lillie U. (Dickey), 245
Seventh District Congressional Convention, 137
Seventh Tennessee Cavalry, U.S.A., 61, 73, 76, 332
Sevier Society, 108
Sewell family, 17
Sewell, Faye Marie, 114
Sewell, Lavera (Thompson), 110
Shady Hill, 277
Shaffer v. Howard, 317
Share, W.E., 269
Sharpe, Wilma (McIntyre), 252
Shatz Brothers, 203
Shaw, C.A.S., 80
Sheets, Effie, 116
Sheffield Branch, 341
Sheffield, E.W., 131
Sheffield family, 16
Sheffield, Mrs., 215
Shelby, Brenda (Malone), 180
Shelby County, Tennessee, 33
Shelby, Isaac, 8
Shelton, Neal, 113
Sherwin, Christopher, 83
Shiloh National Military Park, 135
Shiloh (Pittsburg Landing), 56, 62, 62n, 66, 86, 88, 143
Sibley, Grover, 149
Silverton, Texas, 328, 329, 331
Simmons, Aquilla Q., 340
Simmons, Jim, 116
Simpson, Elsie (Basham), 108
Sipes & Vires, 157
Sipes, Abraham, 59
Sipes, Alfred, 157
Sipes (Cypes) family, 16
Sipes, Hermie, 127
Sipes, John, 59
Sisney, George W., 44, 45
Sisneys, 45
Sixteenth Civil District, 110

Sixteenth Tennessee Cavalry Regiment, 63, 86
Sixth Tennessee U.S. Cavalry, 17n, 51, 52, 53, 54, 55, 56, 57, 59n, 60, 61, 71, 73, 82, 327
Skinner & Company, 156
Skinner, A.W., 40, 46n
Skinner, Absalom W., 341
Smith, 267
Smith, A.E., 120, 121
Smith, Arnelia, 292
Smith, Bud, 292
Smith, Col. Preston, 84
Smith, Dr., 199, 233
Smith, Dr. Ernest, 198
Smith, Dr. J.D., 210
Smith, Dr. John, 198
Smith, Elizabeth, 233
Smith family, 16, 38, 219
Smith, Glen, 109
Smith, G.T., 110
Smith, Hugh, 38, 49
Smith, Irene, 109
Smith, James Louis, 233
Smith, James T. , 38
Smith, Jerry, 270
Smith, Jerry Wilson, 217n
Smith, John L., 58
Smith, Leroy, 267
Smith, Lloyd, 115
Smith, Madison, 58, 233
Smith, Margaret J.D., 38
Smith, Mary, 111, 233
Smith, Mary (McIntyre), 251
Smith, Mary Nelle, 110
Smith, Mrs. Arlie, 218
Smith, Myrtle (Ward), 33, 128, 149
Smith, Richard, 218
Smith, Robert M., 161, 350
Smith, S.W., 38
Smith, Walter, 292
Smith, W.H., 265
Smith, William A., 38
Smith, William E., 58
Smith, William F., 58
Smith, William J. 57
Smith, Gen. William J., 314
Smith, Willard, 109, 110, 180, 346
Smith, W. Lloyd, 108
Smith, Virgil, 292
Snipes, Hermie, 118
Snipes, Jonah A., 118
Snuff Variety Gang, 350
Sol Colston Road, 111, 345
Somerville, Tennessee, 51, 80
South Carolina, 40, 50, 55, 203, 207, 211, 228, 235, 240, 243
South Central Bell, 191
Southern Claims Commission, 53
Southern Confederacy, 85
Southwest Baptist University, 137, 315, 326
Spencer, Elizabeth, 34, 88
Spencer, Harriet, 36
Spencer, R.C., 269
Spirit of St. Louis (train), 187
Spivey, Jack, 294
Spy Jack, 277, 294
Stansel, John W., 256
Stancil family 129
Stanfill, Brother Hallie, 269
Stansell, Arthur, 173
Stansell family, 17
Stansell, J.W., 161
Stantonville Schoolhouse, 141
Stantonville, Tennessee, 141
Star Route (mail route), 345, 346
Starks, Basi, l167, 179
Starks, Elijah, 256
Starr, Stephan Z., 53, 53n
State Highway 199, 110, 117, 267, 271, 281, 298
State of Oklahoma v. State of Texas, 316
Steadman, C.B., 173
Steed, C.H., 131
Steele, Miller, and Company, 198
Stephens Barber Shop, 177
Stephens, Gen., 18
Stephens, J. Ed, 174, 177, 179, 229, 344
Stewart, Antione Jane (McIntyre), 31
Stewart, Coach Dick, 147
Stewart family, 16
Stewart, Martin, 131
Stewart, Tom M., 177, 178
Stock Market Crash of 1929, 173
St. Louis, Missouri, 216

INDEX

Stoll family, 267
Stone's River, 88
Stoltzfus family, 267, 346
Stout, Raymond A., 113, 114
Stovall, Ancell (Walker), 29, 66
Stovall, Mary E. (Beene), 254
Strain family, 267
Strawberry, Arkansas, 273
Stribling, Eveline (Anderson), 28
Stribling, Robert, 25
Sunday School Convention, 135
Sullivan County, Tennessee, 24
Sulphur Springs community, 274
Sulphur Trestle, Alabama, 62
Sumrall, Robbie Neal, 89n, 90n
Sumter County, Georgia, 74
Surratt, John, 114
Surratt, Mary Virginia (Ash), 278
Surratt, Wilma, 113
Swaim family, 17
Swain, Alfred, 60
Swaim, Jane (Croskery), 144
Swaim, John, 144n, 145
Swaim, John R., 112, 119, 120, 142, 144, 168, 198
Swaim, Joseph John, 144
Swaim, J.R. Jr., 144n
Swaim, Pearl, 198
Sweet Lips Baptist Church, 146
Sweet Lips Cemetery, 60, 61, 62, 63, 76, 244, 280
Sweet Lips Creek, 23
Sweet Lips Post Office, 76, 318, 342
Sweet Lips, Tennessee, 73, 195, 212, 243, 317, 342
Swift, Jonathan, 333
Swisher County, Texas, 328, 329, 331

T

Tacker, Buel, 179
Tacker, Elizabeth Jane, 275
Tacker, Elizabeth (Page), 275
Tacker, Evie, 179
Tacker family, 17
Tacker, Joseph Orkerson, 275
Tacker, Kemit, 117
Tacker, Lee, 277, 298, 299
Talbot, Matthew, 261

Talbott, Angie Nora (Wright), 200
Talbott, Diane, 172, 180
Talbott family, 172, 176, 182
Talbott, Faye (McIntyre), 30n, 123, 171, 223, 291n
Talbott, John E., J.D., 87n, 106n, 120n, 297n
Talbott, Luther Edward "Junior," 123, 143, 171, 201, 220n, 223, 224, 281n, 289, 289n, 296n, 330n, 331, 332
Talbott, Newton Perry "Newt," 169, 170, 171, 176, 180, 183, 200, 201, 224, 269, 289
Talbott, Ronald, 172
Talbott Store, 175
Talbott Street, 73, 191
Talbott, Varham (Matlock), 170
Talbott, William Alexander, 200
Talbott, William Perry, 200
Talbott's Grocery, 172
Talleytown, 38
Taney, Chief Justice Roger B., 314
Tar Creek, 24, 25, 28, 29, 56, 68, 86n, 143, 157, 157n, 172, 243, 318, 319, 330, 335, 338, 464, 465
Tar Creek Kennels, 204
Taylor, 218n
Taylor, Diane, 273n
Taylor, J.C., 135n, 138n
Taylor, Martha, 31
Taylor, "old man," 324
Teacher's Institute, 102, 314
Teague, J.B., 121, 128
Teague, Mrs. J.B., 121
Tedford, A.K., 256
Tedford, A. Kennel, 144
Tedford, A.W., 256
Tedford, Eliza (Paralee), 85
Tedford family, 17, 180, 241
Tedford, Frank, 279, 288
Tedford, Gussie, 253
Tedford, Hubert, 279
Tedford, John, 292
Tedford, J.V., 256
Tedford Kennels, 167
Tedford, Margaret Jane, 247
Tedford, Minnie Mae, 203

Tedford, Tom, 256
Tegrum, W.G., 59n
Temple, Sally, 26
Tennessee, 22, 23, 24, 25, 31, 32, 38, 44, 46, 50, 50n, 51, 55, 56, 70, 84, 86, 94, 96, 99, 137, 138, 158, 196, 198, 211, 230, 232, 240, 260, 261, 274, 293, 298, 325, 328, 331, 350
Tennessee Annual Conference, 261
Tennessee Chancery Court, 40
Tennessee General Assembly, 9
Tennessee House of Representatives, 134
Tennessee Mounted Infantry, 61
Tennessee River, 7, 14, 56, 143
Tennessee State House of Representatives, 69, 78, 247
Tennessee State Senate, 83
Tennessee Unionist, 53
Tennessee Valley Authority, 152
Tenth Tennessee Infantry, U.S.A., 61
Texas 137, 148, 254, 316, 328, 329, 330, 330n, 331, 332
The Bank of Finger, 82, 162, 163, 165, 166, 168, 193, 197, 198, 251
The McNairy Guards, 63, 83
The Paris Café, 204
The Regular Baptist Association, 261
The Selmer Post, 135, 135n
The Teacher's Institute, 135
The Weekly Post, 135, 135n, 214n
The Whig Banner, 99, 99n
The Wright Boys, 87
Thirteenth Tennessee Infantry, 62, 87, 88, 246
Thirty-Second Mississippi Regiment, 90
Thirty-Fifth General Assembly, 78, 241
Thirty-Fourth (Reconstruction) Assembly, 241
Thomas J. Womble's General Merchandise, 213n
Thomas, Sarah A., 37
Thomason, Sol, 277, 278
Thompson, Mr. (Finger area mail carrier), 346
Thompson, T.A., 203
Thompson, Capt. Robert M., 80
Thompson, Robert A., 56
Thorington, John H., 72, 73

Tillman family, 17
Tillman, State Senator Manley, 314
Tillmon, David, 156
Tillmon family, 17
Tinsley, Tennessee, 15, 157n, 342, 317, 318, 321, 342
Tippah County, Mississippi, 94
Tippett, Sarah, 29, 30
Tisdale, Eli H., 130, 231, 342
Tisdale family, 17
Tisdale, Robert, 155, 262
Tishomingo County, Mississippi, 90
Townsend, Miss (Texas boarding house owner), 329
"Traveling Home" (song), 141
Treece, Rubee, 114
Trice, James, 25
Troublesome Iron Works, 18
Tucker, Aline, 121, 127
Tucker, Beulah (Harris), 85, 223, 224
Tucker, Dick, 115
Tucker, Dr. Nathaniel A. "Al," M.D., 85, 121, 164, 191, 213, 221, 222, 223, 224, 292, 344
Tucker, Dr. W.C., 222
Tucker, Fred, 266, 270
Tucker, George W., 60
Tucker, Lucy D. (Buckley), 222
Tucker, May, 113, 127
Tucker, Will Clark, 127, 128, 222
Tuckers, 224
Tulia, Texas, 328, 329, 330, 331
Tullis, Melba (McIntyre), 30n
Tupelo, Mississippi, 93, 94, 104, 136, 191
Turner, Buck (entertainer), 350
Tuscumbia Creek, 232
Twenty-First Tennessee Cavalry, 62, 63, 84
Twenty-Second Tennessee Infantry, C.S.A., 61, 62

U

Unidentified Black School, 132
Union, 50, 50n, 51, 52, 53, 54, 55, 56, 58n, 59, 61, 65, 68, 73, 82, 85, 99, 230, 232, 247, 249, 278
Union Army, 48, 50, 55, 65, 73, 78, 81, 144, 342

INDEX

Union City, Tennessee, 74
Union Navy, 55
Union Savings Bank of Finger, 174, 175, 197, 338
Union University, 137
Unionism, 53
Unionists, 61, 68, 69, 70, 71, 78, 248
United States, 89, 97, 162
United States Census (1860), 87, 87n
United States Census (1870), 88, 88n, 89n
United States Census (1910), 279, 279n
United States First West Tennessee Cavalry, 65, 81
   see also: First West Tennessee Cavalry
   see also: Sixth Tennessee U.S. Cavalry
United States Government, 53, 54, 72
United States House of Representatives, 136
United States Navy, 224
United States Supreme Court, 137, 180, 317
University of Nashville Medical School, 214
U.S. Highway 45, 112, 201, 291, 292
U.S. House of Representatives, 137
U.S. Sixth Tennessee Cavalry, 65, 73, 77, 81, 81n, 242, 248, 249, 275

V

Vanderbilt University Medical School, 214n
Vassar, Paul, 132, 291
Venada, Miss Maude, 202
Vaughn, Col. A.J., 87, 87n
Vera Cruz, Mexico, 314
Vickery, 267
Vinson, 267
Vinson, Ruby Dee, 109
Viola Station, Kentucky, 324
Vires, Arthur, 293
Vires, Dewayne, 117
Vires, Euma, 117
Vires family, 17, 321
Vires, Harrison, 209, 270
Vires, Herman, 117, 180
Vires, Hester, 270
Vires, John, 57

Vires, J.T., 117
Vires, Oma, 117
Vires, R.A., 117
Vires, Samuel, 57
Vires, William, 57
Virginia, 25, 34, 39, 44, 237, 244, 274

W

Wade, A., 131
Wade family, 16
Wade, John G., 40
Wade, Kelly 110
Walker, Carroll, 173, 345
Walker, Curt, 254
Walker family, 17, 129
Walker, Frank 173, 254
Walker, Grady 117
Walker, Helen, 117
Walker, Hershel, 254
Walker, J.R., 117
Walker, J.S., 256
Walker, Leanear, 117
Walker, Louisa Caroline, 86
Walker, Malinda Jane (Beene), 253
Walker, Ms., 13
Walker, Murray F., 174, 176, 256, 263, 292, 344, 345, 345n
Walker, Puss, 26
Walker, Samuel L., 59
Walker, Sue, 128
Walker, Taft, 183
Walker, Tobe, 129, 345, 345n
Walker, W.C., 256
Walker, W.H. "Tobe," 161, 174, 263, 264
Walker, William, 39
Walker, William C., 60
Walker, William Parrish, 13
Wall Street, 204
Walsh, C., 29, 157
Walsh, Edwin, 36, 155
Walsh, Elizabeth Jane, 35
Walsh, Elvire, 36
Walsh, E.T., 36
Walsh family, 16, 36, 157
Walsh, Henderson, 36
Walsh, Jack, 36
Walsh, Jefferson, 36
Walsh, Jesse, 36

Walsh, J.F., 36
Walsh, John, 36, 49
Walsh, John L., 36
Walsh, Jonathan, 36
Walsh, J.J., 29, 157
Walsh, Julia, 36
Walsh, Madison, 36
Walsh, Mary, 36
Walsh, Nancy, 36
Walsh, Sarah, 36
Walsh, Thomas, 36
Walsh, T.W., 36
Walsh, Virginia A. (Ingraham), 35, 36
Walsh, William, 25, 36
Walsh, William C., 36
Walsh, William K., 25n, 36
Walters, Nora I. (Beene), 254
Walters, Tom, 329
Wamble family, 331
Wamble, Henry, 325
Wamble, Josiah R., 340
Wamble, Marcus A. "Mark," 331
War Between the States, 23, 26, 27, 31, 40, 43, 43n, 44, 48, 50, 55, 73, 81, 83, 85, 87, 95, 96, 98, 100, 116, 153, 159, 193, 230, 231, 232, 241, 242, 246, 247, 251, 275, 320, 332, 339
War of 1812, 20, 32, 42
Ward, Dennis, 33n, 146
Ward, Dona, 145
Ward, Elizabeth (Hodges), 19
Ward, Esther, 33
Ward family, 16, 33, 146
Ward Family Genealogy, 33n
Ward, Florence (Melton), 145n, 146
Ward, John Brooks, 33
Ward, John G., 145, 161
Ward, Judy, 146
Ward, Lavinia, 32
Ward, Leonard, 33, 33n, 105, 109, 111, 128, 145, 145n, 146, 147
Ward, Luke, 33
Ward, Mary Ann (Loumiza), 33
Ward, Matthew, 33
Ward, Mattie Lou, 127
Ward, M.G., 231
Ward, Millie, 20, 77, 79

Ward, Myrtle, 105, 109
Ward, Nathan Gilbert, 33
Ward, N.G., 79
Ward, Nathan R., 194, 228
Ward, Nathan Richard, 33
Ward, Nicie, 33
Ward, John Clayton, 33
Ward, Saphronia, 33
Warner, Ezra J., 90n, 94n
Warren, Hon. James, 314
Warsham, F.J., 256
Warsham, U.J., 256
Wartrace, Tennessee, 25
Washington City, 100n
Washington County, Illinois, 55, 248
Washington County, Tennessee, 261
Washington, D.C., 136, 313, 316
Washington Valley, 274
Watauga River, 261
Watkins, John, 155, 262
Watts, Amos, 55
Wayne County, Kentucky, 34
Weakley, R., 10
Weatherford, Mrs. Merle (Gibson), 113n
Weatherington, Thomas B., 63
Weaver, Adam, 29, 30, 31, 32, 196
Weaver, Absalom, 30, 31, 229
Weaver, Absalom Sr., 32, 38
Weaver, Absalom W. Jr., 32, 63
Weaver, Adilude (Adilade), 31
Weaver, Ada Emeline, 32
Weaver, Adam, 245
Weaver, Albert, 149, 159, 169, 179, 180, 197, 289
Weaver, Annis, 32
Weaver, Asjona B., 31
Weaver, Catherine Alice, 32, 235
Weaver, Christina "Teny," 30
Weaver, Cordelia H. "Celia," 32
Weaver, Daniel, 32
Weaver, Dedemiah, 30
Weaver, Dovie (Kerby), 22, 330n
Weaver, Elizabeth, 30
Weaver, Elizabeth "Betsy," 32
Weaver, Emily, 31
Weaver, Emma, 32
Weaver family, 16, 29, 318, 319
Weaver, Fanny, 30

Weaver, George, 32
Weaver, George Allen, 32
Weaver, Harris, and Company, 166
Weaver, I.C., 161
Weaver, Isaac, 32
Weaver, Jacob J., 60
Weaver, James, 32
Weaver, James Albert, 32
Weaver, J.B., 160, 264
Weaver, John, 30, 32, 166, 196, 245
Weaver, John A., 31
Weaver, John G., 31, 63
Weaver, John Perkins, 32
Weaver, Joseph Absalom, 32
Weaver, Joseph Harrison, 32
Weaver, Joshua, 31
Weaver, Lafayette D., 31
Weaver, Lavina (Ward), 33
Weaver, Lee Andrew, 83, 161, 165, 166, 168, 174, 175, 176, 177, 196, 197, 207, 218, 245, 330n
Weaver, Margaret, 32
Weaver, Martha, 30, 318
Weaver, Mary, 31
Weaver, Mary A. (Highfield) Womble, 196
Weaver, Mary (McMillan), 245
Weaver, Matthew, 32
Weaver, Nancy, 31
Weaver, Nancy Adilude, 32
Weaver, Robert Lee, 32
Weaver, Robert McMillan, 32, 119, 160, 167, 179, 195, 207, 245, 246, 246n
Weaver, Sarah, 31
Weaver, Sarah Jane, 31, 38, 229
Weaver, Samuel Absalom, 32
Weaver, Sinnai E., 32, 38
Weaver, Susan, 31
Weaver, Susan Elizabeth, 32
Weaver, Tinsley, 46n, 227, 318, 342
Weaver, William, 31
Weaver, William H., 32
Weaver, William Thomas, 32
Weaver, W.T., 131
Weavers, 30
Weaver's Grocery and Café, 177
Webb, Dr., 223
Webb Williamson Hospital, 223

Weber Falls, 326
Webster family, 332
Webster, Daniel W., 332
Webster, Eber T. "E.T.," 332
Webster, Gracie, 22n, 102n, 105n, 109n, 117n, 118, 270n, 277n
Webster, John, 332
Webster, Marcus W., 332
Webster, Nancy, 332
Webster, Rebecca, 332
Webster, William, 332
Webster, William M., 332
Weeks, B.O., 109, 109n
Weeks, Mrs. B.O., 111
Weeks Road, 113
Wells, Abner, 18
Wesleyan Methodist, 262, 268
Wesleyan Methodist Church, 276
Wesleyan University, 99
West, George R., 72, 73
West Point Military Academy, 62, 246
West Point, Mississippi, 74
West Tennessee, 28, 48, 49, 64, 79, 85, 98, 162, 233, 238, 259, 261, 276, 298, 311, 327, 339, 340
West Tennessee Business and Normal College, 93, 98n
West Tennessee Christian College, 134, 139, 214n
Western State Mental Asylum, 217
Western Theater of the War, 86
Westminster Abbey, 313
Westvaco Lands, 21
Wharton Cemetery, 463–464
Wharton family, 267
Wharton, Bill, 256
Wharton, C.R., 83
Wharton, J. Matthew, 200
Wharton, John, 155, 346
Wharton, Johnny, 179
Wharton, Lizzie, 180, 269
Wharton, Pete E., 160, 161, 169, 179, 180, 269
Wharton, William, 168
Wheatley, Carrie (Beene), 253
Whorton, Willodean, 117
Whorton, Yancey, 117
Whig politics, 27, 69

White, Eliza, 247
White family, 17
White, Hugh, 329
White Plains Cemetery, 464–465
Whitehead, Marie F., 241n
Whitehurst, T.B., 348
Whitman family, 17
Whitman, Fiddler S., 57
Whitman, Leberen L., 57
Whitman, Seaborn L., 57
White Plains Cemetery, 24, 28, 157
White Plains, Tennessee, 15, 16, 28, 29, 157n, 246
Whitt, Tom, 320
Whitt, William, 277, 295, 295n
Whitt, Zelphia, 229
Whitt, Zelphia Roberta (McIntyre) Sanders, 248, 295n
Wilhite, Thomas Blakely, 322, 323
Wilkerson, H., 256
Wilkerson, John, 256
Wilkerson, Lt. William, 18
Wilkerson, Mary (Bell), 85n
Wilkerson, Ruby Lee, 128
Wilkes County, North Carolina, 36
Willet, Edward, 244
Willet, Polly (Tedford), 244
Williams, Arthur "A," 348
Williams, David, 105, 256
Williams, Emma Inman, 26n
Williams, Helen W., 30n
Williams, Samuel Cole, 261, 261n
Williams, Tom, 256
Williamson County, Illinois ("Bloody Williamson"), 44, 45, 46, 248
Williamson County, Tennessee, 31
Willow Lane Community, 319
Wills, Brian Steel, 52n
Wilshire and Co., 72
Wilshire, Joe 71, 72, 73
Wilson, Amanda C., 37
Wilson County, Tennessee, 17, 19, 20, 29, 30, 34, 42
Wilson, Dallas, 165
Wilson, Emitt, 320
Wilson, Frank, 148
Wilson, W.H., 142
Wilson, James, 21, 28, 35, 49, 341

Wilson, Jess, 320
Wilson, Litt (Justice of the Peace), 320
Wilson, William, 320
Wilson, President Woodrow, 343
Wilson's Cavalry, 62, 246
Wilsontown Community, 319, 320
Winding Ridge, 235, 274
Wisdom, Dew Moore, 87
Wisdom family, 25, 28
Wisdom, James, 25, 28, 465
Wisdom, John L., 26n
Wisdom, Mahala, 25, 26, 27
Wisdom, Susannah, 28, 465
Wisdom, William Sargent, 25, 26, 28, 83, 99, 465
Wisdoms, 25, 29, 464
Woodward, 267
Woodward, Charles, 284
Woodward, H.D., 160
Woodward, Joe, 284
Woodward, Lela, 283
Wolf, Allen, 270
Wolf, Henry, 60, 60n
W.O. Mitchell and Son General Merchandise, 177
Wolverton, James T., 58n, 59n, 60n
Womble, Allen R., 297
Womble, Carl, 297
Womble and Weaver, 166
Womble family, 16, 319, 331
Womble, Isham, 161
Womble, Isom P., 182
Womble, M.A., 263
Womble, Manley, 245
Womble, Mary, 297
Womble, Mary A. Highfield, 32, 245, 246
Womble, Mary E. (Beene), 297
Womble, Thomas J., 160, 166, 182, 196, 245, 256
Womble, William B., 297
Womble, William E., 245
Wood, C.A., 46n
Wood, Donald, 127
Woods, Judge Levi S., 197
Woods, Moses, 155
Wooten, A.O., 83
Works Progress Administration, 149
World War II, 153, 329, 350

Worsham, W.C., 132
Worthington, A.M., 232, 341
Worthington family, 17
Worthington, Findley D., 232
Worthington, John, 232
Worthington, L.M., 232
W.P. Massey General Merchandise, 161, 162, 193, 287
Wright family, 17
Wright, Major Benjamin 14
Wright, John V., 87, 100n
Wright, Gen. Marcus Joseph, 5, 6, 14, 15, 21, 25, 26, 27, 29, 30, 32, 36, 43, 63, 66, 83, 84, 157, 157n, 158, 210, 231, 254
Wright, Manley, 110
Wright, Newton, 156
Wright's *Reminiscences*, 42n, 43, 43n, 56n, 157n, 210n, 231n
Wynn, Mr. Lon, 195
Wynn, Mrs. Lon, 195
Wynne, N. Gayle, 42

Young, Mary A. Elizabeth "Betsy," 234
Young, Mrs. H.L., 111
Young, Nelius, 292
Young, O. D., 35n
Young, Ovie, 114
Young, Ralph, 287, 287n
Young, Rube, 161, 168, 172, 287, 288
Young, R.W., 256
Young, Sally, 229
Young, Sarah E. "Sally" (Dickey), 244
Young, Sarah "Sally," 181n
Young, Sherman, 165, 167, 178, 179, 257
Young, Thomas, 155
Young, T.V., 105
Young, T.V. Jr., 109
Young, Van, 187
Young, William Sherman, 160
Younger, Clifford, 120, 121, 121n
Younger, Lula (Plunk), 109, 118

Y

Yarbrough, Mary M., 274
Yates, Susan, 32
Young family, 129, 267
Young, A.J., 339
Young, Absolom, 155
Young, C., 173
Young, Clifford, 143, 181n, 296n
Young, Ella, 291
Young, Era, 104
Young, F., 256
Young family, 175
Young, Fonzo, 291
Young, Franklin A., 58
Young, Hobert 109, 111
Young, Horry, 331, 332
Young, James, 181n
Young, James F., 167
Young, J.G., 161
Young, Jim, 179
Young, Jimmy, 256
Young, John, 288
Young, Margaret, 233
Young, Mary, 197

ABOUT THE AUTHOR

JOHN E. TALBOTT was raised in north McNairy County, Tennessee, on Mount Carmel Hill just outside of Finger, Tennessee. He is a seventh generation McNairy Countian and spent his youth in two places: on Mount Carmel Hill and in downtown Finger. Coming from a long line of merchants and farmers, he spent much of his youth in the same store building as did his father and grandfather. He explored the little town and got to know people who began life before the age of the automobile and the electric light and whom were born at home in farm houses and log cabins.

The land and the history made on it fascinated him and inspired him to learn all he possibly could about it. On the pages of this work, he lays out more than twenty-five years of research, interviews, conversations, and walking around in an effort to enlighten the current generations about those past generations before them

Taught in the local schools of McNairy and Chester counties, John is a 1995 graduate of Freed-Hardeman University (B.A., History) and a 2002 graduate of the University of Memphis, Cecil C. Humphreys School of Law (Juris Doctor, Law). He has taught in both the McNairy County and Chester County School Systems and as an adjunct professor in history and world geography at Freed-Hardeman University.

John has been engaged in the practice of law in Henderson, Tennessee, since 2003. He is married to the former Michelle Leigh Smith, a 2001 graduate of Lambuth University, and they have three daughters: Ava Jewel, Claire Elisabeth, and Grace Caroline Talbott. The family resides in Finger, Tennessee within a short distance of where that first generation settled more than seven generations ago.

Other McNairy County titles available from

BRAYBREE
Publishing

A Sacred High Place: A History of Mount Carmel Cemetery and Meetinghouse, McNairy County, Tennessee
by John E. Talbott, J.D. • ISBN 978-0-9671251-9-0

Reminiscences of the Early Settlement and Early Settlers of McNairy County, Tennessee (130th Anniversary Edition)
by Gen. Marcus J. Wright • ISBN 978-1-940127-05-7

Hurst's Wurst: Colonel Fielding Hurst & the Sixth Tennessee Cavalry U.S.A.
by Kevin D. McCann • ISBN 978-0-9671251-2-1

www.ingramcontent.com/pod-product-compliance
Lightning Source LLC
Chambersburg PA
CBHW051532230426
43669CB00015B/2575